Human Systems Development

New Perspectives
on People and Organizations

Robert Tannenbaum
Newton Margulies
Fred Massarik
and Associates

Human Systems Development

Jossey-Bass Publishers

San Francisco • London • 1987

HUMAN SYSTEMS DEVELOPMENT
New Perspectives on People and Organizations
by Robert Tannenbaum, Newton Margulies, Fred Massarik,
and Associates

Copyright © 1985 by: Jossey-Bass Inc., Publishers
433 California Street
San Francisco, California 94104
&
Jossey-Bass Limited
28 Banner Street
London EC1Y 8QE

Library of Congress Cataloging in Publication Data
Main entry under title:

Human systems development.

Includes bibliographies and index.
1. Organization—Addresses, essays, lectures.
2. Organizational behavior—Addresses, essays, lectures.
3. Organizational change—Addresses, essays, lectures.
4. Leadership—Addresses, essays, lectures.
I. Tannenbaum, Robert.
HM131.H78 1985   302.3'5   85-9900
ISBN 0-87589-652-9

Manufactured in the United States of America

The paper in this book meets the guidelines for
permanence and durability of the Committee on
Production Guidelines for Book Longevity of the
Council on Library Resources.

JACKET DESIGN BY WILLI BAUM

FIRST EDITION
First printing: August 1985
Second printing: February 1987

Code 8525

A joint publication in
The Jossey-Bass Management Series
and
The Jossey-Bass
Social and Behavioral Science Series

Consulting Editors
Organizations and Management

Warren Bennis
University of Southern California

Richard O. Mason
University of Arizona

Ian I. Mitroff
University of Southern California

In memory of
Irving R. Weschler
whose spirit is still felt by us
and whose influence is very much present in this volume
and in the profession which he helped to found.

Preface

————————◆·◄◉►·◆·◆————————

This book presents some basic and emerging ideas about people and organizations. It reflects innovative thinking and practice at what constitutes, in our view, the leading edge of two inter-related fields that have evolved during recent decades: (1) or-ganizational behavior (OB), primarily focused on theory and research relevant to the behavior in and of organizations, and (2) organizational development (OD), primarily concerned with the facilitation and implementation of change in human sys-tems, ranging from individuals to complex formal entities.

 Also, this book is a celebration of "the UCLA experi-ence"—a process of discovering, learning, and, we hope, of con-tributing to the field—participated in for more than thirty years by the behavioral and organizational science faculty and stu-dents at the Graduate School of Management, University of California, Los Angeles. The authors of the chapters appearing in this book (with the exception of four coauthors and the au-thor of the epilogue) have been selected from among present and past faculty members and doctoral graduates who at vari-ous times through the years have been associated with this

UCLA Group. Each of these individuals is a widely recognized professional; each has been and continues to be a fruitful contributor to the field's frontiers.

Who Should Read This Book

This book is relevant to a variety of readers. University and college students and professors with interests in the behavioral sciences—and particularly in the individual, small group, large system, and environmental aspects of organizational theory and practice—will find much to challenge their views and perspectives. For both undergraduate and graduate study in universities and colleges, this book is centrally directed to courses in organizational behavior and organizational development, and more specifically to courses in personal and organizational change, human systems management, general management, leadership, human resources management, and behavioral science research theory and practice. This book also can be fruitfully used in courses offered by the more traditional academic disciplines that support and nourish the field of human systems development; namely, industrial, social, and clinical psychology; psychiatry; industrial and clinical sociology; cultural and industrial anthropology; folklore; political science; social philosophy (values and ethics); and economics. In addition to courses in schools of management, business, and commerce, this book can find use in courses offered by other professional schools such as public administration, public health, medical and nursing administration, and engineering.

We hope that *Human Systems Development* will also make important contributions to independent professionals in the areas of individual and organizational change—organizational consultants; specialists in organizational development, sociotechnology, and quality of working life; group facilitators; training specialists; and therapists. Also, thoughtful and progressive managers and staff personnel of organizations (both profit and not-for-profit) will find that various ideas presented here will prove relevant to their thinking and professional endeavors as they strive for excellence in this rapidly changing world.

Overview of the Contents

In this description, the book's contents are presented in sequence; the parts and the chapters within the parts are discussed in the order in which they appear. Readers who use this book, whether professors and students in college and universities or general readers, will, we hope, find this presentation useful in choosing how most fruitfully to approach the book's content. Readers need not start at the beginning and proceed to the end of the book. Each chapter can be viewed as a unit unto itself; no other chapter need be read for any given chapter to be understood. The reader can therefore be guided by his or her own particular needs and interests in making optimum personal use of this volume. However, we would suggest to those readers who desire a general context that, in addition to this Preface, they read Chapter One.

Chapter One, written by the three of us, underscores six basic themes that have been consistent and evolving (through the years) in our work and that of our colleagues—themes highly relevant to research, theory, and practice. These themes involve (1) the human matrix, (2) values, (3) change (at all social levels), (4) behavioral science and the pursuit of research, (5) holistic and systems perspectives, and (6) human experience, personal meaning, and alternate realities. The chapter also suggests that the term *human systems development* might usefully become a designation for an enlarged field that in fact increasingly integrates the concepts and empirical work of OB and OD as well as that of the more traditional contributing academic disciplines. The validity and viability of the enlarged field is evidenced in most, if not all, of this book's chapters as theory, research, and practice—often with case illustrations—are treated as interrelated by the several authors. Chapter One concludes with a reflection on issues considered central to the field's present professional concerns and to its future development.

Part One focuses on the person and on human experience. In Chapter Two, Fred Massarik explores the process of the deep sharing of personal meanings with others and the enhancement of the basic humanness that results. He further describes the phenomenological interview as a device that can be used to draw inferences regarding the experience of others.

Personal meaning is considered in Chapter Three from yet another viewpoint—its breakup, dissolution, and rediscovery—together with the individual and organizational implications of this perspective. Robert W. Hanna, author of this chapter, makes his observations in the context of the current widespread cultural transformation that now involves individuals and organizations. Hanna shows that through an understanding and conscious facilitation of the discovery of both individual and organizational meaning, managers are most likely to be successful in establishing new organizational directions and in eliciting the motivation, commitment, and innovation necessary to pursue them.

Another special aspect of human experience—that of being in transition in an organization—is examined in Chapter Four by Meryl Reis Louis. Steps that can be taken in managing such transitions are examined from the point of view of the individual in transition.

Part Two shifts the reader's attention from the centrality of the individual to that of the organization—and particularly to the processes involved in its design and change. This shift in perspective is facilitated by Robert Tannenbaum's and Robert W. Hanna's extensive consideration in Chapter Five of why major individual change is so troublingly difficult and of how that process sheds light on obstacles frequently encountered in efforts to bring about organizational change. Based on an understanding of the individual and organizational need to hold on, Tannenbaum and Hanna discuss the processes of letting go and moving on and their facilitation, together with implications for organizations, managers, and practitioners.

Another focus on change relates to alternative realities in an organizational setting. In Chapter Six, by Samuel A. Culbert and John J. McDonough, we take a look at how the dominant reality in that setting is constructed and how self-interests lead people to seek modifications in that construction in order to achieve an alignment of their needs with those of the organization. The challenge to managers is to balance the organization's need for stability with the need of individuals to modify the organization's reality in order to make it better support that which each espouses and seeks to contribute.

In Chapter Seven by Louis E. Davis, attention turns to the fundamental process of organizational design involving the need to participatively develop forms and structures and the means of managing them for the purpose of promoting high commitment on the part of members to organizational goals. This has long been a challenge to specialists in the area of sociotechnology/quality of working life. Such issues as the social values used to guide the new organization, the impact of technology and of the environment on the process, and new requirements for effective management are treated in detail.

The growing presence of the meta-problem in a specific environment (domain) of a set of organizations is Eric Trist's topic in Chapter Eight. The meta-problem is a social issue that becomes the common concern of a population of organizations no one of which can individually deal with that issue. In such an instance, interorganizational competence becomes a necessary societal project—competence founded on collaboration rather than competition. Trist presents illustrative cases of ongoing projects with established organizations in existing domains and with innovating organizations in emergent domains. He then proposes intervention strategies that allow interorganizational domains to develop along social processes rather than bureaucratic lines.

The notion that democracy is more than participative management is a challenge to traditional OD. In Chapter Nine, Max Elden asserts that OD values support democracy but that there are few examples of OD practice that have changed power, control, or authority relations to achieve real worker autonomy and self-management. To back up this assertion, Elden offers two cases reflecting worker participation—the first case primarily involving participation in trivial decisions and the second one involving participation in a much more powerful and meaningful mode by way of organizational democracy. Finally, Elden posits some necessary conditions for democratizing organizations.

Yet another approach for managing change is proposed by Jerry I. Porras and Joan Harkness in Chapter Ten. Called "stream analysis," it suggests an organizing structure for diagnosing, planning, and leading a complex change activity, making it possible to get a clear sense of all the change actions occurring, of their interconnections, and of their effects. The authors demonstrate the utility of this approach in an example of a complex change project in which stream analysis was used.

Anthony P. Raia and Newton Margulies conclude Part Two with a progress report on the current field of OD, including a look toward its future. The progress report is based primarily on a number of assessments of the field reported in the professional literature and on conclusions drawn from a survey of articles on OD appearing over the past ten years or so. The look toward the future is based on a Delphi study involving a panel of seventy OD academics and practitioners and buttressed by the authors' assessment of OD's frontiers.

Part Three looks at organizational leadership and the influencing of organizational culture from different points of view, providing additional substance to a research-and-practice focus. Will McWhinney, in Chapter Twelve, holds that the style of leadership used by a given leader is a reflection of the concept of reality espoused by that leader and supported by his or her culture. McWhinney's theory of leadership is based on an understanding of how alternative realities lead to different patterns of leadership. That is, specific alternative realities are displayed and a leadership pattern related to each reality is derived and illustrated.

Leaders subtly, symbolically, and powerfully shape their corporate cultures. The leader behaviors that so influence the cultural fabric of organizations referred to as "the qualitative side of leadership" are discussed in depth by David M. Boje and Dave Ulrich in Chapter Thirteen. These authors draw parallels between leaders who shape culture and ethnographers who study culture. They also describe ways to use ethnographic concepts and behaviors to shape the qualitative side of leadership theory and practice.

With increasing intensity, theorists and practitioners are

devoting attention to the cultures of organizations and how they can be influenced. Central to organizational cultures are myths (stories) and rituals. In Chapter Fourteen, Thomas C. Dandridge offers suggestions concerning the roles myths and ritual can play in the creation, maintenance, and guidance of the organization. Dandridge sees the work of the leader as involving the management of symbols (including stories and rituals). He concludes that the leader follows the organization members in constructing or nurturing symbols that have relevance, while at the same time directing these members by amplifying and reinforcing beliefs that are congruent with the desired identity of the organization.

Conflict within organizations confronts managers (leaders) with one of their greatest challenges. The actual outcomes (positive or negative) of a conflict depend largely on how that conflict is managed. Kenneth W. Thomas and Walter G. Tymon, Jr., in Chapter Fifteen, describe five conflict-handling modes, together with guides as to when to use any of them. They also examine performance appraisals from a conflict perspective. These authors conclude that conflict can often be viewed as an opportunity by the manager and by the organization. The organization must provide managers with tools and settings that enable them to take advantage of that opportunity.

While value issues are confronted in a number of chapters of this book, they are centrally addressed in Chapter Sixteen, by Abraham Kaplan, and in Chapter Seventeen, by William Gellermann. Kaplan focuses on value and the manager or decision maker. Values in decision making are humanly relevant because decisions are always about people, and people are the essential means by which the decision makers' ends may be attained. Kaplan shows that values are presupposed in the subject matter of every managerial decision, which inescapably embodies a judgment as to where the greater good lies. He discusses many facets of this often-neglected area of values.

Gellermann's chapter involves values and ethics for professional practitioners in human systems development. In recent years Gellermann has been coordinating the evolution of a statement of values and ethics for the field. In this chapter he presents the primary ethical issues emerging from work on this statement and specifies areas of agreement and disagreement. Gellermann then delves into value issues that are just beginning to emerge.

Part Four addresses a set of issues relating to theory and method in the behavioral sciences and human systems development. Viewpoints are changing these days, and conventional, quite narrowly constrained approaches absorbed with hypothesis testing are waning, or at least are moving from center stage. Increasingly, as Part Four's contributions reveal, emphasis is placed on a multimethod science responsive to genuine human concerns—in organizations and in practice—rather than one fixated on abstractions or on their elegant refinements. Values cannot be denied nor can the import of disciplined intuition.

Roger D. Evered, in Chapter Eighteen, points out a paucity of research results and argues that it derives not from lack of diligence or the absence of voluminous data, but rather can be traced to undue attention to theory and method that skirt essential relevance to the human condition. In Chapter Nineteen, Abraham Kaplan, elaborating the issue of method in the study of people, quotes Poincaré (with respect to sociology, but the quote applies equally to much of contemporary behavioral science) to the effect that the field "possesses the most in the way of methods and the least in the way of results." In the frame implied by Evered and Kaplan, scientist and observer are intricately and directly involved, and both their judgmental and nonjudgmental analyses serve appropriate and balanced functions in advancing our understanding of significant human phenomena.

It becomes clear that the kind of science envisioned in these pages is not a simple step-like process, each new discovery neatly sitting on top of its equally tidy predecessor. The contributors generally recognize the complex, often "messy" modes of learning about people. In Chapter Twenty, Lee G. Cooper and Harold G. Levine describe an approach they call "guerilla science." And Thomas G. Cummings and Susan Albers Mohrman, in Chapter Twenty-One, examine the sometimes convoluted dynamics of feedback, self-reflection, and unforeseeable action consequences that emerge as we assess outcomes of innovative organization design and systems change. As Peter B. Vaill points out in Chapter Twenty-Two, integration of knowledge remains a goal—though one that is certainly elusive. To move toward it has not been easy nor, to date, particularly successful. Witness experience, for instance, in conceptualizations of sensitivity training, active listening, and the ubiquitous dichotomy of Theory X and Theory Y in motivation within organization systems. The return to trust in process and in the fusion of experience with thoughtful theory reminds us that the science we seek needs to stay in continuing dialogue with the quality of effective practice and of authentic humanness.

The epilogue to this book has been written, at our invitation, by Warren Bennis—an observer through the years of the work of the UCLA Group. He sees at the core of the Group's contributions to the field the restoration and celebration of the self. Indeed, our colleagues' contributions to this book reflect important ferment in the evolving field of human systems development. These contributions do not cover all of the area's conceivable aspects, but they do set forth what we view as challenging concepts and suggestions to enhance the field's theoretical clarity and operational power. Theirs is not a retrospective survey, but rather a look at the present and future.

About the UCLA Group

The UCLA Group (with changing membership through the years) had its origins during the 1949–50 academic year. As a unit, it has always been eclectic in its orientation. Its members have variously focused on issues ranging from the level of the individual to those of the group, the organization, and the encompassing culture. Some have been committed principally to research, others to theory, and still others to practice. Many, perhaps most, however, have been heavily involved in two or all three of these pursuits.

Throughout its history the UCLA Group has made contributions to many areas of the evolving field, including:

- participation in decision making
- leadership and the influence process

- contingency theory
- sensitivity training as an approach to leadership and personal development
- team building
- the facilitation of system (individual, group, and organizational) change and development
- organizational and systems theory
- organizational design, sociotechnology, quality of working life
- organizational mythology (including stories and rituals)
- organizational ecology
- the management of conflict
- the visioning and construction of alternate realities
- research methodology (with particular attention to phenomenology)
- humanistic values as they infuse all of the preceding

While this is not a complete list, it nevertheless reflects the richness and breadth of the work of the Group.

The ambiance of the Group is not easy to convey in words. No doubt each Group member would describe it differently. Considerable attention has been given to the building and maintenance of a learning community committed to mutual confrontation, acceptance and support, the integration of process and content in the movement toward system goals, the valuing of individual differences, the recognition of the importance of both the emotional and the intellectual in the development of the whole person, the linking of thought with action, the willingness to take risks at the frontiers of theory and practice, and the living of the humanistic values that we have espoused. We have often fallen short of these goals, but we have certainly tried to be guided by them.

The individual authors represented in this volume have been—over varying periods of time—active members of and contributors to the Group's unfolding intellectual interests, its action projects, and its ambiance. Each has impacted on the Group and been influenced by it. The colleagues have pursued unique interests, methodologies, and personal styles. And yet, collectively they do hold much in common as evidenced by a subtle unifying thread in their work and by a continuing recognition of colleagueship in their professional careers. All have involved themselves in theory development, research, and practice —not separately, but as highly interrelated and interdependent processes. The individual person functioning in an organizational context is consistently central in their ideas and practical concerns. And an awareness of the roles of values permeates their efforts.

Acknowledgments

Our special appreciation goes to our long-time professional colleague and friend, Warren Bennis, of the University of Southern California, author of this book's epilogue. While at no time an on-going member of the UCLA Group, he has nevertheless served as our collegial consultant and supporter. His seminal contributions to the profession have been most important to our own work.

We want to express our deep respect and gratitude to our UCLA colleagues (and their collaborators) who have joined with us as associates in making this book possible. We also want those other Group members (both faculty and students) not directly represented in this book to know that in this project (as well as outside of it) we have been aware of their valuable contributions to our learning community and, more broadly, to the profession. Through the years, we have needed each other, and we have given to each other—both professionally and personally. That has been of greatest importance.

June 1985   Robert Tannenbaum
                                               Carmel, California

                                               Newton Margulies
                                               Irvine, California

                                               Fred Massarik
                                               Los Angeles, California

Contents

The Authors

Robert Tannenbaum is emeritus professor of development of human systems in the Graduate School of Management, University of California, Los Angeles. He received his B.A. degree in business, his M.B.A. degree, and his Ph.D. degree, with emphases in industrial relations and economic theory, all from the University of Chicago. He was coeditor with I. R. Weschler and Fred Massarik of one of the earliest books on Organizational Behavior (*Leadership and Organization,* 1961), and has authored and coauthored numerous articles in the field of organizational behavior.

Newton Margulies is currently dean and professor of management in the Graduate School of Management, University of California, Irvine. He received his B.S. degree in engineering from Brooklyn Polytechnic Institute, his M.S. degree in industrial management from the Massachusetts Institute of Technology, and his Ph.D. in behavioral science from the University of California, Los Angeles. He has authored and coauthored numerous works in the field of organizational development and has provided consulting services to a variety of organizations in both the private and public sectors. His interests continue to be in the study of organizational change and the variables that affect its implementation.

Fred Massarik is professor of behavioral science and industrial relations and is chair of the behavioral and organizational science faculty in the Graduate School of Management, University of California, Los Angeles. He received his B.A. degree in psychology, his M.A. degrees in anthropology and sociology, and his Ph.D. degree in psychology, all from the University of California, Los Angeles. His international teaching assignments have taken him to Japan, India, Ireland, and West Germany. He has been the president of the Association of Humanistic Psychology and has served as chair for that association's international activities. His current interests are in applied phenomenology and in the assessment of outcomes in group training.

Warren Bennis is Joseph DeBell Professor of Management and Organization at the Graduate School of Business Administration, University of Southern California. He served as president of the University of Cincinnati during most of the 1970s. He has published many books and articles in the field of organizational behavior and is a well-known lecturer on many management topics.

David M. Boje is assistant professor in the Graduate School of Management, University of California, Los Angeles. His major interests are interorganizational relations and transorganizational development. His most recent work is an historical analysis of the relationship between esthetics and technology in the commercial printing industry.

Lee G. Cooper is associate professor in the Graduate School of Management, University of California, Los Angeles. His interests concern the development of psychometric models of human decision processes, and his writings have appeared in many prominent journals, including *Contemporary Psychology, Behavioral Science,* and *Multivariate Behavioral Research.*

Samuel A. Culbert is professor of behavioral and organizational science in the Graduate School of Management, University of California, Los Angeles. He has devoted his attention to the application of sociological and anthropological concepts to management and has written many books and articles on human behavior in organizations. He is a member of National Training Labs and the American Psychological Association.

Thomas G. Cummings is professor of management and organization in the Graduate School of Business Administration at the University of Southern California. He is associate editor of the *Journal of Occupational Behavior* and president of the Western Academy of Management. His research interests include designing high-performing organizations and organizational change and development.

Thomas C. Dandridge is associate professor with joint appointments in the School of Business and the Rockefeller College of Public Affairs and Policy, State University of New York at Albany. He writes in the field of organizational behavior and has special interests in the multifaceted phenomena of organizational culture.

Louis E. Davis is professor of organizational science in the Graduate School of Management, University of California, Los Angeles. He has been chairman of the Center for Quality of Working Life and research fellow of the Tavistock Institute in London. He has been engaged in the study of organizational design since 1949 and has authored numerous books and papers on this subject. The application of his work extends over eighteen countries and has afforded him an international reputation.

Max Elden is professor of organization and work life science at the Norwegian Institute of Technology, University of Trondheim. He has lectured at various universities in Europe and America, and served as visiting research scientist at the Center for Effective Organization, University of Southern California. He has written many articles in the fields of politics, organization, and change.

Roger D. Evered is professor of management at the Naval Post-graduate School in Monterey, California. His research interests emphasize the epistemological issues of management practice, particularly long range planning and futures research. He combines fifteen years of experience with engineering firms with an educational grounding in engineering and management.

William Gellermann received his Ph.D. in behavioral sciences from the Graduate School of Management, University of California, Los Angeles. He has served on the faculties of the University of California, Los Angeles, State University of New York at Buffalo, Cornell University, and City University of New York. Since 1970 he has been an independent consultant in management and organizational development. His clients include a variety of organizations in both private and public sectors.

Robert W. Hanna is associate professor of management and former department chairman at California State University, Northridge. In addition to providing consulting services to many organizations, he has been closely associated with National Training Laboratories and has written in the field of organizational change and development.

Joan C. Harkness is director of operating room services at El Camino Hospital, Mountain View, California. Her experience in health care management and systems development has given her opportunities to consult with organizations in the health care field.

Abraham Kaplan is professor of philosophy at Haifa University, Israel, and visiting professor of behavioral science at the Graduate School of Management, University of California, Los Angeles. He has written widely on philosophical issues influencing organizational life and on significant societal questions. His widely acclaimed book, *The Conduct of Inquiry* (1968), has had profound impact on the study of human behavior and on research orientations in the social sciences.

Harold G. Levine is assistant professor in the Graduate School of Education, University of California, Los Angeles. Trained as an anthropologist, he teaches and writes on research methodology for educational and organizational contexts. He has recently applied these interests to the conduct of ethnographic studies of organizational culture.

Meryl Reis Louis is associate professor in the School of Management and research associate in the Center for Applied Social Science, Boston University. Her major interests include the study of career transitions, work place cultures, and the sociology of social science. She previously served on the faculties of the Naval Postgraduate School, the University of Illinois, and as a visiting professor at the Massachusetts Institute of Technology.

John J. McDonough is professor of management and codirector of the M.B.A. program at the Graduate School of Management, University of California, Los Angeles. His recent research and writing focuses on issues of power and trust in contemporary organizations. His most recent book (with Samuel A. Culbert, 1985), *Radical Management: Power Politics and the Pursuit of Trust,* extends the practice of human relations by providing insights into these phenomena.

Will McWhinney was on the faculty in the Graduate School of Management, University of California, Los Angeles, until 1976. He currently consults on social design and works with the managers of family businesses, combining family systems therapy and business consultation.

Susan Albers Mohrman is research scientist in the Center for Effective Organizations, the Graduate School of Business, University of Southern California. Her research activities and publications have focused on organizational design, innovative organizational systems, and the quality of work life projects.

Jerry I. Porras is currently associate professor of organizational behavior in the Graduate School of Business, Stanford University. He has published widely in both academic and management journals, focusing on planned organizational change and development processes.

Anthony P. Raia is professor of management in the Graduate School of Management, University of California, Los Angeles. He formerly served as assistant dean for executive education and is currently codirector of the Ojai Leadership Laboratories. His interests lie in the application of change theory to organizations, and he has consulted with organizations in both the private and public sectors.

Kenneth W. Thomas is associate professor in the Graduate School of Business, University of Pittsburgh. He has been a research fellow at the Harvard Business School and has served on the business faculty at the University of California, Los Angeles, and at Temple University. He has written extensively on the management of conflict in organizations and has been active in the Academy of Management, American Psychological Association, and the Institute of Management Sciences.

Eric Trist is professor emeritus of organizational behavior and social ecology at the Wharton School, University of Pennsylvania. Professor Trist was a founding member and later chairman of the Tavistock Institute of Human Relations in London. He has been associated as a faculty member with the Graduate School of Management, University of California, Los Angeles, and with the environmental studies group at York University, Toronto.

Walter G. Tymon, Jr., is instructor of management in the Faculty of Business Studies, Rutgers University. His current research interests include the study of conflict, power, and organizational change. Hs is a member of the Academy of Management and the American Institute of Decision Sciences.

Dave Ulrich is professor of organizational behavior in the Graduate School of Management and research associate in the Institute for Social Research, University of Michigan. His research focuses on how organizations can respond to environmental pressures for change. He has also been involved in a variety of change projects in both public and private sectors.

Peter B. Vaill is professor of human systems in the School of Government and Business Administration, George Washington University. He has served on the faculties of the Graduate School of Management, University of California, Los Angeles, and the business school of the University of Connecticut. He has written many articles on organizational development, strategic planning, and the philosophy of science. His current interest is in "high-performing systems" and the development of excellence in human systems of all kinds.

Human Systems Development

New Perspectives
on People and Organizations

1

The Development of Human Systems: Basic Themes

Fred Massarik
Newton Margulies
Robert Tannenbaum

"When did it all start?" If "it" has to do with some kind of explicit approach to the study of people and how they work together toward specified ends, origins are certainly lost in ancient years. We do know, however, that the past five or six decades have witnessed an increasing outpouring of research, formulation of theory, and modes of professional practice (managing, consulting, and teaching) that have shared a common thrust: to enable us *to better understand and/or to effectively influence human behavior in organizational settings.* Many scholars and practitioners, both in this country and abroad, have contributed their creative energies to this continuing and enlarging quest.

From the late 1940s to the early 1960s, Tannenbaum and Massarik, together with a group of academic colleagues (faculty and graduate students) at the University of California at Los Angeles (UCLA), explored certain avenues of thought and action that we first labeled "human relations research and practice" and then later described as "behavioral science ap-

1

proach." This endeavor led to a predecessor volume (Tannen-baum, Weschler, and Massarik, 1961). From the early sixties to the present, our efforts and those of our past and present UCLA colleagues have continued—at UCLA, at other universities, and in the field—as a part of the much broader common thrust.

Through the years, this chapter's authors have increasing-ly become aware of a number of basic themes that have been both consistent and evolving in our work and in that of our col-leagues, many of whom are contributors to this volume. In what follows, we shall address these themes. But before we do so, some introductory but, we think, important observations are in order: (1) The themes discussed are not "pure" types; in spite of their heuristic distinctiveness, they overlap and interlock. They are often highly interrelated and interdependent. Indeed, as presented here, they constitute what one of the contributors to this volume would have elsewhere described as products of a "reconstructed logic" (Kaplan, 1964). (2) The themes are pre-sented by us in what appears to be some kind of logical, linear order. Actually, they evolved—sometimes with purposeful ad-vance deliberation but more often, perhaps, by trial and error, by backing and filling, and as a result of what often seemed to us interminable thought and discussion. Some surely appear clearer to us now, as *themes,* than they did while our work was in progress. (3) We believe that all of the themes are highly rele-vant to research, theory development, and professional practice. However, because of space limitations in the discussion that fol-lows, we will not always, in our comments and examples, relate each theme to each of the three areas of endeavor.

After presenting the themes, we will take a fresh look at the unfolding common thrust of which we have been a part and offer a suggestion with respect to its designation. Finally, we will venture some observations on what we see as significant new directions in this developing field.

The Human Matrix: From Individual to Society

Our permeating and encompassing orientation has framed as central the relationship between the individual and the or-ganization. In a historical sense, classical theories of statecraft and policy have addressed this issue in connection with the relationship between governed and government, citizen and ruler. More recently, but still quite some time ago, F. W. Taylor's (1947) work, hardly seen as heroic by many contemporary writers, is in a sense occupied with this topic. And, more directly relevant, there are the oft-cited contributions of Mary Parker Follett (1924, 1941), Chris Argyris (1957), and Douglas McGregor (1960), to name but a few. In this context, focusing on the individual and organization, certain positions are central to our perspective:

1. We view each individual not as a relatively undifferentiated entity more or less like other individuals (that is, not in statistically modal terms) but with a *clinical and deeply probing recognition of the individual's unique characteristics and dynamics.* We focus heavily on the study of individuals in order to better understand the complexities that make us the unique yet interrelated human beings that we are and ever come to be. And we stress the humanistically oriented value of helping individuals to become more of what they are and what they can come to be. In much of our research, and in basic or small-group training (in prior writings we called it sensitivity training), as well as in individual counseling, teaching, and organizational consulting, this view has served both as theoretical backdrop and as practical beacon. With this clinical perspective, the individual/organization link is examined—not in terms of any one "school," such as psychoanalysis (orthodox or "neo"), nor even in terms of personal construct or Maslowian theory, but, we hope, with eclectic balance.

2. We view organizations not in terms of fixed parameters as such (for example, their size, age, or industry) nor in typological terms but rather as loosely bounded, living, adaptive and changing, unique organisms—perhaps closer to biological than to static, mechanimorphic analogues. Accordingly, we could not drive strongly for any one particular organizational form (whether hierarchical, flat, matrix, or functional), nor for a limiting aprioristic contingency theory. If anything, we seek to examine organizations in terms of dynamic systems concepts, expressed, for instance, in adaptional processes and in sociotechnical systems design.

3. While interrelations between individuals and organizations constitute an important focus, our sphere of concern extends explicitly to take account of small groups and of society at large. *Small groups* have played a special role in the continuity of our efforts. First, there has been our extensive use of sensitivity-training groups as vehicles for individual change. Our earlier work in this area has been reported in our first volume (Tannenbaum, Weschler, and Massarik, 1961) and in subsequent publications (Weschler, Massarik, and Tannenbaum, 1962; Tannenbaum and Bugental, 1963a, 1963b; Massarik, 1970, 1972a, 1972b). Then there have been explicit applications at UCLA, including the Western Training Laboratory, the University Extension Leadership Laboratories ("the Ojai Labs"), the Institute of Industrial Relations' "Sensitivity Training for Managers," and our Graduate School of Management T-group course in leadership principles and practice. Small-group training continues to be seen by us as a powerful process for positive personal and organizational change. Further, we continue to explore the nature of natural, purposive small groups in the daily operations of organizations, both in informal processes and in task-directed activities. Thus, the concept *small group* proves to be of focal significance, both in the sense of change method and as a substantive component of the fabric of living organizations.

Society at large emerges as an enveloping topic of concern, but one that has proved more difficult to approach. We always have been conscious of the broad context within which individuals and organizations, as well as small groups, develop and from which, in some measure, they derive their characteristics. We have been responsive to the notions of *culture* and *environment* but have not attempted major empirical inquiries in the styles of cultural anthropology. On the other hand, the concept *society at large* has usefully drawn our attention to issues such as the following:

• Any given action at an individual, small-group, or organizational level (within these levels themselves and in interaction among them) proceeds within the context of society—its values and views, its technologies and power relationships, and its many other manifestations. Accordingly, each action affects and is affected by this nearly overwhelming but somehow distinctive patterning of persistent forces—forces that often are so pervasive and ubiquitous that we run the risk of taking them for granted.

- Society at large is replete with publics, or what sometimes are referred to as sets of stakeholders (Mitroff and Mason, 1983). Each public or stakeholder stands to gain or lose, benefit or suffer from whatever happens in individual-small-group–organization interactions. There is "no place to hide," and anything that anybody does or whatever is caused to occur in situations involving people has larger consequences, many minor but some surely major.

- Those of us who are concerned with change—purposeful or natural—reaching individuals, small groups, or organizations frequently need to be reminded of those ripple effects (or even massive impacts) on publics or stakeholders in various segments of society. Neither T-group outcomes nor socio-technical redesigns are self-contained events; they emerge from and affect society. In turn, we may choose to conceptually refine society at large into smaller, nested units, such as communities and subcultures. Again, the issue of effects and impacts remains salient.

In concluding this discussion of the human matrix, we underscore the fact that it is the holistic interplay among individuals, small groups, organizations, and society at large that gives impetus to our interests, no matter that a given inquiry or activity may call for severe practical delimitation and concentration on one or another aspect of this interplay.

Values

Throughout the years, a deep concern for values has permeated all that we have done. We have tried to recognize that values are central to human endeavor and that this centrality directly affects what kind of research is envisioned, how it is designed and implemented, how it is interpreted, and how it is put to use (Friedman, 1967; Kurtz, 1969; Smith, 1969). This centrality also is relevant to the behavior, in an organizational context, of individuals (including professional practitioners), groups, and each organizational entity itself. We want the reader to know that we unashamedly label our own personal value bias as humanistic. We have been and are personally committed to research and practice that help individuals to reach as nearly as possible their basic potential. This commitment also extends to the enhancement of the quality of interpersonal and intergroup relations and to the design, management, and functioning of organizations in ways supportive of the growth potentials of their members. It is also important to us that organizations be entities in the service of people rather than the other way around.

Having stated our personal value bias, we hasten to add that we do not see ourselves as rigid in this value stance. We recognize that there are individual differences in value commitment—and cultural differences, as well. And one of our humanistic values involves the acceptance—and the valuing—of such differences. We also recognize that values are not immutable and that their applicability can change from situation to situation; for example, being accepting becomes inappropriate when one is confronted with evil. Also, each person holds to a hierarchy of values, with some taking precedence over others; for example, "Thou shalt not kill" versus service to country in time of war. We are particularly interested in two specific values in a context of our humanistic framework and individual/organization focus:

- *Authenticity*. We are concerned with issues relating to the extent to which a person can be genuinely himself or herself. Concepts such as *openness, self-disclosure,* and the JOHARI-window (a model for explaining and describing interpersonal processes and personal development) fit in this context (Luft, 1969). There are limitations: the issue of optimum privacy is an example. For the most part, "being real" and being in situations (organizations) where being real becomes possible is seen as preferable to the game playing and maskmanship that in our judgment are too prevalent in many personal relationships, in groups and in organizations. And yet the haunting questions of risks to be taken and fine lines to be trod are omnipresent. Further, in interpersonal relations, a person's own values need to be understood by him or her and to be appropriately revealed to others. Difficulties arise when such values are inadequately grasped by their holders or are surreptitiously withheld and hidden from those affected by them. The foundational joint values of thorough *self-knowledge* and appropriate *self-disclosure* run like ever-present twin threads through the labyrinth that is the human condition.

- *Intentionality.* We have particular interest in the purposefulness of life, as expressed both by a person in his or her own existence and by persons who join in common endeavor, as in groups and organizations. While we do not reject behaviorism out of hand, we are unwilling to assume, in either a psychological or a philosophical sense, that all actions are externally determined or that sheer reinforcement or conditioning inevitably carries the day (Skinner, 1972). As to psychoanalysis (whether Freudian or in its various revisionist forms), it also is neither wholly unacceptable nor wholly acceptable; we profess a special attraction to the contributions of C. G. Jung (Campbell, 1971) and to their subsequent elaborations (Singer, 1973). The issue of intentionality emerges in many guises. Whatever their origin, people's goals and purposes are exceptionally important in focusing behavioral science knowledge, and the value of having and seeking goals is an existential given. Holding on to and letting go of goals and of roads leading to them constitute examples of intentionality in action.

At the level of organizations, what is or is not humanistic is subject to some controversy and misunderstanding. Often, the humanistic orientation is misunderstood and distorted. The assumption that our sole value objective was the happiness and job satisfaction of employees, with no consideration given to organizational goals and task requirements, was erroneous. And to many, even now, humanistic orientations are seen as "soft," "weak," and "unrealistic." We think and feel otherwise and assert that humanistic values directly support *both* the welfare of individuals *and* organizational efficiency and effectiveness (Massarik, 1976). We have been involved with sociotechnical systems and with action research—both of which owe a debt to creative concepts and applications rooted in engineering and systems design (Davis and Cherns, 1975a, 1975b). And we are committed not only to individual growth but also to an organization's growth toward a realization of its own positive potential.

Change, Growth, and Development

These value-laden terms have been at the heart of our professional practice—in individual counseling, in sensitivity training, and in organizational and community development. Social change is, of course, pervasive—with or without professional intervention—and is often unpredictable. In our profession, reference is often made to "planned change," but we feel that this usage involves an excessive claim. We, as professionals, deal with complex human beings, with their interdependence, and with the nonhuman aspects of the systems in which they function. We are painfully aware of the frequently turbulent environments that surround these people and the organizational systems within which they are embedded. Little wonder that we are so often faced with surprises. In fact, we constantly move step by step into the unknown. We are involved in an unfolding process, faced with ambiguity, uncertainty, unpredictability; and we are rarely able to have high confidence in what is going to appear at the next step. We have to live with that.

Change can be "good," and it can be "bad." A lot depends on the perspective of the evaluator. The dimension of time can also affect this evaluation: what seems good today may turn out (under changed perspectives) to be an unmitigated disaster tomorrow. And how do we acknowledge the omnipresence of change—and, at times, its necessity—while granting a given system's right *not* to change? These are among the persistent predicaments surrounding the change process.

The terms *growth* and *development* connote movement toward some positive outcome. But what is "positive," and whose "positive" is it? To us, the professional practitioner is not without his or her values. But it is essential that the practitioner be aware and accepting of the values of the system with which he or she works and also be open with the client with respect to his or her own values.

Science and Research

It has been "traditional" to think of "science" (and both sets of quotation marks are necessary) and action as separate and sequential. Considering the history of science, and going beyond an artificially narrow hypothetico-deductive interpretation, one may surmise that even in traditional (read: older and well-chronicled) scientific inquiry, many strategies of investigation coexisted or confronted each other in abundant disarray (Koestler, 1959; Vickers, 1984). Consider, for instance, Newton (distrusting hypotheses), Tycho Brahe (collecting huge amounts of astronomical information, principally as undigested raw data), Darwin (engaged in an apparently obscure collection of animal bones at Galapagos), Einstein (conducting "thought experiments"), and Freud (at intellectual war with Vienna's nineteenth-century medical establishment). Query: did all of them practice a single traditional science? Answer: no way! Science, then, always has been a "House of Many Doors," and simply equating it with procedures involving mechanical hypothesis testing (no matter how sophisticated) never were, and surely are not now, in order.

With this diversity, one needs to re-examine the issue of values that historically have guided investigation and their relevance to the use of findings or, if you will, to action. It is our view that in all instances, including those cited here, a discernible value position was present *at the outset* of each particular program of inquiry. No *tabula rasa* existed in any case, no infinitely responsive blank slate of ever-pure objectivity preceded eventual discovery. The human matrix, of course, encompasses science, as well as any other human effort, and, whatever the consequences, scientists in their professional pursuits are not exempt from the interplay of forces noted, including values. Thus, values are inherently interwoven in science, and we might as well face this circumstance (Feather, 1975; Foss, 1977). We try to recognize that values *are* central to human endeavor and that this centrality directly affects what kind of research is envisioned, how it is designed and implemented, and, perhaps most importantly, how it is interpreted and put to use. Even in this formulation of the preceding sentence, linearity inherent to syntax and to reconstructed logic obscures the dynamic and nonlinear aspects of the research process. Use does not neatly follow design or even interpretation of findings. Action research approaches involve "subjects" (awful word!) in data collection and interpretation and application of results in various simultaneous and "looping" ways—a far cry from the rigid, sequential admonitions found in orthodox research primers. And in the newer nonlinear research paradigms, values interpenetrate what goes on, specifically in the focus on explicit research for positive human growth.

Holistic and Systems Perspectives

Individuals live in systems; individuals are systems. These propositions are hardly new. They are supported by a substantial literature (Berrien, 1968; Buckley, 1968; Ackoff and Emery, 1972) and are frequently cited—sometimes as mere "throwaway" lines, at other times with more substantial content—to refer to complex interactive or self-regulating phenomena. Whatever the detail, it seems clear to us that an eclectic systems view continues to be useful, perhaps essential, to the work of behavioral science scholars and practitioners.

An elaboration is required: We believe that systems approaches at best imply and are fully consistent with *holistic* thinking about human phenomena. True, a system at rest—not considering its dynamics—can be thought of in terms of parts and components. But the system in action does necessarily function as a whole, with the interdependence of both components and processes critical to its mode of operation, survival, and effectiveness. In this fashion, the more appropriate meta-phor is closer to *organism* than to *machine,* and the more suit-able conceptual base is closer to Gestalt theory and field theory (Hartmann, 1935; Koffka, 1935; Köhler, 1969; Mey, 1972) than it is to particularism or reductionism.

If Gestalt theory is adduced in conjunction with systems thought, as we believe it should be, other helpful consequences follow. One may think of the system or of any of its aspects—or of any human phenomenon—in terms of *figure and ground,* at-tending to some of its features while apprehending all else as background. In this manner, recalling the complexity of the hu-man matrix, it becomes possible to select one or another salient manifestation, examining its patterning while not losing the context within which it is embedded. The role of "environ-ment" as ground in various aspects of systems theorizing—focus-ing, for example, on design or energy transformations as figures *within* the system—illustrates this procedure. As in Gestalt imag-ery, focus on ground and figure can just as well be reversed.

There are other specific applications—some with intensive existential power. The pervasive issue of *personal self-identity* enters the picture (Rosenberg, 1979; Goldberg, 1980). In terms of daily existence, there hardly seems anything more firmly given than the "fact" that *I am I,* that there is a core self that constitutes the very essence of my being. Yet there are counter-vailing pressures—in my awareness of others, in my sense of re-latedness, in reaching out, in a search for oneness and unity. My personal identity constitutes a locus of *differentiation*; the countervailing pressures drive toward *integration.* (Elsewhere, Lawrence and Lorsch, 1967, and Lorsch and Allen, 1973, have treated this matter in organizational context.)

The brain and thought processes in general furnish addi-tional applications of this perspective. Brain physiology has been an area of controversy, as well as systematic study, over the centuries (Hart, 1975; Granit, 1977; Furst, 1979). More re-cently, the literature has featured a presumed polarity between right brain and left brain, with the indication that right-brain processes influence nonlinear, creative, and intuitive functions, while the left brain primarily controls linear, abstract, and conceptual thought. Whatever the research evidence (and it appears more equivocal than often assumed), there is little doubt that functions associated with the left brain, whether as physiological structure or in a metaphoric sense, predominate in Western thought. Rationality, rigor, and intellect are the key values, and they tend to hold sway over feeling, emotion, and intuition. In a related matter, there are the relevant dimensions of human response examined in the Myers-Briggs test (among them feeling-thinking and intuition-sensing). Again, various opposites and constellations among these dimensions can be discerned and patterns identified.

We believe that issues associated with right-brain and left-brain functioning, with feeling-thinking and intuition-sensing, can be appropriately explored in terms of holistic and systems perspectives. Significantly, the *whole* brain (as system *and* gestalt) calls for our principal attention—an orientation classically developed in Goldstein's (1959) organismic conceptualizations of brain function. This view need not deter us from zeroing in, for instance, on left-brain activities and on their possible overemphasis in our culture or on insufficiently realized beneficial effects of right-brain dynamics. Or some (not we) might argue just the opposite. The total configuration of feeling-thinking and intuition-sensing (as well as introversion-extraversion and judging-perceptiveness) presents a productive basis for understanding how certain important styles of the person interact and converge (Myers, 1976). But any one dimension may be focused on as figure, while the others for the moment appear as ground. In any case, it is the entire pattern, holistically including its internal systemic ebbs and flows, that deserves consideration.

Experience, Meaning, and Alternate Realities

In spite of the surfeit of theories—grand, of the middle range, or whatever—ultimately, it all comes down to human experience. We believe that much currently "mainstream" behavioral science has moved too far away from the rudimentary but essential truth that as human beings all we have is experience flowing in the stream of time. We need to place a greater emphasis on the experiential as a source of data and depth. William James's "stream of consciousness" and the succession of "life worlds" or "life spaces" in the works of Husserl (1975) and Lewin (1936) come at least a bit closer than many other concepts to capturing the essentially direct and "raw" nature of human experience. Some of our interest areas and research styles are in this spirit.

We are concerned, for example, with improving approaches to the study of human experience, as in empirical reconsiderations of phenomenology, a field with roots in philosophy (Kockelmans, 1967; Psathas, 1973). As researchers and practitioners, we often need to be "inside" the data rather than "outside" in order to generate "knowledge of" rather than "knowledge about." We must recognize that both theory and practice in organizational frameworks are importantly influenced by human conceptions and perceptual constructions of organizational life, based on direct experience as held by those within and without, and not necessarily by "objective" structural factors (Culbert, 1974; Culbert and McDonough, 1980). Leadership likewise often depends on how power is perceived, on definitions of the situation rather than on more obviously visible and prescribed position descriptions. Practitioners can often be of relevance to clients by helping them to break their existing set (definition of reality) and to become aware of alternative possibilities. And so it goes. One may think of numerous concepts conventionally addressed in the behavioral sciences that can be understood in greater depth if they are re-examined in light of fundamental human experiences and resultant perceptions, rather than by overlaid a priori theorizing.

Essential to phenomenological thought and related views are two interlinked processes, the *search for meaning* and the *construction of alternate realities.* Human events, one may suggest, become truly human only if meanings are attributed to these events. Or it may be that the event does not have reality as a *human* experience until it is shaped or recast in terms of meaning by the person involved. Mechanical descriptions of events by third parties (while they are, in a way, experience in themselves for these third parties) do not, we believe, enlighten nearly as much as does the purposeful empathic entry of one person into the other's "life world."

This process of seeking meaning in turn leads us to believe that productive approaches to the field acknowledge and examine the alternate realities of people, especially those of behavioral scientists themselves. The latter versions of reality determine paradigms of research and practice. The very meaning frameworks within which research is designed and practice conducted—namely, the practitioners' and researchers' own alternative realities of the profession, of themselves as persons, and of their roles—profoundly affect the field's intellectual and practical directions. An appreciation of these varying realities, rather than single-minded adherence to any one framework or paradigm, seems to us most helpful in the study and practice of human affairs.

Human Systems Development:
A Call for Reconsideration

Over the years, the terms referring to "the field" (if it is, indeed, a discernible field) have changed. As previously mentioned, at one time (in the late forties and into the fifties), we and others thought of "it" as *human relations*. Subsequently, especially with the impetus of the Ford Foundation (Gordon and Howell, 1959; Pierson and others, 1959), *behavioral science* moved into prominence. Sometimes transmuted into *applied behavioral science,* this formulation has maintained a modest level of currency, especially to characterize practice and applications in areas such as public health and medicine. Undoubtedly most widespread at present is *organizational behavior,* usually referred to simply as OB (Chung and Megginson, 1981; Sashkin, 1984; Steers, 1984). Innumerable textbooks with quite similar content, though varying in style of presentation, have been written in recent years, with all sorts of variations on the theme of OB played out in their titles. In turn, OB has, in some circles, come to be differentiated into "micro" (individual?) and "macro" (larger systems?) components—a distinction of uncertain utility, in our opinion, given the interrelatedness of relevant processes as suggested by the human matrix. And, as is evident, OB is the designation of choice for academic departments concerned with individuals and organizations.

This leaves aside the matter of the more traditional academic disciplines that contribute to and share interest in topics subsumed under the OB label: industrial, social, and clinical psychology; psychiatry; industrial sociology; cultural anthropology; folklore; political science; social philosophy (ethics); and aspects of economics. These are, of course, of continuing significance, even to hard-line OB and surely to any synthesizing field concerned with real people doing real things.

Then there is OD—*organizational* (or *organization*) *development*. Here we find principally a vast array of approaches (interventions, techniques, consultation styles) intended to improve, by sometimes explicit but more often implicit criteria, the functioning of organizations and/or individuals in these organizations. The theoretical base often is less clear than the action orientation, and yet, in spite of (because of?) this, OD is a field of burgeoning activity and vital energy. A new thrust of the past several years, growing out of OD and influenced by systems theory, Eastern philosophies and religions, work in higher consciousness, and notions of alternate realities, is being referred to as OT (*organizational transformation*). People in OT are beginning to evolve a theory base and related intervention methodologies.

At this time, we (and some others) are not fully content either with "the field's" labels and designations or with its process and impact. Our own work, through the years, has partaken of the *behavioral science and* of the *sociotechnical systems* labels. We now believe that the time is right for a new look and for a new disciplinary designation. We think that *human systems development* is now appropriate. Our belief is strengthened by the knowledge that in 1984 a group of representatives from fourteen applied behavioral science groups (primarily in the United States) decided to call themselves the Human Systems Development Consortium. Our rationale for this choice flows, in part, from the substance of the human matrix, from the focus on values and related concerns with growth and development, from the holistic/systems perspective, and from the growing awareness of the relevance of human experience.

We realize that boundaries of disciplines cannot be established by fiat, but tentative delineation of such boundaries can furnish a basis for reflection about a field's substance and about its direction. We may preliminarily think of human systems development (HSD) somewhat in line with the chart shown in Figure 1-1. In these terms, HSD evolves an identity of its own, intimately linked to the present state of the art and to the historical antecedent disciplines interinfluencing each other. It is obvious, however, that this figure constitutes an oversimplification—once more, linearity of the printed page obscures the nonlinearity and confluence of actual flows of influence. A few additional reflections on HSD as an emerging field follow.

It is our strongly held view (1) that some existing boundaries and their specializations have become overly confining or, at least, that they do not serve to contribute to useful action-oriented knowledge (is OB research ever really *used*?) and (2) that action-oriented fields (for example, OD) need to draw more deeply and purposefully from the wells of an ever-accumulating research and theory, with the whole person in the whole organization in the whole society as a suitable core concept. Perhaps HSD may provide an orientation to facilitate this endeavor.

We should emphasize that, in past work as well as in the present line of discussion, *scholarship, practice,* and *teaching* (including the development of high-quality scholars and practitioners) are viewed as a triangle involving continuing interplay and mutual enrichment. For example, the use of groups and teams has spurred interest in theory and study of group dynamics; practical consideration of management and leadership styles has encouraged development of responsive research and measurement techniques; interest in improving productivity has stimulated research on productivity measurement and on the formulation of new organization-change strategies; and conceptualizations of interorganizational behavior have been derived from and in turn inspired theory on networks and network be-

Figure 1-1. Charting Human Systems Development.

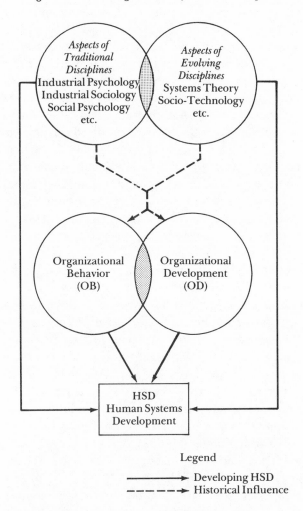

haviors. The three functions do not act in any unchanging sequence. Scholarship does not inevitably precede practice; it can also be the other way around. And simultaneous developments and effects are common.

It is perhaps fairly clear, given the tenor of what has been said, that human systems development is receptive to both qualitative and quantitative research methodologies (Massarik and

Ratoosh, 1965; Lazarsfeld, 1972; Douglas, 1976; Haberman, 1979). Humanistic values, in spite of some stereotypes to the contrary, do not imply a rejection of quantitative procedures. Rather, the crux of the matter is not "quantitative" *versus* "qualitative" or even multimethod or triangulation, but it is the choice of problem and its promise for constructively affecting the human condition. Only if this choice is auspicious does the issue of methodology become relevant. Thus, the burden is on the scholar (nonmethodologist) to suitably define the problem so that it may have near- or long-term human significance. This by no means argues for quick-fix, immediate-payoff research problems but does call for a full, responsible assessment by the scholar of the problem's probable meaning for making life more livable, inside or outside a particular organizational framework. (The judgment may or may not prove correct, of course, but who said it was going to be easy?)

In much of what has preceded, we have pointed to the inevitable presence of nonlinearity, ambiguity, and uncertainty— and continuing change. This has been said with the realization that the needs for predicability and stability appear as equally unavoidable counterpressures. We believe that human systems development and its scholar/practitioners must necessarily address this basic tension. And, beyond, we must face the fact that even favorite objectives—cooperation, team effort, participation, democracy, and the like—are completely intertwined and sometimes counterindicated by conflict, individual drive, acceptance of direction, and hierarchy.

Looking ahead, the time now seems ripe to fundamentally rethink prevailing boundaries and the paradigms of scholarship and practice that they define. Boundaries are, after all, arbitrary, and their meaning emerges from what occurs inside them and at their periphery. Even the term *interdisciplinary* assumes the pre-existence of some specified set of disciplines. But all is fluid, and all is unity. The dichotomies of Western thought, without artificial distortion, have begun to blend with Eastern elements of open voids and all-encompassing completion. East and West, too, may be dichotomies that will blend into one. But, on the way, there will be many steps, many false starts, and lots of small, incremental, technically neat ventures that holographically may reflect the whole while appearing disparate and fragmented. We believe that promising beginnings are in progress.

Some Perspectives on the Future

And where will these beginnings lead us in the future? Once again, no straight-line extrapolations are likely to fit in a world of rapid change, where values, technology, and theories are constantly in flux. When dealing with the future of a field or with a field in transition, predictions include the implicit (or sometimes explicit) reflection on issues that are central to the field's development. Where appropriate, we have tried to identify those issues as both professional concerns and emphases for the future. So, with a combination of hope and some trepidation, we may venture the following possibilities:

In the coming years, we anticipate a gradual convergence between human systems development as a profession and various humanistically oriented approaches to management. While organizational hierarchies are likely to remain one of the key structural characteristics of organizations, even now there is growing awareness of the importance of horizontal and peer relationships, and this dimension of organizational behavior is receiving much more attention as a topic of interest and study and as a critical aspect of organization performance. Relatively new organizational designs, such as the matrix, have grown in popularity and have emphasized the need to understand the more complex dynamics of organizational behavior and relationships. Whatever the future forms may be, and we will undoubtedly see further experimentations with various organizational structures, humanistic orientations will become increasingly prevalent among managers in our society. Some humanistic orientations will necessarily influence the personal and social consequences of organizational decisions, particularly those that promise to exert significant impact on a broad spectrum of publics or stakeholders. In this sense, greater cognizance of the social impacts and responsibilities of organizations and managers is likely.

While there has always been some interest in values and

the influence of values on organizational life, the mid-1980s have seen, in notable measure, a revisiting of this important subject and some overt recognition of values and ethics in company statements—a much more formal and explicit presentation of these values and ethical positions. Such overt statements are likely to become increasingly common in the future, as greater awareness and attention are devoted to values and human circumstances. Top policy makers as well as other managerial decision makers will, of course, continue to vary considerably in their personal styles. This implies that no single value position will emerge or will be all encompassing. So there will continue to be a range of approaches and beliefs about people in organizations and about organizations per se. But the trend, we believe, clearly points to more managers in the future who will hold positions that more closely resemble those of the contemporary (and effective) human systems development professional.

Human systems development professionals, including those based in academia and those who are primarily in professional practice, will no doubt be better trained and educated than they have been in the past. Knowing textbook theory or intervention procedure is simply not enough. This insufficiency is becoming increasingly recognized and is a current concern of the field. As future organizations become more complex, the world of the human systems development professional will in turn become more complicated. Current assessments are already pointing to the need for cognitive and interventional skills that provide greater understanding of these organizational complexities as well as the ability to deal effectively in these new and changing environments. Developing cognitive skills and an ability to utilize new interventional techniques, as well as the personal attributes required of the effective professional, is the educational challenge of the future.

The development of this field and the profession is contingent upon the effectiveness of the individual practitioner. Increasingly, peer review as a means for such quality control, as well as open evaluation by students, clients, and others affected, will become accepted and commonly aspired to. The theoretical and philosophical foundations of human systems development will be strengthened. This will be the case particularly in areas that have become excessively pragmatic or concerned exclusively with immediate or directly visible results. Basic theory of personality, small-group process, organizational dynamics, and the nature of culture and society will be increasingly important to the formulation of the field and to the knowledge base and practice modes of the professional. We hope it will become increasingly unnecessary to periodically rediscover concepts that have been thoroughly studied and established—the 1980s experience with "organizational culture" being a case in point. Numerous writers and practitioners alike have approached the culture concept with little sound understanding of the theoretical foundations previously established in the fields of cultural anthropology and sociology. Thus, after an initial flash of high visibility, it became necessary to re-establish and reincorporate the theoretical roots that had been unnecessarily bypassed.

The profession is already and will continue to become more technologically literate and sophisticated. There is increasing interest, for example, in the use of teleconferencing and computer networking for linking people in the profession and for long-distance work with clients. The technology and, therefore, the potential for communication are unlimited and may have a profound impact on the role of the human systems development professional. The field of human systems development (let us hope) will grow in its internal coherence and integration and in its positive impacts on a wide range of systems, from individual to society. The field will find itself less schizoid than it is presently—drawing hard lines between theory and practice, between quantitative and qualitative research, and between macro versus micro approaches to change. While organizations continue to remain an important focus and important arena for study and practice, work in the small group will recover its vitality. Focus on the individual, the person, will and should (our value position) be of concern, as well as emphasis on societal change and improvements.

Professionals will, of course, continue to specialize, so, as a natural process of choice, there will remain for some time the fields of organizational behavior, industrial psychology, and the like. The basic disciplines will continue to provide their special contributions. We speculate and hope that there will be a declining demarkation between these various forms of social science and less need to create boundaries between the different arenas of practice. After all, the basic intents and the fundamental goal remain the improvement of the human condition.

No Utopias or Eupsychias are expected; conflict at various levels will remain an existential fact. Still, there will be more obvious interdependencies, more open sharing of basic beliefs and differences, all vital and all necessary as the field of human systems development moves toward increasing maturity.

References

Ackoff, R. L., and Emery, F. E. *On Purposeful Systems.* Chicago: Aldine-Atherton, 1972.

Argyris, C. *Personality and Organization.* New York: Harper & Row, 1957.

Berrien, K. F. *General and Social Systems.* New Brunswick, N.J.: Rutgers University Press, 1968.

Buckley, W. (Ed.). *Modern Systems Research for the Behavioral Scientist.* Chicago: Aldine, 1968.

Campbell, J. (Ed.). *The Portable Jung.* New York: Viking Press, 1971.

Chung, K. H., and Megginson, L. C. *Organizational Behavior: Developing Managerial Skills.* New York: Harper & Row, 1981.

Culbert, S. A. *The Organization Trap and How to Get Out of It.* New York: Basic Books, 1974.

Culbert, S. A., and McDonough, J. J. *The Invisible War.* New York: Wiley, 1980.

Davis, L. E., and Cherns, A. B. (Eds.). *The Quality of Working Life.* Vol. 1: *Problems, Prospects, and the State of the Art.* New York: Free Press, 1975a.

Davis, L. E., and Cherns, A. B. (Eds.). *The Quality of Working Life.* Vol. 2: *Cases and Commentary.* New York: Free Press, 1975b.

Douglas, J. D. *Investigative Social Research.* Vol. 29. Beverly Hills, Calif.: Sage, 1976.

Feather, N. T. *Values in Education and Society.* New York: Free Press, 1975.

Follett, M. P. *Creative Experience.* New York: Longman, 1924.

Follett, M. P. *Dynamic Administration: The Collected Papers of Mary Parker Follett.* London: Pitman, 1941.

Foss, D. C. *The Value Controversy in Sociology: A New Orientation for the Discipline.* San Francisco: Jossey-Bass, 1977.

Friedman, N. *The Social Nature of Psychological Research: The Psychological Experiment as a Social Interaction.* New York: Basic Books, 1967.

Furst, C. *Origins of the Mind: Mind-Brain Connections.* Englewood Cliffs, N.J.: Prentice-Hall, 1979.

Goldberg, A. (Ed.). *Advances in Self Psychology.* New York: International University Press, 1980.

Goldstein, K. "Functional Disturbances in Brain Damage." In S. Arieti (Ed.), *American Handbook of Psychiatry.* New York: Basic Books, 1959.

Gordon, R. A., and Howell, J. E. *Higher Education for Business.* New York: Columbia University Press, 1959.

Granit, R. *The Purposive Brain.* Cambridge, Mass.: MIT Press, 1977.

Haberman, S. J. *Analysis of Qualitative Data.* Vol. 2. New York: Academic Press, 1979.

Hart, L. A. *How the Brain Works.* New York: Basic Books, 1975.

Hartmann, G. W. *Gestalt Psychology: A Survey of Facts and Principles.* New York: Ronald Press, 1935.

Husserl, E. *Ideas: General Introduction to Pure Phenomenology.* New York: Collier, 1975. (Originally published 1913.)

Kaplan, A. *The Conduct of Inquiry.* San Francisco: Chandler, 1964.

Kockelmans, J. J. (Ed.). *Phenomenology: The Philosophy of Edmund Husserl and Its Interpretation.* Garden City, N.Y.: Anchor Books, 1967.

Koestler, A. *The Sleepwalkers.* New York: Macmillan, 1959.

Koffka, K. *Principles of Gestalt Psychology.* New York: Harcourt Brace Jovanovich, 1935.

Köhler, W. *The Task of Gestalt Psychology.* Princeton, N.J.: Princeton University Press, 1969.

Kurtz, P. (Ed.). *Moral Problems in Contemporary Society*. Englewood Cliffs, N.J.: Prentice-Hall, 1969.

Lawrence, P. R., and Lorsch, J. W. *Organization and Environment: Managing Differentiation and Integration*. Boston: Division of Research, Harvard Business School, 1967.

Lazarsfeld, P. F. *Qualitative Analysis: Historical and Critical Essays*. Boston: Allyn & Bacon, 1972.

Lewin, K. *Principles of Topological Psychology*. New York: McGraw-Hill, 1936.

Lorsch, J. W., and Allen, S. A., III. *Managing Diversity and Interdependence: An Organizational Study of Multidivisional Firms*. Boston: Graduate School of Business Administration, Harvard University, 1973.

Luft, J. *Of Human Interaction*. Palo Alto, Calif.: National Press Books, 1969.

McGregor, D. *The Human Side of Enterprise*. New York: McGraw-Hill, 1960.

Massarik, F. "Some First (and Second) Thoughts on the Evaluation of Sensitivity Training: A Sensitivity Training Impact Model." *Interpersonal Development*, 1970, *1*, 129-158.

Massarik, F. "The 'Natural' Trainer: A Systematic-Normative View." In W. G. Dyer (Ed.), *Modern Theory and Method in Group Training*. New York: Van Nostrand Reinhold, 1972a.

Massarik, F. "Standards for Group Leadership." In L. N. Solomon and B. Berzon (Eds.), *New Perspectives on Encounter Groups*. San Francisco: Jossey-Bass, 1972b.

Massarik, F. "The Humanistic Organization: From Soft-Soap to Reality." In H. Meltzer (Ed.), *Humanizing Organizational Behavior*. Springfield, Ill.: Thomas, 1976.

Massarik, F., and Ratoosh, P. (Eds.). *Mathematical Explorations in Behavioral Science*. Homewood, Ill.: Irwin, Dorsey, 1965.

Mey, H. *Field-Theory: A Study of Its Application in the Social Sciences*. London: Routledge & Kegan Paul, 1972.

Mitroff, I. I., and Mason, R. O. "Stakeholders in Executive Decision Making." In S. Srivastva and Associates, *The Executive Mind*. San Francisco: Jossey-Bass, 1983.

Myers, I. B. *Myers-Briggs Type Indicator*. Palo Alto, Calif.: Consulting Psychologists Press, 1976.

Pierson, F. C., and others. *The Education of American Business-men.* New York: McGraw-Hill, 1959.

Psathas, G. (Ed.). *Phenomenological Sociology: Issues and Applications.* New York: Wiley-Interscience, 1973.

Rosenberg, M. *Conceiving the Self.* New York: Basic Books, 1979.

Sashkin, M. *Organizational Behavior: Concepts and Experiences.* Reston, Va.: Reston, 1984.

Singer, J. *Boundaries of the Soul.* Garden City, N.Y.: Anchor Books, 1973.

Skinner, B. F. *Beyond Freedom and Dignity.* New York: Bantam/Vintage, 1972.

Smith, M. B. *Social Psychology and Human Values.* Chicago: Aldine, 1969.

Steers, R. M. *Introduction to Organizational Behavior.* (2nd ed.) Glenview, Ill.: Scott, Foresman, 1984.

Tannenbaum, R., and Bugental, J. F. T. "Dyads, Clans, and Tribes." *Human Relations Training News,* Spring 1963a.

Tannenbaum, R., and Bugental, J. F. T. "Sensitivity Training and Being Motivation." *Journal of Humanistic Psychology,* Spring 1963b.

Tannenbaum, R., Weschler, I. R., and Massarik, F. *Leadership and Organization: A Behavioral Science Approach.* New York: McGraw-Hill, 1961.

Taylor, F. W. *Scientific Management.* New York: Harper & Row, 1947.

Vickers, B. (Ed.). *Occult and Scientific Mentalities in the Renaissance.* New York: Cambridge University Press, 1984.

Weschler, I. R., Massarik, F., and Tannenbaum, R. "The Self in Process: A Sensitivity Training Emphasis." In *Issues in Training.* Washington, D.C.: National Training Laboratories–National Education Association, 1962.

2

Human Experience, Phenomenology, and the Process of Deep Sharing

Fred Massarik

The Central Position of Human Experience

The social and behavioral sciences—indeed, most modes of inquiry that regard themselves as scientific—rely on concepts as basic tools of their trade. Whatever their specific purpose, concepts share one common characteristic: they are, perforce, *abstractions,* beneath which ebbs and flows complex reality. Specific concepts, or constructs, obviously are not physical entities or things; they resemble inventions created by scientists or others to organize some kind of underlying raw reality—that proverbial "buzzing, blooming confusion" of life so aptly described by William James. On this basis, concepts exist principally to provide devices for getting out from under this potentially overwhelming chaos and to provide starting points for order and predictability.

The conventional workaday world of science rests heavily on the selection and revision of concepts, on their rigorous manipulation (often but not necessarily by quantitative means), and on the drawing of conclusions, again frequently of a conceptual nature, based on the experimental or observational manipulations noted. All this is well and good, sometimes even exciting; at its best, it is enlightening and importantly contributory to the betterment of the human condition. And even when it is not a matter of "science," much of ordinary life also is transformed into conceptual and symbolic systems. But, in spite of the doubtless utility—nay, essentiality—of concepts as means for making sense in life and science, we need to remind ourselves with renewed wakefulness (perhaps this calls for the sounding of a gong or a flourish of trumpets) that behind all these concepts, whatever their organizing power and sophistication, there stands one pervasive and unavoidable fact: the wellspring of all this is *human experience.*

The basic datum of people's lives *as they are lived* is their experiencing; and, in this perspective, "people knowledge" is necessarily based on human experience as such. While experience is ubiquitous, it has not been a favorite topic or orientation in behavioral science, especially as it has become manifest in the United States during the past several decades. The field of organizational behavior, with occasional exceptions as in aspects of information processing (Taggart and Robey, 1981), likewise has not thoroughly committed itself to the examination of lived and lively human experiencing. If there has been a focus of attention on experience, it is perhaps lodged more typically within the realm of formal philosophy, particularly in classic phenomenology, than in empirical inquiry. I think—and feel—that this is too bad, and I hope that the situation will change. An empirical phenomenology of human systems is needed.

What's the basis for this view? I suppose that it has to do with the question "Is that all there is?" in existence. I should like to urge a qualified "yes" response to this query. It seems to me that, adopting a genuinely radical view in the study of people (radical in the sense of bearing on the field's roots), it is the raw experiencing that goes on within our ever-present stream of feeling and thinking that becomes the *raw* material for subsequent concepts and symbols. Such experience constitutes the ultimate data source of human life as lived, holding in abeyance for the moment our interpretations of life based on external observation. Optimally, the study of experience becomes an area of direct empirical investigation extending far beyond presently existing forms.

Though such direct study as a systematic mode for dealing with human data may not be in the prevailing "mainstream," enclaves of hope emerge. Three examples are noted:

- *Gendlin's approach: the creation of meaning and focusing.* Gendlin (1962) clearly draws our attention to the fundamental nature of experiencing. He, too, finds himself enmeshed in the inherently problematical process of trying to fully describe just what it is that is meant by "experiencing." However, having addressed this issue within the prevailing limitations of language and knowledge, he proceeds to adapt the notion of experiencing (we assiduously avoid the term *concept* of experiencing) to psychological theory and to psychotherapy. Elsewhere (Hendricks, 1984), the redirection of the counsellee's thoughts and feelings to the unfolding events and their immediate experienced reality (together with its relationship to various modes of nondirective or client-centered procedures) emerges as an important modality of personal change. The procedure of "focusing," calling for careful and intentional consideration of specified experience, further pursues this theme.
- *Mahrer's approach to psychology and psychiatry.* Mahrer (1978; Rowan, 1983) makes use of the experiencing process as a major organizing principle for a range of theoretical and psychotherapeutic approaches. In a lengthy, sometimes diffuse book, on occasion moving afield from the focus on experiencing indicated by the title, he examines the breadth of the therapeutic process in the context of humanistic theory and human development.
- *Ihde's experimental approach.* Quite different is Ihde's (1977) work. Ihde, taking an explicitly phenomenological stance, seeks to orient aspects of experimental work, particularly in perception, in terms of various controlled, predesigned modes of experiencing. Although this work is less naturalistic then Gendlin's or Mahrer's approaches, the experiencing process still remains central in it.

In a more applied generic sense, much training/learning effort, particularly in the group-training field (for example, the National Training Laboratories, UCLA's University Extension Leadership Laboratories, encounter groups, and so on) has long held to the emphasis on the experienced "here and now." The issue of phenomenology as a source for the study of present human experience is more complex. This complexity may be traced to the history of the field—a topic quite beyond the bounds of this chapter. In its traditional sense, phenomenology developed as a field of philosophy; indeed, philosophy of quite remote origin. In its most relevant manifestations, considering particularly the work of Edmund Husserl, it grew within the somewhat rarefied atmosphere of the German Academy at the turn of the century. There was little readiness (rather, in fact, there was some explicit opposition) to meld this form of philosophical inquiry with empirical styles of psychological inquiry. Nor were direct methods available at the time for the handling of potential empirical data, notably the complex text and extensive protocol that, for better or worse, emerge as *reports* of human experience. While methods such as theme and content analysis (De Sola Pool, 1959; Hall and Van De Castle, 1966) have had substantial standing for some years, it is only more recently that technologies such as those associated with word processing offer hope for the procedural handling of the necessarily complex textual data.

No one technology or conceptual approach is likely to provide an "instant fix" for the need to improve the level of understanding of human experience. However, both the more abstract philosophical foundation and the recent promising developments in new-paradigm psychological thought (Reason and Rowan, 1981), as well as in data-processing technology, establish foundations for progress. At the conceptual level, it is necessary to take a further look at the nature of human experience, as the basis for required research and action.

The Experience Sequence

"Raw experience" is just that—experience as such, intrinsically, the direct involvement of the person in the event itself.

We shall need to make an explicit effort to examine this raw experience and to develop some typology of its aftermath.

Raw Experience (Experience A). Paradoxically, not much more can be said about raw experience. And yet one is tempted to elaborate on it, as has been the wont of the philosophically oriented phenomenologists. In some sense, in the latter connection lies the road to disaster: One is tempted to dissect and to "explain" in words an event that by its nature resists "wordification." We shall try to avoid this trap here, providing as the basis for this discourse the following working definition:

Raw experience is the experienced event itself, the totality of ideations, cognitions, and sensory impressions, including feelings, as the event itself occurs (Laing, 1967). It is what is happening *now*; while we are experiencing *it* (the event in consideration), we are too busy with experiencing (it) to analyze it or to talk about it. In terms of traditional phenomenology (Husserl, 1975; Spiegelberg, 1965; Schutz, 1970), raw experience refers to *das Ding an Sich*—"the thing (or, more properly, the event) in itself." A related German term is illuminating: *das Erlebnis,* the living and immediate process of involvement in a living experience. The root word *Leben,* "life," is central to the word *Erlebnis,* which connotes the process of involvement with the full life event.

Raw experience is inherently nonverbal. If an experience itself involves words, these words are experienced as part of the pattern, but they are experienced as *such,* not as symbolic reflection. By way of illustration, drinking a glass of milk is raw experience; reading the morning headlines is raw experience. In present context, it is experien*cing* that is central; in the former instance, milk drinking is at issue, in the latter instance, headline reading is at issue; but it is the *process,* not the presence of words, that is focal. *While it is happening,* neither event is expressible.

Immediate Reflection (Experience B). Immediate reflection is a maximally time-proximate internal sensing of raw experience (*A*)—quick follow-on reaction to *A*. Soon after *A* has occurred, immediate reflection (*B*) looks back on *A*. In this connection, *A* constitutes the "target" experience at which *B* aims. Immediate reflection may be both verbal and nonverbal; it potentially involves both some thinking and feeling with respect to raw experience and some initial, often rudimentary meaning attribution. It may constitute an initial attempt to make sense out of what happened at A, quite soon after A has occurred; it may be described as a fairly simple, relatively prompt reaction to what went on at A. While immediate reflection involves some structuring of the target experience, it still remains largely inchoate.

Responsive Reflection (Experience C). Responsive reflection is constituted by a purposeful reflective response to target experience A, at a determinate later time. While, in B, A is denoted implicitly as target experience, the concept of targeting clearly applies more distinctly in C than in B. In B, it is a matter of a quick reaction, while, in C, the process is guided explicitly in an effort to "figure out" what happened at A. Sufficient time has elapsed so that the person who is doing the experiencing can genuinely look back at A, responding to A retrospectively. Typically, this process contains a substantial verbal component, though nonverbal aspects are ever present. In responsive reflection, meaning—responsive meaning—becomes a major concern. A specific effort is made to structure the target experience with some care and to see it in meaningful context. (Later in this chapter we shall reconsider the meaning of meaning.)

Cumulative, or Meditative, Reflection (Experience D). Cumulative, or meditative, reflection (D) involves a purposeful cumulative review—of target experience A as now interpreted, as well as of concatenations of subsequent experiences, including prior immediate reflection (B) and responsive reflection (C) bearing on target experience A. When D occurs, substantial process is generated involving an intensive and thorough backward look at A, its chain of prior interpretations B, C, and so on, and its current meaning interpretation. In this fashion, D may be viewed as a meditation on A and as a significant examination of its nature and ramifications. Substantial verbal but necessarily also nonverbal components appear. Efforts are made to transform the previously experienced nonverbal into verbal terms that can be shared with others. Cumulative, or meditative, reflection results in *meditative meaning*.

Considering the entire process at this stage, we may view

it as an intensive effort to make sense concerning what it was that happened at *A,* our own subsequent thoughts and feelings concerning *A* (that is, *B* and *C* in its various subsequent forms), and a holistic analysis and synthesis of the occurrences, at many levels. From this, the essential aspects of target experience *A* eventually may be gleaned, and we may seek to formulate its *essence.*

For purposes of discourse, we have differentiated the preceding types of experiences in order to consider them as an experience sequence. Such segmentation is convenient for analytical purposes. It does not, however, represent appropriately the intertwined, streamlike character of human experience as lived. The position expressed here does not propose a neat one-two-three-four order of events; it proposes only that some potential sequencing through time may be elucidated from the complex and often convoluted way that real-life experience unfolds. Further, as we reconsider each of the experience "entities" in the experience sequence, we note readily not only that *A* constitutes a potential target experience but that *B, C, D,* and their like may, in turn, also be recognized as potential target experiences. As such, each would generate its own corresponding sequence of *A', B', C', D',* and so on. It simply becomes a matter of deciding what (*which* experience) we wish to explore, then proceeding in its exploration in terms of the sequence.

In summary, the proposed strategy generated by the experience sequence fully recognizes the complex and flowing character of human experience. At the same time, it suggests that a discipline is needed that is analytical (as in differentiation of experience types) as well as synthetic (as in the meditative reflection and in the seeking of essences) to provide a basis for understanding the relevant phenomena and for useful action.

The Concept of Meaning

Because the notion of *meaning* is critical in the study of human experience and in its present examination, we need to interpose this brief reconsideration. Contributions from a variety of viewpoints are elsewhere presented (Ogden and Richards, 1946; Osgood, Suci, and Tannenbaum, 1961; Creelman, 1966), yet, beyond the commonsense and overly abstract definitions, *working* conceptualizations of *meaning* are few and far between. Here, we suggest a fourfold approach, to be viewed *as a whole*, as a basis for practical reconsideration.

Experience, in the sense of the experience sequence discussed earlier, constitutes the essential starting point. It is useless to speak of meaning as bland abstraction: meaning cannot exist by itself; it is necessarily a quality found in experience and only in experience. Meaning (especially in the sense of responsive and meditative meaning and perhaps, in rudimentary form, in immediate reflection) evolves if the person (the experiencer) perceives significantly differentiated antecedent conditions preceding the target experience and/or subsequent anticipations following it. Thus, the experience is lodged in context; the person who is doing the experiencing is conscious of some conditions that appear relevant and that are perceived to have occurred prior to the experience, as well as conditions that are anticipated subsequent to this experience. One might characterize this situation as the person's capacity for knowing where the experience is coming from and where it is going.

One notes that this formulation does not argue for strict cause-and-effect connections as a necessary condition. Rather, the crux of the issue is the person's potential for exploring, in his or her life world, hypothetical connections among discernible factors. For meaning to prevail, the person needs to be able to explore, at a mental or cognitive level, what might be related to what, at least in some rudimentary fashion. The experiencer needs to be able to see possible connections among the forces that he or she views as relevant in the situation as a whole. Some sense of structure (for example, Tolman's cognitive maps, Lewin's life space, Husserl's *Lebenswelt*) exists for the experiencer. One need not assume that this cognitive structuring represents either "truth" or "causality"; rather, it is the presence of perceived structure per se that is critical. This process, particularly as it develops under conditions of ambiguity and stress in the external world, has been described elsewhere as "search for meaning" (Frankl, 1963, 1978) and, in "consistency theories," as an often distortional response (Feldman, 1966). It all amounts to the pervasive need for meaning as an aspect of the human condition and to the creation of meaning—sometimes artfully and with only the remotest connection to external realities—as the basis for comfort or coping.

Associated with the definition of antecedent conditions and subsequent anticipations is the notion of *affect,* or *valence* (Lewin, 1936; Leeper, 1943). The experiencing person feels good or bad about these pre-existing conditions and anticipations. Rarely do meanings exist, at least in daily experiencing, as purely bland and neutral. The very process of structuring experienced events in context, as noted earlier, calls for the mobilization of positive or negative response exceeding some discernible threshold.

The considerations relating to meaning suggest that one may conceive of a continuum or perhaps a typology of meanings, given various combinations of structure in antecedent conditions and subsequent anticipations and the positive/negative affect levels prevailing at various points in the *Lebenswelt.* Without necessarily developing details here, it would seem that various intensities and patterns of meaning may be distinguished in the context of human experience.

"Tuning In": The Phenomenological Interview and Its Variants

We still have found no empirical way to directly observe human experience. We remain dependent on manifestations of various kinds—typically, observation of behavior and/or consideration of verbal productions of the experiencer—by which we draw inferences concerning the other person's experience. This is, of course, an issue steeped in the history of philosophical thought and in commonsense reflection on the process of understanding what goes on in the minds of people. Without reopening here this Pandora's box of argument and speculation, we take account of one of several avenues designed to lead us toward deeper understanding of another human being: the phenomenological interview.

Phenomenological interviewing has been described at

some length elsewhere (Massarik, 1981, 1983). The essential aspects of the phenomenological (or phenomenal) interview may be summarized thus: The interview is characterized by maximal mutuality of trust, the attainment of a genuine and deeply experienced caring between interviewer and interviewee, and a commitment to joint search for shared understanding. Interviewer and interviewee respond to one another as total persons, ready to actively examine and disclose both remote and accessible aspects of their lives, including experiences, present responses, and imageries. The relationship involves fundamental equality and concurring commitment to the quest at hand. The time frame is fluid, unbound by the usual constraints of a therapeutic hour or sometimes even by consideration of night and day. Interviewer and interviewee have, within the limits of their life constraints, free access to one another; ideas explored on one occasion may be temporarily laid aside, only to be re-examined in a changed context later. There is little by way of simplistic question-and-answer exchange; rather, free-form modes of communication and iterative opportunities for review and clarification identify the process. Interviewer and interviewee aspire to enter, with shared commitment and mutual caring, each other's experienced worlds (Massarik, 1981).

Phenomenological interviewing, then, involves mutual sharing between interviewer and interviewee. While the interviewer initiates the process, typically in the framework of a defined role, it involves mutual search rather than question-response cycles or even the less clearly circumscribed inquiry, explicitly from interviewer to interviewee, that sets the frame in depth interviews.

In the phenomenological interview, the interviewer sets aside his or her pre-existing assumptions and enters as fully as possible into a shared search with the interviewee in quest of understanding a phenomenon. This phenomenon is constituted by the experience or experiences of the interviewee. What emerges resembles a natural unfolding of shared experiences, following the model of responsive reflection or—better still—of cumulative (or meditative) reflection. Within this frame of mutuality, the exploration seeks to understand a pattern of events, particularly as experienced by the interviewee. It provides an elucidation of the meaning of the experiences examined in responsive and cumulative reflection and, under the best conditions, the crystallizing of *new* insights and their derived meanings. The emergent process thus generates a deeper understanding of the experiences involved and a significant discovery, for both interviewer and interviewee, of meanings associated with these experiences.

"Deep Sharing": A Process Without a Name?

The phenomenological interview is but one of a genre of interpersonal relationships that involve closeness among two or more participants in the interaction. This generic process through which people affirm one another's personal and social lives remains less distinct and more elusive than we may wish it to be—both in terms of rigorous knowledge and as a means for the enrichment of human well-being. It also is noteworthy that, somehow, this kind of interpersonal sharing and enhancement has received no appropriate label in the literature. Indeed, we may search for approximations, such as "mutually therapeutic relationship," "unconditional regard," and "therapeutic insight." However, in every instance, something appears lacking, or the chosen concept addresses only one aspect of this generic process. Before we attempt a more formal definition of deep sharing, we offer this example:

> A husband and wife are sitting in the living room, late at night after the good TV shows have come and gone. They get to talking—about many things, but especially about how they first met and about what their being together means to them now. They chat about big things and little things, about ups and downs (the dinner out the other evening, the refrigerator apparently self-destructing, leaking water all over the kitchen), about places they have been or plan to visit—Paris five years ago, the Kahala in Hawaii next Valentine's Day—about what it would be like to move to an apartment or condo when the big house gets to be *too* big for just the two.

The following scene provides another illustration:

> "Now I understand it," she said, at first weakly. Then her voice strengthened, and she repeated, "Now I understand it—I really do." She leaned back on the couch, reflecting that it was not like the couch she remembered seeing in books about Freud but rather more like a modernistic recliner. She looked over toward where her therapist sat, at a tiny table immediately to her right. They both smiled, and the therapist (also a woman) joined in. "Now both of us understand it." Then she added: "I hadn't looked at it this way before either; maybe now we know what ought to be happening next."

Finally, consider this passage from Maslow's (1965) *Eupsychian Management*:

> The word Eupsychia can also be taken [to] ... mean "moving toward psychological health" or "Healthward." It can imply the actions taken to foster and encourage such movement, whether by a psychotherapist or a teacher. It can refer to mental or social conditions which make health more likely. Or it can be taken as an ideal limit; i.e. the far goals of therapy, education, or work [p. xi].

The preceding passages point to shared understanding—indeed, to understanding that emerges from sharing. The nature of the setting can vary widely, from a conversation across a dinner table to a psychotherapeutic relationship to the actualization of personal and interpersonal health. That which is shared, if it is named at all, is some *essence of meanings*—meanings in the precise sense proposed in this chapter. There is emerging significance in context with affect and with connections perceived among past, present, and anticipated future experiences. Deep sharing thus may be regarded as a core process that prevails in the enhancement of the person's psychological and social well-being, even as it presently lacks a clear formal label (Lepp, 1966; Edwards, 1982; Gurdin, 1982). Somehow, the structure of scientific language apparently has not caught up. At the mar-

gin, the term *psychotherapeutic,* for instance, is laden with the
burden of mental illness as starting point; that is, it implies an
initial element or some sort of existing malaise that needs to be
ameliorated or eliminated, typically by formal intervention—by
therapy. In turn, this approach adduces the medical model of
patient and doctor, of the doctor healing the sufferer. For all its
merit, the unidirectional nature of this process is evident. "Mutually therapeutic" clearly is a preferred formulation, although
the quasi-medical context of therapy, with its deficiency orientation, remains. Maslow's notion of "moving toward psychological health" or "healthward," especially when interpreted with a
view toward his ideas on self-actualization, comes still closer to
the presently intended position. It lacks, however, in its semantic construction, reference to the fundamentally *interpersonal*
nature of the process involved. At this stage, I am not satisfied
with any of the available designations of this essential and
ubiquitous process, not even with the one presented here—
"deep sharing." Perhaps as a convenient shorthand, it focuses
on a key aspect—the giving to one another, in some mutual
sense, of some important quality.

While the words "deep sharing" do not say it all, one
might extend the phrase to "deep sharing of meanings that enhance our humanness." In more detail, such deep sharing carries those who share through an exploration of their past, present, and anticipated future experiences, together with vivid
involvement in the relevant affect and in the milieu of mutually understood context. It is the genuine sharing of experiences
and of their correlative meanings, including meanings that are
mutually discovered as this process proceeds, that enlivens and
empowers deep sharing as a critically significant aspect of human life.

Deep sharing, then, occurs outside of as well as within
such formal settings as psychotherapy, T-group, encounter
group, and the like—as in such situations as plain folks talking to
one another about things that matter, in the very mundane environments of everyday living. It is the "good stuff" of ordinary
personal and professional life, as it is expressed and evolved in
those interpersonal relationships that enhance our being and

that give us a deeper grasp of what our experiences are all about. Deep sharing serves importantly in helping a person to examine, in joint effort with one or more other people, his or her experiences, in a committed search for meaning. If the initial focus is raw experience, it is this committed search for meaning that moves toward cumulative, meditative reflection. The active interpersonal relationship that develops in deep sharing and that helps deep sharing to develop facilitates the intensive exploration of experience streams. This exploration is not a simple linear process; it evolves contours all its own, at various levels of clarity and confusion and with many layers of alternative realities experienced by the participants. Logic or neatness is not the likely result of this process; instead, complex patterns of meaning are brought forth. Such meaning patterns (considered, for example, by such existentially oriented authors as May, 1983; Frankl, 1978; and Binswanger, 1963) constitute a crucial element in assuring personality growth and change, positive mental health, prevention of suicide and the affirmation of life, and effective relationships in family and organization. To make headway in expanding this beneficent impact, we need to know more about what deep sharing is, what it can become, how it is linked to existing knowledge of human systems, and how it infuses meaning into the experienced realities of our daily lives.

References

Binswanger, L. *Being-in-the-World.* New York: Basic Books, 1963.

Creelman, M. B. *The Experimental Investigation of Meaning: A Review of the Literature.* New York: Springer, 1966.

De Sola Pool, I. (Ed.). *Trends in Content Analysis.* Urbana: University of Illinois Press, 1959.

Edwards, D. G. *Existential Psychotherapy: The Process of Caring.* New York: Gardner Press, 1982.

Feldman, S. (Ed.). *Cognitive Consistency: Motivational Antecedents and Behavioral Consequents.* New York: Academic Press, 1966.

Frankl, V. E. *Man's Search for Meaning.* New York: Washington Square Press, 1963.

Frankl, V. E. *The Unheard Cry for Meaning: Psychotherapy and Humanism.* New York: Simon & Schuster, 1978.

Gendlin, E. T. *Experiencing and the Creation of Meaning: A Philosophical and Psychological Approach to the Subjective.* New York: Free Press, 1962.

Gurdin, J. B. "The Therapy of Friendship." Paper presented at annual meeting of the Society for the Study of Social Problems, San Francisco, September 1982.

Hall, C. S., and Van De Castle, R. L. *The Content Analysis of Dreams.* New York: Appleton-Century-Crofts, 1966.

Hendricks, M. N. "A Focusing Group: Model for a New Kind of Group Process." *Small Group Behavior,* 1984, *15* (4), 155-171.

Husserl, E. *Ideas: General Introduction to Pure Phenomenology.* New York: Collier Books, 1975. (Originally published, in German, 1913.)

Ihde, D. *Experimental Phenomenology: An Introduction.* New York: Capricorn Books, 1977.

Laing, R. D. *The Politics of Experience.* New York: Pantheon, 1967.

Leeper, R. W. *Lewin's Topological and Vector Psychology.* Eugene: University of Oregon, 1943.

Lepp, I. *The Ways of Friendship.* New York: Macmillan, 1966.

Lewin, K. *Principles of Topological Psychology.* New York: McGraw-Hill, 1936.

Mahrer, A. R. *Experiencing: A Humanistic Theory of Psychology and Psychiatry.* New York: Brunner/Mazel, 1978.

Maslow, A. H. *Eupsychian Management.* Homewood, Ill.: Irwin-Dorsey, 1965.

Massarik, F. "The Interviewing Process Re-Examined." In P. Reason and J. Rowan (Eds.), *Human Inquiry: A Source Book of New Paradigm Research.* New York: Wiley, 1981.

Massarik, F. "Searching for Essence in Executive Experience." In S. Srivastva and Associates, *The Executive Mind: New Insights on Managerial Thought and Action.* San Francisco: Jossey-Bass, 1983.

May, R. *The Discovery of Being: Writings in Existential Psychology.* New York: Norton, 1983.

Ogden, C. K., and Richards, I. A. *The Meaning of Meaning: A Study of the Influence of Language upon Thought and of the Science of Symbolism.* New York: Harcourt Brace Jovanovich, 1946. (Originally published 1923.)

Osgood, C. E., Suci, G. J., and Tannenbaum, P. H. *The Measurement of Meaning.* (3rd ed.) Urbana: Institute of Communications Research, University of Illinois, 1961.

Reason, P., and Rowan, J. (Eds.). *Human Inquiry: A Source Book of New Paradigm Research.* New York: Wiley, 1981.

Rowan, J. "Experiencing Mahrer." *Self and Society,* 1983, *11* (1), 1-18.

Schutz, A. *On Phenomenology and Social Relations.* Chicago: University of Chicago Press, 1970.

Spiegelberg, H. *The Phenomenological Movement: A Historical Introduction.* Vol. 1. (2nd ed.) The Hague, Netherlands: Martinus Nijhoff, 1965.

Taggart, W., and Robey, D. "Minds and Managers: On the Dual Nature of Human Information Processing and Management." *Academy of Management Review,* 1981, *6* (2), 187-195.

3

Personal Meaning: Its Loss and Rediscovery

Robert W. Hanna

American business appears to be undergoing a period of dramatic restructuring. It is pressured from the outside by wide-ranging economic changes, massive deregulation, intense international competition, and rapidly advancing technologies, while it is often undermined from within by complacent management, outmoded organizational structures, aging plants and equipment, and high labor costs. Many American industries and organizations have been rudely confronted with the choice between dramatic change and collapse.

In response, new product and service organizations have blossomed as older ones have either declined, retrenched, or reorganized. Along with the excitement, anxiety, frustration, and uncertainty of these dramatic organizational and industrial transitions, there have been many painful dislocations, much stress, and a plethora of new and difficult problems. More than ever, there is a heightened concern for organizational productivity and effective leadership and an intensive search for the latest knowledge and techniques that promise increased motivation, commitment, and innovation.

This chapter provides insight into the complex, interrelated forces at play in our current situation and the way human beings must come to terms with them. Specifically, this chapter advances the premise that we are in a time of wide-scale cultural transformation, of which business organizations are only a part, and that the basic human problem that results is the breakup and dissolution of collective and individual meaning. It is through an understanding and conscious facilitation of the discovery of both organizational and individual meaning that managers are most likely to be successful in establishing new organizational directions and in eliciting the motivation, commitment, and innovation necessary to pursue them.

Cultural Transformation

Since the late 1960s, a number of observers have accumulated evidence suggesting that our culture is in the midst of a dramatic transition. For example, George Leonard (1972), former senior editor of *Look* magazine, wrote in his prescient work *The Transformation* that as a culture we were coming to the end of one line of human development and rapidly moving toward a new one.

> The anticipatory sense of the coming of a new age is shared by soothsayers, astrologers, and others of a visionary turn of mind. At the same time, social observers of various persuasions have examined the possibility of a forthcoming overturn in the way society in the industrial nations is organized. These observers—Daniel Bell, Kenneth Boulding, Herman Kahn, Alvin Toffler, Marshall McLuhan, Jean-François Revel, William Irwin Thompson, and Buckminster Fuller among others— have engaged in the difficult task of describing the world of tomorrow in the language of today. The difficulty shows up in those very terms they have chosen to characterize the future—"post-civilization," "post-industrial society," "Global Village," "super-industrial society". . . .
>   It is my thesis, however, that the current period . . . represents the beginning of the most thoroughgoing change in the quality of human existence since the creation of an agricultural sur-

plus brought about the birth of civilized states some five thousand years ago. . . . I take the term "Transformation" to stand for both the process that spells the end of Civilization and the period during which the process takes place. . . .

Most of our current troubles, from free-floating anxiety to the breakdown of craftsmanship, can be traced ultimately to the lack of a vivid unifying principle or belief system; the biblical dictum that where there is no vision the people perish is by no means merely metaphorical. I believe that the time is overdue for the emergence of a new vision of human and social destiny and being [pp. 1-3].

Leonard cautions that the rough outlines of the new paradigm, or world view, will be filled in not only by the forces of the transformation but also by the forces against it. While he expresses concern that the results could be ominous if the resistances of institutional forces are too great, he does offer the hope that the new vision will be both bold enough and broad enough to mobilize the spirit and energy to succeed.

With the arrival of the 1980s came a more widespread recognition that a major transition was indeed under way. For example, Toffler (1970), who had previously emphasized the personal and social costs of rapid change in his book *Future Shock,* now set out to present a comprehensive picture of a new civilization bursting into existence. In *The Third Wave* (Toffler, 1981), he notes that a civilization develops its own "superideology," a collection of processes and principles that it uses to explain its reality and to justify its own existence. But he sees the support systems of our current "Second Wave" reality (the 300-year-old industrialized civilization) in trouble. For Toffler, the old ways of thinking no longer fit the facts. "The world that is fast emerging from the clash of new values and technologies, new geopolitical relationships, new life-styles and modes of communication, demands wholly new ideas and analogies, classifications and concepts. We cannot cram the embryonic world of tomorrow into yesterday's conventional cubbyholes. . . . Humanity faces a quantum leap forward. It faces the deepest social upheaval and creative restructuring of all time. Without clearly recognizing it, we are engaged in building a remarkable new civilization from the ground up. This is the meaning of the Third Wave" (pp. 2-10).

Like Leonard, Toffler predicted that there will be a struggle between the familiar old order and the uncertain new order. He suggests that the transition period will be marked by extreme social disruption, wild economic swings, political turbulence, violence, and wars and the threat of wars. The clash of the two civilizations will present tremendous dangers. Nonetheless, he remains optimistic that a new society will take shape, and he goes on to outline many of the developments that are or will be taking form.

While Toffler describes the external features of where we came from and where we might be going, two other observers of the transformation focus their attention on the changes taking place within the human being. Marilyn Ferguson (1980) examined the transformational process that she feels both underlies and leads the cultural transition highlighted by Leonard and Toffler. The embodiment of this process is a network of people that she calls the "Aquarian Conspiracy." The conspirators cut across all income and education levels, occupational groups, and professions. Although some are vocal or famous, most are silent and unknown. Their common link is not a political doctrine but the desire to facilitate the turnabout in consciousness of a critical number of individuals, enough to bring about a renewal of society.

The turnabout in consciousness that Ferguson refers to is the state of being conscious of one's consciousness. "You are keenly aware that you have awareness. In effect, this is a new perspective that sees other perspectives—a paradigm shift. . . . Most of us go through our waking hours taking little notice of our thought processes: how the mind moves, what it fears, what it needs, how it talks to itself, what it brushes aside; the nature of our hunches; the feel of our highs and lows; our misperceptions. For the most part we eat, work, converse, worry, hope, plan, make love, shop—all with minimal thought about how we *think*" (p. 68). Ferguson considers it the beginning of personal transformation when one first pays attention to the flow of attention itself. Drawing on a wide range of support, including the most recent developments in modern physics, she posits that the mind is approaching the point of tremendous paradigm shifts, offering the likelihood of creating equally dramatic changes in our civilization. This transition is not in the distant future; it is already in progress. For Ferguson, its outcomes are dependent on how many of us join the conspiracy.

The respected physicist Fritjof Capra also argues that we are in the midst of a vast cultural transformation. In his book *The Turning Point* (Capra, 1983), he offers the basic premise that our society is in crisis because an outdated world view—the mechanistic world view of Cartesian-Newtonian science—is being applied to a reality that can no longer be understood in terms of its concepts. He sees the resolution as a transformation in our thinking toward a new paradigm—a fundamental change in our thoughts, perceptions, and values, already visible in many fields and disciplines. "The sixties and seventies have generated a whole series of social movements that all seem to go in the same direction, emphasizing different aspects of the new vision of reality. . . . This new vision includes the emerging systems view of life, mind, consciousness, and evolution; the corresponding holistic approach to health and healing; the integration of Western and Eastern approaches to psychology and psychotherapy; a new conceptual framework for economics and technology; and an ecological and feminist perspective which is spiritual in its ultimate nature and will lead to profound changes in our social and political structures" (pp. 16–17).

Among the observers previously mentioned, there is much agreement that our world is in a state of crisis and is undergoing an unprecedented transformation—a transformation more readily acknowledged every year. As with any crisis, there is both danger and opportunity. Organizations and their managers can do much to ensure a beneficial outcome. However, they must be willing to attend to the more basic problem for us all during this period—the breakup and dissolution of individual meaning.

The Question of Meaning

In the 1930s, the noted psychologist Carl Jung (1954) made the following observation about people and meaning: "To the extent that a man is untrue to the law of his being and does not rise to personality [individuality], he has failed to realize his life's meaning. Fortunately, in her kindness and patience, Nature never puts the fatal question as to the meaning of their lives into the mouths of most people. And where no one asks, no one need answer" (p. 314). Since that time, much of the guidance and structure of family, traditional religion, and institutional authority, which were the sources of meaning for most, have been lost. In Toffler's terms, the breakup of the Second Wave is dissolving structure in many individual lives before the new structure-providing institutions of the Third Wave are put into place. The evidence is all around us that the question of meaning echoes more frequently and more plaintively through the mouths and minds of many. One has only to read the daily papers or watch the evening news to wonder about the high levels of crime, violence, and child abuse or the increased alcoholism and drug use or the headlong, often empty quest for success and material possessions.

The growing problem of individual meaning has been increasingly reflected in our arts, religion, and psychology since the upheavals of the late 1960s. At the midpoint of the 1970s, Federico Fellini, the film director who captured the euphoric escapism of earlier decades in the film *La Dolce Vita,* saw "a change and loss of psychological cohesion. . . . People are losing their faith in the future. Our education, unfortunately, molded us for a life that was always tensed toward a series of achievements—school, military service, a career and, as a grand finale, the encounter with the heavenly father. But now that our tomorrows no longer appear in that optimistic perspective, we are left with a feeling of impotence and fear. People who can no longer believe in a 'better tomorrow' logically tend to behave with a desperate egotism. They are preoccupied with protecting, brutally if necessary, those little sensual appetites. To me, this is the most dangerous feature of the 70's" (*Time,* 1974, vol. 104 (15), pp. 7-11).

Religion attempts, through its system of beliefs, to give meaning to the age-old sufferings of humankind. As our major Western religious systems have increasingly lost their ability to elicit spiritual experience in their followers, the remaining shell of doctrine is less able to provide a believable means to deal with suffering. With our reliance on drugs for pain, a loss of belief in an afterlife, and church membership increasingly for social purposes, as Kübler-Ross (1969) points out, "we are deprived of the church's former purpose, namely, to give hope, a purpose in tragedy here on earth, and an attempt to understand and bring meaning to otherwise unacceptable painful occurrences in our life" (p. 15). It is this failure of religion that has ushered in not only the various cults but the charismatic, fundamentalist, and Eastern religious movements.

Also, with increasing frequency, a loss of meaning has been noted in the problems that people bring to therapy and counseling. Perry London (1974) described therapy as a social index, since it reacts to the changing ailments of its clients. He noted three shifts in psychological problems occurring during this century, each in response to a different psychological motif dominating Western society. First was psychoanalysis, which dealt with exposing unconscious material and uncovering post-Victorian repression. After World War II, behavior modification, crisis intervention, and marathon therapy attempted to resolve the problems of the "Age of Anxiety." However, since the early 1970s, London notes that "people's preoccupations and needs have shifted from the relief of pain and discomfort to the achievement of meaning and value in life. We have moved from the modest hope of living without fear to the grand need for existential purpose, for positive life goals" (p. 67).

Given the dramatic transformations occurring in our culture, communities, institutions, and organizations, the question of meaning becomes a disturbing problem, both individually and for any collective effort. For some, this transition period offers an opportunity to achieve deep self-fulfillment through unique individual expression as pressures to conform to a narrow set of norms and expectations are reduced. For others, it means being thrust forward into a turbulent future while the foundations for living collapse beneath them. For all, it is a time when cultural meaning is leaking away as basic beliefs, values, and assumptions dissolve before our eyes. Therefore, it becomes our task to continually discover new meaning to replace that which is lost and to resist the pull of depression and debilitating despair. Whether for ourselves or in order to help others, an understanding of both the sources of human meaning and the process of meaning formulation proves helpful to the task.

Sources of Meaning

For many, meaning tends to be a background issue, until there is an abrupt loss. As Weisskopf-Joelson (1967) suggests, "as long as life is meaningful, people tend to think and speak relatively little about its meaning. But as soon as there is a lack or absence of meaning, the problem of meaning plays an important role in a person's awareness and expression" (p. 359). In her comprehensive study of meaning, she provides three general categories that account for what people mean when they say that their lives are without meaning. These categories provide a framework for presenting the general sources of meaning.

Meaning as Explanation or Interpretation of Life. For some, absence of meaning is experienced as a lack of an explanation or interpretation of their lives. To provide meaning, an explanation has to be comprehensive; that is, it has to embrace many or all aspects of life. It has to be an interpretation of both the external and the internal world. As Thomas Szasz (1967) points out, a person needs to believe that his or her existence has meaning. "This need is a consequence of his propensity for symbolizing, and a penalty, as it were, for thinking. The need to find meaning in life has been gratified by belief systems, cosmologies, religions, and philosophies of life. . . . Although Shakespeare suggested, and existentialists reiterate that life 'is a tale told by an idiot, full of sound and fury, signifying nothing,' people must live as if this were not true" (p. 48).

People formulate their explanation of life initially from

the various philosophies or religious traditions of their upbring-
ing and later from those influences and sources that give further
meaning to their life. Weisskopf-Joelson (1967), as well as other
psychologists, has suggested that many therapeutic schools may
be effective for reasons not explicit to the patient or therapist.
That is, they provide an explanation of life via a belief system
that integrates both the private and public world of the patient
and thereby offers life meaning. She also notes that an adopted
belief system must be not only plausible but also congenial to
the individual's own image of life, even if this image is barely
conscious, vague, or unverbalized.

    Meaning as a Purpose or Goal in Life. Victor Frankl
(1969) views humankind's primary concern as a "will to meaning—the basic striving of man to find and fulfill meaning and
purpose" (p. 35). Only when this concern is frustrated does the
individual become either content with power (as developed in
Adlerian psychology) or intent on pleasure (as developed in
Freudian psychology). Charlotte Buhler (1967) sees developed
individuals as having a comprehensive awareness of their own
existence in the present, past, and future. This awareness can
lead to self-realization in self-transcendent goals, which is experienced as a "meaningful life" (p. 85). The search for a comprehensive goal has many expressions. It can consist of shaping
and developing one's own personality, devotion to another,
working for a cause that transcends the self, working in a job or
seeking a career that permits meaningful tasks and activities, or
focusing on an eternal life hereafter.

    Meaning as an Integration of Private and Public Worlds.
Within this category, the responses of people who feel that their
lives are without meaning show that their inner world of
thoughts, wishes, and daydreams is partially or completely separated from the world of outer reality. One can have an active
awareness of an inner world but find little in reality around
which to spin fantasies and wishes. In the extreme, the individual can reject the surrounding world of people and objects as
meaningless, with the risk that this quality then characterizes
one's life. Fromm (1955) described this condition as "alienation." On the other hand, one can take an active stance in the

world of outer reality and give little import and/or attention to one's inner world. In the extreme, the inner guidelines that orient one toward meaningful activity are lost, and we lose a sense of meaning to life. R. D. Laing (1967) has discussed many of the causes and consequences of the "normal alienation from experience."

The need for a linkage between inner and outer worlds for the discovery of a meaningful life is paralleled in the need for linkage between the unconscious and the conscious in the world of the psyche. Rollo May (1969) sees it as our task to deepen and widen consciousness by integrating the "daimonic." He defines the daimonic as that which arises "from the ground of being rather than the self as such. . . . Its source lies in those realms where the self is rooted in the natural forces which go beyond the self and are felt as the grasp of fate upon us" (p. 124). When these unconscious forces are dealt with in consciousness and subsequently integrated toward a higher consciousness, the human being forms personal meaning out of what were previously impersonal and threatening images, feelings, and thoughts. Jung (1970) was a firm believer in the value of a dialogue between consciousness and the unconscious in order to actualize one's potentials in a meaningful life. He felt that during times of great difficulty, our conscious, rational approach must give way to the influence of the nonrational and symbolic. "Reason must always seek the solution in some rational, consistent, logical way, which is certainly justifiable enough in all normal situations but is entirely inadequate when it comes to the really great and decisive questions. It is incapable of creating the symbol because the symbol is irrational. When the rational way proves to be *cul de sac*—as it always does after a time—the solution comes from the side it was least expected" (p. 438).

Many psychologists (Progoff, 1963; Bruner, 1971; Watts, 1970), mythologists (Campbell, 1968; Zimmer, 1948; Murray, 1960), and theologians (Tillich, 1952; Fowler, 1981) have recognized the importance of symbol, dream, and myth as unconscious linking elements contributing to a sense of meaning to life. Whether we pursue meaning through philosophy, goals, or connectedness, they suggest the necessity of an ongoing dialogue with our own inner forces. Regardless of the technique—prayer, meditation, contemplation, working with dreams, or the study of myth—we need to come to terms with the greater horizon of our own deeper and wiser inner self. Doing so facilitates in a conscious way the process of meaning formulation.

Personal Meaning Formulation

Having explored the major sources of meaning, we can now consider how individuals formulate meaning on a day-by-day basis. Here we turn to a phenomenological study of mine (Hanna, 1975) concerning "crisis in meaning"—a period of time in an individual's life when there was a felt loss or lack of meaning. While the major focus of the research was the development of a description of the crisis phenomenon from onset to resolution (summarized in Chapter Five of this book), another outcome, more pertinent here, was the formulation of a conceptual model that clarified the psychological process of meaning formulation and its role in individual development. The key focus of this model is the Personal Construct System, a term similar to what Kelly (1963) described as "construction systems."

> Man looks at his world through transparent patterns or templets which he creates and then attempts to fit over the realities of which the world is composed. The fit is not always very good. Yet without such patterns the world appears to be such an undifferentiated homogeneity that man is unable to make any sense out of it. Even a poor fit is more helpful to him than nothing at all. Let us give the name constructs to these patterns that are tentatively tried on for size. . . . In general man seeks to improve his constructs by increasing his repertory, by altering them to provide better fits, and by subsuming them with superordinate constructs or systems. In seeking improvement he is repeatedly halted by the damage to the system that apparently will result from the alteration of a subordinate construct. Frequently his personal investment

in the larger system, or his personal dependence upon it, is so great that he will forego the adoption of a more precise construct in the substructure. It may take a major act of psychotherapy or experience to get him to adjust his construction system to the point where the new and more precise construct can be incorporated [pp. 8–9].

The Personal Construct System (PCS) is an individual's unique integration of various mental structures (images, values, attitudes, beliefs, and expectations) that comprise the reality of an individual's world and his or her place in it. The PCS is the psyche's mediating device for interactions within itself, with others, and with the environment. This dynamic system is created and continually adjusted by the individual in an attempt to satisfy personal needs and to reduce conflict and anxiety. It is an orderly construction, both personally derived and painfully and repetitiously imposed by enculturation, socialization, and parental training during growth toward adulthood. It is this elaborate and complex system of constructs that provides meaning to the individual's experiences and, therefore, life.

My study of people in meaning crisis suggests that the PCS consists of three basic subsystems vulnerable to disruption and subsequent meaning loss. Each of these interacting subsystems—Philosophy of Life, Story, and Self-Concept—is a storehouse of organized constructs that enable understanding of experience and provide behavioral choices for meaningful interaction in various situations. The three subsystems also parallel the meaning categories suggested by Weisskopf-Joelson (1967) earlier:

1. *Philosophy of Life.* This subsystem contains the constructs that represent one's view of the meaning of life itself. It provides both an explanation of life's purpose (or lack of purpose) and a macroview of the meaning of interactions among people and things in one's relevant environment and the world. The Philosophy of Life subsystem contains basic values, ethics, and beliefs, as well as assumptions and expectations about life and one's place in it. Statements such as

"To everything there is a season," "I see things from an existentialist (Catholic, Republican, conservative, and so on) point of view," "Home and family are the most important things in life," "God helps those who help themselves," and "Don't fool with Mother Nature" are various expressions of this subsystem of constructs. It is the Philosophy of Life subsystem to which the individual turns for the answers to such troubling meaning questions as: What matters most to me? What is the right thing to do? Why are we here? What is the purpose (meaning) of life?

2. *Story.* This subsystem contains the constructs that represent one's view of the meaning of one's own life. It provides a sense of continuity from one's past to the present and into a future in terms of job, career, roles, expectations, and relationships, in such detail and for such a length of time as are individually desirable. The Story subsystem provides purpose and makes sense of one's own life path or direction. It includes goals, aspirations, future life-style, desired activities, achievements and possessions to be attained, skills and capabilities to be developed, and so on. Statements such as "I plan to work at this for another year and then go to law school," "We want to have another child and then move to the country," and "With my MBA and a few more years' experience I can make company president" are various expressions from this subsystem. It is the Story subsystem to which the individual looks for the answers to such meaning questions as: What am I doing? Why am I doing this? Where do I go from here?

3. *Self-Concept.* This subsystem contains the constructs that represent one's view of one's self-meaning. It gives understanding or provides interpretation of one's own feelings, experiences, and behavior. The Self-Concept subsystem includes traits, abilities, personal psychology, present roles, sense of worth, body image, and so on. Statements such as "I am a Capricorn," "I'm a very sensitive person," "I'm still caught in an Oedipal conflict," "I am a good engineer," and "I am brunette and overweight" are various expressions of this subsystem of constructs. It is the Self-Concept subsys-

tem to which the individual looks for the answers to such meaning questions as: Who am I? What value am I? What can I do?

Individuals utilize a construct system that by adulthood is relatively stable (or closed) because of the immense amount of information that is either interconnected, anchored in strong feelings and emotion, or unconscious. Such psychological concepts as tolerance for ambiguity, authoritarianism, and creativity describe characteristics that are influenced by an individual's need for construct stability. Nonetheless, the need for stability is often at odds with the need to integrate new experiences and events and to satisfy newly emerging needs.

The Personal Construct System plays a key role in the larger process of personal meaning formulation. The conceptual model (see Figure 3-1) illustrates this mediating role both within the individual psyche and between the individual and his or her environment. For example, a manager or worker enters an organizational environment containing numerous variables—organizational expectations, tasks, group norms, working conditions and rules—giving direction for action. These external variables are perceived, experienced, and interpreted through the PCS and evaluated for personal meaning—that is, their fit with one's Philosophy of Life, Story, or Self-Concept. Is the action required consistent with or furthering of ethics and beliefs about life? Is the action consistent with or furthering of movement toward the desired future? Is the action consistent with or furthering of abilities, feeling states, or self-worth? In other words, does the action required of me fit my current reality and provide positive experiencing, or, if it doesn't and is uncomfortable (as is much physical and mental work), do I recognize that it still has some value for me or others, now or in the future? As inconsistencies grow and/or negative experiencing increases, meaning is lost—and, along with it, enthusiasm and effort.

The mediating role of the PCS is not only directed outward in extroverted fashion. It also plays a role in understanding and facilitating the expression of our own internal dynamics. For example, as familiar needs emerge into awareness

Figure 3-1. The Construct System as Mediator Between Emerging Needs and Behavior.

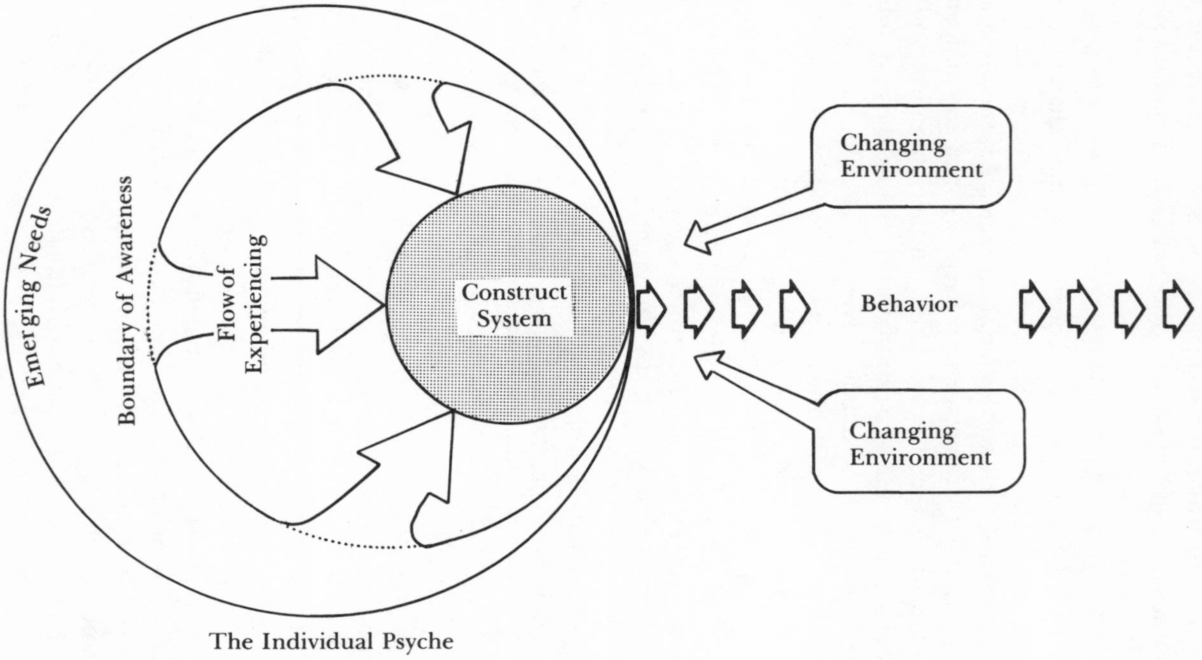

Changing Environment

Behavior

Changing Environment

Construct System

Flow of Experiencing

Boundary of Awareness

Emerging Needs

The Individual Psyche

through a constant flow of experiencing (sensations, feelings, fantasies, ideas, and so on), they are readily interpreted via the PCS, and we consider the likely choices for satisfying them. When I am aware of stomach sensations, certain odors, and internal images of food, I conclude that I am hungry and decide when and where to eat. The familiar needs range from the lower-order biological needs through many of the higher-order needs as described by Maslow (1970) and others. However, periodically, there are also new and largely unfamiliar needs, often representing potentialities, unexpressed capabilities, and developmental requirements that come forth into consciousness from the depths of the psyche during the course of human life (Erikson, 1963, 1968; Jung, 1954; Maslow, 1970). As they are new and are unique to our own individuality and life stage, an understanding of them is often beyond the interpretive abilities of the existing PCS. Their emergence then triggers the conflicts and crises of human development illustrated in the widely read book *Passages* (Sheehy, 1977) and studied by others (Gould, 1979; Levinson, 1978).

Thus, it is through an individual's PCS that he or she attempts to identify continually changing needs and seeks experiences that will provide satisfaction in a constantly changing environment. Life meaning is acquired to the extent that one's PCS provides purposes and goals (and a means of attainment) that are congruent with one's unique and emerging needs for development, whether physical, intellectual, emotional, or spiritual. This results in a sense of satisfaction that lifts us out of boredom and apathy toward enthusiasm and excitement. Conversely, life meaning is lost to the extent that one's PCS is inadequate to provide an understanding and/or acceptance of situations or crises that frustrate emerging needs. This results in dissatisfaction and moves us from frustration and anger toward alienation and depression.

It is the complexity and degree of open-endedness maintained in our PCS, along with one's stance toward inquiry both externally and internally, that determine our ability to identify emerging needs and move toward the experiences that satisfy them. Individuals tend to create some meaning formulation via the three subsystems of the Personal Construct System. When any of the three subsystems fails to maintain a fit between the experience of ongoing events and the satisfaction of emerging needs, individual meaning begins to diminish. Whenever a major reformulation of any of the subsystems is required, individuals are likely to experience some problem with meaning and a concomitant loss of satisfaction and enthusiasm and a decline in performance. The following is a short account of an individual who was struggling with a crisis in meaning related to his work:

Tom is a well-educated and psychologically sophisticated man in his late fifties who recounts what happened after he made a choice to step down from a high-level administrative position and return to his former technical function in the same organization. At the same time, there were role changes occurring in his personal life; his children were grown and leaving home. The organization change proved to be unexpectedly traumatic and painful.

> I began to consider how I would step down or laterally, even with the difficulties. . . . Then, you've effected the change, been rational and conscientious, and the new man is in. You're not going to meetings, and so on. All of a sudden, there rushes over you this sense of feeling like a nonperson. Then there was this subjective sense of "Wow! What am I?" Overnight, your whole pattern of relationships changes—"Who the hell am I?" If the response of co-workers changes or drops out, suddenly you feel like a piece of thread from which all the rest of the fabric has dropped away. There's a tremendous sense of loss, like part of you is flapping around like pieces of raw nerve ending, loose and painful in the air.
>
> The terrible thing about a break in relationship, a break in roles, is not the present, which is unhappy enough, but it's the future that really knocks the props out from under you. Man does not live only with his present and his past. He casts forward like a spider does. He sort of shoots the threads out in front of him toward a future. Then those threads are all broken and he's cast in space,

wondering How will I react? Where will I be? The unknown is always the scariest thing.

I found a couple of people who were very good about listening. It helped me getting through the day and in giving me time to find my own solution. I suggested a new role as elder—to offer the history of how things came about. I also took up yoga, began to read more and build up my skills. I suspect that I'll be able to write again. All of these role incidents have some application to not just the middle years but to the sense of getting ready to change—semiretirement, retirement, where are you now?

As Tom's questions reveal, he experienced his loss of meaning at primarily the Self-Concept and Story subsystem levels. He resolved his crisis by seeking new activities and tasks that put him more in touch with who he was and how he felt and expanded his self-definition beyond a work role. He also had to redefine and come to terms with new Story constructs—a consideration of eventual retirement and beyond. A well-developed Philosophy of Life subsystem provided much assistance to a reformulation of the other subsystems in his Personal Construct System.

In summary, we see that personal meaning is formulated or lost on a day-to-day basis. Meaning for the individual, as always, resides in her or his view of life—a philosophy of life that gives spiritual direction, support in tragedy, and hope in uncertainty; a story whose purposes and goals resonate with the inner themes of emerging needs; and a self-concept that provides the confidence and stability to give and accept love and appreciation in a dynamic world. The challenge that now faces many of us is to discover and reconstruct a meaningful view of life amid the ruins of traditional values and beliefs and to express it in a way that offers benefit not only to ourselves but also to others.

Individual and Organizational Implications

The search for personal meaning today is not only the experience of new outer realities; more importantly, it is an inward journey—a spiritual adventure. As Campbell (1972) sees it, the journey of the hero is the pivotal myth that unites the spiritual quest of ancient heroes with the modern-day search for meaning. Yet he warns us all, heroes and heroines alike, of the dangers of becoming lost in narcissistic excesses or narrow self-fulfillment. "The ultimate aim of the quest . . . must be neither release nor ecstasy for oneself, but the wisdom and power to serve others" (p. 234). Similarly, Frankl feels that self-actualization can be neither the primary intention nor the ultimate destination. If self-actualization is made an end in itself, it contradicts the self-transcendent quality of human existence—the urge of human beings to move toward meanings that are more than mere expressions of themselves. Instead, self-actualization, like happiness, is the effect and the result of meaning fulfillment. Thus, meanings are discovered rather than invented. And when they are discovered, they are of benefit beyond oneself.

Although the search for meaning is a difficult journey, certain individual characteristics can make it a rewarding one as well. First, and most critical, is the necessity of assuming a stance of inquiry—the willingness to explore, to experiment, and to question. The individual must ask, "How can I reconstruct my view of life and react to it in order to discover meaning?" During the inquiry process, there should be a consideration of the important life questions that have been emerging into consciousness. These questions should be converted into forms that move one to a proactive stance. For example, "What is the purpose of it all?" becomes "What is a purpose to life that I can believe in?" or "How can I go about looking for one?" Also, as illustrated earlier, one's questions of meaning point toward the subsystem of constructs that are now inadequate. Meaningful replacements, whether new ideas, beliefs, assumptions, values, or goals, must be sought out and tried on for size—evaluated through the experiencing of them.

This brings us to the second requirement, a willingness to risk—to allow for failure, disappointment, and pain in order that new constructs may be formulated by experimentation with new roles, relationships, behaviors, and situations. Appropriate changes are those that result in the reduction (but not the masking) of formerly painful or negative experiencing and/or the development of pleasurable or valued experiencing. New meaning is then acquired.

Lastly, in our search for meaning, conscious attention must be given to all our experiencing, even the pain. The problem here is our natural inclination to deny or avoid negative feelings. The temptation is to tranquilize them, dull them with alcohol, or distract ourselves from them with television, constant interaction, or repetitious activity. As Ferguson (1980) points out, "denial is a way of life. More accurately, it is a way of diminishing life, of making it seem more manageable. . . . Avoidance is a short-term answer, like aspirin. Avoidance settles for chronic dull pain rather than brief acute confrontation" (pp. 74–75). All three of the previously mentioned characteristics—a stance toward inquiry, a willingness to risk, and attentiveness to all experiencing—are strengthened by the encouragement and support of trustworthy and empathic others.

In addition to the implications for individuals, the search for personal meaning has implications for organizations and management. As always, the key task of any organization is collective accomplishment. However, effective performance in times of transformation is related both to the degree to which the organization's meaning system resonates with the meaning requirements of its members and to the ability of management to facilitate and support the discovery of individual and collective meaning. Organizations, of course, have their own construct systems, expressed through their culture, philosophy, mission, stories, heroes, and rituals. The concern here is to identify those aspects of organizations that facilitate meaning formulation in their members.

Philosophy of Life. As individuals move increasingly toward the values predicted by the observers of transformation in our culture, organizations must create and establish superordinate goals that support these values. Organization members wish to see their firms pursuing goals that provide benefit to the culture, society, the community, and themselves. Such goals define the organizational entity with which organizational members identify and toward whose tasks they are motivated and committed. As Pascale and Athos (1981) point out, the majority of people who work don't have to for economic survival in the short run. Increasingly, they seek, in addition to pay and career opportunities, other kinds of income from their jobs, including work they enjoy, colleagues they like working with, and meaning. . . . It helps enormously if they can see the link between what they do and a higher purpose" (p. 302). If organizations are not successful in this linkage, their members will create a larger meaning outside the organization or in ways that undermine it.

In their comparison of Japanese and American management, Pascale and Athos indicate that Japanese firms tend to be quite successful in their ability to link superordinate goals and values to those of their employees, including the "spiritual values" of service, harmony, cooperation, and humility. Japanese executives take it as their task to attend to much more of the needs of the whole person in their employees, including their needs for meaning. As a result of their studies, they suggest that "what is needed in the West is a nondeified, nonreligious 'spirituality' that enables a firm's superordinate goals to respond truly to the inner meanings that many people seek in their work —or, alternatively, seek in their lives and could find at work if only that were more culturally acceptable" (p. 311).

Ian Mitroff (1983) argues that our old pictures of the world—as well as the methods used for treating problems that were founded on the old pictures—are outworn. He asks, "can we continue to deny any longer that there is a fundamental religious aspect to all organizations—that in their attempt to give purpose and meaning to peoples' lives, to fill up their time, that religious instincts are there no matter how disguised they might be?" (p. 158). Nonetheless, much needs to change to overcome the threat that American organizations perceive not only in spiritual values but in emotional and intuitive values as well.

Story. The search for meaning relevant to the story subsystem requires the creation of a path into the future that best expresses the individual's transcendent goals and emerging needs. Organizations contribute to individual meaning formulation in this subsystem via career development and organization story or myth. Organizations have the power to either support individual story meaning or destroy it through the policies they formulate concerning performance appraisal, career development, career-path movement, geographical transfers, and managerial and human resource development, to name a few. Policies that are implemented inconsistently, secretly, or with little regard for individual differences and changing circumstances create uncertainty and offer organizational members little opportunity to shape a meaningful life path.

Mitroff has proposed the study of organizational stories as a way of better understanding organizational reality. The stakeholders of an organization—those individuals, groups, and institutions who affect or are affected by an organization's plans and actions—are a "part of a complex psychosocial fabric that somehow ties the individual characters together and gives them individual and collective meaning. One of the most powerful integrating mechanisms is stories" (p. 122). To the degree that an organization generates stories that are inclusive of many of its members in a positive way, more individual stories will be given meaning as part of a collective story.

Self-Concept. The search for individual meaning relevant to the self-concept subsystem requires formulating an identity that gives one confidence and a sense of stability and worth and that is continually nourished by a connection to one's changing inner world. Organizations establish the norms and expectations that either foster these inner connections and their expression or inhibit them. Many organizations claim to foster innovation, for example, yet their structures, managerial styles, and reward systems actually inhibit the utilization of the inner connections that underlie creativity. Additionally, organizations develop cultures that either foster or inhibit learning from experience, risk taking, cooperation, tolerance of diversity and ambiguity, the expression of feeling, and taking time for quiet contemplation, all of which are relevant to inner connectedness, creativity, and meaning development. Here again, Mitroff suggests that an organization's interest in its stakeholders be extended not only to its managers' roles but also to the deeper aspects of their personality as conceptualized in Jung's psychological types, the ego states of transactional analysis, and the archetypal patterns in the unconscious.

In conclusion, the evidence presented in this chapter suggests that we have entered an era of transformation. The significant danger to both individuals and organizations is a disabling loss of meaning resulting in confusion and collapse. The opportunity for renewal and growth is also significant and is dependent on the willingness of organizations and their managers to tackle the elemental challenge in the discovery of meaning, both individually and collectively. This chapter suggests some of the places where organizational meaning can overlap with and support the individual quest for meaning, and how, in turn, the individual's discovery of meaning can revitalize that of the organization. A successful outcome will require that attention and effort be directed toward areas of organizational life that are normally taken for granted—organizational culture, myth, and ritual—and aspects of the individual that are often ignored—uniqueness, story, and connectedness to the inner world and emerging needs. However, most challenging of all will be the organizational ability to recognize and incorporate the spiritual dimension of meaning and purpose into the pursuit of collective accomplishment.

References

Bruner, J. *On Knowing.* New York: Atheneum, 1971.

Bühler, C. "Human Life as a Whole as a Central Subject of Humanistic Psychology." In J. F. T. Bugental (Ed.), *Challenges of Humanistic Psychology.* New York: McGraw-Hill, 1967.

Campbell, J. *The Hero with a Thousand Faces.* (2nd ed.) Princeton, N.J.: Princeton University Press, 1968.

Campbell, J. *Myths to Live By.* New York: Viking Press, 1972.

Capra, F. *The Turning Point.* New York: Bantam, 1983.

Erikson, E. *Childhood and Society.* New York: Norton, 1963.

Erikson, E. *Identity: Youth and Crisis.* New York: Norton, 1968.

Ferguson, M. *The Aquarian Conspiracy.* Los Angeles: Tarcher, 1980.

Fowler, J. *Stages of Faith: The Psychology of Human Development and the Quest for Meaning.* New York: Harper & Row, 1981.

Frankl, V. *The Will to Meaning.* New York: New American Library, 1969.

Fromm, E. *The Sane Society.* New York: Holt, Rinehart and Winston, 1955.

Gould, R. *Transformations.* New York: Simon & Schuster, 1979.

Hanna, R. W. "Crisis in Meaning: A Phenomenological Inquiry into the Experience of a Lack of Meaning to Life." Unpublished doctoral dissertation, Graduate School of Management, University of California at Los Angeles, 1975.

Jung, C. G. *Collected Works.* Vol. 17: *The Development of Personality.* Princeton, N.J.: Princeton University Press, 1954. (Originally published 1934.)

Jung, C. G. *Collected Works.* Vol. 6: *Psychological Types.* Princeton, N.J.: Princeton University Press, 1970. (Originally published 1921.)

Kelly, G. A. *A Theory of Personality.* New York: Norton, 1963.

Kübler-Ross, E. *On Death and Dying.* New York: Macmillan, 1969.

Laing, R. D. *The Politics of Experience.* New York: Pantheon, 1967.

Leonard, G. *The Transformation.* Los Angeles: Tarcher, 1972.

Levinson, D. J. *The Seasons of a Man's Life.* New York: Ballantine, 1978.

London, P. "From the Long Couch for the Sick to the Push Button for the Bored." *Psychology Today,* 1974, *8* (1), 62-68.

Maslow, A. H. *Motivation and Personality.* New York: Harper & Row, 1970.

Maslow, A. H. *The Farther Reaches of Human Nature.* New York: Viking Press, 1972.

May, R. *Love and Will.* London: Collins, 1969.

Mitroff, I. I. *Stakeholders of the Organizational Mind: Toward a New View of Organizational Policy Making.* San Francisco: Jossey-Bass, 1983.

Murray, H. A. *Myth and Myth Making.* Boston: Beacon Press, 1960.

Pascale, R. T., and Athos, A. G. *The Art of Japanese Management.* New York: Simon & Schuster, 1981.

Progoff, I. *The Symbolic and the Real.* New York: McGraw-Hill, 1963.

Sheehy, G. *Passages.* New York: Bantam, 1977.

Szasz, T. "Moral Men." In J. F. T. Bugental (Ed.), *Challenges of Humanistic Psychology.* New York: McGraw-Hill, 1967.

Tillich, P. *The Courage to Be.* New Haven, Conn.: Yale University Press, 1952.

Toffler, A. *Future Shock.* New York: Random House, 1970.

Toffler, A. *The Third Wave.* New York: Bantam, 1981.

Watts, A. "Western Mythology: Its Dissolution and Transformation." In J. Campbell (Ed.), *Myths, Dreams, and Religion.* New York: Dutton, 1970.

Weisskopf-Joelson, E. "Meaning as an Integrating Factor." In C. Buhler and F. Massarik (Eds.), *The Course of Human Life.* New York: Springer, 1967.

Zimmer, H. *The King and the Corpse.* Princeton, N.J.: Princeton University Press, 1948.

4

Career Transition and Adaptation: Appreciating and Facilitating the Experience

Meryl Reis Louis

That change is a constant in organizational life is a truism. Academics, consultants, and managers devote much attention to the subject of planned change, of change deliberately introduced toward particular organizational ends. But other forms of change are prevalent—though they have received far less attention. Corporate acquisition, the introduction of new technology, the addition of several new members to an ongoing work group, the establishment of a project team, an individual's promotion, transfer, or move to a different company—each requires individuals to adapt and to cope with a variety of changes. The term *transition* is used here to refer to periods of individual adaptation to any number of such changes. The prevalence of transitions coupled with the magnitude of attendant costs makes the management of transitions a strategic challenge for today's organizational leadership. It is hoped that this chapter will contribute specific conceptual tools to help meet that challenge.

Over the past few years, there has been a growing recognition that there are properties of the experience of being in transition that are common across different types of transition situations. In 1982, for instance, a NATO-sponsored conference on role transitions brought together social scientists working on such diverse transition situations as job change, unemployment, divorce, entering or leaving prison, retirement, immigration, and becoming a parent. The conference organizers note in the preface to the volume of papers resulting from that conference: "In spite of the diversity of role transitions that occur . . . it is important also to realize that many basic psychological processes can be discerned in ostensibly different instances" (Allen and van de Vliert, 1984, p. vii).

Within the organizational sciences, Nigel Nicholson (1984) has been working on a general theory of work-role transitions, while my own past work has looked at the class of transition situations associated with being a newcomer to an unfamiliar work setting (Louis, 1980a, 1980b, 1980c, 1982). The occasion of writing this chapter thus seems an appropriate opportunity to bring together this past work in an integrated look at how transition situations are experienced and managed. For if we—as managers, consultants, academics, and organizational members—are to cope with the myriad changes attendant to everyday organizational life, we must come to appreciate when and how transitions are typically experienced, as well as the tasks essential in making the passage from "before change" to "after change." These, then, are the issues addressed in this chapter.

The main sections of this chapter define and enumerate types of transitions, describe the experience of being in transition and an individual's typical cognitive processes for making sense out of the experience, discuss what individuals must and may do in managing their own transitions, and outline actions that managers can take and approaches that organizations can adopt to facilitate the transitions of organizational members.

Career Transitions: Definitions and Situations

Definitions. As a preliminary step in understanding transitioners' experiences, the terms *career* and *career transition* (CT) will be defined and illustrated. Following Hall (1976, pp. 1-4), *career* will be used here to refer to an accumulation of role-related experiences over time. Further, we will consider that the term *career* may refer to a work or nonwork role. Both objective and subjective elements of roles will be considered. As used here, *career* does not necessarily imply hierarchical or other progression through an organization or professional structure. Any one career or sequence of role-related experiences will be viewed within a framework of several potentially overlapping and interacting life roles. While our definition of *career* specifically includes nonwork roles, the discussion will focus on work roles.

What, then, is a career transition? The term *transition* suggests both the change itself and the period during which a change is taking place. Since the central idea in the previous discussion of career was "role" (that is, the task and other behaviors associated with a position in an organization or social system), we will define career transition as the period during which an individual is changing roles (taking on a different objective role) (Nicholson, 1984), changing orientation to a role already held (altering a subjective state), or experiencing a change in the organizational context or situation in which the role is carried out. In the organizational context, the duration of the period of transition depends in large part on how much difference is experienced by the changer between new and old roles, role orientations, or role situations. Generally, it takes longer to make a transition to an entirely unfamiliar role or situation than to one that is somewhat familiar.

Propositions. The following five propositions form the foundation for this approach to understanding career transitions:

1. During all types of CTs, individuals are faced with a variety of differences between the old and the new—in terms of roles, role orientations, and/or features of the role settings.
2. The more differences there are, and the greater the magnitude of the differences, the more the transitioner has to cope with.
3. The type of transition undertaken is an indicator of the general nature and magnitude of differences with which the individual will have to cope.
4. There is a typical coping process by which individuals inter-

pret and respond to differences experienced during transitions of all types.

5. An understanding of the coping process combined with an analysis of the type of transition undertaken can be used to foresee the needs and facilitate the adaptation of individuals during career transitions.

Typology. When a college graduate begins a first full-time job, when a dentist takes up law, when an engineer enters the managerial ranks, when a middle manager adapts to new policies following an acquisition or merger, when a housewife re-enters the labor force after childrearing years, when an executive retires, and when an engineer adopts a new technology, each undertakes a form of CT. This section catalogues the varieties of CT situations. From the definition of CT as the period during which an individual is taking on a different role or changing orientations to a role already held, we can identify two major categories of transitions: interrole and intrarole. In the former, a new and different role is being adopted; while in the latter, a new and different orientation to an old role is being taken.

Interrole transitions are undertaken when individuals (1) enter or re-enter a labor pool, (2) take on a different role within the same organization, (3) move from one organization to another, (4) change professions, or (5) leave a labor pool.

The occasion of an individual entering or re-entering a labor pool, an *entry transition,* involves a change in roles. The examples of the college graduate entering a work organization for the first time as a regular full-time permanent employee and the housewife returning to work after raising children illustrate the entry transition. A nonwork-role example is that of a person marrying for the first time: the individual is taking on the role of spouse, a new role. In entry transitions in which the new role is embedded in an organizational context, the transitioner must adjust to the reality of the organization, learn how to work, deal with the boss and the reward system, and develop an identity and sense of place in the organization (Schein, 1978, pp. 94–101). Consider, for example, the transition involved in moving from school into the work world. In this transition, various features of the work context differ between the new and old role settings. Differences include the presence and types of supervision and feedback, challenges and autonomy, accountability, task structure, discretion over time, dress, physical setting, status, salary, and role identity.

A second type of interrole transition involves a change of role within the same overall work organization, an *intracompany transition*. In transferring from one department or division to another, for instance, co-workers, tasks, technologies, physical setting, and formal and informal procedures are likely to differ (Brett, 1984; Pinder, 1981). Even when one shifts from a technical role to a managerial role within the same department, responsibilities, authority and reporting relationships, information needs and availability, and work space usually change.

A move from one company to another company represents an *intercompany transition*. In such a transition, the transitioner may have to cope with differences between new and old task requirements, work-group and organizational climate, and industry. In general, intercompany transitions are likely to be more demanding than are intracompany transitions. Traditionally, references to labor turnover refer to voluntary intercompany transitions (Price, 1977).

The fourth type of interrole transition is change in profession, labeled *interprofession transition*. A CT of this type occurs, for example, when a dentist takes up law or when someone moves from the business world to academia. A brief but rich account of an interprofession transition is found in Michael Blumenthal's (1979) description of differences he encountered in leaving as Bendix Corporation's chairperson and chief executive officer to become U.S. secretary of the treasury. In essence, a profession change entails a move to a different culture, or, as Blumenthal says, to a foreign culture. Often associated with a profession change are differences in language used, norms governing interpersonal interactions (for example, different norms for lawyer-client, dentist-patient, businessperson-customer, professor-student relations), codes of ethics, reference groups, professional identities, and societal responses to professional identity.

A final type of interrole CT is an *exit transition*. Exits vary in permanence or duration and in type and source of initiation. A "leave of absence" (sabbatical, pregnancy leave, or travel leave) represents a brief, planned exit, usually of a specified and finite duration. A "withdrawal" represents a long-term or semipermanent leave, usually initiated by the transitioner and often of an indeterminate duration. The stereotypical case is that of a woman who terminates a work role while raising children. A third kind of exit transition is "involuntary unemployment," which by definition is an organization-initiated termination of the individual's employment. It is often unanticipated and necessarily unplanned by the possibly unwilling transitioner; at the outset, the duration of the unemployment period may be difficult or impossible to forecast. "Retirement" represents a fourth and permanent exit from a particular role. It is usually planned by the transitioner, although early retirement may be company initiated and unanticipated by the individual. (For reviews of the sociological and psychological aspects of retirement, see Atchley, 1976, and Friedman and Havighurst, 1954.) In planned exits (generally all except involuntary unemployment), the transitioner usually has the opportunity to select or construct a role to immediately replace the role being left.

In essence, any CT, especially an interrole transition, involves an exit transition as one is leaving an old role or role orientation. Whether or not a new role is entered, the characteristics of any new organizational context are important factors in the transitioner's postexit experience. In most exits, the individual leaves a familiar and meaning-giving organizational culture and role context. In some exits, the transitioner does not then enter a different organization or one with a necessarily well-developed organizational culture. A CT in which an individual leaves but does not take on a new organizational role entails a special set of differences (and stresses) associated with organizational membership. For example, organizational membership may have provided the individual with regular social interaction, a sense of purpose, a place to be, a time structure, and, literally, a reason for getting up in the morning (whether to make a contribution or to avoid a dock in pay for tardiness or absenteeism) (Friedman and Havighurst, 1954; Sofer, 1970; Super, 1957). Research has shown that physiological deterioration, depression, and even death may be associated with withdrawal and retirement (Clark, 1966).

A final set of differences associated with many types of interrole transitions is passage across intraorganizational boundaries. Schein (1971) has identified functional, hierarchical, and inclusionary boundaries within organizations. A newly hired employee crosses all three boundaries: taking on a set of tasks within a functional area (for example, marketing, finance), acquiring a position in the hierarchy (for example, middle management), and finding a place in the organization's information and influence network (usually at a peripheral rather than a central position). Most interrole transitions involve passage across one or more of these boundaries; at a minimum, one's place in the inclusionary system is typically in flux during transition. In sum, each of the five types of interrole transition carries the possibility of many differences between new and old roles and settings.

Intrarole transitions represent changes in individuals' internal orientations to roles already held. Intrarole transitions may involve subtle and gradual changes, in contrast to interrole transitions. And although it is difficult to embark on an interrole transition without consciously being aware of doing so, many intrarole transitions begin without the conscious awareness of the individual. Let's consider several types of intrarole transitions.

An *intrarole adjustment* represents a shift in orientation to a role that an individual makes in response to his or her experiences in the role over time. For instance, Schein (1978) has documented this type of transition among M.B.A. graduates in new work roles, illustrating how complacency can replace enthusiasm and commitment as recruits encounter the realities of corporate life. The M.B.A.s are responding to differences between their actual and anticipated experiences in the role—that is, to surprises. Their in-role, on-the-job experiences have led them to alter their role orientations. The formal role itself does not change in an intrarole adjustment; instead, the transition reflects an internal change. A more positive instance of intra-role adjustment was found in a research laboratory of a large Midwestern university, where the senior professor was seen as a tyrant. He prohibited conversation in the lab during working hours and forbade exchanging information with researchers from other labs. When he went on sabbatical, a new professor, with a more open style, was running the lab. Productivity and personal commitment increased; several people reported experiencing the lab as a fun and exciting place to be. The increase in personal commitment represents an intrarole adjustment. It resulted from a change in working conditions but not a change in role. Often such intrarole adjustments are unanticipated by the individual, who may not be aware of having altered a role orientation.

Merger and acquisition situations precipitate myriad intrarole adjustments, particularly among middle managers in the acquired organizations (Schneider, 1983). Typically, there is a "housecleaning" at the top of the acquired organization; lower-level employees remain largely uninvolved. That leaves those in the middle to interface with the management of the acquiring organization, to translate new policies into operations below, and to shift their own loyalties from old to new management philosophies. Thus, we may expect mergers and acquisitions to occasion intrarole-adjustment CTs, especially among middle managers.

A second type of intrarole transition reflects potential interactions among one's multiple life roles. In *extrarole adjustments,* a change in one life role (for example, a family role) leads to an adjustment in orientation to another role (for example, a work role). The addition of a new nonwork role or a shift in the demands of a nonwork role already held may impinge on a work role, for instance, in several ways. When a professor accepts the editorship of a scholarly journal, he or she may adjust (downward) the time and energy given to other major roles; there may be less time for students, research, family. It may also be that, in the long run, the new role enriches other roles. Similarly, when the first baby of a dual-career couple is born, both adults take on new roles as parents that may lead them to devote less time, energy, and (at least temporarily) commitment to their work roles.

An individual may pour more energy into tasks at work to avoid dealing with difficulties at home; alternatively, problems at home may distract the individual's attention and energies away from the work role. Extrarole adjustments reflect differences in the relative importance of one role in relation to other roles. Here again, the transition in role orientation may occur predominantly at the unconscious level. The potential for interactions among roles makes it important to consider the total "life space" of the transitioner in understanding career dynamics and transitions (Lewin, 1951; Rapoport and Rapoport, 1978).

A third type of intrarole transition occurs in a transition in *role/career stage*. Much work has been done identifying the general stages through which an individual typically passes during an organizational career (Super, 1957; Miller and Form, 1951; Hall and Nougaim, 1968). The first two types of intrarole transition represent responses to unplanned and often unanticipatable experiences in work or other roles. In contrast, this type of transition represents a normal progression through a sequence of stages in the total career cycle. But, even though a stage transition may be predictable, it usually occurs without the individual's conscious effort or awareness. Different issues, personal needs, and organizational opportunities are associated with different career stages. For example, in the typical transition between early and mid-career, the individual moves (albeit gradually) from a peripheral to a more central role in the informal network of the organization. Although role title, responsibilities, and tasks may change in a career-stage transition as they did in an intracompany transition, the career-stage transition is distinct in three respects: (1) it represents a major passage through the career cycle, as compared with a more minor though official change of role and duties; (2) the formal organizational role need not formally change to mark the stage passage; and (3) the changes are more diffuse, pervasive and gradual and less conscious. Each career stage implicitly conveys an image of the expected or normal role orientation. (For a detailed comparison of approaches to career stages, see Hall, 1976.)

A fourth type of intrarole transition, the *life-stage transition*, is based on passage through normal stages in human development. Erikson's (1959) model of the life cycle suggests a series of stages in psychosocial development through which an individual passes from infancy to death. As in models of career stages, different issues predominate at different life stages; issues implicitly guide one's orientation to one's life space and tasks. Although normal psychosocial transitions are expected to parallel and roughly correspond to transitions in career stage, they may separately precipitate reorientation to one's work role. Additionally, certain career-stage transitions presuppose adequate transition in psychosocial stages.

Erikson suggests, for instance, that individuals who at mid- or late adulthood feel they have made a worthwhile and satisfying contribution in their life work may wish to continue to contribute by helping others to develop and by taking on more senior guiding responsibilities (generativity). Other individuals at the same stage may feel discouraged and consider that their efforts have been worthless and that it is too late to start over (stagnation). The popularized phenomenon of the "midlife crisis" (Jacques, 1965) may represent a fight to avoid or deny an experience of stagnation. Experiences of stagnation may result in orientations to work roles substantially different from those resulting from experiences of generativity. The advisability of encouraging individuals to enter new career stages might well depend in part on their resolution of issues in psychosocial development. It is not altogether a one-way interaction, however. The events and outcomes associated with individuals' career-stage transitions significantly facilitate or hinder their psychosocial development. Organizational roles provide a primary arena in and through which individuals test themselves, work through life issues, fulfill needs for challenge, self-development, and interaction, and otherwise construct self-identities.

Any particular transition may contain elements of several types of CTs. For example, a shift from a technical to a managerial role could be experienced as simply an intracompany transition or, additionally, as a fairly major interprofession transition; it could also be considered a career-stage transition. How a particular transition is classified depends on the specific situation and the way in which an individual experiences the situation. Thus, we have seen that there are a vast number of different types of situations that precipitate the experience of being in transition—situations both dramatic and subtle, encompassing organizational and individual changes. Given so many different occasions in which transitions occur, what features are common to the experience of being in transition? And how do transitioners typically cope with their experiences? These questions are addressed in the next two sections, in preparation for discussing how to manage transitions, the subject of the fourth section.

Characteristics of the Experience

Though no two transition situations are identical, and no two people would experience the same transition in precisely the same way, several characteristics are common across most people's experiences of career transitions. By knowing what is "normal" to experience during transition, transitioners can manage their transitions more effectively, and organizations can design means of helping employees adapt to new roles and new orientations to old roles. Differences between new and old roles and role settings are the source of several commonalities. The transitioner may be able to foresee some of these differences before entering the new situation. Other differences emerge only through experiences in and of the new situation and of oneself in the new situation.

The general nature and magnitude of pre- to post-transition differences can be estimated from the type of transition undertaken. For instance, the typical transition from school to work is likely to entail substantial differences between student and worker roles and role settings. In contrast, we would expect fewer and less significant differences for the individual moving from a position as salesperson in Company A to salesperson in Company B, especially if the product line and sales territory are roughly equivalent.

Changes. Several kinds of differences are associated with CTs. Differences in the objective features between new and old situations, referred to here as *changes,* are publicly noticeable and knowable and are often knowable in advance (that is, at the time the transitioner accepts a new position). In moving from systems engineer at IBM in San Francisco to senior consultant at Price Waterhouse in New York, the transitioner knows, for instance, that title, organizational affiliation, office address, co-workers, and supervisor will differ.

Contrasts. Other differences are subjective in nature—that is, they are personally rather than publicly noticed. These differences, referred to here as *contrasts,* are products of the individual's experience in the new setting and role (that is, features identified as figure against the background of a total field). Contrasts emerge both from the objective differences between new and old settings, including changes, and from characteristics of the new setting as perceived by the transitioner. They represent the transitioner's definition or map of the new setting and are person specific rather than inherent in the organizational transition (as are changes). Whether a particular feature of the new situation stands out or emerges as a contrast depends as well on its relative importance to the individual transitioner. For two people undergoing the same objective change in role (for example, graduating from the same law school class and joining the same law firm), different contrasts will emerge.

Thus, differences between settings and characteristics within new settings contribute to the selection of features experienced as "figure" or contrast. For example, how people dress in the new setting may or may not be noticed or be experienced as a contrast, depending in part on whether dress differs between new and old settings. The presence of a difference in dress is a necessary but not sufficient precondition for the noticing of a contrast. Similarly, the absence of windows may or may not emerge as a distinguishing feature of the new setting, depending on the individual and the full set of potential contrasts in the situation. Contrasts are, therefore, person specific rather than indigenous to the organizational transition and, unlike objective changes, are not generally knowable in advance.

A special case of contrast is associated with the letting go of old roles, which often seems to take considerable time as one adapts in the new situation. The letting go associated with career transitions is unlike that in tribal rites of passage and total institution inductions. Typically, no transition ritual erases all trace of the old role before the new role is taken on. Instead, transitioners voluntarily undertake the role change, they change only one of the many roles they hold simultaneously, and they carry into the new role memories of experiences in old roles. The first time the transitioner is involved in almost any activity in the new role (for example, when a professor uses the computer or library or has a manuscript typed at the new university), the memory of the corresponding activity in one or more old roles may be brought to mind. The process is similar, though on a less emotionally charged scale, to the event-anniversary phenomenon that occurs in adjusting to the death of a loved one. As experiences from prior roles are recalled, contrasts are generated. The transitioner may evaluate aspects of the new role using old-role experiences as anchors on internal comparison scales. Or the transitioner may try to incorporate aspects of the old into the new role or resist the new role in favor of the old role.

Given the natural limits of human capabilities for perceptual processing (Miller, 1956), we surmise that there may be some maximum number of contrasts to which individuals can attend simultaneously. In addition, it appears that for individuals in new situations, some minimum number of the contrasts emerge. The contrasts represent subjective differences between new and old settings by which transitioners characterize and otherwise define the new situation.

Surprises. In addition to changes and contrasts, there are differences that arise from discrepancies between an individual's anticipations (tacit as well as explicit) of future situations and experiences and the subsequent real-time happenings. Differences between anticipations and experiences, termed *surprises,* typically stimulate both affective and cognitive reactions. (How surprise triggers such reactions and the processes by which individuals cope with surprise and other transition features are discussed later.)

Surprises differ from contrasts in several ways. Contrasts are subjective appreciations of differences between features of two objective or external worlds—the old and the new roles and settings. Surprises, on the other hand, are subjective appreciations of differences between a personally forecasted experiential world and the individual's subsequent experience of self in the role and setting. Thus, contrasts and surprises differ in both subject (for example, real-world features versus anticipations of experiences) and source (for example, externally generated but personally observed versus self-generated). Surprise may be positive (for example, delight at finding that your office window overlooks a garden) or negative (for example, disappointment at finding that your office window cannot be opened). The subject of anticipation and, therefore, surprise may be the job, the organization, or the self. Anticipations may be conscious, tacit, or emergent; either overmet or undermet anticipations can produce surprise.

Several forms of surprise often arise during career transitions. The first form of surprise occurs when conscious expectations about the job are not fulfilled in the transitioner's early job experiences. *Unmet expectations*, as typically used by organizational practitioners and researchers, refers to *undermet conscious job expectations*. A second form of surprise arises when *unconscious job expectations* are *unmet* or when features of the job are *unanticipated.* Job aspects not previously considered important stand out as important because their presence or absence is experienced as undesirable. As one transitioner said, "I had no idea how important windows were to me until I'd spent a week in a staff room without any." This is an example both of surprise resulting from inadequacy in anticipations and of a contrast, indicating a typical overlap between the two features.

A third form of surprise that may occur during transitions arises when *expectations* (both conscious and unconscious) *about oneself are unmet.* Choice of the new organization is often based on assumptions about one's own skills, values, needs, and so on. During transitions, errors in assumptions sometimes emerge, and the person must cope with the recognition that he or she is different from his or her previous self-perceptions. For example: "I chose this job because it offered a great deal of freedom; now I realize I really don't want so much freedom."

A fourth form of surprise arises from difficulties in accurately forecasting internal reactions to a particular new experience. "What will happen" (the external events) may be accurately anticipated, whereas "how it will feel" (the internal experience of external events) may not be accurately assessed by the individual. How new experiences will feel, as opposed to how the individual expected them to feel, is difficult to anticipate and often surprising. "I knew I'd have to put in a lot of overtime, but I had no idea how bad I'd feel after a month of sixty-five-hour weeks, how tired I'd be all the time." In this example, the facts were available to the individual and were accepted; what was *inaccurately anticipated* and, therefore, surprising was how it would "actually feel," the *subjective experience.* The individual in this example might interpret his experience as "I don't have as much energy as I thought," a form of unmet expectations about self.

A fifth form of surprise comes from the cultural assumptions that transitioners make. Surprises result when one relies on *cultural assumptions brought from previous settings* as operating guides in the new setting, and they *fail.* Van Maanen (1977, p. 20) describes the situation as follows: "A newcomer assumes that he knows what the organization is about, assumes others in the setting have the same idea, and practically never bothers to check out these two assumptions. What occurs upon experience is that the neophyte receives a surprise of sorts . . . in which he discovers that significant others . . . do not share his assumptions. The newcomer must then reorient himself relative to others . . . through a cognitive revision of his previously taken-for-granted assumptions." Since cultures differ between and within organizations (Louis, 1983), a cognitive framework for interpreting meanings in a particular culture must be developed for the specific culture in which it will be used.

A final point about surprise is necessary. Both pleasant and unpleasant surprises require adaptation. However, traditional formulations implicitly treat only undermet expectations or unpleasant surprises. Thus, it is important to include overmet as well as undermet expectations in considering surprises that contribute to transition experiences. In summary, we have seen that surprises may be positive *or* negative; they may result from conscious *or* tacit anticipations concerning the job, the organization, and/or oneself in the new situation.

Traditional views of organizational entry and socialization as well as career transition have focused exclusively on one type of surprise (undermet conscious expectations about the job). However, the picture of the newcomer experience developed here suggests that the predominant traditional strategy of enhancing the realism only of conscious pre-entry job expectations is not adequate. Similarly, traditional strategies aimed at ensuring that conscious pre-entry job expectations are not underfulfilled (unmet) in early job experiences are also not sufficient. Ultimately, both views seek to aid transitioners by reducing the extent of their unmet expectations. Both implicitly deny the near inevitability of the myriad unanticipated and even unanticipatable changes, contrasts, and surprises attendant to any career-transition experience. An appreciation of the types of changes, contrasts, and surprises characteristic of transition experiences is essential for understanding and managing career transitions—one's own and others', whether in the role of manager, co-worker, organizational consultant, or friend. Together they constitute the transitioner's experiential landscape.

Coping with the Transition Experience: Sense Making

Individuals detect and interpret surprises through what can be called a "sense-making process." Sense-making is a recurring cycle of a sequence of events occurring over time. The cycle begins as individuals form unconscious and conscious anticipations and assumptions, which serve as predictions about future events. Subsequently, individuals experience events that may be discrepant from predictions. Discrepancies or surprises trigger a need for explanation and, correspondingly, for a process through which interpretations of discrepancies are generated. On the basis of the meanings that are attributed to surprises, any necessary behavioral responses to the immediate situation are selected, understandings of actors, actions, and settings are updated, and predictions about future experiences in the setting are revised. Updated anticipations represent alterations in cognitive scripts. The cycle as described here focuses on the more rational elements in sense making. It is meant to represent general stages rather than the literal process by which all individuals respond to each experience. Note that meaning is assigned to surprise as an output of the sense-making process, rather than arising concurrently with the perception or detection of differences.

In making sense of or attributing meaning to surprise, individuals rely on a number of inputs. Their past experiences with similar situations and surprises help them in coping with current situations. Individuals are also guided by their more general personal characteristics, including predispositions to attribute causality to self, others, or fate (locus of control; Rotter, 1966), as well as their orienting purposes in the situation and in general. Another input that shapes how sense is made of surprise is the individual's set of cultural assumptions or interpretive schemes. In addition, information and interpretations from others in the situation contribute to the sense-making process.

What special needs do transitioners have during sense making? Let us compare their situation in general with that of individuals making sense of surprise who are not undergoing a transition. The experiences of transitioners differ in three important ways from those of nontransitioners or insiders. First, insiders normally know what to expect in and of the situation. For the most part, little is surprising or needs to be made sense of. Second, when surprises do arise (for example, not getting an expected raise), the insider usually has sufficient history in the setting to interpret them more accurately or to make sense of them on the basis of relevant knowledge of the immediate situation. An insider probably knows, for instance, whether the denied raise is due to companywide budget cuts or is related to job performance and whether it is an indication of how the future may unfold or of a temporary situation. Third, when surprises arise and sense making is necessary, the insider usually has other insiders with whom to compare perceptions and interpretations.

The comparison of transitioners' and insiders' experiences suggests that two types of input to sense making may be problematical for transitioners: local interpretation schemes and others' interpretations. Concerning local interpretation schemes, newcomers probably do not have an adequate history of the situation to appreciate as fully as insiders might why and how surprises have arisen. With time and experience, they may come to understand how to interpret the actions of others and what meanings to attach to events and outcomes in the setting. According to Berger and Luckmann (1967), during the early stages in a new situation, transitioners internalize context-specific dictionaries of meaning used by members of the setting. At the outset, however, they typically are unfamiliar with these interpretation schemes. And, as we saw earlier, transitioners are usually unaware of both their need to understand context-specific meaning dictionaries or interpretation schemes and the fact that they are unfamiliar with them (Van Maanen, 1977).

As a result, those in transition often attach meanings to actions, events, and surprises using interpretation schemes developed through their experiences in other situations; so that inappropriate and dysfunctional interpretations may be produced. For example, what it means to "take initiative" or "put in a hard day's work" in a school situation may be quite different from its meaning in a traditional work setting. Transitioners may attribute permanence or stability to temporary situations (Weiner, 1974); they may see themselves as the source or cause of events when external factors are responsible for outcomes (Weiner, 1974). Similarly, a transitioner's understanding of why a superior responds in a particularly harsh manner may be inadequate. Overpersonalized attributions may result in the absence of knowledge about how that superior typically behaves toward other subordinates. And without relevant background information about, for instance, the superior's recent divorce, lack of promotion, or reduction in scope of authority and responsibility, it is easy to misinterpret situations in the new settings.

The dysfunctional effects of such interpretational errors can be revealed by tracing how individuals' responses are influenced by the meanings they attribute to situations. In a series of studies by Weiner (1974), subjects who attributed events to stable causes ("the boss is always like this") changed behavior more often than did subjects who attributed events to unstable or temporary causes ("the boss is going through a rough but temporary period"). Decisions to stay in or leave organizations and feelings of commitment or alienation would appear to follow from sense made by transitioners of early experiences in the role.

The second type of input to sense making that is problematical for transitioners is *information and interpretations from others* in the situation. In comparison to insiders, transitioners probably have not developed relationships with others in the immediate role setting with whom they could test their perceptions and interpretations. Since reality testing is seen as an important input to sense making, it seems particularly important for transitioners to have insiders who might serve as sounding boards and guide them to important background information for assigning meaning to events and surprises. Insiders are seen as a potentially rich source of assistance to those in transition in diagnosing and interpreting the myriad surprises that may arise during transitions. Insiders are already "on board"; presumably, they are equipped with richer historical and current interpretative perspectives than the transitioner alone possesses. Information may also come through insider-transitioner relationships, averting and/or precipitating surprises. These relationships might also facilitate acquisition of the context-specific interpretation scheme.

The framework presented here suggests that sense made of surprises may be inadequate in the absence of relevant information about organizational, interpersonal, and personal histories. Inputs to sense making from sources in the organization balance the inputs provided by the transitioner (past experiences, personal predispositions, and interpretive schemes appropriate to old situations), which are likely to be inadequate in the new situation. Until transitioners develop accurate internal maps of the new setting, until they appreciate local meanings, it is important that they have information available for amending internal cognitive maps and for attaching meaning to such surprises as may arise during transition experiences.

Managing Career Transitions

Essential Transition Tasks. The same basic transition tasks have been described by people making transitions in and between civilian and military organizations, by people in finance, marketing, production, and other functional areas, by people at different levels in the organizational hierarchy, by people in small, medium, and large organizations, by people in public and private work organizations, and by people undergoing major job changes within the same organization as well as those moving to different organizations. The commonly identified transition tasks are as follows.

1. *Master the basics of the job.* The basics include the formal procedures and technology as well as the tasks involved in the job.
2. *Build an image or role identity.* This signals to others with and/or for whom the person works whether, for instance, he or she intends to "maintain the status quo" or "shake things up around here."
3. *Build relationships.* Relationships must be built first of all with immediate superiors but also with peers or subordinates on whom one must rely in doing the job. It is through these relationships that the needed flow of information and cooperation is ensured and specific expectations are negotiated.
4. *Construct a current interpretation scheme or frame of reference.* A frame of reference is needed that reflects how

and why things are done as they are in the new situation. Core values, norms, and cultural assumptions are encompassed in the frame of reference.

5. *Map the relevant players.* This involves learning names, faces, and roles as well as how people fit together in terms of the formal tasks of the organization and the informal power sources and social networks.

6. *Place oneself within those networks.* Along with mapping networks of players, the transitioner must see where he or she fits in role and work-flow networks and how his or her job relates to the mission of the unit in order to function effectively.

7. *Learn the local language.* Special terms and symbols used by the work group and organization must be decoded. In fact, being able to speak and understand the technical, organizational, and social vernacular is often an indication that the transition is nearing completion and the person is becoming an insider.

8. *Assess how well the job is being done.* Decisions about where to put one's efforts, what to pay attention to, and when and whom to ask for information often reflect one's sense of how well things are running in the department.

Of the basic transition tasks, only the first two, mastering core job activities and developing role identity, bear directly on the job for which an individual is hired. Yet, as this list indicates, the transition entails a much broader set of tasks. Assistance in learning basic job activities is routinely offered through career development; similar assistance in accomplishing other transition tasks—in learning "the system"—is lacking. It is time to focus attention on these other transition tasks and, more broadly, on transition aspects of careers in order to help individuals and organizations better manage transitions.

Diagnosing the Transition Situation. Whether in preparing for one's own transition or in trying to help others, it is useful to take stock of relevant conditions bearing on the transition. Such stocktaking can help flag potential problems, direct one to more information, and otherwise guide the transitioner and/or others in use of resources. In conducting a personal diagnosis of a transition situation, selected characteristics of the transitioner, the boss, the predecessor, key subordinates, other personnel, the new situation, and the overall change ought to be examined. Among relevant aspects of the *transitioner,* one would want to take stock of one's expectations about the job and organization. Additionally, one should conduct a candid self-assessment of such dimensions as patience, tolerance for ambiguity/preferences for structure, preferred modes of communicating, and interpersonal skills. In addition, how one's family is affected by the change has a direct bearing on the transitioner.

In diagnosing the *boss's* potential contribution to the transition, it makes sense to assess how clearly expectations about priorities and standards are communicated, the boss's understanding of and support for the transitioner's position, and his or her reputation for consistency across time and people. Certainly, some of this cannot be ascertained in advance, and much of it is a matter of judgment. Nevertheless, it is useful to take a reading and note any areas that stand out as potential problems. Concerning one's *predecessor,* it is useful to address the following questions in embarking on a transition: Will the predecessor be present to help with orientation? Why is the predecessor leaving? How competent is the predecessor? What is his or her reputation with subordinates, boss, important clients, and counterparts in other departments? Similar issues should be considered with respect to key *subordinates* and *other personnel.*

Another area to assess in diagnosing the transition is the new situation: In what condition is the unit in terms of backlog and resources? What is the history of the position? What is the reputation of the organizational subunit? Is doing the job likely to be a "good" experience? How does the role fit with one's longer-term career plans? And, finally, aspects of the overall change situation need to be considered. For instance, where in the work cycle of the unit does the transitioner's entry come? How sudden was the transition, and what was the impetus for undertaking it? Early on in the transition, then, the individual should diagnose the situation. Such a diagnosis can provide a picture of the overall favorableness of the situation. It can also highlight potential problem sources and resources.

Although some events and experiences are common to every transitioner, people differ in what they prefer and need as they cope with changes in their work situations. For some, the ideal transition is the one that is most challenging; for others, it is the one that is completed most quickly, most comfortably. Knowledge of one's preferences can guide one in seeking out particular tasks, people, and information during a transition. The person who knows that he prefers to have ample time to get on board before undertaking his first major project would manage his transition quite differently, all else being equal, than would the person for whom it is most important to have a challenging assignment the first week. In short, what one personally considers "ideal" in a transition has direct implications for how one manages a transition. Appreciation of such individual differences in preferences and need is critical for those seeking to help people in transition. For the would-be helper, the untested assumption that one's own preferences are universal—that, for instance, everyone wants an opportunity to "sink or swim" by going it alone—may undermine the best of intentions to be helpful.

Facilitating the Transitions of Others

The first part of this chapter offered a description of the experience of being in transition. In the previous section, action steps involved in managing a transition were considered. The perspective taken was that of the individual undergoing the transition. I want to conclude this chapter by discussing organizational and managerial action steps—addressing the question of what can be done to facilitate others' transitions. What approaches, processes, and structures can be adopted by personnel-policy makers, supervisors, and co-workers to facilitate the transitions of organizational members?

The framework presented here for understanding the transitioner's experience suggests that organizational practices that facilitate sense making, appreciation of the local culture, and acquisition of a setting-specific interpretation scheme ultimately facilitate adaptation to the changed situation. In essence, such practices provide the transitioner with particularly relevant and reliable information. What are critical characteristics of organizational practices that facilitate transitions? What qualities should managers and designers keep in mind as they set up transition-facilitating practices? Essential qualities can be derived from the sense-making framework. First, specific information should be made available *in response to* transitioners' needs, rather than in *advance* or merely according to what is considered organizationally efficient. Second, the information should come from an insider, rather than another transitioner; it should come from someone who knows and is willing and able to share with the transitioner something about "how things operate around here." Other transitioners typically do not have this information, and written orientation materials usually do not give it. "In-response" practices facilitate sense making and adaptation more effectively than "in-advance" practices; and practices in which insiders, rather than other transitioners, are the person's primary associates more effectively facilitate adaptation.

In two studies examining these characteristics of transition practices (Louis, 1980b; Louis, Posner, and Powell, 1983), peers as a source of in-response transition assistance contributed to adaptation more than such in-advance aids as supervisors and formal on-site orientation sessions. Further, aids in which insiders (peers and supervisor) were the primary associates were superior to aids in which other transitioners were the primary associates. Peers were superior to all other aids. Peer interactions are *responsive*; they occur in situ both physically and temporally. Peers are *insiders* with whom transitioners share organizational and hierarchical contexts. The perspectives of peers are thus relevant and appropriate as sense-making inputs, and they serve as models for transitioners in building their own local frames of reference. Peers are in the best position to truly empathize and to be seen as "trustworthy" channels and sources of information (Louis, 1980b).

The sense-making perspective suggests that past approaches to managing unwanted employee turnover are inadequate. Past approaches have focused exclusively on new employees' conscious pre-entry expectations about the job. Yet we have seen that surprises arise from tacit and even emergent anticipations and assumptions, as well as from conscious expectations. Expectations are not formed once and for all before one encounters the changed situation; they evolve and are periodically revised as a result of sense made of surprises. Assumptions about oneself (for example, who I am and what I want to do) lead to surprises that have at least as much impact as do expectations about the job. Past approaches favored strategies for managing transitions that provided individuals with more accurate (realistic) initial expectations, such as through a "realistic job preview" when the situation was an entry transition. In contrast, strategies based on this sense-making perspective take as given the near inevitability that transitioners will experience some unmet expectations and surprises. Strategies based on this framework aim to intervene in the cycle as sense is made of all types of surprise.

What this means at the practical level is that, at a minimum, certain secrecy norms, the sink-or-swim, learn-on-your-own philosophy, and sanctions against sharing information among office members are dysfunctional for transitioners and for their employing organizations as well. Each of these restricts possible sources of relevant information. In contrast, fostering links between transitioners and their insider peers or nonsupervisor superiors is beneficial. Superiors can support informal associations between transitioner and co-worker insiders or more formal programs, such as buddy systems, in which insiders receive skills training and serve as guides. Informal sponsor and mentor links between junior and senior members offer other models of relationships through which information, perceptions, and interpretations of events in the organization can be exchanged.

Another potential aid is the appraisal process. Timely formal and informal feedback from superiors to transitioners about their performance may reduce the stress-producing uncertainty of "not knowing how you're doing" and replace possibly inaccurate self-appraisals with data from superiors, which guide transitioners' subsequent assessments of equity in the situation. An early appraisal could foster an understanding of the process and criteria of performance evaluation. With such first-hand knowledge, the transitioner can be expected to make more reality-based self-assessments; in addition, he or she is better equipped to interpret other events related to evaluation, a crucial area in the newcomer's early organizational life. An early appraisal could be treated as a collaborative sense-making session, in which the superior helps the transitioner try on a portion of an important insider's interpretive scheme.

Others can contribute to the earlier transition-adaptation process by appreciating the nature of transition experiences: why it is likely that transitioners may experience surprises; why they are relatively ill equipped to make accurate sense of surprises arising during the early period in the changed situation; and how seeking and receiving information from insiders at work can supplement their own inadequate internal interpretive schemes. Toward that end, college placement, career counseling, executive search, and corporate personnel activities could, as a matter of course, provide individuals with a preview of typical transition experiences and ways to help manage transitions—their own and those of co-workers, subordinates, friends, and spouses.

References

Allen, V., and van de Vliert, E. *Role Transitions: Explorations and Explanations*. New York: Plenum, 1984.

Atchley, R. C. *The Sociology of Retirement*. New York: Wiley, 1976.

Berger, P. L., and Luckmann, T. *The Social Construction of Reality: A Treatise in the Sociology of Knowledge*. New York: Anchor, 1967.

Blumenthal, W. M. "Candid Reflections of a Businessman in Washington." *Fortune,* Jan. 29, 1979, p. 36.

Brett, J. M. "Job Transitions and Personal and Role Change." In K. M. Rowland and G. Ferris (Eds.), *Research in Person-*

nel and Human Resources Management. Vol. 2. Greenwich, Conn.: JAI Press, 1984.

Clark, F. L. E. *Work, Age, and Leisure: Causes and Consequences of the Shortened Working Life.* London: Joseph, 1966.

Erikson, E. H. "Identity and the Life Cycle." *Psychological Issues,* 1959, *1,* 1-171.

Friedman, E. A., and Havighurst, R. J. *The Meaning of Work and Retirement.* Chicago: University of Chicago Press, 1954.

Hall, D. T. *Careers in Organizations.* Pacific Palisades, Calif.: Goodyear, 1976.

Hall, D. T., and Nougaim, K. "An Examination of Maslow's Need Hierarchy in an Organizational Setting." *Organizational Behavior and Human Performance,* 1968, *3,* 12-35.

Jacques, E. "Death and the Mid-Life Crisis." *International Journal of Psychoanalysis,* 1965, *45,* 502-514.

Lewin, K. *Field Theory in Social Science.* (D. Cartwright, Ed.) New York: Harper & Row, 1951.

Louis, M. R. "Career Transitions: Varieties and Commonalities." *Academy of Management Review,* 1980a, *5* (3), 329-340.

Louis, M. R. "Learning the Ropes: What Helps New Employees Become Acculturated?" Paper presented at meeting of the Academy of Management, Detroit, August 1980b.

Louis, M. R. "Surprise and Sense-Making: What Newcomers Experience in Entering Unfamiliar Organizational Settings." *Administrative Science Quarterly,* 1980c, *25* (2), 226-251.

Louis, M. R. "Managing Career Transitions: A Missing Link in Career Development." *Organizational Dynamics,* 1982, *10* (4), 68-77.

Louis, M. R. "Culture: Yes; Organization: No!" Paper presented at meeting of the Academy of Management, Dallas, August 1983.

Louis, M. R., Posner, B., and Powell, G. "The Availability and Helpfulness of Socialization Practices." *Personnel Psychology,* 1983, *36,* 857-866.

Miller, D. C., and Form, W. H. *Industrial Sociology.* New York: Harper & Row, 1951.

Miller, G. A. "The Magical Number 7, Plus or Minus Two: Some

Limits on Our Capacity for Processing Information." *Psychological Review*, 1956, *63*, 81–96.

Nicholson, N. "A Theory of Work Role Transition." *Administrative Science Quarterly*, 1984, *29*, 172–191.

Pinder, C. C. "The Role of Transfers and Mobility Experiences in Employee Motivation and Control." In H. Meltzer and W. Nord (Eds.), *Making Organizations Humane and Productive.* New York: Wiley, 1981.

Price, J. L. *The Study of Turnover.* Ames: Iowa State University Press, 1977.

Rapoport, R., and Rapoport, R. N. *Working Couples.* New York: Harper & Row, 1978.

Rotter, J. B. "Generalized Expectations for Internal versus External Control of Reinforcement." *Psychological Monographs: General and Applied,* 1966, *80* (1) (entire issue).

Schein, E. H. "The Individual, the Organization, and the Career: A Conceptual Scheme." *Journal of Applied Behavioral Science,* 1971, *7*, 401–426.

Schein, E. H. *Career Dynamics: Matching Individual and Organizational Needs.* Reading, Mass.: Addison-Wesley, 1978.

Schneider, B. Personal communication, Dec. 6, 1983.

Sofer, C. *Men in Mid-Career.* London: Cambridge University Press, 1970.

Super, D. F. *The Psychology of Careers.* New York: Harper & Row, 1957.

Van Maanen, J. "Experiencing Organization: Notes on the Meaning of Careers and Socialization." In J. Van Maanen (Ed.), *Organizational Careers: Some New Perspectives.* New York: Wiley, 1977.

Weiner, B. *Achievement Motivation and Attribution Theory.* Morristown, N.J.: General Learning Press, 1974.

5

Holding On, Letting Go, and Moving On: Understanding a Neglected Perspective on Change

Robert Tannenbaum
Robert W. Hanna

The process of change is of central concern to managers and to organization-development professionals. In these critical times, the need for organizational change is ever present. First, adaptation to an environment in rapid flux seems essential for an organization's survival and its potential growth. New knowledge and technologies, fluctuating economic conditions, shifting political realities, growing international interdependencies, the pressures of competition, the quest for peace against the reality of war, the threat of nuclear holocaust, the evolution of new cultural values and perspectives, including the possibility of a major paradigm shift—all these and more impinge constantly on the organization, demanding adaptation, innovation, and, at times, fundamental reorientation. Second, pressures for change emerge from within the organization itself as internal ferment generates new possibilities—for example, gains that might be achieved through structural reorganization, product improvement, cost reduction, or personnel shifts. These pressures cannot be ignored.

In response to these external and internal organizational realities, major attention has been given in recent decades to theories of change, an understanding of the change process itself, and the technology of change. Academic departments in organization behavior focus heavily on this area; professional groups specializing in organization development have arisen and flourished; and managers, assisted by internal staff specialists, are devoting an increasing proportion of their time and energy to managing change. *Planned change, introducing change,* and *intervention strategy* have become accepted and widely used terms.

Major (organizationwide) programs have been started by many organizations. In their early stages, these programs have typically been characterized by the considerable enthusiasm, commitment, and involvement of organization members. High hopes have been held for what might be accomplished, and much positive accomplishment has occurred. Nevertheless, within our experience, few if any of these programs have succeeded in maintaining the powerful thrust and promise of their earliest months or years, nor have they typically achieved the more fundamental objectives they have aimed for. Some have been phased out; others have continued (some for years), but at a much less ambitious and more routine level. For some time now, we have observed these efforts being frustrated, and we have tried to understand why.

Emerging Insights and Speculation

An important breakthrough for us occurred when we became aware of Elizabeth Kübler-Ross, a psychiatrist, and her work with terminally ill patients. On the basis of her observations through this work, she described the stages through which individuals typically pass in the process of dying (Kübler-Ross, 1969). The first stage is that of *denial and isolation.* The dying person is faced with shock—a shock at first receiving the news of the terminal illness. With the shock comes denial. It is what Kübler-Ross calls the "no, not me" phase—a disbelief, a putting-it-off, a forgetting about it. Then comes a stage in which the dying person experiences deep emotions—rage, resentment, envy. Kübler-Ross refers to this stage as *anger*. These emotions are directed both at other individuals and at God. It is the "why me?" phase. Next there is the *bargaining* stage, a period of temporary truce: "Yes, it's happening to me; but if you'll only let me go home from the hospital for a couple of months to be with my children, then I'll come back and be a good patient." The dying person wants time to work through unfinished business. After bargaining comes the *depression* stage, of which there are two phases. The first is called "reactive depression," in which individuals mourn things (including relationships) that are already lost. The second phase is one of "preparatory depression," during which there is silent grief or a mourning of future losses. Individuals symbolically say good-bye to those they relate to, going from those furthest away from them to those dearest to them. The final stage is one of *acceptance*—an achieving of an inner and outer peace: "My time is very close now, and it's OK."

Further insight was achieved when a coauthor of this chapter did a phenomenological study of crises in personal meaning (Hanna, 1975). He collected his data, getting close to individuals who either were going through or had gone through a substantial loss of life meaning. He found that subjects passed through a series of stages similar to those described by Kübler-Ross. First, there is the *onset,* where individuals encounter circumstances that limit or frustrate the satisfaction of some important personal need(s). In an effort to reduce growing discomfort, the individual tries to *evaluate and understand* the situation. However, as his or her view of life proves increasingly inadequate to give value to his or her suffering, the individual's life situation loses meaning. In the *coping* stage, he attempts to avoid his negative experiencing. There is a strong inclination to hang on to the safety of the old, familiar ways of seeing and doing things. Essentially, avoidance and blockage lead to depression and a sense of helplessness. However, if the individual succeeds in moving on to the *search* stage, he begins to reformulate his life direction and to experiment with new modes of behavior and thought. Finally, *resolution* (including renewed life meaning) is achieved when the individual's new behavior, life situation, and/or view of life reduce significantly his sensed discomfort and pain or transform this sense into something of positive value.

Will McWhinney (1980), in his work dealing with organization designing, looks at people in organizations rather than those facing physical death or crises in life meaning. His purpose is to understand the creative organization-designing process following a *disequilibrating event*. He concludes that first there needs to be a *retreat*—a retreat that often begins with anger and feelings of guilt. The retreat involves processes that strip away accrued goals, attitudes, structures, and acceptances of prior beliefs—a letting go, a loosening up of the bindings. Then there is what he calls a *founding*—a rebirth, a turnaround out of which the new ideas, the new creations emerge. Then there is a *return*, which involves a re-engagement of the organizational entity with its environment.

The findings from these and related studies of change are best summarized for us by the four phases reported in an organizationally relevant study by Stephen Fink, Joel Beak, and Kenneth Taddeo (1971). They name the phases they observed as *shock* (the threat to existing structure or fixities), *defensive retreat* (an attempt to maintain the old structure—the holding on), *acknowledgment* (giving up, yielding the existing structures—the letting go), and *adaptation and change* (establishing a new structure and a sense of worth—a moving on).

When the change process is even more broadly viewed, a repetitive pattern of homeostasis (holding on), dying and death (letting go), and rebirth (moving on) emerges with a pervasive universality. There is, for example, the legendary phoenix, a bird represented by the ancient Egyptians as living five or six centuries in the Arabian desert, being consumed in a fire set by itself, and rising in youthful freshness from its own ashes. In the physical universe, there is growing evidence of cycles of implosion and explosion. Year after year, we live through the seasons —fall, winter, spring, summer, and fall again—experiencing these changes in weather and in nature. The cycle is reflected in the world's mythologies and religions. Through the ages, tribes, nations, and cultures have come and gone as new ones have arisen.

The life cycles of organizations have been increasingly noted and studied. And each of us as individuals is acutely aware of our own life cycle—and of our own vulnerability and mortality.

For many years (and, to a considerable extent, even into the present), the primary attention of organizational change facilitators has been on the introduction of change—a diagnosis of the present situation, a decision concerning the goals of the change effort being considered, and a development of strategy and tactics for moving from here to there, followed by appropriate implementation in the field. This has been a future orientation—one starting with an assumption of "acceptance," leading to "resolution," a "founding" or rebirth, and "adaptation and change." What has become increasingly clear to us is that very little, if any, attention has been given to the *working through* of the potent needs of human systems to hold on to the existing order—to that which is—and to avoid the powerful feelings that changed circumstances can trigger. The deeply felt experiencing of "shock," "frustration," "loss of meaning," "anger," "need to bargain," "helplessness," and "depression" has been almost completely ignored (except possibly at a relatively superficial level called "resistance to change"). Thus, the considerable and growing interest in the change process has been one that has not encompassed the totality of that process. It has heavily focused on the *moving on* and has to a large extent neglected or avoided *the need to hold on.*

The Need to Hold On and the Change Process. We came to realize—and through recent years have become more strongly convinced—that this neglect on the part of many of those interested in facilitating change is a critical one. It is a principle reason why so many major change programs have encountered great difficulty in building up momentum and solidly maintaining it over a considerable period of time (compare Kahn, 1982). The need for individuals, groups, and organizations to hold on is powerful (why this is so will be explored in later sections). Not to be aware of this, to ignore it, or to try to override it is to subvert the change process and court failure. Adequate attention *must* be given to the need to hold on and to its working through as part of the total change process.

This need to hold on is not limited to the dying or to

those in crisis but is embedded in the human condition. We can see it in mythology, in the writing of scholars, in literature, and in folk sayings. A selective sampling of these sources is suggestive:

The tenacity of holding on and its sometimes tragic outcomes were fully appreciated by the ancient Greeks. Their literature and mythology are filled with the accounts of those who blindly or stubbornly held on to a pattern of behavior anchored in the human weaknesses, such as pride, vanity, greed, or desire. And when they defied the gods, their punishment was eternal. For example:

- Narcissus, who committed suicide because he could not give up gazing at his unattainable but enrapturing reflection in the water.
- Orpheus, who persuaded Pluto to restore to life his wife, Eurydice, killed by a serpent. The one condition was that he not look behind him before emerging into the upper world. However, he could not resist turning back to look at his wife too soon, and she disappeared forever.
- King Midas, who was so attached to wealth that he got Dionysus to grant his wish that all he touch turn to gold. He lost a daughter whom he loved, and nearly starved to death because all the food he touched would turn to gold.

The psychoanalyst Ernest Schachtel (1959) insightfully explains: "The anxiety of the encounter with the unknown springs . . . from the person's fear of letting go of the *attitudes* to which he clings for safety, of the *perspectives* which these attitudes give him on the world, and of the familiar *labels* for what he sees in the world . . . so man is afraid that without the support of his accustomed attitudes, perspectives, and labels he will fall into an abyss or flounder in the pathless. . . . Letting go of every kind of clinging opens the fullest view. . . . But it is this very letting go which often arouses the greatest amount of anxiety" (p. 195). The eminent physicist Werner Heisenberg (1974) has observed: "When new groups of phenomena compel changes in the pattern of thought . . . even the most eminent of physicists find immense difficulties. For the demand for change in the thought pattern may engender the feeling that the ground is to be pulled from under one's feet. . . . I believe that the difficulties at this point can hardly be overestimated. Once one has experienced the desperation with which clever and conciliatory men of science react to the demand for a change in the thought pattern, one can only be amazed that such revolutions in science have actually been possible at all" (p. 162). James Baldwin (1961) shares this wisdom in his powerful book: "Any real change implies the break up of the world as one has always known it, the loss of all that gave one identity, the end of safety. And at such a moment, unable to see and not daring to imagine what the future will now bring forth, one clings to what one knew, or thought one knew; to what one possessed or dreamed that one possessed. Yet it is only when man is able, without bitterness or self pity, to surrender a dream he has long cherished, or a privilege he has long possessed, that he is set free—that he has set himself free—for higher dreams, for greater privileges" (p. 117). The need to hold on is also reflected in folk and other sayings: "Look before you leap." "There is many a slip between the cup and lip." "Better be safe than sorry." "A bird in the hand is worth two in the bush." "The certainty of misery is better than the misery of uncertainty."

Because the need to hold on is so basic to any change process, it is critical that we understand it much better than we do. We now begin this effort and continue it in the section to follow.

System Identity and the Avoidance of Nothingness. All human systems (individuals, groups, organizations) have boundaries. The boundary of a system (entity) separates what is within the system from what is outside, in its environment. That which is within the boundary gives the system its differentiating character—its identity (its ego or its self-definition). This identity—particularly in its deeper aspects—is experienced by the system as essential to its survival.

As constructed or developed by a system through time, identity is defined by a number of system attributes, or *fixities*. Some overlapping examples of these fixities are the system's world view (its generalized view of reality), purposes, goals, values, beliefs, attitudes, expectations, assumptions, knowledge, skills, modes of behavior or action, and relationships. The attributes of identity of the system range from the boundary itself to the center—or the system's core of identity. Those attributes near the system's periphery are relatively minor and solitary elements, while those at or near the system's core are basic and highly interconnected elements. Those ranging in between take on increasing interconnectedness and greater relevance to the system's identity as they are to be found further from the boundary and closer to the core.

During a change process, we can think of a system letting go of various attributes of its identity. When attributes near the periphery are yielded, what we will call *superficial change* is involved. Such would be the case, for example, when an individual willingly exchanges an old tooth filling for a new one or when an organization replaces its stairs with escalators. Superficial changes are relatively easy to make. When attributes near the core are yielded, what we will call *basic change* is involved. Such would be the case, for example, when a woman yields one of her most central values (for example, her religious beliefs) or when an organization lets go of its long-held antiunion policy. Basic changes are relatively difficult and at times impossible to make.

As a system lets go of attributes closer and closer to its core, it will experience an increasingly greater number of what Keleman (1976, p. 5) has called "little dyings"—not physical death but a giving up of important attributes of the system's identity. Doing so involves facing the unknown (ambiguity, uncertainty), with attendant strong feelings such as fear, anger, and helplessness. At the extreme, letting go of *all* attributes of identity involves moving into nothingness (Novak, 1971)—essentially the real or psychological death of the system. Therefore, as we move from changes that are superficial to those more basic, we encounter more emotional pain and difficulty, and we tend to hold on ever more tenaciously.

Feeling and Emotion and the Need to Hold On

In the preceding section, we emphasized the pervasiveness and tenacity of the need to hold on in *all* human systems undergoing change and the difficulties of altering human-system identity—with all its depth and complexity—as a key factor underlying the need to hold on. In this and the following section, we will focus our attention primarily on one specific human system—the individual. We have three reasons for doing so. First, at the present time, our relevant knowledge and experience are greater at the level of the individual than at other system levels. Second, we believe that this rich knowledge and experience can often have suggestive relevance at other system levels. And third, and perhaps most important, we have a strong belief that all social-system change is mediated through individuals.

We would like to elaborate on the third reason. Certainly, the individual in a group or organization is influenced by the social interactions in which she or he is embedded, and any manager or other change facilitator must be aware of such influences in any change effort. Nevertheless, the nature of any system change and the degree to which it is realized ultimately depend upon the unique responses of the individuals who are involved in the change. No system can effectuate change unless that change is supported—ideally with enthusiasm—by the individual members of the system. Basically, the need of the individual to hold on and the processes for facilitating his letting go and moving on (all in a context of the groups, organization, and larger culture within which he is embedded) must be of central importance to us.

We begin this focus on the individual with the premise that all thinking is accompanied by a parallel stream of feeling (either emotions, undifferentiated feeling, or body sensations). Therefore, all our constructions of reality (from our individual identity to our view of the world about us) are anchored in memory to the various feelings and emotions that accompanied their earlier formulation. This premise has been stated in one form or another by people from many fields of knowledge. A Sufi spiritual master, Hazrat Inayat Khan (1960, p. 142), has observed, "Mind begins to live from the moment that feeling is awakened in it. Neither can the thinking power be nurtured, nor the faculty of reasoning be sustained, without a continual outflow of feeling." A new theory, the Gray-LaViolette model (discussed in *Brain-Mind Bulletin,* vol. 7, nos. 6 and 7, 1982), posits that thoughts are always embedded in emotional codes. Thus, the more abstract the information, the more difficult it is to recall, because it has little grounding in emotionally nuanced memory.

Put another way by psychologist Eugene Gendlin (1962): "Thought is really a functional relationship between symbols and experiencing. . . . We have this or that specific idea, wish, emotion, perception, word, or thought, but we *always* have concrete feeling, an inward sensing whose nature is broader" (p. 11). "A concrete aspect of experiencing accompanies every description, every meaningful thing you say. Above and beyond the symbols there is always also the feeling referent itself" (p. 13). Thus, feeling is associated with every thought and every behavior.

Although this constant flow of experiencing—of feeling and emotion—is usually not conscious, we and others may become abruptly and uncomfortably aware of it when we become engaged in a defense of our significant views (fixities) ranging from those about ourselves to explanations of life itself; thus, the admonition to be cautious in the discussion of three emotionally loaded topics at cocktail parties—sex, politics, and religion. But how do some ideas, behaviors, and situations become emotionally loaded? For an explanation, we turn to Stanislav Grof's (1976) model of how human experience is stored in memory. Grof is a psychiatrist who developed the COEX (condensed experiences) system model on the basis of over a decade of research and analysis of the phenomenology of serial LSD therapy sessions (psycholytic and psychedelic therapy):

> A COEX system can be defined as a specific constellation of memories consisting of condensed experiences (and related fantasies) from different life periods of the individual. The memories belonging to a particular COEX system have a similar basic theme or contain similar elements and are associated with a strong emotional charge of the same quality. *The deepest layers of this system are represented by vivid and colorful memories of ex-*

periences from infancy and early childhood [emphasis added]. More superficial layers of such a system involve memories of similar experiences from late periods, up to the present life situation.

Each COEX system has a basic theme that permeates all its layers and represents their common denominator; the nature of these themes varies considerably from one COEX constellation to another.... Particularly important are COEX systems that epitomize and condense the individual's encounters with situations endangering survival, health, and integrity of the body. The excessive emotional charge which is attached to COEX systems (as indicated by the often powerful abreaction accompanying the unfolding of these systems in LSD sessions) seems to be a summation of the emotions belonging to all the constituent memories of a particular kind [pp. 46-47].

According to the basic quality of the individual charge, we can differentiate *negative COEX systems* (condensing unpleasant emotional experiences) and *positive COEX systems* (condensing pleasant emotional experiences and positive aspects of an individual's past life). Although there are certain interdependencies and overlappings, separate COEX systems can function relatively autonomously. In a complicated interaction with the environment, they influence selectively the subject's perception of himself and of the world, his feelings and ideation, and even many somatic processes [p. 49].

The unconscious thematic emotional content of a COEX system may be propelled toward consciousness by many day-to-day experiences—expressing a new behavior, encountering a new situation, or experiencing a changing relationship or circumstance. Harris (1969, p. 7) calls this a displacement into the past. "The sequence in involuntary recollections is: (1) *reliving* (spontaneous, involuntary feeling), and (2) *remembering* (conscious, voluntary thinking about the past event thus relived)." However, he goes on to state that "much of what we relive we cannot remember." Thus, much of the time, all we are aware of are inexplicable feelings. If these evoked memories are associated with a powerfully charged negative COEX system, we are likely to experience a good deal of anxiety, leading to the engagement of a related defense mechanism (such as withdrawal or denial) to disengage from a conscious reliving or remembering. For example, a young worker may hear through the grapevine that her longtime supervisor, whom she admires and respects, is about to be transferred. She expresses surprise and reacts with anxiety, which she assumes has to do with the uncertainty that this creates about her future and her compatability with a new supervisor. However, her anxiety grows, and within a few days she calls in sick or finds herself completely discounting what she heard as false rumor. Even if the change occurs, by engaging her defenses, she may never have to become aware of the hurt, anger, or possible grief this change has stimulated. Similarly, activated memories of childhood and early adult separations and the associated feelings of rejection, abandonment, and helplessness will probably be suppressed. But there will be a cost. The worker may unaccountably lose interest in her job, feel low on energy, become depressed, or develop physical symptoms until her acceptance of the new (and probably resented) supervisor is well under way. Often these outcomes are attributed to the "stress of change."

All change has the potential to evoke past memories and their associated feelings and emotions via several basic thematic paths:

1. *Change is loss.* Every change in our situation, point of view, or behavior requires us to give up or let go of something familiar and predictable. Our past experiences with loss and how well they were accepted and integrated through a mourning process determine the strength and variety of negative emotions stored away in the unconscious, with the threatening potential to be stimulated by thematically similar change in the present. Some of the emotions and feelings typically associated with loss are anger, guilt, grief, helplessness, hopelessness, and depression.

2. *Change is uncertainty.* All change requires us to move from the known to the unknown. Our past experiences with sur-

prise and ambiguity and how well they were confronted and integrated through external support and patience determine the strength and variety of negative emotions stored away in the unconscious, with the threatening potential to be stimulated by thematically similar change in the present. Some of the emotions and feelings typically associated with uncertainty are fear, panic, dread, and anxiety.

3. *Change dissolves meaning.* All change causes the dissolution of some past meaning, which may or may not be replaced by new meaning. Earlier, we related this aspect to identity, but in the larger sense, it relates to all our constructions of reality. Our past experiences with the loss of meaning in our lives and the attendant confrontations with emptiness, "nothingness," or nonbeing determine the strength and variety of emotions stored away in the unconscious, with the threatening potential to be stimulated by thematically similar change in the present. Some of the emotions and feelings typically associated with meaning loss are confusion, anxiety, frustration, boredom, apathy, and depression.

4. *Change violates scripts.* Scripts are the unconscious life plans we make in childhood on the basis of the injunctions or directives of our parents or other significant authority figures (Berne, 1972). The injunctions, sometimes transmitted nonverbally, are grounded in emotions (usually repressed) such as shame, guilt, and fears of parental abandonment, withdrawal of love, or rejection. Many of our apparent life choices were or are controlled by scripts, and our behavior represents a consistent effort unwittingly to conform to or rebel against the injunctions that created them. For example, I might be working eighteen hours a day, seven days a week because I want to be a millionaire by age thirty. This script may conform to the injunction, "Don't be like your father; make something of yourself." Or it may express rebellion against the injunction, "You'll never amount to anything." In either case, we are trapped by injunctions, and choice is an illusion. Many changes, especially those related to achievement ("Always do better!"), self-image ("Be perfect!"), relationships ("Never

trust anyone!"), and career ("Be successful!"), precipitate a confrontation with our scripts. If the related negative emotions stored in the unconscious are too powerful to experience, we directly or indirectly sabotage changes that violate our script.

What we repeatedly see in our efforts to facilitate basic change at all system levels is the individual need to hold on, linked to painful experiences of the past (particularly those of early childhood that taught us the emotional cost of letting go). As has been pointed out by Freud, Jung, and many, many others, our early childhood experiences become the templates for our adult constructions of reality and for our patterns of response. What is often overlooked, however, is the influence of childhood experience through unconscious painful feelings and critical decisions that still affect our ability to cope with larger system change in the present.

In sum, whenever a new situation or our own evolving growth prompts us to make a change in our construction of reality (identity, world view, philosophy of life), there is a need to hold on. Accepting this need and moving beyond it are dependent on the centrality of our current construction of reality, the strength of the negative emotional charge it is grounded in, and our ability to experience the feelings and emotions that surface in attempting to let go of it. A process by which we can accomplish this movement is the subject of the next section.

The Process of Letting Go and Moving On

For the past eight years, under the auspices of the National Training Laboratories (NTL) Institute, we have conducted week-long workshops for individuals who have been concerned with better understanding and facilitating change. Small-group and organization-development facilitators, managers, therapists, teachers, academicians, and many others have attended these workshops. At the beginning of each workshop, we ask the participants to focus on an area of their lives where a significant need is not being satisfied—one where they feel stuck.

Whether it be in their work, family relationships, creative endeavors, or any other personal involvement, it is the part of their lives where they recognize that change is necessary but where their need to hold on is stronger than their desire for change.

Over the course of the week, through various intrapersonal, interpersonal, and group processes, we offer the participants an opportunity to become aware of the nature and content of that which underlies their holding on. Often, participants become aware for the first time since childhood of painful experiences from the past that are still limiting or negating their options in the present. Many times, individuals powerfully reexperience the painful feelings and emotions of earlier events. Then they remember the critical decisions, beliefs, or assumptions they devised and the injunctions they absorbed from significant others during their formative years that they still permit to control the areas of their lives in which they are stuck today. It is largely from this work, with its successes and failures, that we offer the following insights into the process of letting go and moving on and, in a later section, the facilitation of this process.

The first step in this process is *consciousness raising.* Individuals first acknowledge what it is that they are holding on to and become aware of their own unique set of reasons for holding on. We have found it useful to ask individuals to note their repetitive personal patterns, often using journals for this purpose. We define such patterns as the unchanging complexes of interrelated thoughts, feelings, attitudes, values, and behaviors that become activated whenever individuals find themselves in particular situations, interactions, or relationships. (Underlying these repetitive patterns are the unconscious processes of projection and transference.) An example of such a pattern is illustrated by this journal entry: "Whenever I suspect that a person who is important to me may get angry at something I will do or say, I get anxious. I become placating and willing to compromise my position. Then I feel frustrated and see him as taking advantage of me." We have come to refer to this pattern as *If a, then b,* where *a* (in the example) is the suspicion that an important person may get angry at one's behavior and *b* is the personal response of anxiousness, willingness to compromise, frustration, and "thinking I'm being taken advantage of." Most individuals, after becoming aware of such a pattern, are able to see it as having repeated itself many times, going back to early memories. They begin to wonder why they are enmeshed in such a frequently dysfunctional mode and about the pattern's origins.

At the more superficial levels, there are many roots that anchor the holding on to a pattern of seeing and doing things; the ones most easily generalized and brought to the surface are:

1. Holding on can provide an illusion of security, stability, or predictability.
2. Holding on can provide often obscure secondary gains in painful situations (for example, suffering or illness can attract attention and sympathy, providing an acceptable excuse for avoidance or neglect of conflicts or problems).
3. Holding on can ensure that some personal needs will be met ("it's a living").
4. Holding on can continue the personal and/or social functionality of a way of seeing or doing things ("it gets me through the day" or "people like me for it").
5. Holding on can permit one to avoid the work and frustration of breaking old habits and ingrained patterns.

These reasons for holding on are usually characterized in organizational settings as resistance to change, and counterforces are set in motion to overcome them.

At the deeper, more basic levels, there are other, less identifiable yet more powerful reasons for holding on. These tend to be ignored, overlooked, or avoided, because they are unique to each individual, rooted deep in the unconscious, and have a strong and threatening emotional component. These reasons for holding on fall into three general categories:

1. The influence of childhood injunctions (programming, tapes, and so on) absorbed during the unremitting pres-

sures, humiliations, guilt inductions, and threats of rejection or loss of love in family socialization and societal enculturation.

2. The influence of critical decisions, beliefs, and assumptions —many formulated in one's early years to help bury any overwhelmingly painful feelings and emotions and to avoid the situations, actions, or thoughts that might resurrect them.

3. The influence of catastrophic expectations and the fears, dread, and panic related to the unknown.

To be made conscious and truly understood, these reasons for holding on must first be re-experienced, often painfully and amid anxiety (Gendlin, 1981; Jung, 1968; Miller, 1981).

This brings us to the second step in the process of letting go and moving on—*re-experiencing*. Usually, the deeper and more powerful reasons for holding on are discovered in our workshops during the quiet moments of journal work or meditation and subsequent to listening to others' grappling with their own childhood roots of holding on. The first indicator is usually a vague or uncanny feeling, body sensation, or physical symptom. When this signal from the unconscious is given full attention despite increasing anxiety, and with external support and encouragement, feelings rapidly surface and often erupt into cathartic emotional release. At other times, with the appropriate support, the expression of familiar pain or hurt will go another layer deeper, into a whole new set of feelings and emotion previously too frightening to be experienced. Sometimes immediately, sometimes hours or days after emotional release, awareness gives way to clarity. What becomes not only conscious but truly understood is how an early traumatic experience or unrelentingly painful and frustrating circumstances in childhood fostered a particular belief about oneself, others, or life (for example, "I don't deserve to be loved"; "You can't trust others"; "It's a dog-eat-dog world"). Although this belief, with a related pattern of behavior, once helped in coping with an intolerable situation, it is now seen to significantly limit the ability to make adaptive changes in the present. It becomes obvious that, in order to continually guard against the emergence of this painful "unfinished business," it had been necessary to hold on tightly to a point of view or a way of doing things. So, whatever the benefit, the cost was to remain blind to the limiting beliefs that the individuals lived by and to respond inappropriately in the here and now.

In some instances, one of the deepest reasons for much holding on is reached. Individuals confront the fact that, no matter whether they followed the injunctions they absorbed or rebeled against them, whether they achieved everything that was expected of them or retaliated by seeking failure, their parents never loved them in the unconditional way in which they yearned to be loved as children and, unfortunately, never will. At this realization, the experience is often one of great anger, hatred, even outrage. Then, sometime later, they realize that the parental surrogates in their lives to whom they frequently turn (the lover, the spouse, the friends, the children, the boss) will never love them as they yearned to be loved as children. The resulting experiencing is sadness, grief, loneliness, a sense of hopelessness. At this point, the only saving grace is the knowledge that they can learn to love themselves unconditionally and then give and receive love from time to time in the same way. To the degree that the nature and depth of their re-experiencing can be felt and expressed, they are then freed to begin the process of letting go.

The third step is a *mourning*: a mourning for the loss of the old ways of seeing reality, even though we now know them to be simplistic, distorted, or illusory; a mourning for the lost hopes and expectations that unconditional love could be earned somehow from outside ourselves; a mourning for the outmoded ways of being that were once satisfying, meaningful, or simply familiar. This mourning is expressed with sadness and grief. The death of attachments begins. Sometimes the mourning is accompanied by remorse—a sense of guilt, shame, and sadness for the time wasted, the life that could have been but will never be, the resentments expressed, and the punishments these individuals meted out to those who slighted or failed them. But with forgiveness of others and of themselves come an appreciation and acceptance of what was and is.

The consciousness raising, re-experiencing, and mourning make possible the letting go, involving a lowering of defenses, a vulnerability, and a receptivity. The time is then at hand for the last step—the *moving on* to new possibilities and new ways of seeing things. A unique opportunity becomes available to re-program or reconstruct the singularly negative or limiting ways of thinking from the past or to construct (image) an essentially new reality (a transformation). Techniques such as guided visualization (Korn and Johnson, 1983; Peale, 1982) or directed affirmations (Ray, 1976; Spangler, 1983) are ways to lay down a new track or pattern. With practice, this clears an alternate path different from the well-worn road that has been so reflexively chosen in the past.

The individuals must patiently try to accept the awkward and uncertain attempts to establish the new perceptions and patterns of behavior. We feel it important to emphasize that remnants of the central fixities and patterns to which individuals have long clung will never be fully erased. The fixities are deeply embedded and will continue to be "hooked" by stimuli that involve the individuals in memories of the early and negative life experiences to which the stimuli are related. The first impulse of the individuals typically will be to respond as they always have. But now, having become aware of their recurring patterns, they can recognize that they are on the edge of responding in their usually dysfunctional manner ("Here I go again!"). With such awareness and recognition, they can now choose not to respond in the old way but to activate behavior that is more functional and potentially more effective. Eventually, the positive outcomes will increasingly reinforce the new beliefs or points of view that the behavior is built on.

Facilitation of Letting Go and Moving On

Although our focus in the two preceding sections has been on the individual, we again assert our belief that what has been said about the individual has wide applicability (with appropriate translation) to all human systems. With this in mind, we now broaden our focus to include not only individuals but also the organizations in which they function. To cover in detail the many situational and clinical variables (values, theories, strategies, and methodologies) that might be relevant to the facilitation of letting go and moving on would take us far beyond the scope of this chapter. However, it is possible for us to highlight a few of them that, in our judgment, would be basically relevant to any effort designed for such facilitation.

1. Humanistic values must be omnipresent as guides to the entire change effort. Valuing of and respect for the individuals and for the integrity of the larger system units involved must be central. The level of interpersonal trust must be high. A quest for openness should be pursued, and manipulation should be shunned. To the fullest extent possible, the participation of the individuals and other system elements in decisions involving the change process should be encouraged.

2. The staff professionals responsible for the implementation of the change program should be keenly aware of the role of stability in a context of change. No system can be expected to change in all respects at the same time; to attempt to bring about such change (even if it were at all possible) would be highly anxiety arousing and almost certainly excessively disruptive. Some roots must be firmly in the ground for purposes of security to basic system identity if others are to become loosened. Change specialists must have an acute sensitivity to the system's need to hold on at any given time in relation to its readiness (no matter how tentative) to move on.

3. Realistic patience and a sense of an appropriate time scale must underlie and guide the change process itself. As we know, in this culture we often place a high value on short-run results. We are "Now!" people; we have a tendency to look for quick fixes. But in this aspect of change, there are no magic words. Consciousness raising, re-experiencing, and mourning all involve the powerful need to hold on as well as deep feelings and their working through. Inappropriately "pushing" the client is one of the best ways of ensuring that not too much of value will take place.

4. The processes of consciousness raising and working through, previously discussed, often require or are greatly facilitated by the knowledge, art, and humanity of change specialists.

These persons should be psychologically mature and centered. Ideally, they should themselves have experienced psychotherapeutic and/or related intensive personal-learning processes. They should be clearly aware that they cannot help another to work in areas and depths of feelings that are so anxiety arousing to them that their own perceptions may be dysfunctionally distorted and their potential for effective action inhibited. They must be able to facilitate and comfortably accept the strong emotional expressions of others (guilt, shame, sobbing and crying, anger, outrage, hate, caring, and love), and they need to have an openness and acceptance of their own feelings. They must truly be—and be seen by others as—psychologically strong, calm, competent. This makes it possible for the others to be fully with their thoughts and feelings (no matter how powerful and "irrational") and to be able to express them without retreating into a sense of duty or the need to stay fully in control ("someone else is minding the store").

5. The individuals who will be subject to change in the process should be persons with sufficient psychological strength (a reasonably high sense of self-worth and a considerable tolerance of ambiguity) so as to be able adequately to cope with and to gain from the stresses they will experience in the process. Their courage and willingness to risk are most helpful attributes in initiating and further the unfolding process.

6. There is clearly a great need for support (particularly psychological support) as a system moves through the process, since there is ambiguity in the process, there are deep and unexpected feelings to be confronted, and much that is central to the system's identity is being risked. And, particularly in the latter phases of the process, participants need support in recognizing the need to forgive others for past hurts and oneself for past hurting and the existential reality of being human. Such support must come from the change specialists, from peers in the process, and—in organizational settings—from superiors and subordinates.

Much that has preceded suggests that this basic change process is rooted in anxiety and pain—and it is. But, as it unfolds, it also releases joy, vitality, and meaningfulness. There is a coexisting sense of excitement and an awareness that "we have nothing to lose but our chains"—a feeling of being able to free ourselves from that which binds, constrains, and constricts us, diminishing our organizational productivity and our own sense of vitality. This excitement can be buttressed in the process by an omnipresent image of a future state of being that provides hope or strengthens faith in a positive outcome and also gives meaningful direction to the process as it flows through letting go to moving on.

Implications for Organizations, Managers, and Practitioners

Professionals have now accumulated considerable experience in helping individuals better understand their need to hold on and to facilitate their letting go and moving on. This has been done primarily in one-on-one and group therapy sessions and in group workshops designed primarily for this purpose. To our knowledge, little has yet been done in organizations—except in isolated and small-scale instances—to deal with this critical aspect of change. Additionally, few managers and organizational-change specialists (internal and external) have given special attention—either in theory or in practice—to what we see as a long-neglected aspect of the change process in organizations. Thus, our field is experiencing an exciting new frontier that is wide open for research, field experimentation, and learning. As this frontier is approached, we do have some thoughts and suggestions, growing out of our experience, that may be relevant to others:

1. As in all basic organizational-change programs, the full understanding and support of top management personnel are critical. Since, at this point in time, a focus on the need to hold on would in most cases have to be experimental and innovative and also would have to involve itself in intrapersonal processes not typically sanctioned in organizational-change programs, some risks would be involved. Such an approach should not be initiated without the informed and full backing of those ultimately responsible in the organization.

2. In an organizational context, system interdependencies become more complex. Typically, managers and change specialists give primary attention to the entity that is the target of change. Often overlooked is the fact that, if the target entity does change, this change will have varying degrees of impact on other entities with which it is highly interdependent, which now themselves will be faced with the need to change, with attendant problems around holding on and letting go.

3. The traditional focus on resistance to change will need alteration. This focus, in our view, has typically pointed toward relatively superficial factors interfering with change and has diverted us from seeing as centrally important the deeper need to hold on. Entities would have relatively minor difficulties in effectuating change if the need to hold on were not present.

4. From the most primitive to the most modern cultures, there has always been a recognized need for rituals, rites, or ceremonies to carry individuals from one phase of life to which they have been attached to another that opens up new possibilities for them. It is our belief that mourning is a key facilitating ritual in the process of letting go and moving on—at the organizational level as well as at the level of the individual. We are aware that through the centuries most, if not all, cultures and religions have evolved and institutionalized mourning processes for those who have faced the death of a loved one. From this, we infer that the folk wisdom of the ages has recognized the need for a means of coping with the letting go of a valued relationship and of moving on. We feel strongly that appropriate mourning processes must also be created for use in instances of basic organizational change.

5. There are times when one or more subsystems of an organization or the entire organization needs to die. And yet managers and/or change agents will often use life-supporting technologies to prevent the needed death from occurring. This suggests that individuals in such roles are not themselves above the need to hold on—to an involvement that may be of central importance to their sense of competency and potency, to their professional and personal identity, and to their status and personal income.

In conclusion, we turn our attention to some deeper issues. The professional field of organization development has now been active for about twenty-five years. During this period, it has rapidly expanded in its membership, in the problem areas in which it has gained expertise, and in the number and variety of organizations that have turned to it for its services. With the ever-increasing attention given by managers and change specialists to the facilitation of change in organizations, it is puzzling (as we earlier stated) that so little attention has been given by managers in organizations *and* by the change specialists who serve them to such a critically important area as the need to hold on—together with the related facilitation of letting go and moving on. We have often speculated as to why this avoidance has occurred, and we have concluded that there are at least three fundamental reasons to explain it—reasons that are subtle and that probably lie below the level of comfortable awareness for most people.

First, there is a culturally embedded fear and reluctance to explore elements in the preconscious or unconscious self—and especially to do this in a work setting and with work associates (superiors, peers, and subordinates). The typical person might express her concern as follows: "I really don't know what may be there. And if I do become aware of and reveal something previously unknown to me, will doing so adversely impact my desired image in the organization, and will I either now or later be penalized in some way for what I have revealed? Will I be able to cope with whatever emerges? Maybe it is better to let sleeping dogs lie." And yet consciousness raising is an essential step in dealing with the need to hold on. From the manager's point of view, there is the question as to whether it is appropriate or ethical in a work setting to involve employees in processes that move beyond the ordinary levels of awareness.

Second, there is the culturally grounded and pervasive fear of feelings (loneliness, rejection, unlovability, helplessness, hurt, pain, anger, aggression), particularly of their expression. Most individuals are fearful of their own feelings, and they are threatened by and not sure how to cope with the feelings of others. In our experience, this is true of many managers and change agents alike. And certainly (at some level of awareness), managers must be deeply concerned about the risks involved in sanctioning processes within organizations that might release unpredictable and often powerful feelings. And yet, the re-experiencing of earlier childhood events, together with associated feelings that often erupt into cathartic emotional release, is also an essential step in dealing with the need to hold on.

Third, there is the need to mourn—to work through the dying and death of attachments to elements of personal identity, to aspects of one's view of the reality outside of oneself, to ways of being to which we have clung but that are often dysfunctional for us in the present. To mourn means to face death—little deaths, to be sure, but death, nevertheless—in order to make a rebirth possible. Each of us is ultimately vulnerable, and yet most of us typically blind ourselves to this truth. The anthropologist and political scientist Ernest Becker (1973) points out an impossible paradox: "the ever-present fear of death in the normal biological functioning of our instinct of self-preservation, as well as our utter obliviousness to this fear in our conscious life" (p. 17). While we have no solid evidence to offer, our intuitions lead us to the possibility that the avoidance by managers and change agents of the need to let go and the processes that can facilitate little deaths and rebirths is in part, at least, related to a deep fear that involvement in these processes would bring them too close to a confrontation with their own mortality.

In closing, we can only leave the reader with a gnawing dilemma. We have long been convinced that the area to which we have just given our attention is a seriously neglected one—particularly at the organizational level—in research, theory, and practice. As we stated at the outset, efforts directed at deep change often fail or fall short of desired results because the need to hold on and its working through seem to be so persistently avoided. At a time in history when the demands for change constantly impinge on organizations, this avoidance carries with it most serious consequences. The avoidance is clearly understandable, however, if our conclusions with respect to that avoidance have validity. At present, we have little wisdom to offer as to how this dilemma can be resolved. But we do have faith that, with an increasing and more pervasive understanding of both facets of this dilemma, it will be resolved in the best interests of all participants in organizational life.

References

Baldwin, J. *Nobody Knows My Name.* New York: Dial Press, 1961.

Becker, E. *The Denial of Death.* New York: Free Press, 1973.

Berne, E. *What Do You Say After You Say Hello: The Psychology of Human Destiny.* New York: Bantam, 1972.

Bridges, W. *Transitions: Making Sense of Life's Changes.* Reading, Mass.: Addison-Wesley, 1980.

Bugental, J. F. T., and Bugental, E. K. "A Fate Worse than Death: The Fear of Changing." *Psychotherapy,* December 1984.

Fink, S., Beak, J., and Taddeo, K. "Organizational Crisis and Change." *Journal of Applied Behavioral Science,* 1971, 7 (1), 15-37.

Fried, E. *The Courage to Change: From Insight to Self-Innovation.* New York: Grove Press, 1981.

Friedlander, F. "Patterns of Individual and Organizational Learning." In S. Srivastva and Associates, *The Executive Mind: New Insights on Managerial Thought and Action.* San Francisco: Jossey-Bass, 1983.

Gendlin, E. T. *Experiencing and the Creation of Meaning: A Philosophical and Psychological Approach to the Subjective.* New York: Free Press, 1962.

Gendlin, E. T. *Focusing.* New York: Bantam, 1981.

Grof, S. *Realms of the Human Unconscious: Observations from LSD Research.* New York: Dutton, 1976.

Hanna, R. W. "Crisis in Meaning: A Phenomenological Inquiry into the Experience of a Lack of Meaning to Life." Unpublished doctoral dissertation, Graduate School of Management, University of California at Los Angeles, 1975.

Harris, T. A. *I'm O.K.—You're O.K.: A Practical Guide to Transactional Analysis.* New York: Harper & Row, 1969.

Harrison, R. "Strategies for a New Age." *Human Resource Management,* 1983, *22* (3), 209-235.

Heisenberg, W. *Across the Frontiers*. New York: Harper & Row, 1974.

Jung, C. G. *Collected Works*. Vol. 17: *The Development of Personality*. Princeton, N.J.: Princeton University Press, 1954.

Jung, C. G. *Collected Works*. Vol. 16: *The Practice of Psychotherapy*. Princeton, N.J.: Princeton University Press, 1966.

Jung, C. G. *Collected Works*. Vol. 7: *The Archetypes and the Collective Unconscious*. Princeton, N.J.: Princeton University Press, 1968.

Kahn, R. L. "Critical Themes in the Study of Change." In P. S. Goodman and Associates, *Change in Organizations: New Perspectives on Theory, Research, and Practice*. San Francisco: Jossey-Bass, 1982.

Keleman, S. *Living Your Dying*. New York: Random House, 1976.

Khan, H. I. "Mental Purification." In *The Sufi Message of Hazrat Inayat Khan*. Vol. 4. Netherlands: Servire Wassenaar, 1960.

Korn, E. R., and Johnson, K. *The Uses of Imagery in the Health Professions*. Homewood, Ill.: Dow Jones-Irwin, 1983.

Kübler-Ross, E. *On Death and Dying*. New York: Macmillan, 1969.

Levinson, H. "Easing the Pain of Personal Loss." *Harvard Business Review*, 1972, *9-10*, 80-88.

McCaskey, M. B. *The Executive Challenge: Managing Change and Ambiguity*. Boston: Pitman, 1982.

McWhinney, W. "Paedogenesis and Other Modes of Design." In T. G. Cummings (Ed.), *Systems Theory for Organization Development*. New York: Wiley, 1980.

Marris, P. *Loss and Change*. Garden City, N.Y.: Anchor Books, 1975.

Miller, A. *The Drama of the Gifted Child*. New York: Grove Press, 1981.

Novak, M. *The Experience of Nothingness*. New York: Harper & Row, 1971.

Peale, N. V. *Positive Imaging*. New York: Fawcett Crest, 1982.

Ray, S. *I Desire Love*. Millbrae, Calif.: Les Femmes, 1976.

Schachtel, E. G. *Metamorphosis*. New York: Basic Books, 1959.

Spangler, D. *The Laws of Manifestation*. Findhorn, Scotland: Findhorn, 1983.

6

How Reality Gets Constructed
in an Organization

Samuel A. Culbert
John J. McDonough

As with many who theorize about organizations, our teaching, consulting, research, and writing are intertwined. Seldom are we involved in one without reflecting on the others. In fact, for us, the reciprocity between our consulting and teaching and our intellectual lives is very conscious. For the past fifteen years, we have devoted ourselves primarily to puzzling about the balance that an individual strikes between attending to the interests of the organization and attending to his or her own needs to participate with individuality, meaning, and personal strength. We began with a bias that has withstood the test of our experience: Real organizational effectiveness results from individuals achieving high levels of both organizational contribution and personal meaning. Absent one or the other element, both the people involved and the organizations for which they work have serious problems. To us, no organization succeeds for long when its work requires that people contribute without personal meaning. Conversely, we believe, there is no such thing as personal success when an individual's production does not contribute to his or her organization's well-being.

Others have concerned themselves with the question of

balance and have taken positions similar to the one we take. For example, for years, Argyris has struggled with the issue of personal and organizational mix (1964) and has offered numerous suggestions for helping individuals participate more effectively (1976, 1982). On the other hand, he has outspokenly lamented the difficulties that managers have in changing their practices to include the theories and suggestions provided to them (Argyris and Schön, 1978). Like Argyris, we think that the problem lies not in the intent of managers nor in the diligence of organizational theorists but in the underlying perspective that most managers use in attending to organizational events. To us, their perspective lacks basic understanding about how self-interests determine the ways in which events are portrayed at work.

With this in mind, we have spent literally thousands of hours counseling individuals who were frustrated in working out orientations that mutually benefited themselves and their organizations and in counseling managers who were trying to create systems that might facilitate the "proper" balance. Of course, we found that, for most managers, the "proper" balance meant systems that indulged their own self-interested inclinations while neglecting the self-interests of those who thought differently. Thus, a major part of our consulting and educational activities has been directed toward helping managers see the interrelationships between self-interests and organization pursuits. We help them see how what seems personally appropriate to an individual connects to how that person represents his or her organization's work, represents the work of others, and relates to people and job opportunities every moment of his or her organizational day. We take this approach because we believe that managers who do not understand and respect these connections are ill positioned to make their organizations run effectively. They lack insight into the processes that are most central in determining how their organizations actually run.

In promoting such insight, we find that the most valuable lessons concern the forces and dynamics that affect how reality is constructed in an organization and the role that self-interests play in supporting and changing a construction. These are the topics addressed here. More specifically, we present our perspectives on: (1) the self-interested motives that lead people to perform their jobs and interpret organization events in the particular way that they do; (2) how reality is constructed in an organization and how self-interests lead people to seek modifications in that construction; and (3) the implications of these issues and what managers must appreciate in order to balance the organization's needs for stability with each individual's desire to modify the organization's reality to make it better support what he or she wants to contribute.

Background Theory and Perspective

As one might expect, our insights into the basis of reality in an organization were gradual, with one theme and search for perspective eventually pointing the way to the next. In retrospect, we see three plateaus to our thinking, although, at the time of each involvement, we were so caught up in what we were learning that we weren't necessarily searching for the next. However, in reviewing each, we find that little that we subsequently learned negated what we had formerly concluded.

Our search began with an examination of the organization's reality and the forces that work to indoctrinate and socialize people to the point where they substitute the organization's interests for their own. We saw people acting in self-defeating ways, oversocialized by a runaway corporate mentality that first sought to put the interests of the organization ahead of the interests of the individual and then tried to convince people that these organizationally prescribed ways of behaving were actually good for them. Our investigation culminated in a perspective that described the thought processes that subordinate the individual to the organization and outlined what a group of like-situated people can do to put themselves in a more personally powerful and organizationally constructive frame of mind (Culbert, 1974).

Next, we addressed the other side of the coin. We examined how people are often able to avoid the forces of socialization to pursue their own personal reality with but secondary consideration for the organization's interests. We were fascinated by the issue of individual opportunism and how people are able to pursue self-interests in an organizational culture that seeks to limit and censor self-interested expression. We discovered that many people do not simply stand back and let the organization mold them to its liking. They fight back by manipulating and reframing reality in ways that are designed to make it look as if organizational priorities are solidly behind their own preferred ways of operating. The result, we observed, is an organization culture in which people quickly learn that nothing can be taken at face value and where each individual's work strengths and operating integrity seem to depend on that person's ability to stretch, bend, and subvert the organization's reality to make it fit more closely with his or her personal needs, interests, and operating responsibilities (Culbert and McDonough, 1980).

Having examined the issue of reality in an organization from the perspective of both individual opportunism and the organization's exploitation of the individual, we began to see that the problem runs much deeper than simply the self-indulgences of individuals or the shallowness and insensitivity of organizations. In fact, currently, there appears to be a standoff, with both the individual and the organization righteous in their beliefs that the manipulative and political means they use are justified by the excessive behavior of the other. Individuals are spurred on in their covert efforts to manage and manipulate reality by the fact that organizations operate as if it were their duty to squeeze out the expression of self-interests. On the other hand, organizational managers observe the unchecked flood of self-interests operating and conclude that it would be ludicrous to give more legitimacy to the expression of self-interests than now exists. Consequently, much of their energy goes into attempts to resist this expression and assert more control.

Examining the collision of these two perspectives constitutes the third plateau of our inquiry into the basis of reality in an organization (Culbert and McDonough, in press). We have concluded that the biggest impediment to the achievement of a more effective integration of personal needs and organizational considerations lies in managers' lack of understanding about the pursuit of self-interests at work. Most managers understand very little about the ways self-interests shape the personal realities that orient the people working for them. Most managers understand very little about how people with different personal realities vie with one another in negotiating the realities that govern the disposition of their organization's work.

For years, we struggled to find a terminology that would explain the ever-present and dynamic role that self-interests play in determining the realities that are constructed at work. In discussing self-interests, most managers are inclined to use the term *motivation*. But, for us, using this term places self-interests in a much too narrow context. Managers use it in referring to the self-interests to which they appeal in their efforts to direct a subordinate's efforts and control against deviations from what the organization expects of him or her. They use it in talking about the tactics, strategies, and inducements they can use in "motivating" a subordinate in directions they see important to their organization's progress. And, as we've already stated, we inevitably observe a high overlap between the "organizationally important" directions that are specified and the self-interests of the manager who asserts them. What we have wanted to characterize is closer to what Chester Barnard referred to when he described the connection between the individual and the organization as "the net of inducements and contributions" (Barnard, 1938, p. 140). Our goal has been to utilize a terminology that depicts the integration that an individual achieves between his or her self-interested and self-expressive pursuits and his or her contributions to the organization. We have wanted to portray the self-interests that are part of the fabric of every organizational activity, that are inseparable from an individual's most honest and objective account of each organizational happening.

Eventually, we decided to use the term *alignment*. It became our term for characterizing the unique orientations we see people assuming at work. We define *alignment* as the specific orientation that an individual achieves in linking up (aligning) his or her needs for personal identity, meaning, and success with what that person sees the job as requiring. For us, alignments differ from motivations in that they are intended to characterize the unique orientations that individuals assume by blending together a variety of self-interested motives. The self-interests incorporated in the term *alignment* include the self-interests of performing one's job using those skills that make one particularly effective; the self-interests involved in avoiding tasks that the individual does not feel that he or she is skilled to perform; the self-interests of incorporating those personal and societal values that the individual finds essential to his or her self-esteem; the self-interests involved in utilizing a logic that reflects the way in which one is most comfortable thinking; the self-interests entailed in fitting one's job in with the rest of his or her personal obligations and commitments; and, equally important to all of the aforementioned, the self-interests involved in competently performing the work that the individual honestly believes the organization needs to receive from someone in his or her role and position.

Like Barnard's "net of inducements and contributions," the construct *alignment* is aimed at depicting the *efficiency* that an individual develops in reconciling the pursuit of what is personally meaningful and the work that the individual feels is required by the job. With an "efficient" alignment, any single action has multiple consequences—it simultaneously fulfills many personal needs while advancing the individual toward one or more work objectives. With an "inefficient" alignment, pursuing self-interests and making organizational contributions are two separate activities. The term *alignment* is also useful in characterizing how an individual perceives each organizational event. It is as if a person views organization events through a special lens that orients him or her toward opportunities to contribute organizational product in a personally meaningful way. Alignments provide a frame of reference for instantly recognizing the opportunities and threats entailed in each situation and the importance or dismissability of certain relationships. It is a widely acknowledged fact that people interpret and frame the same events differently (Goffman, 1974). To us, *alignment* is a construct that goes a long way toward a comprehensive explanation of why.

The construct of *alignment* also allows us to differentiate between personal and organizational power. In an organization, *personal power* accrues to those who develop efficient alignments whereby they achieve orientations that successfully integrate the pursuit of their own subjective self-interests with the accomplishment of the job they see needing to be performed. *Organizational power* accrues to those whose alignments, status, and performance correspond to what others in the organization are committed to publicly valuing. Of course, "personally powerful" people are not always successful in getting external acknowledgment for their contributions (we'd say they lack organizational power), and "organizationally powerful" people are not always successful in expressing enough of what is personally meaningful to them (we'd say they lack personal power).

The Construction of Reality

It is now time to present our view of how reality is constructed at work and what each individual faces in getting support for his or her needs to operate efficiently with a high degree of personal and organizational power—a view that features the construct of *alignment* and is based upon the fact that organization events actually appear differently to people with different orientations and motives. In order to better understand how reality is constructed in an organization and what happens when individuals attempt to mold an organization's reality to fit with and support their alignments and resulting orientations, we will describe what might be called "the original organization event": two, three, four, or more people contemplating the founding of an organization.

The Founders' Reality. For the sake of simplicity, begin with these people sitting in a room trying to decide how to exploit a business idea. What they contemplate often starts with externals, such as what market opportunities exist and what way of organizing their efforts will take best advantage of a particular opportunity. Until they strike some key agreements, they are just a group of people spinning scenarios and holding a bull session while trying to predict the future. Once they strike agreements about what they are going to produce, who is going to do what, and how individual efforts will be judged, they become an organization with an "objective" picture of reality. It is "objective" because everyone says that he or she believes it to be true. Of course, what each person agrees to is constrained by considerations of what any particular scenario will do for that individual personally. Each person has a set of "alignment needs" that must be satisfied for that person to lend his or her support to a particular portrayal of reality. In fact, to a large extent, the founding of an organization is acknowledgment that people with different alignment needs have worked out a way of fitting well with one another.

Now, assuming that the organization has been founded, consider what makes it an "organization." In its essence, an "organization" is a group of people with mutual concerns and interests who have struck a set of agreements that lead them to see and interpret events in a similar manner. Some of their agreements will be representations of reality that are based more on rational considerations, such as market demand and technological know-how, than on subjective ones. Some of their agreements will be based more on subjective considerations, such as who wants the job of president and who is willing to temporarily fill in at marketing, than on rational ones. And which is rational and which is subjective will be largely unknown to the participants.

Conversely, "disorganization" takes place when people do not see the same events similarly or when their personal orientations require that they interpret events divergently from one another. What's more, when there is a good degree of "organization," and people do see and interpret events similarly, those who fail to buy into the mainstream of what has been agreed to soon become disenfranchised and treated as outsiders, with most either electing to leave the organization or finding themselves expelled.

Few people enter an organization at its founding. Most enter an ongoing operation and seek to catch on by buying into agreements that are already made. Usually they come with a set of alignment needs compatible with what the founders had in mind, so that the agreements they buy into do not significantly compromise what they believe or want. These people seek a meaningful relationship in which as many as possible of their personal needs are fulfilled. There is some minimum number of needs that must be met or they will not join, and there are some particular needs that, when not fulfilled, cause them either to not join or to join and participate duplicitously. And, of course, there is the need to have a relationship with this organization that is no worse than their best alternative.

Now imagine a newcomer entering the room with the original founders. First, they tell him or her, "Here's how we see our situation, and here's how we see your role." In response, the newcomer reflects on his or her own situation and ways of being effective and says, "I don't quite see it as you have laid it out for me." Mindful of the analysis, tough conversations, and negotiations the group went through in becoming an organization, the group spokesperson answers, "No, I'm afraid you've got it wrong. What you need to see are the following . . ." and then goes on to espouse the company line. Described for the newcomer are the assumptions that he or she was not present to hear discussed and that he or she must be persuaded, rewarded, or coerced to accept. Of course, while many of these assumptions represent valid responses to external market conditions, many also represent accommodations to the needs of one or more founders. They are considerations that needed to be in the original contract in order for one or more founders to buy in. However, these accommodations are not stated as such —they are delivered as rational statements of what is "objectively" required.

For the sake of this example, let us say that the newcomer buys in, or at least says he or she does. Buying in will be based on what flexibility the newcomer sees for pursuing a version of the organization's reality that provides him or her with a job that has personal meaning and the opportunity to be a success and on the alternatives that person sees for a job somewhere else that leaves him or her better off.

In most organizations, newcomers, with their somewhat discrepant views of the organization's reality, eventually take responsible positions and wind up recruiting a second generation of newcomers, who wind up recruiting a third generation, and so on. Thus, most established organizations are populated by people whose reasons for joining are less and less in harmony with the assumptions of the founders and more and more based on what they see as flexibility in the prescribed ways of operating. This flexibility allows them to pursue functions and roles in ways that are personally meaningful to them. In fact, left to their own devices, most people attempt to modify the founders' reality in ways that emphasize and support what is personally and professionally important. And, over time, significant changes and deviations in the founders' reality are institutionalized, and a modified set of operating assumptions emerge.

With each generation, the operating assumptions become more calcified, and the latitudes for asserting personal interests become increasingly difficult to find. This is because there are more people making the same assumptions whose knee-jerk response is to set the newcomer straight. But the reality they are pushing is no longer that of the founders; it is an amalgam that no one in particular actually sees or wholly believes. It is an updated version of the assumptions people must make in their daily operations in order to demonstrate respect for a system that everyone has already agreed to go along with. This reality serves as a constraint on each individual's inclination to pursue his or her self-interests without adequate regard for what others assert are the interests of the organization.

The Dominant Reality. We use the term *dominant reality* to describe the reality that contains the new operating assumptions that get worked out over time. It is the "how do they do it here?" reality that newcomers search out in order to fit in and feel secure. Like the founders' reality, the dominant reality directs daily operations by providing a common frame of reference to which everybody in the organization can relate. It provides the standards that people can use in arbitrating their individual differences and in achieving an integrated approach to operating the organization. Like the founders' reality, it specifies what is going to be produced, how production is to be accomplished, who has what role in production, what constitutes contribution, and how contributions will be assessed and rewarded. *Unlike* the founders' reality, it is separate from what is believed by any individual, although any given aspect may overlap what particular individuals think.

The dominant reality directs relations within the firm by specifying the values, expectations, and assumptions that people who comprise the organization are supposed to hold. It also directs relations with people outside the firm by specifying the basic premises that underlie the conduct of the organization's business. It provides guidelines for representing the organization's products and services, for stipulating who are target customers and clients, for characterizing the organization's position in the marketplace, and for deciding how products and services are to be marketed and promoted.

The dominant reality provides a tangible constraint that people can use in limiting the individualistic aspects of their thinking and performance. It serves as a control against blatantly self-interested interpretations of organizational events and the inclination to exploit each organizational event for one's own personal success. In short, the dominant reality provides order in what otherwise would be a highly idiosyncratic interplay of individual beliefs and actions, and it provides the grounds for people to hold each other accountable.

The dominant reality provides people who have different attitudes, values, and ethics the ability to galvanize themselves around common business practices and relationship codes. For instance, some organizations value and promote team players who create the conditions for others to contribute; others promote star performers. Some organizations require careful portrayals of the entire truth when dealing with clients and customers; others promote glossing over potential problem areas and not mentioning the possibility of a problem until it materializes. The dominant reality presents guidelines for all of this and more.

In providing a common frame of reference, the dominant reality gives people a language for exchanging their individual perceptions. Without it, organizations would be Towers of Babel and would run out of control. People would relate to the same events on different dimensions and use different words with different meanings. Without a common language, there would be virtually no efficiency of effort, for people would have no way to build on one another's contributions or to link to the contributions of those who preceded them.

Without the dominant reality, there would be his reality and her reality. With it, there is his reality, her reality, and the reality that they both accept. The third, or accepted, reality may or may not be one that has validity to either of the people involved, but is the most important reality, for it is the one that each will publicly use in relating to the other's behavior and in "fairly" evaluating what that person contributes.

Because the pressures to have it are considerable, the dominant reality takes on an existence of its own. We have already discussed how it is presented to newcomers and to those who weren't in the room when key agreements were struck. It is presented as a set of "objective" facts and not mere operating givens. Many of the underlying assumptions were conceived at a previous point in time and under different market conditions and by people who are long gone, whose personal needs are no longer a relevant consideration. But talking about these assumptions with an air of objectivity, as if they were shibboleths and absolutes, makes these changed conditions difficult to detect. Thus, extant dominant realities take on an existence of their own, with people talking about what "objectively" exists rather than what has been "agreed to" and could be changed.

Sometimes the dominant reality is the result of power politics whereby people with rank assert their will on those lower down. For instance, a great deal of discussion and heated debate may precede a decision about what a department or work unit ought to produce and who has what role in the production. And often the decision is not what the people who have to implement it independently believe it should be. It is a decision that they must concede because those with rank expressed the intensity of what they thought and wanted. But, after the decision is made, what is to be produced will be accepted as fact, and people who initially disagreed with the role they are now expected to play understand that their evaluation will be based on what others feel entitled to expect.

Most often, however, the dominant reality is the result of give-and-take compromise hit upon as people with different self-interests struggle to decide the meaning that events hold for themselves and others. What gets agreed to and accepted as fact is worked out when a critical number of people, or one or more key people with power, uncover a definition of reality that does enough for what their self-interested perceptions tell them is in the organization's interests. Sometimes people are genuinely swayed by the discussion and adopt the group's conclusion as their own perception. But, more often, people compromise and concede. What they now say is reality is not totally the result of what they actually think or believe needs to be done. It is at least partially the result of their need to get along, to be accepted, or to earn a credit for use on an issue of greater personal importance. Or their agreement may be the result of a recognition that to hold out and not go along would allow others to portray them as an obstacle to the organization's progress. In fact, the group's decision may not have been what anyone thought was organizationally correct; it may have been the best set of agreements that those who participated thought they could reach at that point in time.

Oftentimes, the dominant reality is the result of political agreements struck by people whose different but overlapping motives lead them to agree to describe organizational happenings in a certain way and whose projects and personal interests are furthered by getting others to agree with their descriptions. Thus, to our way of seeing things, a dominant reality is a construction of political expediency and not a reality that has its origins in consensual belief. The origins are in personally convenient compromises that appear to fit in with the needs of the people agreeing to them. Consensual belief is a phenomenon that may or may not take place after an agreement about the nature of reality is struck.

In practice, however, even those who were present when compromise agreements about the nature of the organization's reality were struck talk as if a reality exists that actually reflects how things are (Gendlin, 1962). This way of talking and thinking gives internal stability to an organization. If people were to act otherwise and to speak as if what was accepted as operationally valid were arbitrary and the result of personal expediency, they would open up a big can of worms. All agreements would be seen as variables open for rediscussion, and no decision could be counted on to last with any permanence. Each decision would be vulnerable to unlimited debate, and issues of power and self-convenience would be blatantly visible. This is much too much for today's organization mind to tolerate and would produce great upheaval and personal insecurity. Thus, to a great extent, everyone talks about the organization's reality as if it were fixed and more or less permanent—as if it were a consensual belief.

Each organization has its own dominant reality, complete with a rationale that people can use in justifying what they advocate. Theorists have referred to the statements that comprise such rationales as "reconstructed logics" (Kaplan, 1964) and "ideas in good currency" (Schön, 1971). People use ideas and logics to justify their decisions in the same way that lawyers use previous court decisions to support what they assert. However, unlike the law, organizations do not require that consistency or precedent be observed. Which precedent is followed and which is conveniently forgotten, which rule is bent, which line of the business plan is overlooked—all are options of the people involved and subject to what others, acting on their own values and self-interests, decide to let them get away with.

The dominant reality contains "categories" that, once found out, become determining factors in how people relate to work events. It is analogous to watching Olympic figure skating and finding out that judges separate technical skills and artistry of performance. All of a sudden you find yourself viewing subsequent performances with new standards and new criteria for appreciation. In this way, categories give people their bearings. In an organization, personal thoughts and one's experience of events are merely fragments of one's perception and personal reality until they have referents in categories that the group has agreed are important in the monitoring of these events. Only then do they become part of one's organization experience. In one company, it is servicing the customer; in another, it is protecting cash and maintaining liquidity; in a third, it is gaining market share. It is within these categories that one makes sense of his or her own role in the organization's response.

Organizations not only provide categories; they also provide standards, directions, and ideals that the individual can use in evaluating what an event means to the organization and what specific happenings signify for the accomplishment of its goals. In other words, an organization relies on members to relate their experience to a similar set of categories and to develop a shared sense of what state within each category signifies a desirable situation and what state poses a threat. In fact, we would go so far as to assert that a collection of people become an organization only when they subject their personal experiences to a comparable set of categories with similar value positions and standards. Conversely, the greatest threat to an organization comes from key members relating their experiences to different categories or using different values or standards to state what constitutes an opportunity and what constitutes a threat.

Just as the organization needs constraints to protect itself against any one individual's personal reality running out of control, so the organization needs constraints against its person-made dominant reality getting out of control. For most organizations, at least two such constraints exist. The first is the people who consume the organization's product and/or the marketplace in which the organization conducts its business; the second is the people who currently manage and staff the organization and/or who are available in the professional and labor markets to replace them. Together, these groups act as forces that prevent the organization's reality from becoming too arbitrary or capricious. Organizations with a reality that has got too far out of control lose their ability to relate to customers and to attract capable employees. Of course, organizations with captive marketplaces or with captive labor pools are able to forge realities that indulge those who presently control the organization at the expense of consumers or of their own personnel; when their indulgences become too extreme, it is up to government or labor unions to step in and force a better balance.

We have asserted that the dominant reality is a reality of

agreements negotiated by founders and amended by successive generations of organizational participants. We see it as the result of people attempting to modify organizational givens to produce a definition of reality that characterizes the organization's interests in a way that maximizes the expression of their own. Of course, one's own interests include the organization's viability in the marketplace, competent people to staff the organization, compliance with government regulations, and so on.

The dominant reality is also a reality of compromise, one that does enough for a collection of people who together possess a critical mass of organization power. It is not necessarily a reality that accurately reflects how anyone in particular actually sees organization events. It is a reality that reflects what people with varying positions of organization power have agreed to or, because of other issues of high personal priority, are willing to go along with or, because of lack of power, just plain cannot do anything about. Our point of view contrasts with the more commonly advanced view that, in an organization, reality is consensually arrived at, reflecting a set of perceptions in which most people genuinely believe (Berger and Luckmann, 1966). Certainly, this is what founders are often able to achieve with one another. However, most people are not founders, and many founders, such as individual entrepreneurs, never succeed in getting their reality internalized by anyone else. In our model, no one, in fact, may actually see particular issues in the way that they get defined in an organization, and the organizational view that gets expressed today merely represents a set of compromises that may get reworked tomorrow.

Implications for Management

Now we can return to the "balance" issue raised in the beginning of this chapter and examine what management needs to know in order to manage its operations more effectively. As previously described, we are concerned with management's role in affecting the balance that individuals strike between attending to the interests of the organization and attending to their own needs to participate with individuality, meaning, and personal strength. In discussing this balance with management, we rely heavily on our understanding of the basis of reality in an organization and, in particular, on the use of the concepts *alignment* and *dominant reality*.

The concept *alignment* provides management with a model for understanding how individuals attempt to fuse and integrate their personal needs with the needs of the organization. This concept explains the personal flexibility that is possible prior to an individual fixing on a particular orientation and the routines, response patterns, and biases that are created once an individual decides on one. The concept *dominant reality* provides management with a model for understanding how groups of individuals with different self-interested pursuits negotiate what often gets represented as the "objective" reality of an organization. This concept explains the latitudes and mutability in the way reality gets constructed, as well as the entrenchedness and stabilizing value of those constructions to which generations of people have affixed their alignments.

Together, the concepts *alignment* and *dominant reality* provide management with a model for seeing that, for most individuals, belonging to an organization is tantamount to living with two realities. The first is the reality of the individual and what he or she actually sees existing in the organization. It is created by that individual's alignment—the result of blending that person's needs to contribute, to have a meaningful job, and to get ahead. The second is the dominant operating reality of the organization. It is a reality that can exist independently of any particular individual. It is created through negotiation, using the processes mentioned in the preceding section, by generations of individuals who push their self-interests while acknowledging the organization's needs for effectiveness. Each of these realities produces its own perspective, which, depending on the individual and the circumstances, can be quite different. Recognizing these differences between the dominant reality of the organization and the specific self-interested reality of each individual allows management to appreciate why people experience their conflicts with one another as political events. In organizations, every person has the need to get the dominant reality aligned with his or her personal reality. Thus, a political event becomes any organizational occurrence in which one individual seeks to make his or her self-interested interpretation part of the dominant reality that others in the organization are expected to constructively relate to and support.

Our use of *alignment* and *dominant reality* emphasizes just how tightly the self-interests of individuals and the needs of organizations intertwine. We want management to recognize how hard it is to speak of one without implying the other. For example, if, hypothetically speaking, there are 9,641 elements to the dominant reality, an individual will strive to emphasize those 412 that best reflect what the person has at stake individually and self-interestedly. What is more, that person will seek modifications in those 63 that, in their modified form, would additionally support his or her self-interested pursuits. This is not to imply that this person will ignore the rest. But it is to imply that this person will not go out of his or her way to acknowledge the other elements and will even resist some references to them by others.

We have noticed definite trends in the mismanagement of organizations due to postures inadvertently taken by managers who lack models for comprehending how personal and organizational realities are formed. We have seen managers at the top use their organizational power to impose narrow definitions of reality that exclude the interests of others in their organization, making it difficult for those people to do their job in a self-meaningful way. The result, in the private sector, is that individuals who do not see things as the dominant reality specifies can be forced into positions where they cannot perform competently. These people either quit or eventually are fired. In the public sector, where people have political patronage or civil service protection, we see situations where narrow definitions of the dominant reality disenfranchise groups of people. The result is that people's needs to find organizational support become so acute that their productive efforts are subordinated to the daily political wars in which they find themselves.

On the other hand, we have also observed many situa-

tions where management's inability to articulate the dominant
reality and put adequate constraints on the self-interested pursuits of people who deviate from it has resulted in too many
people operating with divergent pictures of reality that never
correspond or adequately relate to what their associates are
doing. Organizations with this dynamic often undergo what we
call a "rubber-band" effect, where divergences and excesses
build to a point where, for reasons of market credibility and/or
economic strength, the organization must either snap back to a
coherent whole or break apart. Most of the situations we know
about are organizations that were snapped back by managers
who took a very intolerant view toward the self-interested orientations they observed, particularly toward those that differed from their own.

Behind each of these mismanaged situations is the neglect
of two widely recognized "truths" about the subjective nature
of organization, neither of which should be forgotten by managers who seek to operate their organizations effectively. The
first is that people are always looking to perform their jobs in a
way that maximizes the pursuit of their self-interests. The second is that, within organizations, there are an infinite number
of ways to see events, conceptualize problems, and structure
problem-solving activities, and people seek those ways of performing that do the most for their personal situations (which
range from doing what is interesting to doing what will lead others in the organization to judge them successful). Our appreciation of these truths, together with our understanding of the
subjective nature of organizations as depicted in the constructs
dominant reality and *alignment,* lead us to conclude that there
are at least four strategic points at which managers need help in
more realistically operating their organizations:

1. Acknowledging that the way they represent their organiza-
    tion's reality is strongly influenced by their own subjective
    commitments and interests.
2. Providing others with information about their subjective
    commitments so that these others can more accurately

comprehend how the organization actually operates and what they should take account of in forming their own individual alignments.

3. Recognizing that each subordinate has something unique and special to express that that person will not indefinitely subordinate to an externally imposed organizational rationale.

4. Understanding the essentiality of subjective expression and that organizational effectiveness depends on each individual modifying the structure of a situation to create the conditions that allow him or her to contribute with maximum effectiveness.

Operating with an enhanced understanding of the subjective basis of reality, such as the understanding implied in the list above, enables management to perform at a much more realistic level than we see occurring today. More of the factors that actually determine the course of organization events can be considered; more of the factors with which an individual actually struggles in his or her efforts to be effective can be explicitly discussed and not just left to the level of covert manipulation. Management is able to read organizational situations more accurately, create more options for achieving team effectiveness, and more confidently predict the impact of their actions.

We take pains to add, however, that progress depends on managers working with an improved model, not a longer list of violations, "truths," and points to follow. Our consulting alerts us to the facts that managers do not respond enthusiastically to the exposure of their deficiencies and react to prescriptions by eventually either forgetting or misapplying them. Most managers are well aware of their limited understanding of subjective forces. What they seek are increments of insight and prescriptions. What they need, however, are models that restructure their thinking to see that subjectivity and self-interested participation are part and parcel of every organizational action and perception, models that allow them to include this factor in their everyday organizational thinking. It is to this end that our work has been and continues to be directed.

142 Human Systems Development

References

Argyris, C. *Integrating the Individual and the Organization.* New York: Wiley, 1964.

Argyris, C. *Increasing Leadership Effectiveness.* New York: Wiley, 1976.

Argyris, C. *Reasoning, Learning, and Action: Individual and Organizational.* San Francisco: Jossey-Bass, 1982.

Argyris, C., and Schön, D. A. *Organizational Learning: A Theory of Action Perspective.* Reading, Mass.: Addison-Wesley, 1978.

Barnard, C. J. *The Functions of the Executive.* Cambridge, Mass.: Harvard University Press, 1938.

Berger, P. L., and Luckmann, T. *The Social Construction of Reality: A Treatise in the Sociology of Knowledge.* Garden City, N.Y.: Doubleday, 1966.

Culbert, S. A. *The Organization Trap and How to Get Out of It.* New York: Basic Books, 1974.

Culbert, S. A., and McDonough, J. J. *The Invisible War.* New York: Wiley, 1980.

Culbert, S. A., and McDonough, J. J. *Radical Management: Power Politics and the Pursuit of Trust.* New York: Free Press, 1985.

Gendlin, E. T. *Experiencing and the Creation of Meaning: A Philosophical and Psychological Approach to the Subjective.* New York: Free Press, 1962.

Goffman, E. *Frame Analysis.* New York: Harper & Row, 1974.

Kaplan, A. *The Conduct of Inquiry: Methodology for Behavioral Science.* San Francisco: Chandler, 1964.

Schön, D. A. *Beyond the Stable State.* New York: Norton, 1971.

7

Guides to the Design
and Redesign of Organizations

Louis E. Davis

A long-missing area of knowledge is that surrounding the specifics of structuring an organization. Curiously, structural theories and practices are scarce, with the field dominated by a
body of dogma said to be related to the values of society. There
are a number of general theories and general guidelines now
available to the designer of new organizations. Those engaged in
the ubiquitous activity of modifying or changing existing organizations are not in the least concerned with the guidelines or
"principles" of organization design. In changing an organization, the change maker's concerns are almost always with remedying or overcoming a specific organizational problem or defect.
Replacing structures or designing *new* structures seldom enters
their sphere of activity. This is supported by an examination of
the organization-development literature, prepared by professionals and researchers and professedly devoted to organizational change or improvement. The literature noted is virtually
devoid of references concerned with design of organizational
structures, despite the widespread acknowledgment of the fundamental influence of organizational structure on the behaviors
of an organization's members.

What have been the sources of knowledge about organization structure that are specific enough to guide those managers

143

and professionals confronted with the task of designing new organization structures? General concepts and theories have come from many sources, including general systems theory, mathematical biology, and small-group dynamics. Specific organizational guidelines have been painstakingly developed by action-research-based designers of organizations who employ open sociotechnical-systems theory. What follows is both a historical report and a review of learnings concerning structure compiled from and tested in a substantial number of designs of new organizations (Davis, 1983).

Let us begin by considering the historical context. What began in the early 1950s as a search for organizational remedies to overcome the then-visible defects of bureaucracy–scientific management changed within ten years to experimentation with and development of new forms—alternative forms—of organization. By the end of the 1950s, the growing visibility of watershed changes in technology and organizational environment suggested that remedying organizational and job structures likely would be insufficient to meet evolving requirements associated with new technological development. The threat to organizational survival, now so evident, was then hidden from general view. While mechanization continued, it began to be combined with electronic decision making, now called automation. Such sophisticated technology began to change what was required of people in order to achieve desired service or product outcomes. Changes in both the content and the meaning of work were accompanied by deep changes, at first unrecognized, in how people could be managed in these new circumstances. By the 1960s, it was becoming clear that successful operation of an organization was directly dependent on its members' commitment to maximally appropriate action. Settings that now are called high-commitment organizations are characterized by the organization's high degree of dependence on the commitment of its members to take initiatives to adjust, modify, correct, or stop a malfunctioning system as determined by the members. In these circumstances, conventional means available to the organization for controlling and motivating its members to achieve the organization's goals become ineffective.

The changes in the environments of organizations that became apparent were those of growing turbulence, seen by some as instability. This concept was first elucidated by Emery and Trist (1965), Vickers (1970), and Schön (1971) as turbulent texture of the environment, the "loss of the stable state," or environmental instability. Turbulent environments are very slightly, if at all, predictable, limiting severely the possibility of reducing the level of uncertainty surrounding organizations.

In the face of high uncertainty, the ability to survive is threatened. The strategic response of organizational leaders focuses on making adaptability a principal feature of the organization and, thus, on a design requirement for new (or redesigned) organizations. Operationally, emphasis shifts from conformity with predetermined rules to experimentation and learning to increase response capabilities. New forms of organization now are being tested whose goals are both to be successful (efficient) and to increase learning-response repertoires and flexibility of people. Thus, the time, disruption, and stress that usually have accompanied changes to suit new or varying conditions are minimized. In other words, the organization is required to acquire high adaptive capability. In this instance as well, high commitment is required on the part of the organization's members. Thus, there arises the unavoidable need to design organizational forms and structures and the means of managing them that promote high commitment on the part of the members to the organization's goals. The learnings about organizations reported here are extracted from new-design experiences in both high-technology and other settings. Many of these new designs have a high capability of adapting, without distress or disruption, to new, even unpredictable circumstances. As a consequence, the learnings reported are oriented to addressing the realities of the newly evolving era, rather than to remedying the organizational concepts of bureaucracy-burdened scientific management that arose out of (and became synonymous with) the fading industrial era.

The most frequent discussion of the design of new organizations, variously called "new design" or "greenfield design," centers on whether such design is more or less difficult to accomplish than is the modification or redesign of existing organizations. Such discussions are instances both of comparing the incomparable and of confusing the amount of time required with the difficulty involved. Both activities are immensely difficult, but for vastly different reasons. However, the crucial issue for the future lies in the development of tested concepts of organization design. In this regard, the experience of the last fifteen years indicates that the development and testing of concepts required for building organizations that both are highly effective and provide a high quality of working life are taking place primarily in the design of new forms of organization. Redesign, on the other hand, is providing important new learnings about processes and requirements of organizational change. Our present concern focuses on learnings—some tested, some tentative—derived from new designs. These learnings do not fit the academic mold of the social science disciplines. In fact, to approach new forms of organization and jobs, the existing mold deliberately had to be disregarded, since it is so heavily dependent on the long-dominant bureaucracy–scientific-management models of organization.

The learnings acquired from the designs of new organizations are so extensive and diverse that they touch on most scientific, professional, and practical issues of concern to the structuring and operation of organizations and to the behaviors of their members. They challenge currently accepted wisdom—the cherished truths about management, leadership, control, individual and group behavior, motivation, and rewards, as well as training, recruitment, selection, careers, communication, problem solving, role structures, and organizational change. New designs that have broken through the accepted organizational mold of bureaucratic-scientific management are providing new insights and data bearing on organizational psychology and sociology, management, engineering, and architecture. They provide new insights into organizational goal attainment, adaptation, integration, and long-term maintenance. Further, perspectives are provided on the influence of technology on structure and behavior, on organizational vulnerability related to advanced forms of technology, and on the measurement of effectiveness.

Organization Design Process

The first learning that has become visible is that a different process of organization design is required if more effective organizations (having a higher quality of working life) are to be created. The new design process uses a different method of reaching design decisions. It is a process strongly based on participation, in which all the participants are required to approach design from a basis of exposing assumptions and concepts so that the goal of jointly dealing with the multiple objectives can be satisfied. It is a process that integrates world views, various demands to which the organization must respond, and specific needs. It promotes the comprehensive view of the organization as a system and as a working society. Thus, considerable time as well as support and protection are required to permit exploration of values, acquisition of concepts, and the development of alternative world views that may likely challenge the status quo ante.

A number of things are essential for the process to provide desired outcomes. There has to be agreement on values or superordinate goals, embodied in an organizational philosophy statement. A temporary design structure has to be created for the duration of the design period, to provide integration and resolution of conflicting requirements and demands. The scope of the design activities has to be negotiated to bring within the purview of the design team all aspects of organizational structure and operation. Organizational innovations are not likely to be developed without inclusion of the design of technical as well as social systems. The authority of the design team has to be negotiated so that all design decisions are under its control and the implications of all technical, economic, and social decisions will be jointly explored as a basis for making optimal choices. Lastly, top management, through a steering committee, has to provide sanction, support, resources (particularly time), and protection for the design team so that it is free to develop innovative outcomes.

The process requires the appointment at the start of the design of managers who are to be responsible for the success and survival of the prospective organization. The managers (and, in instances where union-management agreement exists, union officials) participate in the process of design and are required to stay through the start-up period to assure adherence to the design during implementation. Lastly, to assure continuity, those appointed to the design team and then to management of the organization should be mature, confident individuals who understand themselves and who do not need to rely either on the power and status of their roles or on control mechanisms as crutches for protection of their positions.

The notion that a deliberate process of organizational design is required is in itself a new development, since no such identifiable process had existed earlier. The "design of organization" was a matter of fitting specific needs into the precast bureaucratic–scientific-management mold that made design synonymous with drawing an organization chart. The major contribution that can now be reported is that, since the early 1970s, a deliberate, systematic, structured, comprehensive process of organization design, tested in a number of complex applications, has become available. To date, the process has been only partially reported (Davis, 1982).

The organization-design process, as does the process of redesign, brings together diverse and often conflicting interests and professionals whose contributions are needed if both a comprehensive and systematic design is to be achieved. Each has a specific role to play in the process. The diverse contributors are brought together on the basis of the structuralist concept of organizational performance and behavior. Briefly stated, this concept holds that both the structure of the organization (roles and relationships) and the organizational climate or environment influence, to a substantial degree, the behaviors of the organization's members and their responses to either organizational or parochial goals.

The roles that the diverse participants play in the design process include not only the provision of deep technical knowledge in their own areas of expertise but also the open interactions among what each perceives as necessary requirements. The consequent and needed clash between competing and/or opposing world views—their correlated concepts and perceived needs and the conflicts that emerge—provides the basis for examining the likely divisive impacts on the prospective organization. Failure to examine and resolve these divisive impacts probably will lead to suboptimal organizational performance and to unsatisfactory consequences for its members. The participants in the design process come to understand that *joint* optimization based on *joint* design of all the features and functions of the organization provides the basis for resolution of conflicts over design choices. It is here that the potential resides for innovation in organizational forms, managerial practices, and worker roles.

The process of integrated comprehensive design has sometimes been called organization-plant design (Lawler, 1978; Davis, 1979), because it includes the design of the technical (transformation) system and its accompanying work system, physical facilities, buildings, organization structure, job content, careers, rewards, training, recruitment, selection, and adaptation (organization-change) mechanisms. Perhaps most important is the world view embodied in the process that the organization is a small or minisociety. Only by designing these aspects jointly are systemic social and technical requirements for achieving outcomes (goals) met optimally. Jointly designing the various technical and social systems generates opportunities for meeting the joint objectives of high organizational effectiveness and superior quality of working life.

The design process begins in a fourfold manner by (1) negotiating with the leadership about their expectations regarding design outcomes to be achieved, (2) establishing a temporary structure for carrying on the process of design (which lasts until the design or redesign is concluded and the new design is activated), (3) requiring the top management and union leadership (where there is a union) to consider and agree on a shared view of the future facing the organization, and (4) agreeing on the social and economic values that will guide both the design process and the subsequent operation of the new or changed organization. Agreeing on shared futures and values requires carefully designed exercises, which lead to development of "internal social policy" that is reported as a "statement of organizational philosophy" (Hill, 1972; Davis, 1980b).

The temporary structure needed to carry on the organizational design process is indicated in Figure 7-1. This structure is

Figure 7-1. Organizational Design Process: Stages and Structure.

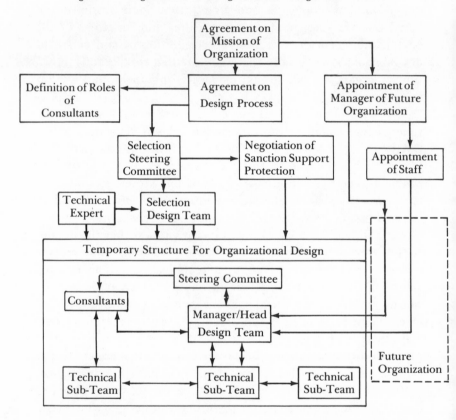

sometimes two-tiered and at other times three-tiered, depending on technical complexity. In the latter instance, design subteams may be required. Important to successful design outcomes are the method of operation and the scope of activities of the design team. The crucial feature is that only the design team as a whole may make the final choices or design decisions regarding the various features of the organization and its technical system.

The various technical, managerial, and social experts who are members of the design team have the dual role of both advising and jointly deciding. This takes the place of their former experts' unilateral design-decision powers, which are now the property of the design team as a whole.

The scope of activities of the design team is unlimited within the bounds of money, product, social, and other policies laid down by the steering committee. The scope includes the design of the production process, equipment, information systems, organization structure, job designs, career paths, measurement and control systems, advancement, rewards, selection, training, discipline, and so forth. Thus, the scope includes all aspects of the creation and maintenance of a work society—its tools, equipment, and physical facilities.

Organizational Philosophy

A second crucial learning is that neither organizational design nor technical design can proceed without agreement on the *social values* that will guide the new organization or society that is being created. Developing a statement of organizational philosophy is the first order of business in the process of organizational design following the creation of the steering committee and design team. The difficult task of elaborating and agreeing on values becomes the earliest activity of the design team and steering committee. The new process of design makes explicit the organizational philosophy, referred to by some as the superordinate goals of the organization (Pascale and Athos, 1981). The resulting impact on design is pervasive, for it serves both as goal and as guide and is a visible reminder that the designers are providing an answer to the question "What kind of society are we proposing to build?"

To recapitulate learnings, what appears to be absolutely crucial is that there be agreement on a basic set of predesign requirements that must be satisfied if design of a new organization is to take place (in contrast to copying). These requirements concern elucidation and agreement on values that will undergird the prospective organization, the use of a process of joint design, establishment of a supportive design structure, and negotiation and agreement on the scope of the process and the authority of the design team. What has been learned is that innovative design is not likely to take place, perhaps cannot take place, unless a deliberate joint design process is established.

Organizational Environment

The design of a new organization—the creation of an institution where none existed before—makes very clear that what is being designed is the organization as a complex of four interacting entities. These four entities may be described as follows:

- A *transforming agency* that converts provided resources into desired products or services, a place where work is done, and a work organization in the first instance.
- An *economic entity* that uses resources and has the responsibility to account for them to private and/or public sources.
- A *small society* in itself that provides to its members rewards, identities, valued relationships, continuity, socially valued roles, and association with the larger society of which it is a part. As a minisociety, the organization acquires the supplementary goal of survival or permanence.
- A *collection of individuals* whose membership in the organization provides the means for satisfying a variety of individually different social and personal goals and expectations. In Western societies, with their emphasis on individualism, the means and process provided for satisfying some, if not all, of the individual's goals and expectations are key to the individual's commitment to the organization's goals.

The design of a new organization reveals that multiple goals exist, whether or not they are formally recognized. There are many stakeholders inside and outside the prospective organization, and these stakeholders generate a multiplicity of goals and expectations to be satisfied. This is what is implied in the statement that the organization is an open system—open to the influences of its environment and having to meet requirements originating in this environment.

Design in the present turbulent environment requires concern not only for success (economic and technical efficiency) but for organizational survival (Emery and Trist, 1973). Given unpredictability and irreducible uncertainty, the survival goal introduces the necessity to design highly adaptive organizations, with a concomitant shift in emphasis from internal stability to continuous change. For the designer, this brings forth the requirement of creating an organization that can learn from its experience and continuously change while doing its work and meeting its goals.

Substantial emphasis must be placed on the design of effective mechanisms for learning, adaptation, and renewal (redesign). Roles and functions need to be designed for the organization's members that will facilitate development of flexible people who can support organizational adaptation.

Organizational Structure

Boundaries. At this moment, very likely the most significant learning emerging from new designs concerns the process of locating organizational boundaries. Placing internal boundaries is very likely the most crucial single act in the design of an organization. Boundary location influences almost all else in organizational structure. It directly affects the units of the organization that are created by the partitioning, influencing what responsibilities are to be assigned to the units. Further, it influences appropriate choice of information, control, measurement, and feedback systems and the basis of interpersonal and intergroup relationships. Inappropriate boundary location largely influences both the number of organizational levels required and management style and, thus, the type of managerial skills required.

Conventional wisdom advises us to place boundaries so that like functions are grouped together, sometimes referred to as organizing by similar technology, or functional organization. This dominant proposition of bureaucracy–scientific management has acquired a vast mythology, largely unverified, extolling the benefits of placing like functions together. This proposition is bolstered by two others: place boundaries so that activities performed in the same time period are grouped together and/or place them so that those performed in the same locale are grouped together. These propositions have come to be known as organizing by time (shift) and/or place.

For the present, the learnings about boundary location have been stated as a set of guidelines or propositions for the designers of organizations. Internal organizational boundaries should be located so that:

1. Within an organizational unit, those responsible for achieving the outcomes can have access to and exercise control over the disturbances or variances that occur in performing work and that may affect the outcomes achieved.
2. Members of a unit can develop some autonomy or a substantial degree of control over their own activities in achieving the desired goals of the unit.
3. Members of a unit can have access to all the information they need to solve the unit's problems and to assess its performance (feedback).
4. The boundaries are between the main transformation processes rather than cutting through a process.
5. The boundaries are located at the completion of a process, product, or subdivision of the product.
6. The outcomes of work activities can be measured at their boundaries in order to provide feedback needed by the members of the unit to regulate themselves.
7. Members of a unit can develop an identity with the product, process, or outcomes.
8. Coordination between activities and people can be accomplished within the organizational unit, leaving integration to managers.
9. Members of a unit can develop face-to-face relationships in carrying out the work of the unit.
10. The requisite skills and activities needed to perform assigned work and to maintain the technical and social systems of the organizational unit are within the boundaries of the unit.
11. The need for external control and external coercion is

minimized. Increased opportunities are available for self-regulation in achieving desired outcomes (Davis, 1982).

Building Blocks. Practical application of the learnings concerning boundary location confront the dilemma that boundaries cannot be located without prior choice of what are to be the "basic building blocks" of the organization. Making this choice in turn depends both on the organizational philosophy and on the chosen technology (Miller, 1959). Without regard to changed circumstances, values, and technology, the most widely used unit at present is still that called for by bureaucracy–scientific management—one person plus his or her task in a specific time period (a work shift). Organizational designers using such units are required to be careful in separating the contents of task-job activities of each unit or person. Carefully drawn job descriptions formally assuring such separation become a concomitant requirement. The results are well known: built-in incapability to cooperate and inhibition of learning. Not infrequently, informal cooperation and learning are rewarded by punishment. Rigid job demarcation leads to a "it-is-not-my-job" syndrome. In placid, less demanding times, the price for all this was somehow affordable. However, the person-task-per-shift building block brings with it suboptimization, organizational rigidity, and inflexible people, resulting in incapability to adapt. Lack of adaptability in a turbulent environment is nonaffordable, for it carries the frightening potential of nonsurvival.

New designs have been particularly useful in identifying the characteristics of organizational units. Ideally, it appears that the basic building block of an organization should be *a miniature version of the organization of which it is a component.* As such, the unit can discharge the responsibilities assigned to it by carrying on its activities in much the same way as the larger organizations. In this sense, an organization is made up of miniature organizations, each responsible for a service, process, or product outcome. Such units have been discussed as follows: "Adaptive organizations require self-maintaining units as their basic building blocks. A self-maintaining organizational unit is one that has the capability to perform all the activities required to achieve its specific objectives under a wide variety of contingencies. It can maintain its internal structure and adapt itself to changing demands impinging upon it from its environment. Such units may exist as groups with supervisors-semi-autonomous teams, or without supervisors-autonomous teams" (Davis, 1982).

Self-maintaining organizational units should not be too large, although successful ones operate that are much larger than previously suggested by small-group theory. This is so even when the units are in the form of autonomous teams without supervisors. Nor should they be too small. Units with fewer than four or five members are too easily disrupted by such events as promotion or absenteeism. Successful units of twenty-five to twenty-eight members exist; however, they have taken very much longer to develop group cohesion than groups of fourteen to eighteen. Self-maintaining units as the basic building blocks require less direction, less coordination, less dealing with problems that they export, and, thus, less supervision and fewer levels in the hierarchy.

Technical Systems

For the practical world of application, the learnings derived from the relationship between technology and organizational design are perhaps the most profound. They call for new commitments on the part of top management, the sanctioners of new design or redesign, and new skills on the parts of both technical and organizational designers. Beginning with the application of technology itself, what becomes evident is that many technical systems can be derived from a single technology, and it is the technical system as designed that has the direct effect on the organizational and job structures. First, the choice of technical systems raises considerations as to who should make the choices and what policy, principles, or desiderata should guide the choice-making process. Second, the response to these considerations is totally affected by an additional learning, namely, that technical-system design cannot, in fact, be completed by technical designers without basic social-system considerations.

The process of designing a derivative technical system requires the designer to answer the question, "How will the machine or system be operated and controlled?" Presently the usual approach is that the technical designer decides who will do what with the machines or system and how these are to fit into the overall functioning of the process or product system. These decisions are, of course, organizational-design decisions that are already foreclosed when most conventional new design or redesign begins. From the point of view of satisfactorily designing technical systems, technical designers are, either unknowingly or reluctantly, "social-system engineers." Thus, we begin to understand why, when we import a foreign technical system or export ours, we also import or export with it the cultural or social assumptions of the country of origin. The twentieth-century belief that science and technology are free of social values can be seen to be a myth that has had enormous negative consequences for Western societies. Returning to practical application, realities, not myths, need to be met.

The above learnings have led to two significant positions. The first is that technological determinism is a put-off, if not a sham. It is a defensive posture adopted by those who either have no policy or desiderata to guide them or are incapable of delving into the joint technical and social issues that must be confronted in technical-system design. In relation to the latter, the concepts of sociotechnical systems provide significant contributions. The second learning is that the processes of technical-system design and organizational design cannot be permitted to take place independently or even separately from each other. The crucial decisions to be made depend on joint considerations. Further, organizational design encompasses the process of embedding the technical system within the social system.

The new process of design can be expected to spread widely, because it addresses reality, aids technical designers in areas where they have been uncertain, and addresses issues presented by the profound changes in the texture of organizational environments. What has been learned *from* new designs, however, is not exclusive *to* new designs. The redesign, modification, or renewal of existing organizations also must deal with the self-same issues that face new design. But, in addition, redesign must face the constraints created by the unique history of each existing organization.

The joint process of designing new organizations in conjunction with "high-technology" or automated systems is proving a significantly useful alternative to independent, isolated technical-systems design. These advanced technical systems not only are composed of sophisticated mechanisms such as are found in assembly robots but are interlocked or integrated (and kept within acceptable control limits) by computer- and microprocessor-driven devices. Such high-technology or automated systems severely change "how the machine or system will be operated and controlled" and thus significantly change the relationship between people and machines. This, in turn, changes the meaning of work. The focus of the work system moves from interaction with machine to system and from predictable actions to selection from a wide response repertoire dependent on events interrupting system continuity. This redefinition of the content and purpose of work and the requirements of the work system was first described in 1971 (Davis, 1971). More and more frequently, what emerges from technical-system design is the necessity to develop "high-commitment organizations."

The design of high-commitment organizations simply cannot be achieved unless joint design is undertaken so that the needed bases for building members' high commitment become part of the design requirements of *both* the technical and social systems. There is no evidence that high commitment can be developed through the design of social systems alone, no matter how innovative these may be. In addition to the lack of access to technical-system choices and, thus, to the underlying requirements of the work system, existing conventional wisdom regarding worker motivation is simply inadequate for dealing with the requirements of high technology.

The consequences of incorporating high-commitment requirements are organizational structures radically different from the forms and precepts of bureaucracy–scientific management. Such structures are still in the process of development and at present are known as "alternative forms of organization" (Davis, 1977). The exploration of and experimentation with alternative organizational structures is at the core of innovative organizational design.

Social Systems

In general, social systems are constituted of the structures, roles, relationships, and functions of groups and individuals directed at the operation of the organization in its various manifestations as a transforming agency, economic entity, small society, and assemblage of individuals. In the most advanced of the new organizational forms, the social system of the organization is a structure consisting of a set of miniorganizations or minisocieties based on an espoused set of social values—on an organizational philosophy (Hill, 1972). Similarly, the social system of each constituent organizational unit is a set of individuals tightly integrated by lateral and hierarchical relationships and by agreed-to social values, cutting across the boundaries of the units. The roles of members encompass elements of all activities of the unit and of the larger organizations, as well as activities focused on the members of the unit as individuals. At the level of the organization as social system, success (effectiveness) and survival seem to be related to those social-system structures that provide:

• Open, visible relationships between managers and the organizational units and their members concerned with decision making, action taking, goal setting, justice, power, status, and rewards. Some have called this "demystification of management." It is more than that, as it is also considerably more than communication, for it involves sharing of functions, participating in decisions affecting the units and their members, and open flow of all useful information to provide advance knowledge as well as feedback.

- Participation of organizational units or their representatives in goal-attainment functions, particularly in goal setting and in organizational control functions, including evaluation and measurement.
- Participation of the organizational units or their representatives in the functions concerned with integration and coordination of the organizational units.
- Both ongoing organizational adaptation mechanisms, such as organizationwide standing change committees, and participation in them by organizational-unit representatives. In effect, what exists is a participative continuing visible process of change.

Optimal social systems can be designed only by jointly designing both the technical and social systems of the organization. This is particularly the case when a high-commitment social system is essential to success.

High Commitment. The differences between developing commitment and developing motivation are very substantial in terms of social-system characteristics. In the high-commitment setting, what has to be done is not specifically known, so that appropriate self-initiated action is crucial to success. What are the requirements for appropriate self-selected, self-initiated action—that is, high commitment of the individual to the goals of the organization? So far, learnings from new designs indicate that the requirements include provision of the means for jointly satisfying both the organization's and the individuals' goals, with opportunities to satisfy some, if not most, of individuals' own goals and expectations. In aid of joint goal satisfaction, a social system is required that is sensitive to individual differences, opportunities for participation, learning, advancement, choice, self-regulation, justice, and equity.

Quality of Working Life. High quality of working life is a fundamental consideration in organizational design if social systems are to be effective. *Quality of working life* refers to the quality of the relationship between the organization's members and the total working environment, with human-requirements dimensions added to the usual technical and economic requirements (Kolodny and Van Beinum, 1983).

Much has been written about the present societal environment to indicate why attention to achieving high quality of working life is essential to organizational and individual effectiveness and survival (Davis, 1980a; Yankelovich, 1981; Levine, Taylor, and Davis, 1984). The important general criteria for high quality of working life, based on a variety of studies, are security; equitable pay and rewards; justice in the workplace; relief from bureaucratic and supervisory coercion; meaningful and interesting work; a variety of activities and assignments; challenge; control over self, work, and workplace; one's own area of decision making or responsibility; learning and growth opportunities; feedback and knowledge of results; authority to accomplish that for which one is held responsible; recognition of contributions—financial, social, and psychological rewards, status, and advancement; social support—the ability to rely on others when one needs to and to be relied upon and the right to expect sympathy and understanding when needed; viable futures (no dead-end jobs); an ability to relate one's work and accomplishments to life outside the workplace; and options or choices to suit the individual's preferences, interests, and expectations (Davis, 1982).

Careers. Effective social systems include the design not only of work systems but of career structures for all members of the organization. Alternative career opportunities and, particularly, participation in career choices are essential both to high commitment and to flexibility (adaptation) of individuals. Alternative organizational structures indicate that further learning is needed concerning the structuring of careers in organizations on the basis of teams and of few layers of supervision and management.

Adaptability. The capability of the social system to adapt seems to be related to the structure of the organization, units, or groups and individuals' jobs or roles. At the organizational level, established standing participative groups or committees recommend changes, providing the operational adaptation function of the organization. Their membership is drawn from the various organizational units and levels. They are permanent entities, continuously engaged in capturing organizational learnings and recommending organizational changes. They are not temporary or ad hoc groups thrown together to help deal with an emergency situation.

Included in structural design is the design of organization-wide systems of information and feedback providing information to all units and levels on the basis of the sociotechnical-systems principle of making information available at the lowest level in the organization needed for decision making (Cherns, 1976). What is seen in such designs is the open flow of all kinds of information relevant to discharging of individual and joint responsibilities of groups or teams and their members. Basic to building adaptability is the choice of self-maintaining groups or teams as the basic units (building blocks) of the organization. Such units, based on the principle of multifunctionalism (Cherns, 1976), have within them most, if not all, of the skills, information, and authorities, including internal reorganization and work assignment, needed to carry on the work of the units.

Individual members of the organization's units have substantial comprehensive roles requiring wide repertoires of responses. They participate in work, problem solving, and improvement activities and exercise substantial self-regulation in their work assignments. Their knowledge of the state of affairs in their teams and in the organization is very large, permitting effective participation in change (adaptation) activities.

Teams. Implementation of self-maintaining organizational units as basic building blocks has led to the extended development of teams that may be either autonomous or semiautonomous. What defines a team, as distinct from a work group, is that its members share the responsibilities and depend on each other for achieving common objectives or goals. A work group, on the other hand, is one whose members share a set of social or authority relationships through reporting to a common supervisor. It is not yet clear whether autonomous teams without supervisors or semiautonomous teams with supervisors are more adaptable to changing requirements imposed by an unstable environment.

A very significant learning holds that, if self-maintaining units are to be effective, their members must require additional competencies beyond the usual work skills. These have come to be known as "social-system skills"—skills in communicating, self-management, conflict resolution, counseling, developing social contracts, and so on. Acquisition of such skills requires supplemental and innovative training approaches.

For autonomous or semiautonomous teams to survive, certain requirements must be instituted and maintained. One such requirement is that the work required to discharge a team's responsibilities belongs to the team as a whole, with the team assigning work to its members on the basis of competence, training needs, absenteeism, breakdowns, and so on. Another is that inputs to a team are controlled by it if it is to be responsible for outcomes. A third requirement calls for an open flow of information to and from each team, coming from management and from other teams. A given team's actions and those of other teams play a deliberate part in the information-transmission (feedback) process.

Management

The various new forms of organization, with their different structural arrangements, lead to altered roles for supervisors and managers. These altered roles require a major shift for managers from directing, assigning, controlling, problem solving, and so on at the center of their organizational units to performing these functions at the boundaries of their units. Boundary management cannot take place unless managers provide the members of their units with the competencies needed for them to function as a team. Supervisorial and managerial roles are restructured to support boundary management. Such management provides buffering or mediation of changes in the environment so that the units are not upset by such changes as they carry on their work. The language used by supervisors and managers in these new forms of organization reflects changed roles. Often heard is: "I can now plan ahead and avoid spending all my time fighting fires." "I can now get out of the trenches and see what is coming and plan ahead so that my people and I are not inundated and always digging out."

The altered roles call for managerial supportive functions, including (1) the building of broad and appropriate response capabilities within the units to meet expected external demands, which requires enhancing the competence of units' members through training and experience; (2) allocating needed resources to be used by units as required in support of achieving their goals; (3) auditing of units' (teams') performance to provide feedback and support; (4) evaluating units' accomplishments rather than the behaviors of their members; (5) developing participation in setting goals and standards; and (6) developing problem-solving capabilities of units' members.

Managers exercise leadership and control so as to further strengthen and maintain the units (teams). Measurement and evaluation approaches are developed that suit managing by objective outcomes (results achieved) rather than responding to behaviors displayed. Similarly, there is greater investment in training and in developing wide response repertoires of members and in providing training and time for team problem solving. Managers control organizational units (teams) rather than directly controlling each individual employee.

Conclusion

Effective methods of organizational design are available that overcome holding the structure of organizations and jobs hostage to independently designed technical systems. The most effective approach available now is that of joint design based on sociotechnical-systems concepts, wherein the technical and social systems of an organization are designed interactively.

The process of design of new organizations makes viable new or alternative forms of organization visible (Davis, 1977). These are organizations consisting of integrated self-maintaining organizational units that are structured and supported to act as self-regulating miniorganizations (minisocieties). These alternative forms of organization are much more responsive to external uncertainty and instability and, within limits, are highly adaptive. They have adequate capacity to change, in large and small ways. These organizations develop flexible and informed members and join them into cohesive units bound together by shared rather than by imposed values, by high commitment, and by participation in a wide variety of functions required to achieve goals and maintain the organization over time.

There is a widespread belief at present that alternative forms of organization are very fragile and therefore will not survive. This will prove not to be so. The few that have failed to survive have left valuable lessons. Most important to early robustness is the presence from the onset of the design process of the manager of the future organization. Combined in these instances are ownership of the design and of the start-up requirements needed for future success. Further, the manager and team that implement the design commit themselves to stay at least through the start-up period and into the early stage of steady-state operation. Lastly, success and survival of alternative forms of organization depend particularly on leadership by mature, confident individuals who understand themselves and who can accommodate a substantial amount of ambiguity. Such managers have only a slight dependence on rules and control mechanisms.

The structures of the evolving alternative organizations provide the means for utilizing a variety of concepts that, while useful in their own right, have never been integrated into the functioning of organizations. Management by objectives instead of by regulation of behavior is a central feature of alternative organizations. Managerial skills in interpersonal as well as group dynamics are essential, as is a high tolerance for ambiguity. An emphasis on individual differences and on managing by counseling and social support is also essential. Managers are required to understand and develop high levels of participation at all levels of the organization. A manager who has acquired organization-development skills would be academically well prepared to begin to manage an alternative organization.

The humanistic values concerning the individual and his or her relationships to organizations so highly prized and expected by the younger generation of employees and managers are realistically applied in the new or alternative forms of organization.

References

Cherns, A. "The Principles of Sociotechnical Design." *Human Relations*, 1976, *29*, 783–792.

Davis, L. E. "The Coming Crisis for Production Management." *International Journal of Production Research*, 1971, *9* (1), 65.

Davis, L. E. "Evolving Alternative Organization Designs: Their Sociotechnical Bases." *Human Relations*, 1977, *3*, 261.

Davis, L. E. "Optimizing Organization-Plant Design." *Organizational Dynamics*, Autumn 1979, *8* (2), 2-16.

Davis, L. E. "Individuals and the Organization." *California Management Review*, 1980a, *22* (2), 5-14.

Davis, L. E. "A Labour-Management Contract and Quality of Working Life." *Journal of Occupational Behavior*, 1980b, *1* (1), 29.

Davis, L. E. "Organization Design." In G. Salvendy (Ed.), *Industrial Engineering Handbook*. New York: Wiley, 1982.

Davis, L. E. "Learnings from the Design of New Organizations." In H. F. Kolodny and H. Van Beinum (Eds.), *The Quality of Working Life and the 1980s*. New York: Praeger, 1983.

Emery, F. E., and Trist, E. L. "The Causal Texture of Organizational Environments." *Human Relations*, 1965, *18*, 21-32.

Emery, F. E., and Trist, E. L. *Towards A Social Ecology*. New York: Plenum, 1973.

Hill, C. P. *Towards a New Philosophy of Management*. New York: Barnes & Noble, 1972.

Kolodny, H. F., and Van Beinum, H. (Eds.). *The Quality of Working Life and the 1980s*. New York: Praeger, 1983.

Lawler, E. E., III. "The New Plant Revolution." *Organizational Dynamics*, Winter 1978, *6* (3), 2-12.

Levine, M. F., Taylor, J. C., and Davis, L. E. "Defining the Quality of Working Life." *Human Relations*, 1984, *37*, 81-104.

Miller, E. "Technology, Territory, Time." *Human Relations*, 1959, *12* (3), 243.

Pascale, R. T., and Athos, A. G. *The Art of Japanese Management*. New York: Simon & Schuster, 1981.

Schön, D. A. *Beyond the Stable State*. New York: Norton, 1971.

Vickers, G. *Freedom in a Rocking Boat*. New York: Basic Books, 1970.

Yankelovich, D. *New Rules*. New York: Random House, 1981.

8

Intervention Strategies
for Interorganizational Domains

Eric Trist

As the 1950s gave way to the 1960s, several of us then working at the Tavistock Institute in London found that the action-research projects in which we were now more frequently becoming engaged, in response to client needs, changed from those primarily concerned with single organizations to endeavors concerned with large-scale social systems involving many and often diverse organizations. That is to say, we had entered the wider field of what we began to call *organizational ecology*. This change in the need for our assistance seemed to reflect a trend in the contextual environment toward increased turbulence (Emery and Trist, 1965). The new condition of society required the identification of a new unit of analysis on the part of the social sciences—the organizational-ecology system (Trist, 1977).

This term is used here in a different sense from its usage in studies carried out in accordance with the population-ecology model and related approaches. These make elaborate use of biological concepts for explanatory purposes, whereas we use *organizational ecology* in a general systems sense to refer to an interdependent set of organizational entities that, in order to survive, must learn in some mutually acceptable way to share the limited resources of a common environment.

167

The idea of organizational ecology led to the idea of organizational or, more accurately if more clumsily, interorganizational domains. The term *organizational domain* means the opposite of what Evan (1966) means by the term *organization-set*. This views an organizational field in terms of a focal organization, whereas the term *domain* views the focal organization in the context of the organizational field, which now becomes the object of inquiry. The term *inter*organizational is used to distinguish it from the usage of Thompson (1967), who employs the term *domain* to refer to the system of relations that any single organization needs to maintain with its transactional environment—a usage that is within the organization-set perspective. By contrast, interorganizational domains are concerned with field-related organizational populations. The perspective is similar to that of Warren (1967). An organizational population becomes field related when it engages with a set of problems or a societal-problem area that constitutes a domain of common concern for its members. The set of organizations is then directly correlated (Sommerhoff, 1950, 1969) with the problem area toward which some action is required.

A complex problem area of this kind is often referred to as a *problématique, metaproblem* (Chevalier, 1966), or *mess* (Ackoff, 1974). The issues involved are too extensive and too many-sided to be coped with by any single organization, however large. The response capability required to clear up a mess is inter- and multiorganizational. Since problématiques, metaproblems, or messes—rather than discrete problems—are what societies currently have to face up to, the cultivation of domain-based, interorganizational competence has become a necessary societal project. The focus of this chapter will be on advanced industrial societies of the Western type. Although it is the very development of these societies that has brought this situation about, they are weak in their interorganizational capability, as compared with their capability at the level of the single organization (although here, also, the higher level of interdependence present in the contemporary environment is rendering traditional bureaucratic models dysfunctional). Debureaucratization of single organizations is necessary but not sufficient. Needed also are advances in institution building at the level of inter-organizational domains—functional social systems that occupy a position in social space between the society as a whole and the single organization. In one perspective, a society may be said to construe itself in terms of domains that tend to actualize themselves in concrete settings. These comprise their locales, which may be sectoral or regional.

An example that combines both is a problématique that has relatively recently emerged as a domain—energy. Another is the declining Northeast of the United States. In an article in the *New York Times,* Rohatyn (1979) describes an organizational proposal that links these two domains in a way that would begin to solve the metaproblem: the creation, through a regional initiative, of an Energy Corporation of the Northeast. The states would participate by subscribing initial capital (a dollar a head), the federal government by guaranteeing loans. The corporation would not be an operating agency but would perform a regulative and developmental function. Facilities would be operated by private parties, who would be asked to invest more than 50 percent of the capital cost of any undertaking. An organization of this type is called a referent organization (Trist, 1977)—a term developed from the concept of reference groups. Such organizations, of which there are several varieties, are of critical importance for domain development. When successful, they develop strong referent power (French and Raven, 1962) not only for their own members but for those in many related organizations in the domain, certain of whose basic aspirations, interests, norms, and values they come to symbolize and validate. Notice that the Energy Corporation of the Northeast is to be regulative, not operational. Moreover, it is to be controlled by the stakeholders involved in the domain, not from the outside. Yet it will not be isolated. The federal government is asked to provide an input, and the private parties would not all have to come from the region. Nevertheless, activities are region centered in the locale of the domain.

The importance of regulation by stakeholders can scarcely be overemphasized, for the danger is considerable that the organizational fashioning, the institution building, the social architecture (a term used by Perlmutter, 1965) required at the domain level in complex modern societies will either take the wrong path or will not be attempted at all. By "the wrong path" is meant organizational elaboration in terms of bureaucratic principles that would extend central power and hierarchical form throughout a domain. This would lead to the corporate state, to a very high degree of totalitarianism throughout the society. If, on the other hand, through fear of this, no attempt is made to weave an appropriate fabric at the domain level, the result can only be further social fragmentation. In the limit, there would simply be large numbers of self-isolating and competing entities, which would, through minimizing their interdependence, prevent the attainment of the degree of organic solidarity (Durkheim, 1964) necessary to hold a complex society together.

These two directions are but two sides of the same penny. They are binary opposites, one being simply the negation of the other. Neither can provide the organizational means likely to lead toward a desirable human future. A lasting societal advance will entail the identification of a set of nonbureaucratic principles at the domain level that will constitute a distinct logical type (in the sense used by Whitehead and Russell, 1910-1913). These principles may be called socioecological, as contrasted with those appertaining either to bureaucratic extensionism or to dissociative isolationism. Socioecological principles imply the centrality of interdependence, entailing some surrender of sovereignty along with considerable diffusion of power. There is no overall boss in a socioecological system, though there is order, which evolves from the mutual adjustment of the parts, the stakeholders. Any overriding purpose that emerges from their sense of being in the same boat would depend on their arriving at a shared understanding of the issues. Any change of direction would be checked back with them.

Socioecological principles enable the organizational life of the society to be strengthened at the domain level in ways that are self-regulating rather than becoming autocratic or remaining ineffectual. If self-regulation is democratic, then the establishment at the domain level of an order that conforms to democratic values is a major project of our times. A level of complexity has now been reached that renders authoritarianism and laissez-faire maladaptive and unviable as societal modes. Facing a future of increasing complexity means trying self-regulation within interdependence, learning how to cultivate the new logical type. We do not have much experience of self-regulation at the domain level. Much evolutionary experimentation (as Dunn, 1971, calls it) will be required.

Developing the argument further is conceptual work that my Australian colleague, Fred Emery, and I began in the 1960s on what we called the "causal texture of organizational environments" (Emery and Trist, 1965), which we have been developing since that time both jointly and independently (Emery, 1967, 1976, 1977, 1982; Emery and Trist, 1973; Trist, 1977, 1980) and of which this chapter is an extension. Distinguishing the contextual environment as supplying the boundary conditions for transactional relations was an important step in the original analysis; for, as the environmental field becomes more richly joined (in Ashby's, 1956, sense), as the parts become more interconnected, there is greater mutual causality (Maruyama, 1963). The denser the organizational population in the social habitat (and the more this itself is limited by the increasing constraints emanating from the physical environment, whose resources are no longer perceived as boundless), the more frequently do the many causal strands become enmeshed with each other. This means that forces from the contextual field begin to penetrate the organization set. This creates what we have called turbulence for the organization, whose internal repertoire may only too easily lack the requisite variety for survival. Ashby's law of requisite variety states that, when a system's response repertoire cannot match increases in variety emanating from the environment, that system's survival is endangered. This is our situation at the present time. The contemporary world environment is characterized by much higher levels of interdependence and complexity than hitherto existed. These have led, in turn, to a much higher level of uncertainty. The consequent variety overload is experienced by the organization and the individual alike as a loss of the stable state (Schön, 1971).

Emery and I distinguished four environmental types, the first two of which (the placid random, Type I, and placid clustered, Type II) describe conditions of relative stability and have become marginal in the contemporary environmental mix. The disturbed reactive environment (Type III) is the world of big industrial organizations and outsize government departments. It is a world in which everything gets centralized—the world that Galbraith (1967) has called the New Industrial State, but which is now becoming the Old Industrial State. For the very success of this world is bringing it to its own limit, thereby creating a very different environment, which is gaining in salience.

The new environment (Type IV) is called the turbulent field. In such a field, large competing organizations, all acting independently, in many diverse directions, produce unanticipated and dissonant consequences in the overall environment that they share. These dissonances mount as the field becomes more densely occupied. The result is a kind of contextual commotion. This makes it seem as if the ground, as well as the organizational figures, were moving. This is what is meant by turbulence. It becomes imperative, therefore, that we find ways through which the regulation and reduction of turbulence can be achieved. The development of self-regulating, interorganizational domains offers one such way. The turbulence emanating from the Type IV environment is reflected in a set of metaproblems, which single organizations are unable to meet. Therefore, an additional response capability is required to produce a multistable system (in Ashby's, 1960, sense) at the domain level. A strengthened set of directive correlations at the domain level is postulated as providing the initial conditions for a negotiated order to evolve. In an action-research study of the Canadian life insurance industry, Chevalier (Chevalier and Taylor, 1983) has called this level the middle ground.

A negotiated order will need to be founded on collaboration rather than competition (Trist, 1977), collaboration being the value base appropriate for the adaptive cultivation of interdependence. So far as this process gains ground, a mode of macroregulation may be brought into existence that is turbulence reducing without being repressive or fragmenting. Its virtue will be that it will have been built by the stakeholders themselves. This is the essence of the different logical type. This change to a new logical type that enables problems of the middle ground to be effectively addressed requires a reversal of the customary relations between competition and collaboration. In a Type III environment, the adaptive governing value in interorganizational relations is competition, which qualifies and constrains collaboration, which, though required to some degree, is a subordinate value. In a Type IV environment, collaboration becomes the primary governing value, which qualifies and constrains competition. This reversal in terms of a theory of logical types has been formally treated by Pava (1980).

If we fail to realize that domains of the middle ground are cognitive as well as organizational structures, we can only too easily fall into the trap of thinking of them as objectively given, quasi-permanent fixtures in the social fabric, rather than as ways we have chosen to construe various facets of it. Domains are based on what Vickers (1965) called acts of appreciation. Appreciation is a complex perceptual and conceptual process that melds together judgments of reality and judgments of value. A new appreciation is made as a new metaproblem is recognized. As the appreciation becomes more widely shared, a domain begins to be identified. It is most important that the identity of the domain is not mistaken through errors in the appreciative process; otherwise, all subsequent social shaping becomes mismatched with what is required to deal with the metaproblem. As an identity is acquired, the domain begins to take a path into the future that points to what courses of action may be attempted. All this entails some overall social shaping as regards boundaries and size: what organizations are to be included, the degree of heterogeneity or homogeneity, and so on. Along with this, an internal structure evolves as the various stakeholders learn to accommodate their partially conflicting interests while securing their common ground. Locales begin to be established.

Four change projects that helped to develop this line of thinking will now be described. The first two are concerned with strengthening collaborative change capacity in established organizations working in already existing domains, the second two with what will be called innovating organizations in emergent domains.

Change Projects

The National Farmers' Union of England and Wales. One early project involved a research team at the Tavistock Institute in the agricultural sector as a whole through the National Farmers' Union (NFU) of England and Wales and many of the organizations associated with it (Higgin, Emery, and Trist, 1960). The NFU is not a trade union of agricultural workers but an association of 200,000 farmers (large and small). The presenting problem was stated as a breakdown in communication between head office and county branches, but the reason for this breakdown turned out to be not so much the unwillingness of either level to talk to the other as a change in the environment in which the NFU was operating. This change was not being communicated, because it was not understood.

Changes taking place toward capital-intensive large-scale industry in the wider society had caught up with farming. On the input side, the farmer now faced the power of a handful of giant, technologically advanced firms that supplied machinery, seeds, fertilizer, and feedstuff, on terms rather more advantageous to them than to the farmer. On the output side, the farmer faced the power of a similar handful of biggies, this time comprising, on the production side, national and international food-processing firms and, on the retailing side, supermarkets and multiple chains, also national and international in scope. Once again, it was they, not the farmer, who largely determined the standards for produce, judging its acceptability to mass rather than local markets. The farmer now had to breed pigs conforming to the standards of the leading meat processors, to grow apples and tomatoes to fit the grades required by the leading greengrocers, and to grow barley approved by the big brewers.

The farmers, large and small, had treasured an individuality of which they saw themselves as one of the last bastions in an increasingly regimented industrial society. Collectively, they had depended on their union to secure government price support quotas that shielded them from market fluctuation. These strategies alone, however, could not defend them against the new threats. Somehow, the farmers had to discover new ways of collaborating with each other in determining the nature and quality of what they should breed and grow. Lest they be too deeply invaded from both sides, they needed to develop countervailing power, which they could do only by evolving cooperative rather than competitive strategies in areas in which they had formerly been autonomous.

This change from competition to collaboration is critical for survival in turbulent environments. In the farmers' case, this entailed the development of agreed marketing, distributing, and even growing and breeding systems, which represented forms of organizational ecology. The arrangements had to be negotiated by the many parties concerned. Only through their participation could interdependent schemes be fashioned and constraints on the individual be accepted that created opportunities for the group. Coercion does not work in this type of situation. Herein lies another clue to a critical feature of systems of organizational ecology, as contrasted with bureaucracies—they involve the evolution of a negotiated order.

Hitherto, in work with single organizations, we had been used to making a diagnosis of the state of the organization. We now were confronted with making a diagnosis of the state of the environment. This proved to be a considerable research undertaking. In addition to the mastery of extensive documentary material and interviews with key individuals in the main organizations associated with farming, it involved us in going on farm walks with quite a large sample of farmers in four different counties, among them representing all the types of farming undertaken in Britain. The intuitive understanding of the issues by some of these grass-roots members gave us, more than any other source of data, the clues necessary for a thorough reconceptualization of the farmers' world.

The union council set aside a whole day to discuss our report, but the novelty of the findings and the enormous problems of implementation required more than a day. The council therefore decided on a step that they had never taken before— to spend a week under social-island conditions, together with the senior staff and ourselves, exploring in depth the problems raised. The deliberations that took place in this setting constituted a genuine search process. A considerable understanding of the emerging issues was reached. The council decided to publish the report and to hold eight regional day-long conferences to discuss it with the membership. As communicative events, these were successful, but they made it clear that further rounds of discussion would be necessary at the local level if a full appreciation of the issues was to be established in the membership as a whole and support generated for major changes. The new mode required full participation.

A crisis regarding leadership succession (not uncommon in such circumstances) then ensued, which caused so much distraction that no local conferences were held. The membership remained confused, and implementation fell far below expectations (and needs). Nevertheless, the new importance of collaboration as an adaptive strategy under increasingly turbulent conditions had been demonstrated. It was also shown that new understanding by a leadership elite alone is insufficient when a basic reframing of problems (Schön, 1980) and fresh appreciation of the issues (Vickers, 1968) have to be made in an organizational population as a whole. The farmers needed to undertake substantial rather than marginal innovation, to use Chevalier's (1980) terms, which would reverse many of their previous values and practices. Widespread membership participation is necessary before substantial innovation can take place.

City and Regional Government. The behavioral scientists involved felt a need not only to understand the processes but to obtain better cognitive maps of large-scale socioecological systems—models that we lacked. We knew that certain people in operational research had made advances in modeling such systems. Accordingly, we negotiated with the British Operational Research Society to set up an Institute for Operational Research linked to the Tavistock Institute. Indeed, we saw our own organization more and more as a system of organizational ecology and believed that, in contending with the problems of its further development, we would learn more about such systems. There was a need to complement the studies made of large-scale organizational-ecology systems in the industrial field by similar studies in the community field and to negotiate arrangements that would lessen the danger of projects being cut short in their initial stages. The first such project, under the leadership of the new institute but including behavioral scientists, was undertaken in collaboration with the lord mayor and council of a medium-sized British city of 300,000—Coventry. This was the first time that a mayor and a social research institute had jointly applied to a foundation for funding. The object of the four-year project was to gain a better understanding of policy-planning processes and to develop new methodologies and strategies for decision making under conditions of complexity and uncertainty. We needed to forge a link between the field of organizational behavior and the planning field.

As Forrester (1971) has said, complexity is counterintuitive. Though this is not true of all its aspects, models are nevertheless useful; otherwise, one gets lost in tracing out the implications of one component system for others. A model was developed called AIDA, for the Analysis of Interconnected Decision Areas. Further work developed a new conceptualization of the sources of uncertainty. This approach was similar to that later introduced in the sociotechnical field by Herbst (1974), called the design principle of minimum critical specification. Means were found of reducing a manifold of solutions to a manageable set of leading solutions and thence of keeping open as many options as possible when decisions had to be taken, under time constraints, to commit resources for a future whose emergent properties could not be predicted (Friend and Jessop, 1969). Improved modes of decision making under conditions of uncertainty are essential for survival under the conditions of a Type IV environment.

On the behavioral side, access was gained not only to members of the city council but also to the caucuses of both political parties, the set of administrative departments, the unions concerned, and groups of voluntary workers out in the wards.

Attempts were made to educate such people in the use of the conceptual tools that had been developed and to provide them with cognitive maps more pertinent to their affairs than those to which they were accustomed. The strategies advocated by the models evolved, however, were not easy to use in face of the anxieties of those concerned.

Since that time, regular seminars and working conferences have been held with an increasing number of mayors and administrative officers of British cities and with chairpeople and executives of some of the then-new regional authorities, so that a learning network has been brought into existence that provides diffusion channels for innovation (Friend, Power, and Yewlett, 1974). The concept of social network is as basic to the understanding of systems of organizational ecology as that of the primary work group is to the understanding of the single organization.

Stringer (1969) called the systems involved in these studies multiorganizations. Friend, Power, and Yewlett (1974) have since introduced the term *reticular* to draw attention to their network character. Managers in such organizations are said to play reticulist roles and to depend on reticulist skills. This represents a substantial change from bureaucratic modes of organization and leadership. Nevertheless, the amount of change that resulted from these studies was limited by the fact that the research team was working almost entirely through official bodies. The constraints operating on the key actors were multiple and severe, though, as Friend and his colleagues have shown, the amount of discretion available could be made considerably greater than that conventionally assumed. This is an important finding, as, in a changing society, established systems must have the capacity to change, and this capacity would appear to be increased by the acquisition of reticulist skills on the part of managers and key staff. Yet, except under conditions of crisis, established organizations tend to limit themselves to marginal change. The introduction of substantial change often requires the bringing into existence of what have been called independent innovating organizations (Trist, 1979). Opportunities were sought, therefore, to engage in action research with such organizations to discover whether they might possess change-producing properties of greater power than their establishment counterparts.

The Jamestown Area Labor-Management Committee. The first project involving innovating organizations in emergent domains concerned the arrest of economic decline. The locale was Jamestown, a small manufacturing town in western New York State with some 40,000 inhabitants and an additional 25,000 in the surrounding urban area. Its traditional industries are metalworking and wood furniture. Engineered products and glass and ceramics were added after World War II, since when uninterrupted economic decline had been experienced. This reached its climax in 1969, when the largest local firm went bankrupt after building a million-square-foot facility. That facility stood vacant until 1974 as a persistent symbol of the inability of the area to attract new industry. Unemployment was over 10 percent. The work force was highly unionized. Labor relations were exceedingly bad; mutual antagonism was deep-rooted and severe. Children were taught not to work in local plants; high schools prepared their best students to go away to college and find careers elsewhere. Though the town's industrial decline reflected the general shift of industry to the South, it was the persisting emptiness of the large closed plant that created a widespread consciousness that its future was precarious. Either decline would continue, or local initiative would begin to make possible some kind of positive future.

Local initiative was taken in 1972, when a young and talented mayor (Stan Lundine, now in Congress) was re-elected with bipartisan support. With the help of the regional director of the Federal Mediation and Conciliation Service and one or two other influentials, he called together the presidents or general managers and union presidents of all plants employing more than seventy-five people to a special meeting to confront the situation and begin a transformation of the labor-relations climate as the basis for future development. The two sides had never before met away from the bargaining table. Within eighteen months, the mayor had succeeded. A new collaborative outlook pervaded the community. Twenty-seven companies and the locals of ten international unions composed what became known as the Jamestown Area Labor-Management Committee (JALMC), which has since established an international reputation as an innovating organization. There are labor and management co-chairpeople and an executive board that equally represents both sides. The mayor remains in an advisory role.

The first task was to prevent further bankruptcies and stem the drift to the South. Five companies were salvaged. Had these gone under, hope to arrest further decline could not have been generated. The investors, some of them local, said publicly that they would not have gone ahead except for the new cooperative spirit created by the JALMC. The mayor played a key role in gaining the support of local banks. In 1974, a major corporation took over the million square feet of empty space as the site for their new diesel plant, stating that the existence and success of the JALMC was the final factor that made Jamestown their choice. That same year, the municipal league made Jamestown an All American City.

My own first visit to Jamestown was in the spring of 1973, when I held a small grant for exploratory research from the National Commission on Productivity and the Quality of Working Life (QWL). At that time, QWL endeavors were confined to single plants; to attempt them at the community level was entirely new. After its initial successes, the committee was not clear what its next tasks should be, and, while they associated QWL with large corporations with assembly lines that induced work alienation rather than with the small job shops of Jamestown, they were willing that, during the summer, I and a graduate student should make a survey of problems common in local plants. This disclosed a major common problem that required immediate attention. The key skills in metalworking and woodworking were developed in-house. The work force was aging—in one plant, the average age was fifty-five. Many of the individuals carrying the key skills would be retiring in a few years. There were no training schemes, which could not be easily afforded by small firms. The long years in dull entry jobs at low pay were causing high turnover, so that the aging skilled work force was becoming sealed off and not being replaced.

Now that the mayor and the committee had produced the conditions that could lead to a positive economic future, its realization would be endangered if the skill stock were not replenished. In reporting this finding to the committee, we noted that in the past there had been a tradition of informal sharing of resources for skills development between firms but that this had lapsed during the years of decline. We suggested that ways be found of reviving this tradition. The committee accepted the challenge. Within a few months, a cooperative skills-development program emerged. The community college, which previously had turned its back on local industry, provided courses to train key workers as instructors, who then carried out the jointly designed programs in the plants. The county manpower authority reinterpreted its rules so that it could provide funds. Several other organizations joined in, so that the committee had created a consortium that pooled their resources. By 1982, 942 workers had graduated from courses covering a wide array of skills, and 325 attended a skills-development dinner.

This would not have been possible had not the city provided funds matched by the Economic Development Authority (EDA) to enable a full-time staff coordinator to be appointed. The legwork had to be done, or nothing would have happened. But it soon became clear that additional staff with the requisite social science skills would be necessary if concrete change programs were not only to be initiated but to be sustained in individual plants and that intensive work at the plant level was the next step for the committee to undertake in order to upgrade performance and enhance the competitiveness of existing and often far from efficient facilities.

The national commission that had provided my original grant declared community-level work out of the scope of its program. Accordingly, I obtained the commitment of two graduate students to go with their families to Jamestown and reside there for a considerable period (one stayed three and the other five years, becoming staff coordinator). I then went with this commitment to the mayor and the two cochairpeople and asked them to go to Washington to secure the necessary funds, which were readily granted directly to the committee.

With the help of these facilitators, in-plant labor-management committees developed in most of the member plants, which set up task forces to undertake agreed projects with visible short-term results. Traditional QWL topics such as work restructuring and semiautonomous work groups were not popular, but the notion of gain-sharing schemes took on in several places, as did the notion of involving workers in product bidding so that reduced costs would enable more contracts to be won. The most dramatic joint innovations took place in layout redesigning (Jamestown plants were old) and product development (new products had to be found in order to avoid severe business curtailment). All these projects saved jobs and were therefore acceptable to the unions as well as to management.

These projects did not move from one part of a given organization to the whole but from part of one organization to part of another. Though the projects themselves were often short-lived (lasting less than a year), the volume, diversity, and complexity of the projects grew in the industrial community as a whole. Moreover, they did not always travel through the consultant-researchers but sprang up spontaneously in firms with which we had had no contact. Repeated projects generated eight identifiable themes. These were compatible with each other and interrelated, composing what Keidel (1980) called a "theme-set" in the organizational community, creating a new industrial culture. This provided a public knowledge and value base to which all had access according to their needs and wishes. In this way, a new concept emerged from the fieldwork, and new modes of intervention were discovered through the interactions that took place between the domain and single-organization levels.

Recently, the committee issued a comprehensive report on its first ten years entitled "A Decade of Change" (Jamestown Area Labor-Management Committee, 1982), updating its earlier five-year report, "Commitment at Work" (Jamestown Area Labor-Management Committee, 1977). These stories give full accounts of the restraining as well as the driving forces and have increased understanding of what has happened in the community and its extended influence elsewhere.

The Craigmillar Festival Society. The second project of this type is concerned with bringing about positive developments when economic decline has proved irreversible. The locale was Craigmillar, a poverty-stricken housing estate of some 25,000 inhabitants on the edge of Edinburgh, Scotland. For many years, unemployment had been around 25 percent among adult males and even higher among women and teenagers. The original industry had long since closed down, and there was a complete lack of social and cultural amenities. Though economic decline proved irreversible, remarkable headway was made in securing and creating social and cultural amenities.

This began some twenty years ago, when a mother and housewife, Helen Crummy, frustrated because her son, who had some talent for music, could get no music lessons at school, began holding a festival in the tradition of Scottish summer folk festivals at which local talent could perform. The locals found that they were as good as many other folks. From this small beginning, a vast development in community arts has taken place, which has become internationally famous. The innovating organization involved has become known as the Craigmillar Festival Society (CFS). Musicals and dramas on issues of local relevance are written and produced and taken touring in the rest of Scotland and in continental Europe. There are a pageant and costumed banquet in Craigmillar Castle, a fair, and a number of street events. The festival now spreads over ten days, with around 75 percent of the local population attending and over a thousand taking some part in the enormous preparations required during the year.

As the resident consultant-researcher, Steve Burgess (an American), has said, "the Festival found a pathway through the arts which awakened the creative capacities latent in the community." With the sense of achievement created by the festival, a negative identity gradually changed into a positive one. Apathy and despair were replaced by engagement and hope in a large number of people. The self-confidence arising from participation in these activities led to the emergence of local leaders of considerable capacity. Within a few years, an area overburdened with elderly and handicapped people and successive waves of slum-cleared families from the inner city (from which any who found the opportunity departed) has produced a lord provost of Edinburgh, a member of Parliament, and several members of the regional and city councils.

In step with this, the CFS has extended its activities from community arts to every sphere of community life. There are now nine workshops (all under the leadership of local residents), which meet monthly on planning, housing, environmental improvements, education, employment, communications, and recreation, as well as the arts. A number of schemes have been developed to meet the special needs of children and the elderly. These leadership talents have been used to secure seriously lacking amenities, such as a high school, a community center, a library, and many improvements in housing and public transport.

Funds obtained from the regional government have enabled the CFS to maintain a small full-time staff led by Helen Crummy as organizing secretary. One of the most notable developments has been the creation of neighborhood workers, local residents who live in the eleven neighborhoods that make up the ward of Craigmillar and who undertake a large variety of social work tasks after being trained by professionals. Their work has helped to reduce the amount of expensive hospitalization for the elderly and the incidence of depressive illnesses. The work with the young has increased school attendance and reduced functional illiteracy and the rate of juvenile crime. Comparisons with a similar area lacking such a key independent organization were in favor of Craigmillar wherever statistics were available.

The ability of the CFS to mobilize external resources as knowledge of its work spread reached its climax in 1976, when it successfully competed for a major three-year grant from the Anti-Poverty Programme of the European Economic Community (EEC), which was later extended for another two years. This funding was provided to encourage the development of pilot schemes to combat common problems that could not be dealt with by conventional methods. It enabled the CFS greatly to extend the scope and raise the quality of its services and to secure more professional assistance. A research dimension was added, which led to my own involvement as a supporting resource for the resident consultant-researcher (Trist and Burgess, 1978). These studies aided the production of a report by the CFS entitled "Craigmillar's Comprehensive Plan for Action" (Craigmillar Festival Society, 1978). The detailed recommendations arose in the various working parties and were put together as a whole by the planning workshop. The document that was approved by the annual convention (which, like the CFS itself, is open to all residents of Craigmillar) is at one and the same time practical and visionary. Its aim is to provide guidelines for continuous negotiation with the various national, regional, and local authorities that are concerned with aspects of community life and also with foundations and other organizations. Regarded by many as one of the most innovative documents produced in the field of urban planning, it contains a philosophy that the CFS gradually worked out from its experience. The basic idea is that of "shared government"—a partnership between voluntary and statutory bodies that would lead to the optimum use of scarce resources, taking into account the specific needs of a given area. The philosophy is eloquently stated in the introduction to the plan:

> This Plan is basically a working document, a kind of green paper, which requires shared government, partnership between the people of Craigmillar and the local and wider authorities and agencies. It contains a vision of life in the years ahead. The vision is the achievement of a viable community with all the necessary ingredients of amenities, facilities and services.
>
> But the action plan includes a very large plus. It is the taking of responsibility by the people of the area themselves in a joint fulfillment of the vision with the outside authorities and wider community. In such a sharing of developing and governing there is revealed a new way which has great relevance for all other similar areas as well as those from which many of the people of the housing estates come, the inner urban areas.

Its basic importance lies in the fact that it
advocates and signifies a change in politics and economics to yield a more fulfilling society [Craig-
millar Festival Society, 1978, contents page].

The values on which the philosophy rests are embodied in a
huge horizontal play sculpture known as "Gulliver, the Gentle
Giant Who Shares and Cares."

Processes of Domain Development

In an analysis of processes found to be important in the
development of emergent domains, two broad classes of non-
establishment organizations may be distinguished—those that
seek to attain their ends through working out means of collaborating with existing organizations and those that seek to attain
them through opposition. Each plays a distinctive role in societal change. The constructive as well as the destructive role of
oppositional groups in the postwar United States has been
studied by Gerlach and Hines (1978). Such groups may be the
source of social movements that lead to broad sociocultural and
socioeconomic change. They will not, however, be discussed in
this chapter, which is concerned with collaborative organizations.

*Independent Innovating Organizations as Referent Organ-
izations.* Independent innovating organizations that seek collaborative solutions, such as the JALMC and the CFS, constitute a type of referent organization of central importance to
Western societies in their present phase of major change. They
have the following common characteristics:

1. A *critical situation* exists that is not being coped with
by traditional means. While a particular incident may act as a
trigger, the crisis will be revealed as chronic, requiring long-
range remedies. There is an organizational vacuum that creates
the social space for a new organization to enter. The initial appearance of a potential referent organization is a major step
toward activating and coalescing the field.

2. The problem to be met is not merely local but is
rather a microcosm of a *major societal problem*—a "mess."

Therefore, effective courses of action that may be taken locally have symbolic as well as actual power. They are quickly perceived as relevant to others in similar circumstances. They soon begin to resonate widely through the social fabric.

3. But the particular metaproblem or mess is *local*. It has a concrete reality as well as a general meaning. This compels those concerned to work at all aspects of it, both short- and long-term, with deep knowledge of the way various factors, which at higher levels may be abstracted into different departments and separate jurisdictions, interact in their own particular setting.

4. The communities concerned have a *negative image*. They are among those who have not made it or will not make it much longer. This negative image is both ascribed to them from the outside and accepted by them on the inside. So long as this internal acceptance of an ascribed identity persists, nothing can happen.

5. The first task of the innovating organization is to refuse to accept this negative identity. Such organizations need to be *independent*—not only of statutory bodies but also of the major local power groups, none of which have coped with the problem. There must be a new cut, a new perspective, a new setting in which effective innovation can develop. A start is made when a few determined individuals who are related to each other through various overlapping networks form a group on their own initiative to do something about what are, after all, their own lives.

6. Because the organization is independent yet netted into many sections of the community, it can secure the *collaboration of key interest groups* who may on other issues be in conflict or indifferent to each other. Because the problem is a major one affecting the community as a whole, all these groups are implicated. A wide support base can be built.

7. Such a support base is a condition of *securing resources*. Without resources, the members of an innovating organization can do no more than talk. To undertake courses of action that will start to clean up the mess, they have to mobilize resources, usually from multiple sources. The most important,

however, involve the *transfer to them of public funds.* They also need to have *some staff of their own,* else courses of action cannot be sustained.

8. The transfer of public funds is a crucial step, since it means that an *alternative power system* begins to come into existence that threatens statutory bodies and local power groups. The innovating organization will survive only if it can show them that its *power is complementary* rather than invasive and if it can develop a *distinctive competence* that demonstrates to the wide set of stakeholders involved that it can deliver in some visible way and to an appreciable degree what has not so far been delivered.

Such organizations do not appear in full form at first. They develop gradually in conjunction with circumstances. As their unfolding takes place, those concerned become increasingly aware of what they have been doing. This self-conceptualization gives them an identity that helps them to explain themselves both to themselves and to others. The reports that the JALMC and the CFS have issued are profound accounts of social learning. Both these organizations are robust—the first has been in existence for more than ten years and the second for more than twenty, in spite of many setbacks and vicissitudes.

Action Learning. The effectiveness of domain development depends on widespread experiential learning in a very considerable number of people, who must sense that they are co-producing the outcome at every step, both with each other and with any third parties involved. This process, which is largely unpredictable and evolves as new needs and factors arise, is referred to as action learning. This is a step beyond action research, which implies discrete problem solving, setting up pilot models under expert guidance and subsequently diffusing them to users in operational systems. By contrast, in action learning, all change is owned by the wider stakeholder group from the beginning and involves reframing, which represents their choices and advance to new consciousness. The term itself was originally introduced by Revans (1973) to refer to a method of experiential learning in management education. Its wider conceptualization stems from my own dissatisfaction with the term *action research* in a number of projects in organizational ecology carried out at York University, Toronto, where an interfaculty group known as the York Action Learning Group has come into existence. Two recent publications give an account of the work of this group and the ideas to which it has given rise (Ramirez, 1983; Morgan and Ramirez, 1984).

Social Networks. Networking is a term that has become much in vogue. Networks constitute the basic social form that permits an interorganizational domain to develop as a system of organizational ecology. Networks are unbounded social systems that are nonhierarchical. They have properties that are complementary to those of the bounded wholes that comprise single organizations and that, in a systems sense, are hierarchical, though not necessarily bureaucratic. In view of their nonhierarchical and open character, networks provide channels of communication that are fluid and rapid. They travel through the social ground rather than between institutional figures. They cross levels and cover the range from private to public. They bring the most unexpected people into relevant contact, so that nodes and temporary systems are formed that become levers of change.

Networks are initiated by proactive individuals who create new role space around themselves. They locate and resonate with other individuals whose appreciations are moving in the same direction as theirs. One of the last projects I arranged before leaving London was a study of the career patterns displayed by managers passing through the Administrative Staff College at Henley-on-Thames. This project was carried out by Rapoport (1970), who discovered three patterns. The first two were expected: the incremental and the metamorphic careers. The third—the tangential (that is, the boundary spanner)—was a surprise, especially as it was found to be on the increase. Those displaying this third pattern were the networkers. This pattern has since been called the reticulist pattern (Friend, Power, and Yewlett, 1974).

A Dutch psychiatrist, van Ravenswaaij (1972), has called such individuals "novelty detectors," after a cell of this type in the brain. In such individuals, new appreciations of emerging metaproblems originate and build up as they interact with other network members, who tend to form a selectively interdependent set. They learn the art of walking through walls. Without carriers of this kind, it is difficult to see how the process of appreciative restructuring can either take place fast enough or go far enough to permit emergent domains to be organized in time and on a scale that will allow the oncoming metaproblems to be contended with.

Search Conferences. Another process that enables shared appreciation to evolve and emergent domains to develop more coherently is the search conference, which has been developed by Merrelyn and Fred Emery (Emery and Emery, 1978) in Australia and which has now been tried out in several different settings in Europe and North America. Searching is the equivalent of appreciating and is carried out in groups composed of the relevant stakeholders. The group meets under social-island conditions for two, three, or sometimes as long as five days. The opening sessions are concerned with elucidating the factors operating in the wider contextual environment—those that produce the metaproblems and are likely to affect the future. The content is contributed entirely by the members, with the staff acting only as facilitators. Items are listed without criticism in plenary session and displayed on flip charts. The material is discussed in greater depth in small groups and the composite picture checked out in plenary. The group next examines its own organizational setting or settings against this wider background and then proceeds to construct a picture of a desirable future, examining relevant constraints and opportunities, with an often surprising amount of agreement. Only when all this has been done is consideration given to action steps—and search conferences are not always ready to proceed with these. Their function is to deal with what Ozbekhan (1971) has called the normative phase of planning. If people can agree on ends in a future time perspective, if a common value base can be established through a process of shared appreciation—by undertaking what Michael (1973) has called "future oriented social learning"—they are likely to come to terms with more of their differences regarding means than they otherwise would. So far as this is done, they can begin to move toward a negotiated order and accept a system of macroregulation that they will have created for themselves. Everything in this approach is based on participation, which is at the root of socioecological regulation.

Conscious Design of Appropriate Referent Organizations. The referent organizations so far mentioned have arisen spontaneously. The needs of domain development in the face of contemporary metaproblems have become so great that their design needs to be undertaken at a more conscious level. This will make them more purposeful, more able to learn from their failures and successes, and more able to seize opportunities.

An example of conscious design that has been suggested by Emery (1976) deals with a particularly important and frequent class of cases—that in which the organizational population is too large to be directly represented in the referent organization and so must be represented by a sample. Emery has suggested that this sampling should be random. If each constituent organization were to nominate an individual able and willing to serve, the sample could be drawn by a procedure modeled on that of jury service. The term of office would be limited, so that careers could not be made in these roles. Special appointments would not be made; neither would there be voting. The panel members would not represent their particular organizations but would be accountable as individuals to the domain. Emery has suggested such a procedure for selecting the members of the industrial councils recommended in a report on policies for the Australian manufacturing industry (Jackson, 1975). The aim is to prevent the domination of such councils by the more powerful inhabitants of the domain and to minimize manipulation by special interest groups. For these councils, Emery thought that thirty to forty members would provide an adequate sample and that any one set, by and large, would be as good as any other.

The work of such councils would be appreciation, not operation. It would involve making critical value judgments concerning the way in which the domain might best develop. Though requiring multiple perspectives, such work is generalist, not specialist, in orientation. Though technical staff would be provided, they, like the panel members, would have only a limited tour of duty. The proposed design reverses the bureaucratic model. It appears likely that the Australian government will bring such councils into being.

Convening the Extended Social Field. A point of special importance is the need of the referent organizations to remain in sensitive contact with the extended social field of the domain. The referent organization cannot make too much of the going itself. The domain community must become part of the learning-appreciation process and must be convened at critical junctures. For example, in Sudbury, a town in northeast Ontario with the nickel industry as its sole economic base, a futures-oriented group called Sudbury 2001 (1979) had arranged a weekend conference of the "think-tank" type, expecting thirty to forty people to engage in a search-type process. But by the scheduled date, major layoffs had taken place at International Nickel, which made real at a new level the question of an alternative future for the community. Eleven hundred people participated in the conference, and the event became a "happening" that led to a step-function change in the level of social learning and community consciousness.

The Jamestown Area Labor-Management Committee holds a widely attended annual conference of a day and a half, which provides a ritualistic occasion for affirmation of achievements and for renewal of commitment. The summer festival of the Craigmillar Festival Society performs a similar function. On one crisis occasion, when it was threatened with withdrawal of regional funds (which would have entailed withdrawal of national and EEC funds), it collected 10,000 signatures in a week, obtained the support of the local press and of the churches, and led a successful demonstration into the council chamber. These events have the character of field events that Emery (1977) has called a "flocking."

Building innovating organizations, stimulating action learning, taking network initiatives, designing appropriate referent organizations, and convening the extended social field are intervention strategies that allow interorganizational domains to develop along socioecological rather than bureaucratic lines.

Such socioecological shaping of the middle ground in a complex modern society is a necessary condition for contending with the metaproblems it confronts and reducing the contextual turbulence that disturbs it. Self-regulation at this middle level would take off excess heat both from the single organization and from macromanagement at the level of the social aggregate. The result would make more likely a balanced and stable organizational configuration that would open the way for a viable human future to evolve.

References

Ackoff, R. L. *Redesigning the Future.* New York: Wiley, 1974.

Ashby, R. *An Introduction to Cybernetics.* London: Chapman & Hall, 1956.

Ashby, R. *Design for a Brain.* London: Chapman & Hall, 1960.

Chevalier, M. *A Wider Range of Perspectives in the Bureaucratic Structure.* Ottawa: Commission on Bilingualism and Bi-culturalism, 1966.

Chevalier, M. "Innovation Strategies in Public Management." In D. Morley, S. Proudfoot, and T. Burns (Eds.), *Making Cities Work.* Boulder, Colo.: Praeger, 1980.

Chevalier, M., and Taylor, G. *New Ground for Enterprise: Managing Critical Issues in the Middle Ground between Government and Private Enterprise.* Toronto: Faculty of Environmental Studies, York University, 1983.

Craigmillar Festival Society. *Craigmillar's Comprehensive Plan for Action.* Edinburgh: Craigmillar Festival Press, 1978.

Dunn, E. *Economic and Social Development: A Process of Social Learning.* Baltimore: Johns Hopkins University Press, 1971.

Durkheim, E. *The Division of Labor in Society.* (G. Simpson, Trans.) Glencoe, Ill.: Free Press, 1964. (Originally published 1893.)

Emery, F. E. "The Next Thirty Years: Concepts, Methods and Anticipations." *Human Relations,* 1967, *20,* 199-237.

Emery, F. E. "Adaptive Systems for Our Future Governance." *National Labour Institute Bulletin* (New Delhi), 1976, *4,* 14-21.

Emery, F. E. *Futures We Are In.* Leiden: Martinus Nijhoff, 1977.

Emery, F. E. "New Perspectives on the World of Work: Sociotechnical Foundations for a New Social Order." *Human Relations,* 1982, *35,* 1095–1122.

Emery, F. E., and Emery, M. *A Choice of Futures.* Leiden: Martinus Nijhoff, 1977.

Emery, F. E., and Trist, E. L. "The Causal Texture of Organizational Environments." *Human Relations,* 1965, *18,* 21–32.

Emery, F. E., and Trist, E. L. *Towards a Social Ecology.* New York: Plenum, 1973.

Emery, M., and Emery, F. E. "Searching: For New Directions: In New Ways . . . For New Times." In J. W. Sutherland (Ed.), *Management Handbook for Public Administration.* New York: Van Nostrand, 1978.

Evan, W. M. "The Organization Set." In J. D. Thompson (Ed.), *Approaches to Organizational Design.* Pittsburgh, Penn.: University of Pittsburgh Press, 1966.

Forrester, J. W. "The Counterintuitive Nature of Social Systems." *Technology Review,* 1971, *73,* 52–68.

French, J. R. P., and Raven, R. "The Bases of Social Power." In D. Cartwright (Ed.), *Studies in Social Power.* Ann Arbor: Research Center for Group Dynamics, University of Michigan, 1962.

Friend, J., and Jessop, N. *Local Government and Strategic Choice.* London: Tavistock, 1969.

Friend, J., Power, J. M., and Yewlett, C. J. C. *Public Planning: The Inter-corporate Dimension.* London: Tavistock, 1974.

Galbraith, J. K. *The New Industrial State.* New York: Houghton Mifflin, 1967.

Gerlach, L., and Hines, V. "Fumbling Freely into the Future." In M. Maruyama and A. M. Harkins (Eds.), *Cultures of the Future.* The Hague and Paris: Mouton, 1978.

Herbst, P. G. *Socio-Technical Design.* London: Tavistock, 1974.

Higgin, G. W., Emery, F. E., and Trist, E. L. "Communications in the National Farmers' Union." London: National Farmers' Union and Tavistock Institute, 1960.

Jackson, R. T. Vol. 1: *Policies for Development of Manufactur-*

ing Industry. Green paper. Canberra: Australian Government Publication Service, 1975.

Jamestown Area Labor-Management Committee. *Commitment at Work: The Five Year Report of the Jamestown Area Labor-Management Committee.* Jamestown, N.Y.: Jamestown Area Labor-Management Committee, 1977.

Jamestown Area Labor-Management Committee. *A Decade of Change: The Ten Year Report of the Jamestown Area Labor-Management Committee.* Jamestown, N.Y.: Jamestown Area Labor-Management Committee, 1982.

Keidel, R. "Theme Set Appreciation: A Multi-Level Approach to Community Development." Unpublished doctoral dissertation, Social Systems Sciences, University of Pennsylvania, 1980.

Maruyama, M. "The Second Cybernetics: Deviation Amplifying Mutual Causal Processes." *Scientific American,* 1963, *51,* 164–179.

Michael, D. N. *On Learning to Plan—and Planning to Learn: The Social Psychology of Changing Toward Future-Responsive Societal Learning.* San Francisco: Jossey-Bass, 1973.

Morgan, G., and Ramirez, R. "A Holographic Metaphor for Guiding Social Change." *Human Relations,* 1984, *37,* 1–28.

Ozbekhan, H. "Planning and Human Action." In P. A. Weiss (Ed.), *Hierarchically Organized Systems in Theory and Practice.* New York: Hafner, 1971.

Pava, C. "Normative Incrementalism." Unpublished doctoral dissertation, Social Systems Sciences, University of Pennsylvania, 1980.

Perlmutter, H. *Towards a Theory and Practice of Social Architecture.* London: Tavistock, 1965.

Ramirez, R. "Action Learning: A Strategic Approach for Organizations Facing Turbulent Conditions." *Human Relations,* 1983, *36,* 725–742.

Rapoport, R. *Mid-Career Development.* London: Tavistock, 1970.

Revans, R. *Developing Effective Managers: A New Approach to Business Education.* New York: Praeger, 1973.

Rohatyn, F. E. "For an Energy Corporation of the Northeast." *New York Times,* June 8, 1979.

Schön, D. A. *Beyond the Stable State.* London: Temple Smith; New York: Basic Books, 1971.

Schön, D. A. "Framing and Reframing the Problems of Cities." In D. Morley, S. Proudfoot, and T. Burns (Eds.), *Making Cities Work.* Boulder, Colo.: Praeger, 1980.

Sommerhoff, G. *Analytical Biology.* London: Oxford University Press, 1950.

Sommerhoff, G. "The Abstract Characteristics of Living Systems." In F. E. Emery (Ed.), *Systems Thinking.* Baltimore: Penguin, 1969.

Stringer, J. "Operational Research for 'Multi-Organizations.' " *Operational Research Quarterly,* 1969, *18,* 105-120.

Sudbury 2001. *A Framework for Action.* Sudbury, Ontario: Sudbury 2001, 1979.

Thompson, J. D. *Organizations in Action.* New York: McGraw-Hill, 1967.

Trist, E. L. "A Concept of Organizational Ecology." *Australian Journal of Management,* 1977, *2,* 162-175.

Trist, E. L. "New Directions of Hope." *Regional Studies,* 1979, *13,* 439-451.

Trist, E. L. "The Environment and Systems Response Capability: A Futures Perspective." *Futures,* April 1980, pp. 113-127.

Trist, E. L. "Referent Organizations and the Development of Inter-Organizational Domains." *Human Relations,* 1983, *36,* 269-284.

Trist, E. L., and Burgess, M. S. *Multiple Deprivation: A Human and Economic Approach.* Linkage Series, no. 3. London: Tavistock Center (Institute for Operational Research), 1978.

van Ravenswaaij, J. F. "Strategies of Change." Paper presented at the World Federation for Mental Health Regional Seminar on Mental Health Strategies of Change, Amsterdam, 1972.

Vickers, G. *The Art of Judgment.* London: Chapman & Hall, 1965.

Vickers, G. *Value Systems and Social Process.* London: Tavistock; New York: Basic Books, 1968.

Warren, R. L. "The Interorganizational Field as a Focus for Investigation." *Administrative Science Quarterly,* 1967, *12,* 396–419.

Whitehead, A. N., and Russell, B. *Principia Mathematica.* (2nd ed., 3 vol.). Cambridge, England: Cambridge University Press, 1910–1913.

9

Democratizing Organizations:
A Challenge
to Organization Development

Max Elden

The abbreviation OD could stand for both "organization development" and "organizational democracy." It does not, of course, and each of these two schools seems completely unaware of the other. At best, they treat each other with indifference, despite the obvious advantages of combining the two fields. Both have the same general democratic and humanistic values and goals. A major common interest of both—enhancing people's efficacy and self-direction in the labor process—could be much better served if the two schools supplemented each other. Since my original formal training was in political science, and I now have more than a decade of experience as an OD (in the combined sense) consultant and action researcher, I am particularly troubled by seeing how each approach could benefit from the other. Organizational democracy could benefit from more applied behavioral science, action research, and practical knowledge about how to make organizations and groups more

Note: The author would like to express appreciation for extensive written comments by Sam Culbert, Tom Cummings, Will McWhinney, and Bob Tannenbaum.

effective. On the other hand, organization development needs a better understanding of democratic theory, power relations, and the dangers of co-optive participation. This chapter is aimed at the latter need—the need for those of us in organization development (hereafter called OD) who are interested in democratization to be less politically naive.

I hope to demonstrate how concepts from democratic theory and field studies of work democracy can enhance OD's contribution to democratizing change. I will assess the limits of OD as a democratizing strategy and suggest how these can be extended. Not all OD is, of course, interested in or intended to promote democratic and humanistic values. I assume, however, that anyone who has read this far is interested in these values. This chapter is intended to improve our chances to realize them.

First, we need some definitions. As Huse (1980, p. 22) has observed, "there exists no single definition of OD to which all practitioners would agree." For my purposes, the most general category is "planned change." OD is an umbrella concept describing the work of behavioral and social scientists and other professionals to increase organizational effectiveness and realize certain values (including human health and welfare, broadly conceived) through planned change. This definition is consistent with most others (such as those analyzed by Huse, 1980, pp. 22-24) but opens up the possibility that other planned-change strategies could be relevant within organizations. One of the main themes of this chapter is that we cannot think of planned organizational democratization within the terms of conventional OD.

Traditionally, most OD concepts and techniques have aimed at improving interpersonal, group, and other social processes, usually among managers or white-collar workers. Lately, however, as most recent texts are quick to point out (compare, for example, Huse's second edition, 1980, with his first, 1975), OD has expanded beyond a management and "process" orientation. It has, for example, developed—under the label of *quality of working life* (QWL)—concepts and techniques for analyzing and redesigning work organization.

I treat QWL as a subcategory of planned change that substantially overlaps OD. QWL means planned change in restructuring work organization. It is well on its way to becoming so widely used that it, too, will soon be difficult to define. Cummings and Molloy (1977) have included such things as autonomous work groups, job enrichment, participative management, flexible working hours, and the Scanlon plan in their analysis of QWL. Within this variety of approaches affecting work organization, I will focus on autonomous or self-managing work groups as defined by sociotechnical systems (STS) analysis (see Elden, 1984, for a definition of QWL based on STS). STS alone is, of course, merely a set of analytical tools, but it has been further developed in relation to particular values. Open-systems planning (OPS), for example, is a more comprehensive approach, aimed at human development (see McWhinney, 1972; Krone, 1975). In Scandinavia, STS has been the theoretical basis of workplace democracy (see Emery and Thorsrud, 1976). Thus, STS and its value-based extensions, which also emphasize autonomy-based structure in work organization, seem to be particularly promising democratization strategies in planned organizational change.

I discuss the meaning of democracy more fully later. For present purposes, we should note that there are two types or levels of organizational or industrial democracy. The first type is representative, or indirect. It aims at increasing worker influence in company policy making so as to bring policies into harmony with worker interests. Worker representation on boards of directors is a typical example. The second type is direct, or participatory, democracy in the workplace. It entails workers' control of the labor process. It aims at reducing alienation and powerlessness by creating organizational conditions that empower people. This approach therefore requires authority structures consistent with self-management and autonomy.

If we ask how OD (or even QWL) contributes to industrial democracy, it is hard to find an answer. Even phrasing the issue this way almost sounds odd. OD values clearly support democracy, but there are few examples of OD praxis that has changed power, control, and authority relations to achieve real autonomy and self-management. Many OD and QWL efforts are highly participative but not necessarily democratic.

Democracy Is More Than Participative Management

The idea of democracy is so confused and misused in planned change that most OD and QWL strategies either actively hinder power sharing and democratization or unwittingly collude in preserving undemocratic organizational forms. One of the most troublesome sources of confusion lies in the way OD tends to equate participation and democracy. The assumption in OD seems to be that an increase in participation translates automatically into increased democracy. Nothing could be further from the truth. Why do so many of us seem to overlook how necessary participation and commitment are for quite undemocratic forms of organization?

Political theorists are careful to distinguish between participation and democracy (see, for example, Pateman, 1970). Participation is a means. Democracy is a value state that can characterize either means or ends. Democratic political theory distinguishes between participation that contributes to democratization (that is, that transforms authority structures in the direction of autonomy, power equalization, and self-management) and that which does not so contribute (that is, involvement in untransformed hierarchical authority structures, such as quality-control circles, problem-solving groups, and participative management). This distinction—essential to theories of political democracy—is overlooked, misunderstood, or completely muddled in discussions of organizational behavior. A recent analysis of the relation between industrial democracy and participative management illustrates the confusion nicely: "The behavioral approach is participative management. It is face-to-face, informal sharing of decision-making at the workplace. It is 'shopfloor democracy.' It is an informal arrangement between managers and subordinates whereby managers—through indoctrination, training, organizational policy, social pressure, or other means—involve their subordinates in consensual decision making about matters of importance to all concerned" (Bass and Shackleton, 1979, p. 397).

Of course, participation is a popular theme in the study of organizational compliance. Participation does pay, but management is seldom willing to pay the price of decreased direct, hierarchical control. The problem in planned change is how to democratize organizations based on unilateral hierarchical authority. Delegating authority is not the same as democratizing it. Participation without autonomy (and especially *with* management "indoctrination") is not democracy, which is one reason why participative management is not necessarily very democratic.

STS is relevant precisely because it requires more than participatory management. STS requires fundamental change of workplace authority structures. This emphasis on peer group or collegial rather than hierarchical authority is necessary to maximize local control over production disturbances ("variances"). STS thus aims at more autonomous (not just more participatory) forms of work organization. Autonomy means that workers make meaningful decisions in the workplace. It means that they have the resources (authority, skills, support) to have the final say over things (see Elden, 1976, 1984; Emery and Thorsrud, 1976; Herbst, 1976; Davis and Cherns, 1975; Trist, 1981; Pasmore and Sherwood, 1978). Thus, STS provides an organizational foundation in the workplace for worker control, self-management, and real "shop-floor democracy."

My first thoughts about work democracy were based on STS and OPS. STS originated in England in the 1950s at the Tavistock Institute (Trist, 1981, is an excellent summary, while Emery and Thorsrud, 1976, provide classic case studies). OPS was developed in part by a group at the UCLA Graduate School of Management in the late 1960s and early 1970s (see, for example, McWhinney, 1972). In 1971-72, I explored these ideas in a new American factory designed expressly on these STS/OPS concepts (especially the idea of semiautonomous groups). This project provides the basis of the first of the following two case studies. My experience with it and my moving to Norway in 1972 led to second thoughts and to a quite different approach to planned change and democratization. I draw on my experience in Norway during the 1970s to describe the second case, which illustrates a different approach to democratizing organizational change. A comparison of these two cases in the concluding section of this chapter creates a basis for evaluating under what conditions OD means organizational democracy. Before presenting these two cases, however, we will need to clarify several different theories or models of political democracy. This will provide a foundation for evaluating the contribution of the two cases to democratizing organizational change.

Three Models of Political Democracy

Participation by itself is a necessary but not a sufficient condition for democratizing working life. The issue is always participation in what? Under what conditions? I have argued that participation in autonomy-based organizational structures contributes to democracy. What do these look like? How are they developed? Part of the difficulty of answering questions such as these is that a naive and simplistic notion of political democracy pervades planned change (including OD, QWL, and STS). In addition to widespread conceptual confusion of terms relating to politics (such as equating participation with democracy), there is a paucity of language and metaphor for understanding what *political* democracy could look like in an *organization.* If we were to consider modern democratic theory, we would find at least three quite different ideas about political democracy. These models can help in evaluating STS as a democratization strategy.

Democracy as Town Meeting (Model I). This could also be called the classical or popular (and populist!) idea of democracy, where everyone comes together to thrash out differences and advance the common good. Pateman's (1970) excellent summary of classical democratic theory focuses on recent formulations (such as those of J. S. Mill and G. D. H. Cole), but the ideas can be traced back to ancient Athens. This is the model that people often have in mind when they think of democracy—a set of values and procedures to ensure equality of opportunity to decide things. It is democratic because everyone participates directly and things are decided according to the principle of one person, one vote. A "town meeting" in theory brings together informed citizens to make rational decisions on the basis of reasoned arguments about what is the best course for the polity as a whole. This is, of course, an idealized picture of town meetings—in practice, they are not quite so participatory or rational (Mansbridge, 1973). Nevertheless, individual rights and freedoms are essential for this kind of open discourse. Participation, as Pateman (1970) makes clear, is both a means and an end: people learn to participate by participating.

There are several problems with this model. It assumes that participatory opportunities are equally distributed in the population. It also tacitly implies that there are sufficiently strong common values to preserve and advance the common good. Finally, it uncritically accepts the proposition that increased information also increases the quality of "democratic" decisions. Systematic empirical studies of voting behavior, however, strongly disconfirm many of the assumptions of popular or town-meeting democracy. Studies repeatedly demonstrate that most voters are not well informed and tend to make decisions on the basis of stereotypes or emotional reactions. Studies of democratic political attitudes reveal wide agreement on democratic values in principle but not in practice (such as: yes, we should have free speech; no, communists should not be allowed to speak at the local school).

How can these findings be reconciled with democratic theory? Is mass democracy a contradiction in terms? Other empirical research shows that the relatively small percentage who participate actively in politics (about 5-10 percent, depending on one's definition of participation) have quite a different set of characteristics, which correspond quite closely to those posited by the classical theory of democracy. Political elites tend to be democrats in both theory and practice. Since they run the political system according to democratic norms, democracy in mass society is still democracy. This revision of classical democratic theory is called "democratic elitism." It fits well with the hierarchical authority structure typical of modern corporations and raises the issue of whether the model of democracy in OD and QWL is implicitly based more on democratic elitism than on participatory democracy.

Democracy as Interest-Group Negotiation (Model II). A second model of political democracy is based on an understanding of politics as a process of negotiation among groups organized to represent particular interests. From this perspective, public policy is determined by groups specially organized to advance particular interests. Their purpose is to influence public policy in directions favorable to these interests. Participation here means being represented by different interest groups reflecting one's various interests. The political function of these groups is to gather together individual interests into an organized form so that they can influence public policy making. In technical political science terms, the function of these groups is to *aggregate and articulate interests* in a form that can be used to persuade formal governmental structures, such as public agencies or legislative bodies, to make decisions favoring the group's particular interests. The main idea is that the political system functions to aggregate and articulate those interests that need to be taken into account in formulating public policy. A political system is democratic because all different interests can be represented (thus, this model is also called "pluralistic").

The main problem with this model is that weak and poorly organized interests do not get represented. Not everyone has sufficient political resources to get their interests aggregated and articulated in the political arena. Indeed, one of the major criticisms of this model as a normative model of political democracy is precisely the tendency of some interests to be excluded systematically from the political arena. Instead of merely competing in the political marketplace, powerful, well-organized interests attempt to control the political agenda. Power has "two faces": on one side, it means to win a conflict that has arisen; on the other, it means to prevent conflicts from arising ("nondecisions"). Defining the agenda is one unobtrusive use of power. Another one is defining situations by control of language, as in the social construction of reality.

The negotiation or "interest aggregating and articulating"

model of political democracy implies that democracy within an organization requires bargaining and negotiating structures. There would have to be more than one interest group for there to be any competition and negotiation. Union-management bargaining is an example of the competing-interest-group model of democracy within an organization. This model suggests that, without unions or some other way of independently and authoritatively aggregating and articulating worker interests, there is little chance for real organizational democracy. Democracy within an organization requires groups sufficiently well established with enough political resources to be able to negotiate.

This model suggests that organization development that would contribute to organizational democracy should help develop structures for aggregating and articulating interests, such as helping to develop labor unions within companies. How much OD has benefited trade unions? In the United States, some companies appear motivated to make QWL improvements as a way of excluding unions. Finally, the model suggests that controlling the definition of what is important may be a significant source of power. If advancing one's interests through negotiations is a sign of power, then being able to determine the agenda for negotiation would be a sign of even more power. Since OD is in the business of generating new possibilities, this model would suggest that control of the change process could itself be an important political resource. Thus, how OD itself is organized and managed would have substantial implications for democratization. Control of change processes is even more central in the third model.

Democracy as Community Mobilization (Model III). A third way of thinking about political democracy is as a way of building up (through consciousness raising, community organizing, protests, and so on) the resources necessary for people to have an impact on the conditions that determine their lives. The main idea can be traced back to Marx and the proposition that individuals do not develop their full human potential in total isolation. Nord's perceptive summary of Marx shows that political empowerment and full development of individual power depend on a *social process*: "Individual self-actualization could not occur without the actualization of the species. . . . Human nature developed through the total configuration of relationships in the social system. . . . Marx stressed the need for a social system in which all members developed together. To him an appropriate social system was a necessary condition for human development" (Nord, 1977, pp. 77-78). In other words, solidarity is a prerequisite for mobilization.

The central tenet of this approach is the power that the individual derives from membership in a larger collectivity or movement. Individual empowerment contributes to and is, in turn, nourished by the development of a larger social collectivity. At the extreme, Marxism could be interpreted as requiring collective development as a precondition for individual potentiation. Individuals alone as isolated atoms cannot overcome conditions that produce powerlessness, alienation, and other limits on human empowerment. Democratizing means activating, organizing, and mobilizing all people—especially those relatively poor in political resources—often in the form of a movement that either becomes institutionalized or takes over existing power structures. In Third World countries, struggles for national liberation or literacy and consciousness-raising campaigns are examples of a mobilization strategy. Community organizing projects in politically weak communities or groups in Europe and America are other examples.

Political learning is central in this model. To achieve the goal of solidarity, people require shared vocabulary, reality definitions, and ways of thinking. These develop through a learning process (liberation through consciousness raising) in which people work together to create a shared social understanding of their individual experiences. This learning process must necessarily be actively managed by the participants themselves; it is based on their making sense of their experience on their own terms and thus requires highly democratized pedagogical forms. Applied to the kind of study needed to understand and change one's own work situation, this process requires participant-managed research for action rather than expert-dominated planned change, such as OD (see Brown and Tandon, 1983).

This model of political democracy raises deep and significant questions about both the form and the content of all types of OD as democratization. According to this model, organizational change would be democratizing to the extent that it increased political resources among the relatively powerless. Moreover, this should occur through a participant-managed learning process. The participants' definition of reality, their language and concepts, their way of thinking should be the basis of learning. Democratization in this model means mobilizing for change through participant-managed learning where the content of the learning is making *political sense* of *personal experience*. This model raises the question of whether even STS can democratize unless it is based on worker-managed organizational learning.

Political Democracy and Organization Development

The preceding three quite different models of political democracy suggest that the contribution of organization development to democratizing working life could occur in three quite different ways. Furthermore, the three models are by no means mutually exclusive. Indeed, the democratizing effects of OD would probably be stronger if it were *not* limited to only one model. Yet what is most striking about OD and organizational democracy is how little a typical OD project resembles any one of the three models. There appears to be a big gap between OD and QWL, on the one hand, and real political democracy, on the other.

The concept of democracy in OD and QWL, to the extent that there is one, is Model I. It aims at individual enlightenment and a town-meeting form of democracy, where more information and better reasoning will produce agreement about what is in the best interests of the system as a whole. Unfortunately, regardless of how much participative management there may be, companies do not (and probably cannot in a market economy) practice any form of political democracy. In practice, there is no town meeting. Management has the final say. So even if OD were to attempt to be democratizing, it would at best be such a weak case of Model I that the result would be more "democratic elitism" and less "participatory democracy."

Such speculation notwithstanding, we can at least conclude that little OD—especially as it is known in America—seems to involve Model II and III forms of political democracy. Where are reports of OD projects controlled by workers or trade unions? How does OD contribute to increasing the political resources of relatively powerless organizational members? Such questions about OD as a political enterprise can be fruitfully addressed if we do not limit ourselves exclusively to American OD experience (see Faucheux, Amado, and Laurent, 1982, for an informed and informative assessment). I therefore present two case studies in which I have been deeply engaged. Both are based on projects in industrial companies. Both have a basis in STS ideas about work organization. Both attempt to use planned change to democratize working life. There are also important differences. The first case describes a new factory start-up in the western United States in a large progressive but nonunionized corporation. The second case describes a project in an aluminum plant in Norway where the trade union asked for help in combatting the negative effects of advanced computerization. The two cases illustrate two quite different ways of organizing and managing a change process intended to be democratizing.

A Case for Democratization—First Thoughts. This project was part of a long-term collaboration in the early 1970s between a large international conglomerate in the consumer-products industry and an action-research team at the UCLA Graduate School of Management. The team's task, under the leadership of Will McWhinney, was to design and help start up a new, highly participative production facility. I joined the team in mid-1971 to help with the start-up. In addition to consulting, I was also able to complete a series of research studies on work democracy. The results led me later to wonder whether QWL, even in its most democratically promising use of STS, was part of the solution or part of the problem in democratizing work life.

The new plant was located in a predominantly agricultural region in the western United States several hours' drive from a major metropolitan area. It was a small (about 250 employees), highly specialized (only production and warehousing) facility run by managers recruited from throughout the corporation. They were bearers of a strong corporate culture, and moving up in the corporation usually meant moving to another part of the country (if not to another country). Workers were recruited locally and for the most part did not have prior industrial experience. There was no trade union, and the corporation did not want one.

The design of the new plant (best described in McWhinney, 1972, but see also Elden, 1976) was a radical version of a now more widely practiced form of STS- and OPS-based total systems design (see, Jayarom, 1976; Denison, 1982; Hackman and Oldham, 1980; Cummings, 1978). A striking feature was the design's strong emphasis on participation in autonomous groups and worker-manager task forces. Autonomous work groups were to be responsible for matched pairs of highly automated production lines (five groups or "teams" per shift, or twenty teams on a four-shift rotating basis). Each team was to be autonomous in making all basic production planning and control decisions in its part of the production process. In effect, the team was to take over all supervisory functions. In addition, the teams were to have control over recruitment, pay raises, work assignments, training, and other personnel functions. Pay was to be based on competence ("pay for skill"), as determined in part by each team through "peer evaluation."

Few organization designs even today go much further to foster worker autonomy and participation. This design did so. It created participatory opportunities for workers in managerial decision making. Problem-solving task forces were to be created so that workers and managers could cooperate in coping with issues involving more than a single team.

Participation was not intended just to get the work out or to solve interteam problems. The consultants sought to promote deep learning, development, and empowerment. The plant was designed to meet management's criteria; the design also seemed to provide a basis for extending an OPS approach to work democracy. Participation was to be a way of empowering workers by gradually increasing their task competence through extensive on-the-job training. This training was also designed to be an experience in self-management. As workers learned new skills, their task competencies would increase, and the boundaries of their autonomy would expand to encompass more challenging tasks. In this manner, they would gradually take over additional managerial tasks. Self-management would empower and lead to more self-management. In this way, it seemed that a single design based on STS could develop a new type of factory organization that was high on both performance and democracy.

The design was developed in collaboration with plant management and corporate headquarters. Workers were trained in technical skills and in group-process and communication skills. Since managers were experienced with the fairly complex automated equipment, while workers were not, each team was assigned a manager in the beginning.

I collected data during the plant's first year partly through my consulting but mostly through interviews, participant observation, small action studies, and a comprehensive survey. The survey was based on standardized QWL items (such as peer leadership and support, perceived influence, opportunity to participate, and so forth), supplemented by items focused on power, control, authority, and other political dimensions—including off-the-job political attitudes such as "political efficacy" (a widely used measure of feelings of potency in relation to the polity; see Elden, 1976, 1981, for details). A simple linkage analysis divided the QWL items into two distinct clusters, but only one of these linked with power and political items. This cluster contained all the organizational and QWL variables linked to power, control, and authority (such as perceived influence, opportunity to participate, support for self-management, and the like). It contained all those variables that were important if the STS design were to contribute to democratizing industrial authority structures. The other cluster contained no power variables—only group morale, "feeling good with co-worker," and general job-satisfaction variables—and did not link with any external political behavior variables.

I called the first cluster the *democratization* (power-sharing) indicator and the second the *humanization* (social-satisfaction) indicator. These two indicators helped me to see how the design, which was intended to be democratizing and had been implemented to management's satisfaction, did not, in practice, contribute much to work democracy. It turned out that the same STS design could be implemented to emphasize either humanization or democratization. Management was much more interested in the design's potential for increasing effectiveness and productivity than in its potential for empowering and democratizing. Analysis of participant-observation data revealed how much management retained control where it counted while at the same time supporting work-group self-management (see Elden, 1976). Data came from a team that was officially self-managing in that its manager had formally left the team. Nevertheless, management still controlled the most important production decisions. The more important a decision, the more likely that it was made unilaterally by management; the team made many decisions daily, but none of them were very important. The same pattern occurred in personnel decision making. The team could generally decide who worked where, but decisions such as pay and promotion were made by management. The difference was clear when management and team judgments conflicted. Under these circumstances, workers felt that management either kept returning the decision to the team for "rethinking" (that is, for team thinking that corresponded to management thinking) or set up problem-solving task forces that tended to block worker interests.

Worker-manager task forces bogged down on issues where workers and managers could be expected to have conflicting interests. On other issues (for example, designing a peer evaluation system or participating in setting plantwide production goals and building the annual budget), this form of participation provided an effective opportunity to exercise influence. One example of workers and managers disagreeing was the issue of sick-pay benefits. Workers could accumulate sick leave during the year, but unused portions could not be transferred to the next year. From the workers' point of view, these benefits simply evaporated at the end of each year. Workers wanted to accumulate them. Management disagreed. In a unionized plant, this would have been a typical issue for negotiation. Here, however, there was no union or other mechanism for authoritatively aggregating and articulating workers' interests; workers were unable to negotiate. The personnel office started up a joint worker-manager task force, but it petered out. As one of the workers on the task force said to the personnel officer: "We don't have a union; you don't have to listen to us."

In summary, the OPS design was never adequately implemented. As a result, what should have democratized only humanized. Most of the design's potential for really empowering workers was in the heads of the consultants, while the design's implementation was in the hands of management. Management wanted the design's production advantages without its political costs. Management wanted to increase such things as flexibility, motivation, productivity, and quality without diminishing hierarchical control. Management got what it wanted, and workers were not dissatisfied (high job-satisfaction scores, low turnover, little interest in unionization). *The design resulted in a lot of participation but little democratization.*

At best, participation meant a form of 'sandbox government" where workers had the least control over the few but very important decisions and the most control over the many but largely trivial or routine decisions. Perhaps no more could be expected where organization development is limited to an elitist (Model I) concept of political democracy.

A Case for Democratization—Second Thoughts. The Norwegian project started when national officials in the politically powerful Norwegian Chemical Workers Union (NKIF) asked researchers for help in coping with the effects of technological change. The union had two goals. The first was to acquire more general knowledge about how technology affected its interests so that it could develop more informed and effective union policies (especially for both local and national bargaining with management). The second goal was to increase local union activism in negotiating the implementation of technological change. Norwegian unions had pioneered a new form of collective bargaining called "technology agreements," which gave them formal rights to influence technological change. This could mean a de facto veto, but too little was known about how the new agreement would operate. The NKIF wanted research that would help realize the potential for influence created by the technology agreements.

Over a period of almost four years, the research team performed a variety of research and development activities, including technological and economic forecasting, drafting position papers for debate at national conventions, designing and implementing training programs, and cooperating in numerous local development projects. I will describe one of these local projects as a way of illustrating an approach to democratizing organizational change that departs significantly from our first case. This will necessarily be brief (for a more complete description, see Levin, 1982; Elden, 1982).

The first problem was to design a project to produce knowledge both of a general character about the effects of technological change on union interests and of a specific character usable on the local level. An extensive computer-based literature search did not help much, for at least two reasons. First, there was little research on issues most of interest to the union. We found numerous citations on issues of primary interest to management (such as productivity) or where union-management interests coincided (such as reduction in number of jobs or changes in job content) but almost none on issues of primary interest to the union (such as effects of technological change on worker solidarity). Generally, social science research, especially in the area of organization behavior and organization development, seems much more concerned with problems facing management than those facing unions. Second, abstract general propositions alone seldom, if ever, are sufficient to produce local action. The project required research that would both inform about how technology could affect union interests (general propositions about the consequences of technological change for unions on both national and local levels) and activate local unions in exercising their rights under the technology agreements. The result was a project based on "participatory research" rather than OD (see Levin, 1982; Elden and Taylor, 1983; Brown and Tandon, 1983).

The project was carried out in an aluminum-smelting plant with some 1,200 employees that had been established in what twenty-five years earlier had been a small farming community. The work force, many of whom had moved to the community because of the opportunity for employment, was very stable and virtually 100 percent unionized. The project was very much a union activity, under the leadership of the locally elected "technology shop steward," backed up by the local union board and a group of interested workers called the "technology study group." The union invited us to visit the company, informed management (which otherwise was not much involved—a striking reversal of roles compared to most planned-change projects), designed and carried out the study, and used the results (in part to stop implementation of a new computer-based production planning and control system). The project produced both actionable knowledge and action, even though it was not a case of action research.

The project took shape at a two-day workshop organized by the local union. Another researcher and I met with the technology steward, the technology study group, and other union officials to help define and plan what should be done. First, we tried to give meaning to the Norwegian phrase "good-quality total working environment" by summarizing a half-dozen or so QWL ideas found in Norwegian labor legislation and national labor-management agreements. The workers then readily developed seventeen well-specified criteria. These were much more situation specific, relevant, and meaningful than we outside "experts" could have produced. Next, in reviewing the history of technological change in the company, the workers (many of whom had been there since day one) realized that there had been three main phases of technological change during the twenty-five-year history of the company. The union had access to company job descriptions for each of these phases. Designing the research was now easy.

Objective data on changes in job descriptions could be analyzed according to the workers' seventeen QWL criteria for each of the three phases of technological change. In addition, the union's technology study group interviewed other workers (both individually and in small groups) from different parts of the plant with different kinds of experience from different periods. It took the technology study group more than a year working part-time to complete its analysis and write a report.

The conclusions were clear. Technological change had increased production (both quantitatively and qualitatively) and improved some QWL factors (especially the physical working environment) but also decreased the number of workers and the workers' possibility for discretion, control, learning, and social contact in work. From the union's point of view, new technology eliminated or de-skilled work and undermined worker solidarity. The study implied that these consequences resulted more from a lack of planning than from management policy.

This implication reaffirmed the value of collective bargaining to control what the union saw as negative effects of technological change. We should note here that union interests coincided with management's only in part. Like the sick-leave-pay dispute in the first case, technological change created a situation where workers' interests conflicted with management's. There were at least three important results.

In the first place, the project produced local knowledge actually used by the people who produced it. When management proposed a new computer system for production planning and control, the union effectively blocked it pending a study of the proposed system's total effects. The project could be seen as a form of organization development for the local union. New structures were created (the technology steward and the technology study group). The local union increased its repertoire of action possibilities. Local officials were better able to cope with management's initiatives and therefore more active in trying to cope. The project clearly met its goal of activating people locally to exercise their rights in technological bargaining. But it is not accurate to interpret the project primarily as OD for the local union, since improvements in the union's organization were more a precondition for rather than a result of the project. The project is interesting for our purposes because it demonstrated an empowering change strategy—participative research—that produced actionable knowledge and increased union power vis-à-vis management. Participatory research is not typical of OD but rather supports Model III–type democratization.

In the second place, new knowledge was generated in a highly participant-controlled manner. This process of participative research led to a research report written by workers but of sufficient quality to warrant publication in a research monograph series (see Elden, 1982, for an analysis integrating the workers' research report with reports from other studies by professional researchers on the same issue). The project clearly met its other goal: it produced new knowledge that contributed to general propositions concerning the QWL effects of technological change.

In the third place, and for our purposes most significant, the project resulted in positive experience in self-organizing for self-study and self-managed change. The participatory research process resulted in an increased ability to aggregate and articulate interests. At minimum, a significant force undermining worker solidarity and union interests was blunted. Further technological change in the company is unlikely without serious consideration of what the workers have shown to be important QWL consequences of new technology.

This project contributed to organizational democracy in at least two important ways. First, it increased union knowledge, which in turn increased the union's power base in negotiating with management. From the point of view of labor-management relations, the project functioned under a Model II, or pressure-group, type of democracy, by increasing the ability of labor to aggregate and articulate its interests vis-à-vis management. The use of OD in service of trade unions may be uncommon, but it does not necessarily require a fundamentally different model of planned change than is typical for most OD.

The second way the project contributed to OD as organizational democracy was by suggesting another model for planned change in working life. Seen in traditional OD terms, the "client" in the second project took over so much of the consultant's job in making an organizational analysis and applying the results that the terms *client* and *consultant* do not seem appropriate. The project was well planned, organized, and managed, but not by us outside experts. We were very much on the sidelines. Our role was certainly a long way from that of experts in charge of change. The project was such a do-it-yourself form of planned change that I hesitate to call it OD. This may say something about me, but I think it says something more significant about OD. How many OD professionals would call a homegrown organizational change effort not involving professionals an OD effort?

What strikes me about the second case was how the project was so totally controlled by the participants. We had sporadic contact, usually at their initiative and then mostly as discussion partners responding to issues as they defined them. The new knowledge was generated by the workers in their language, on their terms, and helped them to mobilize themselves. This form of worker-controlled inquiry and definition of the situation implies a Model III, or mobilization, approach to democracy. This approach to democratizing planned change through participative research where the client becomes the consultant requires quite a different type of planned change than we saw in the first case.

Planning Organizational Democracy: Some Necessary Conditions

Under what conditions can OD lead to organizational democracy? Although OD has democratic values and ideology, the concept of democracy is so poorly understood in planned organizational change that high participation is automatically equated with increased democratization. OD does not differentiate between empowering and co-opting forms of participation but rather uncritically accepts all participation as a form of holy communion. Yet participation without autonomy does not democratize. And autonomous work groups alone without any supporting structure such as a trade union are not sufficient. The STS strategy in the first case was thus limited to "democratic elitism" in a Model I type of democracy. This form of democracy retains and reinforces hierarchical authority structures, which make autonomy-based organizational forms difficult to develop.

The second case illustrates how elements of Model II and Model III forms of political democracy can be used within a company to promote planned organizational democratization. Although the two cases are from two different industries in two different countries, the most significant difference for our purposes is the difference in conceptions of planned organizational change. There are American unions as strong as the NKIF, but there is not much OD in America like that based on *worker-managed organizational change* of the kind described here (lest the NKIF case be dismissed as an exception, see also the other cases presented in the *Journal of Occupational Behavior* (1983, vol. 4, no. 1). The "do-it-yourself" and "control-it-yourself" approach of participative research contrasts sharply with the typical OD approach in at least three significant ways (see also a slightly different and more comprehensive analysis by Brown and Tandon, 1983).

First, workers study their own workplace on their own terms. They decide what to study, gather the data, analyze it so that it makes sense to them, and create explanations of their work world so that they can better control it. The whole process of inquiry itself becomes autonomy enhancing. An outside expert may help participants design their own research, but they develop their own "local theory." Generating actionable knowledge is no longer the monopoly of highly trained researchers. *Worker-managed inquiry strengthens worker autonomy.*

Second, workers decide how to use the results of their research. The second case illustrated, among other things, that OD as organizational democratization does not necessarily follow traditional OD proverbs, such as the necessity of top management support. The generation of knowledge in the NKIF case was not grounded in the company's managerial authority structure (note that such projects do not necessarily require a trade union—see, for example, Borum, 1980; Toch and Grant, 1982). Democratizing OD must in part be based on a conflict model of organization rather than exclusively on a harmony model.

Third, our role of outside experts was quite different from that of the typical change agent, who is responsible (ultimately and unavoidably to management) for solving certain problems. We were no longer "experts in charge of change." We had to relinquish (not just share) control of the research and change process. Since we no longer monopolized creating new meaning or determining the agenda of acceptable action, the progress of the OD effort was no longer measured by how well our interventions got them to learn "our" theory. Our role was to help them invent their own theory. In short, their inventions were more important than our interventions. The first case was expert-based *intervention*. The second case was participant-managed *invention*. Regardless of which model of democratization OD might pursue, to the extent that it is imposed from without, it will not enhance democracy. The problem with the first case was not the quality or amount of OD. More OD would not have been more democratic, because it was limited to a Model I type of democracy (for example, no union) and because the underlying model of OD was itself not democratic. OD in the NKIF case meant so much "client" control that the distinction between client and consultant disappeared. Ultimately, the client system was its own best consultant.

In conclusion, at least two conditions are necessary for OD to democratize. First, there must be some way of worker interests being authoritatively represented—as, for example, through a union or a workers' council. Second, OD itself needs to be reconceptualized. Democratization implies not just implementing certain forms of organization, such as semiautonomous groups, but real participant control over organizational self-study and change. OD as planned organizational democratization requires worker-managed organizational change supported by a power base not totally dependent on managerial authority.

References

Bass, B., and Shackleton, V. J. "Industrial Democracy and Participative Management: A Case for Synthesis." *Academy of Management Review,* 1979, *4* (3), 393-404.

Borum, F. "A Power-Strategy Alternative to Organization Development." *Organization Studies,* 1980, *1* (2), 123-146.

Brown, L. D., and Tandon, R. "The Ideology and Political Economy of Inquiry: Action Research and Participatory Research." *Journal of Applied Behavioral Science,* 1983, *19* (3), 277-294.

Culbert, S. A. *The Organization Trap and How to Get Out of It.* New York: Basic Books, 1974.

Cummings, T. G. "Self-Regulating Work Groups: A Socio-Technical Synthesis." *Academy of Management Review,* 1978, *3* (3), 625-634.

Cummings, T. G., and Molloy, E. S. *Improving Productivity and the Quality of Work Life.* New York: Praeger, 1977.

Davis, L. E., and Cherns, A. B. (Eds.). *The Quality of Working Life.* (2 vols.) New York: Free Press, 1975.

Denison, D. R. "Sociotechnical Design and Self-Managing Work Groups: The Impact on Control." *Journal of Occupational Behavior,* 1982, *3,* 297-314.

Dunn, W. N., and Swierczek, F. W. "Planned Organizational Change: Toward Grounded Theory." *Journal of Applied Behavioral Science,* 1977, *13* (2), 135-157.

Elden, M. "Democracy at Work for a More Participatory Politics: Worker Self-Management Increases Political Efficacy and Participation." Unpublished doctoral dissertation, Department of Political Science, University of California, Los Angeles, 1976.

Elden, M. "Political Efficacy at Work: The Connection Between More Autonomous Forms of Workplace Organization and a More Participatory Politics." *American Political Science Review,* 1981, *75* (1), 43-58.

Elden, M. (Ed.). *Good Technology Is Not Enough.* Trondheim: Institute for Social Research in Industry, Norwegian Institute of Technology, University of Trondheim, 1982.

Elden, M. "Quality of Working Life: A Definition." *QWL Journal* (in press; manuscript dated January 1984).

Elden, M., and Taylor, J. C. "Participatory Research at Work: An Introduction." *Journal of Occupational Behavior,* 1983, *4* (1), 1-8.

Emery, F., and Thorsrud, E. *Democracy at Work: Report of the Norwegian Industrial Democracy Program.* Leiden: Martinus Nijhoff, 1976.

Faucheux, C., Amado, G., and Laurent, A. "Organization Development and Change." *American Review of Psychology,* 1982, *33,* 343-370.

Hackman, J. R., and Oldham, G. R. *Work Redesign*. Reading, Mass.: Addison-Wesley, 1980.

Herbst, P. *Alternatives to Hierarchies*. Leiden: Martinus Nijhoff, 1976.

Huse, E. F. *Organization Development and Change*. St. Paul, Minn.: West, 1975; 2nd ed., 1980.

Jayarom, G. K. "Open Systems Planning." In W. G. Bennis, K. D. Benne, R. Chin, and K. E. Corey, *The Planning of Change*. (3rd ed.) New York: Holt, Rinehart & Winston, 1976.

Krone, C. "Open System Redesign." In J. B. Adams (Ed.), *Theory and Method in Organization Development*. Arlington, Va.: National Training Laboratories, 1975.

Levin, M. "Building Trade Union Influence over Technological Change." Paper prepared for the tenth annual World Congress of the International Sociological Association, Mexico City, August 1982.

McWhinney, W. *Open Systems and Traditional Hierarchies*. Paper presented at the International Conference on Quality of Working Life, Arden House, Columbia University, New York, September 1972.

McWhinney, W., and Elden, J. M. *Reticular Society: New Institutions for a Post-Industrial Democracy*. Paper presented at the Center for the Study of Democratic Institutions, Santa Barbara, Calif., 1972.

Mansbridge, J. "Town Meeting Democracy." *Working Papers for a New Society*, 1973, *1*, 5-15.

Nord, W. "A Marxist Critique of Humanistic Psychology." *Journal of Humanistic Psychology*, 1977, *17* (1), 75-83.

Pasmore, W. A., and Friedlander, F. "An Action Research Program for Increasing Employee Involvement in Problem-Solving." *Administrative Science Quarterly*, 1982, *27* (3), 343-362.

Pasmore, W. A., and Sherwood, J. J. *Sociotechnical Systems: A Sourcebook*. La Jolla, Calif.: University Associates, 1978.

Pateman, C. *Participation and Democratic Theory*. Cambridge, England: Cambridge University Press, 1970.

Toch, H., and Grant, J. D. *Reforming Human Services: Change Through Participation*. Beverly Hills, Calif.: Sage, 1982.

Trist, E. *The Evolution of Socio-Technical Systems: A Conceptual Framework and an Action Research Program.* Issues in the Quality of Working Life: A Series of Occasional Papers, no. 2. Toronto, Ont.: Ontario Quality of Working Life Centre, Ontario Ministry of Labour, June 1981.

10

Managing Planned Change: A Stream Approach

Jerry I. Porras
Joan Harkness

Managing a complex organization requires attention to a wide variety of organizational factors. Are supplies and materials available at the right spot and time? Is the schedule being met? Are people working efficiently? Do people have the information they need to do their job correctly? Are machines and equipment functioning well? Do people know what their jobs are? These issues and many more like them are continuously addressed by managers as they proceed through a typical workday. Ideally, the organization is operating in a relatively steady or quasi-equilibrium state. Yet this is seldom the case. What happens when the organization's environment begins to change, with concomitant alteration in the demands it places on the system? In this, the more typical situation, the organization's responses must be more adaptive in nature and specifically geared toward dealing with the ever-changing world. The process of planned change in organizations is a way of life rather than the exception to an otherwise steady-state condition.

Note: The authors wish to thank Coeleen Kiebert for her contributions to the project upon which this paper is based and to thank Loretta Dutton, who was a key person in the planned change that took place.

Managers must deal with change, yet few rigorous tools exist for systematically assessing the needs of the organization as a whole and then for planning action on the basis of an integrated view of these needs. The purpose of this chapter is to propose an analytical framework, called *stream analysis,* as one approach to managing change and to demonstrate its utility by describing a complex change project in which it was used. A community hospital operating room undergoing a long-term organization-development process was the site for this example. It was managed by a director familiar with stream analysis who wanted to apply this tool to the active management of change, a use for which it was not originally intended. Initially, stream analysis had been developed as a research tool for decomposing organization-development interventions (Porras, Harkness, and Kiebert, 1983a).

A Model of the Managing Process

Managers, through their behavior, manage or affect four key sets of organizational elements: (1) the organizing arrangements, (2) the social factors, (3) the technology, and (4) the internal physical setting of the organization. These four variables constitute the organizational environment in which each employee lives and works. Consequently, these are the factors that strongly impinge on the employee and, to a large degree, determine his or her work-related behavior. Employee work-related behavior, in turn, affects not only the psychological state and development of the employee but also the overall performance of the organization.

The management process can therefore be conceptualized as the selection and/or performance of behaviors affecting the four key organizational elements. The employee process consists of the individual's work-related behavioral response to the existence of or change in the four organizational elements and its consequent impact on both the individual's own psychological state and the organization's performance. Needless to say, a feedback loop exists in which both employee behavior and individual/organizational outcomes turn around and affect management behavior. This overall process is depicted in Figure 10-1.

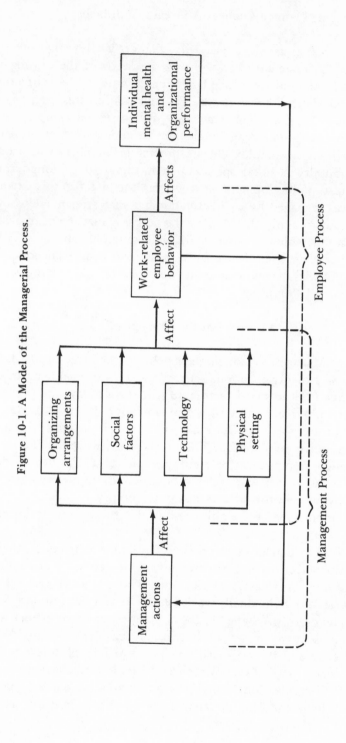

Figure 10-1. A Model of the Managerial Process.

The four organizational elements are the key leverage points for managers and, as such, become the important factors for planned change (Friedlander and Brown, 1974; Margulies and Raia, 1978; Steele, 1973). A clear description of the content of each element is therefore in order. The organizing arrangements consist of the formal structure of the organization (the organization chart and all formal definitions of roles), the organization's policies and procedures, its administrative systems (short- and long-range planning systems, cost-control systems, information systems, order-processing systems, and so on), its formal reward system (salaries, bonuses, profit-sharing plans, promotions, perquisites, benefits, and so on), its formal evaluation system, and its purpose, mission, and goals. The social factors consist of the organization's culture (beliefs, values, assumptions, norms, symbols, myths, history, stories, customs, rituals, and particular language), its interpersonal, group, and intergroup processes, individual attitudes and behavioral skills, informal communication networks, informal status and influence patterns, and, in general, the human processes of the organization. The organization's technology includes the tools, equipment, and machinery used to produce the organization's product, technical expertise of people, design of jobs, workflow design, technical procedures, and technical systems. Finally, the organization's physical setting consists of the building or buildings in which the business of the organization takes place, the division of space into its specific uses, the characteristics of the spaces, and the characteristics of the ambience (noise, light, temperature, air quality, and so on). Through their decisions and actions, managers can and do affect each of these organizational elements, which, in turn, then affect the behavior of the employee. In adapting to changing environmental conditions, therefore, the four elements are the levers for planned change available to the manager.

Reviews of the literature appear to indicate that few change projects actually affect all four of these elements (Cummings, 1978; Porras and Berg, 1978; White and Mitchell, 1976). Although one would expect that, at some point in the life of any comprehensive program, each of these key variables would be affected, this does not appear to be the case. This may explain the failure of many change efforts. Why are so few change programs truly eclectic across these four elements? A variety of reasons exist. Perhaps one of the most compelling concerns the ambiguity inherent in any complex change process. In most situations, it is often unclear when intervention activities should shift focus from one key element to another. Typically, then, the manager of a change process frequently continues to use the intervention techniques that are most familiar rather than those that are most appropriate. When it is unclear which factors in the organization it is most critical to affect at any point in time, what the interconnections between factors and between interventions are, or exactly which factors are being affected, it is no wonder that leaders of change processes choose to do the most familiar. The stream-analysis approach speaks to this deficiency —an ambiguous sense of all the change actions occurring, of their interconnections, and of their effects—by proposing an organizing structure for diagnosing, planning, and leading a complex change activity. Our purpose is first to describe this approach and then to demonstrate its use as a managerial tool in a hospital operating room planned-change process.

Stream Theory

Stream theory is based on the premise that all activities occurring in a planned-change process can be conceptualized as a stream of intervention actions flowing over time. This could be thought of as similar to a set of water molecules flowing together across the landscape in a pattern we call a stream. If the individual change activities making up the overall intervention are categorized according to the key organizational element they affect (organizing arrangements, social factors, technology, or physical setting), then they might be conceived of as similar to different currents flowing in the same stream at the same time. Each current would have its own particular characteristics but would be flowing in concert with all the other currents in the same stream. Figure 10-2 shows four parallel change streams or currents flowing together through time, each reflecting all

Figure 10-2. A Stream Representation of Organization-Development
Interventions.

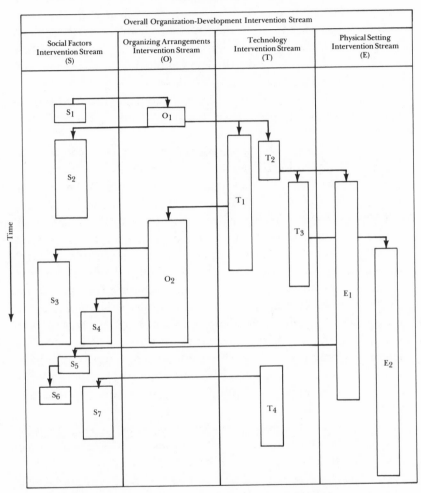

the intervention activities focused on one of the organizational
elements. By identifying the particular focus of any change activity, placing it in its proper stream and temporal position, and
then representing its time duration, we can begin to decompose
the actions taken in a complex organization-development project and achieve a clearer understanding of its particular dynamics.

Since an OD intervention typically is a building process in which one activity rises out of a previous activity, a final step, the identification of interconnections between activities, provides additional information on the change-process dynamics. A single intervention can precipitate one of a series of activities, either planned or unplanned. By making appropriate interconnections between events across or down streams, one begins to get a more focused picture of interdependencies in the total organizational-change process, either as it is taking place or post hoc.

A brief example may help sharpen this perspective. Consider an organizational change that introduces a new computerized billing system (both an organizing-arrangements and a technological intervention). This type of change will trigger the need for physical space in which to house the computer and associated equipment, a physical-setting change activity. Concurrently, a structural change might take place involving the creation of a computer-specialist group, which, in turn, might lead to a social-factor intervention of team building for that group. Further technological change might include job design and the creation of technical and job-procedure manuals. Figure 10-3 could be a stream chart representing this process. Note that the length of time taken to perform each change activity is represented by the size of each activity block and that activity blocks are placed in proper temporal order, with their appropriate interconnections.

There are several advantages to depicting a change process in this manner. First of all, even though this example shows only a relatively simple group of interventions, it may well be that several other sets of activities happening simultaneously also affect the process depicted. Conceptualizing planned change as consisting of four parallel streams of action can provide a systematic method for assessing the effects of these external (to the intervention) factors and responding accordingly. Second, since the manager attempts simultaneously to lead the change process and to keep the organization operating as effectively as possible, a difficult bind typically develops. Clearly, it is imperative that managing the change process not be so overwhelmingly

Figure 10-3. An Example of the Stream Approach.

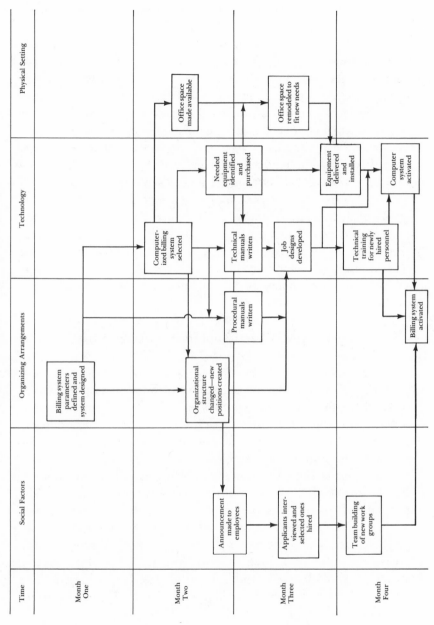

complex either that the normal organizational functioning is neglected or that the manager avoids any involvement in the change activity. Needed, therefore, is a method for achieving an enhanced understanding of changes occurring in the system so that managers can do both tasks effectively. The stream-analytical approach can potentially serve that function.

Stream analysis is used in three ways to manage planned organizational change: (1) in diagnosing the current state of the system, (2) in planning changes focused on solving problems identified in the diagnostic process, and (3) in tracking actions taken to change the system. The next section shows how this approach was used to plan and execute activities necessary to accomplish a relatively small-scale change in a hospital operating room. The detailed example could easily be expanded to describe a more complex situation, but, for purposes of clarity, we will attempt to demonstrate these principles in a concise form without sacrificing any of the richness inherent in real-world problems.

Stream Analysis as a Tool for Managing Change

An Operating Room Example. The operating room department (OR) of a large community hospital had outgrown its original facilities because of changes in the environment, technology, and the organization itself. Over a six-year period, ever-growing community demands for up-to-date medical care increased the number of surgical procedures performed from 6,000 to more than 11,000. These changing conditions precipitated a prolonged and complicated renovation and expansion program of the physical facilities in the OR. Floor space tripled, outpatient areas doubled, and the number of operating rooms increased from ten to fourteen. Office, supply, and instrument areas were also expanded and modernized. The organization structure was changed, and numerous activities aimed at improving the human processes in the system took place (Porras, Harkness, and Kiebert, 1983b).

The project described here was in the instrument and supply areas of the OR called the center core. It occurred approximately three years after the beginning of the larger process described previously. The final stages of construction had provided a highly sophisticated instrument-processing and supply-distribution facility, in addition to the four new operating rooms. This resulted in a pressing need to change the role of the nonprofessional employees called nursing assistants (NAs) and to develop the proper conditions to support them.

Managing the NAs had always eluded the formal organizational structure of the OR and was considered a long-term, unsolvable problem. Yet the new procedures, supply systems, instrument-washing technology, and increased workload now made viable management of the NAs supercritical. The OR director decided to use stream analysis as a way of managing changes in the center core. Her approach involved: (1) consideration of the situation from the four-streams perspective, (2) selection of actions according to how they might alter problems reflected on each of the streams, (3) anticipation of how a particular action might trigger follow-on actions and what those actions would be, (4) development of an overall action plan, and (5) tracking of actions actually implemented using the stream framework.

Diagnosis. The materials management coordinator, an individual who had worked closely with NAs for a period of years and had experienced the operating difficulties firsthand, joined with the director to determine the dimensions of the situation. The initial analysis centered around the NAs' position in the OR's organizational structure. The NA job, considered an "entry-level position," required no basic skills, afforded little or no opportunity for advancement, and paid relatively low wages. No specific policies or procedures to govern an NA's work existed, making an assessment of performance and reliability difficult. Job functions were, in general, relatively undefined, although they did include transporting patients, running errands, handling supplies, and washing instruments. Numerous small tasks, mostly spur-of-the-moment, resulted in a sporadic work pace. The formal organizational structure further minimized the status of the NAs, who appeared at the very bottom of the organization chart and reported directly to almost everyone in the OR. It is no surprise, therefore, that absenteeism and turnover were high, morale low, and job performance even lower.

These observations, along with several others, were categorized and placed in the appropriate spots on a stream chart, resulting in a representation of the problems existing in the current situation. After the main points had been placed in their appropriate streams, connections showing the interrelationships between issues were made. Figure 10-4 reflects the *accumulated* state of affairs prior to any intervention. It is important to note that this diagnostic chart does not depict events over time and goes back only far enough to identify the issues most relevant to the present state of the system.

Although the complex set of issues shown in Figure 10-4 existed, the specific events triggering action were only a subset of those shown. Construction of the new facilities had allowed for both mechanization of instrument-room functions and development of a new case-cart system to manage surgical-supply availability to the operating room. These two technological innovations resulted in job-function changes for both nurses and NAs. For example, the case-cart method of providing supplies for each surgical procedure, or case, required an important shift of responsibility from nurses to NAs. This change created a time conflict in the performance of another important NA task, that of patient transport.

Timing in the flow of patients and supplies through an operating room is critical. Changing to a case-cart system meant that NAs would have to be in two places at once: bringing supplies into the operating room for the next case while at the same time transporting a patient for that same next case from the nursing unit to the OR. Since the number of case "turnovers" numbered from forty-five to fifty a day, with as many as seven or eight rooms turning over at the same time, performing these two tasks simultaneously would require almost double the number of NAs on the staff.

The stream diagram in Figure 10-4 also does not contain all the issues existing at the time of diagnosis. Rather, it shows only those considered most critical by the director and coordi-

Figure 10-4. Stream Analysis Used for Diagnostic Organizational Problems.

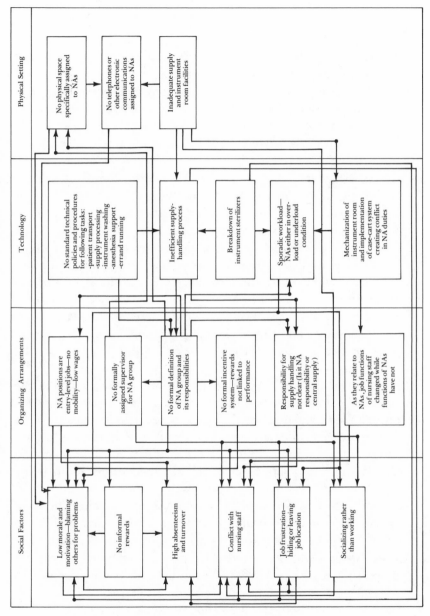

nator. Even so, the diagram is fairly complex and highlights a potential trap in the use of this approach. Too much may be included, resulting in such complexity that the diagram is of no use. Care must be taken to capture only the most important events and keep the process manageable.

An analysis of the stream diagram yields several general observations. First, most of the arrows shown flow into the social-factors stream. The deep problems of an organization often manifest themselves in the human area. The stream diagram provides some verification for this. Second, most of the arrows going into the social-factors stream come out of the organizing-arrangements stream, implying that, at least for this organization at this time, organizing issues were at the root of many of the difficulties in the social area. Third, most of the arrows going into the organizing-arrangements stream come from the technology stream. It appears that technological problems were highlighting the deficiencies in various aspects of the organization's structure. Finally, there also appeared to exist a considerable number of intrastream interconnections in both the technology and physical-setting streams. Problems in these areas tended to be the root causes of other problems in the same areas.

Planning. The next step in the process was to take the most central issues in the initial diagnosis and develop plans for action. Since organizational change is an organic process, planning more than a few steps into the future should be undertaken with caution. Although every effort must be made to identify as many actions as possible, expectations about being able to complete them all in the exact manner planned should be held in check. Figure 10-5 shows the initial plans developed by the director and coordinator, plans based on solving only the major problems picked out of all those identified in the diagnostic stage. Note that a time dimension is included in this diagram, showing the expected beginning and ending points for each activity and a series of lines describing the interconnections or triggers between the various actions planned.

As a first step in dealing with the key issues of uneven workload and inefficient use of NA time, a new patient holding

Figure 10-5. Stream-Analysis Framework Used for Planning Intervention.

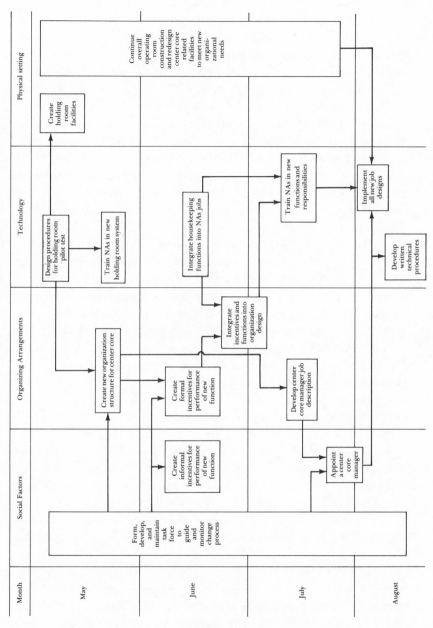

room was proposed. This room would provide a quiet environment in the immediate vicinity of the OR, could accommodate six to eight patients, and would allow the NAs to transport patients well in advance of case preparation time. Availability of NAs for exchanging case carts and assisting nurses in changing over from one case to the next could then be assured. Further analysis revealed an underutilization of housekeeping personnel whenever they worked within the OR. Janitors (or porters, as they were formally titled) spent only 30 percent of their time performing two major functions—mopping floors and carrying out soiled laundry between cases. Assumption of responsibility for these functions by the NAs would consolidate the two roles (porter and NA) into one and eliminate significant labor hours. Furthermore, the major janitorial tasks would help fill up those times of low activity and even out the workload for the NA.

Since implementing these changes required attention to all four streams, the director and coordinator both felt that it would be advisable to form a task force representing expertise in each stream, assuring a wide range of input. Such a task force could create an organizational design for the center core that would address the needs across each stream. The task force selected consisted of the director, who represented both the organizing-arrangements and social-factors streams and was the final decision maker; a head nurse and the materials management coordinator, who provided expertise in both the technology and organizing-arrangements streams; the construction coordinator, who represented the physical-setting stream; and the staff development coordinator, who provided input and support for training and skill development in the technology stream. In addition, since the change effort would involve three other departments as well—housekeeping, personnel, and management engineering—these managers were also requested to take part in planning the implementation process. It was further planned that the task force would first work on its own effectiveness before trying to generate any concrete action. Once this was done, effort would be focused on developing a design for the new organization to deal with the demands for additional service and the need for a managerial framework for center-core activities. A major part of this effort would be to bring all four streams to bear on integrating the NAs into the organizational structure in a way meaningful to them as well as effective in the overall scheme of things.

Since the task force would have as one of its goals the creation of a new organizational structure, the task-force activity in the social-factors stream would trigger a new organizational structure in the organizing-arrangements stream. Figure 10-5 represents this by connecting the two with an arrow. In the technology stream, the development of the holding room would trigger both the technical training of the NAs (technology stream) and the creation of holding-room facilities (physical-setting stream). In general, then, the planning process takes place by recognizing interconnections between boxes in the diagnostic chart and planning interventions that will deal with both the problem identified in the box and the need implied in the interconnection. Furthermore, it must be recognized that actions often trigger the need for other actions not anticipated or implied by the problem diagnosis.

Formation of the task force occurred immediately upon conclusion of the initial planning process by the director and coordinator. The stream analysis done up to this point was shared with the task force. Laying out the current situation in its streams (Figure 10-4) provided a useful introduction into the situation. Discussion and analysis of this chart, along with the planning chart (Figure 10-5), provided direction and focus and served to move the task force along quickly. Members of the task force concentrated on the streams that included their areas of expertise, bringing their ideas and proposals to the larger group for discussion. Using Figure 10-5 as a basic guide, the task force developed the details of the change effort.

Implementation. Initial discussion in the task force identified early on that one of the most significant implementation problems would be in the social-factors stream—the NAs' acceptance of and cooperation in the change process. An approach to dealing with the problem was the development of more effective work incentives and rewards. Since these would have to provide a means of enhancing the self-esteem of the

NAs, the final structural design included upward mobility for them. A two-level job structure was devised, with the higher-paying level requiring broader skills and increased responsibilities. The two levels not only included more difficult functions, such as anesthesia support and equipment care, but also contained the housekeeping chores previously held by porters. Another important aspect of this structural change was the creation of a new title for the NAs, which more closely described the work that they would be doing. Since NAs not only assisted nurses but directly supported physicians, patients, and other nonprofessional staff as well, their title was changed to operating-room assistants (ORAs). The designations ORA I and ORA II corresponded to the two new job levels. These changes were expected to provide the NAs with a clearer identity in the organization, a chance for advancement, and a validation of their worth.

Before any of the plans could be implemented, procedures had to be developed for integrating all these new tasks into a working system. After thorough study of all four streams, the staff-development and supply coordinators, along with the director, worked out the details of a preliminary work-flow design for case turnover and patient transport. Management engineering and the construction coordinator worked on providing temporary quarters for a holding room, while the head nurse coordinated efforts to organize a holding-room pilot program. When all the procedures were worked out to the satisfaction of the task force and the pilot program for the holding room had been implemented and validated, it was time to include the NAs in further development of the system. A process for sharing the new design with all affected personnel was then developed.

The preliminary work-flow design, along with proposed changes in organizational structure, was presented to all NAs at a group meeting. They were asked to try out the new job design by working in pairs with members of the nursing staff. All agreed to do it. Daily meetings were set up for evaluating and adjusting the system. Because of their extensive knowledge of the NA environment and their eagerness to learn new skills, a smooth-running system was created by the new ORAs within two weeks. The daily meetings became a permanent part of the system, providing for feedback, problem solving, and overall departmental communications. These daily meetings served to further the ORAs' feelings of identity and value within the organization.

Simultaneous with this effort was an attempt to gain final approval for a permanent holding room. Since physician support for the concept had been acquired and the goal of providing more service for less had been met, the proposal for modification of office space to contain a permanent holding room was approved by administration. Once the organizational framework encompassing the center core had been clearly laid out, the needed technical training was provided for. This left one final and vital intervention—the selection of a manager for the center core. The task force had expected that the ORAs would perceive this as a positive move but not as much more than that. The reaction was far beyond their expectations. Having a head nurse appointed as their manager brought about the ORAs' final validation as an important, integral part of the OR. Their pride and self-esteem, reinforced through this final action, was demonstrated by their enthusiasm, cooperation, and esprit de corps. The result was that the initial implementation of a critical new system occurred without interruption or compromise of patient care.

Tracking. Since implementation of the plans yielded a series of activities, some planned and some unanticipated, a stream diagram was useful in a third way—tracking the intervention activities actually implemented. This tracking document allowed the director to understand the change process more clearly and at the same time manage it more effectively to produce the desired long-term results. It showed the progress of the action plan over time, a particularly important function in this instance, because a controlling time factor existed in the physical setting—the end of construction by July 30.

Developed as the intervention unfolded, the stream diagram resulting from tracking the change activities is shown in Figure 10-6. The director regularly mapped out each action performed and classified it into its appropriate stream. The task

Figure 10-6. Stream-Analysis Framework Used for Tracking OD Interventions.

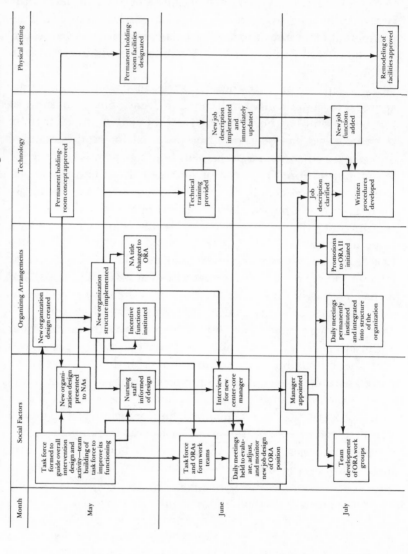

force would then refer to the stream diagram to check and analyze progress, comparing it to the original plans and noting the impact of each activity on other activities. This greatly enhanced their ability to proact rather than react, producing a smoother change process. The diagram shown here captures the most salient points so as to provide the essence without getting bogged down in all of the detail.

Tracking across the four streams also permitted spotting holes or weaknesses in the change process as it unfolded. A hole is a nonevent—a situation in which an intervention activity should have occurred but did not. Often, this was signaled by the occurrence of that missing event at some time after it should optimally have occurred. An example of this shown in Figure 10-6 is the social-factor activity of informing the nursing staff of the new organization design. In retrospect, this should have been done earlier than it was, as signaled by the reactions of the nursing staff, who resented not having been told at the same time as the NAs. Since they regarded their status as higher, they believed they deserved at least equal treatment.

A comparison of Figures 10-5 (planning chart) and 10-6 (tracking chart) shows that, although many of the planned actions were carried out, not all were actually performed, and some were not performed in the prescribed order or at the anticipated point in time. Certainly, this is consistent with the very nature of any planning process. But one of the key benefits of all plans is that they force the implementers to consider the reasons for not taking or for delaying certain actions. It is through this confrontation of plan with reality that wiser choices of action are made.

A further comparison of the two figures reveals that there were several unanticipated actions taken, some even very early on in the process—for example, presentation of the new design to both the NAs and the nursing staff. These actions were determined to be necessary for the cooperation and involvement of the two groups. Somehow, they were missed in the planning process. However, in the future, one could expect that actions such as these would be anticipated and planned for early on. This is a simple example of the type of learning that can result from carefully tracking the change process and then comparing the actual events to those that were planned.

The impact of all this real-time analysis was that the members of the OR could learn about the dynamics of their own change process and use this learning to better manage their future efforts at improving the system's functioning.

Conclusions

The stream-analytical approach proved to be a beneficial management tool in the situation described here. It was used first as a diagnostic device, then as a planning aid, and finally for tracking and managing the actual change process. In all three cases, the approach helped the manager as well as the organizational members to think more clearly about the change situation and, as a consequence, make wiser action choices. Implied in the process is a model for implementation of change by managers. The steps in this model are:

1. Lay out the existing situation and its more recent historical roots in the four streams.
2. Consider what actions will be necessary to deal with the problems represented, as well as with the interconnections between problems.
3. Plan tentative initial actions in each stream, projecting into the future as many steps as seem reasonable.
4. Form a task force and use it to flesh out and alter, if appropriate, the broad actions planned by the manager.
5. Implement the action plan.
6. Track the change process using the four-streams approach to help identify and solve problems in the implementation of the action plan.
7. Keep the stream data generated as a historical data base for assessing effectiveness and understanding the dynamics of change in the system.

Following these steps could help managers simplify the complexity of most change activities and lead them to more effectively direct the process of organization development.

References

Cummings, T. G. "Sociotechnical Experimentation: A Review of Sixteen Studies." In W. A. Pasmore and J. J. Sherwood, *Sociotechnical Systems: A Sourcebook*. La Jolla, Calif.: University Associates, 1978.

Friedlander, F., and Brown, L. D. "Organization Development." *Annual Review of Psychology*, 1974, *25*, 313-341.

Margulies, N., and Raia, A. *Conceptual Foundations of Organization Development*. New York: McGraw-Hill, 1978.

Porras, J. I., and Berg, P. O. "The Impact of Organization Development." *Academy of Management Review*, 1978, *3* (2), 249-266.

Porras, J. I., Harkness, J., and Kiebert, C. "Stream Analysis: A Method for Decomposing Organization Development Interventions." In D. D. Warrick (Ed.), *Current Developments in Organization Development*. New York: Scott, Foresman, 1983a.

Porras, J. I., Harkness, J., and Kiebert, C. "Understanding Organization Development: A Stream Approach." *Training and Development Journal*, March/April 1983b, 382-401.

Steele, F. *Physical Settings and Organization Development*. Reading, Mass.: Addison-Wesley, 1973.

White, S. E., and Mitchell, T. R. "Organization Development: A Review of Research Content and Research Design." *Academy of Management Review*, 1976, *1* (2), 57-73.

11

Organizational Development: Issues, Trends, and Prospects

Anthony P. Raia
Newton Margulies

The focus of this chapter is on organizational change and development. It is partly a progress report and partly a forecast of the future of an emerging field that at this time can be best described as a kaleidoscope of theories, approaches, techniques, and practices. Compared to most other disciplines, organization development (OD) is still an adolescent, and, like most adolescents, it has suffered growing pains. These have ranged from the usual identity crises to periods of criticism and self-doubt. This is perhaps as good a time as any to examine these developments and to assess the future of the field. As a matter of convenience, we will first examine the issues and trends that have emerged over the past decade or so, drawing rather heavily from the literature. We will then explore the prospects for the future.

Issues and Trends

In one of the first reviews of the OD literature of the early 1970s, Friedlander and Brown (1974) noted the need for a balance among rationalism, pragmatism, and existentialism in organization-development efforts. The focus at that time was

246

primarily on methods such as job design and enrichment, or what the authors called technostructural approaches, and on those that intervened in human processes. They also identified two emerging themes: (1) the characteristics of successful versus unsuccessful interventions and (2) the distinctions between the multiple interventions of a total system and ad hoc single interventions.

White and Mitchell (1976) analyzed the literature in terms of (1) the recipient of change, (2) the level of expected change (conceptual, structural), and (3) the nature of the relationships—whether they were intrapersonal or interpersonal. They reported that most OD efforts attempt to change attitudes or behavior of either individuals or groups, with a focus on relationships—intrapersonal (the individual) or interpersonal (with peers). These authors also questioned the quality of research, noting that most of it is field research, that most changes are reported in percentages without statistical comparisons, and that the data are generally collected and reported by researchers who are committed to the success of the effort.

In an update of the Friedlander and Brown review, Alderfer (1977) noted the following trends: in terms of research, (1) more sophisticated evaluation designs, (2) newer and better measuring instruments, and (3) the emergence of more sophisticated theories of change and development; in terms of practice, (1) an increase in the application of OD methods and techniques in public and not-for-profit organizations, (2) the emergence of some new techniques, and (3) greater concern about the interface between the organization and its environment. Alderfer also noted that the humanistic values of OD may be incompatible with organizational values that stress productivity and efficiency.

Porras and Berg (1978a, 1978b) identified a number of issues and trends in two separate reviews. These included (1) an increase in the use of survey feedback and process consultation and a decrease in the use of the managerial grid and (2) an increase in laboratory training, but with more of a task focus and less emphasis on process. With reference to a review of the OD research, they noted (3) that a change in process may not cause a change in outcome, (4) that task-oriented variables were affected less by OD interventions, and (5) that there was little systematic evidence supporting the efficacy of organization development.

Burke and Goodstein (1980) provided perhaps the most comprehensive review of the field as it moved into the 1980s. Utilizing a variety of sources and references, they identified a number of problems that need to be addressed, including:

1. resolving the dilemma between OD values and the concern for "bottom line"
2. developing a theory-based practice
3. measuring and documenting the impact of OD interventions
4. dealing with the poor quality of practices and practitioners, as well as the lack of adequate controls in the field
5. increasing the credibility of OD
6. dealing with the changing nature of workers and their motivation to work
7. unifying the theory of OD
8. dealing with its "faddishness"
9. organizing and managing the OD function in organizations
10. dealing with the impact of economic uncertainty, energy shortages, and environmental turbulence and uncertainty

With reference to emerging trends and prospects for the field, the authors also noted:

1. an increase in the application of systems theories and approaches
2. increasing use of OD to improve productivity and profitability
3. an increasing concern for improving the quality of working life
4. the development of more effective and systematic methods of organizational diagnosis
5. a willingness to deal with the issues of power and influence in organizations

6. an increase in the application of OD in nonbusiness organizations and domains
7. the unification and codification of theory and practice
8. the achievement of sustained, long-term change
9. more comprehensive, broad-scale interventions
10. the use of contingency theories of OD
11. more emphasis on the integration of women and minorities into organizations
12. the use of OD to improve organizational designs
13. an increase in the application of OD in international, multinational, and multicultural organizations and settings
14. the use of OD in long-run forecasting and strategic planning

Finally, in the most recent review available at the time of this writing, Faucheux, Amado, and Laurent (1982) assert that OD in the United States is becoming quality of working life (QWL), noting that many of the recent books in the field reflect a systems perspective, sociotechnical-systems analyses, and/or QWL approaches. They also note that OD research has been generally poor but has improved significantly with the advent of QWL studies beginning in the late 1970s. Furthermore, they believe that culture blindness, ethnocentrism, and the claim of universality may have plagued the field. The authors conclude that, after some twenty years of OD, the sociotechnical-systems approach offers a new paradigm and that QWL reflects a social movement. They also point to the need to cope with interorganizational domains and the need to stress the cultural and cross-cultural context of organizational change.

These reviews are both interesting and useful in that they represent a "status report" or snapshot of the field at different times over the past decade. It should be noted, however, that they were provided by different sets of authors, each with a different perspective and set of biases. Their orientations ranged from laboratory method of sociotechnical systems to quality of working life. Some of the reviews dealt with issues, some with trends, and a few with both. Some emphasized either research or practice; some emphasized both. Collectively, they represent a reasonable overview of OD during this time period.

A Survey of the Literature

In an attempt to more systematically identify and synthesize the issues confronting the field, we conducted a literature survey of approximately fifty articles published in a wide variety of journals over the past decade or so by some thirty-five different authors (Raia, 1982). The issues are summarized and discussed under the following general headings.

Paradigms, Models, and Theory. As one might suspect, most of the criticism in this area comes from academia. There appears to be a great deal of concern on the part of some academics that OD has not yet been scientifically defined, that there is no clearly identifiable and systematic body of knowledge as there is in other respectable disciplines. Furthermore, given that many different definitions currently exist, OD seems to have lost its identity as a science or an art. A number of academics are calling for new paradigms or models. They see the existing ones as being unrealistic and/or inappropriate: They are oversimplified versions of organizations and people; they tend to ignore the political realities of organizational life; and they do not reflect systems thinking or a systems perspective. As we will discuss later, we tend to disagree with much of this criticism.

Research and Assessment of OD Efforts. Related to the previous criticisms, but shared by both academics and practitioners, is a great deal of concern about evaluating the effectiveness and value of OD as an approach to change. Academics tend to be more concerned about the nature and quality of research in the field. They are concerned about poor research designs, about studies that seem to be redundant or have not been properly validated, about the lack of theory-based research, and about the fact that the effectiveness of OD is not being systematically studied. Practitioners, on the other hand, are concerned about the lack of objectives and the fuzziness of end results of OD efforts, about the lack of relevant criteria that can be used to assess the impact of OD, and about the fact that OD has not yet proved itself in terms of costs and benefits. Despite some recent progress in this area, we tend to agree with most of these criticisms.

Interventional Technology and Applications. There has been a great deal of criticism about interventional strategies and the application of OD technology by academics and practitioners alike. Many feel that OD has fallen short of its promise to address a wide range of problems and to deal with the total organizational system. The focus is generally on interpersonal relationships; many efforts seem to hinge on one device or one technique; there is an overemphasis on personal and on cultural changes without consideration of economic and technological factors. Others feel that the technology is nothing more than a tool kit, a bag of tricks to be played on the organization. They are concerned that many interventions are not tailored to fit either the problem or the organization, that they are not based on sound diagnosis. Our own view is that many of these criticisms are "old hat" and no longer true. The interventional technology has expanded rapidly and is still growing; new strategies, new approaches, and new methodologies abound; and the means for doing sound organizational diagnosis are available. Despite these advances, however, some justification for these criticisms still exists. The field does tend to be driven by the technology, many interventions are not based on sound and appropriate diagnosis, and some OD efforts are not tailored to meet the needs of the client system. We believe that these issues are due more to the shortcomings of many OD practitioners than to the shortcomings of the field.

OD as a Profession. There has been some concern, especially among academics, about the need for professionalism in the field. The status, expertise, self-discipline, and ethical codes that exist in other professions, such as medicine and law, do not exist in OD. There is no certifying agency, there are no standards for training and developing OD practitioners, and there is no systematic body of professional knowledge. We, too, see this as an issue, but one that cannot be resolved until some of the others have been addressed.

Organization and Management of the OD Function. This issue is of concern primarily to practitioners. Some feel that OD is often written off as a personnel function and, hence, is tangential to other activities. Furthermore, internal consultants often have other responsibilities that keep them from doing OD.

Some see a need to enhance the image and credibility of the function by linking it to key power figures in the hierarchy. Others advocate relating the OD effort to the organization's reward and penalty system. In our experience, these issues are very real and need to be addressed in the context of any given situation.

Values and Ethics. There has been and continues to be a great deal of concern among both academics and practitioners about OD values and ethics. Some see a basic conflict between the humanistic values of OD and organizational values that stress efficiency, productivity, and the "bottom line." Others see and experience an inconsistency between the values espoused by OD consultants and their actual behavior, and some are concerned about what they see as the lack of "informed consent" among participants in OD efforts, the misuse of confidential data by consultants, and the potential invasion of privacy that exists in many OD efforts. It is our view that the current set of OD values does *not* conflict with the values held by most modern organizations. There is a considerable amount of experience and technology available to improve both productivity and the quality of working life. Our concern, once again, is that most of these issues result from the shortcomings and behavior of OD consultants rather than from any conflict in values between the discipline and the organizations it serves.

Practitioners and Consultants. As indicated earlier, a number of the preceding issues can be traced to the shortcomings and biases of OD practitioners and consultants. Many have not been properly trained. They often have limited knowledge and experience, lack appropriate skills, and/or apply a limited number of techniques in a "tool-kit" or "bag-of-tricks" manner. Some are seen and experienced as having a poor sense of self and needing to "get their stuff together" before they can work effectively with client systems. Equally as important, perhaps, a number of critics have been concerned about the values, ethics, and/or behavior of some OD consultants. We share many of these concerns and see the training and development of practitioners as one of the keys to the future of the field. More will be said of this later.

Miscellaneous Issues and Criticisms. A number of critics have argued that OD is a fad or that it has little credibility in most organizations or that it is difficult to apply in bureaucracies and in the public and not-for-profit sectors. We believe that these are no longer relevant issues. The field has been operant for over twenty years now and is still growing. It has credibility in an increasing number of organizations, and the demand for OD has increased dramatically in public and not-for-profit organizations over the past five years or so. Another set of issues centers around the roles of and relationships between internal and external consultants and between OD consultants and their clients. The advantages and disadvantages of using internal versus external consultants have been argued extensively in the literature. Our own experience tells us that larger, longer-term projects require both. Issues around consultant-client relationships are also well documented. As with any set of relationships, these come with the territory and must be worked out in "real time," in the context of a given engagement.

A Summary Perspective

The preceding represents a collection of independent views of the field of organization development over a period of time. Many of the earlier issues seem to have been resolved, and new ones have taken their place. Some of the old ones remain to haunt us. In retrospect, the field has undergone some dramatic changes and has made considerable progress since the early 1970s. We would summarize this progress as follows:

There has been some success in dealing with many of the issues that plagued the early development of the field. These include (1) an expanded theory base, (2) an increase in both the quantity and quality of research, (3) considerable improvement in the assessment of OD efforts, and (4) more universal application of systems thinking and broader, longer-term OD projects. A variety of new approaches and strategies have emerged, including Gestalt, laboratory methods that go beyond T-groups, sociotechnical-systems analyses, and open-systems planning, to name only a few. There has been an increasing emphasis on and success in job design/redesign and QWL projects, as evidenced by the work of such people as Hackman and Oldham (1980), Walton (1978), and Goodman (1979) and the QWL projects of Louis Davis throughout the 1970s and 1980s. The values of OD have been modified to include a greater appreciation for and emphasis on efficiency and the "bottom line," as evidenced by the increasing number of productivity-QWL projects in the United States during the last five years or so.

There have been increased applications of OD in the non-business sector, especially in health care, emergency medical systems, and hospitals. There has also been a significant increase in the application of OD in multinational and multicultural settings. A wide variety of new methods and techniques continue to flood the field, including quality circles, career planning, semiautonomous work groups, the rebirth of assessment centers, stress-management programs, and the reincarnation of MBO (management by objectives), to name only a few. Unfortunately, from our perspective, at least, the field continues to be "technology driven."

Consistent with what has been happening in management and organization theory, there has been a shift in the level or unit of analysis from individuals, groups, and organizations to the organization-environment interface, interorganizational relationships, and transorganizational development. Many new conceptualizations and "fresh eyes" are now available. These include natural-selection models (Hannan and Freeman, 1977; Aldrich, 1979; McKelvey, 1982), resource-dependence models (Pfeffer and Salancik, 1978), nonrational models (Cohen, March, and Olsen, 1972; Cohen and March, 1974), self-designing systems (Hedberg, Nystrom, and Starbuck, 1976), and loosely coupled systems (Weick, 1976). Each is new and different, and each can help us to expand our view of organizational change and development. There is renewed and increasing interest in the concept of organization culture, including the development of some useful conceptual and analytical frameworks (for example, Deal and Kennedy, 1982). Related to this, there is also an increase in the use of language, metaphors, symbols, and myths to diagnose and facilitate organizational change (for example, Pfeffer, 1981).

Issues of power and politics are no longer avoided in the field. We have recently seen the development of OD models that include the concepts of power and politics (Pettigrew, 1975; Cobb and Margulies, 1981), strategies for changing the political subsystem of an organization (Tichy, 1983), and suggestions for improving the political will and skill of OD consultants (Margulies and Raia, 1984). There is an increasing interest in and better conceptual tools for dealing with the issues related to the management of organizational transitions (Beckhard and Harris, 1977; Kimberly and Quinn, 1984), implementation and institutionalization processes (Zucker, 1977; Goodman, Conlon, and Bazerman, 1978), and long-term organizational change (Goodman and Associates, 1982). There has been a continuous redefinition and expansion of the role of OD practitioners and consultants, which was narrowly focused on process facilitation, to include Weick's (1982) conceptual theory and the political orientations of Margulies and Raia (1984).

Finally, a word about technology. The continuing proliferation of sophisticated technology in a variety of fields, including microelectronics, information, and computer hardware and software, will provide a major focal point for OD efforts in the future. The change-management efforts that are driven by new technological developments are likely to challenge all of us to become more aware of the potential impacts of technological change. Projections are that organizational configurations and the nature of management in the future are likely to emerge from the requirements and demands of new technology.

A Study of the Future of OD

In the first section of this chapter, the issues confronting the field of organization development were extrapolated from the literature—specifically, from those writings that have been devoted to this focus. In this section, we are presenting in summary fashion a perspective on the future of the field, derived primarily from the results of a recent study with that focused intent.

There have been a number of different views and differing opinions about the future of organization development as a field. In the recent past, some theoreticians speculated that, in fact, organization development was in the throes of a steady demise. Some more recent views, based on a Delphi study, seem to indicate otherwise (Shepard and Raia, 1981, 1982). This study provided a detailed empirical basis for this projection. The research, which was completed at UCLA, looked at the various issues confronting organization development in the future and at various possible futures for the field.

The Delphi study was conducted in three different iterations with a panel of seventy organization-development academics and practitioners, including both internal and external consultants, some based at universities and others with OD practice as their primary occupation. The practicing professionals employed a variety of approaches to organization development. The overall profile represented both men and women, with various levels of experience in the field and emphasis on different arenas of application in both public and private organizations of various sizes.

In general, the study projected an increase in the demand for OD activities in the future (see Figure 11-1). The greatest increases in demand seem to be in organizations that have not yet made maximum use of OD technology. For example, these include health care organizations and organizations primarily in the high-technology research and development arenas. It appears that there will be less demand in manufacturing and educational institutions, including colleges, universities, and school systems. Additionally, it appears that the greatest demand will be in large multinational organizations that are confronted by the complexities of change, geographical dispersion, and the need to function in multicultural settings.

The study also dealt with the perceived effectiveness of OD technology, the perceived level of professional skills being employed by practitioners, and the perceived quality of research currently being conducted in the field. The panel indicated a relatively low level of perceived effectiveness (see Figure 11-2). There was some concern that, with increase in demand by the year 2000, organization development will not be effectively applied or utilized so as to maximize the outcomes of established technologies.

**Figure 11-1. Organizational Trends Expected to Affect
Future Demand for OD.**

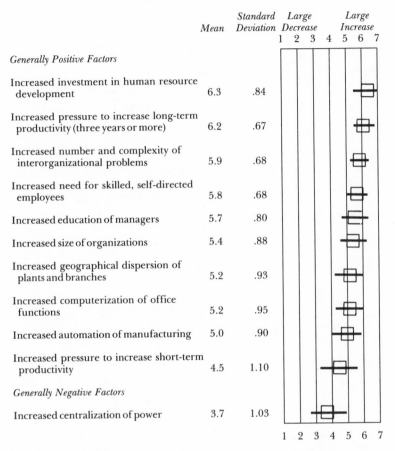

	Mean	Standard Deviation	Large Decrease 1 2 3 4	Large Increase 5 6 7
Generally Positive Factors				
Increased investment in human resource development	6.3	.84		
Increased pressure to increase long-term productivity (three years or more)	6.2	.67		
Increased number and complexity of interorganizational problems	5.9	.68		
Increased need for skilled, self-directed employees	5.8	.68		
Increased education of managers	5.7	.80		
Increased size of organizations	5.4	.88		
Increased geographical dispersion of plants and branches	5.2	.93		
Increased computerization of office functions	5.2	.95		
Increased automation of manufacturing	5.0	.90		
Increased pressure to increase short-term productivity	4.5	1.10		
Generally Negative Factors				
Increased centralization of power	3.7	1.03		

As indicated in Figure 11-3, the panelists also seemed to believe that increased dissemination of information about the effectiveness of OD programs might, in fact, change this existing perception. Moreover, they indicated great concern over the quality of professional training and the need for increased sharing of OD practices and outcomes, which are now considered proprietary by many organizations. There also seems to be a significant need for modifying and developing theories of organizational change and development that fit various industries, cultures, and organizational types.

Figure 11-2. Evaluation of OD's Overall Effectiveness and
Future Demand for OD Services.

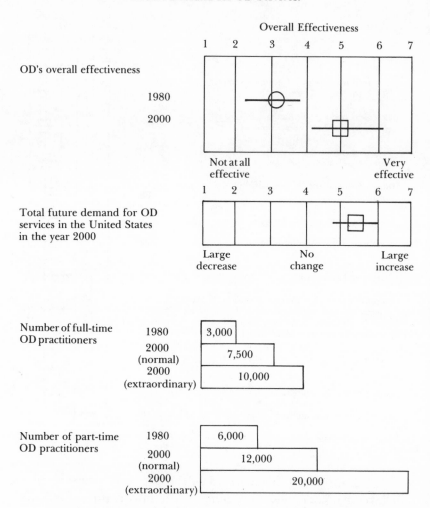

With regard to the quality of organization-development efforts and the training of OD professionals, the study indicated the need for the development of a set of "core skills" that should be designed and utilized in the training of practitioners (see Figure 11-4). The reasons, as established by the panelists, include the need to increase the level of practitioner competence,

Figure 11-3. Predicted Impact of Efforts to Increase Demand
for OD Services.

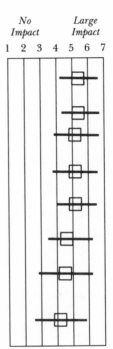

	No Impact				Large Impact		
	1	2	3	4	5	6	7

Increase advocacy and dissemination of information
about the effectiveness of OD programs

Increase the quality of professional training

Increase corporate sharing of OD practices and
research now considered proprietary

Increase development of OD theory to fit different
industry and organization contexts

Increase the quality and quantity of OD research
and evaluation

Increase greatly the number of competent
OD practitioners

Increase the ease with which clients can
identify competence in OD practitioners
(accreditation)

Establish a quality, well-enforced code of
ethical practice

the need to provide experience-based professionals who can use new technologies effectively, and the need to improve the overall image of the field. While some panelists disagreed with this general thrust, the primary reasons for this disagreement center around the inability of the experts to agree on which particular skills would be most useful as a core set.

The major categories of core skills include general consultation skills, such as organizational diagnosis, process consultation, and the design and execution of intervention strategies. Additionally, many of the core skills evolve around a basic knowledge of organizational behavior, including organizational theory, group dynamics, organizational design, communication

Figure 11-4. Factors Affecting Establishment of Set of Core OD Skills.

The Proposition

A set of core skills should be designed for the field	Agree	78%	
	Neutral	10%	
	Disagree	12%	

	Mean	Standard Deviation	Importance of Factor
			None 1 2 3 4 Very high 5 6 7

Reasons for Establishing a Set of Core Skills

To increase the level of practitioner competence in the field — 5.35 — 1.35

To provide good grounding so that practitioners can then pick up and use new technologies with understanding and skill — 5.14 — 1.40

To provide a rational basis for the systematic design of a curriculum — 4.71 — 1.36

To socialize new OD practitioners to the field and to establish a lifelong learning set — 4.47 — 1.53

To improve the field's public image and indirectly to increase the demand for OD services — 4.33 — 1.51

To protect individual clients from harm and organizations from financial loss — 4.29 — 1.71

Reasons Against Establishing a Set of Core Skills

Established core skills may become a means to restrict entrance to the field — 3.84 — 1.98

OD experts cannot agree on a set of core skills that can be taught in a reasonable amount of time — 3.56 — 1.73

Much useful OD work can be done by specially trained OD paraprofessionals who do not need training in OD core skills — 3.21 — 1.71

Established core skills would tend to stifle creativity and exploration in the years while the field is still young — 2.92 — 1.79

The field is richer if each academic program invents its own set of core skills to fit its perception of demand and its teaching resources — 2.92 — 1.82

theories, and other like subjects. There was also considerable emphasis on the development of interpersonal skills as a basis for effective consultation with clients. The two most critical, in our opinion, are (1) individual development specifically in conceptual and analytical ability and (2) the ability to theorize and build models that are experience based. The study seems to indicate that knowledge of research and evaluation was seen to be a vital area for development of the future OD practitioners. It is our view that the field has been exceptionally sparse in the development of new conceptual models and theories of change. For the most part, practitioners have become more interested in application, with very little reflection and theory building based on the outcomes of their interventions. One reason for this is that research skills and theory-building skills are generally neglected in educational programs directed at the training of OD professionals. Unfortunately, this area of development has been left primarily to the academicians, and the separation between theory and practice continues to be exacerbated. Given the complexity of organization-development practice and the need for organizational change in the future, the development of these skills as part of the basic education of future OD professionals is essential.

Related to the question of basic education for OD professionals is the panel's estimate that only 20 percent of all those currently practicing organization development as a profession have received excellent training; 36 percent were judged to be acceptable, and, more importantly, 43 percent were judged to have received inadequate training and supervised practice. There was a general feeling that too much of current practice involves incompetent responses on the part of OD professionals. This includes a sometimes narrow and inaccurate diagnosis of the situation, the utilization of incorrect interventions, the application of improper OD technologies, and, most importantly, an incorrect and inaccurate understanding of the organizational realities confronting the client system. The impact of such behaviors can be critical—not only for the client per se but also for the image of the field. Given this perspective, there is a strong need to develop more effective educational and training programs. In general, the panel seemed to concur that university-based programs tend to be more effective than those offered commercially or those conducted in-house.

The panelists also expressed concerns about the quality and quantity of organization-development research (see Figure 11-5). Overall, there are moderately negative perceptions about

Figure 11-5. Quality and Quantity of OD Research.

Type of Research		Mean	Standard Deviation	Low 1 2 3 4 5 6 7 High
Implementation research	Quality	3.83	1.32	
	Quantity	3.84	1.38	
Assessment research	Quality	3.08	1.35	
	Quantity	2.77	1.33	
Evaluation research	Quality	3.01	1.15	
	Quantity	2.90	1.15	
Theory-building research	Quality	2.90	1.44	
	Quantity	2.51	1.27	

the quality and quantity of research on the implementation of strategic interventions. In addition, there is agreement that the field has been clearly deficient in evaluating the impacts of OD efforts and in accumulating empirical information leading to improved theories. The panel stressed the importance to the field of continued development of an empirical base for evaluating the multiple impacts of organization-development interventions (see Figure 11-6). In general, the work of OD practitioners reported in the journals was seen to be somewhat qualitative and anecdotal in approach. The field has not made use of more rigorous quantitative techniques for evaluating the various impacts and variables associated with organizational change and development. Several suggestions designed to improve organiza-

Figure 11-6. Importance of Progress in OD Research.

	Mean	Standard Deviation	Importance None to High (1 2 3 4 5 6 7)
Type of Research			
Assessment research	5.13	1.49	
Implementation research	5.11	1.52	
Theory-building research	5.09	1.65	
Evaluation research	4.79	1.49	

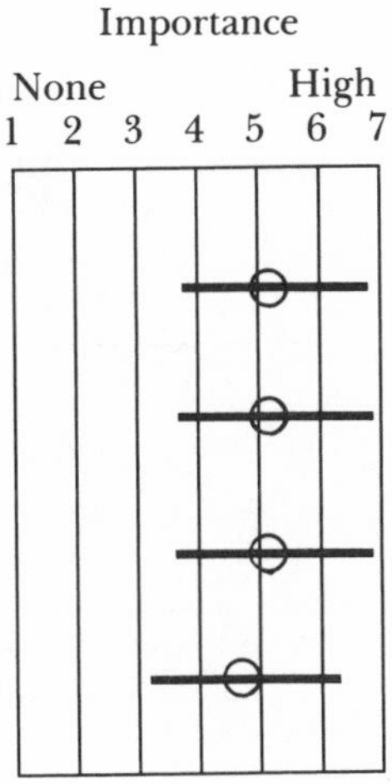

tion-development research were identified. For example, there was reasonable agreement that there needs to be increased motivation for organizations to participate in and to support research efforts. In addition, even when research information is available, organizations tend to protect such data because of real or imagined competitive advantages that they feel would be lost in the publication of the work. The study also indicates the need to encourage the development of academic researchers who also understand the organizational change and development process.

With regard to theory and research, the most critical need seems to be the improvement of the overall education of OD professionals, such that there is a greater appreciation for the quality of empirical data associated with their practice. If, in fact, research can be viewed as an integral part of an OD learning process rather than as a separate and distinct (sometimes adversarial) one, both the quantity and quality of available research information may be enhanced. There also appears to be some concern that a large number of current OD practitioners come from the less quantitative disciplines and, therefore, do not appreciate or understand the value of more sophisticated quantitatively oriented research designs.

Finally, as indicated in Table 11-1, the panelists identified several high-priority research projects that could enhance OD theory and knowledge. These include emphases on the na-

Table 11-1. Activities with Potential to Improve OD Research.

	Potential Contribution to OD Research	
	Mean[a]	Standard Deviation
Finding ways to increase motivation for organizations to participate in OD research	5.81	1.22
Increasing financial resources for OD research	5.64	1.36
Finding ways to encourage organizations to share OD project data they now consider proprietary	5.64	1.36
Improving the quality of training for academic OD researchers	5.39	1.27
Sponsoring careful planning of OD research agendas	5.19	1.33
Improving research measurement processes and procedures	5.19	1.34
Establishing OD centers that combine practice, teaching, and research	5.16	1.47
Enlisting the support of industry trade associations in OD research	5.03	1.39
Investing effort in operationalizing theoretical concepts of change	4.91	1.54
Improving research designs for external reliability	4.79	1.31
Increasing the number of academic OD researchers	4.75	1.69
Improving research designs for internal reliability	4.66	1.30
Increasing research training for OD practitioners in OD master's degree programs	4.64	1.45
Developing simplified evaluation research modules that most OD practitioners could use with little formal training	4.59	1.73
Publishing textbooks on OD research and evaluation	4.29	1.43
Improving statistical procedures used to analyze OD intervention data	4.23	1.65
Establishing new journals to publish all varieties of OD research	4.02	1.56

[a]A seven-point Likert scale was used, with 1 representing the lowest contribution and 7 the highest.

ture and impacts of various organizational designs, the settings and contexts for different OD interventions, ways of implementing new plant design and start-up, the effective training of OD practitioners, new models of organizational change, and OD's impacts on and relationships to strategic planning.

Prospects for the Future

In recent years, there has been a growing interest in and concern for the development of models and methods that enable systemwide change. Methods that encompass the socio-technical-systems approach and have a total organizational focus are common. At the operational level, however, many of the efforts at total system change really incorporate the methodology that has been proliferated that is directed at either the individual, the group, or the small organization. While the analytical tools are available for viewing organizations as larger systems, the operational tools for change and development have not developed at an equal pace.

Although these approaches have been common, they are likely to expand with the continuation of the philosophy of decentralization, which has resulted in the breakup of many large organizational systems. An example in this regard is AT&T's recent divestiture. It is also clear that many organizations will continue to grow as a result of acquisitions and mergers, particularly in the newer fields and in industries related to information, biomedical engineering, microelectronics, and computers. In these cases, continued emphasis will be placed on the OD technology that will facilitate the coexistence of different cultures. There is also likely to be continued emphasis on international and multinational organizations. With rapid changes in communications technology and travel and the differential in the costs of labor and technology, this development is highly probable.

What seems clear is that there is a new avenue for study and a new phenomenon emerging from the dispersion of larger systems. For example, the emergency medical system (EMS), while in some sense an organization, is in reality a network of various organizations with different self-interests and different functions that make up the total delivery service of emergency care. In the EMS system, there are relationships among ambulance companies, base-station hospitals, paramedical units, state and local agencies, and the American Medical Association chapters in particular areas. This multifaceted organization may be described as a *social network*. Network behavior is of growing interest in the social sciences and will in the near future become an interest in the field of organization development. The techniques for network analysis are not yet developed enough for organization-development practitioners to make use of them, but this seems to be an area of great promise. Furthermore, the understanding of network behavior and the management of networks, as well as the processes of network change, will also become an area of growing interest and an increasingly important part of organization-development technology.

New Conceptual Developments for the Field. A number of new conceptualizations or models that have appeared in the literature may be of some assistance to the field of organization development. For example, there are a number of *nonrational* models and also a number of *adaptive* models. Nonrational models recognize that there are severe limitations on the complete rational cycle of choice in organizations. "Garbage-can" models, for example (Cohen, March, and Olsen, 1972), view organizations as streams of problems, solutions, participants, and choice opportunities that intermingle and produce a decision of some sort. Decisions, then, are not due to certain unambiguous and rational processes. Cohen and March (1974) have also viewed organizations as organized anarchies, where preferences of organizational members are often problematical, where technology is unclear, and where participation in the system is random and fluid. Adaptive models have also appeared in the literature. Self-designing systems are an illustration of an adaptive model. Hedberg, Nystrom, and Starbuck (1976) view self-designing systems as organizations that are designed on the basis of fluidity and mobility rather than permanence. In addition to this aversion to permanence, in order to adapt through self-design, the organization must unlearn yesterday. Self-

designing organizations value improvization rather than fore-
casts, look for opportunities rather than dwell on constraints,
value impermanence rather than permanence, experiment rather
than seek final solutions, and encourage rather than discourage
contradictions. Loosely coupled systems (Weick, 1976) are another form of adaptive model. In loosely coupled systems, relationships among members are sudden rather than continuous,
occasional rather than constant, negligible rather than significant, indirect rather than direct, and eventual rather than immediate. These raw conceptualizations challenge the field and
raise a number of interesting questions. For example, how can
we better integrate these perspectives, conceptual models, and
methods and apply them to the theoretical mainstream? What
are the limits of rationality in our field? How can we create and
maintain a balance or a healthy tension between rational and
nonrational organization-development processes?

*The Movement Toward the Process of Organizational
Transition.* The area of organizational transition tends to be of
growing interest to the field of organization development. A
variety of approaches and perspectives seem to currently exist
in the literature. One approach tends to emphasize the detailed
planning process for the implementation of change over some
significant period of ambiguity and flux. This is essentially the
approach of Beckhard and Harris (1977). The value of this perspective is that it emphasizes the necessity for detailed planning
of the implementation of the change process from one state to
the next and that it recognizes the distinctive longer-range period of organizational transition that is not generally common to
other approaches to organization development. This approach,
in essence, conceptualizes the management of the transitional
state.

The Kimberly and Quinn (1984) volume *Managing Organizational Transition* presents a number of other perspectives
that more clearly differentiate common approaches to organizational change and development from the newer perspectives
on organizational transitions. In essence, the core or central
ideas that emerge in this volume are (1) that organizational transition differs from organizational change in the sense that transi-

tional management requires *fundamental* and *major* changes in organizational culture or strategic positions and (2) that organizational transitions emphasize the importance of environmental scanning and the fact that organizations are indeed imbedded in an active and reactive environment. Organizational transition promises to be both a new direction and an addition to the field of organization development. It emphasizes the need for technology that incorporates a process of environmental scanning and basic culture change into the technology of organization development, which may require new approaches and methods to help manage the transitional state.

Power and Politics in Organization Development. The field is likely to increase its awareness of and interest in the dynamics of power and organizational politics and their impact on the processes of organizational change and development. There is a growing perspective that organization development is, in fact, a political process in and of itself. Consequently, the need for conceptual tools to better understand the nature of political systems and the role of the organization-development professional in analyzing and changing them will be of paramount importance. Some additional ideas around the changing role of the OD professional will be presented later. At this point, it is sufficient to say that theories of political action and theories of change that encompass the political system of the organization will become more and more prominent and important to the professional development of the field in the coming years.

Cultural Analysis as a Facet of Organization Development. There is a renewed interest in organizational culture as an important facet of the field of organizational behavior and as an important ingredient in understanding the processes of organizational change. Culture has recently become not only a factor in the process of change but the *target* of change itself. Previously, we have discussed the growing importance of transition management, defined as a major fundamental change in the organization. Culture change fits into this category. With this renewed interest, there is also some impetus for the development of refined tools for the analysis of culture dimensions that have been largely peripheral for some time. For example, our increased knowledge about the use of organizational myths, symbols, and metaphors has suddenly added increased understanding and dimensionality to the definition and nature of organizational culture. These areas are discussed in some detail elsewhere in this volume.

Redefinition and Expansion of the Role of OD Professional. Traditionally, the role of the OD consultant has been rather narrowly focused on counseling and/or facilitating data collection, diagnosis, and planned-change processes. Now, however, we see a clear need for a redefinition and expansion of the role of OD practitioners. This would include, for example, the function of *conceptual therapist*. The conceptual therapist provides a conceptual framework not previously applied to a given situation. He or she articulates confusion and acts as a grammarian, giving people rules for tying together and labeling parts of their experience; he or she also consolidates, edits, and repunctuates the language given to him or her and gives it back in different form. The conceptual therapist directs attention, asks questions, manages language, tells stories, and does a myriad of other activities besides facilitate. The role of the OD consultant can also be expanded to include activities that may best be described by the phrase *power broker*. The idea that organization development can be thought of as a power-equalization process and, indeed, that change often requires the redistribution of organizational power means that the OD professional is often in the center of such efforts and in this sense is in the role of power broker. He or she uses power and influence to facilitate the redistribution of organizational power to the ultimate benefit of the organizational system and its members.

We have tried to indicate briefly the possible new directions for the field of organization development. The label itself may undergo some change as we proceed to the next decade. These changes are really modifications to a field that is becoming more solidly grounded in the conceptual and empirical base from which such emerging developments can come to fruition. We project continued and exciting changes in the field, ones that will add to both the depth of theoretical understanding and the effectiveness of professional applications.

References

Alderfer, C. P. "Organization Development." *Annual Review of Psychology,* 1977, *28,* 197-223.

Aldrich, H. E. *Organizations and Environments.* Englewood Cliffs, N.J.: Prentice-Hall, 1979.

Beckhard, R., and Harris, R. T. *Organizational Transitions: Managing Complex Change.* Reading, Mass.: Addison-Wesley, 1977.

Burke, W. W., and Goodstein, L. D. (Eds.). *Trends and Issues in OD: Current Theory and Practice.* San Diego, Calif.: University Associates, 1980.

Cobb, A. T., and Margulies, N. "Organization Development: A Political Perspective." *Academy of Management Review,* 1981, *6* (1), 49-59.

Cohen, M. D., and March, J. G. *Leadership and Ambiguity: The American College President.* New York: McGraw-Hill, 1974.

Cohen, M. D., March, J. G., and Olsen, J. P. "A Garbage Can Model of Organizational Choice." *Administrative Science Quarterly,* 1972, *17,* 1-25.

Deal, T. E., and Kennedy, A. A. *Corporate Cultures: The Rites and Rituals of Corporate Life.* Reading, Mass.: Addison-Wesley, 1982.

Faucheux, C., Amado, G., and Laurent, A. "Organization Development and Change." *Annual Review of Psychology,* 1982, *33,* 343-370.

Friedlander, F., and Brown, L. D. "Organization Development." *Annual Review of Psychology,* 1974, *25,* 313-341.

Goodman, P. S. *Assessing Organizational Change: The Rushton Quality of Work Experiment.* New York: Wiley-Interscience, 1979.

Goodman, P. S., and Associates. *Change in Organizations: New Perspectives on Theory, Research, and Practice.* San Francisco: Jossey-Bass, 1982.

Goodman, P. S., Conlon, E., and Bazerman, M. "Institutionalization of Planned Organizational Change." In B. M. Staw and L. L. Cummings (Eds.), *Research in Organizational Behavior.* Vol. 2. Greenwich, Conn.: JAI Press, 1978.

Hackman, J. R., and Oldham, G. R. *Work Redesign.* Reading, Mass.: Addison-Wesley, 1980.

Hannan, M. T., and Freeman, J. "The Population Ecology of Organizations." *American Journal of Sociology,* 1977, *82,* 929-965.

Hedberg, B. L., Nystrom, P. C., and Starbuck, W. H. "Camping on Seesaws: Prescription for a Self-Designing Organization." *Administrative Science Quarterly,* 1976, *21,* 41-65.

Kimberly, J. R., and Quinn, R. E. (Eds.). *Managing Organizational Transition.* Homewood, Ill.: Irwin, 1984.

McKelvey, W. *Organizational Systematics: Taxonomy, Evolution, Classification.* Berkeley: University of California Press, 1982.

Margulies, N., and Raia, A. P. "Developing a Political Perspective for the OD Professional." *Training and Development Journal,* 1984, *38* (8), 20-26.

Pettigrew, A. M. "Toward a Political Theory of Organizational Intervention." *Human Relations,* 1975, *3,* 191-208.

Pfeffer, J. "Management as Symbolic Action: The Creation and Maintenance of Organizational Paradigms." In L. L. Cummings and B. M. Staw (Eds.), *Research in Organizational Behavior.* Vol. 3. Greenwich, Conn.: JAI Press, 1981.

Pfeffer, J., and Salancik, G. R. *The External Control of Organizations: A Resource Dependence Perspective.* New York: Harper & Row, 1978.

Porras, J. I., and Berg, P. O. "Evaluation Methodology in OD: An Analysis and Critique." *Journal of Applied Behavioral Science,* 1978a, *14,* 151-173.

Porras, J. I., and Berg, P. O. "The Impact of Organization Development." *Academy of Management Review,* 1978b, *3* (2), 249-266.

Raia, A. P. "Issues and Trends in OD." Unpublished manuscript, Graduate School of Management, University of California at Los Angeles, 1982.

Shepard, K., and Raia, A. P. "Report to the Delphi Panel." Unpublished manuscript, Graduate School of Management, University of California at Los Angeles, 1981.

Shepard, K., and Raia, A. P. "The OD Training Challenge." *Training and Development Journal,* 1982, *36* (4), 90-96.

Tichy, N. M. *Managing Strategic Change.* New York: Wiley-Interscience, 1983.

Walton, R. "Teaching an Old Dog New Tricks." *Wharton Magazine,* Winter 1978, pp. 38–46.

Weick, K. E. "Educational Organizations as Loosely-Coupled Systems." *Administrative Science Quarterly,* 1976, *21,* 1–19.

Weick, K. E. "Management of Organizational Change Among Loosely-Coupled Elements." In P. S. Goodman and Associates, *Change in Organizations: New Perspectives on Theory, Research, and Practice.* San Francisco: Jossey-Bass, 1982.

White, S. E., and Mitchell, T. R. "Organization Development: A Review of Research Content and Research Design." *Academy of Management Review,* 1976, *1* (2), 57–73.

Zucker, L. G. "The Role of Institutionalization in Cultural Persistence." *American Sociological Review,* 1977, *42,* 726–743.

12

The Realities of Leadership

Will McWhinney

I begin with a tale. I have been working with the government of a Middle Eastern country to devise a governance system for two model cities constructed by American civil-engineering firms. A temporary organization has been created to supervise the transition from construction to operation of the living cities. This organization has a dual structure, with each position of responsibility filled by both an employee of the construction firms, with the general title of manager, and a member of the local population, with the general title of director. Thus, firms provide a program manager, managers, and deputy managers, while the local people, who are being trained to operate and maintain the cities, have the equivalent positions of director general, directors, and deputy directors. Although these titles are intended to illustrate the equivalence of the positions, the actual roles are quite different. The managers are action oriented—they make things happen; while the directors' role is more that of authorizing actions. These roles are appropriate for the moment, for they reflect the roles the participants have actually been playing.

The choice of names—manager and director—intrigued me. The program manager said that the naming had evolved accidentally: their own titles were pre-established, and the nationals often used the director titles. I don't believe in acci-

273

dents. The naming seemed to parallel a profound difference in the organizational views of the two cultures. To satisfy my curiosity, I searched for a person who would have insight into both the American and the host cultures, and I located an Armenian who had traveled the world in engineering projects. He called my attention to the role in the British colonial governments of the director general—the crown's representative in the colony, the personification of the government, the British presence. And it was with the British that this kingdom had had its first contacts with modern management and governance.

Pursuing this clue led me to see that the two organizations—the construction contractor and the new governance group—provide very different forms of leadership. One, the directorship model, is based on a monistic world view. The director's role is to carry out the dictates of the monarch as his or her extension. The other, the management model, is based on a pluralistic world view. The manager's role is to allocate properly the resources for which he or she is responsible, indicating a strong relationship among the world view, the form of leadership, and the form of organization. This observation heightened my sensitivity to the deep connection of our behavior with our world views and, more specifically, with our concepts of reality, identifying the systematic relations between the views of reality one holds and the leadership style one uses. The articulation of this relation forms the basic thesis of this chapter. Explicitly, the *styles of leadership* used by leaders are a reflection of the *concepts of reality* held by those leaders and supported by their cultures.

From this thesis, a theory of leadership is derived, based on an understanding of how alternative realities lead to different patterns of leadership. My purpose here is to develop this theory and to display the leadership styles that emerge from an examination of the alternative realities that occur in a society. The power of this theory is evident in the great range of leadership styles that it uncovers. Most significantly, this model includes monistic styles that I identify with charismatic, prophetic, and entrepreneurial leadership—types seldom included in a list of styles. The power is also revealed by an examination of the relation between the followers' styles and the types of organization that emerge. The theory also leads to new insights into bureaucratic structure and the relation of leadership to creativity, topics that will not be examined here.

Alternative Realities

Some years ago, in an attempt to understand the sources of conflict that lead to major issues in human society, I came to the conclusion that the source of much human conflict is the differing views of reality held by the parties. Following Lawrence LeShan's (1976) *Alternative Realities,* I developed a typology of alternative realities espoused by people in Western cultures, if not in all cultures. This proved to be a useful model for studying conflict. Discussion of this conceptualization led to a corresponding model of alternative forms of leadership. In order to display these new insights about leadership, I first need to introduce in skeletal form the realities model. A fuller presentation of this model is given in McWhinney (1984).

LeShan identified four concepts of reality, based on historical and psychological insights. In an attempt to further delineate their qualities, I developed a theoretical model from which to derive the properties of these realities. The model is represented by a two-dimensional field selected so as to distinguish sharply the characteristics LeShan attributed to his four realities (see Figure 12-1). My formulation did not exactly at-

Figure 12-1. Alternative Realities.

	Unity ⟵⟶ Multiplicity	
No Free Will	Unitary (clairvoyant)	Sensory
Free Will	Mythic	Social (transpsychic)

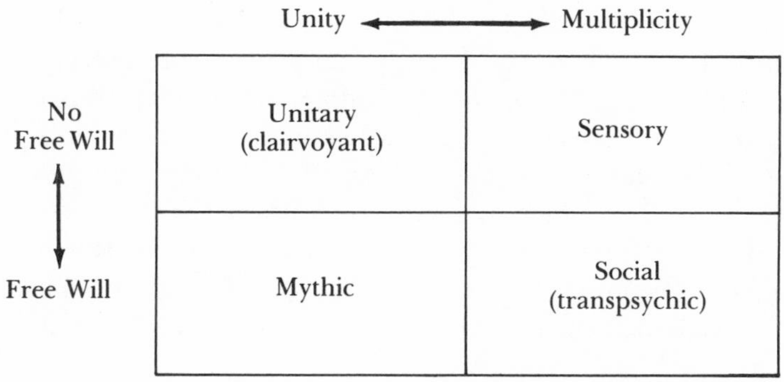

tain this goal, but it did extend his concept in a fruitful manner. To indicate the distinguishing differences, I have changed two of the names he gave to the realities.

The first of the dimensions is the monistic-pluralistic dimension mentioned earlier in relation to the difference between director and manager in the Middle Eastern city government. Properly, there are only two points on this dimension, for it is a dichotomy of one and many. However, I am treating it as varying continuously from unity to "almost a unity" (coexisting with at least one "other world") to being divided into an infinity of things and objects.

The second dimension is *freedom of will*: the freedom to make the world the way we wish it to be. At one extreme, we feel that there is no freedom whatsoever—everything is predetermined by a supreme being or natural laws. Such a concept of reality may be held by a deeply spiritual person as well as by an empirical scientist. At the other extreme, we believe that there is total freedom of will, that we can accomplish anything we wish. We can see this view expressed in solipsism and, more moderately, in the creative artist and charismatic leader. We can envision various degrees of freedom along a continuum between the extremes.

The extreme regions of these two dimensions define four types of realities, with intermediate strength of beliefs lying between the extremes. The characteristics of these four world views are deducible more or less formally from their positions on the underlying dimensions. These characteristics are sufficiently close to those proposed by LeShan that I use his name for two quadrants. The others I renamed to suggest less extreme forms than did LeShan's names (shown in parentheses in Figure 12-1). There are a great many personal characteristics deducible from the model, providing rich descriptions of the stereotypical person who has chosen or was born to live close to one of the realities. Some of these characteristics are indicated in Figure 12-2, which is a reproduction of the feedback sheet for the Realities Inquiry, a paper-and-pencil instrument designed to measure the relative strength of a person's beliefs. (Interested readers may obtain copies of the Realities Inquiry

Figure 12-2. Descriptions and Positions from the Realities Inquiry.

Name_____   Date _____

feel very much a part of everything I am involved in. I am loyal, likely to stay in the organizations which I have joined. Trust in something beyond myself, in an idea, an organization, in God, is important to me.

feel the world to be a complex, continuous single event. All divisions, classifications and separations are arbitary.

When things are going well I feel joy, connected and, at times, very peaceful, at one with with world.

The first question for me is what to do, not a lot of whys.

hold deeply to the truth, not worrying about other's values; the worst thing is people being divisive, wanting to tear things apart.

like to be practical and immediate, to get work done whether I am in charge or following another's direction.

I see the world as filled with an infinity of things. History and the future are important to me. I want to know about the world, to understand it and to anticipate what will happen.

I read, analyze and validate what I think, using facts and the opinions of other people.

I like to know how things work and what causes what.

I feel good when I know where I am, what is coming up for me and when I know I can handle it. I like feeling competent, grounded.

The important criterion for me is "does it work?"

I take an objective view of the world. Either, I tend to like the sciences and technology, believing they are very useful, or I am very much into the senses, enjoying an intensity of visual, tactile and taste impressions.

The world is a wondrous place in which I can organize and create just about anything I want. It's just a matter of intent.

I am self-starting and believe if something good is to happen for me that I ought to go out and make it happen.

I am playful, I enjoy power, but some people see me as caprious, a bit unreliable.

I am very concerned about how I act because I know I can make a difference in the lives of others.

I am inventive. I like to take charge, to create new activities, businesses, events, and so on.

My world is richly connected; everything seems to be relatable to everything else, but everyone sees the connections differently.

I am very much aware of the variety of needs that we all have. Sometimes I can see each person in his or her separate needs; sometimes all I can see is the over-all picture of a country or mankind.

I like being involved in deep change— in my life, or in society's. But being so involved I sometimes find the world heavy

I can feel awe and majesty and excitement. I am not often serene or peaceful.

Moral issues bother me. I am not sure of where my responsibilities begin and end.

I am an inquirer. I like big issues and questions, and I work at understanding other people.

UNITARY

SENSORY

MYTHIC

SOCIAL

Source: Copyright Enthusion Inc., 1981.

from the author.) Other characteristics, less relevant to the present discussion, are displayed in Appendix 12-1. No one could exist who lives and behaves exclusively within any of the extreme positions; there must be some admixture of determinism and free will and some practical realization of plurality. So these stereotypical descriptions are of people whose behavior is dominated by one concept of reality, with other beliefs determining their behaviors to much lesser degrees.

In addition to a few characterizing comments, I will describe each type in terms of five aspects particularly relevant to the leadership behavior that a person holding those beliefs would display: (1) concepts of change, (2) modes of action, (3) criteria for choosing an action, (4) sense of responsibility, and (5) relations to other people. Following are characteristics of people who behave from these four views of realities, including those related to the five aspects.

Sensory. I begin with the sensory reality, for it is the most familiar. It is what we most often associate with the term *reality.* It is the belief system that allows us to have confidence in the permanence of "stuff" and the common laws of nature. It is essential to our bodily survival and our creature comforts. Examples of the sensory person include the empirical scientist and the engineer but also the practical person on the street and the gourmand—all those who are primarily interested in sensing what is "out there."

> *Concepts of change.* In the extreme, there is no possibility of making changes in the sensory world—it is all predetermined. There would be no reason to select any particular redirection. For the practical sensory person, change is reification, making what must be.
> *Action mode.* This is anticipation in order to select among futures.
> *Criterion.* Does it work?
> *Responsibility.* Lacking free will, there is no moral responsibility. However, the observed behavior indicates a response to a "technological imperative," to doing what must be done, effectively and efficiently.

Relation to others. The basic relation is one of use. A relation is chosen on the basis of how well it will contribute to one's work. Like all relations, if viewed in
the small, it will appear self-serving; if viewed on a
grand scale, it appears to make contributions to humanity.

Social. The social reality, in combination with the sensory, forms the pre-eminent American reality. The social reality
is based on values, not the "stuff" of the sensory world. Persons
holding to a social world view are concerned with the relations
among the values held by themselves and others. The near-pure
social viewpoint leads to paralysis, for one can never decide
among conflicting evaluations of alternatives. Social reality supports an interest in social philosophies, moral causes, and engagement with others for shared anguish and enjoyment.

Concepts of change. Change is fundamental to the social
belief, for there is a continual need to rebalance the
values. For a person of a social world view, change is
the essence of life—in the natural course of life and
death, in social movements, and in grand evolution.
Action mode. The mode here is interactive.
Criteria. Is it fair? Does it support interdependence?
Responsibility. The joint condition of free will and
pluralism creates a world in which there are a multitude of individuals with volitions of their own, each
able to affect the world according to his or her power.
Thus, each is responsible for the other. This is the reality of moral responsibility.
Relation to others. Shared valuing is central to the social
reality. Thus, relations with others are the source of
value, of liveliness. Engagement per se is valued, whether in harmony or in conflict.

Mythic. The mythic reality is monistic and free of prede-
termination. In the extreme view, it leads to solipsism, to a belief that "I am the only existing being" and that "I have total

free will to create the world as I wish." In less extreme form, I might hold as a mythic that "I have unique power over a domain as large as the world (or restricted to my person)." The theme is "I can make anything happen—within the domain I control." The image of one who has a strong mythic reality includes such descriptions as unpredictable, creative, playful, self-centered, daemonic. The mythics of great power are the "creators" of the world, as artists and spiritual and political leaders. Creations in all domains—science, politics, religion—come from a mythic view. Mythics are symbol makers, giving meaning to experience.

> *Concept of change.* Paradoxically, there is no change in the pure mythic world, for it is always the created world that is. The mythic creates in the moment the total existence—present, past, and future. In less extreme beliefs, change may be recognized, but it is of little importance if it applies beyond one's domain. To the observer, the mythic person may be involved in unending, unpredictable, and chaotic change. It is destructive, even life threatening, for the mythic to be forced to accept change within his or her own domain. Mythics are the least likely to be "organization men."
>
> *Action mode.* The mythic's action mode is proactive and self-starting.
>
> *Criterion.* Does it expand, enliven my domain?
>
> *Responsibility.* There is total personal responsibility for one's acts, and one is thus responsible for the world (or one's domain). Conversely, the mythic has no concept of morality in the sense of taking care of the other, for there is no other. At one extreme, the mythic carries the burdens of the world; at the other, the mythic is totally independent of what goes on beyond him- or herself.
>
> *Relation to others.* Interrelations such as seen by the social or sensory are meaningless. The mythic creates the other as a character in his or her dream. Conversely, by

that act of creation, the (nonmythic) others in a mythic's presence are reified and given meaning. I believe
that this ability to create the other is the basis of the
power of the charismatic leader.

So simple a typology as this does not provide enough variety to
show the difference in personalities that can be described even
by a single reality. As Wilber (1983) points out, a mythic person
may operate from a primitive level that might be better labeled
"magical." There, the behaviors are manipulative, as in voodoo,
based on the assumption that the part, a symbol, can control
the whole. Alternatively, a mythic reality may encompass the
world view of one at a spiritually advanced level, such as Gandhi
or the poet William Blake.

Unitary. Like the mythic, the unitary reality supports
very different personalities. In the extreme in which one maintains the perfect unity of reality, we find deeply spiritual people
who accept the world as it is. We might say that the person of a
unitary belief needs the oneness. But that belief is hard to sustain. With the slightest suspicion that there may be a split in the
universe, that it is not a unity and that there may be a dark side
as well as the light, many different personal responses emerge.
The basic world view of the unitary is of continuity, community, flow, immediacy. LeShan labeled this view "clairvoyant"
in recognition of the access the unitary has to the totality of
time and space. However, with the acceptance of some dichotomy, the peace, freedom from choice, and unifying love of humanity are undermined, leaving the unitary open to feelings
of doubt, fear, and guilt. Those who hold a generally monistic,
if not perfectly unitary, position are of central interest to this
study, for the unitary world view underlies the bureaucratic personality and the followership of the monistic leaders.

Concept of change. There is no change in a unitary world.
Everything that will be already is. That which others
might call change is clarification, harmonization, or
the exposition of the utopia that is inherent in the
universe.

Action modes. For the unitary, this is primarily going
with the flow of events.

Criterion. This is not a meaningful concept with the pure
unitary. But to one who accepts the possibility of the
other, the criterion is, "Are you one with us?"

Responsibility. To remain at one and to support others
in so doing is the basic responsibility to the unitary.
There is no concept of wrong except that which violates the unity, that is, a heretical act.

Relation to others. The unitary perceives an undifferentiated community. All expressions of relation are but
conveniences.

These descriptions of the four alternative realities are
given in terms of the archetypes, of people who view reality
from nearly pure, polar viewpoints. Most people do not come
close to being extreme types, and most believe in aspects of
more than one reality. My observations, supported by the Realities Inquiry, indicate that most people work from two and
some from three of these belief systems. The resulting personalities and modes of engaging with the world are thus combinations of the qualities of the different realities. What particular
qualities are called up at any moment depends on all manner of
stimuli. Studies of related personality constructs suggest that
the preference for realities is, in part, inborn. Another influence
on one's choice of reality base is its relative acceptability in
one's social setting: childhood experiences, training, and the
presence of threats and opportunities also affect what we consider to be real at any moment and thus affect how we act.

It is hard to distinguish between acts that arise from some
combination of reality views and those chosen alternatively
from one or another reality, but the latter seem to be more
common. I frequently observe acts that are themselves stereotypical of one or another of the realities described above. This
is so even though the person has indicated on the Realities Inquiry that he or she favors more than one reality. In fact, as I
will show, some of the most interesting leadership styles arise

from behavior that seems to flip between sources in different realities. I sense that the assumptions of a particular reality dominate our choices, just as our perception of the famous silhouette that may be seen as either two women or a vase or the perspective drawing of a cube flips from one to the other interpretation. In spite of the fact that I habitually draw on more than one concept of reality, at any one moment I may act on the assumptions of a single reality.

This model of alternative realities has proved to be a fecund generator of hypotheses in diverse topics: for example, in identifying different bases for esthetic judgment and for different modes of creativity. My original application of it to leadership studies came from the question of how one would select the team of people to resolve complex social issues. This application has been tested in comparisons of the predicted behaviors with those of prominent leaders and in the assignment of personnel to tasks in various organizations. Its empirical validity is under study (see McWhinney, 1984).

Varieties of Leadership

This exploration of leadership phenomena proceeded by mapping leadership behaviors onto the behavioral characteristics of alternative realities and then attaching style names to those behaviors in accordance with common usage. For example, a leader operating on rational, empirically based evidence, making decisions according to pre-established criteria, would appear to be working out of a combination of unitary and sensory realities. Such a combination we recognize as what is commonly called *task leadership.* This combination has also been identified as *authoritarian.* I choose not to use this latter term, because there is another set of more strongly unitary behaviors that seems to better characterize the authoritarian leader.

I will display the mapping progressively, beginning with the broad style distinctions that parallel the director and manager roles highlighted in the tale with which I began this chapter. I will then present the styles that emerge from the four single, relatively pure concepts of realities, followed by the mapping that arises from leaders behaving out of two realities and, finally, out of three. The mapping isolates more than a dozen distinct leadership styles, significantly transcending our popular American view that there is a much more restricted menu from which we choose and act. At each level of complexity, there are styles that provide new insights into leadership processes.

Directors and Managers

American and much European sociological and administrative thinking has been based on a pluralistic world view. This view holds empirical phenomena and values to be real. According to the theory presented here, it leads to what I label a *managerial concept of leadership*. Its premises include the delegation of responsibility, clearly defined roles, expertise based in scientific (empirical) knowledge, efficient causality, and the fundamental economic assumption that the values placed on objects and activities differ among individuals. It is described in Weberian bureaucracies as well as the open systems, matrix, and networklike organizations emerging in the last quarter of this century. The leaders of such organizations are managers, regardless of whether they are called directors, executives, or presidents.

Much of the rest of the world (and parts of Europe in earlier times) bases its thinking on a monistic world view, taking neither facts nor values nor any boundaries to be real. From the monistic perspective arises a very different view of organizations and their direction, which has been largely ignored in contemporary Western theories of leadership used within a business and administrative context. Ralph Stogdill's (1981) second edition of *Handbook of Leadership,* which cites over 3,000 articles, still makes no discernible reference to monistic styles. With the recent surge of interest in entrepreneurial behavior, there is now a focus on the charismatic and other monistic forms as so elegantly developed in Burns's (1978) *Leadership.* The monistic realities call for a *directorial concept of leadership*. Its premises include an exclusive value system, total loyalty to that system, status based on knowledge of the dogma, formal causality, and the denial of the assumption of individuality and differing valu-ings. The organizational forms include traditional tribal and vil-lage structures, feudal hierarchies, theocracies, and the related bureaucratic forms. The directors are representatives of the sys-tem or of its senior leadership (kings, founders, entrepreneurs). They are extensions of the leader, standing for him or her in representations to the people. They are not in distinct roles but are personally responsible to the leader for their conduct.

The ways in which the monistic and pluralistic views are acted out are, of course, dependent on the strengths of the posi-tions and the other variables, particularly expressed free will. These are detailed in the following sections on specific leader-ship styles.

Leadership from a Single Dominant Reality

Initially, I present a brief description of the stereotypical styles that follow from the four alternative realities. Table 12-1 presents the characteristics of each leadership type in an organi-zational setting. To a large extent, the characteristics indicated here are derived from those of the underlying world view with which each style is associated. I have backed these derivations with anecdotal illustrations and references to the work of other investigators.

Technological. Leadership based on a dominant sensory style is not a familiar one, yet on examination I can find a few examples. This leadership depends on the technological impera-tive, that is, on the follower knowing what must be done from a scientific viewpoint. Leader and followers share in their obedi-ence to the objective science. Such a leader manages by classi-fying goods and events in his or her domains of responsibility and assessing the accuracy with which scientific procedures are followed. (In contemporary Western societies, "scientific" has become equated with "rational.") One place in which this style appears to be appropriate is in the management of a scientific laboratory in which the prime skill used is the ability to estab-lish facts. If the purview of management includes the behavior of the subordinate, the technological style could produce a to-

Table 12-1. Leadership Styles Based on Single Realities.

	Authoritarian	Charismatic	Technological	Integrative
1. Major purpose	Clarifying and conforming to values and rules of establishment	Creating belief in and commitment to leader's own belief systems	Discovering-testing scientific facts	Developing shared value systems
2. Objective	Directing efforts within belief system; maintaining the status quo	Reifying one's ideas; system is not bounded and thus not optimal; sky's the limit	Obtaining clear evidence regarding the given task	Providing conditions for flexible, adaptive movement toward group goals (not bounded)
3. Type of organization	Hierarchical: authority structure	"Star" form, with flexible assignments for subordinates	Project; varying with task; small units only	Open systems, task and process structured
4. Goals in resolving conflict	Preventing divisiveness	Creating unity	Supporting a common world view based on scientific principles and data	Resolving issues of fairness
5. Means of dealing with internal conflict	Denying conflict—no open interpersonal differences; destroy the enemy	Overcoming conflict via excitement and commitment	Rationalistically resolving conflict; systematic and logical	Exposing and organizing efforts to resolve interpersonal problems in a broad context
6. Future and planning	Utopian; short-term planning for an unchanging world	A device for creating hope and a sense of possibility; flexible; long-range but highly unstable	Maximum adaptation via knowledge, anticipation, and clarification of alternatives; as long-range as the data permit	Visioning toward possible futures, adaptive and long range, aims at openly creating a future
7. Supervision style	By the rules; paternalistic	Leader little involved except around issues of trust	Informing, measuring, and evaluating	Encouraging, exploring, listening
8. Ideal follower behavior	Reliable, loyal, knowing the rules; imitative and supportive of supervisors	Trustworthy to leader, carrying out orders, uncritical, flexible; the "true believer"	Informed, skillful, capable of carry-through; can take delegation well; assured	Direct, confronting, informing, courageous, open, conscious
9. Reality base	Unitary	Mythic	Sensory.	Social

tally humane and effective management. The leader who holds some degree of social reality beliefs will caution that the sensory science is not sufficient to account for the subordinate individual's value choices. But this is so in all these descriptions, for we must realize that our evaluations are coming from our personal realities.

Integrative. Of the four styles based in a single reality (in this case social), the integrative is the most familiar. It is the equivalent to the subordinate-centered leadership at the upper end of the scale originated by Tannenbaum and Schmidt (1973). It is the extreme allocative style, for it is based entirely on the value judgments of the participants, as opposed to the technological allocations that are based on an objective science. The integrative manager's job is to take into account the values, needs, feelings, and emotions of all subordinates and of those in related operations in coming to decisions and assigning work.

Charismatic. Of all the possible contributions of this theory of leadership styles, the inclusion of charismatic style will be the most important. In spite of the centrality of charisma to political governance, spiritual development, and business entrepreneurship, it has been almost totally neglected by behavioral scientists. (Weber, 1947, included charismatic organizations among the major types, but most students of his work have focused only on his contribution to bureaucratic theory.)

Charismatic leadership is based in the drive to create the world as one desires it to be; that world could be a new enterprise, an art form, or the globe's entire expanse. The direction is entirely from an inner source. It has no objective base or form upon which the follower can count, so the leadership is highly personalistic. The leader-follower relationship must be one based in loyalty to the leader, for there is no process by which the follower can come to expect rewards beyond the feeling of being created by the leader. There is no question of morality or responsibility from outside, though the charismatic may derive from his or her culture a view of the world that others would call deeply moral or immoral. Wagner, Socrates, Gandhi, and Hitler were all charismatic leaders. The common characteristic is the ability to create symbols that capture the imagination and allegiance—the charismatics are magicians of high or low quality. A concomitant characteristic is high creative energy, a drive to reify oneself, a drive that is sensed by nonmythics as libidinous, from the shadow side, or, at very least, unfathomable. Berlin (1980, pp. 14–15) characterizes the charismatic political leader in his description of the wartime Churchill:

> In 1940 he assumed an indomitable stoutness, an unsurrendering quality on the part of his people. . . . He idealized them with such intensity that in the end they approached his ideal and began to see themselves as he saw them: "the buoyant and imperturbable temper of Britain which I had the honour to express"—it was indeed, but he had a lion's share in creating it. So hypnotic was the force of his words, so strong his faith, that by the sheer intensity of his eloquence he bound his spell upon them until it seemed to them that he was indeed speaking what was in their hearts and minds. . . . He created a heroic mood and turned the fortunes of the Battle of Britain not by catching the mood of his surroundings but by being stubbornly impervious to it, as he had been to so many of the passing shades and tones of which the life around him had been composed.

Charisma is not always associated with greatness. Probably all mythics of high energy are, to some degree, charismatic. My sample of those who have taken the Realities Inquiry indicates that most of those who are leaders in work life show a far greater than average belief in the mythic reality. The mythic inclination is also common among the women in my sample who have moved into positions of responsibility in recent years; it is easy to recognize the charisma among them.

Authoritarian. I use the term *authoritarian* in a narrow sense to label the unitary leader whose basic role is the interpretation of "the word." The word may be a holy writ, an administrative code, or a tradition passed down through ritual procedures. The role is totally depersonalized—one is chosen for it in accordance with one's ability to speak "ex cathedra." The role is played by civil court judges, umpires, and particularly religious leaders such as the Roman Catholic pope and the Tibetan lama. Pope John Paul II succinctly characterized the authoritarian position in stating, "The unity of the church signifies and demands that we submit our conceptions and doctrine and our pastoral projects to the teachings of the church represented by the Pope and the bishops" (Schanche and Torgeson, 1983, p. 18). The authoritarian style is the extreme opposite of democratic leadership. It bears noting, however, that, conversely to our common use of the term, the authoritarian is devoid of overtones of personal control or dictatorship.

The less extreme unitary—that is, the person who accepts some free will and whose unity is a significant world but not the whole universe—may be what I called *director*. Certainly, this is a monistic style in which the leader directs the subordinates in his or her interpretation of regulations and writs. The director, like the administrator, denies the individual (including him- or herself) in favor of the system of which he or she is a part.

Leadership Styles Based on Two Dominant Realities

It should not be surprising that styles based in two dominant realities are more familiar, for a double dominance is typical in American society—at least as measured by the Realities Inquiry. These styles are also of greater interest, for they exhibit more complex behaviors, are more difficult to predict from knowledge of their world views, and are more important to the operation of our society. These six basic types are described in Table 12-2. That they can so sharply characterize important classes of leadership is a positive indicator of the theory's power.

Task Leader. The task leader style is familiar as the left end of the Tannenbaum-Schmidt continuum, or as the 9-1 position on the Blake grid (Blake and Mouton, 1964). It is based on a balanced unitary-sensory world view, incorporating an orthodoxy not present in the technological style. The focus stays on the task, but the leader gains authority beyond his or her science. The task style gives less weight to individuality and values, plac-

Table 12-2. Leadership Styles Based on Two Realities.

	Styles Based on Adjacent Realities				Styles Based on Opposing Realities	
	Task	Participative	Facilitative	Prophetic	Entrepreneurial	Consultative
1. Major purpose	Carrying out established goals in relation to external	Proper allocation of human and physical resources	Bringing out energy and skills of the participants	Bringing the word of authority to the members	Realizing a personal image	Using subordinates to effect policy
2. Objectives	Logically exercising power to achieve organizational goals	Managing optimally for resource use—short and long term	Optimal sharing of production of ideas and responding to member's values	Obtaining compliance with "the word"	Reifying one's ideas in the "real world"	Best ideas to achieve organization's goals
3. Type of organization	Hierarchical; task	Functional	Open system	Tribal	Charismatic, growing into hierarchy	Hierarchical task
4. Goals in resolving conflict	Task accomplishment	Short- and long-run effectiveness of operations	Open communication and emotional support	Conformity to "the word"	Causing the issue to disappear	Shared perception of imposed policy
5. Means of dealing with internal conflict	Requiring conformity to policy	Negotiating to find shared values	Active counseling to involved parties	Establishing true word and rejecting heretics	Wiping out the power base of the opposition	Clarification of issue with involved parties
6. Future and planning	Explicit temporal and resource allocations	Plans designed to optimize present and future achievement	Expansive exploration of possibilities	Strong bias toward assuring future performance	Same as charismatic, but steadier goal orientation	Informed movement toward established goal

7. Supervision style	Clarification of goals, technology, and planning	Supportiveness in connecting people	Evocative facilitation	"Shepherding"	Hard-driving, achievement-oriented	Responsive and demanding, with danger of double bind
8. Ideal follower behavior	Technically competent; accepts organizational demands	Cooperative and analytical	Independent, open, and inner-directed	Trustworthy, loyal; accepts rules and suspends judgment	Self-abnegating; flexible and responsible	Informed, open, and accepting of authority
9. Reality bases	Unitary-sensory	Sensory-social	Social-mythic	Mythic-unitary	Mythical-sensory	Social-unitary

ing more on conformity. Based on the Realities Inquiry and similar measures, the unitary-sensory world view appears to be the most common style found in the upper management of heavy industry, banking, and the law and accounting professions.

Participative. Perhaps, if the term *participative* were not already so loaded with connotation, this style might simply be called "manager." It is founded in pluralism, in both the uniqueness of the individual and the incomparability of personal values. Thus, the participative leader operates from the two pluralistic reality bases: sensory and social. I subtitle this style "practical" to indicate the commitment to sensory fact that the integrative leader does not appreciate. The participative leader plays a role midway between the "facts of the situation" and the values of those involved—9-9 on the Blake grid (Blake and Mouton, 1964). It is a difficult balancing act, so it is typical to find the leader tending in any decision toward one or the other world view, even if, over time, he or she represents both. For some managers, this style will be played out in an economic setting, with primary concern for the value of goods. For others, it will be played out in a social context, with primary concern for realizing human values. This style, too, is common among American managers, particularly in service industries and in work that depends on interpersonal contacts.

Facilitative. I am not sure whether the type that combines social and mythic is ever an organizational leader. I don't have a clear exemplar. One can make some guesses based on the qualities of the two realities: social-mythic leaders might be creative and accepting in their relation to subordinates but not constructively directive. If anything, they are "managers of meaning," perhaps leading a group of rather independent creative or research workers. The examples I have of this world view, including myself, are teachers, writers, and artists who, in most cases, do not work within formal organizations.

Prophetic. It has been interesting for me to conjure up images of a person who has both mythic and unitary beliefs. One image that arises is of charismatics who act as *conduits of truth,* from a divine or worldly authority. As mythics, they would see themselves as unique conduits, having "the word."

The classic case is Moses bringing the Ten Commandments, but there are a multitude of lesser prophets, teachers, and guides that inhabit palaces, schools, and offices—wherever those of unitary belief congregate. A second image is based on a sample of two people who "tested" as unitary with a lesser mythic score. They were both creative, entrepreneurial lawyers. They appear to be examples of those who reorganize and reformulate within a structure—in this case, legal code and process. They lead not by symbol making but by clarifying, bringing order to a situation. They do not fit the prophetic mold, yet there is a similar outcome from their work. That two such different ways of life are associated with similar views of reality is a cautionary indicator of the frailty of the theory as a predictor, but it also attests to its generative power.

The remaining two pairs, unitary-social and mythic-sensory, are particularly interesting, for they call for jointly maintaining opposing belief systems. The maintenance of contradictory, paradoxical views seems to be a common property of powerful systems—the Chinese yin-yang, the Hegelian dialectic, the monistic-pluralistic, and the dark and light sides of life seen in classical myths. The leadership styles based in these dual realities are appropriately complex and intriguing.

Consultative. Acting from a social belief, a consultative leader seeks advice and senses the ideas and feelings of others. Then, at some point, the leader switches to a unitary mode and makes decisions that fit within the monistic structure. This behavior can be effective in strongly hierarchical organizations in which roles are well defined, but the switch can raise problems for the subordinates if the point at which it occurs is not anticipated. Subordinates may continue to express opinions after the switch is made, so that what was once accepted into the leader's thinking becomes heretical. This style of leadership can produce what Bateson (1972) identified as "double binds." Such behavior, which in the family or corporation may produce schizoid behavior, in society can begin by eliciting the highest moral ideals and end in a reign of terror, as have so many political revolutions. This style was much discussed in the 1950s but is less favored today, perhaps because of this difficult aspect.

The switch from behavior based in the social reality to

that based in the unitary probably is a response to security needs. I have found no evidence of a leader moving in the opposite direction; that is, from basic authoritarian leadership to the integrative style.

Entrepreneurial. For the entrepreneurial leader, there is a path from the solipsism of dreams to the birth of new symbols to the creation of new empires—political, economic, or ideational. The dream is moved toward the empire, toward reality in the usual sense of the word, through steps taken in the sensory realm. The entrepreneur dreams in a mythic consciousness but enters the sensory world to protect the dream and implants that dream of the possible on an existing framework of practice. The entrepreneurial style is a pairing of charismatic and technological leadership and exhibits qualities of both. It draws the primeval energy of creation into the sensory world without the constraints of moral sanctions; it is unpredictable in its inception and as obvious as hard fact in its execution. The entrepreneur is often a "pathfinder," as Harold Leavitt has described the style.

Entrepreneurs exhibit spontaneous self-creation, imagining themselves able to do or produce all manner of things, but they may collapse if they cannot maintain power within their domain. We see this characteristic in the "roller-coaster" careers of repeated success and failure of inventors, financiers, and impresarios. Following failure in the "real" world, the mythic side may re-emerge in fantasy, patently protected against sensory evaluation. Perhaps this is a description of Nixon's path out of the White House.

Leadership Styles Based on Three Realities

The ability to come from three (or all four) views of reality greatly increases the complexity of one's leadership style. The range of behavior presented by variations in the weightings and in the application of belief in various situations is so great as to make generalizations of these types significantly more difficult. So far, I have learned more by looking at what these richer styles avoid than by what they accept. For example, I find in American society many people, otherwise open, who reject the beliefs and values of the unitary reality; from that, one can predict something of their leadership styles—for example, resistance to dogma. Some groups, such as those trained in the professions, reject the mythic reality, and we find their leaders strongly maintaining the existing symbology.

Looking at what a leader rejects leads me to consider leadership style in terms of the culture in which it is operative. I have noted in my sample that the most effective leaders in corporate society are those who accept all but the unitary reality; this clearly would not be true in a strongly religious society. I suspect that there was almost no acceptance of social reality in traditional Spanish life, and there certainly are societies where charismatics and entrepreneurs are suspect—for example, Norway. At some point, the effects of personal style become indistinguishable from responses to the dominant social demands.

In many traditional societies, including those of classical Greece and China and the Plains Indians, the developmental path of humanity was to gain awareness of and comfort with all four realities—variously labeled "seasons," "signs," or "winds." I see in those people who work out of three (or four) realities an increase of appreciation for and complexity of responses beyond that of people with a more focused world view. However, I do not yet know whether the broader world view always leads to better leadership. The relative advantage between leadership developed out of such traditional models and a more focused view is a question of social theory beyond the scope of this chapter.

Conclusion: Directing Managers and Managing Directors

The ideas presented in this chapter represent an expansion in the space of alternative forms of leadership that can be accommodated within a single theoretical framework (see Figure 12-3). In so doing, it brings attention to forms that have been neglected (for example, the prophetic) and provides a powerful means of discriminating among the varieties identified. Whereas existing models are based in diverse assumptions run-

Figure 12-3. Leadership Styles on a Map of Realities.

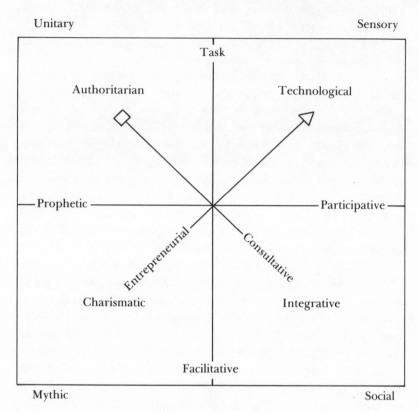

Unitary   Sensory

Mythic   Social

ning from economics, logic, and magic to accidents of history, the present study uses a single underlying ontological model. From the use of a single base, we gain elegance and simplicity of explanation. We also are provided a basis for looking at the connection between the leadership styles and the forms of organization with which they are associated.

For me personally, the greatest value of this formulation is the understanding I have gained of the diverse motivations that may underlie behaviors that have appeared perverse, even threatening to me. It gives me access to the existential anxieties that are aroused in leaders and followers—and myself—as we inevitably confront diverse world views.

Appendix 12-1. Alternative Realities.

Unitary		Sensory
Everything is one; boundaries are arbitary. Space and time are a continuum. Events simply are. No involvement in the past or future.	Connectivity	All objects are separable. They affect each other by direct contact and according to general laws. Time and space are separate dimensions.
No free will: no doing or wishing to do. Things which happen, happen.	Will	No free will, though there are alternative paths one can follow.
Going with the flow.	Action	Anticipation allows selection among features.
Direct experience of oneness; knowledge is gained by direct intuition of the oneness. Senses provide only false information.	Sources of knowledge	All valid information comes directly or indirdirectly via the senses. All is testable and verifiable.
No meaning to causality, since it is all one. The central question: What?	Causality	Cause precedes effects. Action occurs only through physical forces and contact. Central questions: How? and How to?
Connectedness, serenity, joy, peace. No existential anxiety or aloneness.	Emotion	Groundedness, confidence, the well being from taking action. Fear of death.
No moral opportunity. A single valued world. Divisiveness is only evil.	Moral judgement	No moral judgements. Criterion: Does it work?
"We know we are at home in the universe."	Sources of meaning	Workability: "I can see the effects." Grounded in facts.
Experienced only as cleansing of what is.	Change	Selecting among established futures.
Relativistic physics, law, maintaining authority structures, devotion.	Uses	Survival, creature comforts, everyday commerce. Empirical science and technology.

Any part can stand for any whole. No difference between objective and subjective or between things and symbols. Once a connection is established, no space/time separation.	Connectivity	Separable entities, but boundaries are chosen according to the purpose they are being used for.
All connections start with acts of will. All things have power (mana) to create connections among anything in the universe.	Will	Free will in each sentient being. Everything can effect everything else, so at the level of the cosmos there is predetermination.
Proactive; self-starting.	Action	Interactive: transformational.
Oneself, since all can be created by one's intention.	Sources of knowledge	Through observation, but also through direct awareness as part of a whole. (Recognizes the possibility of ESP and so on).
All is willable. No accidents: everything has meaning. Nothing is falsifiable. Central question: Do I want it?	Causality	Strong focusing can bring to bear forces of the cosmos onto a local situation. Central question: Why? as well as How?
Playfulness, capriciousness, humor, and powerfulness to create.	Emotion	Awe, humility, majesty, greatness. Love and anxiety: can't fully experience oneness.
Total moral responsibility for one's acts, since others are not recognized as active agents. No concern for wishes of others.	Moral judgement	Since we can choose, we are subject to moral and ethical demands: golden rule. Recognizes the morality and rights of the other.
The creative potential of the living will. Life and death are phases of one's being.	Sources of meaning	Own choicefulness in articulating a moral world. Awareness of separation and integration.
No change, just creation.	Change	The normal interactive modes produce change.
Play, art, dreaming, invention. Taking charge—charisma.	Uses	Inquiry, philosophy, policy, ethics. Social organization.

Mythic		Social

◀──────── Monistic ─────────┴────────── Pluralistic ────────▶

(Right margin, vertical: ↑ ─ ─ ─ Deterministic Behavior ─ ─ ┼ ─ Free Will ─ ─ ─ ↓)

Appendix 12-2. A Selection from the Realities Inquiry.

The major portion of this task is doing a brief piece of writing. Then you are asked to respond to some multiple-choice questions.

Before you get into writing, take time to settle comfortably into your chair, put away distractions, and relax. Take a few deep breaths.

Now, in your mind's eye, picture two characters. You can make them up or you can think of people you have known. One should be a leader, a person you might call a president, king or queen, manager—whatever you find easy to think about. The other should be a person of wisdom whom you might want to call a sage, an adviser, or earth mother.

Once these characters are established in your mind and you feel that you know how they would think and behave, write about some sort of encounter they might have or a situation they might be in together. Write anything you want and use any form you like. It needn't be particularly long, "clever," or polished.

You may use the following pages of the booklet for your writing. If you require additional pages, use loose sheets and insert them in the booklet. Take twenty minutes or so to write. When you are finished or time is called, go on immediately to the questionnaire.

Please don't turn to the questionnaire until you have completed your writing.

Questionnaire

As you respond to these questions, try to stay connected with the feelings and thoughts you had as you were writing. Remember to think of yourself as "Author" as you answer the questions.

Each of the questions on the following pages has four possible responses. Select the one that comes closest to matching your thinking. If it matches *very* closely, circle the 9 in the scale on the right. If it is close but not very close, circle a 7 or 8.

Then select the response that is furthest from matching your thinking. If it is *completely* unlike the way you think, circle a 1. If it doesn't match but you don't feel so strongly about it, circle a 2 or a 3.

Then look at the remaining items, rate the degree to which each matches your thinking, and circle the appropriate numbers.

But *please*, don't have any ties! Each of the four responses to a question should get a rating different from the others. If you find yourself rating two the same, look again. Chances are that you don't really feel just the same about them.

Example

	Least Like							Most Like
When filling out a questionnaire ←								→
a. I take it as a challenge.	1 2 3 4 5 6 7 8 9
b. I sort of enjoy doing it.	1 2 3 4 5 6 7 8 9
c. I struggle with some answers.	1 2 3 4 5 6 7 8 9
d. I always wish it were longer.	1 2 3 4 5 6 7 8 9

1. I think a leader's prime strength lies in
   a. the authority that's gained by being especially in tune with the purposes and goals of a group.   1 2 3 4 5 6 7 8 9
   b. the authority that derives from deep knowledge of a situation and an understanding of the consequences of alternative actions.   1 2 3 4 5 6 7 8 9

		Least Like							Most Like

c. personal charisma, the
ability to generate a
sense of direction and
confidence among one's
followers.   1   2   3   4   5   6   7   8   9

d. the ability to build an
environment of mutual
confidence and respect
among followers.   1   2   3   4   5   6   7   8   9

2. The writing I did pursues
the question
a. Why? What was the un-
derlying purpose of the
problem or situation?   1   2   3   4   5   6   7   8   9
b. Who? Who had the
power to cause some
particular events to
happen?   1   2   3   4   5   6   7   8   9
c. What? What actually
happened?   1   2   3   4   5   6   7   8   9
d. How? What caused the
events to happen?   1   2   3   4   5   6   7   8   9

3. People I identify most
with
a. take the world as it is,
appreciating without
changing it.   1   2   3   4   5   6   7   8   9
b. enjoy creating the sit-
uations they are in.   1   2   3   4   5   6   7   8   9
c. get meaning from de-
veloping and changing
themselves.   1   2   3   4   5   6   7   8   9
d. get meaning from see-
ing their efforts being
effective.   1   2   3   4   5   6   7   8   9

References

Bateson, G. *Steps to an Ecology of Mind.* New York: Ballentine, 1972.

Berlin, I. *Personal Impressions.* New York: Viking Press, 1980.

Blake, R. R., and Mouton, J. S. *The Managerial Grid.* Houston: Gulf, 1964.

Burns, J. M. *Leadership.* New York: Harper & Row, 1978.

LeShan, L. *Alternative Realities.* New York: Ballentine, 1976.

Lipnack, J., and Stamps, J. *Networking.* Garden City, N.Y.: Doubleday, 1982.

McWhinney, W. *Resolving Complex Issues.* Venice, Calif.: Enthusion, 1983.

McWhinney, W. "Alternative Realities." *Journal of Humanistic Psychology,* 1984, *24,* 7-38.

Schanche, D. A., and Torgeson, D. "Pope Jeered, Harassed in Nicaragua." *Los Angeles Times,* March 5, 1983, p. 18.

Stogdill, R. *Handbook of Leadership.* (2nd ed.) New York: Free Press, 1981.

Tannenbaum, R., and Schmidt, W. H. "How to Choose a Leadership Pattern." *Harvard Business Review,* 1973, *51,* 95–102.

Weber, M. *The Theory of Economic and Social Organizations.* (A. M. Henderson and T. Parsons, Trans.) New York: Free Press, 1947.

Wilber, K. *Eye to Eye: The Quest for the New Paradigm.* Garden City, N.Y.: Anchor Press/Doubleday, 1983.

13

The Qualitative Side
of Leadership

David M. Boje
Dave Ulrich

Leadership is one of the most researched topics in organizational behavior, yet only recently has pressure to study the dynamics of leadership stimulated researchers to turn to qualitative methodology (Morgan and Smircich, 1980). Several researchers (Argyris, 1960; Dubin, 1976; Davis and Luthans, 1979) are demanding that the study of leadership focus on observable leader behaviors rather than only survey perceptions of behavior. Using qualitative methods, researchers garner insights into the human conditions in organizational settings by focusing attention on contextual details and subtle nuances that may escape surveys and structured interviews (Van Maanen, 1979). To date, the majority of leadership studies have devoted more attention to replication, using survey instruments that gloss over many important subtleties of leadership. Managers often respond to this quantitative leadership research by stating that findings grossly oversimplify their reality (Livingston, 1971). It is ironic, therefore, that quantification is often advocated as a tool for managers to improve decision making and organizational processes (Brown and ReVelle, 1978). We propose that the study of the qualitative side of leadership will enhance understanding of leadership processes. We argue for this position by (1) briefly indicating the lack of qualitative research in historical leadership studies, (2) presenting reasons for pursuing qualitative leadership research, and (3) offering specific uses of ethnographical techniques for leaders in practice.

Leadership Studies and Qualitative Research

Leadership research began with the study of great leaders such as Winston Churchill, Douglas MacArthur, and John Kennedy. Researchers believed that a trait model would emerge to isolate personality attributes of successful leaders (Mann, 1959; Stogdill, 1948, 1974; Payne, 1974). While a few personality factors were found to be related to effective leadership, the popularity of this line of research declined, because different key traits were found in various studies. In the late 1940s, the study of leadership analyzed behaviors: What do leaders do? What behaviors distinguish effective and noneffective leaders? While many models of leader behavior have been proposed (Lewin, 1944; Pfeffer, 1977; Tannenbaum and Schmidt, 1973), the most researched models are the Ohio State approach (Weissenberger and Kavanagh, 1972; Kerr and others, 1974; Schriesheim, House, and Kerr, 1976; Schriesheim, Kinicki, and Schriesheim, 1979) and the Michigan approach (Katz and Kahn, 1952; Kahn and Katz, 1960; Likert, 1961).

Analysis of the Ohio State approach, which is similar in technique to the Michigan approach, reveals how the qualitative side of leadership was overlooked. Early investigators began with a list of specific leader behaviors (for example, inspecting sites, writing reports, hearing complaints) and attempted to determine how performance and time spent in these activities related to leader effectiveness (Hemphill and Coons, 1957; Halpin and Winer, 1957). From this list, efforts were made to formulate general behavioral dimensions that would fit all leaders using quantitative factor analyses of leader behavior description questionnaires (Hemphill and Coons, 1957; Fleishman, 1957). If there had been sufficient dimensions to capture the complexities of leadership, the qualitative side of leadership probably would not have been ignored. However, only two factors were identified: initiation and consideration. Two other dimensions in the original scheme were dropped: social awareness (sensitivity and awareness of social interrelationships and pressures in and outside of the group) and production emphasis (behaviors intended to motivate the group to greater activity by emphasizing the mission or job to be done). Korman (1966) concludes that leadership studies of initiation and consideration provided little prediction of leader effectiveness. Oldham's (1976) work suggests a more appropriate set of leader behaviors than those employed in the Ohio State approach: "one of the probable reasons for the previously inconclusive results is simply that improper leader activities were focused on" (p. 66).

The need to study other leader behaviors may explain the popularity of Mintzberg's (1973) structured observation work. It broadens what is included in "leader behaviors," finding that leaders must interact constantly with staff, attend seemingly endless meetings, engage in diverse boundary roles, and spend a high percentage of their time in face-to-face communication. One problem in Mintzberg's approach is that it counts behaviors rather than attempting to understand their contextual importance. As Pondy (1976) asserts, it is more important to understand the contextual meaning of leader behaviors for subordinates, to identify the most critical leader behaviors (Calder, 1977).

The contingency research on leadership does link behavior to context, but it studies a limited range of behaviors. Fiedler (1972), for example, departs from trait and behavioral models by asserting that group performance is contingent on the leader's psychological orientation and on three contextual variables: group atmosphere, task structure, and leader's power position. Fiedler's model has been the subject of criticism (Schriesheim and Kerr, 1977): How valid is the least-preferred-co-worker instrument in measuring psychological orientation? To what extent do leaders influence subordinates' perception of structure (environment) and task? A second example of contingency research makes the link between leader behavior and its context even clearer. The path-goal approach (House and Dessler,

1974; House and Mitchell, 1974; Schriesheim and VonGlinow, 1977; Downey, Sheridan, and Slocum, 1976; Schriesheim and Schriesheim, 1978) builds on expectancy theory and suggests that leaders guide subordinates' behaviors (path) to attain both subordinates' and leaders' valued outcomes (goal). Unlike Fiedler's model, path-goal theory does not presume leaders' motivational state. Rather, leaders must develop an appreciation for the context of the organization and the motivational forces of subordinates.

In brief, leadership research is only now beginning to redefine behaviors central to effective leadership, focus on the context and meanings of behaviors in organizations, and examine subtle and qualitative leader controls. Historical antecedents of these current research efforts include examples of qualitative work by Whyte (1955), Dalton (1959), and Goffman (1961) and theoretical development of qualitative work by Schutz (1967), Glaser and Strauss (1967), and Garfinkel (1967). Current leadership research that deals with qualitative issues includes charismatic leader behaviors (House, 1977), symbolic leader behaviors that shape corporate cultures (Peters, 1978; Deal and Kennedy, 1982), and language created and used by leaders (Pondy, 1976; Daft and Wiginton, 1979).

Why Study the Qualitative Side of Leadership?

To understand more subtle leader behaviors, we propose the use of qualitative methods—in particular, ethnography—as a leadership tool to improve organizational culture. The goal of ethnography is to discover how people use cultural knowledge to organize their behavior and make sense of their experience (Lofland, 1971; Pelto and Pelto, 1978; Sanday, 1979; Spradley, 1980). To do ethnography, ethnographers must immerse themselves in a culture until it becomes their culture. Ethnographers try to catalogue all activities, cultural objects, historical information, and ceremonies and rituals of the culture they are studying. They learn to distinguish relevant information from irrelevant. Finally, ethnographers develop behaviors for entering cultural settings with minimum disruption of the essential processes. We believe that one of the reasons leaders and leadership researchers have relied more on quantitative than on qualitative methods is the same reason ethnographers prefer to study foreign cultural settings, rather than their own turf: It is difficult to see nuances in a culture that is taken for granted. Further, it may be easier for leaders and leadership researchers to depend on the quantitative methods drilled into them in business schools than on the qualitative methods that are difficult to teach, let alone learn.

To understand the value of the qualitative side of research, we now review the forces moving leadership research toward ethnography and the differences between how leaders and many leadership researchers categorize leader behaviors.

Leadership and Ethnography. Several forces are pushing leadership research toward ethnography. First, as reviewed earlier, surveys often measure perceptions, not behavior. Measuring perceptions of initiation or consideration, for example, does not necessarily reflect what leaders actually do. Second, most studies that go beyond perceptions and study leadership behavior have been crude attempts to count how many times a behavior has been performed; for example, how often someone has answered the phone (Mintzberg, 1973). While such description helps one understand leadership roles, it does not capture dynamic qualities of leader behavior, nor does it explain alternative behaviors in which leaders may engage to improve leadership practice. Third, although theories of leader behavior necessitate observing behavior, whenever a researcher enters a dynamic setting, the setting is disrupted. The discipline that has devoted most attention to how to observe a setting with a minimal disturbance of essential processes is ethnography (see, for example, Erikson, 1967). Fourth, fully studying contingencies of leadership (for example, Fiedler's theory or path-goal theory) requires awareness of many nuances. Understanding subtleties of symbols, culture, and language will require that leaders use ethnographic skills.

Leadership in Practice Versus Leadership Research. To understand the full impact of the qualitative side of research, we need to distinguish leader behaviors from leadership research.

Categories used in leadership theory and explanation, such as initiation structure and consideration, are embedded in a social science language system and may not be appropriate when projected onto organizations. The problem of imposed versus in-use categories has been formulated by ethnographers as the emic-etic distinction (Price-Williams, 1974): "The 'emic' approach describes a phenomenon in terms of its own units. The 'etic' approach imposes a measurement external to the phenomenon" (p. 95). Leadership researchers are prone to use an etic approach, wherein the researcher imposes a set of categories on a leader's behavior. Unfortunately, many leader behaviors are overlooked with this approach, and thus an emic approach may be more appropriate. There may be an interplay between emic classifications used by leaders to describe their behavior and the etic classifications used by researchers. The etic system of the researchers, such as "concern for task" versus "concern for people," is becoming the emic system of managers as they undergo graduate and other training programs. As researchers ask questions about leadership based on these simplistic categories, we may find that our training and questioning create a reality that leaders verify by acting on the basis of this schema.

Distinguishing emic and etic research is valuable for separating leader behaviors from leadership research. Much leadership research attempts to fit an organization's categories of behavior into a researcher's scheme. The emic alternative teases out the embedded system in each organization through an in-depth, culturally sensitive ethnographical analysis. Naturally, one might wonder whether comparison across settings will become too difficult if we attend to the idiosyncrasies of each organization. That possibility is real, but we believe that the pitfalls of generalizing categories of limited relevance to many settings are a more severe handicap for any science (see Susman and Evered, 1978).

To study the social reality that leaders establish, we propose studying the culture and context in which leadership occurs. As a beginning, we need to study language. Words have meaning only in the context of sentences. Similarly, Pondy (1976) asserts that specific leader behaviors have meaning only in the context of a set of social rules or grammar. To research this grammar and to understand organizations with the same framework, we propose studying emic categories of leader behavior and language. Examples of leaders using language to create an organizational culture and reality are numerous. At IBM, the slogan "IBM means service" motivates employees to better serve customers; stories abound at IBM of employees who did not serve the customer and were chastised as a result. At General Electric, the culture implied by the slogan "Progress is our most important product" may have helped GE focus on becoming a technology leader. Leaders such as Tom Watson, Jr., at IBM, Robert E. Wood at Sears, Roebuck, Alfred Sloan at General Motors, and Ray Kroc at McDonald's fulfilled their roles in part by creating language and symbols. By using such examples, we hope to illustrate the importance of leaders' language in influencing and changing behavior of individuals in organizations. Through creating stories, leaders link together a changing set of players into a more stable social order. Through innuendo and language, leaders may initiate events that give direction to others.

This description of leadership behavior differs significantly from traditional studies of leadership using surveys and other quantitative techniques. It requires development of emic categories of leader behavior that coincide with leadership in practice. The approach that we propose also differs from that proposed by Mintzberg in that we are proactively encouraging leadership researchers to understand a socially constructed world. Symbols, metaphors, and language become the focus of research. As researchers trying to understand the leader's role in creating symbols, we need to learn from ethnographers, who are skilled in understanding and creating cultural contexts in which actions occur. By learning some of the skills associated with ethnography, leaders should be more able not only to understand their organizations but also to create social symbols that direct an organization in directions consistent with leaders' desires. Through effective use of symbols and metaphors, leaders may be able to begin to enact changes in directions consistent with their own values and ideals. By better understanding ethnography, we can better understand leadership research and practice.

Ethnographical Techniques for Leaders

As discussed earlier, ethnographers study how people use cultural knowledge to organize their behavior and to make sense of their experience—to see the world as others do. Ethnographers must be aware of how they translate, simplify, generalize, and otherwise gloss another's world through their own cultural heritage. Rather than try to suspend their culture (an impossible objective), ethnographers are taught to record their own biases and feelings along with what they observe about others and how their biases and feelings adjust over time. We believe that general guidelines for ethnographers may apply to leadership researchers and leaders. By examining tactics that ethnographers recommend for studying their own cultures, we may identify areas relevant to leaders who want to understand the qualitative side of their organizations. The qualitative approach gives research added insights into the organization phenomena. While not all of these guidelines apply to every situation, we explicitly review how leaders and leadership researchers may use qualitative methods to assess organizations.

Develop Trust and Honesty. The humanistic approach emphasizes development of congruent and honest values as a prerequisite to leadership. Ethnographers would also encourage the researcher to be congruent and honest with self and others. In many situations, leaders might want to develop this honesty by sharing appropriate information with subordinates, keeping confidences when appropriate, and being available for employees to interact with.

Develop Informal Networks. The ethnographer needs to get close to many members in familiar settings. These key informants should have access to people and events outside the ethnographer's current life space (Edgerton and Langness, 1971; Pelto, 1970). Key informants give information on many facets of the work setting. Leaders can also develop networks within organizations. Lifson (1979) talks about the Japanese organization as one in which managers have broad-based information networks. These networks allow for information to flow to and from managers on a variety of information needs. Ethnographers use personality to "win over" members of the organization. Ethnographers and leaders need to use charm (Johnson, 1978) and empathy (Whyte, 1955) to become close to the members of the organization. Ethnographers need to be willing to use a "quid pro quo" technique. While gathering information, the ethnographer needs to be willing to share insights with the informant. These insights may be about the observations that are being made and about the individual's personal history. Information trading is an important resource for the ethnographers and may be an equally valuable resource for leaders and researchers.

   Understand Employees' Language. Just as ethnographers need to learn the language of the culture being studied, leaders need to learn the language of the workers. This serves a number of purposes. First, leaders can compare their language system with the employees' to assess possible differences. Second, leaders can use appropriate language and symbols to communicate effectively. Third, leaders can learn what symbols to create to better direct the behavior of the employees. Researchers also may benefit by understanding language nuances of the research site. Ethnographers compare the language and practices of several groups within the social setting (Glaser and Strauss, 1967, p. 292). By looking at different groups—their language system and patterns of behavior—ethnographers and leaders can see unique qualities of work groups. Comparing variations in the language of different groups in a setting provides researchers and leaders insights into the operations of important symbols (Daft and Wiginton, 1979). Ethnographers and leaders can learn to gather stories from different subgroups, allowing them to develop insight into the cultural fabric of a setting (Byington, 1978; Wilkins, 1978; Boje, Fedor, and Rowland, 1982).

   Performances vary from one context to the next. For example, people will take on a role in a board meeting that they will not perform in a department meeting. Ethnographers have just begun to realize how organizational performers set up the context in which certain performance qualities become more or less acceptable (Bell, 1976; Zetlin and Sabsay, 1980). Leaders and researchers need to learn some of the same skills and be equally sensitive to various settings.

Be Patient in Understanding Cultural Changes. Sanday (1979) emphasized the need to work with a group of workers for at least one year before understanding the nuances of the system. Leaders and researchers may also need to spend extensive amounts of time to learn the subtle factors affecting behavior in the organization.

Have Employees Maintain Time Logs. Mintzberg (1973) analyzed time logs of chief executive officers and found that these officers performed tasks in rather short time frames, with many verbal activities governing the day. Similar analyses could be done with employees. Time logs could be kept for a week or two; then leaders could sit down with employees to assess the data gathered. Using these time logs could serve as a basis for job descriptions, managerial development programs, and career counseling.

Meet with Employees Away from the Office. Ouchi (1981) discusses the need for Japanese executives to occasionally meet with employees away from the work setting. By so doing, employees and managers can share information and get to know each other more completely. The same activity may help other leaders. Meeting away from work pressures may open avenues of trust and communication.

Withdraw Periodically to Assess What Is Happening. Ethnographers spend more time thinking about the events than they do observing. Since leaders work in hectic jobs with little time for reflection, allocating time for reflection may help leaders realize what strategies could be appropriately used. Researchers also need to pause periodically to reflect on the overall purpose of their research.

Learn to Be a Sensitive Observer. Much of the information gathered by qualitative methods comes from direct observation. Leaders need to learn to observe and pay attention to cues in the environment. The questions used by Lofland (1971) provide a good foundation for leaders' observation: What acts seem to recur among all participants? What acts seem to have more importance to the participants? What are the phases of the acts that occur? What meanings are the participants attributing to the activities that are occurring? What phases of meaning are developed? Who are the key individuals in developing the meaning constructs? What are the patterns of participation that are used by the group? What are the relationships that are used by the members of the group? Are these deep, cyclical, or informal relationships?

Take Accurate Notes. Ethnography is intricately linked with journal writing. Leaders could be asked to write a diary of what they do every day on the job. As a part of that diary, leaders could do personal assessments of their performance and identify areas where improvements could occur. Through content analysis, the diary could periodically be assessed to determine major themes that leaders perceive in the work setting.

Look for Unobtrusive Signs of Activity or Inactivity. Unobtrusive measures can be used by leaders and researchers to identify signs of performance or nonperformance and traces of employees' activity (for example, who interacts with whom on breaks and rest periods). Leaders, like ethnographers, can use these unobtrusive measures to collect information.

Leaders who seek the sensitivity of ethnographers can engage in some or many of these activities to become more aware of an organization's culture and thus more able to create an alternative culture. As leaders learn to understand and apply these and other qualitative techniques and processes, they will be more sensitive to and aware of the work setting. Since leaders deal with people in complex social settings, understanding leadership must be incorporated with the process of understanding people at work. Qualitative methods have recently been used extensively to provide better understanding of the process of people at work from a theoretical perspective. As leaders learn to apply those skills, the effectiveness of organizations should also improve.

Implications for Theory and Practice

Leaders are the cultural guardians of organizations. They create and maintain the attitudes, habits, beliefs, and traditions that make each organization unique. By focusing on the qualitative side, leaders can begin to create cultural fabrics that bind people together, that motivate people in the setting, and that provide people with a sense of belonging and continuity. Organizations as cultural microcosms must adapt to a changing environment. Since leaders stand as sentries of organizations, they must be able to respond to a changing world. To make those necessary changes may require that leaders rely on more than the traditional quantitative techniques. The qualitative side of leadership may help leaders to integrate an organization's culture into a changing setting. Along with others (Berlew, 1979; Deal and Kennedy, 1982), we advocate qualitative study of leadership. Leaders learning from ethnographers may be a concrete starting point for such future research.

References

Argyris, C. *Understanding Organizational Behavior.* Homewood, Ill.: Dorsey Press, 1960.

Bell, M. J. "Tending Bar at Brown's: Occupational Role as Artistic Performance." *Journal of Western Folklore,* 1976, *35,* 93–107.

Berlew, D. E. "Leadership and Organizational Excitement." In D. K. Kolb, I. M. Rubin, and J. M. McIntyre (Eds.), *Organizational Psychology.* (3rd ed.) Englewood Cliffs, N.J.: Prentice-Hall, 1979.

Boje, M., Fedor, D. B., and Rowland, K. M. "Myth Making: A Qualitative Step in OD Interventions." *Journal of Applied Behavioral Science,* 1982, *18* (1), 17–28.

Brown, K. S., and ReVelle, J. B. *Quantitative Methods for Managerial Decisions.* Reading, Mass.: Addison-Wesley, 1978.

Byington, R. "Strategies for Collecting Folklife in Contemporary Urban/Industrial Contexts." *Journal of Western Folklore,* 1978, *13,* 185–198.

Calder, B. J. "An Attributional Theory of Leadership." In B. M. Staw and G. Salancik (Eds.), *New Directions in Organizational Behavior.* Chicago: St. Clark Press, 1977.

Daft, R. L., and Wiginton, J. C. "Language and Organization." *Academy of Management Review,* 1979, *4,* 179–191.

Dalton, M. *Men Who Manage.* New York: Wiley, 1959.

Davis, T. R., and Luthans, F. "Leadership Reexamined: A Behavioral Approach." *Academy of Management Review,* 1979, *4,* 237-249.

Deal, T. E., and Kennedy, A. A. *Corporate Cultures: The Rites and Rituals of Corporate Life.* Reading, Mass.: Addison-Wesley, 1982.

Downey, H., Sheridan, J., and Slocum, J. "The Path-Goal Theory of Leadership: A Longitudinal Analysis." *Organizational Behavior and Human Performance,* 1976, *16,* 156-176.

Dubin, R. "Theory Building in Applied Areas." In M. Dunnette (Ed.), *Handbook of Industrial and Organizational Psychology.* Chicago: Rand McNally, 1976.

Edgerton, R., and Langness, L. L. *Methods and Styles in the Study of Culture.* San Francisco: Chandler, 1971.

Erikson, K. T. "A Comment on Disguised Observation in Sociology." *Social Problems,* 1967, *14,* 366-373.

Fiedler, F. "Personality, Motivational Systems, and Behavior of High and Low LPC Persons." *Human Relations,* 1972, *25,* 392-412.

Fleishman, E. A. "A Leader Behavior Description for Industry." In R. M. Stogdill and A. E. Coons (Eds.), *Leader Behavior: Its Description and Measurement.* Columbus: Bureau of Business Research, Ohio State University, 1957.

Garfinkel, H. *Studies in Ethnomethodology.* Englewood Cliffs, N.J.: Prentice-Hall, 1967.

Glaser, B. G., and Strauss, A. *The Discovery of Grounded Theory.* Chicago: Aldine, 1967.

Goffman, E. *Asylums.* Garden City, N.Y.: Doubleday, 1961.

Halpin, A. W., and Winer, B. J. "A Factorial Study of the Leader Behavior Descriptions." In R. M. Stogdill and A. E. Coons (Eds.), *Leader Behavior: Its Description and Measurement.* Columbus: Bureau of Business Research, Ohio State University, 1957.

Hemphill, J. K., and Coons, A. E. "Development of the Leader Behavior Description Questionnaire." In R. M. Stogdill and A. E. Coons (Eds.), *Leader Behavior: Its Description and Measurement.* Columbus: Bureau of Business Research, Ohio State University, 1957.

House, R. J. "A Path-Goal Theory of Leader Effectiveness." *Administrative Science Quarterly*, 1971, *16*, 321-338.

House, R. J. "A 1976 Theory of Charismatic Leadership." In J. G. Hunt and L. L. Larson (Eds.), *Leadership: The Cutting Edge*. Carbondale: Southern Illinois University Press, 1977.

House, R. J., and Dessler, G. "The Path-Goal Theory of Leadership: Some Post Hoc and a Priori Tests." In J. G. Hunt and L. L. Larson (Eds.), *Contingency Approaches to Leadership*. Carbondale: Southern Illinois University Press, 1974.

House, R. J., and Mitchell, T. R. "Path-Goal Theory of Leadership." *Journal of Contemporary Business*, 1974, *3*, 81-97.

Johnson, A. W. *Quantification in Cultural Anthropology: An Introduction to Research Design*. Stanford, Calif.: Stanford University Press, 1978.

Kahn, R. L., and Katz, D. "Leadership Practices in Relation to Production and Morale." In D. Cartwright and A. F. Zander (Eds.), *Group Dynamics*. (2nd ed.) New York: Harper & Row, 1960.

Katz, D., and Kahn, R. L. "Human Organization and Worker Motivation." In L. R. Tripp (Ed.), *Industrial Productivity*. Madison, Wis.: Industrial Relations Research Association, 1952.

Kerr, S., and others. "Toward a Contingency Theory of Leadership Based upon the Consideration and Initiating Structure Literature." *Organizational Behavior and Human Performance*, 1974, *12*, 62-82.

Korman, A. K. "Consideration, Initiating Structure, and Organizational Criteria: A Review." *Personnel Psychology*, 1966, *19*, 349-362.

Lewin, K. "The Dynamics of Group Action." *Educational Leadership*, 1944, *1*, 195-200.

Lifson, T. B. "An Emergent Administrative System: Interpersonal Networks in a Japanese General Trading Firm." Working paper, Harvard Business School, 1979.

Likert, R. *New Patterns of Management*. New York: McGraw-Hill, 1961.

Livingston, J. S. "Myth of the Well-Educated Manager." *Harvard Business Review*, 1971, *49*, 79-89.

Lofland, J. *Doing Social Life: The Qualitative Study of Human Interaction in Natural Settings.* New York: Wiley, 1971.

Mann, R. D. "A Review of the Relationships Between Personality and Performance in Small Groups." *Psychological Bulletin,* 1959, *56,* 241-270.

Mintzberg, H. *The Nature of Managerial Work.* New York: Harper & Row, 1973.

Morgan, G., and Smircich, L. "The Case for Qualitative Research." *Academy of Management Review,* 1980, *5,* 491-500.

Oldham, G. R. "The Motivational Strategies Used by Supervisors: Relationships to Effectiveness Indicators." *Organizational Behavior and Human Performance,* 1976, *15,* 66-86.

Ouchi, W. G. *Theory Z: How American Businesses Can Meet the Japanese Challenge.* Reading, Mass.: Addison-Wesley, 1981.

Payne, R. *The Great Man: A Portrait of Winston Churchill.* New York: Coward, McCann & Geoghegan, 1974.

Pelto, P. J. "Participant Observation." In P. J. Pelto (Ed.), *Anthropological Research.* New York: Harper & Row, 1970.

Pelto, P. J., and Pelto, G. H. *Anthropological Research: The Structure of Inquiry.* (2nd ed.) Cambridge, England: Cambridge University Press, 1978.

Peters, T. J. "Symbols, Patterns, and Settings: An Optimistic Case for Getting Things Done." *Organizational Dynamics,* 1978, *14,* 67-81.

Pfeffer, J. "The Ambiguity of Leadership." *Academy of Management Review,* 1977, *2,* 79-91.

Pondy, L. R. "Leadership in a Language Game." In M. McCall and M. Zombardo (Eds.), *Leadership: Where Else Can We Go?* Durham, N.C.: Duke University Press, 1976.

Price-Williams, D. R. "The Problem of Categories." *Ethos,* 1974, *2* (2), 95-114.

Sanday, P. R. "The Ethnographic Paradigms." *Administrative Science Quarterly,* 1979, *24,* 527-538.

Schriesheim, C. A., House, R. J., and Kerr, S. "Leader Initiating Structure: A Reconciliation of Discrepant Research Results and Some Empirical Tests." *Organizational Behavior and Human Performance,* 1976, *15,* 297-321.

Schriesheim, C. A., and Kerr, S. "Theories and Measures of Leadership: A Critical Appraisal of Current and Future Directions." In J. G. Hunt and L. L. Larson (Eds.), *Leadership: The Cutting Edge.* Carbondale: Southern Illinois University Press, 1977.

Schriesheim, C. A., Kinicki, A. J., and Schriesheim, J. F. "The Effect of Leniency on Leader Behavior Descriptions." *Organizational Behavior and Human Performance,* 1979, *23,* 1-29.

Schriesheim, C. A., and VonGlinow, M. "The Path-Goal Theory of Leadership: A Theoretical and Empirical Analysis." *Academy of Management Journal,* 1977, *20,* 398-405.

Schriesheim, J. F., and Schriesheim, C. A. "A Test of the Path-Goal Theory of Leadership Across Multiple Organizational Levels in a Large Public Utility." Unpublished manuscript, College of Business Administration, Kent State University, 1978.

Schutz, A. *The Phenomenology of the Social World.* Evanston, Ill.: Northwestern University Press, 1967.

Spradley, J. P. *Participant Observation.* New York: Holt, Rinehart and Winston, 1980.

Stogdill, R. M. "Personal Factors Associated with Leadership: A Survey of the Literature." *Journal of Psychology,* 1948, *25,* 35-71.

Stogdill, R. M. *Handbook of Leadership: A Survey of Theory and Research.* New York: Free Press, 1974.

Susman, G. I., and Evered, R. D. "An Assessment of the Scientific Merits of Action Research." *Administrative Science Quarterly,* 1978, *23,* 582-603.

Tannenbaum, R., and Schmidt, W. "How to Choose a Leadership Pattern." *Harvard Business Review,* 1973, *51,* 95-102.

Van Maanen, J. "Reclaiming Qualitative Methods for Organizational Research: A Preface." *Administrative Science Quarterly,* 1979, *24,* 520-526.

Weissenberger, P., and Kavanagh, M. J. "The Independence of Initiating Structure and Consideration: A Review of the Evidence." *Personnel Psychology,* 1972, *25,* 119-130.

Whyte, W. F. *Street Corner Society.* (Rev. ed.) Chicago: University of Chicago Press, 1955.

Wilkins, A. L. "Organizational Stories as an Expression of Management Philosophy." Unpublished doctoral dissertation, Stanford University, 1978.

Zetlin, A. G., and Sabsay, S. "Characterizing Verbal Interaction Among Moderately Retarded Peers: Some Methodological Issues." Unpublished paper, Mental Retardation Research Center, UCLA Neuropsychiatric Institute, University of California at Los Angeles, 1980.

14

Organizational Stories and Rituals

Thomas C. Dandridge

From its various perspectives, this book is about the worlds of individuals and how these worlds are shaped into sufficiently similar views to form a common system. The purpose of this chapter is to present ideas about the roles that ritual acts and organizational stories can play in the creation, maintenance, and guidance of the common system. To the extent that individuals agree in defining an organization, the organization has an identity. In the case of a corporation, this "defining" is legal; the corporation has a separate legal identity. In practice, however, we intuitively know that the organization has an identity only as we perceive it operating. "In a particular situation the set of meanings that evolves gives a group its own ethos, or distinctive character, which is expressed in patterns of belief (ideology), activity (norms and rituals), language and other symbolic forms through which organization members both create and sustain their view of the world and image of themselves in the world" (Smircich, 1983). In operation, an organizational culture emerges that has a defining quality analogous to the personality of an individual. It may not be empirically definable, but it is evident in the operation and the nature of our expectations of the organization (Schwartz and Davis, 1981). Louis (1983) likens an organizational setting to a Petri dish. "Some organizational settings may 'bear' (in the sense of supporting the development of) elaborate cultures, while, in others, no appreciable culture may develop. In the latter case, the settings may be characterized by more purely instrumental involvement of members and individually-oriented behaviors" (p. 46). Even the "sterile" organizations that Louis refers to involve a set of expectations and, hence, a type of culture. In every case, as she notes further, "the organization provides the setting or milieu in and through which cultures may develop . . ." (p. 47).

Pfeffer (1981) discusses consensus on identity as one way of defining organizations. He suggests a way of defining boundaries or determining identity "by the degree of acceptance of a distinguishing ideology, perception of the world, or distinctive organizational paradigm" (p. 13). The resulting understanding provides members of the organization with a sense of belonging and identity. The understanding works for both insiders and outsiders. In particular, the resulting commitment of members aids in guiding their activity. Management bears the responsibility for creating and shaping this "person," guiding its character, and, in total, nurturing the organization's culture. In the fulfillment of this responsibility, the work of a manager becomes the management of symbols, more than production scheduling or accounting. The result of this symbol management is social consensus, on which operational activities depend. Pfeffer states that "It might be predicted that shifts in power and control occur, and the organizational coalition becomes unstable or begins to fall apart primarily when social reality construction and sense-making activities have been neglected and ignored within the organization" (p. 15).

Some of the tools useful in accomplishing symbol management are the organization's rituals and stories. The richness of detail or the depth to which we comprehend the unique organizational identity is largely determined by the stories we select to tell about the organization and the rituals enacted. As they communicate this richness, they act as symbols. The term symbols is used here in distinction to the term signs. Signs are seen as serving a static function of talking *about* something or taking the place of what they represent. "Symbols go beyond this static function as they actively elicit the internal experience of meaning . . . they help to translate an unconscious or intuitively known internal world of feelings into the comprehendable terms of our visible reality" (Dandridge, 1983, p. 71). Using Langer's (1953) concepts, a *discursive* language provides a linear description to point out a subject or to talk about attributes of the subject. Signs are discursive; for example, a stop sign. A *presentational* language, in contrast, presents an experience in total. It draws out for the participant more than is superficially observed in the words or actions per se. Music as seen on a page is an example of discursive language, while the presentational language and the symbolism are evident in the music as experienced. Symbols as defined here are a different *level* of communication—not a substitute for rational discursive language but an additional tool. There is thus no issue of truth or falsehood to a story as it is used as a symbol. That is in contrast to the way we frequently use the word *myth* to mean an unfounded story that someone else may believe, while we know better. As the leader focuses on *meaning* rather than on rationality, he or she attends to the symbolic quality and is prepared to use the symbol in management.

As we explore the nature of symbolism, we need to recognize the complexity of the concept and the difficulty in grasping it. Morgan and others (1983) note three broad issues that contribute to this difficulty. First, symbols vary greatly in their complexity. Second, their creation may be either conscious or unconscious. Third, symbols vary in the extent to which they are shared and the extent to which different people experience the same item as symbolic. These concerns, especially the latter, will be discussed further as we consider the stages in the evolution of a symbol.

This chapter is intended to raise the reader's awareness of stories and rituals as organizational symbols and to aid in a consideration of the potential to *manage* symbols. Symbols do exist, and they have varying effect on the definition and operation of organizations. It is part of the art of leadership to make use of them responsibly and effectively. The chapter focuses on stories and rituals in particular as two potent symbolic elements, acknowledging that other types of symbols also are effective.

Rituals can include routine events, such as coffee breaks, as well as annual events, parties, or once-in-a-lifetime anniversary celebrations. Vinton (1983) has drawn an important distinction between ritual and procedure. "While there are procedural aspects to rituals, rituals hold much deeper meanings. . . . Procedures are simply accepted ways of accomplishing certain tasks. A ritual, on the other hand, is a medium of culture creation whose crucial feature is the message it contains" (p. 104). She emphasizes the presence of ritual in a quotation from Campbell (1972): "The function of ritual . . . is to give form to human life, not in the way of a mere surface arrangement, but in depth. In ancient times every social occasion was ritually structured and the sense of depth was rendered through the maintenance of a religious tone. Today, on the other hand, the religious tone is reserved for exceptional, very special, 'sacred' occasions. And yet even in the patterns of our secular life, ritual survives" (p. 43). Ritual provides a "safe place" to learn norms and behavioral skills that are important to the organization; it provides a medium for learning at an appropriate speed and context. The importance and the power of learning through *doing* are particularly evident in rituals.

Stories are symbols as they contain a summary of a variety of events that lead to one perception. The story carries, contains, or represents a broader data base and is a succinct summary of that data base and its meaning. Eoyang's (1983) point about symbols applies well to stories: stories "can be more concise than the meanings that they represent; that is to say that the expression of meaning can be compressed in space and time through symbolic representation" (p. 110).

Symbol Audiences

Symbols may be used effectively with any of three different audiences. The identity of the organization is important with each of these audiences, and sophisticated use of symbols can encourage different perceptions by each of these different audiences. One audience is the general public, including the consumers of the company's product or services. Burton Clark's description (1970) of the saga, or organizational history, of three unique small colleges in the United States was one of the early studies of stories of organizations and their impact on the "consumer" (the prospective students). A celebration of the anniversary of a company's founding may be designed to impress the consuming public, with stories told that carry an image that confirms how long and how ardently the company has served the local community, the consumer, and the nation. On the 100th anniversary of Exxon in 1982, the company published a hardcover book of stories and pictures of the company's history (Bailey, 1982). The description of the founder, John D. Rockefeller, portrays him as a shrewd but generous man. "The guiding example was John D. Rockefeller, who even as an enterprising teenager with an income of $300 a year, regularly donated part of his earnings to churches and other charitable institutions" (Bailey, 1982, p. 99). The ruthless activities for which he is reportedly responsible and that are alleged to be a part of the assembly of the Standard Oil Company are not mentioned. Elsewhere, stories are told of how he supposedly ordered the burning of a factory belonging to a widow because she refused to sell out to him.

A second external audience is other companies, including suppliers and competitors. On Ford's 75th anniversary, a Ford-built rocket was launched from Cape Kennedy, and 1,708 copies of the original Model T, made of sterling silver and gold with diamonds for headlights and operating brake and steering mechanisms, were sold at $5,000 apiece or given to key customers and suppliers. (The number produced matched the number of Model Ts produced in 1903.) General Electric had an entire catalogue of memorabilia available for their branches and distributors to give to representatives of other firms on the company's 100th anniversary (Dandridge, 1979). The catalogue states: "Centennial Program Activity over the past few weeks has produced a demand for a selection of distinctive GE100 commemorative devices that can be used to recognize employee contributions and achievements internally, and serve as valued mementos for VIP customers, civic and governmental leaders and other external influentials." Outside the corporate world, the traditional "rivalry" of the Army-Navy football game represents an interorganizational ritual of long standing. It serves as an example of how stories and rituals can define the interface between two organizations, including them both in the enactment.

The third audience, the one of primary concern here, is the membership of the organization itself. The study by Clark (1970) cited previously and works by Rohlen (1970, 1974) were among the first to describe symbols intended to influence new or existing organization members. Rohlen's works focus on the use of stories and ritual to manage employees in a variety of Japanese companies. Trice, Belasco, and Alutto (1969) saw ceremonials as "an essential element of all social systems" and defined them as "distinct sets of system practices, procedures and techniques—which are accepted and desired by system members" (p. 41). They list data on the symbolic aspect of familiar items in organizational life, such as the exit experience and the performance review. These activities are rituals, as they have cultural meaning or significance to participants beyond their explicit task-related intent (Moberg, 1981). Eating patterns, such as who eats together or has coffee together, are often ritualized and present messages. For a manager to *stop* asking his secretary to make and serve coffee certainly has symbolic meaning in today's work world. Such a decision on the part of the manager is an example of symbol management, just as the decision to *enforce* such a duty as part of the secretary's job carries a symbolic message. Again, the corporate personality is constructed of such decisions on the part of the managers and the employees. In some cases, managers may be faced with more than the familiar routines and activities of work. Unique events or settings provide possibilities for symbol management. A *Wall Street Journal* article (Browning, 1983) described Americans' experiences with "Fung Shui" when operating an office in Hong Kong. The idea of Fung Shui is that if objects such as a building or furniture are located so that they are in harmony with nature, they can bring good fortune to the users, but if they are not, disasters can occur. People trained in Fung Shui can be hired to analyze an office's omens and to make recommendations for location of furniture or inclusion of special items, such as tanks containing specific types of fish that can absorb the bad luck that may be present. Mirrors may be recommended to deflect bad luck emanating from other nearby property. Foreigners often initially hire a Fung Shui adviser "to put Asian customers at ease, or to please local staff members." Browning notes that these same foreigners may later be drawn to the practice, as "it is based on the idea that people should live and work in harmonious surroundings." The ritual can be seen to act on managers and employees alike, whether through representation of an underlying value for harmony or through a belief in the magic connected with the practice. It is quite possible that the practice works purely because those who use it *believe* it will work, and that is the core of the concept of any effective symbol.

Symbol Functions

A key to using symbols in leadership is understanding the functions they can serve in the organization. One way of categorizing these functions is as *descriptive, energy controlling,* or *system maintaining* (Dandridge, 1976, 1983). Purely as description, we get very different pictures of two companies from the following brief stories:

> The owner of the company liked to claim that he was the only businessman in New York who could be driven right to his office door; the elevator in his building was large enough to accommodate his limousine, which took him to the twelfth floor.
> At a recent stockholders' meeting, the president arrived in bermuda shorts, riding up the aisle on a motorbike.

A more convincing and more concise sense of the organization is provided by such description than by discursive description.

In each case, the leader himself is the center of a story that is then nurtured as representing relationships or values.

Under the category of *energy controlling,* there are several functions with which managers may be particularly concerned. First, the rituals or stories can be used to attract new members who have values that are of particular worth to the organization. In the same way, current members can be inspired by the act or story. A study by Martin and Powers (1983) provides empirical evidence of this function. They found that, "First, stories caused commitment. Second, stories caused more commitment than other means of communicating information, such as statistics" (p. 103). As a second form of energy control, a person in isolation can re-experience a feeling or inspire himself or herself by repeating a ritual act or thinking of a story. Third, rituals in particular can provide acceptable means of venting feelings. Office parties and interdepartmental athletic events are examples. Obviously, stories or acts can be counterproductive in their impact, attracting the wrong applicants or promoting destructive venting if they are not attended to by the manager or selected with care. Thus, the leader serves as he or she selectively nurtures symbols and times their use.

Finally, symbols can function to guide an organization and its members during a time of change or to stabilize the organization, providing barriers to change. Wilkins (1983) emphasizes the importance of stories in a stabilizing function: "The stories are important indicators of the values participants share, the social prescriptions concerning how things are to be done, and the consequences of compliance or deviance. The stories may also indicate the social categories and statuses which are legitimate in the organization, and are thus an important guide to what kinds of people can do what. Such information is crucial for the successful participation of organizational actors" (p. 82). As noted earlier, we make rituals of promotions and employment terminations, often as much for those left behind as for those who move.

Wilkins and Martin (1979) provided a classification of symbols' functions similar to that provided earlier. They concluded that there are three functions served, particularly by organizational stories, which are to: "(1) generate commitment to an organization's policies and philosophy of management, (2) help participants make sense out of what they know about the organization, and (3) serve as control mechanisms, helping the organization regulate its members" (p. 44). These three functions are of particular concern to leaders. Organizational stories, from this perspective, are critical tools for the art of leadership. Deal and Kennedy (1982) describe three similar functions, in this case of ritual. Rituals release tension, guide behavior, and display or describe the organization's culture, keeping "values, beliefs, and heroes uppermost in employees' minds and hearts" (p. 63). Thus, these authors affirm rituals as other functional tools of leadership. A different categorization of symbol functions is provided by Eoyang (1983), considering their functions in communication: (1) They can provide a "compressed" presentation of meaning: they are a concise shorthand carrying meaning. (2) They can be manipulated more easily than the original thoughts. (3) Their character aids storage and retrieval of information. (4) Since they can be reproduced, communication can be reliable. (5) They enable articulation of abstractions.

The categories of functions described by these authors are not as separate in use as they have been made here for describing them. A story can serve any of the functions at different times or multiple functions at the same time. As an example, Pfeffer (1981) notes that the executive succession process can be symbolic and serve a variety of functions for several audiences. "The occasion of executive succession provides numerous opportunities to manage the creation of meaning within organizations. The fact of involuntary succession, much like organizational redesign, provides symbolic ratification of the intention to change organizational operations, and presumably, the effectiveness of those operations. Scapegoating . . . occurs in organizations other than sports organizations. . . . This creation of the belief that the position is consequential is particularly important when the position incumbent is to be used as a scapegoat for organizational difficulties later on" (p. 39). In this description, we see the potential use of both ritual and story to nurture a symbol, internally as well as for external relations. The scapegoating may be done largely to "show" something to an outside audience about the internal values of the organization. A manager in a highly visible position can be fired to separate the company from values or activities that the manager can be shown to represent, and this can be displayed to employees as well as external audiences. In the process, description, catharsis, and system-stabilization functions all are served.

It should also be noted that, as multiple symbols coexist in an organization, they may present inconsistent or conflicting messages. The symbols of the informal system may be likely to conflict with those of the formal system, especially at times of low morale. The manager may do well to simply avoid nurturing symbols that consistently present conflicting messages. If the management style has been highly autocratic all year, a "family" Christmas party may serve only to highlight that style by the contrast.

A separate but closely related issue in the use of symbols by leaders is the source of the story or ritual. Little research has been done on the originating process for a symbol. It appears less likely that an effective symbol can be created new, of whole cloth, than that managers can selectively nurture or starve stories or acts as they emerge. Nurturance can mean embellishing a story, adding authenticity through leader association, or printing it. None of this has to have any basis in scientific evidence, as was noted in the beginning of this chapter, when it was pointed out that stories or ritual are *different* from discursive communication. This nurturance can include explanation of what the story should mean, emphasizing desired values. On the other hand, the most effective way to *starve* a symbol may be providing factual evidence to the contrary, "explaining" it in scientific terms, or showing the underlying psychological features of the user. Instant discontinuance of an active ritual should be done with caution. If the ritual has potency, the discontinuance itself takes on meaning. Such a case provides an example of the complexity of symbols and their management. As meaning and symbol potency vary among participants, the leader must use care in reinforcing or changing them. The fact that the ritual has no value to the leader does not assure that it has no value to other members or outsiders.

Stages of Belief in a Symbol

The impact of a story or ritual as a symbol is dependent partly on the way in which it is perceived by those participating in it, both as leader and as respondent. This perception, or level of belief, follows a pattern that can be regarded as the life cycle of the symbol (Dandridge, 1984). The four stages proposed as part of this cycle are as follows: (1) absolute belief in the potency or reality of a story or ritual, with no conflicting data known; (2) belief in the face of conflicting beliefs or evidence to the contrary; (3) belief only when all data are included only in scientifically verified descriptions; (4) belief in an underlying value or principle and acceptance of the story or act as a symbol, since it serves as a medium for identification with this value.

We may use belief in Santa Claus as an example of the four stages. Small children have an absolute belief in the existence of Santa Claus, with no question even occurring to them for years that anyone else believes otherwise or that it is even possible to believe otherwise. This is a stage-one relationship to a symbol. At some point, the child meets peers who question this belief. The child then moves to stage two, continuing to believe in spite of growing evidence to the contrary. This *choice* to believe is on one side of the line, facing the choice to *not* believe, and is thus the entry to stage three, in which only that which is verifiable is accepted. Still later, the *enjoyment* of believing, and the connection to underlying values that Santa Claus represents, can lead the person to fervently *act as if* there is a Santa Claus, allowing this "as if" belief to motivate and guide behavior. Louis (1983) supports the idea of this "chosen belief" as she states, "In contrast to participation in a culture of birth, participation in an organizational culture is more temporary and more a matter of voluntary choice" (p. 49). Pfeffer adds the idea that the leader is equally subject to the symbols that he or she supports: "management and politicians fool themselves as well as others with their symbolic acts. If one sits in a magnificent office in a magnificent structure . . . one not only convinces others that one is in control and has power over organizations . . . one is also likely to convince oneself" (p. 47). Deal and Kennedy (1982) acknowledge the same point, but with concern: "managers need to be fully aware of the ritualistic element of their own culture and not allow themselves to be captured by the magic of what they do day to day" (p. 83). If being captured means becoming a victim of the ritual, then this warning may be appropriate. The other authors still acknowledge the value of a powerful tool well used, and deliberate stage-four choice of symbols permits such use.

We may consider these four stages from the perspective both of the "influencer," usually the manager, and of the respondent. We should recognize in passing that the roles may be reversed at times as employees invoke company ritual or remind the leader of a story that, serving as a symbol, influences the behavior of the leader. An influencer with a stage-one type of belief would not comprehend why respondents are not influenced by the ritual or story; there is no alternative to believing. A stage-two influencer would be aware of "heathens" or of errant beliefs of the competition or detractors from the company and might foster stories of what happens to nonbelievers. A stage-three influencer would not personally ascribe to any practice or story that did not have a factual or rational base but might manipulate others as he or she saw the usefulness of others' beliefs. The personnel director at Mattel Toy Company reported that at one time he found that a large number of applicants for work believed that they were going to be like the elves in Santa's workshop. This was true for production workers in particular but seemed true for many others as well. His response was to include statements in the orientation for new employees and in job announcements that encouraged belief in the "fun" of working in a toy company and the joy the product provided. The stage-four influencer would selectively nurture or modify symbols as creative tools but personally experience the influence as well. Peters and Waterman (1982) appear to support operation at this stage in the pursuit of managerial excellence as they state: "We reason by stories *at least* as often as with good data. 'Does it feel right?' counts for more than 'Does it add up?' or 'Can I prove it?' " (p. 55).

Similar differences can be found if we shift our focus to the perspective of the respondent. A respondent with a stage-one or -two basis for his or her beliefs would be highly susceptible to influence through symbols, as long as the stories or acts were consistent with this pre-existing position. We like to believe that the Russian people are managed through the selected information and stories they are allowed by their news media and that only data that support desired beliefs or confirm existing stories are provided. The typical approach to work in this country places employees in a stage-three orientation as they are rewarded for rational behavior based on factual information. At work, we often do not expect symbolic content and may disregard the possibility. A person with this orientation would be difficult to influence with symbols. In stage four, the respondent finds that added involvement, inspiration, or satisfaction is possible if he or she fully participates in the ritual or acts as if the story is true. Rather than laughing at the company song as foolish, this respondent joins in. It is this stage of leadership and membership that Peters and Waterman found in excellent companies.

The interaction of influencer and respondent varies, depending on the stage of each in regard to the symbol in question. Figure 14-1 provides a matrix showing the relationship of the respondent and the influencer and indicates the combinations with the greatest and least potential for managerial influence. (See Dandridge, 1984, for more detailed presentation.) The *H* indicates extensive managerial potential, while *O* indicates that the orientation of the influencer or respondent makes influence through symbols unlikely. As the relationships represented here are between individuals, a management dilemma is emphasized: How can we use symbols effectively in groups? This can most easily be done by selecting employees with a given orientation (the selection process of the Marines is an

Figure 14-1. Relationship of Respondent and Influencer.

Respondent's Stage

		1	2	3	4
Influencer's Stage	1			O	
	2			O	
	3	H	H	O	O
	4	H	H	O	H

example) or by fostering a companywide attitude that appreciates stories and ritual, such as described by Wilkins (1978) for "Company Z."

Conclusion

Stories and rituals are proposed here not as an end in themselves but as a potentially effective tool in the effort toward excellence in leadership. With care in the selection and telling of simple stories or the performance of ritualized acts, a manager can build a consistent identity for the company or for his or her portion of it. The leader is not a prisoner of the organization's culture but is its careful designer and caretaker. The leader follows the members in constructing or nurturing symbols that have relevance but at the same time directs respondents by amplifying and reinforcing those beliefs that are congruent with the desired identity of the organization. An effective leader can become aware of stories and rituals as symbolic elements of any organization. In managing these elements, the leader lets the symbols take part in managing the company. Symbols are tools of managers, just as are financial analysis, management information systems, and theories of organizational change and leadership that are based on purely factual empirical results.

It is consistent with the theme of this chapter to use symbols to provide a summary. Metaphorically, we may consider an organization as being built or as growing. Discursive language tools help build organizations. Leaders shape human, financial, and material resources and weld them together into a structure. Our presentational language of stories and rituals grow organizations. Leaders nurture seed events, drawing out their significance, providing fertile soil for symbol development, and weeding out symbols that present conflicting values. The culture then flowers and grows on its own, with the leaders defining its direction.

Using weaving as a symbolic representation of a company and its continuity, the profit or the "bottom line" may be represented by the warp threads, running lengthwise through the material and providing the stability of the fabric. The production and marketing technology, the human and production resources, and the control systems are the woof, woven across the warp and providing the pattern and the texture of the fabric as it emerges. Both together provide the unity. The stories, rituals, and other symbols provide the color and the "feel" of the material produced.

References

Bailey, R. H. *Century of Discovery*. New York: Exxon, 1982.

Browning, E. S. "Some Chinese Simply Won't Make a Move Without Fung Shui." *Wall Street Journal*, Dec. 19, 1983, p. 1.

Campbell, J. *Myths to Live By*. New York: Viking Press, 1972.

Clark, B. *The Distinctive College: Antioch, Reed, and Swarthmore*. Chicago: Aldine Press, 1970.

Dandridge, T. C. "Symbols at Work: The Types and Functions of Symbols in Selected Organizations." Unpublished doctoral dissertation, Graduate School of Management, University of California at Los Angeles, 1976.

Dandridge, T. C. "Celebrations of Corporate Anniversaries." Paper presented at annual meeting of the Academy of Management, Atlanta, Ga., August 1979.

Dandridge, T. C. "Symbols' Function and Use." In L. R. Pondy and others, *Organizational Symbolism*. Greenwich, Conn.: JAI Press, 1983.

Dandridge, T. C. "The Belief Stages of a Symbol: When Symbolism Works and When It Can't." Paper presented at the Conference on Organizational Culture and the Meaning of Life in the Workforce, University of British Columbia, April 1984.

Deal, T. E., and Kennedy, A. A. *Corporate Cultures: The Rites and Rituals of Corporate Life*. Reading, Mass.: Addison-Wesley, 1982.

Eoyang, C. "Symbolic Transformation of Belief Systems." In L. R. Pondy and others, *Organizational Symbolism*. Greenwich, Conn.: JAI Press, 1983.

Langer, S. K. *Feeling and Form*. New York: Scribner's, 1953.

Louis, M. R. "Organizations as Cultural-Bearing Milieux." In L. R. Pondy and others, *Organizational Symbolism*. Greenwich, Conn.: JAI Press, 1983.

Martin, J., and Powers, M. E. "Truth or Corporate Propaganda: The Value of a Good War Story." In L. R. Pondy and others, *Organizational Symbolism*. Greenwich, Conn.: JAI Press, 1983.

Moberg, D. J. "Job Enrichment Through Symbol Management." *California Management Review*, 1981, *24* (2), 25-30.

Morgan, G., and others. "Author: Please Provide Chapter Title." In L. R. Pondy and others, *Organizational Symbolism*. Greenwich, Conn.: JAI Press, 1983.

Peters, T. J., and Waterman, R. H., Jr. *In Search of Excellence: Lessons from America's Best-Run Companies*. New York: Harper & Row, 1982.

Pfeffer, J. "Management as Symbolic Action: The Creation and Maintenance of Organizational Paradigms." In L. L. Cummings and B. M. Staw (Eds.), *Research in Organizational Behavior*. Vol. 3. Greenwich, Conn.: JAI Press, 1981.

Rohlen, T. "Sponsorship of Cultural Continuity in Japan: A Company Training Program." *Journal of Asian and African Studies*, 1970, *5* (3), 184-192.

Rohlen, T. *For Harmony and Strength: Japanese White-Collar*

Organizations in Anthropological Perspective. Los Angeles: University of California Press, 1974.

Schwartz, H., and Davis, S. M. "Matching Corporate Culture and Business Strategy." *Organizational Dynamics,* 1981, *10,* 30-48.

Smircich, L. "Organizations as Shared Meanings." In L. R. Pondy and others, *Organizational Symbolism.* Greenwich, Conn.: JAI Press, 1983.

Trice, H., Belasco, J., and Alutto, J. A. "The Role of Ceremonials in Organizational Behavior." *Industrial and Labor Relations Review,* 1969, *23* (1), 40-51.

Vinton, K. E. "The Small Family-Owned Business: A Unique Organizational Culture." Unpublished doctoral dissertation, Graduate School of Business, University of Utah, 1983.

Wilkins, A. L. "Organizational Stories as an Expression of Management Philosophy: Implications for Social Control in Organizations." Unpublished doctoral dissertation, Stanford University, 1978.

Wilkins, A. L. "Organizational Stories as Stories Which Control the Organization." In L. R. Pondy and others, *Organizational Symbolism.* Greenwich, Conn.: JAI Press, 1983.

Wilkins, A. L., and Martin, J. *Organizational Legends.* Research Paper No. 521. Palo Alto, Calif.: Graduate School of Business, Stanford University, 1979.

15

Structural Approaches to Conflict Management

Kenneth W. Thomas
Walter G. Tymon, Jr.

Conflict seems to be inevitable wherever the following three conditions exist: (1) two or more people have somewhat different beliefs, needs, or preferences; (2) they are interdependent (that is, decisions need to be made that affect them all); and (3) resources are limited (so that not everyone can be satisfied). With this in mind, it is easy to see why conflict is to some degree a fact of life in organizations. Indeed, conflict is *designed* into organizations, where people are assigned different but interrelated responsibilities, and budgets and other financial controls limit the use of organizational resources.

In recent years, as organizations and societies have become more aware of interdependencies and resource limitations, interest in conflict has grown. In a survey by Thomas and Schmidt (1976), managers at different levels reported a strong and growing desire to learn more about conflict and its management. The managers reported that skill in managing conflict had become more important over the past decade. Estimates of the proportion of their time spent dealing with conflict were sizable, ranging from 18 percent (for chief executive officers) to 26 percent (for middle managers). Academic interest in conflict has also grown. Since the time when Schmidt and Tannenbaum (1960) wrote about the "Management of Differences," conflict has developed as a major area of research among organizational scientists. It is now routinely included as a chapter topic in organizational-behavior textbooks, for example.

As research evidence has accumulated, one central consensus has emerged: conflict itself is intrinsically neither bad nor good. Rather, it has the potential for being either. It is thus unfortunate that the word *conflict* has negative overtones, for it is as appropriate to see conflict as an *opportunity* as it is to perceive it as a danger. Consider, for example, the following four dimensions of conflict outcomes (Thomas, 1982):

1. *Quality of decisions.* Conflict can immobilize decision making and can result in unworkable compromises. On the other hand, it often aids decision making by causing problems to surface and bringing different perspectives to bear upon an issue. Research shows, for example, that open conflict increases the potential creativity of group decision making (Hall, 1971) and can be used to produce high-quality decisions on complex or unstructured problems (Mason, 1969; Mitroff and Emshoff, 1979).

2. *Working relationships.* Conflict can create mistrust and antagonisms that scar relationships and reduce the ability of people to work together. However, it can also be an opportunity to work through misunderstandings and improve or deepen relationships.

3. *Individual satisfaction.* Frustrations and stress from unresolved conflicts can reduce satisfaction and thus impair the ability to work and reduce an individual's commitment to an organization. At the same time, conflict provides a means for people to voice their frustrations and to change or improve the things that dissatisfy them.

4. *Time and energy.* Conflicts can consume large amounts of time and energy, creating significant opportunity costs for an organization in terms of other tasks and decisions that are neglected. On the other hand, conflicts and competition can sometimes energize individuals and groups to work

harder at organizational tasks (for example, see Deutsch, 1971; Blake and Mouton, 1961).

While conflicts have the potential for these positive or negative outcomes, the *actual* outcomes of a conflict seem to depend largely upon how that conflict is *managed* by the people involved in the conflict. Thus, the focus of this chapter is on conflict management. More specifically, the chapter concentrates, first, on the general strategies or behaviors that can be used by individuals to manage the conflicts in which they are engaged and, second, upon the structural conditions that shape those behaviors.

Five Conflict-Handling Modes

Conflict is often defined as a kind of behavior—as mutual interference, escalated hostilities, and so on. It seems more useful here to think of conflict as a *situation* or *condition,* namely, "the condition in which the concerns of two or more parties appear to be incompatible" (Thomas, 1978, p. 56). This definition allows us to separate conflict from the behaviors that people use to deal with it, so that we can consider different behavioral "conflict-handling modes." In *The Managerial Grid,* Blake and Mouton (1964) described five management styles in terms of two underlying values of the manager: concern for production and concern for people. Associated with each style was a preferred behavior for handling conflicts with subordinates. In the last twenty years, a number of extensions or reinterpretations of this scheme have been introduced by other scholars, who attempt to focus more exclusively upon conflict behaviors and their underlying dimensions (for example, Thomas, 1976; Ruble and Thomas, 1976; Hall, undated; Rahim and Bonoma, 1979).

Much of the work of one of the current authors has involved the model shown in Figure 15-1. Rather than classifying behaviors according to underlying values or personality, this model focuses upon the individual's intentions in a given situation. (An empirical comparison between this scheme and others

Figure 15-1. Two-Dimensional Model of Conflict Behavior.

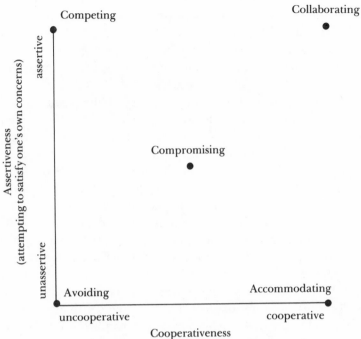

Source: Adapted from Ruble and Thomas (1976).

is presented in Thomas and Kilmann, 1978). As shown in Figure 15-1, the conflict-handling behaviors of an individual can be described in terms of two basic underlying dimensions of intent: *cooperativeness*—attempting to satisfy the other person's concerns—and *assertiveness*—attempting to satisfy one's own concerns. These two basic dimensions serve to define five different conflict-handling modes: (1) *Competing* (being uncooperative, assertive) is an attempt to arrive at a win-lose outcome that favors oneself. Competing behaviors involve various uses of power to force the other to concede—argument, authority, threats, and so on. (2) *Accommodating* (being cooperative, unassertive) is the opposite of competing, seeking to satisfy the other's concerns at the expense of one's own. Accommodating can take various forms, including selfless generosity, obeying orders that one disagrees with, and yielding to superior force. (3) *Avoiding* (being uncooperative, unassertive) neglects both one's own and the other person's concerns by not raising or addressing the conflict issue. Avoiding can take the form of diplomatically sidestepping an issue, postponing it, or simply withdrawing from a threatening situation. (4) *Collaborating* (being cooperative, assertive) is the opposite of avoiding, attempting to work with the other person to find a solution that fully satisfies both one's own concerns and those of the other. Collaborating might involve exploring a disagreement to learn from each other's insights and arrive at an optimal decision or confronting and trying to arrive at a creative solution to an interpersonal problem. (5) *Compromising* (intermediate in both cooperativeness and assertiveness) seeks an expedient middle-ground position that provides partial satisfaction for both parties. Compromising falls between competing and accommodating, since it makes more concessions than competing but fewer than accommodating. Likewise, compromising addresses an issue more than avoiding does but does not explore it in as much depth as collaborating does. It can take such forms as splitting the difference or exchanging concessions.

Two studies by Ruble and Thomas (1976) have demonstrated the meaningfulness of this scheme for classifying conflict-handling modes. Using techniques involving factor analysis and semantic differential ratings in conflict situations, individuals were found to perceive other people in terms of two basic dimensions that closely paralleled assertiveness and cooperativeness. In addition, individuals' placement of the five conflict-handling modes along these two dimensions corresponded closely to the model. Thus, there is strong evidence that this model captures categories that people use to interpret each other's behavior in conflict situations. Initially, two-dimensional models of conflict behaviors were used primarily to identify and recommend collaboration (also called "problem solving," "integrating," "confrontation," or "synergy") as a constructive approach to conflict management. Collaboration involves the following steps (Thomas, 1979): (1) confronting the conflict; (2) identifying the underlying concerns of the parties—getting beneath the positions they have taken to the underlying facts or needs that have led them to take those positions; (3) posing the conflict as a problem—namely, is there a way that both parties' underlying concerns can be reconciled or satisfied? (4) problem solving to find alternatives that would satisfy both parties; and (5) selecting the most jointly satisfactory alternative. (For more on collaborative approaches to conflict, see Filley, 1975; Eiseman, 1978; Likert and Likert, 1976.)

Collaboration appears to have a number of advantages. For example, people who are seen as collaborative appear more likely to be liked and respected (Ruble and Thomas, 1976), so that working relationships are improved (Burke, 1970; Renwick, 1975). It is also directed at increasing the satisfaction of the conflict parties and strives to reach creative, integrative decisions. However, collaboration has costs in terms of the time it takes. There are also a series of limiting conditions to its effective use, including the skills and motivations of the conflict parties and whether the conflict issue will permit win/win outcomes. Accordingly, when groups of chief executive officers of organizations were asked to identify uses of the conflict-handling modes (Thomas, 1977), they generated a list of uses for *each* of these modes (shown in Table 15-1). The list suggests that each conflict mode can be a useful managerial tool in appropriate situations. The general conclusion we have reached is that the optimal conflict-handling mode varies from situation to situation. Effective conflict management requires that one understand the conflict issues involved in a given situation, the concrete ways in which conflict-handling modes can be acted out in that situation, and the consequences of those behaviors. We now turn to an example of this type of situational analysis.

A Case Example: Performance Appraisal and Feedback

Despite the enormous energy that has been put into designing various performance-appraisal systems, appraisal and feedback remain problematical activities for supervisors. They involve the sensitive, emotionally charged issue of the subordi-

Table 15-1. Uses of the Five Conflict-Handling Modes.

Mode	Uses
Competing	1. When quick, decisive action is vital—for example, in emergencies. 2. On important issues where unpopular actions need implementing—for example, cost cutting, enforcing unpopular rules, discipline. 3. On issues vital to company welfare when you know that you are right. 4. When people take advantage of noncompetitive behavior.
Collaborating	1. To find an integrative solution when both sets of concerns are too important to be compromised. 2. When your objective is to learn. 3. To merge insights from people with different perspectives. 4. To gain commitment by incorporating concerns into a consensus. 5. To work through feelings that have interfered with a relationship.
Compromising	1. When goals are important but not worth the effort or potential disruption of more assertive modes. 2. When opponents with equal power are committed to mutually exclusive goals. 3. To achieve temporary settlements to complex issues. 4. To arrive at expedient solutions under time pressure. 5. As a backup when collaboration or competition is unsuccessful.
Avoiding	1. When an issue is trivial or when more important issues are pressing. 2. When you perceive no chance of satisfying your concerns. 3. When potential disruption outweighs the benefits of resolution. 4. To let people cool down and regain perspective. 5. When gathering information supercedes immediate decision. 6. When others can resolve the conflict more effectively. 7. When issues seem tangential or symptomatic of other issues.

Table 15-1. Uses of the Five Conflict-Handling Modes, Cont'd.

Mode	Uses
Accommodating	1. When you find that you are wrong—to allow a better position to be heard, to learn, and to show your reasonableness.
	2. When issues are more important to others than to yourself—to satisfy others and maintain cooperation.
	3. To build social credits for later issues.
	4. To minimize loss when you are outmatched and losing.
	5. When harmony and stability are especially important.
	6. To allow subordinates to develop by learning from mistakes.

Source: Thomas (1977).

nate's contribution and ability. Moreover, they involve the confrontation of predictable differences of perception between superior and subordinate. For example, there is a tendency for superiors to attribute low performance to subordinates' personal characteristics (habits, skill deficiencies, attitudes, and so on), while subordinates are more likely to attribute low performance to events outside their control (DeVries and others, 1980). There is also a well-documented tendency for subordinates to see their own performance as better than the superior sees it (Meyer, Kay, and French, 1965). Thus, there is a fairly strong tendency for the superior to see greater need for subordinate improvement and development than does the subordinate. Given these differences, the five conflict-handling modes provide a way of organizing research findings on the alternative behaviors used by supervisors and their consequences.

Competing occurs when the superior tries to force upon the subordinate the evaluation that the superior regards as accurate. Many performance-appraisal systems encourage this sort of behavior by requiring the manager to prepare a written appraisal prior to meeting with the employee (Miner, 1974). When the performance feedback session is held, the superior is thus placed in the position of having to defend an assessment to which he or she is already committed. Accordingly, managers report that the formal appraisal system causes them to "save up" items where improvement is needed in order to be able to defend their assessment more convincingly during the feedback session (Kay, Meyer, and French, 1965; Thompson and Dalton, 1970). Research clearly suggests that this type of feedback behavior tends to threaten the subordinate's self-esteem. As noted earlier, there is a significant tendency for subordinates to perceive their own performance as higher than the superior's assessment of that performance. In a field study, Meyer, Kay, and French (1965) concluded that this was true for 82 percent of the subordinates they interviewed and that the feedback session was thus likely to be a deflating experience for these employees.

When the supervisor adopts a competitive posture, subordinates are often placed in a no-win situation. If subordinates do challenge an unflattering assessment, they are likely to receive even more criticisms from the supervisor in defense of that assessment. This, in turn, will serve only to increase the threat to their self-esteem. Meyer, Kay, and French (1965) found that employees who received an above-average number of criticisms during the feedback session showed less goal achievement ten to twelve weeks later than those who had received fewer criticisms. This occurred despite the fact that these employees had not previously been poorer performers than the other employees.

Avoiding occurs when the superior attempts to sidestep giving appraisal feedback altogether or gives it in a brief and perfunctory manner. Avoiding may represent an attempt to prevent or minimize the negative consequences described earlier. It can also be interpreted as an attempt to conserve the time and energy associated with this sensitive process. This avoidance motive appears to be a factor in the relatively brief amount of time spent on performance-appraisal feedback. In one study of 1,450 managers, for example, almost all the managers were appraised only once a year, and the length of the appraisal interview in 60 percent of the cases lasted less than half an hour. In addition, 25 percent of the managers said that their appraisal covered only some, or even none, of the important aspects of their jobs (Cellucci and Lombardo, 1978). In fact, appraisal feedback is sometimes given in so perfunctory a manner that subordinates are unaware that a formal appraisal has taken place. When subordinates and their superiors are asked whether formal appraisal discussions have been held, subordinates are less likely to say yes. Porter, Lawler, and Hackman (1975) coined the term *vanishing performance appraisal* to describe this phenomenon.

Avoiding may reduce some of the negative consequences associated with competing—threat to self-esteem, hostility, damaged working relationship, dramatic productivity drops. And, as noted, it is likely to conserve time and energy, at least in the short run. However, avoiding represents a neglect of the performance-appraisal feedback process. The superior's expectations and assessment are not presented in detail to provide guidance for the subordinate's development. In addition to hindering development, the resulting uncertainty and ambiguity can be a considerable source of stress for the subordinate (Kahn and others, 1964).

Compromise and *accommodating* both refer to superiors raising their formal assessment of the subordinate's performance above what they feel is accurate. The difference is a matter of degree. Compromise involves giving a rating that is somewhere between the supervisor's and the subordinate's views of what is appropriate, while accommodating refers to a complete yielding to the subordinate's views or desires. The tendency of superiors to raise performance-appraisal ratings in anticipation of feedback sessions was dramatically demonstrated in an early experiment by Stockford and Bissell (1949). These researchers obtained the ratings made by supervisors in a company in which ratings had traditionally been kept secret from subordinates. After these ratings were made, supervisors were told that they would now have to conduct feedback sessions with subordinates on their appraisals, and they were given the opportunity to "reevaluate" their subordinates, if necessary, prior to those feedback sessions. The researchers found that the mean rating of 60 on the evaluations increased to a mean of 84 in anticipation of the feedback sessions, a very significant jump. This same tendency has also been documented in more controlled laboratory experimentation (Fisher, 1979).

Like avoiding, compromise and accommodating can prevent or reduce some of the negative consequences associated with managerial competing in performance appraisal and feedback. However, compromise and accommodating also have significant costs, since they involve the relaxation of the superior's standards. In the more extreme case of accommodation, the superior fails to address (and thus to help correct) areas of performance where deficiencies are apparent. The superior may thus allow problems to grow into difficult or intolerable situations. One study of firing behavior by managers, for example, found that, while competing managers were quicker to fire low performers, both accommodating and competing managers found it necessary to fire more subordinates than other managers (O'Reilly and Weitz, 1980).

Collaborating is a process that attempts to reach a shared understanding of the subordinate's present performance and the path toward future development. To achieve this goal, collaborating requires a different quality of interaction between manager and subordinate than do the other conflict-handling modes. In every other conflict mode (with the possible exception of avoiding), both superior and subordinate tend to enter the feedback session with an overall assessment of the subordinate's performance. This assessment is a conclusion that is based upon the facts they have access to, as well as their insights and needs. In the case of competing, compromising, and accommodating, these conclusions become the focus of the interaction: Both individuals take a position based upon their own or the other's conclusion or a position that falls between the two conclusions. The underlying facts, insights, and needs are used, if at all, to justify these positions.

In collaborating, by contrast, conclusions need to be suspended in order to reach a common understanding. This process requires an honest dialogue in which both parties share the facts, insights, and needs that are relevant to understanding and guiding the development of the employee's performance. This part of the process requires an openness to new information and involves learning by both parties. Only when these facts, insights, and needs have been discussed and accepted is an overall assessment and development plan agreed to. This new set of conclusions is likely to be quite different from and more comprehensive than the conclusions reached by either party alone. Furthermore, both parties are likely to be more firmly committed to these decisions than to decisions that result from other conflict-handling modes. A great deal of research indicates that positive outcomes from performance appraisal are associated with encouraging the subordinate to participate in this type of collaborative discussion. In a review of the performance-appraisal literature, Cederblom (1982) found that the superior's encouragement of participation by the subordinate was consistently related to such positive outcomes as the subordinate's favorable attitudes toward the appraisal process and the superior and subsequent performance improvements by the subordinate (for example, Burke and Wilcox, 1969; Burke, Weitzel, and Weir, 1978; Greller, 1975; Nemeroff and Wexley, 1977).

To summarize this example, the five conflict-handling modes provide a rather parsimonious way of organizing available research on supervisory behavior during the appraisal and feedback process. When combined with empirical findings on the consequences of these behaviors, this analysis yields rather clear normative implications. Collaborative behaviors are shown to result in more improvement in performance, a more favorable attitude toward the appraisal process and the superior, and less threat to the subordinate's self-esteem. Where employee development and the maintenance of morale and work relations are sufficiently important, collaborative performance appraisals thus clearly appear to justify the somewhat greater time investment required for this type of process.

A Structural Approach to Conflict Management

From an applied perspective, of course, identifying a preferred conflict-handling behavior is only the first step. What remains is the task of intervening to bring about an increase in the desired behavior. There are two basic ways of approaching this task (Thomas, 1976; Kilmann and Thomas, 1978). The first involves thinking of conflict episodes as discrete *processes*—as sequences of events that occur from time to time in the organization. One may attempt to change conflict behavior by intervening in this stream of conflict events. These "process interventions" include various forms of direct involvement—as mediator, adviser, peacemaker, or some other role. The second approach requires thinking of the conflict-handling modes as occurring in the context of various *conditions* (for example, individual abilities, norms, and an organizational design). The configuration or structure of these conditions can be seen as shaping the conflict behavior that occurs within it. Thus, one may also attempt to change conflict behavior by making a variety of "structural" interventions to reshape these surrounding conditions. Alterations can be made in the cast of characters, social norms, reward systems, operating procedures, and so on.

Our focus here will be upon the structural approach as a way of increasing the frequency of desired conflict-handling modes. Both forms of intervention have their place in an organization. By intervening directly in conflict events, process interventions can often have a more immediate and precise effect upon a given episode of conflict behavior. On the other hand, structural interventions are likely to have more lasting, systematic effects in an organization, continuing to affect all the episodes that occur in a given setting. Thus, from a cost-benefit standpoint, while process interventions are likely to be best suited to occasional critical incidents, structural interventions will likely be most efficient in managing recurrent or widespread conflict phenomena (such as the rather predictable conflict issues involved in performance appraisal).

A number of recent structural models of conflict management have been developed (see, for example, Brown, 1983; Likert and Likert, 1976). The one used here (from Thomas, 1976) is shown in Figure 15-2. Derived from a review of empirical research, it focuses upon those parameters of a situation that directly shape the behavior of the individual parties to a conflict. The model identifies four general sets of parameters: (1)

Figure 15-2. Structural Model of Dyadic Conflict.

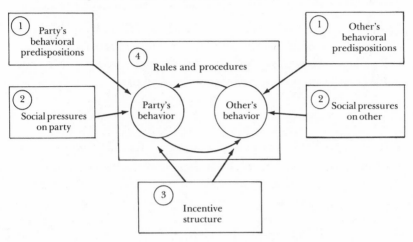

Source: Thomas (1976).

each person's behavioral predispositions, (2) social pressures up-on each person, (3) the incentive structure for the parties, and (4) the rules and procedures within which the parties interact. The following is a brief overview of each set of factors.

Individual Predispositions. Although individuals can show considerable flexibility in responding to different conditions, there are also some central tendencies or consistencies in their behavior (see, for example, the findings of Gormley and Edelberg, 1974, on assertiveness). These "predispositions," in turn, appear to reflect a number of individual characteristics, including skills, motives, assumptions, and attitudes. The organization can exert considerable influence over the distribution of these characteristics through its criteria for selection, promotion, and placement. Assessment centers, for example, use a number of evaluation exercises that involve the handling of conflict situations. Questions about cooperative work relations are also common in reference letters and performance appraisals.

Training provides a mechanism for modifying or supplementing conflict-management skills and insights. For example, established training instruments are available to help individuals learn their own behavioral predispositions in conflict situations and the probable consequences of these predispositions (Thomas and Kilmann, 1974; Hall, 1969; Rahim, 1983). Training modules have also been developed to teach specific tactics, including the collaborative tactics of active listening or some of the competitive and compromising tactics involved in bargaining.

Although there are few definitive data on the topic, available studies suggest a significant potential for beneficial effects of selection and training on conflict management. In a selection study using assessment-center ratings, for example, Graves (1982) found evidence that managers who rated high on conflict-management skill were likely to be both more effective and more rapidly promoted in their subsequent jobs. Likewise, the previously mentioned survey by Thomas and Schmidt (1976) indicated a strong interest by managers in receiving training on conflict and its management.

Social Pressures. This second factor refers to forces exerted upon the conflict parties by the other members of their social system. Broadly, each party may be exposed to social pressures from various individuals or groups concerning proper behavior—expectations of how that party "ought" to behave. These sets of expectations form the social "rules of the game" within which the parties interact. Much of the initial research on this topic focused upon sets of localized pressures upon conflict parties. For example, Thomas and Walton (1971) found that individual executives' emphasis upon collaboration had an impact upon their subordinates' collaborativeness during interdepartmental conflicts. Likewise, negotiators who represent the interests of groups were often found to be subject to strong pressure from their constituents to take competitive stands during negotiations with other groups (see, for example, the laboratory research of Blake and Mouton, 1961). This research has been helpful in suggesting sets of localized interventions targeted to expectations in specific settings. Individual supervisors' expectations can be altered or reinforced through selection and training, for example, while constituent pressures can be modified through a variety of intergroup interventions (see Blake, Shepard, and Mouton, 1964; Beckhard, 1969).

Other research has focused upon broader, organization-wide expectations that shape conflict behavior. Litwin and Stringer (1968), for example, examined conflict behavior as one aspect of an organization's overall "climate." Likewise, Blake and Mouton (1964) proposed that prevailing patterns of conflict-handling behavior were part of an organization's predominant style of management. Elaborate systemwide change programs have been developed by Blake and Mouton (described in Blake and others, 1964) and by Likert (1961, 1967) that are directed in large part at systematically producing collaborative norms in organizations.

Quite recently, a large number of organizational researchers have begun to examine such organizationwide norms in terms of organizational cultures (for example, Deal and Kennedy, 1982; Kilmann, 1984; Louis, 1980). Although not focused explicitly upon conflict, this approach promises to yield considerably more understanding of the origins of the shared belief systems and norms that shape conflict behavior in organizations and of the rituals, stories, and socialization processes that maintain these behavioral patterns.

Incentive Structure. This third factor explains individuals' conflict-handling behavior in terms of what will be instrumental for satisfying their concerns. Although an individual may have some general predispositions and be subject to others' expectations of how to behave, there are also sets of strategic considerations that provide incentives to behave differently in different conflict situations in order to achieve preferred conflict outcomes. The term *incentive structure* is used in a very broad sense to refer to what is at stake for the conflict parties in their relationship and how the satisfaction of each party's concerns is linked to the satisfaction of the other's concerns. More specifically, the model identifies two central aspects of this incentive structure for each party: (1) the size of the stakes involved and (2) the extent to which there is commonality of interest between the concerns of the two parties.

The size of the stakes for each party refers to the importance, to that party, of his or her concerns that depend upon the behavior of the other party. Essentially, the more an individual depends upon the other in some way for the satisfaction of important concerns, the greater is that individual's stake in the relationship with the other. Other things being equal, an individual is expected to be more assertive in those relationships where stakes are highest. In such relationships, a person is more likely to invest the time and energy required to obtain satisfactory outcomes (Thomas, 1976). The second variable, commonality of interest, refers to the degree to which the concerns of the two parties are mutual or shared, on the one hand, or incompatible, on the other. The latter condition is generally referred to as "conflict of interest" (Axelrod, 1970). A great deal of evidence indicates that commonality of interest generates cooperative behavior, while conflict of interest produces uncooperative behavior (Axelrod, 1970; Deutsch, 1949; Sherif, 1958).

Figure 15-3 shows how these two variables are believed to interact to shape each party's conflict-handling modes (Thomas, 1976). Other things being equal, collaborating appears most likely to occur when stakes are high for an individual and there is strong commonality of interest between both parties. In such situations, the individual is motivated enough to invest the time and energy required for collaboration and is also likely to regard the other party as an ally—someone with sufficiently similar concerns to be trusted in working together to resolve an issue. Other combinations of stakes and commonality of interest encourage other conflict modes. When the stakes are high but strong conflict of interest exists, an individual is more likely to take a competitive stand. Avoiding is likely to occur when conflict of interest is present but stakes are low—where issues represent relatively minor annoyances. Accommodating is most likely where stakes are too low to justify assertive behavior but there is sufficient commonality of interest to be concerned for, and defer to, the other party's wishes. Finally, compromise appears somewhat more likely to occur in situations that are intermediate in terms of stakes and commonality of interest.

Stakes and conflict of interest in conflict issues are often the results of organizational design decisions. Commonality of interest, for example, depends in large part on the specific re-

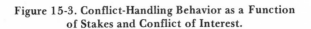

Figure 15-3. Conflict-Handling Behavior as a Function
of Stakes and Conflict of Interest.

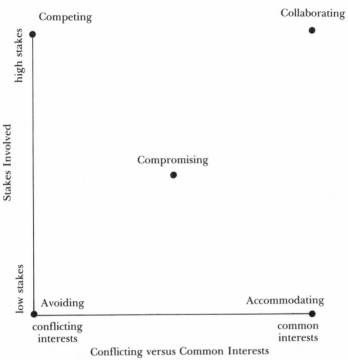

Source: Adapted from Thomas (1976).

sponsibilities delegated to different individuals, whether they
are housed in the same or different departments, and the performance criteria used to evaluate them. Likewise, an individual's stakes in an issue depend largely upon job description, the
delegation of responsibility, the visibility of negotiations and
outcomes, and the workings of control, evaluation, pay, and
promotion systems. Thus, these and other factors may be altered
when they appear to be creating dysfunctional effects upon
conflict-handling behavior. Collaboration can be increased between highly interdependent workers, for example, by designing group-based pay systems to provide significant stakes and
commonality of interest (see Blau, 1955; Lawler, 1973). Likewise, avoiding and accommodating on key issues may be reduced

by fixing accountability, establishing controls, and tying outcomes to performance evaluation (raising stakes).

Rules and Procedures. The final set of structural conditions concerns the organizational rules and procedures that bear upon the conflict parties' negotiations. These rules and procedures make up the established decision-making machinery that serves to shape and constrain the behavior of the individuals who interact within it. Decision rules frequently emerge to cover sensitive conflict issues (Thibaut and Kelley, 1959). Whether they take the form of informal agreements, precedent, or formal organizational policy, they specify which alternatives are to be chosen or avoided when certain issues arise. Such rules have the advantage of settling conflict relatively quickly. However, they have the disadvantage of reducing discussion of the merits of alternative decisions on future cases. Rules thus provide a relatively easy method for an organization to manage conflicts but run the risk of suspending critical discussion and proliferating into cumbersome masses of red tape (for example, Merton, 1957).

Negotiation procedures, on the other hand, dictate not the content of a decision but rather the manner in which it is to be made. Like decision rules, these procedures may be based upon informal precedent or elaborately formalized regulations. Procedures might involve such things as the frequency and location of meetings, whether records are kept, and the number of people present and their roles. Procedures can influence conflict-handling behavior in a number of ways, many of them unintended. Channeling all interdepartmental negotiations through department heads, for example, may reduce the likelihood of collaborating by moving negotiations away from the individuals with enough facts to be able to engage in problem solving. Keeping formal records or allowing constituents to be present may encourage competing by raising the stakes and encouraging negotiators to "grandstand" for constituents' benefit. Holding infrequent meetings may be efficient in terms of saving negotiating time but may also allow hard feelings to build, allow people to forget the facts involved in specific issues, and allow issues to accumulate so that stakes and conflict of interest appear magnified (Thomas, 1976). (More specific considerations regarding negotiation procedures can be found in Brown's 1983 discussion of the structuring of conflict "interfaces.")

Implications. Briefly, then, the structural model indicates that conflict-handling behavior in organizations is shaped by at least four very different types of parameters: by individual skills and predispositions, by social pressures and organizational culture, by the incentive structure of a given conflict situation, and by rules and procedures. Individually, each of these factors is likely to be helpful in diagnosing the sources of conflict-handling behavior and in suggesting structural changes to modify that behavior. However, there is one implication of the model that we wish especially to emphasize. According to the model, conflict behavior is shaped by the configuration of *all four* sets of conditions. Thus, no single factor is likely to be sufficient to explain behavior or to produce behavioral change. Changes in any one factor may easily be overwhelmed or negated by other, ignored factors. Thus, effective change will usually require a systematic examination of all four sets of factors and the establishment of a *congruence* among them. Collaborative behavior in a given setting, for example, is likely to occur most reliably when the conflict parties have the necessary collaborative skills and predispositions, interact within a culture that encourages problem solving, experience strong collaborative incentives, and interact under rules and procedures that facilitate problem solving.

Example Revisited:
Structural Issues in Performance Appraisal

To illustrate the potential application of the structural model, we return to the example of performance appraisal and feedback. Much of the research that bears upon the sources of dysfunctional behavior in performance appraisal has been concerned with single causal factors. As noted earlier, the structural model provides a framework for organizing the conclusions of these separate studies into a more comprehensive or holistic view of the barriers to collaborative behavior and for indicating the systematic program of changes that may be required to increase collaboration in that setting.

Managerial Predispositions. The need for training in collaborative methods of performance appraisal has been noted repeatedly. A number of researchers have noted that managers often feel awkward and ill at ease in performance interviews (for example, Kikoski and Litterer, 1983) and that involving employees does not necessarily come easily or naturally to managers (Cederblom, 1982; DeVries and others, 1980; Rosen, 1967). However, it has also been noted that performance-appraisal training is still uncommon and often receives a low priority in supervisory training (Gallegos, 1983).

Specific training recommendations have included skill training and the correction of important perceptual biases. Gallegos (1983) and Kikoski and Litterer (1983) have provided a detailed description of specific collaborative skills for performance appraisal, including providing constructive feedback, paraphrasing, reflecting feeling, and other interviewing and listening skills. In addition, Ilgen, Fisher, and Taylor (1979) found that supervisors are strongly biased in overestimating the quality of the feedback they provide to subordinates. This bias seems related to the marked tendency of individuals to overestimate their own collaborativeness compared to others and to underestimate competitive elements of their behavior (Thomas and Pondy, 1977). Thus, role plays and feedback seem to be required to correct these misperceptions, demonstrate the need for improvement, and show managers how improvements can be made.

Social Pressures. It is important here to recall that a collaborative approach to performance appraisal tends to require more managerial time and energy than other conflict-handling modes. Gallegos (1983) noted, therefore, that top management must place a high priority upon a collaborative appraisal and feedback process if it is to take place. Supervisors were observed to perceive the appraisal process and human resource development in general as of low priority compared with capital resources, budgets, and short-run production—even though upper management often paid lip service to the importance of performance appraisal.

Other researchers have observed that collaborative norms regarding performance appraisal must be consistent with the other norms that make up the organization's culture. Collaboration during performance appraisal needs to build upon the patterns of collaboration, participation, and trust fostered in everyday relations between superior and subordinate (Beer, 1981; DeVries and others, 1980; Ilgen, Fisher, and Taylor, 1979). If top management attempts to implement a participatory and collaborative approach to goal setting and appraisal in an organization with a traditionally "top-down" or autocratic culture, then performance appraisal is likely to be viewed as awkward, manipulative, or even meaningless (for example, McCall and DeVries, 1977).

In short, then, it appears that an organization's culture must emphasize a complex of related norms and values in order to support collaborative performance appraisal. These norms and values include the importance of employee growth and development, shared responsibility between manager and subordinate, and participative decision making, as well as a general norm of collaborating when differences appear.

Incentive Structure. Many of the specific conditions related to this factor involve the distinction between a *developmental* and an *evaluative* focus for performance appraisal and feedback. Thompson and Dalton (1970) note, in effect, that a developmental approach to performance appraisal creates commonality of interest by shifting attention to the positive-sum aspects of organizational work life. Appraisal and feedback sessions tend to become future oriented, with both parties working together to build upon the subordinate's ability. In contrast, Thompson and Dalton conclude that an evaluative emphasis is more likely to generate conflict of interest between superior and subordinate by directing attention to comparisons of relative ability among subordinates. As noted earlier, these comparisons are more likely to lead to areas of disagreement that involve substantial threat to the subordinate's self-esteem. Thus, the incentives for collaborative behavior appear to be especially strong when the superior sees employee development as the main purpose of performance reviews.

A key question for building collaboration then becomes,

"What creates strong developmental incentives in an organization?" Hyde (1982) argues that human resource development has become more critical to most organizations, with the increasing technological intensity in many industries, greater emphasis on innovation, and the requirement for greater skill diversity to make rapid adjustments to changes dictated by the environment. We would add, however, that developmental incentives are likely to vary considerably among firms. For example, a strong developmental emphasis is likely to be present in organizations with rapid growth—where the need to develop subordinates for higher positions is apparent to superiors. The developmental emphasis is likely to be even stronger when tight labor markets make it difficult for these organizations to hire skilled managers from outside the organization.

A number of specific human resource decisions under the more direct control of the firm can be used to reinforce the developmental incentives bearing upon the superior. Formal reward systems that assess and significantly reward the development of subordinates are an obvious measure. In addition, however, the superior will have little incentive to develop subordinates unless those subordinates have been selected and trained for the ability to develop (for example, Cummings and Schwab, 1973) and unless career ladders or other opportunities are provided to allow subordinates to continue to use their increased skills. Developmental incentives would also be expected to be greater where management decisions favor the promotion of internal candidates over the hiring of external candidates to fill vacancies.

Rules and Procedures. Considerations concerning this last set of factors range from specific features of performance-appraisal procedures to entire appraisal systems. A consistent conclusion drawn by performance-appraisal researchers is that employee development cannot be effectively discussed and promoted in the same interview in which employee evaluation is discussed. Beer (1981), for example, has explained the need to separate these two activities in terms of the incompatibility between the behaviors involved in the superior's roles of judge and helper. Employee performance and attitude toward superiors have been reported to improve when joint-purpose interviews were changed to separate development and salary interviews (Beer, 1981; Cederblom, 1982; Meyer, Kay, and French, 1965).

The conflict perspective also suggests two obvious procedural means of reducing some of the dysfunctional, zero-sum aspects of evaluation. Comparisons are more likely to be injurious and arouse defensiveness when superiors are forced to rank their subordinates or assign them percentile scores (Thompson and Dalton, 1970). Such procedures ensure that some subordinates come out at the very bottom—whether or not their work is acceptable. Using rating scales will at least reduce some of this threat to self-esteem. Second (as noted earlier), we would add that superiors are more likely to be viewed as competitive when they are forced to defend an evaluation to which they are already committed. Many appraisal systems require the manager to submit an evaluation to his or her superior for approval before presenting it to the subordinate being reviewed, thus reducing the manager's flexibility during the appraisal session. In such cases, giving managers more flexibility is a prerequisite for allowing them to listen and make the session more collaborative.

In addition, management-by-objectives (MBO) systems have been recommended as a more comprehensive attempt to create collaborative performance-review processes. (For an overview of MBO, see Carroll and Tosi, 1973.) In addition to building in some degree of subordinate participation and directing attention to employee development, MBO has the potential for considerably reducing the amount of conflict experienced during the evaluation process. When used successfully, MBO results in consensual goals that are stated in specific, verifiable form. In effect, the superior and subordinate agree upon operational rules for the next evaluation, so that there is less room for disagreement. This, in turn, generates less uncooperative behavior to interfere with the developmental focus of MBO.

However, it is also worth re-emphasizing that the structural model provides a framework for explaining why MBO systems often *fail* to achieve collaborative performance-appraisal and feedback sessions. Thus, superiors may lack the necessary skills, the prescribed participative/collaborative behavior may be incompatible with organizational norms and culture (Kerr, 1976; Carvalho, 1972), and/or the manager may have no real incentive to aid in employee development.

To summarize, then, collaborative appraisal processes do not occur in a vacuum. Rather, they require a number of specific enabling conditions. The structural model provides a useful scheme for diagnosing these conditions and suggesting the coordinated set of interventions that might be required to correct them. Thus, the model helps to explain why collaboration, despite its substantial benefits in performance appraisal, is not more prevalent in organizations and why a comprehensive approach to change is likely to be far more successful than piecemeal remedies.

Summary and Conclusion

In this chapter, we have noted the interest of academics and practitioners in the topic of conflict and have presented some concepts and models from the literature on conflict management. The chapter is centered upon two such models: a two-dimensional model of conflict-handling behaviors available to individuals and a structural model of the factors that shape conflict-handling modes in a given situation. Together, these two models provide a potentially powerful means of analyzing behavior and intervening to manage that behavior.

Because conflict has too often been treated as an isolated topic, we have also applied these two models to the specific issue of performance appraisal. This issue was chosen as an example because of its importance, because it has not traditionally been analyzed in terms of conflict, and because enough research has been conducted on it to allow us to draw empirically based conclusions. But the same sort of analysis can be performed for other organizational issues that cause recurrent interpersonal problems for managers—aspects of the budgeting process, sales contacts, collections, strategic planning, and so on. We believe that such applications will benefit both the conflict models and the substantive areas to which they are applied. The models are broad frameworks that need more research findings on specific issues to flesh them out and to further test and develop them. In turn, the models provide a means for organizing existing research studies on a given topic into a whole and for directing future theory and research. Above all, perhaps, the models force us to recognize the complexity of behavioral options available to individuals in difficult interpersonal situations and the complexity of factors that must be taken into account to steer that behavior in constructive directions.

References

Axelrod, R. *Conflict of Interest.* Chicago: Markham, 1970.

Beckhard, R. *Organization Development: Strategies and Models.* Reading, Mass.: Addison-Wesley, 1969.

Beer, M. "Performance Appraisal: Dilemmas and Possibilities." *Organizational Dynamics,* 1981, *9* (3), 24-36.

Blake, R. R., and Mouton, J. S. "Reactions to Intergroup Competition Under Win-Lose Conditions." *Management Science,* 1961, *7,* 420-435.

Blake, R. R., and Mouton, J. S. *The Managerial Grid.* Houston: Gulf, 1964.

Blake, R. R., Shepard, H. A., and Mouton, J. S. *Managing Intergroup Conflict in Industry.* Houston: Gulf, 1964.

Blake, R. R., and others. "Breakthrough in Organization Development." *Harvard Business Review,* November-December 1964, *42,* 133-135.

Blau, P. M. *The Dynamics of Bureaucracy.* Chicago: University of Chicago Press, 1955.

Brown, L. D. *Managing Conflict at Organizational Interfaces.* Reading, Mass.: Addison-Wesley, 1983.

Burke, R. J. "Methods of Resolving Superior-Subordinate Conflict: The Constructive Use of Subordinate Differences and Disagreements." *Organizational Behavior and Human Performance,* 1970, *5,* 393-411.

Burke, R. J., Weitzel, W., and Weir, T. "Characteristics of Effective Employee Performance Review and Development Interviews: Replication and Extension." *Personnel Psychology,* 1978, *31,* 903-919.

Burke, R. J., and Wilcox, D. S. "Characteristics of Effective Employee Performance Review and Development Interviews." *Personnel Psychology,* 1969, *22,* 291-305.

Carroll, S. J., Jr., and Tosi, H. L., Jr. *Management by Objectives: Applications and Research.* New York: Macmillan, 1973.

Carvalho, G. F. "Installing MBO: A New Perspective on Organizational Change." *Human Resource Management,* 1972, *11* (1), 23-30.

Cederblom, D. "The Performance Appraisal Interview: A Review, Implications, and Suggestions." *Academy of Management Review,* 1982, *7,* 219-227.

Cellucci, T., and Lombardo, M. "A Survey of Managerial Performance Appraisal Practices." *Center for Creative Leadership Newsletter,* 1978, *5,* 3.

Cummings, L. L., and Schwab, D. P. *Performance in Organizations.* Glenview, Ill.: Scott, Foresman, 1973.

Deal, T. E., and Kennedy, A. A. *Corporate Cultures: The Rites and Rituals of Corporate Life.* Reading, Mass.: Addison-Wesley, 1982.

Deutsch, M. "A Theory of Cooperation and Competition." *Human Relations,* 1949, *2,* 129-152.

Deutsch, M. "Toward an Understanding of Conflict." *International Journal of Group Tensions,* 1971, *1,* 42-54.

DeVries, D. L., and others. *Performance Appraisal on the Line.* Technical Report No. 16. Greensboro, N.C.: Center for Creative Leadership, 1980.

Eiseman, J. W. "Reconciling 'Incompatible' Positions." *Journal of Applied Behavioral Science,* 1978, *14,* 133-150.

Filley, A. C. *Interpersonal Conflict Resolution.* Glenview, Ill.: Scott, Foresman, 1975.

Fisher, C. D. "The Transmission of Positive and Negative Feedback to Subordinates: A Laboratory Investigation." *Journal of Applied Psychology,* 1979, *64,* 533-540.

Gallegos, P. M. "Communicating Performance Results." *Journal of Systems Management,* 1983, *34,* 25-31.

Gormley, J., and Edelberg, W. "Validity in Personality Trait Attribution." *American Psychologist,* 1974, *29,* 189-193.

Graves, J. P. "Successful Management and Organizational Mugging." In R. Katz (Ed.), *Career Issues for Human Resource Management.* Englewood Cliffs, N.J.: Prentice-Hall, 1982.

Greller, M. M. "Subordinate Participation and Reaction to the Appraisal Interview." *Journal of Applied Psychology,* 1975, *60,* 544-549.

Hall, J. *How to Interpret Your Scores from the Conflict Management Survey.* Conroe, Texas: Teleometrics, undated.

Hall, J. *Conflict Management Survey: A Survey of One's Characteristic Reaction to and Handling of Conflicts Between Himself and Others.* Conroe, Texas: Teleometrics, 1969.

Hall, J. "Decisions, Decisions, Decisions." *Psychology Today,* 1971, *5* (11), 51-54, 86-87.

Hyde, A. C. "Performance Appraisal in the Post Reform Era." *Public Personnel Management Journal,* 1982, *11* (4), 294-306.

Ilgen, D. R., Fisher, C. D., and Taylor, M. S. "Consequences of Individual Feedback on Behavior in Organizations." *Journal of Applied Psychology,* 1979, *64,* 349-371.

Kahn, R. L., and others. *Organizational Stress: Studies in Role Conflict and Ambiguity.* New York: Wiley, 1964.

Kay, E., Meyer, H. H., and French, J. R. P. "Effects of Threat in a Performance Appraisal Interview." *Journal of Applied Psychology,* 1965, *49,* 311-317.

Kerr, S. "Overcoming the Dysfunctions of MBO." *Management by Objectives,* 1976, *5* (1), 13-19.

Kikoski, J. F., and Litterer, J. A. "Effective Communication in the Performance Appraisal Interview." *Public Personnel Management Journal,* 1983, *12,* 33-42.

Kilmann, R. H. *Beyond the Quick Fix: Managing Five Tracks to Organizational Success.* San Francisco: Jossey-Bass, 1984.

Kilmann, R. H., and Thomas, K. W. "Four Perspectives on Conflict Management: An Attributional Framework for Organizing Descriptive and Normative Theory." *Academy of Management Review,* 1978, *3,* 59-68.

Lawler, E. E., III. *Motivation in Work Organizations.* Monterey, Calif.: Brooks/Cole, 1973.

Likert, R. *New Patterns of Management.* New York: McGraw-Hill, 1961.

Likert, R. *The Human Organization.* New York: McGraw-Hill, 1967.

Likert, R., and Likert, J. G. *New Ways of Managing Conflict.* New York: McGraw-Hill, 1976.

Litwin, G. H., and Stringer, R. A., Jr. *Motivation and Organizational Climate.* Cambridge, Mass.: Harvard University Press, 1968.

Louis, M. R. "Organizations as Culture Bearing Milieux." In L. Pondy and others (Eds.), *Organizational Symbolism.* Chicago: University of Chicago Press, 1980.

McCall, M. W., Jr., and DeVries, D. L. *Appraisal in Context: Clashing with Organizational Realities.* Technical Report No. 4. Greensboro, N.C.: Center for Creative Leadership, 1977.

Mason, R. O. "A Dialectical Approach to Strategic Planning." *Management Science,* 1969, *15,* 403-414.

Merton, R. K. *Social Theory and Social Structure.* Glencoe, Ill.: Free Press, 1957.

Meyer, H. H., Kay, E., and French, J. R. P. "Split Roles in Performance Appraisal." *Harvard Business Review,* 1965, *43* (1), 123-129.

Miner, M. G. *Management Performance Appraisal Programs.* PFF Survey No. 104. Washington, D.C.: Bureau of National Affairs, 1974.

Mitroff, I. I., and Emshoff, J. R. "On Strategic Assumption-Making: A Dialectical Approach to Policy and Planning." *Academy of Management Review,* 1979, *4,* 1-12.

Nemeroff, W. F., and Wexley, K. N. "Relationships Between Performance Appraisal Characteristics and Interview Outcomes as Perceived by Supervisors and Subordinates." *Proceedings of the Academy of Management,* 1977, 30-44.

O'Reilly, C. A., and Weitz, B. A. "Conflict-Handling Styles and Managers' Use of Sanctions." Working paper, School of Business Administration, University of California at Berkeley, 1980.

Porter, L. W., Lawler, E. E., III, and Hackman, J. R. *Behavior in Organizations.* New York: McGraw-Hill, 1975.

Rahim, A. *Rahim Organizational Conflict Inventory-II.* Palo Alto, Calif.: Consulting Psychologists Press, 1983.

Rahim, A., and Bonoma, T. V. "Managing Organizational Conflict: A Model for Diagnosis and Intervention." *Psychological Reports,* 1979, *44,* 1323-1344.

Renwick, P. A. "Perception and Management of Superior-Subordinate Conflict." *Organizational Behavior and Human Performance,* 1975, *13,* 444-456.

Rosen, A. "Performance Appraisal Interviewing Evaluated by Proximal Observers." *Nursing Research,* 1967, *16,* 32-37.

Ruble, T. L., and Thomas, K. W. "Support for a Two-Dimensional Model of Conflict Behavior." *Organizational Behavior and Human Performance,* 1976, *16,* 143-155.

Schmidt, W. H., and Tannenbaum, R. "Management of Differences." *Harvard Business Review,* 1960, *38* (6), 107-115.

Sherif, M. "Superordinate Goals in the Reduction of Intergroup Conflict." *American Journal of Sociology,* 1958, *63,* 349-356.

Stockford, L., and Bissell, H. W. "Factors Involved in Establishing a Merit Rating Scale." *Personnel,* 1949, *26,* 94-116.

Thibaut, J. W., and Kelley, H. H. *The Social Psychology of Groups.* New York: Wiley, 1959.

Thomas, K. W. "Conflict and Conflict Management." In M. D. Dunnette (Ed.), *Handbook of Industrial and Organizational Psychology.* Chicago: Rand McNally, 1976.

Thomas, K. W. "Toward Multi-Dimensional Values in Teaching: The Example of Conflict Behaviors." *Academy of Management Review,* 1977, *2,* 484-490.

Thomas, K. W. "Introduction: Conflict and the Collaborative Ethic." *California Management Review,* 1978, *21* (2), 56-60.

Thomas, K. W. "Conflict." In S. Kerr (Ed.), *Organizational Behavior.* Columbus, Ohio: Grid, 1979.

Thomas, K. W. "Manager and Mediator: A Comparison of Third-Party Roles Based upon Conflict Management Goals." In G. Bomers and R. Peterson (Eds.), *Conflict Management and Industrial Relations.* Boston: Kluwer-Nijoff, 1982.

Thomas, K. W., and Kilmann, R. H. *The Thomas-Kilmann Conflict Mode Instrument.* Tuxedo, N.Y.: Xicom, 1974.

Thomas, K. W., and Kilmann, R. H. "Comparison of Four Instruments Measuring Conflict Behavior." *Psychological Reports,* 1978, *42,* 1139-1145.

Thomas, K. W., and Pondy, L. R. "Toward an 'Intent' Model of

Conflict Management Among Principal Parties." *Human Relations,* 1977, *30,* 1089–1102.

Thomas, K. W., and Schmidt, W. H. "A Survey of Managerial Interests with Respect to Conflict." *Academy of Management Journal,* 1976, *19,* 315–318.

Thomas, K. W., and Walton, R. E. "Conflict Handling Behavior in Interdepartmental Relations." Research Paper No. 38. Division of Research, Graduate School of Business Administration, University of Southern California at Los Angeles, 1971.

Thompson, P. H., and Dalton, G. W. "Performance Appraisal: Managers Beware." *Harvard Business Review,* 1970, *48* (1), 149–157.

16

Values in Decision Making

Abraham Kaplan

Decisions are not made all at once; they are arrived at. A decision is the outcome of a process in which alternatives are weighed until one is finally singled out. Decision makers make up their minds, which before were unsettled. Their minds are set at rest by a process of deliberation. Thus, to decide means to come to a conclusion; conclusions imply antecedents. A decision, therefore, is more than simply a choice; choices can be made arbitrarily. When Caesar crossed the Rubicon, he declared that the die was cast. He meant that the act was irretrievable, not that chance had had a hand in it. To defy the orders of the Roman Senate was a decision; Caesar crossed the river deliberately.

In every decision, the choice is expected to make a difference; the decision is taken because of that expectation. To count out "Eeeny meeny miney mo" produces a choice but not a decision. A decision is being made only when it is intended to realize a potential good, or goal. In short, every decision implicates values. For managers, values are doubly ineluctable. Values are presupposed in the subject matter of every managerial decision, which inescapably embodies a judgment as to where the greater good lies. Values are presupposed also because, whatever the subject matter of the decision, the manager manages people. He or she can do so only by linking decisions to motivations. A motive is an internalized value serving as a guide to action. Not even the impersonal scientist is free of values. Objective decision making, like objective inquiry, does not presuppose that values have been eliminated. If they were, there would be no reason for conducting inquiry and nothing for the decisions to be about. Objectivity means, rather, that values have been made explicit and taken into account in the process of inquiry or of deliberation.

The manager is a person with values of his or her own. He or she may be caught between the values of family and of work and in both contexts may face decisions relating to the budgeting of both time and money. As a manager, his or her values define his or her conceptions of a "fair" wage and of a "fair" profit, as well as his or her readiness to take risks, to adopt a "minimax" or some other strategy. On the larger social scene, the manager may participate in decisions on how much of the national resources to allocate to consumer goods and how much to capital investment or on whether to cut off the tail of the distribution of goods and services or to raise the peak—to provide more housing or to expand the space program. Management wades in values; every manager can scoop them up by the bucketful.

That value considerations abound is beyond dispute; whether they are worth considering is another matter. Many people take it for granted that values are in principle beyond rational treatment. For my part, I endorse the dictum of Socrates that the unexamined life is not worth living. More to the point is my conviction that the unlived life *is* worth examining. No one can pretend that values, whether personal or social, are today so secure or even so discernible as to need no examination. In the end, examination may not help, but prejudging its outcome is unworthy of human capacities. Unexamined values constitute *customary* morality, as distinct from the *reflective* morality arrived at after examination. The two are distinct, but they do not necessarily differ. Values enjoined by custom may also be those to which deliberation leads. Rejection of customary morality does not mean rebellion against it. Rebellion is conformity in reverse, equally determined by the customary values, which rebellion simply negates. In moral autonomy, values are what they are because of the moral agent's own decisions, not anyone else's, whether these have been accepted or have been replaced by their opposites.

Customary morality is adhered to because of the force of habit in the individual and because of the social forces imposing conformity. It is also sustained by the quest for certainty and the impulse to escape from freedom. To be told the difference between right and wrong is reassuring, even at the cost of one's being continually exhorted to do what is right. Recurrent guilt is easier to bear than sustained anxiety. To know for sure what is right and what is wrong is especially comforting. These are matters on which few people are content to play the odds. Yet, as Aristotle pointed out, ethics is concerned with things that are for the most part so, things quite capable of being otherwise; this defines the domain of probability.

Customary morality confuses being good with being goody-goody, focusing on sex behavior, speech, dress, and other matters of propriety. It goes beyond respectability only here and there—for instance, with regard to drugs (other than caffeine, nicotine, and alcohol). Its conception of "business ethics" localizes moral issues in deviant behavior such as bribery, unfair competition, and false advertising, but not always in widely accepted practices such as the treatment of women and minorities. Customary morality, moreover, is occupied far more with vices than with virtues. The modern Mrs. Malaprop, Billie Dawn in *Born Yesterday,* unintentionally describes very well the presupposition of customary morality to the effect that this country and its institutions belong to the people who *inhibit* it. Morality is generally thought of as submission to a set of prohibitions.

Moral issues are perceived as being localized in the conflict between duty and desire. This may be true of the conflicts in adolescence. Maturation is acquiring the capacity for controlling impulse, postponing gratification to more appropriate circumstances, or redirecting it to more appropriate objects. In maturity, moral problems arise from conflicts among duties and from conflicting desires as well. Sin, said a Hassidic master, is whatever one cannot do wholeheartedly. The question is what to do when the moral inclination is divided against itself.

Customary morality separates facts from values, assigning facts to science and technology and values to a realm of their own, not subject to the governance of reason. The separation has been generalized to a pervasive cultural dualism in which facts belong to weekdays and values to Sunday, facts to work and values to "personal" life, facts to the world of action, with its harsh realities, and values to the domain of feeling, with its noble ideals. The result is that the real world is deprived of aspiration to the ideal, while ideals are left without a grip on reality. The pernicious impact of this dualism is apparent in the complex of attitudes toward automation and computerization. On one side is the notion that the technology is its own justification—to be assessed, that is, on the basis of technological parameters only. On the other side is the attitude that the technology in and of itself is dehumanizing. This charge overlooks the circumstance that Frankenstein is the name of the man, not the monster. But the defense against the charge remains largely on the level of fantasy, in which the robot is given a personality. *Star Wars'* R2D2 has the innocence of Adam before the Fall, naming the animals that parade before him. The problem for values posed by technology was recognized by John Dewey over half a century ago, long before nuclear energy and electronic data processing became realities. American pragmatism recognized early that modern society has allowed the intellect to transform means but has strongly resisted its impact on ends. Today there is widespread recognition of the need to discover not just better ways of doing things but things better worth doing. Dewey's thesis to the effect that a culture that permits science to destroy traditional values but distrusts its power to create new ones destroys itself, now seems prophetic.

In the perspectives of cultural dualism, values are taken seriously only after they are recast in what is thought to be a scientific mold. This procedure exhibits *scientism* rather than a genuinely scientific temper. Characteristic of the dualism is a polarity in which one side is preoccupied with moralistic preachments while the other side applies a pecuniary calculus to evaluate the "bottom line" for any decision. Scientism is sustained by what might be called the *utilitarian fallacy,* the assumption that every decision can be evaluated in terms of some single parameter—such as profit, productivity, efficiency, or in a word, "utility." One of the early utilitarians tells us that when he felt that the time had come for him to marry, he chose his wife by listing all the eligible women of his acquaintance, arranging the names in order of desirability, then proposing down the list till he was accepted. He does not tell us how he decided it was time for him to marry, how he arrived at the relative desirability of the eligibles, nor how his future wife responded to being told that he loved her more than all but $N - 1$ other women.

Utility theory as such does not rest on the utilitarian fallacy. The theory describes the geometry of the value space but says nothing about the location of any specific values in the space. The utilitarian fallacy is committed only when utilities are assigned to values in terms of some one parameter, with the implication that the assignment provides a justification of the valuation being made, rather than the other way around. The classical model of "economic man," like all scientific models, does not purport to be anything other than an idealization. What would be fallacious would be to assume that the model provides norms for economic behavior rather than to recognize that the worth of the model depends on its appropriateness to such norms. In particular, it is dangerous to assume that utilities are measurable in monetary terms. Models of maximizing utilities are taken to define rational decision making. Such definitions are not arbitrary, are not sheer matters of convention. They call for justification themselves, justification that demands going beyond purely mathematical considerations. Scientism mistakes the desiderata of particular scientific techniques for necessities of scientific method in general. Logic does not dictate, for example, that wherever values depend on more than one factor, there is always a suitable set of weights by which the worth of all the factors taken together can be reduced to a single magnitude. Valuations might be made instead on the basis of *configurations,* as we judge the beauty of a face or the quality of a life-style. The worth of separate components might be derived from *holistic* judgments as much as conversely. Mathematically, vectors are as legitimate magnitudes as scalars. Values need not be one-dimensional, even if the one dimension is given as abstract a label as "utility."

Usually intertwined with the utilitarian fallacy is a mystique of quantity, which tacitly assumes that, in rational decision making, what is imponderable is irrelevant. Equally unwarranted is the mystique of quality, which assumes just the contrary, that everything measurable is irrelevant. Aristotle formulated a realistic alternative to both mystiques: "It is the part of an educated man to require exactness in each class of subjects, only so far as the nature of the subject admits." This is the thrust of Dewey's condemnation of the traditional utilitarian theory of rational decision making in terms of pleasures and pains, viewing it as an intricate calculus of inaccessible and indeterminate results. Matters are not improved when the hedonical basis is replaced by scientism's substitute, "utility."

Something inaccessible to one person might be accessible to another. Ours is the age of the expert, in every endeavor from making love or raising children to making war or raising a standard of living. Today, there are experts on values, as on almost everything else. The trouble is that there are too many experts—they do not all agree. "If you don't know jewels, know your jeweler," runs the slogan. How this is to be done, and whether the one is any easier to do than the other, the slogan does not say. Philosophers have long been looked to for moral instruction. A philosopher is generally seen as someone who is not quite with it but who knows where it's at. Socrates claimed that he knew only his own ignorance, but other philosophers have had no hesitation in advising decision makers, whether householders or kings. A distinguished writer on the history of morals plausibly concludes that the inventor of anesthetics has contributed more to human happiness than all the moral philosophers from Socrates on down. *Philosophy* means "the love of wisdom"; I have had occasion elsewhere to suggest that here, as with other sorts of love, the professionals may be the ones who know least about it. Increasingly widespread in legislatures, professional associations, hospitals, and other such organizations are ethics committees. As expressions of moral aspiration, such committees are to be commended. The examined life implies an examiner. The question is how the examination is conducted. A code of ethics cannot be regarded as the set of correct answers by which examination papers are to be graded.

The division of labor these days is defining a new role: the consultant as priest and prophet—one who lays down the moral law and exhorts his or her hearers to keep the law. It is one thing to *counsel* a client, helping him or her arrive at decisions; it is quite another to *advise* the client, transmitting the consultant's decisions about the client's problems. Both counsel and advice have a place in decision making. Where values are at issue, it is chiefly counsel that is called for, even if expertise were beyond dispute. There is a sense in which values are facts, and all that is problematical is the determination of the facts. We may mean by a value something valued, rather than something sustained by an evaluation. The difference is that between prizing something and appraising it favorably, what the market will fetch and what it is really worth. In the first sense, a value is whatever somebody values; in question may be only whether that person does in fact value it, not whether it is indeed valuable. To determine what somebody's values are is not easy, even if the somebody is oneself. What a person says that he or she values, though a significant datum, is an unreliable one. Self-deception is familiar; unawareness is even more widespread. Lip service is notorious; if conventional morality is demanding, it is a tyranny tempered by hypocrisy. The credibility gap is especially great with regard to values professed by society as a whole. The sanctity of life, for example, certainly commands consensus in what we say, but what we do is something else. More than a dozen countries have a lower rate of infant mortality than does the United States; traffic deaths and homicides are horrendously frequent. Substances found by the surgeon-general to be life threatening not only are readily available but even enjoy government subsidies. Whether widespread criticism of military expenditures signifies a commitment to the sanctity of life or an isolationist self-interest is far from clear. The same is true of resistance to the use of nuclear energy.

The unreliability of what one says as evidence for what

one values is heightened by the not uncommon tendency to be more proud of vices than of virtues. Many managers more readily admit to being tough and unyielding than to being compassionate and humane. Corporate philanthropies are represented as investments in "goodwill" or "public relations," which they may be; but the representation may also serve to discount any impression of softness or sentimentality on the part of those who decide on such expenditures.

Values are not constituted by fleeting thoughts and feelings, but only by those that we are prepared to act on. The wishes expressed in dreams, Freud pointed out, may be shameful, but it is important that they remain only dreams; for the most part, we do not act out our fantasies. To look lustfully may be to commit adultery in our hearts, but this is a very different place from the bedroom; in the domain of values, this difference makes all the difference. Actions considered by themselves, however, may be as misleading as fantasies or verbalizations with regard to the values being pursued. What the actor believes must also be taken into account. Someone may reach for sugar not because he or she likes sweets but because he or she mistakes the sugar for salt. Actions, beliefs, and values are bound up in a triad: each can be inferred from the other two, but it takes both of the others. Methodological difficulties result from the circumstance that only actions are directly observable; these are difficulties, however—not impossible hurdles.

When we succeed in determining what people value, the outstanding fact that emerges is that they value different things. "Different strokes for different folks" is empirically undeniable. It is true not only on the world scene but also within each society, as cultural heterogeneity defends itself from the melting pot. In the days of British rule in India, the government tried to put down the practice of burning widows on the husband's funeral pyre. A deputation waited on the viceroy, reminding him of Britain's promise not to interfere with local customs. "Right!" he replied, "but we British have the custom of hanging those who burn people alive." What are we to do when customs conflict? There is a widespread inclination to deny that there are any differences to start with in what people value.

When Bertrand Russell was jailed as a pacifist in World War I and was asked to state his religion, he said, "Atheist!", to which the kindly bailiff replied, "Oh, well, we all believe in the same God, anyhow!" Value systems, like cuisines, owe their taste and flavor as much to differences as to samenesses; common to all soups is only water.

Denial of differences in values is sustained by a line of argument I call the *eudaemonian fallacy*, from Aristotle's word for well-being, conceived as the aim of all action. The fallacy consists in an equivocation between a broad and a narrow sense of words used to designate some basic value, words such as *happiness, self-satisfaction, pleasure*, and *profit*. In its broad sense, each word can cover all pursuits, but only because the word has been emptied of any content. In its narrow sense, the word has a content but for that very reason is no longer universally applicable. We know nothing about a person when we are told only that he seeks happiness or maximum utility unless we know what makes him happy or to what he assigns utility. If we assume certain answers, there is no reason to suppose that the assumptions fit everyone equally. Everyone seeks "pleasure" if "pleasure" means only whatever pleases, for then the generalization reduces to the tautology that we all please to do whatever it pleases us to do. But if "pleasure" means, say, sensory gratification, hedonists are probably in the minority and are certainly not all-inclusive. Everyone is "selfish" in the sense that each person's values are tautologically *his* or *her* values; but whether all that is valued is a certain state of oneself or includes that of others as well is another matter entirely. We all seek what we expect will profit us; whether "profit" means the excess of selling price over cost or the welfare of the soul varies from person to person and from situation to situation.

Diversity of values is a datum for every empirical theory of value. Diversity in itself, however, does not entail conflict. Different values may be able to coexist—Jack Spratt and his wife lived happily together on fat and lean. But values define norms, and norms everywhere tend to acquire normative force. "This is how we do things" easily becomes, "This is how you, too, ought to do them!" Conformist pressures embody the notion that the opposite of unity is disunity, rather than plurality. Different values may be able to coexist not only empirically but also logically. When values differ, it does not follow that one must be better and the other worse; they might simply not be comparable. To argue whether a Beethoven quartet is better or worse than a Rembrandt portrait is pointless, not because there is no arguing about tastes or because beauty is in the eye of the beholder but because different standards are relevant to each of the two.

Pluralism is the recognition that different values do not necessarily conflict. Pluralism does not imply, however, unrestricted permissiveness, as though "You pays your money and you takes your choice." There may well be norms that justifiably restrict our pursuits. What is being called for is responsible and rational decision making in place of arbitrary choice. How can such decision making be carried out? The conventional reply is likely to be a species of sloganeering, urging the application of familiar formulas. In this vein, morality is often alleged to consist in "nothing more than living by the Ten Commandments." Four of the ten, however, have a religious content rather than an ethical one, being concerned with monotheism, idolatry, profanity, and the sabbath. Moreover, among thousands of students, I have found virtually none who could specify all ten of the commandments, the most common number being five (including the ritualistic ones). Everyone remembers the prohibition of adultery and murder, but very few remember the injunction against bearing false witness. Only a few more recall the commandment to honor father and mother and the prohibition of stealing. "Thou shalt not covet" is usually remembered only with reference to the neighbor's wife.

The formula, even when recalled, must be interpreted. Few people, in the West at any rate, would agree with Proudhon that property is theft, but what exactly confers the right of ownership is subject to moral as well as legal uncertainty. Putting one's parents into communities for the aged may be less a way of honoring them than of condemning them to life sentences at solitary confinement. "Love thy neighbor," to take another formula, has a very different meaning today than it once did, since, in modern urban life, each of us has 20,000 "neighbors" living within one mile of us. As this example reminds us, differences arise not only in interpreting formulas but also in applying them to new situations. That is why so little is gained by exhortations to return to "the old-fashioned virtues" and to established values and why the credibility gap between the generations is so great precisely in the domain of values. Medical technology, to take another example, now makes possible the prolongation of life in circumstances previously unthought of and therefore poses moral issues not previously considered.

Scientism has its formulas as well. The common appeal, for instance, to the principle of "the greatest good for the greatest number" assumes a single maximum for two different functions. There is no difficulty in deciding between two policies that benefit the same number of people while one confers a greater benefit, or between two policies that confer the same benefit while one extends the benefit to more people. Unfortunately, the choice is almost always between two policies one of which confers a greater benefit but to fewer people than the other. The clash between quality and quantity in education, medical care, transportation, housing, and much else is glossed over by the formula, not resolved.

Formulas must be examined as carefully as the values they purport to define. Customary morality condemns all examination as revealing a lack of faith in our values. On the contrary, it is the condemnation that is lacking in faith, as though the values will not survive rational scrutiny. Hypochondriacs are unwilling to see the doctor for fear of what might be found. In the preface to his *Critique of Pure Reason,* Immanuel Kant persuasively argued that when values attempt to escape assessment by reason, "they inevitably awaken a just suspicion of the soundness of their foundation, and they lose all claim to the unfeigned homage paid by reason to that which has shown itself able to stand the test of free inquiry." Values secured from examination are inevitably left to unthinking tradition ("policy"), blind prejudice, and naked power. At most, reason may be invoked as rationalization of decisions already reached. Not uncommon is the confusion of *reasons* with *causes*, since both answer to the "why" of an action. "I was brought up to believe . . ." specifies a cause but does not provide a reason.

Intermediate between causes and reasons are what might be called *indications*—cues that, when validated, are signs of worth without themselves providing justifications. "There is no one who does not eat and drink," said Confucius, "but few there are who really know flavor." We can responsibly accept the judgment of the few without knowing their reasons, provided it has already been established that they have good taste. Familiar indications are the price of a wine or a perfume, the fame of a painting, the prize awarded a book or a movie, and the canonization of a saint. Making a judgment of value implies the existence of reasons for the valuation. The judgment embodies a decision, which, as we have noted, presupposes an antecedent process of deliberation. Value judgments are like verdicts in a court of law. In the aggregate, these make up the body of law that, retrospectively, they are said to apply. The dictum that the law is what judges say it is has its counterpart in the domain of value. The values of a person or group are those it judges to be of value—provided the judgment was arrived at by due process. The distinction between values and reasons, however labeled, is of enormous practical importance, for it is possible to agree on values without agreeing on the reasons for them, and vice versa. A nation might seek peace because this is the will of God or because peace is in the interests of the revolution; two nations might be at war in defense of the faith even though they espouse the same religion. Specific decisions call for agreement only on the values to be pursued, not on the reasons for pursuing them. Differences in reasons, however, sooner or later will lead to differences in values; if they do not, the reasons do not really differ.

The characteristic reasons that are invoked define different value styles. For some decision makers, decisions are typically justified by reference to the decision makers themselves—their personal goals, ideals, and principles. This "personal" style contrasts with the "systemic" style, in which the reference is to some externally given set of values, such as "company policy."

A third style, the "situational," focuses neither on persons nor on institutions but on concrete particulars. All three styles rest in turn on one or another fundamental ground. For centuries, this ground has been religious. The religious ground, because of its comprehensiveness, puts decisions in perspective. It also provides depth as well as scope; dealing, as it does, with ultimate concerns, it directs attention to the centrality of commitment in the moral life. Religious claims to certainty are weakened, however, by the variety of the claimants. Insofar as the claims of religion transcend experience, they must rest in the end on dogmas, propositions for which, in principle, no reasons can be given, though the propositions are not self-evident. Ours is a time, it has been said, in which we have ceased to believe without ceasing to be credulous. This age of science is also, ironically, an age of superstition. We have set foot on the moon while astrology flourishes, broken the genetic code while food fads abound, and probed the unconscious while mystical cults proliferate. If values are to be grounded in religion, the inescapable question is, whose religion? And how is the false prophet to be distinguished from the true man of God?

For many people, the overtly religious ground has given way to conscience, an internalization of religious authority. "The Word is very near to you, in your heart," says Scripture. Morality does presuppose the internalization of values; it lies in the decisions we ourselves make, not in what is imposed on us from without. Conscience, however, is at least as diverse as is religion. If conscience is God-given, Freud remarked, it was an uneven and careless piece of work. Each of us feels that we ourselves have too much conscience while others have too little or have strangely distorted ones. What is worse, conscience may be divided against itself; instead of resolving inner conflicts, it might well reflect them.

In many parts of the world, values are grounded in ideology. The reduction of morals to politics rightly emphasizes the importance to morality of the moral community. To a large extent, however, political ethics is a secularization of religious ethics, with a corresponding eschatology of Paradise Lost and to be regained, a body of sacred writings, a roster of prophets, a

priesthood, indisputable obligations, and ex cathedra pro-
nouncements on disputed matters of faith. The political ground,
therefore, is subject to the same critique of dogma as is religion
proper. In addition, the political ground of morality is vulnerable to the criticism that it limits morality to a defense of
power. For democracy, to ground morals in politics is to argue
in a circle, since democratic ideology subjects political authority
to a moral test: power is justified only if it governs with the
consent of the governed and is used to secure certain unalien-
able rights.

Where religion and politics do not hold sway, morality is
often perceived as a matter of feeling. Emotivism is the contemporary version of the eighteenth-century idea that a distinctive
moral sentiment serves as the ground of moral judgment (the
position of David Hume and Adam Smith, for example). Modern emotivism turns to feeling not to provide something for
reason to work on but on its own account. Ideologically, the
romanticist revolt against industrialization has won out. In the
perspectives of cultural dualism, what Max Weber called the rationalization of the economic enterprise is attacked today just
because of its rationality. Feeling is first, says the poet; for
some, feeling is all in all. Feelings *are* facts, often of cardinal
importance in decision making, both as data and as infusing the
process of deliberation. A common failing of scientism is that
it overlooks feelings, even dismisses them as irrelevant or unim-
portant. Equally misconceived is the scientistic attempt to argue
people out of their feelings. The attempt is misconceived not
because feelings have no cognitive roots but because the cognitions involved do not change readily with a purely cerebral, un-
processed flow of information. What is sound in emotivism is
the insistence that values must be *felt* to be valuable or they are
not being valued. All the species of value rest on the *intrinsic
value* of something experienced to be valuable. There must be
an *experience* of something satisfying, or nothing can be judged
to be satisfactory. To have feelings is not unmanly; it is part of
being human. Feelings are a *necessary* condition for life, or anything else, to be worthwhile.

The feeling of worth, however, is not a *sufficient* condition for value, as emotivism supposes. To be judged worthy of the feeling, something experienced as satisfying must continue to be satisfying in the long run, under an open set of conditions. No food would deserve a gourmet's approval if it always tasted bad, but it might taste good and still be indigestible or even poisonous. This example also illustrates the importance of cultivating moral sensibility, as we do taste. Gourmet foods do not always appeal to the uninstructed palate. The question is how to tell whether the palate is being instructed or is being corrupted. Emotivism must acknowledge, for instance, that a manager facing the decision whether to fire someone may arrive at a poor decision either because the manager is sentimental or because he or she is callous. What constitutes these failings cannot be explicated by reference to the feelings alone; at issue is whether the feeling is appropriate to its object.

The notion that feelings are self-validating helps maintain a vicious circle of taste. Always satisfying only current taste, whatever its level, works to maintain taste at that level. A cartoon depicting an Elizabethan tavern has one writer saying moodily to another, "That Bill Shakespeare has the right idea—just give the public what it wants!" Not all publics are so lucky. If there were no arguing about tastes, there would be no ground for judgments of value. Wine connoisseurs, tea tasters, industrial designers, and interior decorators, however, all have a good deal to say in recommending one product over another. Even if differences in intrinsic value were beyond dispute (does chocolate taste better than vanilla?), such differences are not typical of moral disagreement. To regard positions on issues such as abortion, capital punishment, pacifism, and euthanasia as a matter of taste is itself morally repugnant.

Feelings are not encapsulated, so dissociated from the outside world that what we know of the world is irrelevant to them. Feelings *are* sometimes cut off from reality, but, if so, so much the worse for them. There is a well-known euphoria experienced by divers and pilots subjected to loss of oxygen. It is called "the rapture of the deep"—its victims die with a smile. Such rapture may have intrinsic value in the last moments of life; there is not much else to be said for it. Feelings of anxiety, too, may be cut off from reality. On the other hand, in the presence of real danger, a fearless person either does not know what is going on or else does not care. In either case, such a person is scarcely able to make sound decisions. In the analysis of decision making, the contrast to be drawn is not between reason and emotion but between rational and irrational emotion. Feelings unquestionably enter into decisions, but as part of the problem, not its solution.

A decision might owe more to the self-needs of the decision maker than to the task needs of the problem confronting him or her. For instance, that heroic measures are called for may be a conclusion reached only because of a secret desire to be a hero. The personal hidden agenda may be more decisive than the agenda that is open and shared. That is poor decision making, not a paradigm for the analysis of value judgments. How value judgments are to be validated is subject to another complication. A value judgment may be *reporting* a valuation or *making* one. It may affirm that someone has a certain value or that something is indeed valuable. A value judgment, in short, may have a descriptive function or a normative one. How the judgment is meant in a particular case may be uncertain. Value judgments often suffer from this "normative ambiguity." The judgment that a certain behavior pattern is "normal," in the descriptive sense, can be validated by statistical frequencies; in the normative sense, it may implicate an entire theory of psychology, politics, or economics.

A distinction can be drawn between *inherent* and *instrumental* values, the inherent being those valued for their own sake, while the instrumental are valued only for bringing us inherent values. All intrinsic values are inherent, but not conversely. Music, for instance, is an inherent value, while listening to it has intrinsic value; the phonograph has only instrumental value. Inherent value is the value of an end; instrumental value, that of a means. The value of music is instrumental, therefore, if it is used as therapy or from motives of snobbery. Means are validated by the ends to which they lead. What validates ends? Whether something is a means to an end or is itself an end depends on how it is being considered—the same man may be both a son and a father. An end might be appraised by considering it in relation to still further ends to which it is a means. The desirability of integrated schools, for instance, might be evaluated in terms of the resulting quality of education, sense of community, and the like. Ends can also be weighed on the basis of the means they call for—appraised, that is, by their conditions as well as by their consequences. What would be the cost of attaining an objective may be a crucial element in its appraisal as better or worse than other possible goals. Every end, in short, is enmeshed in a whole network of ends, what John Dewey called the "means-ends continuum." Values, like sorrows, come not singly but in battalions. That ends are given implies not that they are beyond appraisal but that their value is taken as established. This is only an assumption, and it might turn out to be false. The means on which evaluation initially focuses—those relevant to the given ends—are like a patient's presenting symptoms; they initiate the inquiry, but they do not determine what eventually must be taken into account.

Every evaluation rests on values that are not then and there brought into question. This does not mean that there never can be argument about them. They are undoubted but not indubitable. No problem at all can be formulated unless something is taken to be unproblematical, to provide the terms of the problem. But problems can be formulated mistakenly and may need to be recast in other terms. The statement of given ends is, in the context, a bare assertion; that does not make it a dogma, impossible ever to question. Action embodies an endless sequence of means and ends, but evaluation of decisions does not generate a vicious regression. A scientific assertion rests on evidence. That such and such *is* the evidence may itself need substantiation. The chemical analysis of a substance is made with reagents assumed to have a known composition. The reagents might have to be analyzed in turn and then used in *that* analysis. Continuing to insist on another step smacks more of paranoia than of scientific caution. Chemists do not profess an unquestioning faith in labels, but neither do they despair of ever determining what is in their flasks.

The objectivity of values depends on referring them to a

context, which is usually provided, without examination, by the process of evaluation itself. The context may be a *personal* one, that of the evaluator. It may be a *standard* context, fixed by the purpose of the evaluation. It may be the *ideal* context, calling for the most comprehensive and discriminating assessment of conditions and consequences. The question whether a movie is a "good" one may be asking whether the speaker would enjoy it; on the other hand, it may be asking whether it would be a box-office success, or whether it would be suitable for distribution by the State Department, or whether it would be educational in a school setting, and so on. It may be raising the issue of cinematic worth, as this would be judged by competent film critics. The process of evaluation is equally subject to procedural norms in all three sorts of cases.

Bertrand Russell concludes his *History of Western Philosophy* by speaking of the "subjectivist madness" of our time. The retreat to subjectivity is characteristic of the age. When the domain of fact is experienced as nightmare, it is not surprising that values are also taken to be a dream. "Why should you care about the world outside?" asks a character in a modern play. "For me the only reality is imagination, the world inside myself." The play is set in a madhouse, the mise-en-scène of much contemporary theater; but sanity itself has been made subjective. The claims of reality against fantasy have been asserted on behalf of delusional systems themselves. *Absolutism* posits final and unconditional ends that stand outside the means-ends continuum and thus resist evaluation save by fiat. Absolutism does not recognize that the value of ends is qualified by what consequences they have in turn and that ends are shaped by the means used to attain them. When ends are thought to justify any means while needing no justification themselves, they are betrayed by the means, and by their own consequences. Terrorism and the revolution triumphant provide tragic examples. Absolutism often reveals itself in the establishment of fixed priorities—first I will attain power, national liberation, financial security, or whatever, *then* I will pursue peace, justice, or love and leisure. Tomorrow never comes. Pursuits do have their preconditions, to be sure, but what lies always in the future robs every present of meaning. It is also true that sometimes radical solutions are called for and extreme measures must be taken: to pull a tooth or a trigger halfway is folly. But, for the absolutist, extremism is an end in itself. In this ideology, the good war justifies the cause.

There are values that have proved themselves so successfully by their conditions and consequences in such a variety of contexts that they can effectively function as if they were absolutes. Moral principles are such *relative absolutes.* That love is better than hate and truth better than falsehood may be taken as axiomatic. Yet, even here, there may be exceptions. Truth is precious and divine, but Hillel reminds us that we are nevertheless to compliment every bride on her appearance. The best of measuring rods must be made of substances whose coefficient of thermal expansion is always greater than zero; though serving as standard, the rod still needs to be standardized. The thrust of contextualism is not that there are no absolutes but that they, too, are relative. Decisions must respect particulars as well as principles. At bottom, decision making rests on good judgment, in the sense given to it by Kant: the faculty of applying general principles to particular cases. The faculty cannot be dispensed with, he pointed out, for if we had rules for the application of principles to cases, we would need judgment in applying the rules. To ask whether ends justify means is like asking whether commodities are worth the price—in the abstract, the question is pointless. The example has an additional relevance: the demand for the commodity affects the price. The decision maker and his or her deliberations are themselves important components of the values he or she is appraising. "Don't admire anything!" may be good advice for someone entering an antique shop, but sharing the joys of collecting may be worth more than another bargain acquisition.

Among the most important means for the attainment of any person's ends are other people. This is the fundamental linkage between moral values and management. Effectiveness in the pursuit of ends demands coordination of many efforts. Decisions are typically made not for an individual but for a group. Here we face a dilemma. Action by a group on behalf of

specific ends calls for organization, but organizations have ends
of their own, distinct from and sometimes antithetical to the
ends for which they were organized. The dilemma is that the internal ends may interfere with the external ones, but these cannot be attained without organization. Labor unions may impede
production; schools, with their lectures, assignments, and exam-
inations, interfere with education; police and courts pervert justice; the military establishment pose a threat to national security. I am confident that many people share my views on the
dangers of organization; I wish we could get together and do
something about it!

In a democracy, the values of the group are construed dis-
tributively rather than collectively; they are localized in the
individual citizens, not in the state. Yet means must often be
collective: education, health, and personal security, for instance,
are usually pursued through public instrumentalities. Kennedy's
injunction "Ask not what your country can do for you, ask
what you can do for your country" runs counter to democratic
ideology. Governments are instituted to secure certain rights for
the individual; members of the government are servants of the
people, not the other way around. But collective effort can
achieve nothing unless individuals are loyal to the collectivity,
even, under some circumstances, to the extent of putting its
welfare above their own. Responsibility for collective decisions
remains, in any case, with the individuals participating in the
decisions.

Protection of the individual, whether from the state or
from lesser aggregations of power, notoriously calls for eternal
vigilance. "Power does not corrupt," Bernard Shaw remarked;
"men corrupt power." Yet power lies chiefly in organizations
whose individual members may be virtually powerless to control them. An organization may have values that are not those
of any of its members, just as the individual members may pursue ends contrary to those of the organization. The sales force,
production engineers, and shop stewards may be more concerned with their own special interests than with the welfare of
the company. On the other side, an organization may deem it
the cardinal virtue of its members not to make trouble; this is

what often defines a "good student," an "able soldier," a "trustworthy employee," and a "capable manager."

Strategies are available for dealing with differences in the values of interacting individuals in special cases. An apple can be fairly divided between two eaters if one cuts it into two parts and the other has first choice. Whiskey can be fairly distributed among a set of drinkers by giving each glass, as the whiskey is poured, to the first person to say "When!" Taxes on property can be fairly assessed if each homeowner makes the assessment of his or her property but is required to sell it at that price if a buyer offers. "Fairness" in these instances consists in allowing each individual's values to be decisive. Whether that is truly just and, just or not, whether such a method exists in general are not easy questions to answer. Social philosophies purport to answer both questions, but ideologies themselves are subject to diverse and often conflicting valuations. Realities, moreover, may make a mockery of ideological claims. The essential difference between capitalism and socialism, it has been said, is this: capitalism is the exploitation of man by man; in socialism, it's just the other way around!

A combination of a religious ethic, an equalitarian ideology, and Middle Eastern culture patterns gives Israeli decision making a distinctive quality, which I have tried to capture in three principles: (1) every right is transformed to a privilege; (2) every privilege is denied; and (3) every denial is negotiable. Foreign business people have complained that in Israel a contract is less a commitment than an occasion for negotiating. If the contract itself is to be negotiated, it should follow that in Israel the process of negotiation is endless. It is.

Among the values with which managers are most likely to be concerned are those connected with work. These values are said to constitute the "work ethic"; in the usage I have adopted, it is a question not of "ethics," which deals with *why* something is of value, but of "morals," which specifies *what* is valuable. The value of work—more accurately, its disvalue—is often prejudged by contrasting work with play: work is "whatever a body is obliged to do," as Tom Sawyer put it, not something we might do because we enjoy doing it. Whitewashing the fence was work for Tom but play for his friends. Yet maturation demands the recognition of necessities, things we are obliged to do whether we like doing them or not. Philosophers such as the Stoics and Spinoza took the recognition of necessity to be the definition of freedom. When the child's polarities are carried over into the cultural dualism of the adult world, professional life is deemed to be no better than a necessary evil, while personal life is uneasily felt to be superficial and unworthy. There can be no doubt that, for the overwhelming majority of humanity, work is nothing but toil, at best a deadening succession of empty operations for trivial ends. In much of the world, industrialization has not yet been achieved, so that work is mostly a matter of muscular effort. In the postindustrial societies, though there is more brainwork, most work is still as much routine drudgery as it ever was. The advantages enjoyed by workers in the developed nations are chiefly that conditions of work have improved. Work has been made shorter but seldom more meaningful. Sociologists have noted that Americans are among the most leisured people on earth, but scarcely the most leisurely, lacking what elsewhere is known as *serenidad* ("serenity") and the enjoyment of *dolce far niente* ("the sweet art of doing nothing"). We work at playing, escaping from its rigors only by resigning ourselves to the role of spectators.

For decision makers, work has values that others can find only in play, if even then. It is a challenge that, when met, provides a sense of achievement, a value that can be derived from the shared responsibilities of participative management, as Rensis Likert has pointed out. Work can express caring for others, a contribution to external interests with which the worker has identified; managers can be truly devoted to the welfare both of the company and of its employees. Work can fulfill what Thorstein Veblen called "the instinct of workmanship," yielding the joys that come from creating, producing, and exploring as much and as well as we know how. Work can provide a basis for self-respect and for acceptance by others, as in the Israeli kibbutz or the Japanese corporation. Whether, in a particular context, work in fact has these values depends on the entire set of values with which work is implicated in that context.

Values in decision making are fundamentally humanistic, because decisions are always about people, no matter what else they are about. People are the essential means by which the decision maker's ends can be attained. The most important part of every human being's environment, said Spinoza, is other human beings. This is certainly true, at any rate, with regard to the environment of every manager. What Kant formulated as the most fundamental of categorical imperatives is that no one is to be treated as a means only. To do so is what Martin Buber called relating to that person as "it" rather than as "thou." There is also the alternative of "you," where people are not ends but where there is a recognition, nevertheless, that they also might be, and deserve to be, ends. There is nothing immoral in treating people as customers, clients, or contacts, as resource or manpower. What is immoral is to treat them as if they could never be anything else. It is one thing to have people stand in lines when there is really no help for it. It is quite another thing routinely to force them to do so as an economy measure. Incomparably more serious is the dehumanization by discrimination, treating a person not as an individual human being but as an instance of an irrelevant abstract category. The dehumanization remains even if the discrimination is being practiced in reverse, in the expectation of thereby redressing prior wrongs.

For human beings, people are inescapably the measure of all things. Nothing else can be of worth if people themselves are worthless. There is a self-defeating illogic in housing computers in carpeted, air-conditioned quarters while remaining indifferent to the sensitivity of human beings to psychological shocks and to the emotional climate of the place of work. The operating characteristics of machines are undeniably important to the decision maker, but only so that decisions can ultimately leave human beings free to do what only human beings can do. Machines are increasingly capable of making decisions; values are the work of humans. A question that thereby becomes crucial to our decisions is what manner of people are coming to be—the people responsible for the decisions and those affected by the decisions. Only some of the values implicated in any decision can be settled by calculation. The most fundamental questions transcend calculation, because they include evaluations of relating to people in a calculating way. The issue is not only what kind of world is in the making but also what kind of person one is becoming in arriving at one decision rather than another. This is the issue faced in the recognition that values are an expression of character. Our values are embodied in *how* we make decisions as well as in *what* decisions we make. Some values are imposed, shaping an *involuntary self,* the person that we are because we have no choice—peon, taxpayer, or soldier in an unjust war. Other values characterize the *peripheral self,* which lives a life neither imposed nor freely chosen, the life of the commuter, the worker on the assembly line, or the office slave. Only a few values are rooted in the *authentic self,* the locus of freedom and autonomy, expressed in love and creation and experienced as joy.

General Patton is supposed to have said about his soldiers, "I don't want them to love me; I want them to fight for me." Many managers might say the same, only replacing "fight" by "work." But why should others fight or work for *them*? Management might be defined as so relating people to their work and maintaining such conditions of work as maximally to engage the authentic self of the worker, minimally the involuntary self, and only as much of the peripheral self as technology makes necessary. Effective managerial decision making thus presupposes caring for those affected by the decisions, not as a matter of sentiment but as taking into account what is essential to the optimal carrying out of the decisions. The manager's own values, embodied in the style of his or her decision making, may express instead the character of a despot or slave driver. Decision making may become an occasion for the exercise of power, as in other human relations what passes for caring may in fact be controlling, possessive, and smothering. Caring for others does not mean being namby-pamby with regard to our own values. "If I am not for myself, who will be?" asked Hillel. Some values are *competitive,* resting on each person's affirming his or her own interests. Other values are *cooperative,* depending on mutually supportive effort. Still other values are *pluralistic,* their pursuits proceeding on parallel and independent paths.

Generalizations about the relative worth of each of these species of value owe more to ideological preconceptions than to contextual analyses of specific cases. Caring may not always be possible nor, indeed, appropriate. Respect for others, however, is, in my opinion, a relative absolute. It implies, first of all, respect for their otherness, rather than overlooking the differences that make them other or, worse, denying their right to the differences. Projecting onto others our own values may be fulfilling to us, but it fails to establish a link with *their* motivations. What looks like sharing decision making with them may be no more than engineering their consent to decisions we alone have already arrived at.

Respect for others also means allowing them a margin for error. The policy of "One mistake and you're through!" may provide an incentive for the involuntary self but precludes the services of the authentic or even the peripheral self. Disagreement in the process of decision making (or even after the decision has been made, for that matter) need not be taken as the mark of a moral failing. It is possible to accept values that we do not share—that is, to recognize that others value them and to acknowledge the right of the others to their own values. If acceptance in this sense is confused with adopting the values, we must either betray our own values or institutionalize hypocrisy. On the other hand, not all values are acceptable. It is sometimes necessary to dissolve a marriage, terminate employment, or go to war. Respect for others, finally, is embodied in the capacity for delegation of authority. Being "helpful" to others does not necessarily help them. "Helpfulness" may imply the inability of the other to make the right decisions or to carry them out. Often, this is a self-fulfilling prophecy. Delegation is important not only for the manager but also for subordinates. Effective management has much in common with psychotherapy: even the most insightful therapist can only hold the ladder; the patients must climb it for themselves.

Making a decision is inseparable from responsibility for it; the buck stops wherever deliberation does. Common in our time are *virtual decisions*—decisions in all but name—such as those made by military "advisers" and often, in the civilian sector, by consultants. Virtual decisions allow for a kind of ventriloquism, as though it were someone else who arrived at the decision. With regard to values, there is a widespread projection of responsibility onto such institutions as the family, the church, and the school for personal values and government, business, the media, and the military for social values. Projection is reinforced by disguising decisions as acts of God. Ethical and legal systems agree that those who pursue a particular end are responsible for all the consequences reasonably to be expected from the means used to attain the end, even if, in the particular case, the consequences were unintended or unforeseen. To be responsible is to be answerable, to be subject to being brought to account. A community of obligation enters into the context of the decision, for, as Thomas Hobbes put it, covenants without swords are but words.

The terrorist tactic of shifting responsibility for the fate of hostages onto those who reject the terrorists' demands manifests the question-begging illogic of naked power. There may be more subtlety but no less sophistry in shifting responsibility for industrial pollution, military waste, and governmental incompetence onto anyone and everyone except the members of the corresponding bureaucracies. Responsibility may be indirect (as of the bartender who previously served the drunken driver) or vicarious (as of the parent or guardian of the juvenile vandal). Responsibility is all the more undeniable by those who directly and personally share in making the relevant decisions. Such denial is more often tacit than explicit. To the many diagnoses of the moral crisis of our time might be added this one: it is a crisis of indifference, of moral isolationism. Being involved, however, is far more likely to be antecedently given than to be consequent upon a decision. Though the tree of knowledge of good and evil is not of our own planting, it has borne for us a bitter fruit. If we do not, like Adam, think to run and hide, we may yet come to know enough to choose wisely.

17

Values and Ethical Issues
for Human Systems Development
Practitioners

William Gellermann

This chapter is intended as a contribution to the ongoing process of increasing ethical consciousness and ethical practice within the organization and human systems development (OD/HSD) profession. It is written from the perspective of a person who has been closely involved with the profession for more than twenty years and who, beginning in 1982, has been coordinating the development of *A Statement of Values and Ethics for Professionals in Organization and Human System Development* (Gellermann, 1982, 1983, 1984a, 1984b, 1984c). More specifically, the objectives of this chapter are to examine the values underlying the practice of OD/HSD; to identify the primary ethical issues that have arisen in the process of developing the *Statement of Values and Ethics* and to summarize the range of positions that practitioners have taken on those issues; and to encourage readers to clarify their consciousness of their own positions on those issues, to guide their own behavior by that consciousness, and to join actively in the process of increasing ethical consciousness and practice throughout the profession. Before moving further, it will help to review the background out of which my part in the discussion has emerged.

Background

One of the recognized primary indicators of a profession's existence is that it has a generally accepted code of ethics. Therefore, for those of us who do consider organization and human systems development (OD/HSD) a profession, it is important that we acknowledge that general acceptance of an ethical position by OD/HSD practitioners does not exist—and then do what it takes to create a position that can be generally accepted.

The acknowledgment began for me during a conversation in 1981 with Dan Kegan, a lawyer who is also an OD practitioner and researcher. He told me about a survey he had conducted of OD practitioners that concluded that OD was not a profession, because, among other things, it did not have a code of ethics (Kegan, 1982). (At the time of the survey, most people referred to the field only as organization development. As discussed later, the field's definition appears to be expanding to encompass all human systems development; however, since the Kegan survey focused on OD, that is the reference used at this point.) Don Cole, executive director of the OD Institute, responded to the Kegan survey by drafting a first version of a code and publishing it in the institute's newsletter, asking for comments. I responded, and Don asked if I would coordinate an effort to draft a code for the institute. I said that I was interested in drafting a "statement" but that "code" was too rigid for where I thought we were; I wanted to create something that would be acceptable throughout the profession. Several years later, after numerous drafts of a statement and endorsements of the process for developing such a statement by Certified Consultants International, the National Training Laboratories (NTL) Institute of Applied Behavioral Sciences, the OD Institute, the OD Network, and the Human Systems Development Consortium (leaders and representatives of fourteen OD/HSD-oriented groups, primarily in the United States), we have an experience and data base for discussing values and ethical issues in OD/HSD.

The process of creating the statement has included drafting a version, sending it out to people for comments and suggestions, redrafting on the basis of the responses, and then repeating the process. There have been more than eight drafts of the statement, and more than 100 people from over ten countries have been involved so far. The process is expected to continue, with increasing participation by people throughout the profession.

The Statement. The July 1984 draft of the statement (Gellermann, 1984c, p. 1) begins with an introduction stating that "Organization and Human System Development (OD/HSD) is an emerging profession rooted in human values and relevant theory whose purpose is to help individuals, organizations and other human systems achieve excellence. . . ." It then identifies its purposes as increasing professional consciousness and responsibility among OD/HSD professionals, enabling those professionals to make more informed ethical choices, and contributing to enabling the OD/HSD profession to achieve excellence in its own functioning. The remainder of the draft statement consists of a preamble and sections on assumptions and ethical guidelines. The guidelines are grouped under four main headings: "Responsibility for Professional Development and Competence," "Responsibility to Clients and Significant Others," "Responsibility to the Profession," and "Social Responsibility." (In time, we expect to develop an ethics clearinghouse for the profession.) The central offices of the OD Institute, the OD Network, and Certified Consultants International may be contacted for information about the current draft of the statement.

The Issues Discussion. An essential companion document to the statement is the "Issues Discussion." When suggested changes in the statement involve an issue on which significant difference of opinion seems likely, the differences are described in this document. An example of this type of issue is "Do we place high value on democratic decision making?" (This topic is discussed later in this chapter, under "Content Issues.") The statement is explicitly an evolutionary document, not fixed and final; I expect that in time we will achieve substantial consensus on the statement and the "Issues Discussion" combined.

Values and Ethics. Before continuing this discussion, it will be helpful to differentiate values and ethics. The term *values* refers to those qualities or things (such as behaviors, results, beliefs, and attitudes) that are considered desirable, important, or worthy. For example, dependence, independence, and interdependence are alternative values. In contrast to values, *ethics* refers to standards of judgment and conduct. For example, "fully informing participants in any activity initiated by me as to its sponsorship, nature, purpose, implications, and any significant risks associated with it so they can freely choose their participation" is a standard of conduct. And the standards that we use in guiding our behavior, consciously or unconsciously, are our ethics.

By referring to these examples of values and ethics, we can also make the point that values are more fundamental than ethics and provide the implicit foundation for ethics. For example, the ethics of "fully informing participants . . . so they can freely choose their participation" tends to be based on the independence value (rather than the dependence value). And other standards may also be based on that same value, as in the case of "encourage and enable my clients to provide for themselves the services I provide rather than foster continued reliance on me." One further point: The values and ethics that most concern us are the ones that guide our actual behavior, rather than the ones we talk about. This chapter is based on the assumption that, by discussing our values and ethics, we will enable ourselves to bring our actual practice into alignment with what we say by clarifying what we want our values and ethics to be.

Areas of Agreement on Values

Some areas of agreement on values are clearer than others, but I will identify the ones on which I think substantial consensus exists. In my view, most practitioners would agree with the value areas identified, even though they might not agree with the details of my discussion of each one. The following are the values that I see as central to OD/HSD practice.

Consciousness of Values. This is a metavalue, since it involves valuing values and answering questions such as "What's most important?"—particularly in regard to choices about results desired, means of achieving them, and the costs associated with those means.

Excellence. In Search of Excellence, the title of the book by Peters and Waterman (1982), rang a sympathetic chord in the hearts and souls of most OD/HSD practitioners I know. And I think that was because, although the word *excellence* had not been widely used within the field prior to that book, it captured the spirit of what most of us are about. For me, it means more than effectiveness and efficiency, although it includes those. And it means more than the literal meaning of the word, with its roots in excelling, surpassing, and outdoing. The meaning that is relevant to us, I think, is closer to the spirit of "be the best *you* can be," rather than "be the best" (in the sense of better than everyone else). It means people doing the best they can, individually and collectively, with their potential.

System Effectiveness. This refers to achieving desired results. In the early days of OD practice, it was sometimes overlooked because of the field's emphasis on process. It is now clearly a primary value, although there are issues about what to include in the category of desired results and whose desires to consider in identifying them. (For example, see the discussions following under "Stakeholder Orientation" and "Quality of Life.")

System Efficiency. Achieving desired results at minimum cost was also sometimes overlooked during the early days of OD practice, again because of the attention given to process. It, too, is now a widely shared value. However, what to recognize within the costs of achieving results is still an issue.

Holistic, Systemic View. This involves valuing from the point of view of systems as wholes. For example, an organization is a system comprising interdependent individuals and groups as subsystem levels within it; simultaneously, the organization is an interdependent subsystem within a higher-level socioeconomic system. The holistic view recognizes interdependencies among all system levels. And holistic valuing tends to be all-win rather than win-lose, which means valuing the purposes of all levels, including subsystems and more inclusive systems, rather than valuing only from the organization's point of view. (For more about all-win, see the discussion under "Collaboration.") Systemic valuing shows itself in the increasing acceptance among practitioners of the next value.

Stakeholder Orientation. Although related to the systemic view, this is different in that it focuses attention on all those who have a stake in the organization's results, including stockholders, customers, employees, labor organizations, suppliers, and the larger community. In addition to considering the interests of all stakeholders, I think most OD/HSD professionals strive to value those interests equitably. Doing that in practice is difficult, however; and, at least in part because of that difficulty, the *equitable* valuation of stakeholder interests does not seem to be a generally shared value. (In fact, practitioners who are paid by one group of stakeholders sometimes have an understandable tendency to give greater value to the interests of that group.)

Competence. Having the necessary knowledge and skill to achieve desired results efficiently, by people within both the profession and client systems, is valued highly. But the profession's values go well beyond job competence, as is indicated by some of the other values mentioned here, especially human potential and personal growth.

Human Potential. There seems to be a general assumption that individual human beings have unique potentials for contributing to collective achievement, and value is given to the full realization of their potentials. For example, Tannenbaum and Davis (1969) say, "We are struck by the tremendous untapped potential in most individuals yearning for discovery and release" (p. 8). In my view, most OD/HSD professionals share that view and place great importance on bringing potential into full realization within their client systems.

Quality of Life. This value contrasts with mechanistic values that tend to treat people as objects to be used in the service only of system purposes and without regard for personal purposes. One manifestation of this value is the quality of working life (QWL) work being done in many organizations. In addition to this broad value, there are a number of related values that focus on individual human beings: (1) Individuals should be valued as persons, not just as means for achieving organizational results. Tannenbaum and Davis (1969) wrote of this when they referred to movement away from avoidance or negative evaluation of individuals toward confirming them as human beings (p. 7). Among other things, it means caring about them personally, including their concerns, hopes, and desires, as well as their productive strengths and weaknesses. (2) Individuals should be valued as whole persons, not just as employees or performers of particular jobs. By recognizing the whole person, OD/HSD practice seeks to enable and empower people to express their full potential in their jobs and in their lives generally. For example, this is reflected when an organization supports a person's development even when it may mean the person's eventually leaving the organization. (3) Personal growth is valued as well as growth of job-related competence. Organizations may question whether it is their responsibility to encourage growth that does not directly serve their purposes, but OD/HSD practice tends to be based on the assumption that, when people's full growth potential is not attended to, the portion that is organizationally relevant is likely to suffer. There may even be a widely shared judgment that ignoring or hindering personal growth simply because it does not serve organizational purposes is morally wrong. (4) Human differences and individual uniqueness are valued. Some organizations may be threatened by difference, but OD/HSD practice tends to support the acceptance and utilization of differences in the service of organizational creativity and flexibility, as well as out of respect for individual authenticity.

Authenticity. In general, this value refers to being true to oneself in the moment and in relation to the full realization of one's potential over time. From the perspective of OD/HSD practice, it refers to supporting or creating the conditions that make that truth possible. A number of more specific values are consistent with this general value. One of these is integrity. For some practitioners, this value is based on the assumption that there is a self to which each person can be true, but this is not yet a generally shared assumption. However, for almost everyone, integrity in the sense of honesty and candor is generally shared. I find it useful to identify honesty and openness separately.

Honesty—accurately expressing what one thinks and feels—is generally accepted as a value among practitioners themselves and as a guide to the kind of systems norms they seek to support or create. I find it helpful to differentiate openness from honesty, since it is possible to conceive of people being absolutely honest about what they express without being completely open. It is the difference between speaking the truth and speaking the whole truth. Within the profession, there is a clear preference for openness as well as honesty. However, some people seem to advocate openness without qualification. Others qualify openness by taking into account conditions such as the usefulness and relevance of what is being expressed. For example, leveling about something that a person or larger system cannot change, leveling beyond a system's ability to cope with the amount of information, or leveling about things that are likely to harm a relationship may be unnecessarily destructive and harmful. Furthermore, all "openness" is not truly "open," as in the cases of name-calling and judging in ways that do not clearly admit that the expression is a statement about the speaker, not about the object of the speaker's expression. For further discussion of this, see Morton (1966). Another specific value, empathy and listening with understanding, might be called receptive openness, since it refers to actively receiving the expression of others and understanding them from their point of view. It means not distorting other people's meanings with your own and not reacting defensively. It is essential for authentic relationships.

The value of appropriate and effective communication of feelings as well as thoughts recognizes that feelings are facts that informed decision making must consider. It also recognizes that feelings are an essential element in the formation of human relationships over and above the minimal mechanistic task relationships required to get work done. Tapping into the deepest levels of human potential and motivation is generally recognized as requiring communication about feelings, even from the point of view of serving the organization's purposes alone. And when quality of life is also valued, communication about feelings is essential. However, it is important to differentiate communicating about feelings from reacting to feelings, since communicating about and recognizing feelings is not the same as being blindly controlled by feelings, one's own or those of others. That is the reason for including the words *appropriate* and *effective* in the description. They emphasize communication that serves the higher values underlying individual and organizational purposes.

Finally, the value of appropriate confrontation is a logical consequence of all the specific values that are part of the authenticity value. It is grounded in recognizing that difficulties, differences, and conflict are facts of organizational life and that problem solving, productivity, creativity, quality of life, personal growth, and many other organizationally desired results require honest, constructive confrontation. Failure to confront appropriately is generally recognized among OD/HSD practitioners as being dysfunctional for system effectiveness.

Process as Well as Task. According to this value, the processes by which work is performed are considered to be as important as the task activities directly connected with production. For example, when a group works on decision making, *process* includes such things as how people listen, argue, fight, withdraw, and generally support or undercut one another, whereas *task* tends to refer only to communication specifically about the decision.

Autonomy, Freedom, Responsibility, and Self-Control. Generally speaking, this value has been expressed in the statement as "Human beings are . . . rightfully responsible for and capable of making choices, taking charge of their lives, and functioning autonomously within a context of interdependence," although it is recognized that some human beings are not capable of this (Gellermann, 1984b, p. 2). Some people raise questions about whether people do, in fact, have "free choice," but I think most practitioners agree that they enhance free choice by acting as if it exists, and, therefore, they tend to value it. Doing so tends to empower individuals, and—when their purposes are aligned with those of the organization—it also empowers the organization.

Independence and Interdependence. These values are represented in the statement's position that "A major aim of Organization and Human System Development is to help the system become conscious of and able to fulfill its purpose by: (a) enabling the system as a whole and each part within it to understand their purposes and interdependence with one another . . . (and) (b) helping individuals within the system accept responsibility for their lives (and) recognize the extent of their freedom and their power to choose the way they live their lives within the system . . ." (Gellermann, 1984c, pp. 2 and 3). The idea of independence within a context of interdependence is also implicit in the quotation from the statement given in the preceding discussion of autonomy.

Authority, Power, and Influence. In what may seem to be a contradiction to the independence and freedom values, authority, power, and influence are valued when they serve system effectiveness and do not unnecessarily limit independence and freedom. However, there is wide difference of opinion about what this means in particular situations, especially about the conditions under which limiting independence and freedom is "necessary." Generally speaking, authority of knowledge and skill is preferred over authority of position, and influence is preferred over coercive power. In some crisis situations, however, even coercive power may be necessary; for example, an urgent need to repair a major piece of equipment may require a manager to compel people to work (although, ideally, they would be willing to do so without compulsion).

Collaboration. In its simplest terms, this means people working with each other for a shared purpose rather than against one another for different purposes. It does not necessarily exclude competition, since it recognizes and values the possibility of friendly competition in the service of the greater organizational good. It seeks to minimize win-lose competition, which requires a loser for someone to be a winner, and seeks to maximize all-win competition, in which winning, even by one, is valued because of what it means for all. (For example, many Olympic athletes view their competition from an all-win perspective, and they decry the media's overemphasis on gold medals.) In cases of competition for scarce resources, emphasis is on working together to find alternative resources that serve everyone's needs and, when that is not possible, to resolve the differences on the basis of those higher values that are shared by the individuals involved in the competition. (For an extensive discussion of experience with this value, see *Working Together* by Simmons and Mares, 1983.)

Trust. The kind of system that is created out of all of the preceding values involves a high level of trust among all members of the system. This is particularly true in cases of conflict and competition. At the moment the conflict or competition is recognized, the presence or absence of trust determines whether people direct their energy and attention to working with each other against the problem in an all-win way or against each other in a win-lose way.

Risk Taking. Valuing the willingness to assert oneself and to take a stand is a logical outcome of many of the other values, including system effectiveness, competence, human potential, quality of life, authenticity, autonomy, independence and interdependence, and collaboration. With those values, particularly when functioning in systems that do not share them, practitioners need to behave in ways that are risky and to encourage others within their client systems to do the same. Not to value risk or to value avoidance of risk instead would tend to work in opposition to those other values.

Systems Development, Growth, and Transformation. This cluster of values is grounded in several of the other values but is different from them. It is grounded in such values as human potential and personal growth, but it goes beyond them to value the collective growth and development of the system in ways that bring into being the fullest realization of individual potential in the service of the whole. This involves the ongoing creation of a system composed of human beings. At some points, this creation process can involve a change in form, literally a transformation, that is analogous to the change from caterpillar to

butterfly, as when an organization shifts from a hierarchical, bureaucratic form to a more egalitarian, democratic form. The unsettled period of transformation may appear to move in opposition to the excellence value, but there are a rapidly increasing
number of practitioners who value transformation, because they
see it as essential for creating systems capable of achieving at
the highest levels of human aspiration.

Context Issues

The issues discussed in this section do not actually involve values and ethics, but they are essential to our discussion,
because they establish the context within which the content
issues of values and ethics are meaningful.

1. *Do we conceive of ourselves as a profession and as
professionals?* Most practitioners implicitly seem to consider
themselves professionals, but some qualify that view. For example, one person says: "We are a social movement of which parts
aspire to professional status. Accrediting members is a minimal
requirement of a professional association, and only a few of the
present organizations qualify" (Gellermann, 1984a, p. 41).
Others hold that OD/HSD will not be a profession until (1) it
has a set of standards that defines professional practice and provides a base for censure for harmful practice and (2) it is clearly
involved in relating theory and practice. Others are concerned
that, by becoming a profession, we will put ourselves above our
clients or "become a regulatory clique that controls entry and
practice like medicine" (Gellermann, 1984a, p. 41).

Most practitioners seem to accept that OD/HSD is an
evolving, emerging profession; that it does not have to make the
same mistakes as other existing professions; that the process of
developing a statement of values and ethics is part of its consciously becoming the kind of profession its practitioners want
it to be; that the profession needs some boundary clarification
to protect itself and its clients (but how much and in what ways
is still an open question); that it is possible to become a profession in ways that make the world better for everyone, not just
the profession, including ways that enable others to do what

OD/HSD professionals do without putting the professionals above their clients; and that it is possible to be both a professional and a person without getting so caught up in the role that one's sense of self is lost.

2. *What is our field*—organization development (OD), human systems development (HSD), applied behavioral science (ABS), or something else? Since OD/HSD practitioners tend to work primarily with organizations as clients, many of them prefer *organization development* as the name for their field. However, a substantial minority prefer *human systems development,* and still others prefer other names (Gellermann, 1984a, p. 42). Although organizational clients may comprise the bulk of the profession's practice, I see an emerging acceptance of *human systems development* as the name for the field, since that will enable all people who work with human systems, ranging from individuals and families to communities, societies, and even transnational systems, to be included within it.

3. *Is developing a statement of values and ethics worthwhile?* Most practitioners seem to agree that it is worthwhile to develop a statement. Their reasons for this include: (1) it is individually clarifying, (2) it clarifies a widely shared view, (3) it can give clients an idea of what to expect from a professional, (4) it can provide guidance for professional education, and (5) the statement-development process is evolutionary and not static. Differences of opinion are not so much about whether to develop a statement as about the nature of the statement.

4. *What kind of statement do we choose to develop?* The statement can be of different kinds, including aspirational, educational, and regulatory. An *aspirational* statement is a general description of ideals toward which professionals can strive. In contrast, a *regulatory* statement is much more precise; that is, it is specific enough to be buttressed by rules that govern behavior. And an *educational* statement, though less precise than a regulatory statement, seeks to describe and explain professional norms precisely enough so that it can be used in preparing practitioners to resolve the ethical dilemmas they experience in their practice.

In my judgment, a regulatory code is clearly not feasible

for the profession now, although existing organizations may develop their own regulatory codes if they so choose. For the profession generally, we need to crawl before we walk, and that involves achieving consensus first on an aspirational code and then on an educational one. Ideally, regulation in our profession will be self-regulation, and, therefore, until we have a clear educational code and materials to support it, it seems premature even to talk about a regulatory code with externally imposed sanctions.

Content Issues

The issues discussed in this section are those that, in my view, are central to the profession's consciously developing widespread agreement on values and ethics among its members throughout the world.

1. *Are our ethics too culturally specific? Is our thinking oriented primarily to practice in the United States?* In responding to a questionnaire about the statement (Gellermann, 1984a, p. 43), a substantial majority accepted it as not being too culturally specific. Most of them recognized that it did have a cultural bias, but they thought that the words were still acceptable as a base for aspiration by OD/HSD professionals throughout the world. Respondents from Africa, Norway, India, Japan, Great Britain, and Germany considered the words as more or less acceptable, with minor modification.

Others disagreed. A respondent from Saudi Arabia said, "The typical Arab has trouble understanding how anyone cannot be 'all he can be.' To suggest something different is to suggest that God (as they see Him) has overlooked someone. People don't become; they are." Others pointed out that some cultures require behavior that would seem to be counter to the statement, such as bribery and the subordination of women. Someone else (from Great Britain) said, "The whole concept is alien to some cultures even in our own country. But I can't see how this can be avoided."

If the profession is going to develop an ethical stance that is acceptable across cultures, it seems essential to acknowledge cultural bias and to view the creation of such a stance as a continuing process of communication between, among, and even within cultures. Some specific ways in which cultural differences may be provided for have been recognized in the statement (Gellermann, 1984c), including: "When cultural conditions preclude following these guidelines, we accept responsibility for the consequences of our action or inaction and will seek to be clear about the guidelines we choose to guide our action in their place" (p. 10). "Obtain consultation from OD/HSD professionals who are native to and aware of the specific cultures within which I work when those cultures are different from my own" (p. 5). "Be aware of my own personal values, my values as an OD/HSD professional, the values of my native culture, the values of the people with whom I am working, and the values of their cultures; involve the client system in making relevant cultural differences explicit and exploring the possible implications of any OD/HSD intervention for all the stakeholders involved" (p. 5). Further discussion of how cultural differences affect the evolution of the profession's ethical stance follows in the section headed "Frontier Issues."

2. *Should we include among the aspirations of OD/HSD "helping organizations align their purposes with the welfare of the earth and all its people"?* Responses to the questionnaire were strong and varied widely, ranging from "I like the idealism there. Who knows where the aim for the stars will take us" and "Yes. Definitely" to "Pretentious and irrelevant do-goodism," "Come on! I for one have no messianic complex," and "too grandiose." Since there was substantial opinion both for and against the wording mentioned, the words in the statement were changed to read "helping people align both individual and organizational purposes with the welfare of all the people of the earth and their environment" (Gellermann, 1984c, pp. 3 and 8).

The issue is still open. The primary question, I think, is: Does the OD/HSD profession, as a profession, have a global aspiration? In view of the fact that the systems with which we work are open systems and are, therefore, ultimately subsystems within the global system, I consider a global perspective essential. Even though our clients may not see the connection, it is appropriate for us to take a leadership role on the issue whenever we can do so effectively. I should mention, though, that I do not consider it necessary to stress that connection with all clients under all conditions. I do think that we are uniquely qualified as a profession to maintain a global perspective and to assert it when it might make a positive difference. And I think that, as a profession, we can aspire to make the world as a whole a better place, though most of us could not do so individually.

3. *Do we value fundamental human rights? If so, what ones?* Most respondents to the 1983 questionnaire (Gellermann, 1984a, p. 44) accepted that "An OD professional places high value on . . . fundamental human rights," but a few wanted to eliminate reference to fundamental human rights. Several supported the idea of incorporating the United Nations' "Universal Declaration of Human Rights" into the profession's ethical position, including one person who said that "using it may be a step toward 'world cultural bias' rather than 'U.S. bias.' "

For reasons mentioned earlier, I would like to see us move toward a "world cultural bias" by making a commitment to fundamental human rights of the kind identified by the United Nations' declaration, including rights to life, liberty, and security of person; freedom of thought, conscience, and religion; freedom of opinion and expression; and freedom of choice. In general, I would like to see us understand and take a strong position in support of the United Nations' declaration—and then intentionally use that position to guide our practice. That the declaration does represent a generally acceptable world view is indicated by the fact that it was adopted by the United Nations in 1948 by a vote of 48 to 0, with 8 abstentions (Poland, Byelorussia, Czechoslavakia, the Ukraine, Yugoslavia, South Africa, Saudi Arabia, and the Soviet Union). It includes a preamble and thirty articles, ranging in focus from Article 1, "All human beings are born free and equal in dignity and rights . . . ," to Article 5, "No one shall be subjected to torture or to cruel, inhuman or degrading treatment or punishment" (Williams, 1981).

4. *Do we place high value on "wide participation in organizational affairs, confrontation of issues leading to effective*

problem solving, and democratic decision making"? Most practitioners who responded to the 1983 questionnaire (Gellermann,
1984a, p. 45) accepted that wording, but many wanted to recognize explicitly that democratic participation is not practical
under all conditions. One person argued against that, however,
by saying, "Don't qualify a true statement. Everyone knows
that compromise is at times necessary." Others said: " 'Placing
a high value' does not mean a practicing professional will insist
on democratic process as the only means in every situation."

The view of the people who support using the word *democratic* are in
agreement with Marvin Weisbord, a partner in a leading national
consulting firm, who said at a recent OD Network conference,
"The only thing we bring to the party that other specialists
don't is a commitment to democratic processes for achieving
desired results." Comments from those who disagreed included:
"The emphasis on democracy as an end is misplaced." "I don't
think we are trying to make all organizations into 'democ-
racies,' and this statement creates that image." "Excludes many
OD people." "Drop democratic decision making. It is not universally relevant to effective problem solving or decision making." "I don't like the statement—it commits to an ideology
with which I am only sometimes aligned. But I'd rather have it
stand than add anything to it."

The view of the people who would like to drop the reference to "democratic decision making" and shift the emphasis to
"participation" and "involvement" may be summarized in the
words of one respondent who said: "Equating democratic decision making, which has a strong popular identity as a political
process, with involvement and participation is inaccurate and
can create unnecessary resistance among clients. . . . Participation and involvement are sufficiently justified by 'effective
problem solving,' improved decision making, and 'organizational
excellence.' . . . Our democratic values should be secondary or,
better yet, a nonissue."

Is it sufficient to drop "democratic decision making" and
assume that it is recognized by other words? Part of the preference for doing so seems to come from confusing the vision of
democracy with the current reality of political process. Disillusionment with that process can understandably leave people with

doubts about democracy. However, if we view democracy as government of, by, and for the people, then, in spite of its limitations in practice, we can choose it as an ideal to guide us. Even granting that, however, some people still rate other values higher, such as excellence and efficiency. But I believe it is possible to have excellence and efficiency with democracy and, in the long run, impossible to have them without it. (For evidence that supports the possibility of democracy coexisting with excellence and efficiency, see Mason, 1982, and Simmons and Mares, 1983.) Democratic decision making means substantially more than "voting" and "political process." It involves enabling and empowering people to participate in making the decisions that affect their lives. Viewed in that way, the OD/HSD role involves helping to provide the structures, procedures, knowledge, abilities, and information needed for people to participate as fully and effectively as possible.

Current reality may limit our opportunities for democratic decision making, given the priority of the excellence and efficiency values, but we can still value democracy by encouraging participation and involvement in the present and striving to broaden democracy in the future. The issue of explicitly valuing democracy is still open. OD/HSD professionals generally seem to seek democratic participation whenever it is practical because of its power to motivate and contribute to excellence—and because they value free choice and self-determination. But to what extent do they see empowering people to control their own lives as central to their role? To what extent are they willing to subordinate the freedom and self-control values to the organizational excellence value, and vice versa? And, ultimately, are both democracy and excellence achievable without subordinating either value? I think they are, and I think that realizing that truth, in the sense of bringing that truth into being, is one of the primary challenges faced by the profession.

Frontier Issues

This section will discuss issues that have arisen most recently in the evolution of the statement and that have a depth to them that seems just beginning to be revealed. They are among the most fundamental issues on the frontier of defining what the OD/HSD field is all about.

1. *Do we want to develop general agreement among OD/ HSD professionals throughout the world on a statement of values and ethics? And, even if we do, is it possible, given the fact of major cultural differences?* Hofstede (1980) has reported the results of a study of 116,000 employees of a single multinational corporation in forty countries around the world. On the basis of statistical analysis of the data, he identified four primary dimensions that he used to describe and differentiate the cultures of those forty countries: power distance (the degree to which unequal distribution of power in institutions and organizations is accepted by people throughout a society); uncertainty avoidance (the degree to which people feel threatened by and seek to avoid uncertain, ambiguous situations); individualism-collectivism (the degree to which people are supposed to take care of themselves and their immediate family or, at the collective extreme, the degree to which they expect their relatives, clan, organization, or other in-group to care for them in exchange for absolute loyalty to the group); and masculinity (the degree to which people hold masculine values, such as assertiveness and acquisition of money and things, and *not* caring for people and the quality of life).

To illustrate what those dimensions mean more specifically, consider these differences in attitudes of people who are low and high on the power-distance dimension (Hofstede, 1980, p. 46):

Low	*High*
a. Inequality in society should be minimized.	a. There should be an order of inequality in which everyone has a rightful place.
b. All people should be interdependent.	b. A few people should be independent; most should be dependent.
c. Hierarchy means inequality of roles established for convenience.	c. Hierarchy means existential inequalities.

Or, on the individualism dimension (Hofstede, 1980, p. 48), consider the following:

Low	*High*
a. Identity is based on the social system.	a. Identity is based on the individual.
b. "We" consciousness is primary.	b. "I" consciousness is primary.
c. Belonging to organizations is emphasized; membership is the ideal.	c. Individual initiative and achievement are emphasized; leadership is the ideal.

In spite of methodological criticism of his study (Goodstein and Hunt, 1981; Hofstede, 1981), Hofstede's results clearly suggest that substantial cultural differences exist along the four dimensions he identified. And, more importantly for our discussion, his results indicate that certain values that seem central to OD/HSD may be more reflections of the U.S. culture that gave birth to OD/HSD than they are a sound basis for establishing a global perspective regarding OD/HSD values and ethics.

The fact of U.S. difference is indicated by the following results reported by Hofstede (1980, p. 49): on power distance, the United States ranked below average (fifteenth out of forty countries), but not as low as several other wealthy countries; on uncertainty avoidance, it ranked low (ninth); on masculinity, it ranked above average (twenty-eighth); and on individualism-collectivism, it was the single most individualist country of all those studied (fortieth).

I see two alternatives for dealing with cultural differences in developing professional ethics on a global scale. The first might be called the pluralist alternative; that is, one in which countries or clusters of countries with similar cultures develop common statements. Ideally, all of those statements would follow a similar format, so that similarities and differences could be readily identified. The second alternative might be called the universalist alternative; that is, one in which a substantial consensus is developed around a single common statement, but with recognition of and allowances for cultural differences, such as those mentioned in the discussion of content issue 1.

The way the second alternative might come about can be illustrated by the contrast between the primary "I" consciousness of individualist cultures and the primary "we" consciousness of collectivist cultures. As I see it, OD/HSD tends to transcend that apparent conflict by viewing it not as "either I or we" but as "both I and we." And within the "both-and" perspective, the orientation is to find or create all-win results that work for both the individual and the collective, rather than one or the other. In any case, I expect that the discovery or creation of one of those alternatives (or something else) will be an exciting experience. I would like to see us undertake it as a contribution both to our own development and to global peace and the constructive resolution of differences.

2. *To what extent, if any, do we recognize responsibility for helping organizations and other human systems to provide for the equitable distribution of the fruits of their productivity among all of their stakeholders?* For example, if an OD/HSD professional facilitates an employee-participation program that results in a substantial increase in productivity, does he or she have a responsibility for encouraging the equitable distribution of that increase? Some people would not even consider the question. Others would say no. Still others would say that the employees who contributed to the increase should get some part of it, but opinions vary widely about how much.

The exact nature of this issue is still vaguely defined, since it can extend beyond sharing productivity increases to the question of how to establish equity in salaries and wages and compensation generally. I know of many organizations in which managers as well as workers feel they are not fairly treated by the existing compensation system, but they feel powerless to change it. They talk as if they still want to contribute to the best of their ability; but, in my judgment, their motivation must inevitably be affected, with substantial loss in productivity, creativity, and satisfaction as a result. This issue also extends beyond compensation to the question of how to establish equity for customers, stockholders, suppliers, governments, communities, and all of a system's stakeholders in sharing the fruits of its productivity. In my opinion, equitable sharing is an ethical issue of primary importance for the OD/HSD profession. However, as I see it, our role is more one of facilitating decision making about equity than one of prescribing what is equitable.

3. *To what extent, if any, do we recognize "love" in the practice of OD/HSD?* The July 1984 draft of the statement (Gellermann, 1984c, p. 2) includes these words: "A major aim of Organization/Human System Development is to help the system become conscious of and able to fulfill its purpose by . . . creating and supporting a climate within which freedom, equality, mutual trust, respect, and love prevail." Those words are adapted from a policy statement developed by senior executives in a medium-sized computer company (Kollmorgen) (Kiefer and Stroh, 1983, p. 27). Many people in our field explicitly or implicitly refer to love, as in Robert Tannenbaum's question, "Does this path have a heart?" But some do not want to refer to love. For example, one person reacted to the 1983 questionnaire with a note saying: "Define love. It sounds like 1960s flower children. Churchified. Pollyannaish." Another said: "I suggest deleting the word *love.* The other characteristics (for example, trust, openness) are ones that the profession values in organizations and, as a logical extension, values in society at large. Love is not necessary for effective organizational functioning. Because it does not stem from our professional values, it seems inappropriate to include it with the others" (Gellermann, 1984a, p. 47).

Some of the concern about referring to love seems to stem from the feeling that it will not be acceptable to our clients, so that, even though we may value it, we shouldn't talk about it. However, Alban and Hughes suggest that it is we, more than the people who are our clients, who are hesitant to work at the heart level (Diagonali, 1984, p. 2). Are we? Can we achieve what we consider to be truly important if we do not intentionally align our efforts with the "energies of the heart"?

4. *To what extent, if any, do we recognize a spiritual dimension in the practice of OD/HSD?* Responses to the May

1983 statement suggested including the following words as one of the assumptions underlying the guidelines: "Human beings are . . . interdependent economically, socially, culturally, and spiritually and are responsible for the choices they make within that context" (Gellermann, 1984c, p. 2). The spiritual reference was added because one person identified "starting a spiritual increment" as one of the central purposes of the profession as he sees it. Another person specifically suggested including *spiritual* in the words quoted above. In contrast, two people asked, "Is this a profession or a religion?"

Just as some people's experience with democratic political process can leave them with an aversion to democracy, the experience of others with established religions can leave them with an aversion to religion. Regardless of how practitioners feel about "religion," they may still be able to acknowledge that there is a spiritual dimension to the practice of OD/HSD. As an example of how spiritual consciousness is beginning to appear as an issue, two highly experienced practitioners, Billie Alban and Sheldon Hughes, in a presentation to the New York OD Network (Diagonali, 1984), talked about their discovery "that managers are indeed looking for a deeper spiritual base upon which to build." They invited the OD professionals present at the meeting "to be inspired, emboldened and encouraged to infuse our training and consulting practices with our hearts, minds, and spirits" (p. 2).

As I see them, the key questions underlying this issue are: Do we acknowledge spirit as an aspect of reality with which OD/HSD practice must deal? And, if so, how do we deal with it? As a first step toward answering these questions, I find Wilber's (1983) ideas clarifying. To paraphrase him: We need to recognize that mind can adequately look at and map sense data because it transcends them; it can adequately look at and map intellectual data because they are its own creation; "but it cannot adequately look at and map spirit because spirit transcends *it*" (p. 70). The challenge for us as a profession, as I see it, is to find or create ways of data gathering and communal affirmation in the realm of the spirit that will enable us to move ahead together.

Conclusion

Building on the foundation of the general areas of agreement about values described in this chapter, I am confident that the OD/HSD profession will be able to resolve the issues that have been discussed—and others that emerge as the field continues to evolve. Even more importantly, I expect its members to clarify their shared sense of mission in the world and, as a result, to acquire an increased sense of professional identity. As I see it, that mission involves supporting the development of the highest levels of excellence to which the members of organizations and other human systems aspire—levels that I believe will far surpass most people's present levels of aspiration. Among the conditions that will make achievement at those highest levels possible are that OD/HSD professionals throughout the world accept the belief that it is possible and that they then join with one another in committing themselves to bringing that vision into being. And central to that outcome is achieving clarity about the values and ethics that the profession chooses for guiding its members along the way.

References

Bayles, M. *Professional Ethics.* Belmont, Calif.: Wadsworth, 1981.

Chalk, R., Frankel, M., and Chafer, S. *AAAS Professional Ethics Project: Professional Ethics Activities in the Scientific and Engineering Societies.* Washington, D.C.: American Association for the Advancement of Science, 1980.

Diagonali, J. "December NYODN Meeting." *New York Organization Development Network Newsletter,* February 1984, pp. 2-4.

Gellermann, W. "Ethics and Organization Development." *EXCHANGE: The Organization Behavior Teaching Journal,* 1982, *1,* 26-32.

Gellermann, W. "A Statement of Values and Ethics for Organization Development Professionals." *Organization Development Journal,* 1983, *1* (1), 35-44.

Gellermann, W. "Issues in Developing a Statement of Values and Ethics for Organization Development Professionals." *Organization Development Journal,* 1984a, *2* (1), 39–47.

Gellermann, W. "A Statement of Values and Ethics for Organization Development Professionals." Unpublished paper, February 1984b.

Gellermann, W. "A Statement of Values and Ethics for Professionals in Organization and Human System Development." Unpublished paper, July 1984c.

Goldman, A. *The Moral Foundations of Professional Ethics.* Totawa, N.J.: Littlefield Adams, 1980.

Goodstein, L., and Hunt, J. "Commentary: Do American Theories Apply Abroad?" *Organizational Dynamics,* 1981, *10* (1), 49–62.

Hofstede, G. "Motivation, Leadership and Organization: Do American Theories Apply Abroad?" *Organizational Dynamics,* 1980, *9* (1), 42–68.

Hofstede, G. "Do American Theories Apply Abroad: A Reply to Goodstein and Hunt." *Organizational Dynamics,* 1981, *10* (1), 63–68.

Kegan, D. "Organization Development as OD Network Members See It." *Group and Organization Studies,* 1982, 7 (1), 5–9.

Kiefer, C., and Stroh, P. "A New Paradigm for Organization Development." *Training and Development Journal,* 1983, *37* (4), 26–35.

Mason, R. *Participatory and Workplace Democracy.* Carbondale: Southern Illinois University, 1982.

Morton, R. " 'Straight from the Shoulder'—Leveling with Others on the Job." *AMA Personnel,* November-December 1966, 65–70.

Peters, T. J., and Waterman, R. H. *In Search of Excellence: Lessons from America's Best-Run Companies.* New York: Harper & Row, 1982.

Simmons, J., and Mares, W. *Working Together.* New York: Knopf, 1983.

Tannenbaum, R., and Davis, S. "Values, Man and Organizations." *Industrial Management,* 1969, *10* (2), 67–86.

Wilber, K. *Eye to Eye: The Quest for the New Paradigm.* Garden City, N.Y.: Anchor Press/Doubleday, 1983.

Williams, P. (Ed.). *The International Bill of Human Rights.* Glen Ellen, Calif.: Entwhistle Books, 1981.

Wooten, K., and White, L. "Ethical Problems in the Practice of Organization Development." *Training and Development Journal,* 1983, *37* (4), 16–23.

18

Transforming Managerial
and Organizational Research:
Creating a Science That Works

Roger D. Evered

"Science is an organized activity. Hence it operates according to
some managerial principles. A unified science of management
implies a management of science, a science of science, a self-
reflective science." So says C. West Churchman in his book
Challenge to Reason (1968, p. 116). Churchman's insightful
comment challenges us to examine the special role that managerial and organizational research plays in the societal endeavor
called *science*. Hence, this chapter is intended to stimulate reflection—and dialogue—on the fundamental nature of research
in the field of organization and management. In particular, I
want to draw attention to the importance of what might be
called the "meta-issues" of research, in contrast to either the
methods of research or the results of specific research studies.
By *meta-issues* I mean the implicit, or tacit, value assumptions
we habitually make about what good research should be; or, in
Thomas Kuhn's terms, how our own "normal science" is constituted and what is involved in its transformation.

The value assumptions we collectively make prescribe the
epistemology we use. What are the implications of our tacit
value assumptions for doing research in our field? Is it not pos-

sible that alternative value assumptions and epistemologies would be more effective for creating healthier organizations and management practices? By "healthier," I mean more conducive of human contribution and development, as well as more productive, workable, and satisfying. Our task, as researchers, is to develop and maintain continuous discourse processes for critically (that is, reflectively) evaluating the value assumptions we hold about the nature of our own particular version of "science." This chapter will therefore be useful if it contributes to the discourse that is already under way among organization and management professionals on issues that are variously labeled "philosophy of science," "epistemology," "metascience," "alternative paradigms," and what I am calling "the meta-issues of research." I believe that dialogue, in the context of a commitment to improvement, will lead to steady improvement in the quality, usefulness, and societal impact of research and that willingness to discourse on pertinent questions is more valuable than prescriptions and a priori solutions.

In the following pages, I want to critically draw attention to the relevance of the dominant paradigm we use for dealing with the actual activity of managing in real organizations, which I take to be the focal phenomenon of interest in our field. My criticism is of the reigning paradigm itself, which the social sciences have collectively, myopically, and in some ways disastrously bought into. My intention is to bring more sharply into awareness some of the features and implications of the prevailing positivistic/rationalistic paradigm, to suggest ways to avoid its dysfunctional consequences, and to present a vision of what is possible for management and organization research. In particular, I want to draw the critical distinction between *science* and *praxeology* (or *prax-science*), the latter being neither technology in the sense of instrumental technique nor science in the familiar, restrictive sense.

One Researcher's Viewpoint

Each of us engaged as professional researchers in organization and management holds views about "science," what constitutes good "research," and how "knowledge" relates to management practice. Some of these views are personalistic, and some are shared by the research community and even labeled "objective"; but, either way, they are subjective. What I shall do in this chapter is present one researcher's view of these issues with the intention of generating discussion and thereby improving management practice and real-world organizations. The thrust of my chapter derives from the following assertions:

Society Is in Trouble; Organizations Are Not Working. Society in the broadest sense reveals itself as a panorama of messes—wars, unemployment, injustice, terrorism, drugs, accidents, alienation, environmental pollution, conflicting ideologies, technological complexity, and the threat of nuclear annihilation. The combined effects of these messes seem to grow in severity every year. Most of our societal problems are fundamentally problems of human organization and management, whether we are thinking of episodic events (such as the Three Mile Island nuclear accident) or of ongoing phenomena (such as unemployment). The problematical messes of society, the so-called problématiques, have a clear origin in managerial/organizational practice. The variety and complexity of societal messes are apparently richer than our wisdom, skill, and capacity to create appropriate organizational forms and to administer them. The organizations and institutional forms we currently have are not adequate for the task we collectively face; and I have the sense of rapidly running out of time. Am I the only one who experiences the urgency to create new kinds of organizations and new ways to manage them?

Our existing organizations—industrial, educational, political—work only in the superficial sense of producing certain desired outcomes (products, graduates, regulatory policies, and so forth). But, in a more profound sense, they do not work. Most organizations that I know support inequities, injustices, and incongruencies. They tend to promote conformity, dependency, alienation, personal irresponsibility, dehumanization, and collective myopia. The core human needs to express oneself, contribute, participate, make a difference, be valued, be treated justly, relate authentically, and experience one's true nature (rather than one's beliefs about it) are seldom met by our existing organizations. For whatever reason, the workplace is not commonly experienced as a source of joy and meaning and personal worth, a place where one can be genuinely honest. Society is in trouble, and our organizations are not working.

Practitioners Need Help. Notwithstanding the relative primitiveness of our current organizations and the array of complex societal problems, men and women do live and work amid them. They do the best they can with what confronts them, and what confronts them is frequently incomprehensible, alienating, or overwhelming. Given this reality, today's practicing managers need support, insight, and empowerment. How much of our research provides these?

Managers often operate in intricate and complex organizational settings and must deal with situations that seem to grow more entangled each year. The character of the situations confronting today's manager seems to be changing in the direction of more "complexity, uncertainty, instability, uniqueness and value conflicts" (Schön, 1983, p. 14). As the problems grow bigger and more complicated, so do the chances for and consequences of ineffective management. The prospect of a nuclear war between the two superpowers represents the ultimate example. Clearly, today's management practitioners need all the help they can get.

Our Social Sciences Have Not Helped Them. The mainstream, or "normal," science we have been religiously using has been dismally ineffective in assisting managerial practitioners or in convincing policy makers that the social sciences have anything useful to offer. Positivism may provide precise facts about how the world is (or was!); but on the topic of change and transformation, it is virtually silent and, therefore, useless. The time is surely overdue for us in organization and management research to tell the truth about our collective research that is based on the positivistic paradigm. The accelerating volume of published studies over the past twenty-five years has not in aggregate much altered the condition of society or the managerial and organizational world that is purportedly being studied. It does not seem to have changed anyone's thinking or influenced practitioners in any discernible way. The mainstream traditional science paradigm, on which most of those studies are based, seems to be seriously flawed. It is no longer shocking to hear a colleague in the social sciences say that "only the promotion-and-tenure interests of the researcher are being served by most of the published journal articles" or that "as soon as I get tenure, I can stop writing meaningless articles and do something worthwhile."

Our Social Sciences Actually Contribute to Our Problems. Why are our social sciences not contributing to the real world of practitioners? My current awareness of the social sciences leads me to think that they are actually generating problems rather than assisting in their resolution. The "science" that we have become wedded to is couched in language that traps us into conceptualizing social and organizational realities in prescribed ways. Processes become reified, change is seen as externally caused, explanation substitutes for doing, knowledge generation is separated from the doer, analysis takes precedence over synthesis, a billiard-ball model of cause and effect is presumed, reality is assumed to have the same structure as our logic, and objectivity hides its own assumptive base.

The practitioner's world is ruled by situational particulars, engagement, conjecture, possibility, and action—the very items that our science (with very rare exceptions) entirely ignores, implying that the paradigm of our science is epistemologically invalid. The damage we do with the prevailing social science paradigm derives from the fact that it is believed, revered, worshiped. As organizational researchers, we are coconspirators in buying into it. Our holy cow is the paradigm underlying our science, and it produces unholy problems. Most of the time, we are worsening the very situation we are trying to resolve.

Our Conception of Science Must Be Revised. We need to transform the conception of science and technology that we inherited from the physical sciences. Physics and engineering are not useful models for the social sciences to follow. The epistemological assumptions for dealing with inanimate systems are just not powerful enough to cope with societal or human systems. Two requirements follow: (1) we must let go of our current conception of positivistic/rationalistic science, and (2) we must develop alternative and inherently more effective modes of knowing (such as collaborative inquiry, phenomenology, and action research). We must redefine science in more authentic and pragmatic ways while we simultaneously let go of our obsession with positivistic science as something sacred and magical. The American obsession with positivistic science and technical rationality is at the expense of society itself—at least as I know and value it. The revision of the epistemology underlying the social sciences generally, and managerial/organizational research in particular, is therefore a matter of considerable urgency.

The Total System That Supports "Science" Must Be Reformed. Transformation of our conception of science, while cognitively possible, cannot be created or sustained without transformation of the total sociocultural/politicoeconomic organizational system that maintains the enterprise we call science. It is necessary that we study the total surrounding system (field) of support and gain appreciation of what that system is composed of, how the pieces fit together and feed each other, and what it would take to unfreeze that dynamic system so that it could sustain a more fruitful form of social science.

The actual organizational system that surrounds the personal and interpersonal process of knowledge generating would include professional conferences and journals, curriculum development, research sponsorship, institutional reward procedures, the book publishing industry, professional norms and expectations, the economic realities of academia, the conditions required for creative work, and societal shifts in values and culture, as well as the perceived utility of the organizational sciences. The four critical gatekeeping functions of this surrounding infrastructure system are research sponsors, faculty tenure committees, journal editors, and the media, which jointly sustain the prevailing societal norms and assumptions about science. The essence of my point is nicely captured by the following quotation:

> What social scientist does not know that government funding pervades our disciplines? Who does not know that the way to get funds is to propose to do something innocuous—that is, politically

harmless—by using a veritable steamroller of "hard science" methods that predetermines almost everything that can be "discovered" in the "research"? Who does not know that the surest way to administrative favor, promotion, professional fame, and personal fortune is to develop a web of grantsmanship contracts in the maze of government agencies, to milk agencies, to bribe graduate students into doing your work for you? Who does not know that government agencies making those determinations of what the young people will study are all too often the failures of the academic world? Who does not know major instances in which the "findings" of such research projects were literally corrupted to make sure they were politically right but scientifically lies? Who does not know how research grants are "managed" to further imperialistic strategies of the various academic cliques? Who does not know how the professional organizations and journals are "managed" in the same way? Who does not know that 95 percent of what fills our journals is there for careerist purposes and has no significant value to science or to our society? . . . State funding and bureaucratic controls have combined with the rhetoric of absolutist science to turn most of what passes as social science into myth and fraud [Douglas, 1979, p. 62].

In Order to Reform Our Science, We Need to Build Reflectivity into the Organization and Management of the Scientific Enterprise. By *scientific enterprise,* I mean the total macrosystem and community (as identified earlier) that operates and maintains the prevailing conception of science in our field. What I am here proposing is that this macrosystem be developed to provide an ability to be organizationally and managerially self-reflective. Organizational self-reflectivity refers to the ability of an organization (in this case, the whole organization of the scientific enterprise in our field) to look at itself critically, to raise questions about what it centrally does, and to generate meaningful responses to these questions. The self-reflective function of an organization is important for the health, performance, and vitality of an organization. It provides an institutional means to overcome myopia, whether at the level of the individual, the group, or society itself. A self-reflective and, therefore, healthy organization would have at least the following attributes:

- The capacity to examine its own assumptions and to raise pertinent critical questions about its own functioning and reason for being.
- The willingness to continuously challenge the question of how to know whether it is performing adequately.
- The ability to assess its own health, including its own criteria for health, on a continuous basis.
- The willingness to explore, to test by engagement, and to continuously transform itself.
- The encouragement of both intraorganizational and boundary-spanning dialogue.
- The tolerance of dissent, criticism, and self-doubt.
- The willingness to expose itself to the opposite (entertain the other).
- The orientation to search continuously for improved ways of understanding its own nature (core learning).

It is precisely this self-reflective capacity that needs to be developed within our science. Organizational vehicles are required for generating self-reflective dialogue within the scientific community on the meta-issues of our science. This implies a large-scale, long-term, organization-development effort on the organization and management of science itself.

In the following pages, I shall explore the prevailing scientific ethos, the role of values in the development of science, and how mainstream social science got to be positivistic. Since my viewpoint is that there is something seriously amiss with the epistemological base of managerial/organizational research, it is appropriate to begin by articulating that base. My criticism is foundational, so I shall begin with a clear statement of that foundation (see Evered, 1976; Evered and Louis, 1981). Subsequently, I shall discuss what is involved in creating a more viable, or effective, epistemology (or epistemologies). My aim is not to produce a new hegemony but rather to demonstrate the inherent attractiveness of alternative paradigms derived from action-based learning (see Morgan, 1983, p. 393).

Value-Free: The Immaculate Conception of Science and Technology

The ideal of an objective, value-free, researcher-independent science has been one of the core driving forces of Western societies, especially America in its past fifty years. The creed that surrounds and supports this ideal is along the following lines:

> There is a world out there that exists independently of us. It is unified, ordered, and structured in some particular way. It is possible to infer its structure from empirical observation and to represent its structure with the appropriate symbols, especially mathematically. That is to say, data about the world can be logically reconstructed into laws, reflecting the presumption of a morphological correspondence between the structure of logic and the structure of the world out there.
>
> Statements made about that world can be tested for their truth value, which is to say that the correspondence between the presumed logic of the statement and the presumed timeless structure of some selected part of the world out there can be tested. The neutral, value-free researcher may use any professionally approved empirical method. The gathering of sense data and the testing of truth statements must be carried out according to precise rules and procedures that are sanctioned by professional peers. Validation of the research findings is accomplished by other neutral, value-free researchers using similar tools of measurement and logic. Findings that are reproduced by others are then assigned the title of "laws of nature," with the attributes of universal and timeless statements about the world, unless or until other research demonstrates credible anomalies to these "laws of nature." Facts, findings, and laws so generated are held to be context free; in particular, they are held

to be independent of situation or human interpretation.

The scientific ethos that supports this enterprise to discover (uncover) the objective truths about the world out there requires institutions (academies) and persons (researchers) whose only interest is in the discovery of the external order.

Particularly interesting are those truths that describe the causal connections between entities, such as between causal agents (input factors) and effects (outcomes). *A* causes *B*. When such cause-effect connections can be credibly demonstrated, empirical objective science has, in fact, provided a reliable technique for causing a particular outcome. Thus, empirical objective science yields an instrumental logic, a technical rationality for producing desired outcomes reliably. This technical rationality based on objective science provides a repertoire of surefire methods for production, control, dominance, and, if necessary, coercion. Technical rationality provides the expertise to "manage" outcomes.

Each of the leading professions—medicine, engineering, education, and business management—is presumed to benefit from the use of science-based technical rationality. The doctor, the engineer, the educator, and the manager become technicians whose "practice" consists of applying the techniques, procedures, and methods derived from objective, value-free science. As these professions become more mature, they become more objective, more technical, more certain. They move away from the primitive prescience notions of craft, art, intuition, skill, and wisdom.

Education in each of these four professions is increasingly more technical and is based on the core model of first acquiring objective knowledge and subsequently applying that knowledge. Education therefore consists of acquiring the best techniques of the field, so that they may later be applied in practice. The term *techniques* refers to any complex or standardized means for attaining a predetermined result.

Likewise, the management of each of these four professions is increasingly more technified.

The use of explicit methods, rational organization structures (what Weber termed bureaucracies), and computers produces the accelerating movement toward a fully technified management system. Organizations of the future will be managed increasingly by "managers" who have been trained to use the latest science-based techniques that may be applied to any area of social, economic, or administrative life. The process is limited only by the amount of scientific research done in the field of organization and management. Practitioners, whether managers, teachers, doctors, or engineers, will increasingly need the services of professionals to provide technical expertise in specialty areas. Professionals put science-based technique at the service of the practitioners. The greater the range and technical depth of the professional, the more he or she will be needed by the practitioner, and the greater will be the benefit to the organization and to society. More science leads to more techniques, which lead to a more functional society. All that is required is to maintain the critical mass of professionals who can convince each other that this is *not* a social construction of reality but an objective, value-free science.

The preceding litany is riddled with fallacies, fantasies, and illusions; it is what has been called the "objectivist illusion" (Habermas, 1973, p. 315), "one-dimensional thought" (Marcuse, 1964), and "technical anesthesia" (Ellul, 1964). It is also Comte's vision of a "positive science." It is a mythology that has increasingly dominated Western cultures for the past hundred years, though it is only in the past few decades that the larger societal implications have become apparent, at least to some. It is precisely this concern about the societal consequences of this positivist epistemology that underlies this chapter.

Let us next take a deeper look at the relation between science and human values. After looking at the value-free assumptions of mythical science, we can look at the value-laden reality of the sciences, especially the social sciences, and even more especially the managerial/organizational sciences, where human action in human settings is central.

Science and Values

The general question of the relation of science to values is complex, pervasive, inescapable, and essentially unending. This is not merely a quaint philosophical puzzle but a matter of deep human concern with far-reaching implications for society and its future. Our understanding of science and scientific research and their perceived value to society develops from continuous critical attention to our implicit value assumptions. According to Wartofsky (1968, p. 404), the relation of science to values involves three separate issues:

1. Is value amenable to scientific study, and may the object of such study be taken as either natural/physical or human/social fact? Is there a science of value?
2. What values are exhibited *in* science? This is a question concerning the sociology of science or the study of the *ethos* of science.
3. What is the value *of* science? What larger interests does it subserve or subvert? How is the worth of science itself to be judged?

Of particular relevance here is the second item: the values *in* science and the issues of the sociology and ethos of science.

Numerous social scientists have addressed the relationship between science and human values, most notably perhaps Dilthey, Rickert, Marx, Weber, Lewin, Dewey, Allport, Kaplan, and Mitroff. Kaplan (1964, p. 377) particularly has systematically explored the role of values in the behavioral sciences. He identifies six different ways in which values play a part in the scientific enterprise:

1. Values as subject matter (for example, the values that managers hold).
2. Values in the ethics of the profession (for example, research ethics).
3. Values in the selection of problems (for example, choice and definition of research topics).

4. Values and meanings (for example, researchers' interpretations of observed behavior).
5. Values and facts (for example, criteria for determining what is and what is not a fact).
6. Objectivity and values (for example, sociology-of-knowledge issues).

Most pertinent here is item 6: objectivity and values, encompassing sociology-of-knowledge issues.

The Physical Sciences. The development of Western science reflects the need for valid, reliable knowledge about the world and the quest for systematic processes that transcend the idiosyncratic, the unconfirmable, the arbitrary, the mendacious, and the dogmatic. The scientific method implies a positive valuation of observation, logic, and experiment. Norms have evolved regarding skepticism to claims, evidence and experimental testing, impartiality and fairness, separating one's own feelings and beliefs from "the facts," and consistency, truth, and confirmation. By virtue of the presumed universality and timelessness of these norms, science is intended to transcend personalistic beliefs, local prejudice, and narrow interest. The values of science (that is, within science) become part of science itself.

Almost all of us who share these values of science take pride in our participation in and contribution to their enactment in the research studies we do, the professional relationships we develop, and the scientific institutions we construct. The scientific ethos is valued by us, particularly the ethical norms that imply impartiality and temporary detachment from one's own beliefs and values—other than one's beliefs and values about science itself. *Value-free* implies a consistency and intersubjectivity in the underlying values in science, rather than an absence of values. It implies *consensus* with the values of the scientific community, rather than "objectivity."

Historically, the development of the scientific ethic provided a means to overcome the domination of ignorance, superstition, religion, and princes. The success of science in the natural, or physical, sciences provided technologies that significantly improved humanity's physical and economic conditions. Science became positively valued for its *by-products,* in addition to its *methods.* In the physical sciences, "science" became so highly valued, as a method of generating knowledge, as a store of knowledge about the world, and as a necessary condition for producing material goods, that it almost appeared at times to have the aura of magic, religion, and power that it had earlier overthrown. Only in the last decade or so has the value *of* "science and technology" become questioned. Some of the consequences of "science and technology" are now viewed as societally threatening (Evered, 1978). Additionally, some fundamental conceptual concerns have arisen regarding the presumed "objective" nature of the physical sciences. Heisenberg (1958b), for example, has said that, at the subatomic level, the notion of an objective reality is quite meaningless. And, at the astronomical level, the problems that black holes pose for one's notions of objective science are well known.

Notwithstanding the profound value issues underlying the physical sciences, for all practical purposes they could be ignored. Not so in the social sciences, where value issues may *not* be overlooked and must necessarily be attended to.

The Social Sciences. In moving from the physical sciences to the social sciences, fundamental value choices must be made. For example, one of the following value positions must be assumed: (1) There is only one kind of science, which is the same for all fields. The physical and social sciences are therefore identical modes of inquiry, except that the latter is less developed than the former. The physical sciences represent the ideal, which the social sciences strive to attain. (2) The two domains, physical and social, are fundamentally and inherently different in their nature, since the social sciences must deal with the new elements of human action, language, and consciousness. We must therefore develop a new mode of inquiry that is appropriate to the social realm. The epistemology of the physical sciences is too primitive to cope with the complexities of the social realm.

Given the power and awe of the scientific method in the physical sciences, it is not surprising that it should have become directly applied without appropriate modification, elaboration, or extension to the social realm. The aping of the physical sciences has been, in my opinion, an intellectual disaster and a societal drain. We are left with a mode of inquiry that has all the trappings of rigor, precision, and quantification but that is without relevancy to or grounding in the realm of human action in living human systems. Despite its claims of value-free objectivity, positivistic social science might be characterized as a technology based on the *assumptions* of positivism, *faith* in the Comtean world view, and an *obsession* with mental imperialism —all held together with diverse humanizing Bandaids.

The limitations of the current social sciences are well established, both theoretically and in practice. Criticism of current social science epistemology has been penetrating, extensive, relentless, and enduring. Most damning of all, perhaps, is the *rational* criticism of positivism by the logical positivists themselves, most notably the famed Vienna Circle: "There is rational agreement about the inadequacy of the original Positivist understanding, knowledge and meaning" (Bernstein, 1971). Yet it continues to be practiced, supported presumably by a surrounding institutional context that enacts and empowers the "science = good" halo effect from the physical sciences. Deficiencies in outcome of positivistic social science are sometimes taken as evidence that we need more facts, more powerful inference techniques, more rigorous methods. In my view, however, the deficiencies arise from the Comtean world view itself.

The uncritical adoption of the epistemology of the physical sciences into social inquiry was initially perpetuated by Comte (borrowing from Condorcet and Saint-Simon) in the 1830s, in the enthusiastic wake of the French Revolution. Comte set down the blueprints for a "positive" science that presumed to guarantee scientific objectivity in the human/ social realm. He used the term *positive* to refer to *actual* (versus imaginary), *certainty* (versus undecidedness), *exact* (versus vague), *useful* (versus vain), *relative validity* (versus absolute validity) (Habermas, 1971, p. 74). Comte is "the forerunner of all subsequent positivist movements in the social sciences—

movements which, while protesting their indifference to considerations of human value, have always done so on the basis of a
rather fervent faith in the liberating value of their enterprise"
(Matson, 1966, p. 35).

Comte sets down three principal doctrines of his Positivism, as summarized by Schön (1983, p. 32): "First there was
the conviction the empirical science was not just a form of
knowledge but the only source of positive knowledge of the
world. Second, there was the intention to cleanse men's minds
of mysticism, superstition, and other forms of pseudoknowl-
edge. And finally, there was the program of extending scientific
knowledge and technical control to human society to make
technology, as Comte said, 'no longer exclusively geometrical,
mechanical or chemical, but also and primarily political and
moral.' " Comte's prescriptions for a "positive science of society" rest on a set of value-laden assumptions about science and
society. The task of his social science was to collect social facts
and establish laws of the regularities of social objects and
events. He prescribed a "social factist" science. His vision of a
positive science was the universal enlightenment and emancipa-
tion of humanity. His procedures were aimed at applying "objective" scientific method to the rationalization of human
conduct (social engineering). Comte's prescription is virtually
indistinguishable from those of F. W. Taylor and B. F. Skinner.
Any present-day researcher who does research based on positivistic assumptions (for example, behaviorists) necessarily buys
into the Comtean values and world view—which is to say,
Comte's visions, hopes, speculations, motives, prescriptions,
assertions, prejudices, convictions, categorical imperatives, even
passions and dogma. On such human values is "objective,"
"value-free," and "rational" positivism based. Above all, the
positivistic scientist exhibits *faith* in the Comtean value system.

The Comtean world view (that is, positivistic social science) purposefully leaves out a number of critically important
features of most social/organizational/human phenomena. Specifically, it omits the motives and purposes of both the researcher and the organizational actor (the "object" of study); the process of interpreting and evaluating events and facts; the signifi-

cance of the actor's "phenomenal world," "life structure," "situation definition," or "problem setting" in determining actions; the reality of self-observation, self-reflection, and introspection on the part of either the researcher or the actor; communication and exchange between the researcher and the actor—that is, the possibility of collaborative interaction; and the realities of human action, language, and consciousness. It is difficult to see how an epistemology that systematically excludes any of these factors could ever generate meaningful knowledge that pertains to the practice of management. These factors can no longer continue to be systematically excluded from our science; we have to develop ways of building them back into our science-defining concepts and methods. We are obligated, I believe, to evolve new epistemologies that are both phenomenally relevant and methodologically precise. It is also sobering to remind ourselves that the methods of science cannot, *ever*, resolve the epistemological problems for us, which Gödel so elegantly demonstrated in 1931 (Gödel, 1962).

Values in the Organizational and Managerial Sciences

The problems of the social sciences are most particularly acute and urgent in the managerial/organizational sciences. Though we are perhaps the last of the social sciences to encounter the epistemological issue, we are likely to be the first to be compelled to provide a resolution. The demand for relevancy, based on the consequences of irrelevancy, is most keenly felt in the managerial world, which the managerial/organizational sciences seek to address. In an earlier paper, I wrote: "There is a crisis in the field of organizational science. The principal symptom of this crisis is that as our research methods become more sophisticated, they have also become increasingly less useful for solving the practical problems that members of organizations face. . . . What appears at first to be a crisis of relevancy or usefulness of organizational science is . . . really a crisis of epistemology" (Susman and Evered, 1978, p. 582).

The assumptions underlying the traditional "objective" science paradigm lead to a view of the managerial practitioner as primarily a user of science-based techniques. Problem solving is reduced to applying technical procedures to achieve pre-established objectives. Action is merely the implementation and demonstration of techniques whose objectivity and generality derive from statistical procedures and controlled experiments performed elsewhere. The more the organization and its people can be technified, the greater the effectiveness of the techniques.

Reality Versus Technical Rationality. Regrettable as it may seem for those who espouse the values of value-free science and the technical rationality that derives logically from it, there do seem to be limits to the technification and rationalization of a living system. The people who make up a typical organization may be malleable to some extent and to an extraordinary degree for short periods, but, in the end, the reality of the living system asserts itself as contradictory to technical rationality. Human beings seem to exhibit, at least occasionally, behaviors that arise from sources other than science-based technical rationality—imagination, curiosity, pain, playfulness, perversity, deception, randomness, boredom, collaboration, love, self-expression, personal survival, thoughts about the future, and a wide range of needs for affiliation, power achievement, esteem, body functioning, and self-actualization. Additionally, people have important differences in their fundamental beliefs about the nature of reality, humanity, meaning, God, and so forth. Often, small distinctions in fundamental values are accompanied by massive emotional differences and behaviors, as witnessed by the current battles between different sects in the Middle East.

In addition to value conflicts, people in living organizational systems generate uncertainty, volatility, and turbulence that technical rationality is ill equipped to deal with, since it is designed for certainty, order, and stability derived from a world that is assumed to be structured, ordered, stable, and tidy. Real people in actual living organizations do seem to mess up the mind-set of the technical rationalist, who is more attached to his or her simple, tidy, universal mind-set than to the actual messiness and complexity of situational reality.

There are at least three other aspects of reality that are particularly irksome for the positivistic science/technical rationality mind-set, because its methods cannot deal with them. First, an essential truth about reality is that every situation is in some way unique or distinctive. You cannot step in the same river, situation, or organization twice! Second, appropriate action is based in part on how the situation is defined (especially by the actor), and this depends on historical development of the situation (including its actors), how the situation is framed in language, and the declared commitments of actors. Knowledge of replications of previously observed relationships between actions and outcomes is not sufficient and may be irrelevant. Third, when theory is separated from practice, researcher from practitioner, and knowing from doing, the effect is to reduce the practitioner's competence to handle situations without the use of professionals with technical expertise. The consequence of objective research and technical rationality is the fostering of helplessness and dependency in the practitioner, in the sense that the practitioner is deprived of the essential means to directly learn. He or she becomes instead an operator of techniques rather than a *proficient*, learningful practitioner. (The root meaning of *proficient* is "making progress," from the Latin word *proficiens*. The word *profit* has the same root.)

The reality that practicing managers in live organizations face daily is composed of the characteristics of real people, which do not nicely fit the neatness of technical rationality. Instrumental techniques derived from scientific research performed elsewhere comprise only part of the changing situations that the practicing manager must work with. It can never be *all* of any given situation, unless there are no people there, and then only if stasis and certainty can be guaranteed. Reality has a habit of being richer than the technicians' models, and omniscience is still a way off. I take great comfort in that!

One way of thinking about the modern manager's job is as that of a mediator between technical rationality (techniques), on the one side, and living reality (people), on the other. We might surmise that as the crunch grows between the growing range and power of science-based technical rationality and the "complexity, uncertainty, instability, uniqueness, and value conflicts" of the people who inhabit organizations (Schön,

1983, p. 14), we would expect to find mounting pressures on the practicing manager. Already we find growing scientific interest in such topics as burnout, stress, and alcoholism. Such practitioner stress is clearly apparent within the medical profession. Since the Flexner report in 1910, medical education has been ordained to consist of two years of acquiring scientific knowledge (facts), followed by two years of applying that knowledge in a clinical setting (internship). A prescription such as this carries many assumptions about the nature of knowledge, how it is obtained, and how it is used—and especially about the relationship between the practitioner and the researcher. Medical education is an excellent illustration of the positivist science/technical rationality world view and its benefits and liabilities. Since 1910, the volume of scientific facts to be absorbed has grown overwhelmingly, and the clinical-practitioner side has degenerated into a dependent second-class activity. Practicing doctors have commonly become dispensers of scientific products, and the link between the doing and the learning is almost lost. Simultaneously, the incidence of doctor burnout, stress, and alcoholism grows yearly.

Additionally, there is great concern in medical schools over the quality of medical education, as there is in management schools regarding the quality of management education. Arguments are commonly made about the increasing amount of technical knowledge that a student must learn and about the fact that any amount of technical knowledge will not make a practicing manager. The general management skills of the practitioner-manager may still be taught in many curricula, but the pressure grows to replace them with more technical or scientific subjects. And what gets degraded in the process of training in technical rationality is the *art* of management.

A core problem for knowledge that pertains to the art and practice of management (and, indeed, any of the professions) is the artificial split between the acquisition and the application of knowledge. The fact that universities are based on the premise that "knowledge" can be produced (by research), disseminated (by teaching), and then applied (by practitioners) further underscores the difficulty of creating practitioners' knowledge on the basis of practitioners' actions. The suspicion grows that the intrinsic structure of academia may actually preclude the creation of a true praxis science based on practitioner action.

Alternative Paradigms for Inquiry. A number of alternative inquiry paradigms have been or are developing in the social sciences in an attempt to overcome the glaring epistemological deficiencies of Comtean (positivistic) social science. They are variously conceived and labeled—*action research* (Lewin), *anthropology* (Kluckhohn), *collaborative inquiry* (Torbert), *cultural science* (Dilthey), *dialectical inquiry* (Esterson), *dialogical research* (Randall), *ethnomethodology* (Garfinkel), *human action science* (Torbert), *new paradigm research* (Reason and Rowan), *organization development* (Bennis), *participative research* (Elden), *participatory research* (Hall), *phenomenology* (Schutz), *pragmatism* (Dewey), *praxis* (Marx), *reflective research* (Schön), *symbolic interactionism* (Mead), *verstehen* (Weber). Currently, the field of organizational science can be characterized as having two uncomfortably fitting parts: a major paradigm (Comtean positivism) that produces ever more peripheral knowledge with increasingly high precision and methodological rigor and a number of alternative paradigms that can generate pertinent knowledge, using quasi-methods that are frequently imprecise, vague, and difficult to articulate. What we need to develop is a new kind of science that combines the precision and methodological standardization of Comtean science with the relevancy and action-groundedness of the alternative paradigms now in use.

Human Action Science. What might this "new science" be like? The new science that seems to be emerging is likely to be more action centered, value based, collaboratively contexted, experientially rooted, situationally responsive, praxis oriented, and self-reflective than the current image of our "normal" (positivistic, objective) science. It is likely to incorporate the American "pragmatic" thinking of Peirce, James, Dewey, and Mead; the European "critical" thinking of Marx, Dilthey, Weber, Marcuse, and Habermas; and the "emergent meaning" notions of Bergson, Smuts, Husserl, Heidegger, Langer, and Polanyi. For convenience, and without yet being able to specify it, we can label this new science *human action science*. The study of human action science would then be properly called *praxeology* (*praxis,* "action," + *logos,* "discourse"), a term first used by the economist Von Mises in 1933 (Von Mises, 1949). Though rarely used in America (possibly because it sounds somewhat medical!), the term is in current use in Europe, especially France. Possibly the term *prax-science* might be more politically acceptable in the United States.

The term *praxis* has, of course, a long vintage. "The Greek term 'praxis' has an ordinary meaning that roughly corresponds to the ways in which we now commonly speak of 'action' or 'doing,' and is frequently translated into English as 'practice.' . . . *'Praxis'* in the formal (Aristotelian) sense signifies the disciplines and activities predominant in man's ethical and political life. These disciplines, which require knowledge and practical wisdom, can be contrasted with *'theoria'* because their end is not knowing or wisdom for its own sake, but doing—living well" (Bernstein, 1971, p. ix). The notion of praxis seems to have lain dormant until the mid-nineteenth century, when it became a central concept for both Hegel and Marx (and later Dewey), though each developed it somewhat differently. Nowadays, we usually think of praxis in the way Marx developed it, as reflectively (critically) doing what is necessary to get work done, practical action at the place of work, self-corrective inquiry in the dialogue of work. The term *praxis* is clearly close in meaning to the "new science" I am trying to define, but, because of the historical and political baggage associated with its various shades of meaning, it seems unwise to use the terms. I propose to use *prax-science* until a superior term is found.

Research in the Organizational and Managerial Sciences

Knowledge. In our normal everyday discourse, we talk of *research* as knowledge producing, *teaching* as knowledge dispensing, and *practicing* as knowledge using. I believe there is much inherent mischief in this terminology. Though to talk this way seems natural, it is, I assert, a language trap that has become unwittingly institutionalized. So let us try to undo the mischief by getting back to some basics. In my view, the future health and viability of society rest on our collective ability to constructively address this core language/epistemological topic and to find more effective and fruitful resolutions of these specific questions:

1. What do we mean by knowledge in the organizational sciences?
2. How is knowledge related to action by persons in organizational settings?
3. How do we assess the usefulness, value, and relevancy of knowledge?
4. How might we set up functional procedures for "coming to know," such that our coming to know would make a difference?

It occurs to me that these questions, in one form or another, have an extraordinarily long vintage—at least 2,500 years. They have been the focus of thought of some of the greatest minds of history: from Aristotle, Plato, and Socrates through Kant, Hume, and Hegel to Marx, Husserl, and Whitehead. Of special pertinence to the organizational sciences are the writings of Dewey, Lewin, Lasswell, Barnard, Kaplan, Churchman, Simons, Habermas, Giddens, Argyris, Schön, and Weick. The works of these writers constitute the core of our collective wisdom about the nature of knowledge and human action in the social field. Yet it is probably true that the mainstream majority of organizational scientists consider the collective wisdom of these writers to be "too philosophical" and, therefore, irrelevant and peripheral, whereas a concerned minority are likely to see these writers as relevant and central. This split in the field between those who view philosophy (metascience) as irrelevant and peripheral and those who view it as centrally relevant is surely an important fact for us to work with. It is only a slight exaggeration to say that science (physical, social, and managerial/organizational) proceeds in sublime ignorance both of the assumptions that form its epistemological base and of the collective wisdom of these writers.

This leads to a real dilemma. Why is this accumulated col-

lective wisdom so unattended to by our field? Will the results of
our deliberations here be added by organizational scientists to
the set of "what need not be attended to"? In short, *what are
the conditions under which our field will attend to its epistemological base?* I suspect that a major factor that determines
whether a scientific field attends critically to its epistemological
presumptions is the sociopoliticoeconomic system that supports
it. The problem is to transform or generate anew the infrastructure that can enable critical re-evaluation to occur—which is
what our academic and/or intellectual institutions should be
doing.

What precisely do we mean by knowledge? In common
with the other core concepts of life (goodness, truth, beauty,
love, justice), knowledge defies precise definition, as the extensive literature on epistemology attests. According to a widely
accepted formal definition, *knowledge* means "justifiable true
belief"; that is, knowledge is a *statement* about some aspect of
the world that is in some way supportable. While the difficulties
in this definition are many, they are greatly exacerbated in the
human sciences, where issues of history, culture, language, symbols, free will, and human action considerably complicate the
relatively simple (!) problem of knowledge for the natural sciences.

More broadly conceived, knowledge refers to *any com-
municable cognition (statement) that influences human behavior. Knowledge* is therefore more like a verb than a noun. Or-
ganizational-science knowledge is about what is real in the social
domain as well as in the physical domain. What is real is what
has effects, both socially and physically. There are probably
differences in knowledge quality depending on which evidential
processes are evoked to justify a belief. One of my beliefs is that
we have arrived at a level of maturity and awareness in the organizational sciences of realizing that some knowledge of great
usefulness cannot be justified by the more formal and rigorous
scientific procedures. Other procedures for justifying a demon-
strably useful belief are required, though they have yet to be
developed.

The paradox is that the most certain knowledge we have

is that based either on intuition and feelings or on commitment and promise; yet these kinds of knowledge are difficult to communicate and share in a credible way. In contrast, scientific knowledge in the strict sense is merely a general statement that has not yet been refuted or disproved. Its generality, universality, and often statistical quality provide dubious information for any *particular* situation—which is precisely what the practitioner must work with. So we have this paradox: intuition yields certainty that is difficult to communicate credibly; science produces precise probability statements of uncertain applicability that are readily communicated.

There seem to be three basic ways of handling intuitive knowledge in the organization and management field. The Chicago approach holds that intuition is a primitive, prescience mode of thought, from a time before the modern methods using logic were developed and best exemplified by operations-research techniques. The dual-brain approach holds that thought requires a balanced integration of the logical, linear left brain with the intuitive, nonlinear right brain. How these are integrated remains the essential mystery. The Harvard approach holds that organizations are living systems (rather than technical artifacts), such that the core managerial thought processes require intuition, perception, interpretation, judgment, purpose, and commitment. Rational methods and logic techniques are secondary aids to the human thought processes of the practitioner—what Barnard termed the "non-logical mental processes" of the practicing manager (Barnard, 1938, p. 302).

The idea of the usefulness of knowledge raises questions of usefulness *to whom?* and *for what purpose?*, questions that, although not new, are inadmissible in the strict scientific ethos. Presumably, any given knowledge can serve multiple purposes, to different degrees. The knowledge that a manufacturing facility is about to be closed down would be differentially useful to, say, the production manager, union leader, investor, and local merchant. Also, knowledge can be differentially useful over time. It may be of no immediate use but vitally important subsequently, or vice versa. Some uses change over time or with new people. Must the requirement for knowledge change accordingly? Is it appropriate that we continuously respond to the sponsors' knowledge needs? Is knowledge to be generated only where the dollars are? And are the amount and kind of knowledge generated determined by the available funds? The answer is yes only if knowledge is conceived of as a commodity to be purchased. Is this the only way of judging the value of knowledge? How are we, in fact, to assess the *future* usefulness of the knowledge?

We need to be extremely careful about the language we are using when discussing the problem of the usefulness of knowledge. Language traps us into structuring the problem in a particular way, which not only predisposes us to particular kinds of thoughts and solutions but also precludes other, perhaps better ways of thought and solutions. We are, for example, so used to talking dualistically about knowledge producing (research) and knowledge using (application) that we may come unconsciously to see them as two separate activities requiring two separate institutions. We therefore preclude the possibility that knowledge can be generated at the workplace by the worker, at the managing place by the manager, at the office place by the "officer," at the "do place" by the doer.

The nature of our language leads us to see knowledge as a *thing* that we may *have* (acquire, possess). It is difficult to talk about knowledge as a verb, as a *doing*; and we flounder around with clumsy terms such as *knowledge-generating* to try to capture an activity of felt importance that we do not yet have language to articulate. As soon as we have made knowledge a thing, our language predisposes us to use it as the subject of a verb doing something to the object of the verb (knowledge is power, works wonders, conquers all, knows no bounds, and so on). There is, moreover, a notable language fit between the way we have to describe knowledge and its usefulness, on the one hand, and the nature of our sociopoliticoeconomic system, on the other. The concepts of property rights, division of labor, and economic exchange lead rationally to the notion that knowledge, like other things, can be made (in a knowledge factory), owned, used, purchased, delivered, even stolen. Some folk produce "it," while others use "it," with a seemingly natural economic exchange between them. Knowledge is spoken of as a commodity. In reality, however, knowledge may have an entirely different character. Knowledge may be like an interactive skill that inheres in a transaction, more like *knowing how* than *knowing what*. This is similar to the traditional distinction between *knowledge of* and *knowledge about.*

It is again worth noting that any empirical scientific study that yields findings demonstrating the "thing-ness" of knowledge is probably demonstrating the role of language in framing problems in familiar ways. It is evidence only of the prevailing social (that is, artificial) reality system and serves again to remind us of the essential emptiness of positivistic empiricism for understanding social reality. Even more noticeable is the isomorphism between the assumptions we make about *science* and the assumptions we make about *management.* Positivistic science, with its split between researcher and the object under study (often called the subject), is a remarkable fit with the world view of top-down rationalistic management, with its split between management and workers (managerial subjects). Like the positivist, the top-down rational manager seeks impersonal detachment while using the subjects for his or her own purposes. Both seek control over the situation, while maintaining their impersonal detachment from it. Positivistic science and the Weberian bureaucratic structure managed by a technocratic elite were made for each other. Conversely, to change one (either "science" or "management") is to require a change in the other. The ideas of Follett, Roethlisberger, Lewin, or Barnard about management and organization necessarily imply changes in the appropriate science to generate the required knowledge. Organizational change necessarily implies a change of science, with its accompanying epistemological shift; it also necessitates a change in the organization's language.

The inescapable conclusion from my own explorations is this: There are important ties among (1) the terms we use about "knowledge" (for example, reification), (2) the research epistemology we adopt (for example, positivism), (3) the organizational structure of management systems (for example, bureaucracy), and (4) the societal structure of the scientific enterprise itself (for example, factory model). The growth of such notions as participative management, management by objectives, T-groups, Theory-Z organizations, quality circles, computer conferencing, and process consulting generates new organizational structures that must inevitably lead us away from positivism as the core knowledge paradigm. In any society, its sociopolitico-economic organizational structure and its epistemology must fit together and change together. One of the grand ironies of this is that as long as organization scientists continue to hold fast to positivism as the knowledge-producing paradigm, they thereby *prevent* the development of new concepts for managing and organizing. To hold fast to the positivist paradigm in organizational science is to inhibit the development of new organizational forms and to preserve the existing sociopoliticoeconomic structure. Thus, in our field, positivism seems to be research in the service of the status quo.

Knowing. The whole notion of knowledge in the organization and management sciences has grown increasingly suspect. More and more of us are gaining these insights: that knowledge as a thing is a lie; that knowledge derives from action; that the meaning of knowledge comes from its context and situation, so that the idea of universal and timeless statements of truth seems absurd; that knowledge is more like evocative metaphors than it is like a description of the physical world; that knowledge detached from action has no relevance to practicing managers in living systems; and that our knowledge often gets in the way of our knowing or, rather, of our coming to know.

We need to transcend the way we have been framing our language about knowledge. We need to get beyond what we think we know, to gain awareness of that which is currently beyond organized awareness. We need to get beyond "knowledge" as a heap of things (facts) and move on to "knowing"—that is, the active *process* of knowing. My assertion is that research in the field of organization and management is not about knowledge per se but about the way we get our knowing. Learning is not about altering *what* we know but about the *way* we come to know. More precisely, research and learning are activities in the context of how we do our knowing.

Knowing and Action. The paradox is that the knowledge we have interferes with our doing know*ing.* We need to adopt a more agnostic position and act from a position of not knowing if we are to learn how to actively do knowing. Knowing is a deliberately chosen act that requires a commitment by the actor (learner) to find out, to notice, to be open to what is not yet known, acting out of a context of a clear purpose, goal, or vision. Knowing is reflective action in the service of a purpose.

So what is action? *Action taking,* along with *problem solving* and *decision making,* is a central notion in the field of management. But whereas problem solving and decision making have received extensive treatment in our literature, very little can be found on action taking. This may reflect the proclivity of the academic for thought and away from action, in sharp contrast to practicing managers, who seem to prefer action over thought. It is noteworthy that, whereas the managerial/organizational sciences are fairly neglectful of "action" (with some notable exceptions, such as organization-development practitioners and some case writers), some of the most famous names in the social sciences have given focal attention to it. Marx, Weber, Dilthey, and Lewin each made action the centerpiece of their theorizing.

Bernstein (1971) made a thorough critical study of the concepts of praxis and action in four action-based philosophical positions: Marxism, existentialism, pragmatism, and analytical philosophy. The works of Bernstein (1971) and Habermas (1971 and 1976) are the best fundamental analyses of praxis and action that I have found. A recent collection of papers edited by Reason and Rowan (1981) contains many insightful references and comments on the notion of action. Other writers who have interesting things to say about action include Parsons and Shils (1951), Hampshire (1959), Polanyi (1964), Jantsch (1975), Hall (1977), Feyerabend (1978), Argyris and Schön (1974), and Weick (1983, 1984). Most recently though, Habermas has developed his praxis notions into a systematic and powerful theory of communicative action, based on the paradigm of language-in-use (Habermas, 1984). Barnard (1938) appears to be one of the few who have explored the notion of managerial action. He distinguishes between efficient actions and effective actions; between physical actions and social actions; between process and effect; and among acts, actions, and systems of actions. Characteristically, he also relates action to purpose, to needs, and to communication.

At root, *managerial action is a communication, or sequence of communicative acts, in a particular organizational context.* It is intended to mobilize and utilize resources to produce a desirable effect. The individual who is taking action (communicating with intent to produce an effect) will usually be acting (communicating) on behalf of others (organizations, groups). The action research cycle, which is intended to simultaneously produce a desirable effect and promote learning from the process by collaboratively tailoring an action to the particular situation, consists of diagnosing, action planning, action taking, consequence evaluating, specifying learning, and then returning to the beginning of the cycle. The more knowledgeable the organizational actions *prior to* taking action (diagnosing and action-planning stages) are, the more effective is the action taken. Also, the more knowledgeable the organizational actors are *after* taking action (that is, the better learners they are), the more knowledgeable they will be for the next action occasion. For any particular action sequence, we can therefore distinguish among reflection prior to action, during action, and after action.

Types of Knowledge. Let us focus on an individual actor taking action in a particular organizational setting and confronted by some particular situation. For whatever reason or purpose, the individual must act, take action, do something. Useful knowledge is any information that enables one participant to act more effectively, appropriately, or meaningfully than he or she otherwise would. Our participant has potentially several different kinds of knowledge available, as indicated in Figure 18-1.

1. *Universal knowledge.* The participant has a body of generalized, context-free knowledge obtained by traditional science methods—facts, data, measurements, theories, meth-

Figure 18-1. The Varieties of Managerial Knowledge.

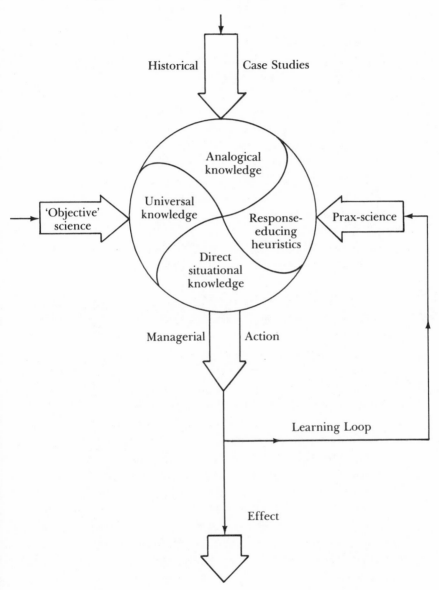

ods, models, techniques. This is knowledge obtained by others using standardized methods and generally accepted procedures. It is knowledge that is widely accepted as universally and timelessly true, although the particular situation may or may not be related to those truths.

2. *Direct situational knowledge.* The participant has some direct personal knowledge of particulars of the situation confronted, as well as skills for collecting data, interpreting, appreciating, judging, evaluating, and diagnosing. The participant knows something about the temporal-spatial embeddedness of the situation he or she confronts; that is, its relatedness to other events in time and space. Knowledge takes the form of direct personal situational knowing and contextual awareness (as opposed to universal or context-free facts).

3. *Analogical knowledge.* The participant has a body of knowledge concerning other, similar situations or cases. This may have been obtained from mentors, consultants, case studies, relevant historical events, or advice from peers. Judgment is required to assess the degree of similarity between the situation faced and those held to be similar. Essentially, this is knowledge derived from and imparted by the experience of others in interacting in similar situations or, more generally, from relevant history.

4. *Response-educing heuristics.* The participant also has a set of skills, rules, programs, routines, algorithms, and heuristics that can be called into play for guidance in testing or stimulating the situations so as to obtain further relevant information about the situation. The actor knows how to prod the situation in various ways so as to provoke a response from which one actor can learn. And the actor knows how to notice, see, and hear the response that the situation yields. He or she knows how to create quasi-situations in which surprises, anomalies, and interesting contrasts may show up. Our organizational actor has a repertoire of useful miniprograms for educing responses. He or she does not know what the response will be but does know how to generate a response. This response-

educing knowledge deals with how individuals learn to learn and how they become proficient at their focal practice. It implies learning how to interact with a complex situation, especially that complex web of social and political interactions that constitutes the art of management. Closely related to this kind of knowledge are the notions of praxis (Marx), learning by doing (Dewey), action research (Lewin), clinical research (Goldstein), personal learning (Polanyi), field stimulation (Salancik), clinical method (Piaget), reflective conversations with the situation (Schön), and what the earliest scientists used to call the "interrogation of nature in the experiment" (Habermas, 1971, p. 175). This kind of knowledge is characteristic of the practitioner and is just that kind of knowledge that technical rationality and instrumental logic are designed to disregard.

What is important here is that there are distinct kinds of knowledge that connect with managerial action in different ways. There are many important differences among these four kinds of knowledge; I would like to point out just one. In the first kind of knowledge, universal knowledge, the research that generates this knowledge is split from the doer. It is done elsewhere by others. In contrast, the fourth kind of knowledge, response-educing knowledge, provides the doer with an ability to do his or her own learning. Providing response-educing heuristics augments the manager's ability to generate knowledge; in contrast, providing science-based universal knowledge reduces the manager's ability to generate knowledge. Response-educing heuristics empower the manager; science-based universal truths disempower the manager. The argument leads us to the conclusion that the kind of knowledge that the practitioner needs, uses, and generates has the quality of a useful metaphor rather than a universal, timeless fact. It suggests that the business we are in, as organization and management researchers, is creating pragmatic metaphors, heuristics, and symbols, rather than trying to make truth statements about the world. In this sense, we are pragmatic artists rather than scientists.

Knowledge from Action. There is growing awareness that

something is incomplete or missing with the "spectator knowledge" that traditional positivism has developed to such a sophisticated level. What is missing is the component of *human action* that constitutes the core of a practitioner's world. The realization grows that an important kind of knowledge comes from actions by the practitioner. Researchers are rediscovering the works of Marx, Dilthey, Weber, Lewin, and Piaget, each of whom placed action at the center of their epistemologies. The field of organization development, now almost thirty years of age, is based on Lewin's action-research epistemology—"if you want to understand something, try to change it"—which he first articulated in 1943. Recent writings by Thorngate (1976), Torbert (1972, 1976), Argyris and Schön (1974), Schön (1983), Weick (1983, 1984), and Starbuck (1983, 1984) indicate a renewed interest in the notions that action produces knowledge and that a science based on this principle is likely to produce knowledge that has more impact than that produced by positivist science. What we need to develop is a theory *for* action, rather than a theory *of* action, and to evolve that theory from action itself.

The Argument for Creating a New Kind of Science

The argument thus far has been as follows: Objective, value-free science is neither objective nor value free. Positivism is an epistemological fraud. Nevertheless, it is capable of generating some knowledge, and especially techniques, that may be useful but that must always be peripheral to the practitioner's core activity. The practicing manager (or any other kind of practitioner) needs other kinds of knowledge than that which can be generated using the positivist paradigm. Technical rationality that derives from positivistic science will steadily drive out other forms of knowledge generating (Marcuse's argument). There are long-run societal liabilities for our overdependency on positivist science. An important class of knowledge for the practitioner is what I have called "response-educing heuristics," which enable the practitioner to create a reflective conversation with the relevant situation. Response-educing heuristics enable the practitioner to actively inquire, to learn, to increase personal skills at dealing with a variety of particular situations, and to move to increase situational proficiency.

At the heart of any practitioner's job is taking action. This is especially so for the practicing manager. We need to develop a new kind of science (prax-science) that is based on and directly contributes to managerial action, in situ. We must get beyond the traditional syndrome of "acquire knowledge—apply knowledge" that is embedded in our educational system. The new kind of science will be based on the realization that *action produces knowledge,* especially the kind of knowledge that practitioners value. The academic community has had it the wrong way around; we have been looking where the action isn't! As researchers, we are in the business of creating metaphors, heuristics, and symbols that produce fruitful human action. Making truth statements is a peripheral, sometimes related activity. In its essence, management research should be more like finding out how to coach the practitioner than descriptively mapping the cosmos. Coaching is performed as a communicative act in a language that is readily understood by the actor. What it will take to create a more workable science, prax-science, will be three things: people doing it, a professional network of people doing it, and a surrounding infrastructure of support.

Guidelines for Improving Research Relevance

As we get beyond the idea of a manager as a technique-pushing operative in an impersonal organizational machine and begin to acknowledge that what makes the crucial difference is the manager's skill, know-how, judgment, wisdom, and learningfulness (what we might generally term the manager's *art*), we begin to sense the limitations of our positivist research. When we align ourselves with the realities of the management practitioner's world and what it takes, in terms of knowledge, to enable him or her to act more effectively, constructively, and improvingly, we begin to glimpse a requirement for a different kind of research. The outline of a new research paradigm emerges that differs substantially from the traditional positivist research most of us were trained in.

From the viewpoint and arguments presented, it seems probable that the kind of new science we need to develop would support more research that would (1) be based on in situ *action* of the practitioner; (2) arise from the direct *collaboration,* dialogue, and relationship between the practitioner and researcher; (3) acknowledge the *uniqueness* and concreteness of the particular situation, including the particular actors and particular researcher (it follows directly from this that research cannot be replicated—replication is a nonsalient artifact); (4) *evolve method* during the course of the research process (a priori prescriptions of methods are inappropriate constraints on the actual phenomena); (5) *produce change* in the organization in the sense that a clear shift or transformation occurs; (6) yield useful *learnings for all parties* involved—improved action-taking heuristics for the practitioner and new ways of generating action heuristics for the researcher—the new knowledge residing in the revised activities, skills, and values of the parties involved; (7) cause all the parties to proceed with more *self-reflection* before, during, and after action taking; and (8) *empower the practitioner* to act more effectively, meaningfully, learningfully, improvingly, and humanly.

None of these points is new. However, taken collectively and taken seriously, they constitute the basis for a different kind of science. They challenge the way we have been going about our business of research in management and organization. (Almost everything in the *Academy of Management Journal* is inconsistent with these eight characteristics of "good research.")

Specifically, I suggest that what is required in the field of organization and management is to develop (1) a commitment by the community of professionals/scholars/practitioners in our field to overhaul and revise the epistemology of the social sciences; (2) new organizational/institutional vehicles for developing a new kind of prax-science; and (3) a way to do action-based research in our field that will lead to more functional, fruitful, workable, and human organizations. This implies a commitment to do whatever is necessary to find out how to do research in our field that actually makes a difference to management practitioners in real-world organizations.

The issue is this: *Are we actually going to do anything about improving the relevancy of the collective research in our field? And, if so, what might we do to move in that direction?* What heuristics do *we* have that could improve our job as research practitioners? It is, after all, our collective responsibility to organize and manage the "scientific" enterprise in such a way that our research studies really do make a difference to the way in which society itself is organized and managed.

And if not now, when?

References

Argyris, C., and Schön, D. A. *Theory in Practice: Increasing Professional Effectiveness.* San Francisco: Jossey-Bass, 1974.

Barnard, C. J. *The Functions of the Executive.* Cambridge: Harvard University Press, 1938.

Bernstein, R. J. *Praxis and Action.* Philadelphia: University of Pennsylvania Press, 1971.

Churchman, C. W. *Challenge to Reason.* New York: McGraw-Hill, 1968.

Douglas, J. D. "Future Perils." *Society,* 1979, *16* (5), 57-63.

Ellul, J. *The Technological Society.* New York: Vintage, 1964.

Evered, R. "A Typology of Explicative Models." *Technological Forecasting and Social Change,* 1976, *9* (3), 259-277.

Evered, R. "Some Human Consequences of Technology." *Humanitas,* 1978, *14* (1), 97-123.

Evered, R., and Louis, M. R. "Alternative Perspectives in the Organizational Sciences: 'Inquiry from the Inside' and 'Inquiry from the Outside.' " *Academy of Management Review,* 1981, *6* (3), 385-395.

Feyerabend, P. *Against Method.* London: Verso, 1978.

Gödel, K. *On Formally Undecidable Propositions.* New York: Basic, 1962.

Habermas, J. *Knowledge and Human Interest.* Boston: Beacon Press, 1971.

Habermas, J. *Theory and Practice.* Boston: Beacon Press, 1973.

Habermas, J. *Communication and the Evolution of Society.* Boston: Beacon Press, 1976.

Habermas, J. *The Theory of Communicative Action.* Vol. 1. Boston: Beacon Press, 1984.

Hall, E. T. *Beyond Culture.* New York: Anchor, 1977.

Hampshire, S. *Thought and Action.* Notre Dame, Ind.: University of Notre Dame Press, 1959.

Heisenberg, W. *The Physicist's Conception of Nature.* London: Hutchinson, 1958a.

Heisenberg, W. *Physics and Philosophy.* New York: Harper & Row, 1958b.

Jantsch, E. *Design for Evolution.* New York: George Braziller, 1975.

Kaplan, A. *The Conduct of Inquiry.* San Francisco: Chandler, 1964.

Marcuse, H. *One Dimensional Man.* Boston: Beacon Press, 1964.

Maslow, A. H. *The Psychology of Science.* New York: Harper & Row, 1966.

Matson, F. *The Broken Image.* New York: Anchor/Doubleday, 1966.

Morgan, G. *Beyond Method.* Beverly Hills, Calif.: Sage, 1983.

Parsons, T., and Shils, E. *Toward a General Theory of Action.* Cambridge: Harvard University Press, 1951.

Piaget, J. *The Place of the Sciences of Man in the System of Sciences.* New York: Harper & Row, 1974.

Polanyi, M. *Personal Knowledge.* New York: Harper & Row, 1964.

Reason, P., and Rowan, J. (Eds.). *Human Inquiry: A Source Book of New Paradigm Research.* New York: Wiley, 1981.

Schön, D. A. *The Reflective Practitioner.* New York: Basic Books, 1983.

Starbuck, W. H. "Organizations and Action Generators." *American Sociological Review,* 1983, *4,* 91–102.

Starbuck, W. H. "Acting First and Thinking Later." Paper presented at the fifth workshop on radical design of organizations, Naval Postgraduate School, Monterey, Calif., May 1984.

Susman, G. I., and Evered, R. "An Assessment of the Scientific Merits of Action Research." *Administrative Science Quarterly*, 1978, *23*, 582-603.

Thorngate, W. "Must We Always Think Before We Act?" *Personality and Social Psychology Bulletin*, 1976, *2*, 31-35.

Torbert, W. *Learning from Experience: Toward Consciousness.* New York: Columbia University Press, 1972.

Torbert, W. *Creating a Community of Inquiry: Conflict, Collaboration, Transformation.* New York: Wiley, 1976.

Von Mises, L. *Human Action: A Treatise on Economics.* Chicago: Regnery, 1949.

Wartofsky, M. W. *Conceptual Foundations of Scientific Thought.* London: Macmillan, 1968.

Weick, K. "Managerial Thought in the Context of Action." In S. Srivastva and Associates, *The Executive Mind: New Insights on Managerial Thought and Action.* San Francisco: Jossey-Bass, 1983.

Weick, K. "Perspectives on Action in Organizations." In J. W. Lorsch (Ed.), *Handbook of Organizational Behavior.* Englewood Cliffs, N.J.: Prentice-Hall, 1984.

19

Understanding Method
in the Study of People

Abraham Kaplan

In the quarter-century since I ventured opinions on the conduct of inquiry, I have been increasingly occupied with inquiries into conduct. Abstract speculation is one thing; concrete practice is another. "Gray, dear friend, is all theory, and green the golden tree of life." Theory about theory is doubly colorless, and the tree of knowledge is as gold and green as any other living growth. The distinction between the reconstructed logic of the philosopher of science and the logic in use of the working scientist is more significant for me now than it was when I first became aware of the difference.

The conduct I have been observing with somewhat more care than is usual in everyday encounters is that of people in small groups. The contexts of my observations were designed primarily not for the sake of inquiry but for executive training and personal growth. Insofar as this is science, it is of the sort usually called "applied science." The label is a misnomer, since it implies the antecedent existence of an explicit theory whose generalizations are being applied. It is hard enough to understand concrete particulars without presuming to have at hand abstract and general explanations. People knew how to start fires and how to put them out long before anyone had a theory of combustion; their knowledge could scarcely have been called "applied chemistry." In matters such as leadership, organization, communication, and decision making, even practical knowledge still leaves much to be desired. Pursuit of such knowledge is not to be invidiously contrasted with scientific inquiry. Practical interests have played an important part in the scientific enterprise throughout its history. Modern science arose when practitioners and philosophers ceased to distinguish themselves from one another, as they had been distinguished in the ancient cultures of Greece, India, and China. Archimedes and Galileo owed important discoveries to the thought they gave to engines of war, while Newton owed much to his interest in navigation when Britannia ruled the waves.

Pure science has often preceded its applications, as non-Euclidean geometry preceded relativity and the mathematical theory of groups (which has only the name in common with the study of human groups) preceded quantum mechanics. But so-called "applications" have also preceded theory. The theory of probability arose from the treatment of problems of gambling, and the statistical theory of the design of experiments stemmed from a concern with the relative merits of fertilizers. An appropriate image for "pure" science might be that of the Buddha seated on a water lily floating in serene whiteness on the surface of the pond while its roots reach into the mud below.

A more significant distinction than that between "pure" and "applied" science is one between basic research and research relevant only to a limited set of contexts. Even for the latter, the limits cannot be fixed a priori. To be intellectually respectable, science need not represent a useless expenditure of time and energy by members of the leisure class. That a preoccupation is also an occupation, by which someone earns a living, and that it has social utility as well does not deprive it of scientific worth.

In the decades that have elapsed since my observations became more than casual, differences in patterns of inquiry into conduct have become more marked. On the whole, the "hard" sciences have become harder and the "soft" softer. I wish it had been the reverse, in both directions. In the same period, I have also wished, with as much futility, I'm afraid, that the world had grown more unified politically and more diversified culturally, instead of the other way around. Managerial decisions have come to rely more and more on such hard disciplines as operations research, linear programming, game theory, utility theory, and a whole array of computerized mathematical models. The study of small groups relies on scales, "instruments," and other modes of collecting data that lend themselves to statistical treatment. Most such reliance is laudable, but the drunkard's search is all around us—there are hunters under every streetlight, because it is lighter there. The need is not for more lampposts but for more searchlights that can be directed where our problems demand—even the practical problems.

Scientism is rampant in our time: science has been turned against itself. The outer marks of successful inquiry have been borrowed as plumage for unscientific and even antiscientific enterprises. Scientific theories have been extended far beyond what the theories have established or even concerned themselves with. There is much talk in psychology today of "energy fields," for example, in a sense that has nothing to do with either Maxwell's fields of force or Einstein's mc^2 as in an earlier day there was talk of "animal magnetism" in a sense that had nothing to do with Gilbert and Faraday's discoveries about magnetism, or with animals, either, for that matter. To take another example, the ancient dualism of reason and emotion has been given renewed popularity today by being equated with the difference between logic and intuition and couched in terms of neuroanatomy (the right and left hemispheres of the brain), as though the vocabulary itself provides both meaning and truth.

The soft approaches have increasingly sought to conquer under the sign of "humanism," with little more than faith to sustain them. Occult doctrines have been refurbished. There are quasi-sciences that acknowledge the requirements of scientific method but whose results are either wholly negative, such as those of psychic research, or highly questionable, such as those of parapsychology. Pseudosciences disdain established criteria of evidence and inference, relying instead on the jargon of one or another esoteric tradition, as is done by astrology, palmistry, and the metaphysics of meditation and metempsychosis. Both quasi-sciences and pseudosciences, as well as disciplines, such as alchemy, combining features of both, have played a part in the history of science, not always in the role of villain. In the human sciences, no sharp line divides the ancient theory of humors and the theories of nineteenth-century phrenologists and physiognomists from the modern characterologies of Adler, Jung, and Freud. It is not easy to maintain scientific integrity and yet take care not to block scientific progress by an excess of conservatism. Especially noteworthy in the human sciences are the tactics of defensive exclusion and defensive incorporation: "Everyone ought to work on what *I* do, and in *my* way" and "No one should work on what *you* do, and certainly not in *your* way." Standards of selection of problems and methods follow choices already made rather than guiding choices to start with. Approaches are seen as rational only because they serve as rationalizations.

There are fashions in science as there are in dress and manners. Scarcely anything done by the researcher is wholly determined by objective needs and constraints. Art is not alone in expressing its culture; science, too, reflects the style of the times. This is more than a matter of passing fads, though these are common enough in studies of human behavior. At work are more subtle, pervasive, and enduring features of cultural style. The antithesis of hard and soft approaches in behavioral science is a facet of the polarities our culture perceives between technology and the human being, between means and ends, between facts and values. These polarities are not grounded in an objective duality. They reflect, rather, the dualistic metaphysics of the culture, its world view. Psychologists have seen in them expressions of contrasting temperaments, like those William James characterized as "tough-minded" and "tender-hearted." Whatever the roots of these polarities, they flower in scientific inquiry.

A common focus of the current antithesis between hard and soft approaches is the attitude toward mathematics and computer technology. On both sides, preferences and preconceptions, not to say prejudices, are expressed as a noble adherence to methodological principles, an adherence demanded by intellectual integrity. A mystique of quantity endows numbers with nearly magical powers, though the specific quantities measured may be irrelevant to the problems at hand or, at best, of secondary importance. Doctoral candidates in clinical psychology are almost everywhere required to write a dissertation around statistical findings. Yet, for example, the statistical distribution of incest, homosexuality, and rape is not necessarily the most significant information concerning pathologies in sexual relations. Students of organizational behavior may be required to focus on productivity, absenteeism, and turnover, because these are measurable magnitudes, rather than on qualitative differences in managerial style or cultural norms, even though these may be more directly relevant to the problems, say, of effecting organizational change. How easily something can be measured does not necessarily correspond to how significant it is in specific inquiries.

Equally groundless is the countervailing mystique of quality, which repudiates quantitative data just because they are quantitative. In this mystique, everything most distinctively human will forever elude weights and measures. Since Kant, at the end of the eighteenth century, it has been generally recognized in methodology that being measurable is not an intrinsic attribute but depends, rather, on our mathematical insight, technical ingenuity, and, above all, understanding of what we propose to measure and why. Every quantification undeniably leaves something out—measurement presupposes selection; but what quantification does include it characterizes more fully than any purely qualitative description could. Quantifying something does not reduce it to a number but sharpens our awareness of what it really is. Utility theory illuminates what it means to value something, and game theory illuminates what constitutes a rational decision; neither theory pretends to say all there is to be said about its subject.

Early in the century, the French mathematician Henri Poincaré characterized sociology as a science that possesses the most in the way of methods and the least in the way of results. A distinguished present-day sociologist, quoting the remark, adds that Poincaré could not fairly say so now. It would be fair, however, to note the preoccupation even today with methods of studying human behavior. We have not yet altogether freed ourselves from the myth of methodology, that only "the right method" is lacking to elevate our study to full scientific status; that "the right method" will do so is, of course, a tautology, if results are what make it "right."

The myth of methodology is a particular instance of a more general outlook widespread in our culture—the belief in technique. What was once Yankee ingenuity in the invention of mechanical contrivances has been broadened, in popular perspective, to generate the conviction that nothing is unattainable if we take thought how to get it. "How-to" books are perennial best sellers—how to lose weight or quit smoking; how to make love, raise children, or save a marriage; how to make money or be a successful manager. No doubt a book will soon appear called *Three Steps to Spontaneity,* and another will be advertised, "Be a leader—follow these rules!" Legitimate concern with small-group behavior is not immune to corruption by the prevailing fashion of trusting in technique. Especially seductive are techniques in which the researcher happens to be skilled already. The effect constitutes the "law of the instrument": give a small boy a hammer, and it turns out that everything he sees needs pounding. That each scientist has distinctive skills that he or she is eager to use is unexceptionable; difficulties arise when problems are formulated to suit the scientist's skills rather than fitting the skills to the needs of the problem. Research on organization development, for instance, calls for different emphasis in the small-group process than does a focus on personal growth. Researchers at the Tavistock Institute study people in *groups,* while those at Bethel, the classic center of T-group learning, study *people* in groups.

Individual differences in cognitive style are more significant in shaping the conduct of inquiry than reconstructed logic takes into account. Each style has its potentialities and its limitations. The question for methodology is not which style is best but whether a particular inquiry meets the demands for its own style. Important contributions to science have been made by specialists and by generalists, by experts in quantification and by those skilled in qualitative description. Work in small groups reveals marked differences in the styles of group leaders, trainers, or facilitators (the labels themselves point to characteristic styles). There are differences in the extent to which the observer is also a participant; in the frequency and directiveness of interventions; in the degree of structuring of the group process; and in reliance on nonverbal activities, on games and exercises, and on other special techniques. The early doctrinaire positions on how groups should be conducted has given way to the increasingly widespread recognition that (almost) "everything works."

A feature of cognitive style that has claimed my attention is the researcher's "canonical number," the number with which he or she feels intellectually comfortable, so that when confronted with any dissonant multiplicity, old distinctions are collapsed, and new distinctions are introduced until what is given has the chosen canonical number of components. Numerosity is sometimes objectively determinate (setting aside inevitable vagueness in our categories), such as the number of planets, of chemical elements, or of candidates on a ballot. Typically, however, the researcher's canonical number is projected onto her or his subject matter. How many ways there are to skin a cat depends more on the skinner than on the cat. The history of ideas readily provides examples. Those whose canonical number is zero, the nihilists, repudiate categorization altogether, usually on behalf of some nonconceptual mode of cognition contrasted with analysis, such as Bergson's "intuition" or Zen's "seizing reality with bare hands." Monists, such as the idealist Parmenides and the nineteenth-century materialists, reduce everything to one underlying reality, a reduction said to be the aim of all scientific explanations. Dualists demand two categories, such as Descartes's mind and body or Plato's world of ideas and world of the senses. Trinitarians include Aristotle, with his golden mean between two extremes, and Hegel, with his dialectic of thesis, antithesis, and synthesis. Pluralists favor some larger number of categories, as do the Greek atomists and the modern empiricists. Thinkers such as William James and Bertrand Russell are radical pluralists, recognizing even infinities.

People usually have more than one canonical number. Often their second choice is as revealing as the first. In Kant's thought, triads are very common, but each has four components. Movement from a particular canonical number to some specific other number may be characteristic. John Dewey, for instance, repeatedly takes polarities such as thought and feeling, theory and practice, and the school and society and endeavors to show that the two are or ought to be, at bottom, one. The relevance of canonical numbers to the understanding of human behavior can be illustrated by the cognitive styles of personnel directors. A director who is a radical pluralist insists that every human being is different from every other; one must consider each individual as an individual. A pluralist, while acknowledging significant differences, adopts a limited set of categories into which individuals can be classified, usually on the basis of personality tests and their associated typologies. A trinitarian might divide applicants into those who cannot follow orders, those who can, and those who are able to provide their own direction. Dualists are common in our society, arguing, for instance, that there are workers and freeloaders, the task of the personnel director being to separate the sheep from the goats. Often dualists rely on a pair of pairs. Needed are, say, skill and motivation; those who have neither are to be rejected; those who have only skill must be motivated, while those with motivation only must be trained; applicants with both skill and motivation are eligible for managerial positions. Monists invoke an underlying human nature common to all; only when this is rightly understood can we make optimal use of our human resources. Nihilists are likely to feel that the whole personnel division is a total waste; just put people to work and announce a simple incentive plan: "One mistake and you're through!"

The prevailing fashions in science, together with the individual scientist's cognitive style, reinforce the tacit assumption that some one method is "the" scientific method. Writing on the rules of sociological method, Emile Durkheim warned that at best one can establish only provisional rules, since methods, too, will change as science advances. Even in the most rigorous of sciences, mathematics, the concept of "proof" has undergone significant changes. In small-group practice, there has been a marked movement during the last several decades away from "touchy-feely" techniques and deliberate feeding of hostility. The participant-observer has come to participate in correspondingly different ways.

The autonomy of the scientific enterprise is continually threatened. In the Eastern bloc, political science and economics are explicitly subservient to the state. In Islamic countries, as well as in the United States, religious ideologies impose themselves, even in the natural sciences—for instance, in the recurrent efforts to require the teaching of creationist biology. Autonomy from other disciplines *within* science also continually needs to be reaffirmed. Many students of human behavior—though not as many as several decades ago—still injudiciously imitate the externals of the hard sciences. They are as anachronistic as blacks who try to "pass" or Jews who live the lives of amateur gentiles.

No phase of inquiry can be singled out as the starting point of scientific investigation—we can begin only where we are, Charles Peirce emphasized. In studies of human behavior, we are still caught up in the tasks of conceptualization: we do not yet know what we are talking about, let alone what to say about it. Artificial taxonomies abound; few of them, if any, are generally recognized as providing typologies, systems of natural classes embedded in the subject matter, such as the typologies conceived by Darwin and Mendeleyev.

The paradox of conceptualization is that concepts are validated only by how well they lend themselves to successful theory, but it takes a good theory to provide the concepts in the first place. The viciousness of this circle, as of others in methodology, is broken by successive approximations. We theorize as best we can within a given conceptual structure, which in turn is improved, or replaced altogether, as a result of our theorizing. Concepts cannot be refined and polished while knowledge stands still; zero growth in either meaning or truth entails zero growth in the other as well. The search for "correct" definitions is as ill conceived as the search for absolute truth. All concepts have a dynamic openness of meaning; they become closed in one direction or another as inquiry continues, while new uncertainties open up. It is not only the definitions of *humanity, mind,* or *self* that have changed with time; we think differently about these things from the way that we once did because we know more about them.

The interdependence of concepts and theories implies that concepts also have a systemic openness of meaning. We cannot claim to understand exactly any part of a science unless we understand all of it. This is not to say that no psychoanalytical idea, for example, can be adopted without subscribing to the whole of psychoanalytical theory. It is impossible, however, to explicate an idea without subscribing to something or other. An orthodox psychoanalyst and a behavioral psychologist not only assert different things about, say, anxiety; *anxiety* means something different to the one than to the other. Meanings are seldom explicitly defined, except in very restricted domains of the mathematical disciplines. By far the simplest way to convey the difference in the shades of red designated by *carmine, cerise, crimson, magenta, puce,* and *scarlet* is to exhibit samples of each. Meanings are also conveyed by descriptions of what is being designated. To explain what is meant by *aardvark, agouti, anteater,* and *armadillo,* it may be more appropriate simply to describe the beasts than to give the Latin taxonomical designations. Everywhere, even in the most exact sciences, we must ultimately rely on direct presentation of something meant. "Anxiety," a psychology student explained during his oral examination for the doctorate, "is what I am feeling now."

Meanings are often most usefully explicated by specification of the features of the denotation that are meant to be taken into account, probable indicators of the term's applicability. For most of the concepts of the behavioral sciences, there is virtually no alternative to this process of specification of meaning. Terms are not formally defined but become sufficiently well understood to serve their purpose when characteristic profiles of the things to which the terms apply are specified. The specifications selected by the researcher and the probabilities assigned to each reflect a provisional judgment of what is likely to be relevant and how significant it will be in anticipated contexts of inquiry. *Hostility,* to take an example important in small-group behavior, is sometimes contrasted with *aggressiveness* and is sometimes replaced by *aggressiveness,* when the contrast is with *assertiveness.* What is meant by *hostility* need not be captured in an exactly equivalent defining phrase; specifications of meaning can be more useful. For instance, hostility is likely to be displaced—directed not against those who stand in the way but against those who are conveniently placed to serve as targets. Hostility is likely to be disproportionate, markedly exceeding what is needed to remove opposition. It tends to become an end in itself, so that possibilities of preventing conflict, or of nonviolent resolution of conflict when it occurs, are rejected out of hand. A person being hostile is often unaware of the hostility or perceives it only as a perfectly reasonable insistence on his or her rights. Acts of hostility are likely to be uncontrolled, not flowing from deliberate and rational choice but breaking out involuntarily.

Concepts of managerial styles provide another example of the usefulness of specifications of meaning rather than verbal definitions. I have found it helpful to distinguish three managerial styles (when I am not a radical pluralist, I am a trinitarian). A "leader" takes a stand, makes his or her own decisions; the leader's choices are expressions of his or her values. In relating to others, the leader tends to rely on personal communication. The organization is an extension of his the leader's personality ("Welcome to my team!", "Just call me Jane," "My door is always open"). New members of the organization are given an orientation, a picture of what the leader has in mind for the organization and for them—the leader's vision of their common destiny, the utopia toward which they will strive. What the leader expects from them, above all, is loyalty, unquestioning implementation of his or her will. The "leader" is seen by people with other styles as a ruthless, narrow-minded, self-centered fanatic.

A very different managerial style is that of the "administrator." The administrator's decisions are determined by what he or she interprets to be company policy. The interpretation is the administrator's, but the policy has an external source ("I don't like it any more than you do, but that's what we gotta do"). He or she acts on the basis of directives and expects others to do the same, forever issuing memorandums to staff and subordinates. In this organization, new members are given an indoctrination—instruction in the established principles and procedures ("Take this book home and sleep on it; let it be your bible; it will answer all your questions—and be sure you study the supplement that will be issued next week!"). Goals are specified in an unending sequence of quotas, objectives, and schedules. The quality most valued in subordinates is reliability. The "administrator" is often seen as rigid, hidebound, and bureaucratic.

A third managerial style is exhibited by the "executive." The executive's response is to the specific circumstances of the continually changing situation. He or she is interested only in "the facts of the case," putting emphasis on prompt, periodic, and detailed reports. Newcomers are given neither orientation nor indoctrination but are gradually absorbed ("Look around a while; see where you'll fit in best, and tell us what you think you would like to do"). Goals are set only in general terms, by long-range programs and guiding ideals. What is called for are the qualities of flexibility, self-reliance, and good judgment. The "executive" is likely to be seen as pragmatic, opportunistic, and unprincipled.

A central concept in the study of human behavior is that of the "self," on which, paradoxically, the small-group process throws light. In the early decades of this century, theorists such as Gordon Allport, Harry Stack Sullivan, and Franz Alexander drew attention to the fluidity and internal multiplicity of the self. The assumption of an antecedently given unitary and unchanging personal identity is highly dubious. Belief in its existence is an instance of what philosophers have called the fallacy of misplaced concreteness. The search for one's identity may continually fail, not because the identity is so elusive, but because an identity has not yet been achieved. The search itself may impede the attainment, as do self-conscious quests for pleasure, happiness, or wisdom.

Components or aspects of the self, subpersonalities, might be called "personae" (in a sense not pre-empted by Jung). Relations among the personae are writ large, as Plato recognized, in the relations among the members of a group. Personal identity, like group identity, emerges from the understanding and acceptance by one another of the members of the group, the personae. Pathologies develop when self-contained cliques form; morbidity is extreme when each persona goes its own way, and the group is effectively dissolved.

Communication in small groups, as well as in larger organizations, points to the inadequacy of the simplistic distinction between the "conscious" and the "unconscious" mind, even when a third category, the "preconscious" or "subconscious," is added. The flow of information in the self, as seen in the large, is far more complex. Every message circulating in the system is read by someone, at least the original writer or the initial receiver. But no message is read by everyone—there is always someone who does not get the word. No member of the organization, least of all in its administration, knows everything that is going on, and no one is totally uninformed. Every communication, moreover, has its own circulation list. In the self each persona, and in an organization each working unit, processes only the information of particular relevance to its own operations. Furthermore, what the processing consists of varies. Information received may be barely noted and then discarded; it may be stored for later retrieval; it may be put on the agenda for immediate consideration; it may be acted on, set aside, or countered. Within the self as within the group, the question is always who says what to whom, when, and with what effect.

Self-deception is an ineluctable datum of group life; what is learned in groups above all is that we do not always see ourselves as we really are. On the assumption of a unitary self, self-deception is a contradiction in terms, as Sartre has argued. How can I believe what at the same time I know to be false? The contradiction is resolved if the believer and the knower are different personae. The surprising thing is not that we perpetuate illusions about ourselves but that we know ourselves as well as we do. The concept of "sincerity" needs corresponding modification. No member of the group can speak for the whole group, not even the group leader, whether self-appointed or otherwise designated. A particular persona may be quite sincere yet cannot be taken as spokesperson for the entire assemblage of personae. Ambivalent feelings are as common in individuals as differences of opinion are in groups. What passes for honesty in interpersonal relations may be truly honest in itself yet simultaneously serve as camouflage for hostility. Frankness may conceal all the more effectively just because it is genuine. The nude encounter groups that were once fashionable in certain quarters demonstrated that nakedness is only another cover-up.

The resistance of the group to intruders and to what is perceived as censure by the staff member is in the structure of the self paralleled by the mechanisms of defense. To say that someone is being "defensive" is not properly a criticism; it specifies a function. A significant tautology about human behavior affirms that without defenses we are defenseless. If the statement that one is being defensive is made as an accusation, the reply could be, "Of course I'm defensive—I'm being attacked!" The question is whether the attack is real and, if so, whether the defense against it is effective. Shortcomings in personal defense systems resemble those of national defense establishments. They may be geared to fight over again the last war, or even the one before that, rather than to face impending dangers; in individual psychology, these are the pathologies of fixation and regression. The defenses may take too large a share of the gross national product; in the psychic economy, so much effort may be expended on defenses that little remains for the satisfaction of other needs and wants. The defenses may elude civilian control; the person may be in the service of his or her defenses rather than the other way around, an inversion that can be carried even to the point of self-destructiveness.

The group comes to have a character not simply because of its composition, but only as its various members influence the direction that the group takes. Every leader is alone until followed. Even God did not create his people; they became his when he redeemed them from bondage. The model of the self as a group accommodates nicely what existentialism has emphasized as essential to being human. The human being is an existent with "transcendence" as well as "facticity": with an undecided future as well as a determined past. A person is what he or she is becoming; integrity is being true to the self in the making. The punishment for pretending to be a saint, said the Hassidic master Simchah Bunam, is that eventually one really gets to be one. This is the plot of Max Beerbohm's tale *The Happy Hypocrite* and R. K. Narayan's novel *The Guide*. Many might add, "It is the story of my life."

Empirical science is by definition experiential. It might be better to speak of "observational" science. In the study of human behavior, the difference between experience and observation has become blurred in recent times. There is an emphasis on the importance of direct experience in respects that can be justified, if at all, only on political grounds, not on methodological ones. There is widespread acceptance of an "axiom of direct experience," which states that direct experience is both a necessary and a sufficient condition of knowledge. The assumption that direct experience is necessary for knowledge underlies the insistence that only blacks, women, youth, and other victims of discrimination can understand the problems faced by the corresponding groups. The proposition is tautologously beyond dispute if to "understand" means to share an experience. It is plainly false if to "understand" means to know the conditions of an occurrence and to be able to predict its consequences. Culture consists, at bottom, in the capacity to learn from the experience of other members of the society. Judges need not have been criminals nor psychiatrists insane. But it might help—direct experience is the ultimate reservoir from which all knowledge draws.

Direct experience is not sufficient for knowledge. We have all spent lifetimes in a gravitational field, but this is not enough to make us Newtons. Natives might know less about the language they speak fluently than does an inarticulate foreign linguist. Direct experience is an opportunity for knowledge, not the knowledge itself. We take advantage of the opportunity when the experience is made an occasion for reflective observation. That is the scientific significance of small-group processes.

In the study of human behavior, many of the data come from listening—speech is the most revelatory behavior of all. What passes for listening in everyday life is not observing in the scientific sense, any more than is the seeing of everyday life. The amount that goes unheard, that is misheard, and that is misinterpreted is one of the most striking of the data that emerge from small groups. Moreover, just as the visible spectrum is only a fraction of the range of radiation, what we usually hear is, at best, a part of what is being said. We listen to the words but not to the music—the intonation, stress, rhythm, gesture, posture, and much else. These have their effect on the listener, but only the trained observer can reliably distinguish signal from noise and correctly interpret the signal.

The observer needs more than training; knowledge also is needed. Data are not observed if they are not meaningful; only theory gives data meaning. *Data* designates not a class but a relation; we can identify only data relevant to some hypothesis or other. Useful hypotheses, on the other hand, can be formulated only on the basis of the data. The circle, the paradox of data, parallels the paradox of conceptualization. Like the latter, it escapes being vicious by the application of successive approximations. Without hypotheses to make them meaningful, data are invisible. In small groups, the common misuse of pronouns, for example, usually goes unnoticed. The speaker means "I" far more often than the word is used; "we" is often a wholly unwarranted generalization; "you" is often a projection and "they" an evasion. Such ventriloquism may serve various purposes, such as denying responsibility, softening conflict, or engineering consent. It is because of invisible data that hidden agendas remain hidden. The most successful cipher is one that conceals not only the message but even the fact that a cipher is being used. There are also cryptic data: data observed but dismissed as having no significance. In the human sciences, the best example is data of the psychoanalytical theory of dreams and of slips of the tongue, both long dismissed as random or "accidental." Small-group processes provide other examples. "It was only a joke" and "I was just curious" are invoked over and over to camouflage significant motives. It is extraordinary how often such an explanation is accepted—but the acceptance itself may also be a camouflage.

Observations are made with the mind, not by the senses alone. In an insightful dictum, there is more to seeing than meets the eye. This "more" has sometimes been condemned by reconstructed logic as a contamination of the data, a condemnation flowing from what Nietzsche called "the dogma of immaculate perception." The purity of the data can be preserved only at the price of sterility. Just as we see not colors and shapes but objects—trees, stones, and stars, all the choir of heaven and furniture of earth—so also do we observe human behavior as meaningful conduct, not as sequences of muscular contractions and skeletal movements. These *are* observable, as are colors and shapes, but these observations, too, presuppose meanings. The physical events constitute acts; the data for the sociologist and psychologist are actions, acts that have meaning for the actor as well as for the observer. A wink may be a reaction to something in the eye or an invitation; the student of human relations had better know which.

For the observer to deny himself or herself the resources of meaning is both futile and pointless. Science is not impersonal, if this means the exclusion of any distinctively human capacities. What is personal is excluded only insofar as it is idiosyncratic, not insofar as it implicates the observer's mind—or heart, either. So-called impersonal observation dehumanizes both the observer and the observed. The impersonality of the Nazi experimenters on human beings did not make them better scientists, only worse human beings. The subservience of science to church and state, as well as the ethnocentricity of observers of human behavior, gives substance to the ideal of scientific detachment. The ideal has been misconceived. It is one thing for the scientist to be detached from his or her conclusions—that is, to welcome the truth, however unpleasant it might be. It is quite another thing for the scientist to be detached from the subject matter and methods. Just as an open mind is not an empty one, objectivity is not indifference. Detachment in a sense that contrasts with participant observation is something else again. This may well serve useful purposes in inquiry—for instance, to facilitate transference in the psychoanalytical situation. It can be justified, however, only by the specifics of the context of inquiry, not by any general methodological principles. That the observer of a group is a participant in the group process does not invalidate her or his observations. On the contrary, it may make the observations more sound and meaningful, contributing to both the reliability and the validity of the data.

Errors of observation are as certain as death and taxes, but life goes on. Especially frustrating are the iatrogenic errors —the illnesses produced by the medical treatment. Thorstein Veblen identified the "trained incapacity" of the observer, the inability to see something because the observer is schooled to see something else. The law of the instrument applies to instruments of observation as much as to any other. Psychoanalysts easily forget, Freud warned, that sometimes a cigar is just a cigar. Observers of small-group behavior who are trained in organization development or in any other specialty have comparable lapses of memory. Recognizing error enables one to take it into account in processing the data—if, for instance, the values of the observer are introducing a systematic and subtle bias. It is better, if possible, to cancel out the error—the theory of adversary proceedings, which might be applicable to the study of conflict situations. Best of all is to insulate observation from identifiable sources of error. It was long ago established, for example, that Caucasian interviewers in the inner city obtain less reliable data than do black interviewers; the same might be true of data on sexual discrimination gathered by men rather than by women.

Errors of observation are likely to be outnumbered and outweighed by errors of interpretation, but uninterpreted observations, if they could exist, would be worthless. For inquiry into conduct, interpretation is all in all. The dimension of meaning is what makes human conduct out of what would otherwise be animal behavior, significant only for the physical and biological sciences. Acts have their meaning, just as do actions, or they would not be scientific data, but actions have meaning for the actor as well as for the observer. To understand what people do, we must grasp what they mean to be doing. This is not always apparent in what they say. The difference between manifest and latent content applies to all communication, not only to psychoanalytical symbolism. It is the difference between the meaning of what is said and the point in saying it. The meaning belongs to the words and can be retrieved from dictionaries. The point belongs to the speaker and his or her hearers in just that context and can be grasped only by knowing the people and their situation, not merely the language. As a small group carries on, its members achieve more than understanding of what is being said; they also begin to understand one another.

Getting the point is not the same as figuring out what it is, even when we figure correctly. If we did not find a joke funny to start with, we are not likely to laugh after it is explained. Understanding is a matter of direct experience; what is being understood presents itself as an observable, not as a hypothetical construct. This is what underlies the emphasis on intuition in understanding people. Getting the point is not making an inference, but it *is* inferential. It is the uncertain residue of habitual inference. The previous inferences may have been mistaken, or they may be misapplied in the particular case. Intuition is of great heuristic value but of little probative force. Like all modes of knowing, intuition, too, rests on experience, and no amount of experience can provide an absolute guarantee against error.

Characteristic of intuition is the circumstance that the process of inference takes place outside the focus of attention, perhaps outside of awareness altogether. We can know without knowing how we know. But, for the purposes of science, we must know *that* we know, and *this* knowledge can be validated only by nonintuitive processing of the observational data. Otherwise, intuition is indistinguishable from confident but uncritical self-deception. Certitude, however intensely felt, does not entail certainty.

Empathy is the intuitive grasp of what another is feeling. The view that people can be understood *only* empathically rests, as John Dewey has amplified, on a confusion between knowing something and experiencing it. We can know that something was meant to be funny without feeling inclined to

laugh at it; we can know the alcoholic content of wine without ·
getting drunk and even without tasting the wine. Conversely,
the meaning of the experience may rest on quite other grounds
than what we think we thereby know—confidence tricksters
notoriously look and sound completely trustworthy. In anthropology, Bronislaw Malinowski has warned, empathy usually
amounts to guessing what somebody is feeling; there are bad
guesses as well as brilliant insights. We do not have knowledge
until we can distinguish between them. Those whose views on
methodology derive from what they think are the methods of
the hard sciences aspire to doing without interpretation altogether. Behavioral psychology, however, is not the same as doctrinaire behaviorism. What we observe, admittedly, is behavior;
but the data of observation have meaning to those behaving as
well as to the observer. Interpretation is nothing other than the
process of arriving at the meaning. What must be avoided is not
interpretation but misinterpretation—projecting meanings that
are not grounded in what is being observed.

Projective interpretation is mind reading in a pejorative
sense. Such interpretation is forced on the subject in spite of
protestations, as though the subject either does not know what
he or she is thinking and feeling or will not admit what it is.
"*I* tell my patients who they think they are," says the psychiatrist in Dürrenmatt's play *The Physicists.* Psychic processes
are sometimes repressed or suppressed. Methodologically, however, the presumption must be that, by and large, people know
what they mean and are expressing it. Ethnocentrism and subjectivity make any other presumption dangerous. In any case,
denials are additional data to be taken into account. Responsible interpretation of dreams cannot be made with a gypsy
dream book; the dreamer's own associations are indispensable.

What the speaker says that he or she means is not decisive by itself. Interpretation is validated by a number of considerations. A particular interpretation may have a high antecedent
probability, such as the likelihood of a veiled sexual interest. It
may contrast with other interpretations already established
("But yesterday you said . . ."). It may be more comprehensive
than its alternatives, resting on a range of signals, the music as

well as the words ("Did you know you were smiling the whole time you were telling us that?"). It may command widespread acceptance by other hearers; a Yiddish proverb runs, "When two say drunk, the third should sleep it off." The continual flow of meaningful data must be continually checked. Checking may take the form of mirroring the message, repeating it in one's own words and asking the other whether that is what he or she meant to say. The reply does not settle the question. What someone thinks he or she means may be no less problematical than what others who know him or her think is meant. "I had heard of you by hearing of the ear," Job concludes, "but now my eye sees you, wherefore I abhor my words, and repent." Repentant or not, every observer is an intimate of sin; but God might have expressed himself more clearly to start with.

Here is the shortcoming of applying to interpersonal communication the depersonalized model so useful in the mathematical theory of information. In that model, coding by the transmitter and decoding by the receiver are separable and independent processes. In the life of dialogue, however, there is a continuous interaction between them. What is happening is not the transmission from one point to another of an antecedently existent and determinate message but the emergence of a shared meaning, by which each person gets the point of the encounter then and there, in all its specificity. The interchange is not just communication but a species of communion by which alone, as Martin Buber elaborated, each participant in the dialogue first becomes a person.

When people misunderstand one another, that "they don't speak the same language" is not an explanation but a restatement of the fact. The fault is neither with the medium of communication nor with the speaker or the hearer. What happens is a property of the whole system. This is why the small group has such importance for inquiry as well as for practice. We cannot understand people unless we understand how people come to understand one another by being with one another. The objection is sometimes made that the small group is an artificial situation. So it is, as are all situations designed to facilitate observation—which is to say, experiments. The laboratory cannot be contrasted with "life." *Artificial* does not mean *unreal*; on the contrary, the artificial circumstances may be such as to encourage the participants to be, for once in a way, real people. We may allow ourselves to be more truly ourselves among strangers in a laboratory setting than among those with whom we have for long entered into a tacit agreement to rest content with one another's conventional falsehoods. A laboratory situation carries with it, however, risks of introducing its own errors; the colors seen under a microscope may result from the strain used to heighten visibility or from the chromatic aberration of the lens. More data are needed on the effect on small-group behavior of the particular participant observer. Organization development owes something to the developer as well as to the composition and context of the organization; just what and how much is owed is as yet unclear.

Different observers have different presuppositions, make different assumptions, formulate different hypotheses—in a word, they adopt different approaches to human behavior. Observers emulating the hard sciences may look to the rewards reinforcing certain responses. Psychoanalytical perspectives may bring into relief genetic considerations, especially of factors below the level of awareness. Humanistic psychologies may focus on the domain of moral and spiritual crises, while ideologies turn instead to economic pressures and political constraints. Other schools of thought—such as phenomenology, existentialism, and gestalt—are also expressed in characteristic approaches. Nor are participants free of their own presuppositions. Vices are often more credible and more readily acknowledged than are virtues. The remark "There's something about you I find very appealing" may evoke the suspicious "Just what are you after?", while "For some reason, I don't know why, you turn me off" is responded to with "Thanks for leveling with me." Hostility and self-seeking are taken to be more genuine than their opposites. A manager may more easily characterize himself as "a tough bastard" than as a sensitive, caring human being, though he may be as much the one as the other.

A certain role-playing exercise is instructive. A personnel director interviews a job applicant; a man and wife meet at home after work; a young man and woman make each other's acquaintance at a singles bar. Each performer is paired with an alter ego, who is instructed to say what the ego is really thinking and feeling. The conventional myth, usually enacted by the egos, is that employer and applicant care only for the good of the organization; that husband and wife only love and honor one another; that the young people seek only innocent companionship. The alter egos invariably enact a countermyth, that employee and applicant pursue only the narrowest and most immediate self-interest, that marriage is a state of only contemptuous hostility, and that men want only sex while women aim only at parasitism and entrapment. Genuine loyalty and aspiration, commitment and caring, loneliness, insecurity, and the need to be needed—these realities are as much obscured by the countermyth as by the conventional myth.

No methodological principles predetermine which general approach to the study of small groups is to be adopted. A sensitive practitioner and skillful observer in any of the perspectives is likely to be more effective and to arrive at more significant findings than someone making a heavy-handed and mechanical application of techniques deriving from other approaches. What is methodologically objectionable is not the doctrine adhered to but being doctrinaire. An approach is viewed as "scientific" only when, to paraphrase George Homans, nature, however stretched on the rack, still has a chance to say no. None of the approaches, nor their counterparts in the physical and biological sciences, can pretend to literal exactness. Theories are not pictures aspiring to photographic realism; they are maps by which we can find our way, in thought as well as in action. What we take to be literal are the maps embedded in our basic presuppositions. Other maps are regarded as being, at best, only suggestive metaphors. One person's trope is another person's truth.

Figures of speech range from mythopoeic analogies to mathematical models. All of them have their uses. Oedipus is no less respectable than a mass point; Weber's ideal types no less real than Boltzmann's ideal gases. Understanding that is participative as well as predictive depends on the symbolism's meaning to the people being observed as well as to the observer, and on its latent meanings even more than on its manifest ones. Language, the witticism runs, was given to people to enable them to conceal their thoughts.

A master, reproached for speaking always in parables, answered with a parable: A man, having built and furnished a new home, showed it to a visitor, who asked, "If you don't want people to look in, why have windows? If you do want them to look in, why have curtains?" The reply was, "One day someone who loves me will come by, and together we will draw the curtains aside." This is not a bad image of the small-group process at its best. Here we see the usefulness of anecdotal empiricism. One or two instances rarely suffice to ground a generalization in a domain as variable as human behavior, but a single case can be evocatively symbolic. An attractive young woman who was nevertheless insecure about her appearance was advised by the group to place over her mirror where she could see it each morning the inscription "You were expecting maybe Queen Victoria?" Anxieties that one cannot be taken for a queen are not widespread; self-doubts because of presumed shortcomings in appearance or other qualities are almost universal. There are few Don Quixotes among us but many who suffer from quixotic romanticism in politics or in personal relations. There is another contribution of the revelatory anecdote. It shifts attributions from the character of the person to a quality of a behavior pattern and anchors the abstract quality in concrete actions. It is one thing to say, "You are a hostile person," something else to say, "You are full of hostility," and still better to point out, "Tuesday you attacked Tom, yesterday Dick, and now both Harry and Joan." One cannot be a different person, and it is hard to see how one can give up an abstract quality. One can, however, stop doing specific things. When it is the identity itself that is being brought to account, one might well rejoin, "How would it be if I started all over and arranged to be born in Weehawken?"

Several specific instances, even if not a considerable number, may begin to exhibit a pattern. Actions can be explained by reference to the pattern even if we cannot predict which particular form the actions will take. An action that fits the pattern falls into place; it makes sense. Persistent patterns of action are habits, and a network of habits makes up character. "That's the kind of person he is" is not a tautologous explanation. Indeed, it might be false: not every action is in character, and, moreover, the character may be inchoate or conflicted. Nevertheless, a pattern explanation might be more useful than an unending search for a universal proposition from which the particular case can be deduced. Pattern explanations need not rest on assumptions about motivations. On the contrary, motives can be inferred from patterns. A function might be assigned to an action in terms of the pattern into which it fits; this can be said to be the purpose served by the action. Purposes are not always motivated; explanations in biology, for instance, are functional but not motivational. The function of the kidney is to eliminate wastes; it adds nothing to say that this is why nature evolved it. Insistence on motivational explanations in human affairs leads to such absurdities as the conspiratorial and the bedroom theories of history. Unanticipated and unintended consequences may nevertheless fall into patterns. That people gamble in order to lose money, that criminals commit crimes in order to be punished, and that adolescents rebel in order to be rejected may be more acceptable explanations of the deviant behavior than their conventional opposites.

Which explanations are favored, even which data are taken into account, is affected by the researcher's values—*true* and *significant* are, after all, terms of appraisal. Values enter into our presuppositions and infuse the norms governing the conduct of our inquiries. As we are human, nothing human is foreign to us; in the study of behavior, the student is inevitably engaged with what is being studied. The place of values in science, especially in the human sciences, continues to be troubling. The troubles cannot be done away with by eschewing values altogether. That this can and should be done is what Gunnar Myrdal, anthropologist and social critic, has rightly condemned as an untenable neutralism. The scientist is not and ought not to be neutral in choosing the problem, in respecting empirical evidence and rational argument, in insisting on autonomy, and in preserving intellectual and moral integrity. It is not values that corrupt the scientific enterprise but biases—prejudicial, unreasoned, and uncritical values—just as it is not interpretation but projective interpretation that is unscientific.

That values in their very nature cannot have an objective ground is itself a bias in favor of authority, tradition, or sheer self-assertiveness. Values not only sustain inquiry, they can be sustained by it, if they are made explicit and put to the test. Even if there were ultimate values that were beyond testing, final ends that could not be appraised as means having their own consequences, the issues in which the scientists are caught up concern only penultimates—not absolutes, but ends of action relative to a given situation. We seek a nonviolent resolution only of this conflict or that one, not perpetual peace; sensitivity to and caring for particular persons, not omniscience and universal benevolence. We live always, in the meantime, in our own corner of the world. Inquiry, too, however wide its reach, is set always in a particular and limited context.

Neutralism is not the same as being nonjudgmental, listening to the expression of a feeling without responding that the speaker should or should not have that feeling. Unless listening is nonjudgmental, there will soon be little of significance to be heard. "Judge not lest ye be judged" applies to the relations between persons, not only to the relations between a person and God. Approval may be as inappropriate as disapproval. Whether or not one is being weighed in the balance may be more important than whether or not one is found wanting; the jurisdiction of the court may be the most basic point in dispute.

To be nonjudgmental means not to betray one's values but only to set them aside as not relevant then and there. Even evangelical bearers of good tidings must know how to listen, or they will have nothing to proclaim. We can accept views with which we do not agree—hear them, understand them, acknowledge that others have a right to them, and continue to live together with the others on the basis of values that *are* shared. This does not imply that we have thereby changed our own opinions or abandoned our own values. Human relations are difficult precisely because people are different from and differ with one another. If I can live only with those with whom I agree, I may not be able to live even with myself.

Nonjudgmental responses have an important place, but their place is not everywhere. It is important to be able to accept what we do not agree with, but not everything is acceptable. For each of us, there are attitudes, and actions embodying them, that lie outside the bounds of what we can live with. Democrats and Republicans can accept one another; both find terrorists unacceptable. A psychiatrist accepts a variety of sex patterns with which he or she does not agree; this does not imply that he or she would listen nonjudgmentally to a sadistic killer. To learn to be nonjudgmental does not mean to become morally indifferent. It means learning that people who are different from us have the right to live their own lives in their own way and that, with our differences, we can yet live together in mutual respect.

It is not easy to discover what a person's values are. The values to which one gives more than lip service can be inferred from action only if we know something of the actor's beliefs. A person may take one action rather than another not because he or she values the outcome of the first action more than that of the second but because he or she believes, perhaps mistakenly, that it will have the preferred outcome. Values, beliefs, and actions are linked: from any two of them, the third can be inferred. Presupposed is knowledge of the two that is logically independent of assumptions about the third; there is the trap that can make calamity of such inferences. We cope with the danger, as so often in science, by successive approximation—in this instance, approximation to a pattern in which beliefs, values, and actions all have their place.

Sameness of values is often taken for granted, as though people differed only in the means they choose in order to attain the same ends. But the means themselves embody values. Differences remain unless ends are defined so abstractly as to be empty. That someone is seeking "happiness" tells us nothing about that person, unless it is specified what sorts of things make him or her happy; the same is true for "pleasure" and "self-realization." We all seek to maximize our utilities; differences in our assignment of utilities make all the difference. Utility theory relates to values as geometry does to the shapes and sizes of specific things. The assumption of sameness of values has the comforting implication that no values are unacceptable and that all conflicts can be resolved in a manner satisfying to all parties. Such a belief sustains irresponsibility and courts disillusionment or self-destruction. In World War II, the United States Navy had to construct airfields quickly on a number of Pacific islands, using local labor. It was found that the islanders were working only four days a week, idling away the other days. Accordingly, their wages were doubled, whereupon they worked only two days a week. Their values and motivations demanded a certain income—and nothing beyond it.

Differences in values do not rest only on differences in culture; they can also be found within relatively homogeneous populations. Open-ended questions are completed in a variety of ways. Work, for instance, is described as a necessity or as a fufillment, as toil and trouble or as a challenge; nature is something to be appreciated and enjoyed, explored and understood, or controlled and exploited; people are basically good or else contemptible, fascinating and complex or simply diverse; relations between the sexes are joyous or a battle, frustrating and overrated, complicated and mysterious, or rapidly changing. Differences become more marked when priorities are assigned.

Attention has been increasingly focused on the inquirer's own values, as research shares the concern of many other professions with their professional ethics. For a time, small groups organized for personal growth, teaching, and research became disreputable, as in some quarters the activity took on the character of an evangelical movement. Screening of sponsorship, staff, and participants was minimal; professional competence in the field is still only loosely defined. This is not entirely an unmitigated evil. When a discipline attains the status of having its own academy, it runs the risk of becoming routinely academic. The frontiers of research inevitably have their fringes as well.

The autonomy of the scientific enterprise does not free it from social and moral responsibility. The pursuit of truth, like the pursuit of any other value, must take its place among other pursuits. Values are not isolated from one another, nor can any value lay claim to overriding all the others in all circumstances. In the human sciences, standards are crystallizing to free procedures from deception, manipulation, and other forms of exploitation of human resources, including the researchers themselves as well as their subjects. So far as the dangers of the small-group process are concerned, both my own observations and the uniform reports of my colleagues convince me that fears of "breakdowns" owe much more to displaced anxieties than to realistic grounds.

Beneficial effects, too, may fall short of popular expectation. The study of small groups brings into relief the nature of learning. Not only is the study itself a process of learning about human behavior; that same process is its subject matter. What the study discloses first of all is a point often overlooked by enthusiasts—that there is no such thing as instant learning. Insight, to be sure, is sudden, and it plays an important part in understanding people, especially oneself. But insight requires a period of preparation and an even longer time to become incorporated in habitual responses. Equally ill conceived is the faddist notion of instant intimacy. Virginity can be lost in a few moments, but a lifetime might barely suffice to attain true intimacy with another human being.

The recognition that learning need not be immediate can reinforce the capacity to make nonjudgmental responses. Hearing something about oneself—"feedback" in one of its several senses—need not be promptly rejected or agreed to. Instead, it can be reflected upon and made the subject of considered judgment. "How about that!" may be a more appropriate response than either "You're wrong!" or "I'm sorry!" It is, at any rate, a more philosophical response. The unexamined life, said Socrates, is not worth living; learning in the small-group process rests on the conviction that the unlived life is worth examining.

Learning about feelings calls for more than the uninhibited expression of feeling. The act of expression may provide quick catharsis, but the resulting temporary sense of relief does not mean that we have made sense of the feeling. To think so is to repeat the mistake of the axiom of direct experience. Understanding our feelings—as Spinoza, Freud, and others have seen—

relieves us of their compulsion. The converse, however, is not true: being relieved does not imply that we have made sense of the feeling. Expression of feelings is a necessary condition for understanding them, for they must first be observed in order to be analyzed and interpreted. But expression alone is not a sufficient condition for understanding—data do not explain themselves. Still less does acting out of feelings imply understanding them; on the contrary, such action may seriously impede learning, or prevent it altogether.

The learning sought for by the small-group process is integral learning, comprising both experiential and conceptual components. The soft approaches tend to disparage the conceptual side of learning; the hard approaches tend to overrate the effectiveness of the purely conceptual. Both components generate types of knowledge. One can know how to ride a bicycle and know the laws of motion; know someone and know something about her; hear time's winged chariot hurrying near and know that all people are mortal. Each kind of knowledge is power of a sort, and each has its own limitations. Integral learning has the farthest reach, but, as Spinoza concludes at the very end of his *Ethics,* all things excellent are as difficult as they are rare.

Learning is often painful; the experiential component of integral learning may make it especially so. The pain can serve a useful purpose, heightening awareness of what is ineffective in our behavior. Pain in some measure is the inevitable concomitant of learning; growth means losing something of what we once were. I do not share, however, the metaphysics or theology that sees something constructive in pain in and of itself. The bitterness of the medicine does not make it more medicinal. The small-group process draws attention to the dangers of the belief in the converse, that if a medicine tastes bitter, it should not be taken. Most groups have their Florence Nightingale, the group member who rushes in with ointment and Band-aids, often even if there has been no injury. Being "helpful" does not always help one to learn, as all children know. The memorable title of an essay on this theme is "Chicken Soup Can Be Poison."

The small-group process has a unique advantage: it makes

possible vicarious learning on an experiential level. Learning does not take place only for the participants in a dramatic encounter in the center of the stage. Onlookers may be feeling more intensely and observing more clearly. Such vicarious learning may account for the cultural importance of ideology and art, ceremony and ritual. Communicants may be more spiritual than the priest; pupils may be teaching more than the teacher.

The quandaries in which people find themselves not only present problems to be solved. They also confront us with predicaments, quandaries that are insoluble yet inseparable from the human condition. Even here, however—perhaps here most of all —learning has a place. As knowledge grows, we learn to solve problems; learning to cope with predicaments marks the growth of wisdom. "When skies are hanged and oceans drowned," the poet writes, "the single secret will still be man." These words of e. e. cummings are not a cry of despair; they celebrate, rather, the limitless potentialities of the human being for growth—and for learning.

20

Guerrilla Science:
An Epistemology for the
Applied Behavioral Sciences

Lee G. Cooper
Harold G. Levine

Knowledge has always come from the interplay of thought and evidence. Evidence is ubiquitous. Our contemporaneous experience, our history and memory, the outer world and the inner world offer evidence to confront our thoughts. Scientific knowledge is but a subset of knowledge and must, therefore, follow a subset of the methods of gaining knowledge. The basis of scientific knowledge is epistemology. This chapter describes the difficulties with parts of prior epistemologies and presents an epistemology that does not fall short of its task.

Some have said that the phrase *guerrilla science,* which we have used to title this chapter, has the chilling ring of terrorism and terrorists. Nothing could be further from the heart of our work. Nothing could be further from the traditional use of *guerrilla* in science. In 1880, Thomas H. Huxley (1893) juxta-

Note: The authors appreciate the comments and suggestions on earlier versions of this chapter that were provided by Samuel Culbert, Fred Ellett, David Ericson, Abraham Kaplan, Fred Massarik, John McDonough, Will McWhinney, Robert Tannenbaum, and Anthony Tinker.

posed the terms *guerrilla* and *science* in his essay "Science and Culture." He invoked the memory of Joseph Priestley while dedicating the Scientific College, funded by the Josiah Mason Trust, in Priestley's home town. Huxley characterized Priestley by saying, "Priestley's life leaves no doubt that he, at any rate, set a much higher value upon the advancement of knowledge, and the promotion of that freedom of thought which is at once the cause and consequence of intellectual progress" (Huxley, 1893, pp. 134–135). And he characterized Josiah Mason by saying:

> Finally having reached old age with its well-earned surroundings of "honor, troops of friends," the hero of my story bethought himself of those who were making a like start in life, and how he could stretch out a helping hand to them.
>
> After long and anxious reflection this practical man of business could devise nothing better than to provide them with the means of obtaining "sound, extensive, and practical scientific knowledge." And he devoted a large part of his wealth and five years of incessant work to this end [p. 138].

Of the educational revolution that had led to the occasion of his address, Huxley said:

> For us children of the nineteenth century, however, the establishment of a college under the conditions of Sir Josiah Mason's Trust, has significance apart from any which it could have possessed a hundred years ago. It appears to be that we are reaching the crisis of the battle, or rather the series of battles, which have been fought over education in a campaign which began long before Priestley's time, and will probably not be finished just yet.
>
> In the last century, the combatants were the champions of ancient literature on the one side, and those of modern literature on the other; but, some thirty years ago, the contest became complicated by the appearance of a third army, ranged round the banner of Physical Science.
>
> I am not aware that anyone has authority to

speak in the name of this new host. For it must be
admitted to be somewhat of a guerrilla force, composed largely of irregulars, each of whom fights
pretty much for his own hand [pp. 135–136].

The battlefield analogies in Huxley's essay presage our use. But
such analogies are apt when dealing with issues of power derived from the sociology of scientists. Rather than aligning with
modern terrorists' exploitation of civilian populations, our
analysis recalls the ancient Maccabees and their use of time and
space to help equalize power. The epistemology we present is
friendly toward researchers acting independently on similar sets
of commitments and values. We hope it will be of use to behavioral researchers and other scientists whose inquiry is guided by
a sense of commitment to the delivery of human services and/or
the understanding of human interaction.

When one walks into academic domains that are remote
from one's accustomed avenues, there are certain paths that are
much safer than others. We try, where we can, to walk on the
lines. Literally, we seek to build on lines of development for
which other scholars bear or share responsibility and credit. The
works of Abraham Kaplan and Frederick Suppe have been our
primary foundation in the philosophy of science. It was Kaplan's (1964) *The Conduct of Inquiry* that convinced us that the
philosophy of science is the responsibility of scientists, no matter how removed they are from philosophy departments. This
book provided and crystallized frameworks for knowledge that
largely transcend the limitations of the philosophy of science
that Suppe called the "Received View." It is Suppe's (1977)
weighty tome *The Structure of Scientific Theories* that articulated the residual problem. In the fine workings of the received
view, the distinction between theory and observation has not
been tenably drawn. To serve the role that the theory-observa-
tion dichotomy could not fulfill, we offer a single dimension,
with pure thought at one extreme and pure evidence at the
other. The creative tension between these extremes becomes a
catalyst, and the commitment of scientists to solving problems
and learning becomes the motive force for building knowledge.

In particular, the commitment of behavioral scientists to improving the delivery of human services becomes a central element in the development of a human system science.

To assert a philosophy of science is but a small part of a philosophical defense. Evidence from many sources bears on philosophical theorizing as well as scientific theorizing. We present our defense publicly so that independent scholars can judge its utility for their own inquiries.

We begin with a brief introduction to the macromethodology that we propose. In the next section, we deal mostly with scientific terms and definitions. We report why operational definitions of terms are inadequate and how they were replaced by reduction sentences, which partially define terms. We also report how no tenable distinction has been drawn between theoretical terms and observational terms. The following section presents the epistemological problems that accompany changes in the definitional form. It proposes that scientific beliefs can be based on statistical inference, direct observation, and reliable measurement. Scientific knowledge, however, is based on the accumulation of evidence in a scientific domain, not on a single relation. We then go on to apply the epistemology that we have developed to classroom settings and the development of scientific knowledge concerning learning disabilities. We conclude the chapter with a brief discussion of the forces that press for rationality in the growth of scientific knowledge.

A Macromethodology

Science, according to the *Oxford English Dictionary,* is the state or fact of knowing, or, in a more restricted sense, the branch of study that is concerned either with a connected body of demonstrated truths or with observed facts systematically classified and that includes trustworthy methods for the discovery of new truth in its domain. A macromethodology is a method of doing science—a philosophy of science. There are three criteria for the evaluation of a macromethodology: (1) it must be logically consistent; (2) it must be a reconstruction of the activity of scientists—an accurate record; and (3) it must provide a basis for scientists to address the problems of the domain. This chapter describes a macromethodology and how it satisfies these three criteria. While the macromethodology may be broadly applicable throughout the domains of science, the questions that drive this macromethodology arise primarily from the applied behavioral sciences. Applied behavioral sciences cover many domains of activity: counseling and therapy of many kinds, organization development and change efforts, ongoing management, program evaluation, consumer behavior, and education. We ask, "How is it that independent groups of applied behavioral scientists are able systematically to accumulate knowledge in domains without many of the resources of the established scientific community?" The answers we see are in the activities of applied behavioral scientists that share much in common with a guerrilla's use of time, space, and power to achieve hard-sought objectives.

Time. Guerrilla wars are not won overnight. They require a sustained commitment over time. This means that guerrilla scientists had better have or develop means of sustaining themselves in their scientific efforts. Applied behavioral scientists have certain advantages that do not necessarily accrue to all kinds of scientists. By delivering human services (for example, therapy, consulting, or teaching), applied behavioral scientists can often earn a living while they remain immersed in the phenomena or evidential flow of their science. Every scientist need not have a faculty post at a university or a position in a research institute. Applied behavioral science can progress as an outgrowth of professional practice. But sustained commitment is at best a necessary, not a sufficient condition for progress in science.

Space. For guerrillas, the wise use of space is very important. Guerrillas are small groups or individuals working independently or interdependently. The ability to work in separate parts of the domain simultaneously has at least two important advantages. First, since guerrilla scientists may be sustained by the services they deliver locally, they are not as dependent as armies on the central infusion of resources. To understand the second advantage, we need to introduce Shapere's (1977) formal use of *domain* (compare Suppe, 1977). Items of information become associated together as bodies of information when the following conditions obtain: (1) the association is based on some relationship between the items; (2) there is something problematical about the body so related; (3) that problem is an important one; and (4) science is "ready" to deal with the problem (Shapere, 1977, p. 525). Such bodies of information Shapere calls *domains*. That the boundary of a domain may be fuzzy or that the division and coalescence of domains into subdomains and superdomains may not be clearly regulated has no detrimental impact on our discussion.

We might think of domains as battlefields in science and subdomains as particular sets of problems in the battlefield. The wide spread of the activity of guerrilla scientists increases the likelihood that the breadth of problems of the domain will be encountered. While this does not assure that the problems will be solved, there is still an advantage to encountering the problems—problems that are not encountered have very little chance of being solved. Art psychotherapists, for example, now work in outpatient and inpatient settings in psychiatric and general hospitals, therapeutic schools, residential treatment centers, private practice, and many other venues. They work with child, adolescent, adult, and geriatric populations separately and in conjoint settings. With a common commitment to the delivery of human services, an extremely broad array of problems is confronted. If guerrilla scientists develop effective communications systems, their independent results can be linked as a net over wide expanses of the domain. The communications systems of the local and national art-therapy communities are leading to very rapid professional and scientific development.

Power. Power comes to scientists from inside and outside science. The external sources of power come from the alignment of resources in the environment with the interests connected to the domain. Power inside science is derived from epistemology, which is concerned with the basis of knowledge. The language and methods of science are elements in an epistemology. These elements must be connected in a logically consistent manner if there is to be the accumulation of knowledge—if science itself is to exist. It has been changes in the epistemology of science that have returned scientific power to the clinic, the field study, and the classroom.

Changes in the Philosophy of Science

In 1969, the University of Illinois convened a symposium to address the question "What is the structure of a scientific theory?" The main proponents and critics of the traditional view of scientific theories and advocates of the major alternative views presented their positions and debated opposing views. The implications of these discussions for applied behavioral sciences became clearer with the publication of the second edition of the proceedings (Suppe, 1977). This volume presents not only the position papers and a summary of the discussion but also a critical introduction and afterword by Suppe. The latter two sections are of book length and together document the traditional philosophy-of-science view, the critique of this view current at the time of the symposium, and the "rather dramatic developments in the philosophy of science since the 1969 symposium" (p. iii). Our very abbreviated remarks in the sections on "The Received View" and on "Weltanschauung Approaches to Science" are based mainly on Suppe's writings.

In order to understand some of the motivation behind the development of the received view, metaphysics must be briefly discussed. *Metaphysics* really means ontology. Ontological assumptions deal with the ultimate nature of reality. Is reality composed of one kind of stuff? Is that stuff mental or material? A monist would assume that all things are one. A materialistic monist would assume that matter is the only kind of stuff; a mentalistic monist would assume that reality is a construct of the mind. Dualists would assume that reality is both mental and material. Ontological assumptions are neither selectively supportable nor refutable within science. One does not need to assume an ontological position to be a scientist. The only value of an ontological assumption for a scientist is in the questions it prompts. For example, a materialistic monist as applied behavioral scientist might ask, "How is it that life evolves from what I assume is only matter?"

The Received View. The received view is the product of

logical positivism—the predominantly Germanic movement that sought to cleanse philosophy of abstract metaphysical speculation, which did not allow for empirical specification. It was strongly influenced by Whitehead and Russell's (1910-1913) *Principia Mathematica,* which attempted to reduce all of mathematics to logic, and, in its final form, was intended to be suitable to explicate all scientific theories. Gödel (1931) published a theorem that demonstrated that there were formally undecidable propositions in *Principia Mathematica,* so that Whitehead and Russell fell short of their goal (compare Luchins and Luchins, 1965). The scientists, mathematicians, and scientists-turned-philosophers of the Vienna Circle and Reichenbach's Berlin School were convinced by the brilliant, though flawed, arguments of *Principia Mathematica.* The result was the original version of the received view, which held: "A scientific theory is to be axiomatized in mathematical logic. . . . The terms of the logical axiomatization are to be divided into three sorts: (1) logical and mathematical terms; (2) theoretical terms; and (3) observational terms which are given a phenomenal or observational interpretation. The axioms of the theory are formulations of scientific laws, and specify relationships holding between the theoretical terms. Theoretical terms are merely abbreviations for phenomenal descriptions (that is, descriptions which involve only observational terms)" (Suppe, 1977, p. 12). A theoretical term was explicitly defined in terms of what is measured of specified phenomena or their properties, and correspondence rules were used to formalize the relationship of the two. This procedure enabled proponents of the received view the opportunity to purge scientific theory of metaphysical entities, since these entities were not considered to be either phenomenal or observational.

Once metaphysics had been eliminated from theory, philosophers began to ask whether it could not also be stricken from the language of science. The issue was how the terms of a scientific language would be related to the phenomenal world so as to be verifiable empirically. One could directly accept a person's description of phenomenal experience as an observational term or allow only a physicalistic language, where one speaks of the observable properties of material things. At the time, standard doctrine held the mistaken impression that a person's reports of sensory experience were error free and thus presented no verification problem. Nonetheless, physicalism won out, and the received view restricted observational terms to material things and their observable properties.

A major modification of the received view resulted from the recognition by Carnap (1936, 1937) that the explicit and complete definitional form did not work for dispositional terms. Using Suppe's example of the dispositional term *fragile*, we have: "An object x is fragile if and only if it satisfies the following conditions: for any time t, if x is struck sharply at t, then x will break at t" (1977, p. 18). The truth of the phrase "an object is fragile" rests on the truth of the conditional phrase "for any time t, if x is struck sharply at t, then x will break at t." This conditional phrase is considered true whenever the antecedent (if x is struck sharply at t) is true *and* the consequent (x will break at t) is true. But the phrase is also considered to be true whenever the antecedent is false (compare Quine, 1953). Thus, an object is considered fragile if it is not tested. This ridiculous state of affairs is true for *all* operational definitions, which prompts Suppe to comment in a footnote: "It seems to be characteristic, but unfortunate, of science to continue holding philosophical positions long after they are discredited. Thus, for example, Skinner's radical behaviorism, which insists on operational definition came into prominence and dominated behavioral psychology well after most philosophers had abandoned the doctrine of operational or explicit definitions; taxonomists today strongly insist on operational definitions for taxa" (p. 19).

It should suffice that operational definitions are logically inadequate, but they are also practically inadequate. The dictum that a concept must be synonymous with the set of operations used to measure it does not allow for measuring the same concept by different means. Different ways of measuring lead to different concepts, according to operational definitions. Physical sciences could not progress without different ways of measuring the same thing, and neither could social sciences.

The received view replaced the explicit definition with the *reduction sentence,* which partially defines a theoretical term by specifying sufficient but not necessary conditions for a particular instance to be considered an application of a theoretical term. Using the previous example, this means that for the object x at time t, striking it sharply implies that it will break if and only if it is fragile. This allows a nonfragile item that is not struck still to be nonfragile—avoiding the logical flaw called the "contrafactual conditional," while also allowing for other ways of measuring fragility. If the object were twisted sharply, it would break if and only if it were fragile. All kinds of tests for fragility could be included by further reduction sentences, each adding partially to the meaning of the concept. The meaning of concepts, terms, or constructs is open. It grows as we learn more and relate a construct to other constructs.

But even these progressive revisions of the received view could not completely rescue it, because no tenable distinction has been drawn that distinguishes theoretical terms from observational terms. The coup de grace is administered in a series of direct attacks by Putnam (1962) and Achinstein (1965, 1968), reported by Suppe (1977). They demonstrate that the features of direct observation that are intended, in the received view, to differentiate observable from theoretical terms do not hold. Observation, Achinstein notes (in Suppe, 1977, p. 81), has the following characteristics:

1. How many aspects of an item, and which ones, I must attend to before I can be said to observe it will depend upon my concerns and knowledge.
2. Observing involves paying attention to various aspects and features of the item observed but does not always require recognizing the kind of item being observed.
3. It is possible to observe something even if it is in a certain sense hidden from view—for example, a forest ranger observes the fire even if he can see only smoke—so observing an item does not necessarily involve seeing or looking at it.
4. It is possible to observe something when seeing an intermediary image—for example, when looking at myself in a mirror.

5. It is possible to describe what I am observing in the sky as either a moving speck or an airplane.

The first and second points indicate that observation is preconditioned by theoretical cognition and intention. The third and fourth points deal with the role of implicit causal theories in observation: one infers fire from smoke, and one assumes the image in the mirror is nondistorted. The fifth point emphasizes the conscious choices an observer has regarding description. All point toward the "theory ladenness" of observation (that is, observational terms are tainted with theoretical terms as antecedents). These characteristics do not show that the observational-theoretical distinction is undrawable but rather show that "the distinction has not been successfully drawn, and what is more, cannot be drawn in any plausible way on the basis of ordinary usage of terms in natural scientific languages. The only way the distinction could be drawn is artificially in a reconstructed language, and doing so would introduce an unwarranted degree of complexity into the analysis. Furthermore, even if the distinction is drawn satisfactorily it will mark no philosophically significant or epistemically revealing distinction. Finally, the distinction fails to capture what is distinctive either of theoretical terms or observation reports in science. The observational-theoretical distinction obviously is untenable. As such most of the epistemological interest of the Received View is lost. Insofar as the observational-theoretical distinction is essential to the Received View, the Received View is inadequate" (Suppe, 1977, pp. 85–86).

Although a good deal of further criticism of the received view is provided in Suppe and elsewhere, it suffices to say that the view that construes scientific theories as axiomatic calculi in which theoretical terms are set apart from observational terms and given meaning by operational definitions is no longer taken seriously.

Weltanschauung Approaches to Science. If science does not proceed as the received view would hold, how does it proceed? Kuhn (1970) holds that science consists of periods of normal science interrupted by occasional scientific revolutions. Normal science "means research firmly based upon one or more past achievements, achievements that some particular scientific community acknowledges for a time as supplying the foundation for its further practice" (Kuhn, 1970, p. 10). The theory or collection of theories that the scientific community shares is called a paradigm or disciplinary matrix. Normal science proceeds by elaborating the paradigm and solving the puzzles raised by it. Eventually a puzzle that is unsolvable within the paradigm arises, causing scientists to consider alternative theories. "The revolutionary proliferation of alternative theories continues until one of them emerges as victor, and a new scientific community coalesces around, and gives allegiance to, that theory—at which time normal science reemerges" (Suppe, 1977, p. 636). Kuhn maintains that this is not only an accurate record of the history of science but also how it *ought* to be. Feyerabend (1963), according to Suppe, doubts that "normal science" really exists. He believes that science ought to progress via a proliferation of competing, incompatible theories.

Despite differences in what Kuhn and Feyerabend say "ought" to occur in science, their epistemologies are very similar and similarly problematical. To both of them, scientific knowledge is based on nothing more than the sociological or psychological agreements among a group of people who call themselves scientists. These positions confuse battlefields with armies. The styles of definition, or correspondence rules, that Kuhn espoused became more and more like the received view as Kuhn modified his position to respond to his critics. But how are we to evaluate progress in "normal science"? Armies can choose their parts of the battleground and the problems they address. Kuhn shortchanges the role of rationality in the growth of scientific knowledge. Choosing to occupy a small part of the battlefield is analogous to choosing to engage only a select few of the problems of the domain. This does not foster rational growth of knowledge. There should be an advantage that accrues collectively to the scientists in the clinics, field settings, and classrooms who broadly encounter the problems of the field.

There is also growing skepticism that Kuhn's historical view of the cycling of science between normal and revolutionary periods is an accurate portrayal of history. But most basic to the criticisms is that Kuhn espouses an epistemology so subjective that "it makes discovering how the world really is irrelevant to scientific knowledge" (Suppe, 1977, p. 648). What is needed is an epistemology, tailored to applied behavioral sciences, that does not rest ultimately on subjective agreement and an untenable distinction between theoretical and observational terms.

An Epistemology for Applied Behavioral Science

The "standard epistemological view" of knowledge is as a "justified true belief." That is, one knows a proposition is true if and only if: (1) the proposition is true; (2) one believes that it is true; and (3) one has adequate evidence for believing that it is true. In addition, Suppe (1977, p. 717) argues that it has been at least tacitly assumed in most recent epistemological writings that part (3) embodies what has come to be known as the "K-K thesis" (Hintikka, 1962): (4) one's knowing a proposition entails that one knows that one knows the proposition. This thesis, in effect a kind of philosophical "reflexivity," implies that one cannot know the "truth value" one assigns to theoretical propositions about real-world phenomena unless one also knows the "truth value" of the *claims* that are made as to the veracity of these same theoretical propositions. Thus, the evidence used to justify one's belief in the truth of one's theory must be equivalent to and, indeed, a *guarantee of* the truth of one's *claim* to knowledge. Acceptance of the K-K thesis presents insurmountable obstacles to advancement in the observational sciences for two reasons. First, as we have already argued, the meaning of theoretical terms would need to be entirely observational in nature. As a result, it would be impossible to regularly specify all exact correspondence rules that link observational dimensions of the phenomenal world to theoretical terms. Second, the level of certainty is so demanding that even rigorous statistical tests fail to satisfy the criterion.

What we are suggesting is an epistemology that avoids the K-K thesis and involves a separation between the roles of scientific belief and scientific knowledge. Inferential statistics, direct observation, reliable measurement, and prior knowledge become the evidential bases of scientific belief. Confidence in scientific beliefs can be increased by additional confirming evidence or decreased by disconfirming evidence. Although confidence can increase without limit, the truth of the beliefs need not be completely justified at a particular point in time.

Scientific knowledge comes not from single beliefs but from the network of relations in a scientific domain. While there will be alternative explanations for a single belief, the richness of a network can allow us to assess our justified true belief (that is, scientific knowledge) in the relations of a domain.

The Bases of Scientific Beliefs. Inferential statistics have often been presented as if they provided enough evidence to assert that a proposition is true. But statistical inference has inherent weaknesses. A basic test of a hypothesis is subject to two kinds of error. Type I error is the probability of rejecting a null hypothesis when one should not. The level of this type of error is routinely set at one out of twenty or one out of one hundred. While one may be willing to assert a belief in a proposition if one is wrong only one time out of one hundred, this is far too liberal a criterion on which to assert the truth of the proposition. Of course, if this were the only serious threat to accepting a proof, one might be satisfied by setting the acceptable level of Type I error at some very extreme value, say one chance of error out of ten billion, and tolerate the residual uncertainty. Even in elementary statistics classes, we were all taught about Type II error, the probability of failing to accept a correct alternative explanation (hypothesis). The Neyman-Pearson lemma for uniformly most powerful tests establishes for us the standard procedures for testing a hypothesis so as to minimize the probability of Type II error for all possible alternative hypotheses. These procedures ensure, in general, that the more certain we insist on being, the less powerful are our statistical tests at detecting a true alternative hypothesis. So, while inferential statistics can provide an adequate basis of scientific belief, it is not rational to use them solely as a basis of "scientific" truth.

Shapere (1977; compare Suppe, 1977, pp. 689–691) presents an analysis of observation in which he rejects the received-view notion on a theory-neutral observational language but still avoids the relativism of observation explicit in the weltanschauung view. According to this analysis, the starting propositions of these two positions are "plausible, and appear to constitute adequate criteria for any philosophy of science": (1) Observation must be independent of, neutral with respect to, the theory to be assessed. (2) Observation, if it is to be relevant, must be interpreted. These basic principles are compatible with many approaches to applied behavioral science, including applied phenomenology. The willing suspension of disbelief prior to the onset of a phenomenological encounter of some sort, termed "bracketing," is an embodiment of the spirit of proposition (1). The mulling over of events after an encounter with the phenomena, termed "sifting," is in the spirit of proposition (2). It leads to an interpretation that need not be preordained by theory. Shapere demonstrates that accepting these propositions does not lock us into the received-view or weltanschauung analyses.

As we discussed earlier, we observe more than we can actually see. A traditional argument showing the limitations of observation comes from astrophysics, where a whole theory of instrumentation (for example, radio telescopy) interposes itself between the eye and the phenomena under "observation." The infrared radio telescope now in earth orbit, sending signals back to earth, is hardly equatable with seeing. Any reliable measurement provides at least as sound a basis for scientific belief as do statistical inference and direct observation.

The writings of Fiske (1979) on reliability deserve comment. He juxtaposes the study of characteristics of persons to the study of behaviors and, in discussing the study of the characteristics of persons, implies that such studies are of low reliability. Although he speaks of these two types of studies as if they were worlds apart—the former roughly corresponding to the building of response-response (R-R) laws and the latter roughly corresponding to the building of stimulus-response (S-R) laws—applied behavioral science uses both kinds of studies. In particular contexts where the focus is on behaviors, the relatively short duration of actions, the recognizable onset and termination of behaviors, and the low level of abstraction of the terms referring to those behaviors each acts to foster the reliability of observation and/or measurement.

The study of the characteristics of persons is portrayed by Fiske as focusing on entities, processes, or states of longer duration. A primary use of this kind of study in applied behavioral science entails the summarization of an individual's history as it applies to a current context. Stimulus-response approaches are ill suited for such efforts. The relatively low interrater agreement cited by Fiske (1979, p. 735) does not typify the reliability of the broad class of methods for the development of response-response relations. Generalizability theory (Cronbach and others, 1972; Shavelson and Webb, 1981), construct validity (Cronbach and Meehl, 1955), latent trait theory (Lord and Novick, 1968), and general multimeasurement approaches to causal modeling (Bentler, 1980) all entail entirely reasonable (and very powerful) approaches to the establishment of scientific belief.

One restraint on the utility of information, if not the reliability, that deserves more attention is what is termed "method variance." In the study of characteristics of persons, method variance refers to the component of information that results not directly from the phenomena but from how the phenomena are measured or assessed. In the study of behaviors, method variance refers to the unique component of information contributed by a particular observer (for example, the teacher, therapist, or consultant). In general, applied behavioral scientists should attempt to keep track of the impact of their choices on the phenomena under study. It is important to record one's assumptions and presuppositions. Comparing this record to the record of the phenomena (for example, the charts or diaries) can help the therapist, consultant, or teacher to see, over many cases, what he or she is contributing to the "observed" phenomena. The goal is to better understand the problem once the influence of the behavioral scientist is discounted.

The Role of Theory. Theory is the device by which scientists accumulate information in a domain. At different levels of

abstraction, theoretical statements allow for a parsimonious representation of the state of scientific belief in a domain of inquiry. In Jungian psychology, for example, a high-level theoretical statement might be that personality is manifested in two
functions—how an individual perceives and how an individual
processes information about the world—and in whether one
looks inside or outside oneself for such information. In a sensitivity training context, a related theoretical statement might be
that individuals whose thoughts dominate their feelings will gain
more appreciation for others' feelings if they are simultaneously supported for the quality of their thoughts and confronted
for their absence of feeling (Taylor, 1977).

In an organization-development context, a high-level theory might say that an organization must periodically regenerate
its reason for being or cease to exist (Mittler, 1974). This theory
results in a set of diagnostic signs for three cyclic states of organization life. Such statements in a domain are part of a relational network. In the network, there will also be some reduction sentences, which partially define constructs or concepts in
terms of reliable information; statements of direct observation;
statements relating the results of research efforts to theoretical
constructions; and statements relating other theories to ones
currently under consideration.

But any theory has inherent problems. Shapere (1977)
recognizes three kinds of theoretical inadequacies. The first is
incompleteness. If the network of relations that covers the domain is thought of as a mesh or sieve, incompleteness refers to a
hole or break in the mesh—an area of the domain that is not
covered as completely as others. A theory of orienting style
(Taylor, 1977) may give a very useful explanation of the temporal changes brought about by differing normative profiles of
group members, but it provides no account of possible permanent changes in personality structure. The second theoretical
inadequacy is *oversimplification*. A sieve is a three-dimensional
object, yet the phenomena one wishes to cover with a network
may well have four dimensions or more. As an individual changes
in response to the normative profile of a group, the normative
profile of the group may also change. The theory may be over-

simplified by not attending to the change in group profile over brief periods of time. An organization is a multigroup, multifacet structure. Different parts of the organization may be in different substages of the regenerative cycle at a given point in time. Any major division may oversimplify the process occurring at sublevels to a certain extent. The third kind of inadequacy Shapere calls *black-box incompleteness*. This refers to the fineness of the mesh or sieve. No matter how fine, the mesh is never closed, and something may always pass through.

The Basis of Scientific Knowledge. The past reliance on operational definitions can be viewed as being based on an unworkable premise that all scientific knowledge is stipulative. Our overconfidence in hypothesis testing can be viewed as being based on an unworkable premise that all scientific knowledge is inferential. A more general premise is that all scientific knowledge is relational. This conforms to our everyday experience, since belief and knowledge—scientific or not—are relations of one sort or another. Most of what we know about worldly objects comes from our history of relations with them. Most of what we know about things that we cannot see comes from how they relate to things that we can. Inference is a particular relation that we sometimes use as a basis for knowledge. It is not that such a relation is disallowed as a basis for scientific knowledge; rather, it is the primary or exclusive use of it that will lead to difficulties in science.

Consider the possibility that knowledge and truth do not accrue to a particular relation in isolation. Toulmin (1953; compare Suppe, 1977, pp. 127-155, 670-682) went so far as to say that theories and other representational devices are neither true or false, but statements about their scope or range of applicability are. While we do not go this far, it is useful to recognize that many of the relations in a network address the issues of scope or range of applicability of the theory. In applied behavioral science, we do not expect relations such as $E = mc^2$. Rather, our assertions are restricted to certain kinds of people in certain kinds of situations. From the diversity of people and circumstances we can build up rich networks of relations in a scientific domain.

The relational network in a domain carries the largest burden as a basis for scientific knowledge. Evidence from all sources can increase or decrease our belief in the propriety of an asserted relation. Confirming evidence and disconfirming evidence have equal status in terms of their impact on belief in the network. Both are partial, weak, fallible, local, and temporal. However, evidence does flow in a network from areas of higher concentration to areas of lower concentration. If we know that an analytical method is proper, this increases our belief in unusual or unexpected results in some application. If we know what results are proper, our belief in new methods increases if they produce these results. A relational network may stem from a simple statement of high-level theory. While high-level theory may be valued for its elegance and simplicity, the relational network is valued for its complexity and intricacy. The abundance of confirmed relations between constructs is what allows us to overcome the inherent weakness of a single experimental/research result in isolation.

Competitive support and parsimony also have roles in the establishment of scientific knowledge. It is rare, yet possible, that competing theories are specified in ways such that all the evidence relating to one theory can be evaluated against all the evidence relating to the other theory. If this occurs in richly articulated domains, the theory offering the better total explanation ought to be accepted. For explanations with equal support, the more parsimonious one is favored. But competitive support and parsimony are often oversold. Garner, Hake, and Ericksen (1956) built a system called "convergent operationism" from the sense that competing theories could be evaluated by a series of "crucial experiments" that would result in one final contest. This final experiment would supposedly crucially eliminate all but one theory. But, in reality, there will still be an infinite number of alternative explanations for the result in the final experiment. Whole networks may at times be compared to other networks, but sequential elimination by successive experimentation is untenable. In young domains, such as the behavioral sciences, parsimony is easily misused. It is thus that theories of memory without organization or choice without values might be advanced in the name of parsimony prior to having the appropriately specified alternative theories for competitive evaluation.

Theories in a domain become scientific knowledge when the overwhelming burden of evidence supports the asserted relations. This does not mean that there must be no disconfirming evidence. If this were so, we would attribute more value to such evidence than it deserves. Disconfirming evidence serves to limit the range and scope of the relation. Once the entire network has reached an extreme level of confirmation, the theories in the network are considered to be lawful relations. These lawful relations may be used as evidence in support of largely hypothetical relations in other domains if a basis for the generalizability of the theories is established. One may judge the completeness of a domain by the resolution of the problems that characterize it. The professional who is aware of the completeness of a scientific domain may rationally judge when there is sufficient confidence in the asserted relations to use them as a basis for experimental practice, when there is enough confidence to establish policy. Applied behavioral scientists may act on the basis of scientific beliefs and, in the process, gain the evidence that helps scientific belief become scientific knowledge.

The Role of the Practitioner: Teachers as Scientists

Though practitioners may not normally regard themselves as "researchers," there are several reasons why their efforts are ideally suited to contribute to science. In the first place, the standards of professional responsibility that guide the practitioner are consonant with the best principles of scientific inquiry: learning as much as possible about the phenomenon in question and generalizing this knowledge to broader sets of circumstances; maintaining well-kept records of one's efforts and results; and adopting a stance that values "listening to" over "listening for" and "looking at" over "looking for." Second, as noted earlier, applied behavioral scientists, as groups of people working in a particular subject area, have access to a far greater population of individuals and situations than any "researcher" is likely to obtain and, therefore, are more likely to be able to observe the full range and diversity of the behavior in question. The various professional societies and publications of the applied behavioral scientists are the fundamental mechanisms for the support and dissemination of these efforts.

An implicit consequence of recent thinking in philosophy of science is that the epistemological base for conceptualizing "traditional" social science is no different from that which underlies applied behavioral science. In fact, philosophy of science is currently modeling the very process that that discipline claims as its subject matter: the justification of scientific practice and knowledge. Science *is* increasingly coming to be practiced by the applied behavioral scientists. Though such scientists typically phrase their research questions in terms of what *works,* and why, and are often eager to try *to make* something work, they do come upon evidence pertaining to one or more domains of knowledge. The more traditional scientist confronting this same or related evidence through his or her research question is most often concerned with what is *happening* and why. Under the received view, with its seemingly inviolate distinction between observational and theoretical terms, its operational definitions and extensive controls, its "covering-law" explanations and axiomatized theoretical propositions, and its crucial tests and universalist "proofs," efforts of applied behavioral scientists were often outside the process by which knowledge was considered "justified." However, postpositivistic science recognizes domains of scientific interest where theory and observational fact are not always distinguishable and are, in any case, mutually interdependent, and where the role of theory is as crucial to scientific belief as it is to scientific truth. The well-trained applied behavioral scientist, as much as any "pure" researcher, is both a user of and a contributor to theory and, hence, to science. We wish to illustrate more explicitly how this might be done by using the example of teachers of retarded learners. (We use the definition of mentally retarded learners given by the American Association on Mental Deficiency (1973, p. 5): individuals who possess significantly subaverage general intellectual functioning as well as deficits in adaptive behavior, both of which are manifested during the development phase of the individual's life.)

Any well-trained teacher is a professional whose work combines both observational and communicational skills in the classroom with the best of current instructional and learning theory. Some of the main points of the theory that informs the efforts of both teachers and academicians toward retarded learners are listed here (Ellis, 1979; Gearheart and Litton, 1975; Kolstoe, 1972, 1976; MacMillan, 1977).

1. Learning is directly related to mental age. The general laws of learning that apply to "normal" children apply to retarded children as well.
2. While performance is initially haphazard, once the child understands what to do, it tends to occur at the same rate as with normal students of similar mental age.
3. Thought processes of retarded students are described as concrete, discrete, unrelated, immediate, and obvious.
4. Retarded learners have poor discrimination abilities, so that similar materials and competing stimuli impede learning.
5. Transfer of training is extremely limited and may regularly occur only when transfer is by identical elements rather than by principle.
6. Self-teaching or autoinstruction is typically deficient.
7. Incidental learning seems deficient, though the role of cultural and experiential factors is unknown.
8. Learning strategies are more likely to be characterized by avoiding failure than by seeking success.
9. Retarded learners are also socially inept, which has a further effect on their learning by narrowing the opportunities for learning or by confusing the learners because of misconstruals of the task demands.

These statements clearly are not a set of logically derived or formulated propositions. Rather, most express relations between hypothetical and evidential entities, processes, or states. These items clearly relate to one another, are of importance and current concern among researchers, and are problematical in that all, in some way, attempt to explain what distinguishes retarded learners from normal learners while attempting, sometimes implicitly, to account for these differences. They seem, therefore, to conform to Shapere's (1977) definition of a domain in scientific inquiry. Since "proof" for any of the elements in this domain is lacking—indeed, seemingly contradictory information is available for most—they comprise the corpus of scientific beliefs for most of those who work with retarded learners.

How might classroom teachers contribute to the elucidation of this domain? Since we have argued that the efforts of teachers and other applied scientists have an epistemological status no different from that of "pure" research, the question can be rephrased in more general terms: "What are the scientific problems connected with a domain and with the theories that help constitute that domain?" In general, there are three sorts of scientific problems: domain problems, which involve clarification of the elements within and the boundaries of the domain; theoretical problems, which concern the level and type of explanation of phenomena within the domain; and problems of theoretical inadequacy, which refer to the thoroughness of the theory itself. Teachers of retarded learners, in their "new" role as applied behavioral scientists, are in an ideal position to contribute to our knowledge about this domain.

Domain Problems. In large part, the history of research in mental retardation parallels that in psychology in general (Brooks and Baumeister, 1977). Consequently, one of the major topics in mental retardation research is learning, particularly as studied behaviorally. Self-monitoring, incidental learning, generalization, discrimination abilities, and other elements of this domain have been characterized behaviorally and most often studied under experimental or quasi-experimental conditions. Teachers have the opportunity to add a naturalistic perspective to the study of these aspects of learning and to refine or reconceptualize them on the basis of their observations and interventions. Perhaps it will be necessary to expand the domain to include metalevel cognitive abilities (Brown, 1975; Flavell, 1971; Flavell and Wellman, 1977) or other phenomena that have yet to be understood adequately in laboratory settings but that appear to affect everyday performance.

Theoretical Problems. Two kinds of explanatory theories

in science are compositional and evolutionary (Shapere, 1977). A compositional theory explains by recourse to constituent parts of the individual units studied within the boundaries of the domain and regularities that govern these separate parts. Evolutionary theory, on the other hand, resorts to the development of individual units within the domain. Deciding on which perspective best fits the domain items in question, if, indeed, one can be said to be a best fit at all, is itself an important problem. Certainly, it is a problem that is implicit in studying learning abilities of mentally retarded students. Teachers who often have the same students over a period of several years and who, in any case, maintain files and records of the children's progress (especially now that individualized educational programs and evaluation are typically mandated by law) are perhaps best able to make judgments and collect data relative to a "developmentalist" versus "atomist" explanatory framework.

Theoretical Inadequacies. As mentioned earlier, Shapere (1977, pp. 557-565) discusses three types of theoretical inadequacies: incompleteness, oversimplification, and black-box incompleteness. A theory can be considered complete or incomplete relative to the body of information within a domain or, more usually, within a subdomain. In the area of mental retardation research, recent findings indicate that the laboratory-based tasks by which we typically evaluate such cognitive abilities as memory may be quite different in terms of their underlying structure from memorial tasks found under "everyday" conditions (Levine, Zetlin, and Langness, 1980). In addition, long-term observations of retarded learners reveal quite sophisticated social skills, high and enduring motivation toward specific goals as well as complex, shifting strategy selection in pursuit of these goals, widely varying performance incentives, and common use of symbols (for example, abstract thought) and fundamental deductive logic in problem solving. Current theory does not adequately provide for these manifestations of cognitive functioning.

We can identify two different types of oversimplification. The first results from making assumptions about the units in the domain or their behavior when evidence is lacking, contradictory, or inadequate. The debate over whether trainable mentally retarded learners (those whose IQs fall in the 36-55 range) can profit from academic subjects is one such issue. There are some who maintain that trainable mentally retarded learners will always remain trainable, not educable, and therefore should be taught with nonacademic curricula (Burton, 1974). Others maintain just the opposite and cite research to show that complex cognitive skills such as reading can be taught (Brown and Perlmutter, 1971). The second form of oversimplification results from having general agreement among most researchers that they *do* possess the adequate evidence or theory (usually as part of another domain or theory rather than the one of immediate concern) for dismissing certain "background information" as irrelevant to the issue at hand. In fact, this claim is a hypothesis that may prove to be quite erroneous as further research accumulates. The history of classroom research shows increasing recognition of the diversity and multiplicity of variables that affect learning outcomes: contextual variables affecting tasks and task presentation and individual variables, such as motivation and the students' perception of the demands made upon them, teacher expectations, and the like.

Incompleteness as discussed earlier is a "known" quantity —that is, the researcher knows what has been omitted and realizes its crucial role in the theory or domain. Black-box incompleteness refers to a state in which the attributes of some more microlevel phenomenon may play a role in explanation, but just how and even whether it does so remains unclear. In mental retardation research, this problem is a major one. For many individuals labeled as mentally retarded, we are unable to pinpoint the underlying cause; even when this is possible, we cannot usually characterize the specific neurophysiological (or other) effects on the individual's cognitive abilities. The result is a true "black box," which is often glossed over, disclaimers to the contrary, by speaking of *the* trainable mentally retarded child as if there were some homogeneous group of such children. In addition, it is unclear whether any lack of academic progress for the individual student is solely related to mental inadequacy or is equally traceable to other problems, such as lowered teacher expectancies and/or lowered student motivation, inappropriate teaching strategies or instructional programs, or inappropriate social behaviors in the classroom by teacher and student alike that are not conducive to learning (for example, teachers coddling those students engaging in infantile behaviors).

Thus, there are a number of ways in which teachers as applied behavioral scientists will make contributions to domains of scientific interest. Methodologically, these contributions will come about through the classroom application of such research techniques as observational and diagnostic accounts of students focusing on description, comparison, and explanation, simple frequency counts of characteristic behaviors, "natural" experiments (Sechrest, 1970), unobtrusive measures (Webb and others, 1966), accounts of unique or otherwise puzzling phenomena, and the like. Increasingly, $N = 1$ experiments (Dukes, 1972; Hersen and Barlow, 1976) and interventions will become the common currency of action-oriented research. Teachers can be expected to specify and measure the outcomes of new curriculum materials of teaching strategies as they try to *make* education *work* for their students. Results of this intervention must be compared with other such attempts by the same teacher, other teachers in the school, or similar efforts reported in the literature. The teacher-researcher will look for commonalities, whether they be related to the contexts in which the techniques were employed, to the students themselves, to the kinds of tasks for which the new teaching method seemed particularly suited, or to the outcomes. Finding the commonalities is only the first step. They must be related to the statements within a domain, and ultimately they must address one or more of the problems inherent to or subsumed within that domain. Their research, like that of "pure" behavioral scientists, will neither prove nor disprove a theory. Rather, perseverance in their work with the problems of retarded learners will inevitably lead to evidence that (1) increases belief in an asserted set of relations, (2) decreases belief in those relations, or (3) demonstrates the inadequacy of current theorizing and provides the basic data for a new set of relations.

Rationality in the Growth of Scientific Knowledge

"Science is not a static enterprise; rather its concepts, interests, presuppositions, theories and other representational devices are dynamically evolving" (Suppe, 1977, p. 670). How can we be responsive to the dynamic character of scientific knowledge and yet avoid the view that science is whatever armies of scientists say it is? Sometimes armies are dominant enough to make their conventions seem like law. But this is an ultimately subjective view of science. It makes what is real simply a matter of doctrine or definition.

It seems to us that the following conditions are collectively sufficient for rational growth of knowledge. First, a commitment to scientific realism is unavoidable. This amounts to asserting the reality of even hypothetically unobservable constructs and seeking to know their character. But, as Kaplan (1964, pp. 306-310) indicates in his insightful discussion of scientific realism and instrumentalism, simply asserting the reality of one's constructs is not enough. Our understanding at a given point in time is open and partial. Using partially understood constructs in order to better learn their meaning implies the use of instrumental approximations as building blocks—as means toward realistic ends. But scientific realism creates a proper pressure for closure even if closure is unattainable.

The second condition concerns coverage of the scientific domain. The engagement of applied behavioral scientists in problems in all parts of the battlefield is an important ingredient. The clinical setting helps ensure that applied behavioral scientists confront the problems of the domain rather than select a problem of interest. When efforts at professional development coincide with the efforts of scientific development, great synergy can result.

The third ingredient is communication. The social/professional organization of applied behavioral scientists is very important for progress in science. By sharing problems, perspectives, and accomplishments, networks of behavioral scientists can overcome the inherent weakness of individuals. Communication systems help ensure that professional experience leaves an accumulating residue. That residue is a rich record that allows others to build upon past learning. Each increment can indeed be small. But the collective efforts help to guarantee the rational growth of scientific knowledge.

References

Achinstein, P. "The Problem of Theoretical Terms." *American Philosophical Quarterly*, 1965, *2*, 193-203.

Achinstein, P. *Concepts in Science.* Baltimore: Johns Hopkins University Press, 1968.

American Association on Mental Deficiency. *Manual on Terminology and Classification in Mental Retardation.* (Rev. ed.) Washington, D.C.: American Association on Mental Deficiency, 1973.

Bentler, P. M. "Multivariate Analysis with Latent Variables: Causal Modeling." *Annual Review of Psychology*, 1980, *31*, 419-456.

Brooks, P. H., and Baumeister, A. A. "A Plea for Consideration of Ecological Validity in the Experimental Psychology of Mental Retardation." *American Journal of Mental Deficiency*, 1977, *81*, 407-416.

Brown, A. L. "The Development of Memory: Knowing, Knowing About Knowing, and Knowing How to Know." In H. W. Reese (Ed.), *Advances in Child Development and Behavior 10.* New York: Academic Press, 1975.

Brown, L., and Perlmutter, L. "Teaching Functional Reading to Trainable Level Retarded Students." *Education and Training of the Mentally Retarded*, 1971, *6*, 74-84.

Burton, T. A. "Education for Trainables: An Impossible Dream?" *Mental Retardation*, 1974, *12*, 45-46.

Carnap, R. "Testability and Meaning." *Philosophy of Science*, 1936, *3*, 420-468.

Carnap, R. "Testability and Meaning." *Philosophy of Science*, 1937, *4*, 1-40.

Cronbach, L. J., and Meehl, P. E. "Construct Validity in Psychological Tests." *Psychological Bulletin*, 1955, *52*, 218-302.

Cronbach, L. J., and others. *The Dependability of Behavioral Measurements: Theory of Generalizability for Scores and Profiles.* New York: Wiley, 1972.

Dukes, W. F. "N = 1." In R. E. Kirk (Ed.), *Statistical Issues: A Reader for Behavioral Science.* Monterey, Calif.: Brooks/ Cole, 1972.

Ellis, N. R. *Handbook of Mental Deficiency, Psychological Theory and Research.* Hillsdale, N.J.: Erlbaum, 1979.

Feyerabend, P. "How To Be a Good Empiricist: A Plea for Tolerance in Matters Epistemological." In B. Baumrin (Ed.), *Philosophy of Science—The Delaware Seminar.* Vol. 2. New York: Interscience, 1963.

Fiske, D. "Two Worlds of Psychological Phenomena." *American Psychologist,* 1979, *34,* 733-739.

Flavell, J. H. "Stage-Related Properties of Cognitive Development." *Cognitive Psychology,* 1971, *2,* 421-453.

Flavell, J. H., and Wellman, H. M. "Metamemory." In R. V. Kail, Jr., and J. W. Hagen (Eds.), *Perspectives on the Development of Memory and Cognition.* Hillsdale, N.J.: Erlbaum, 1977.

Garner, W. R., Hake, H. W., and Ericksen, C. W. "Operationism and the Concept of Perception." *Psychological Review,* 1956, *63,* 149-159.

Gearheart, B. R., and Litton, F. W. *The Trainable Retarded: A Foundations Approach.* St. Louis, Mo.: Mosby, 1975.

Gödel, K. "Über Formal Unent-scheidbare Sätze der *Principia Mathematica* und Verwandter Systeme." *Monatschefte für Mathematik and Physik,* 1931, *38,* 173-198.

Hersen, M., and Barlow, D. H. *Single-Case Experimental Designs: Strategy for Studying Behavior Change.* New York: Pergamon, 1976.

Hintikka, J. *Knowledge and Belief.* Ithaca, N.Y.: Cornell University Press, 1962.

Huxley, T. H. "Science and Culture." *Collected Essays.* Vol. 3. London: Macmillan, 1893.

Kaplan, A. *The Conduct of Inquiry.* San Francisco: Chandler, 1964.

Kolstoe, O. P. *Mental Retardation: An Educational Viewpoint.* New York: Holt, Rinehart and Winston, 1972.

Kolstoe, O. P. *Teaching Educable Mentally Retarded Children.* New York: Holt, Rinehart and Winston, 1976.

Kuhn, T. S. *The Structure of Scientific Revolutions.* (2nd ed.) Chicago: University of Chicago Press, 1970.

Levine, H. G., Zetlin, A. G., and Langness, L. L. "Everyday Memory Tasks in Classrooms for TMR Learners." *Quarterly Newsletter of the Laboratory of Comparative Human Cognition,* 1980, 2, 1-6.

Lord, F. M., and Novick, M. R. *Statistical Theories of Mental Test Scores.* Reading, Mass.: Addison-Wesley, 1968.

Luchins, A. S., and Luchins, E. H. *Logical Foundations of Mathematics for Behavioral Scientists.* New York: Holt, Rinehart and Winston, 1965.

MacMillan, D. L. *Mental Retardation in School and Society.* Boston: Little, Brown, 1977.

Mittler, E. "Organizational Regeneration." Unpublished doctoral dissertation, Graduate School of Management, University of California at Los Angeles, 1974.

Putnam, H. "What Theories Are Not." In E. Nagel, P. Suppes, and A. Tarski (Eds.), *Logic, Methodology, and Philosophy of Science: Proceedings of the 1960 International Congress.* Stanford, Calif.: Stanford University Press, 1962.

Quine, W. V. O. *Methods of Logic.* New York: Holt, Rinehart and Winston, 1953.

Sechrest, L. "Experiments in the Field." In R. Naroll and R. Cohen (Eds.), *A Handbook of Method in Cultural Anthropology.* New York: Columbia University Press, 1970.

Shapere, D. "Scientific Theories and Their Domains." In F. Suppe (Ed.), *The Structure of Scientific Theories.* (2nd ed.) Urbana: University of Illinois Press, 1977.

Shavelson, R. J., and Webb, N. O. "Generalizability Theory: 1973-1980." *British Journal of Mathematical and Statistical Psychology,* 1981, *34,* 133-166.

Suppe, F. (Ed.). *The Structure of Scientific Theories.* (2nd ed.) Urbana: University of Illinois Press, 1977.

Taylor, V. O. "Change of Orienting Style During Laboratory Training: A Jungian Perspective." Unpublished doctoral dissertation, Graduate School of Management, University of California at Los Angeles, 1977.

Toulmin, S. *The Philosophy of Science—An Introduction.* London: Hutchinson, 1953.

Webb, E. J., and others. *Unobtrusive Measures: Nonreactive Research in the Social Sciences.* Chicago: Rand McNally, 1966.

Whitehead, A. N., and Russell, B. *Principia Mathematica.* (2nd ed., 3 vols.) Cambridge, England: Cambridge University Press, 1910-1913.

21

Assessing Innovative Organizational Designs

Thomas G. Cummings
Susan Albers Mohrman

In the past decade, American organizations have increasingly attempted fundamental and often large-scale changes in their designs. Many of these changes involve alterations in structure, work design, management style, and human resource systems, which aim to counteract some of the deeply rooted principles of bureaucratic organizations. Quality circles and other participative approaches blur the distinction between manager as "decider" and worker as "executor" and challenge the conception that responsibility for quality, productivity, and work methods lies with specialized groups. Increased emphasis on the use of teams such as self-managing work groups, designed according to sociotechnical concepts, as a central organizing principle reverses the trend toward increasingly fractionated jobs and division of labor based on sophisticated specialization. Cooperative union-management efforts address problems in the workplace in a collaborative, as opposed to a strictly adversarial, manner.

These approaches both expand the arena of concerns of American organizations and underscore traditional business values. The quality-of-work-life movement, for example, attempts to mobilize worker commitment to valued organizational outcomes, such as efficiency, productivity, and competitiveness. It also emphasizes human outcomes as a legitimate and necessary organizational responsibility (for example, Nadler and Lawler, 1983; Walton, 1973). In part a pragmatic response to the declining competitiveness of American organizations in a worldwide economy during the early 1980s, current organizational innovations are also an attempt to address altered societal and work-force values and expectations (for example, Yankelovich, 1981; Mohrman and Lawler, 1984). What began as isolated workplace experiments (Cummings and Molloy, 1977) has become a major questioning of the tenets and traditions of American organizational life (for example, Ackoff, 1981; Ouchi, 1981; Reich, 1983). Organizations such as Motorola, Honeywell, General Motors, and Procter & Gamble (for example, Simpson, 1982-83; Beckhard, 1983) have begun to embark on nothing short of a change of culture, implying fundamental alterations in behavior and values of organizational members and transformation of organizational structures and systems.

This flurry of activity has rarely been the product of rigorous research about how to make organizations more effective. Rather, it has been stimulated more by a burgeoning popular press full of descriptive accounts of innovative approaches, with very little "rigorous" evaluation of results or in-depth analysis of the change process. Are these innovative approaches working? Are they making a difference in organizational performance? Are their benefits worth the substantial costs of implementing them? Managers who are deciding whether to try out some of these new approaches want answers to these questions. Those who have made the decision to innovate search for ways of thinking about the evaluation process.

This chapter provides an approach to assessing innovative organizational designs, such as the introduction of participative approaches to management and work design. These change programs are "messy" in that the goals, the particular changes, and the implementation process are tailored to specific organizational situations. This tailoring process requires considerable learning about and modification of the change program during implementation. Traditional evaluation methods assume that the innovation is a discrete, describable set of components whose impact can be measured and assessed. They do not capture the reality of organizational change programs and discourage innovators from systematically evaluating their efforts. What is needed is a research and evaluation framework that stresses organizational learning and innovation rather than program assessment. Such a framework is developed in this chapter.

Complex Organizational Changes

There is a tendency to conceptualize organizational-design innovations as relatively discrete, describable changes. Managers, who are accustomed to purchasing technological equipment and systems, often seek to purchase and install managerial and behavioral-change "packages" that are fully described, include specified implementation steps, and are well documented as to the improvement in organizational performance that can be expected. Management by objectives (MBO) programs, supervisory training packages, work-redesign projects, pay-incentive systems, and quality circles are among the approaches to organizational improvement that have been "put in place" in many organizations. Even social-process approaches, such as team building, third-party conflict resolution, and process consultation, often tend to be viewed as packages that can be purchased to solve operational and management problems.

Reviews of some of these change programs (for example, Cummings and Molloy, 1977) suggest that, in actuality, the implementation of these innovations is not as simple as the term *install* implies. In fact, implementation is a complicated and organization-specific process. Many innovations fail to affect organizational performance simply because they are never implemented successfully. The program often has to be altered and refined in order to fit the organizational context. Furthermore, one change, such as a new work design, often leads to others, such as extensive supervisory and employee training to understand and be able to manage the changes. All of these issues make it difficult to assess the impact of these workplace innovations on organizational performance.

A growing number of change projects are aimed at wide-ranging changes in organizational design. Quality-of-work-life programs, for example, set in motion multigroup problem solving. Structures are established to enable union and management to work cooperatively on matters of mutual concern. Lower-level employees are encouraged to generate solutions to their work-related problems. Many production systems are redesigned or designed from scratch to encourage involvement of workers in problem solving and decision making. Utilizing sociotechnical principles, such organizations are designed jointly to optimize human and organizational outcomes and, by implication, to provide meaningful work. They often include innovative reward systems, such as gain-sharing and profit-sharing plans.

There continues to be pressure from practitioners to package these changes as a sequence of identifiable steps and describable components. A large number of consulting firms promote "packages" and materials for implementing such "programs" as union-management projects, quality circles, and gain-sharing experiments. Case studies of some programs, however, underscore the complexity, unpredictability, and difficulty of successful implementation (for example, Goodman, 1979; Nadler, 1978). Organizations vary in their hospitality to these innovative approaches. What is appropriate in one setting might not fit with the people or the technology in another. Time and again, we have learned that what at first seems to be a change in one aspect of an organization, such as the reward system, actually sets in motion forces to alter other, interrelated aspects of the organization, such as the distribution of responsibility and authority and the sharing of information (Mohrman and Lawler, 1984).

This has led to approaches to organizational design that contain multiple interventions designed to simultaneously affect related aspects of the organization. Organizations such as Motorola and Honeywell are recognizing that changes in their management culture can best be achieved by addressing structural issues, reward, promotion, and selection issues, and development and training issues simultaneously. These conscious attempts to fundamentally alter organizational design often occur in parallel with technological advances such as automation in both the blue- and white-collar sectors of the organization.

In addition, many of these change programs occur in a turbulent economic environment, amid layoffs and cutbacks. There is growing recognition that the pattern of staffing and promotion and of increasing wages and benefits of the last three decades cannot be sustained in the future. This stimulates questions and experimentation concerning new structures and motivational practices in organizations. At the same time, many organizations are embarking on large-scale "programs" designed to improve quality and productivity, with interventions designed to increase teamwork and move decision making downward in the organizational hierarchy.

There is increasing realization that complex organizational change is not achieved through packaged approaches. Similarly, it is becoming apparent that there is no simple answer to the question: "Do these new organizational designs really make a difference?" Evaluation methods must fit with five salient aspects of organizational-design innovations if they are to be effective.

Simultaneous Interventions. Multiple, simultaneous interventions make it difficult to specify the change program or to isolate the aspects of it that are producing observed results. As we have seen, some of the simultaneous interventions may be related to one another, as in the case of supervisory training to support employee-participation groups. At the same time, unrelated interventions, such as the introduction of automation, may also be introducing change into the organization. This phenomenon is described in the evaluation research literature as "multiple treatment interference" (Cook and Campbell, 1979; Wortman, 1983). It confounds the interpretation of conventional research results.

Applicability to Context. Interventions are tailored to the particular organizational context. Team building, for instance, may be conducted quite differently in different organizational settings, depending on time, space, and technological constraints. Quality circles may be comprised of intact work groups in one organization, whereas volunteers from several work groups may constitute a circle in another. Furthermore, the goals of the same intervention may vary from location to location. Participation groups may be established in one company in order to foster two-way communication between management and workers; in another, the groups may be expected to generate cost savings and productivity improvements. Because change programs are adapted to the local setting, a quite different sequence of events may be described by the same generic term, such as "job enrichment," "participative management," or "quality circles." In addition, generalization from the success of a program in one setting to its likelihood of success in another is difficult. Given the desirability of local adaptation, it is questionable whether general applicability is an important concern.

Ongoing Refinement. Effective implementation of organizational change is characterized by ongoing refinement of the intervention. Aspects of the initial intervention may change as the organization finds that its organizational systems are incompatible with some of the changes that were originally envisioned. An organization that sets out to create flexible production teams by cross-training individuals and giving them responsibility for scheduling work and monitoring its progress may discover that the work is too complex to permit effective cross-training. The organization may continue to try to vest more responsibility in the team but may abandon the hope for flexible use of team members. During implementation, the original intervention may set additional changes in motion. For example, an organization that is trying to implement a quality-improvement effort may find that it must develop better quality measurement and feedback systems and must alter its reward systems to reinforce explicitly high-quality performance.

From the perspective of those who advocate rigorous statistical evaluation of innovative programs, the ongoing change and adaptation of the initial change program violate the "integrity" of the program being evaluated (Judd and Kenny, 1981; Wortman, 1983). Organizational members are motivated to avoid failure by quickly addressing unanticipated consequences, by eliminating elements of the change that do not appear to be working, and by providing support for promising additional design features and implementation activities. Although these modifications make perfect organizational sense, they provide a dilemma for the evaluation process, since it is unclear just what is being evaluated.

Change, by its nature, is necessarily a dynamic process. One extensive investigation of organizational innovation has found that it generally takes at least fourteen months after conceptualization to get an innovation implemented and upwards of three years for it to begin to bear fruit (Kanter, 1983). Many change processes are terminated before the fruit-bearing stage. It is difficult to determine an appropriate time period for observation and measurement in order to declare the innovation a success or failure. In the rapidly changing times in which we live, it is probable that major organizational disruptions will occur during implementation, introducing alternative explanations for the causes of whatever observed results do occur. In our own experience with implementing innovative organizational designs, we have found major disruptions, such as turnover of the top manager, introduction of new, centralized data systems, merger and divestiture, and major up- or down-sizing, to be the norm rather than the exception. This brings into question the plausibility of rigorous, controlled evaluation.

Organizational Learning. Successful implementation of organizational change involves considerable learning by organization members. New organizational designs can operate effectively only if people understand the design and what is expected of them in their redefined roles. They must also develop the skills and acquire the information necessary to enact the new roles successfully. Implementing organizational designs frequently requires a questioning and alteration of basic assumptions regarding the exercise of authority, the appropriate initiation of ideas, and the motivation of people. This implies learning new behaviors.

Formal training programs can begin the learning process, but, beyond that, much of it takes place by trial and error. Organizations are frequently traversing uncharted waters, with little possibility of imitating existing models. In fact, each implementation step becomes the content of the learning. Successful change depends on the creation of a "learning community" in which organizational members start with some ideas about a new way of doing things and gradually refine their understanding of what it is they are trying to do and how best to carry it out. The nature of the change as well as people's shared understanding of it are in an *ongoing* process of transformation. In our experience, those who advocate organizational change generally underestimate the amount of learning required to implement it effectively (Mohrman and Cummings, 1983).

Organizational learning during the implementation process is facilitated by the collection of information. In order to refine and tailor the change process, organizational members must be reflective and examine evidence of how well the implementation is going and how well the new design is working. Thus, ongoing processes closely resembling evaluation procedures facilitate organizational learning. Indeed, data collected from any evaluation process are potentially useful for learning how to implement organizational designs.

Goals and Values. Organizational change programs generally have multiple goals, and are guided by diverse values. Goals may include organizational outcomes such as profit or productivity, human outcomes such as satisfaction, growth, and development, and organizational-process outcomes such as improved communication, problem solving, and long-term environmental adaptation. Some of these goals may be stated, while others may be implicit. Some are readily measurable, and others are not. Some goals may be instrumental to the attainment of others; for example, improved problem solving may contribute to increased productivity. In our experience, organizations frequently begin innovative approaches, such as quality circles or sociotechnical redesigns, with improved productivity as a primary objective. They learn quickly, however, that employee growth and development are complementary objectives. In fact, failure to value and emphasize the latter often results in failure to successfully implement and institutionalize organizational-design innovations. Thus, goals develop and change over time, particularly when the organization learns that the values inherent in the change program conflict in important ways with the values underlying the current management philosophy. Thus, we have witnessed more than one organization begin simple experiments to improve quality or productivity and gradually expand its goals to a more far-reaching alteration in "culture"—the patterns of behaviors and shared assumptions that characterize the way it does business.

Continual reshaping and clarifying of goals and values necessitate a rather fluid approach to the evaluation of change programs. The process is actually circular—as organizational members examine information about the implementation and functioning of the program, they develop more realistic expectations of what it is able to achieve and, simultaneously, a better understanding of the scope of change necessary to allow new practices and behaviors to be assimilated into the organization's normal functioning.

The five aspects of the change process described here have strong implications for assessing organizational-design programs. In the next section, we contrast the assumptions and framework of traditional methods of evaluation with an approach that is more compatible with the realities and behavioral requirements of implementing innovative organizational designs.

Program Assessment: Two Views

Program assessment involves collecting information that enables evaluation of changes that organizational members carry out. Collection of data itself can be expected to affect the change situation through the reactions it evokes in the individuals being evaluated (Campbell and Stanley, 1966). The assessment process sets up predictable behavioral dynamics that have consequences for the validity and usefulness of the evaluation results. In the following pages, we will address the characteristics of two approaches to assessment, as well as their behavioral dynamics and consequences.

Traditional Program Assessment

Program assessment developed as a strong academic discipline at a time during the 1960s and 1970s when our society embarked on large numbers of social, educational, and medical programs aimed to improve the delivery of services in our country. The underlying principles and conceptualization of assessment were borrowed from experimental psychology (for example, Campbell and Stanley, 1966; Riecken and Boruch, 1974; Cook and Campbell, 1979). Key tenets of evaluation research are rigorous experimental control, reliance on the power of statistical measurement, and emphasis on replicability of results. Although assessment techniques of a more qualitative nature were advocated by some researchers, mainly in the disciplines of cultural anthropology and sociology, strong quantitative assessment formed the underpinnings of most empirical assessment work. Similarly, despite the cautions of some researchers (for example, Suchman, 1967) that the "formative" evaluation of the stages of program definition and implementation was as important as the "summative" evaluation of overall program effects, most attention has been paid to the latter. Modification of the defined program and failure to implement it adequately were not treated as phenomena whose impact on program outcomes should be studied and understood; rather, they were considered to be "error" to be statistically controlled.

The primary goal of this approach to program evaluation is to provide useful, policy-relevant information (Wortman, 1983). It helps decision makers answer the resource-allocation question: When faced with limited resources and many potential uses for them, what uses are likely to have maximum positive impact on desired objectives? Evaluation research answers this question at a macro level. It provides evidence as to the likelihood of positive effects for the population of cases (for example, organizations, groups) as a whole, not for the individual case.

The key to good evaluation design is random assignment of cases, such as organizations or work groups, to receive the treatment or change program. Observed results in this "experimental group" are compared to the results in units that did not receive the treatment, which are generally referred to as the "control group" (see Figure 21-1). Random assignment assures that peculiarities of individual cases are distributed in the comparison groups by chance rather than by design, thus ruling out the alternative explanation that the treatment was effective

Figure 21-1. Traditional Evaluation Design.

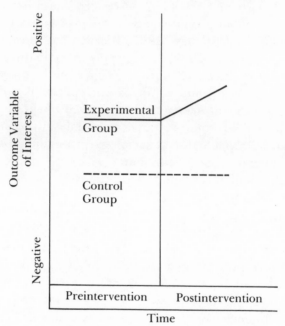

because of the self-selection of groups who were in some way unusual. Thus, in theory, a policy maker could feel more secure in answering the question: "*In general,* is this treatment (change program) likely to have a positive impact?" Moreover, because of the quantitative approach to measuring impact, a policy maker can compare the magnitude of the impact of one treatment with that of another.

As pointed out, this approach is largely concerned with broad questions of resource allocation among various priorities. Where should society place its limited service-delivery dollars? For private-sector organizations, the analogous decisions might be made by the tóp executives of a large, multiunit organization, who must decide which programs and approaches to encourage in the various units and which resources to make available. A random group of organizational units would be encouraged to try out a new approach. Outcomes in this group would be compared to a control group that did not try the new program. On the basis of the results of this evaluation process, other units would be encouraged or discouraged from implementing the approach. This use of evaluation experiments in organizations has been suggested by various academics (for example, Staw, 1977) and is employed by various large organizations with relatively sophisticated in-house research capability. In general, program evaluation is carried out by neutral outsiders, who are believed to be objective observers and skilled measurers of change.

Traditional program assessment averages the impact of change programs across a group of experimental cases. Thus, in the experimental group, the treatment may positively affect outcomes in some units but not others. If a statistical comparison of change in outcomes shows more positive change in the experimental than in the control group, the treatment is declared successful. More recently, the magnitude of positive impact is weighed against the costs of implementation to determine whether the treatment is both effective in an absolute sense and cost effective.

For the administrator or manager of an individual unit such as a plant, a small business unit, or a regional office, the results of such an analysis provide only general guidance in making resource decisions. Average results in the population of units studied do not give a probability of success for the individual unit. Furthermore, the focus on outcome measures does not provide a good understanding of the elements comprising the design of the program or of the implementation process. Unless there is substantial qualitative description of the change program as it unfolded in the most successful units, the administrator has little to go on in determining whether his or her situation is conducive to effective implementation. A considerable amount of subjective judgment is required to determine the likelihood of compatibility of the change program with a particular organizational context, the probable cost of implementation, and the likelihood that the treatment will "take" (be implemented successfully) in the setting.

This traditional evaluation model is best suited to a change program that is fully developed and specifiable. It assumes, for instance, that all experimental units implement essentially the same program and utilize similar implementation procedures. To the extent that this is not the case, error is introduced into the evaluation results. This may not be a fatal error, however, if there are enough cases so that the idiosyncrasies of particular cases are washed out by the similarities across multiple cases. Nevertheless, even proponents of this evaluation strategy caution against drawing conclusions about the efficacy of a change program when it is in developmental stages (Wortman, 1983; Cronbach and others, 1980). Once developed, however, there is a belief that evaluation research can provide "right" answers about the impact of a program.

Behavioral Dynamics of Traditional Evaluation. The underlying model of traditional program assessment is essentially that of an experiment. Organizational members who are implementing the change are very much in the role of subjects in the experimental design. The experiment is defined and executed by the researcher or evaluator, with the behavior of the individuals and the resultant impact on organizational functioning as the dependent variables. Subjects in psychological experiments often react to the experimental situation in ways that may result in erroneous learning (Orne, 1962; Wortman, 1983). "Evaluation apprehension," for example, is probably a major threat to validity, since the subjects in the experiment are unlikely to be able to differentiate between the impersonal evaluation of a treatment and the evaluation of them as organizational implementers.

Subjects in an experiment may also respond to the experimenter's expectations. They may deliberately bias their behavior or questionnaire responses to try to confirm or disconfirm the hypothesis that they believe underlies the experiment (Orne, 1962). Members of the control group, for instance, may be inclined to bias their own data because they feel left out of the change program. They may not see a benefit to their unit as a result of the data-collection efforts. Advocates and sponsors of the organizational change are likely to feel committed to it and to have a strong interest in how the evaluation turns out. They are likely to be the most threatened by the evaluation process and to have reason to portray the innovation as a success. We have encountered numerous examples where program sponsors or managers who have been encouraged by their superiors to try out a program described the change program in glowing terms despite external evidence that little implementation had occurred and little in the way of positive results had emerged from the process (for example, Mohrman and Novelli, 1984).

Administrators or managers who have publicly advocated the change process and who feel personally responsible for its success or failure may anticipate repercussions affecting their own careers if it fails. The "trapped administrator" (Campbell, 1969) may prefer to avoid the evaluation process altogether, to limit data collection, or to whitewash the results. During the early stages of implementing a change program, evaluation is often experienced by organizational members as an unnecessary and time-consuming intrusion. This is precisely the time when it is most important for managers to be collecting information about how the program is progressing and responding with sensitive implementation strategies. The "trapped administrator," on the other hand, may respond by escalating commitment to the change (Staw, 1977), increasing pressure on employees, and increasing resources and time applied to the change. This may be counterproductive, if rethinking and redirection—tailoring the change program—are required, rather than redoubling efforts in the same direction. Commitment should be to the *process* of improving the organization rather than to a particular program.

The assignment of the change program to units on a random basis or even the soliciting of "willing" units to participate in the research may set in motion another behavioral dynamic. Organizational units may agree to accept the treatment not because they are committed to its success or its goals but because they may receive special benefits through participation (Wortman, 1983). For instance, we have experienced departments who are willing to try out "participative management" because the larger corporation will provide them with extensive management training if they do. Similarly, an organizational unit may see the evaluation research itself as valuable, because it needs a systematic organizational diagnosis. In both these cases, the "program" is merely the excuse for the real goal of the decision makers and is likely to be discarded as soon as the other benefits are derived.

Consequences of Traditional Program Assessment. Ideally, a rigorous experimental evaluation design results in valid data that are helpful to managers and administrators in deciding whether to commit resources to a change program. To the extent that the behavioral dynamics discussed earlier operate, the research may fall short of this goal. It may actually result in erroneous learning. The resources spent on such evaluation might be better utilized for developmental purposes.

The characteristics of organizational-design innovations described earlier make good experimental evaluation design unlikely. The existence of multiple, simultaneous interventions, tailoring the change program to the particular situation, and ongoing refinement and modification of the design during implementation all work against tight experimental control. Yet these are the characteristics that seem to be essential to the effective implementation of organizational change. Rigorous experimental evaluation actually works against successful change if it results in poor implementation because the organization hesitates to "tamper with" the innovation. This may discourage the rich variations that naturally emerge in different organizational settings (Mohrman, Ledford, and Lawler, 1984) and may lead to homogeneity of change programs rather than to programs tailored to fit a specific situation.

The characteristics of traditional program assessment are summarized in Table 21-1, along with expected behavioral dynamics and their consequences. We will now describe an alternative approach to program assessment, which is more suited to assessing organizational-design innovations.

The Feedback/Adaptation Model of Organizational Assessment

The goal of this approach to assessment is to provide organizations with information helpful in tailoring and adjusting a

Table 21-1. Traditional Program Assessment.

	Characteristics	Behavioral Dynamics	Consequences
Goal:	Resource allocation and policy decisions	"Trapped administrator"	Resource inefficiency
For Whom?	Societal and institutional-level decision makers	Escalation of commitment to treatment	Incomplete or poor implementation of designs
		Evaluation apprehension	
What?	Fully developed programs		Erroneous learning
		Distortion of data	
Who?	Outside neutral party Objective observer		Homogeneity of change programs
How?	Experimental design Random assignment		
Measures:	Goals/outcomes largely quantitative		
Assumptions:	Objective real world static Right answers		

change program to the situation. This model expressly fits the aspects of organizational change listed earlier in this chapter. Change was depicted as varying across locations, changing through time, requiring constant adaptation to a changing context and environment, having varied and changing goals, and requiring ongoing learning on the part of organizational members. Change does not exist as a program with its own reality that retains an integrity across organizations. Rather, it exists only as enacted in various organizational settings.

The enactment of a change program is itself a dynamic process. A program will vary depending on how long it has been functioning. For example, we might examine the introduction of a gain-sharing plan (Doyle, 1982) into a manufacturing plant. A gain-sharing plan has two basic design elements: an economic formula for distributing part of the improvement in economic performance to employees and mechanisms through which employees can participate in improving performance. Many aspects of such plans might change over time. The design of the plan itself, including its economic formula, its participative mechanisms, or the frequency of payout, may be modified. During the first years, the payout may be too large, with insufficient retained earnings to permit capital improvements. This may lead to a modification in the economic formula for distribution of gain. Employee understanding of the plan will probably increase, including knowledge of the performance and of the areas in which the employee's own actions can have a favorable impact on the measures. At first, supervisors and managers may play a more central role in employee problem-solving processes than they do after employees have learned more about the business. Supervisors and managers may alter their ways of dealing with the work force as they experience and come to expect responsible, results-oriented behavior from individuals at all levels. These are but a few of the dynamic aspects of such a change process. The key point is that there is not a simple answer to the question: Is a gain-sharing plan an effective way to increase organizational performance? Even within the same organization with the same plan, effectiveness will vary over time, the plan will change, and the elements that are responsible for the results will differ in different time periods.

Given such a changing, dynamic process, it would be difficult to try to identify a period when it is possible to say: "The change program has been successfully implemented, and it is time to evaluate whether it helps." Even if the time were to arrive when a program is relatively stable, it is clear that the organization needs to assess how it is working long before then if it is to do the modifying and tailoring that are so often necessary during implementation.

The feedback/adaptation assessment model does not view organizational-design innovations as packages designed by experts and put in place in organizations. Rather, the true designers are the organizational members. They become aware of ideas and innovations from the behavioral science and practitioner communities and decide to try them out (Notz, Salipante, and Waters, 1976). They must first put them in the context of their own values, goals, technology, and contextual constraints and fashion an approach that makes sense to them. In short, they design the specific change program themselves.

Assessment is an ongoing process, whether formal or informal. As soon as organizational members begin to implement their changes, they collect data concerning how things are going. As they run into obstacles, they adapt the program to overcome them. Thus, there is a constant cycle of feedback and adaptation, which may ultimately result in the innovation looking very different from what was originally anticipated. Through such an adaptation process, the original change program may even be abandoned in favor of changes that embody quite different principles.

The hypothetical plant that implemented the gain-sharing plan referred to earlier might serve as an example of this feedback and adaptation process. After several years, the plant may discover that it cannot, as currently designed, continue to improve productivity sufficiently for the plan to pay out to employees. Most of the major production problems have been solved, and the plant is functioning smoothly at a steadily improving rate, but not quite well enough to yield enough gain to be shared. This may result in low morale and disillusionment on the part of employees who liked the plan, enjoyed participating in productivity-enhancement processes, and liked the financial payout. Rather than abandon gain sharing altogether, the plant may decide to automate parts of its production process and utilize employee problem-solving skills to help with implementing and debugging the automated processes. It may also train operators in the technical skills necessary to maintain automated equipment, thus reducing the need to rely on contract maintenance. In the end, the plant may be substantially more productive than before because of the automation or the gain-sharing plan, and the economic gains that are paid out may be substantial. Given such a scenario, it seems pointless to ask whether it was gain sharing or automation that resulted in the productivity improvement. Various changes combined to produce those results.

Although the feedback/adaptation model describes a process that happens naturally, it is frequently not done well. We see many examples of premature abandonment of change programs because of lack of results. Often, a program is abandoned before successful implementation of the design components. In some cases, this reflects a judgment that successful implementation has too many costs associated with it; in others, managers appear unaware that effective implementation was not achieved. In yet others, organizational members do not develop a good understanding of the obstacles and problems that are encountered and are unable to develop strategies for overcoming them. Often, key people are unaware that a change program is in trouble until it is already dead.

To establish an effective feedback/adaptation assessment process, it is necessary to design a system for collecting feedback data and for tailoring the change program. At first, the implementation process must be carefully monitored to determine whether the program components "take"—that is, whether they are successfully implemented. If not, additional implementation steps or altered designs might be instituted. In addition, organizational members should track performance indicators. They should monitor the short-term impact of the program on performance goals. In this way, they become aware of unanticipated consequences and of performance decrements caused by utilization of resources during implementation. Corrective action can be taken before it is too late. In addition, long-term trend data are useful in making overall assessments of the approach. Such long-term data might lead the organization to alter course significantly or to add major design components to the change program. For example, because of long-term trend data, the gain-sharing plant described earlier realized the necessity of making major alterations in its capital-equipment and production processes in order to sustain productivity improvement.

The ongoing process of feedback and adaptation can be performed by a design team, working closely with other organizational members to sense both the successful and problematical aspects of the change program. This group must be trusted by the rest of the organization, have access to relevant information about the program and its effects, and have enough power to make necessary modifications. Ultimately, the organization as a whole must learn to manage change. This requires that organizational members learn together and that they develop a shared definition of how things will be done differently. They must establish a "learning community" as a component of successful organizational change.

Behavioral Dynamics of the Feedback/Adaptation Process. This approach to assessment is relatively new, and there is not much literature or experience upon which to draw in describing the behavioral dynamics. We have worked with several organizations that are utilizing this approach, and we will describe the dynamics that we have experienced in them.

The major behavioral manifestation of this assessment approach is a feeling of "ownership" and, consequently, control of the change process. Organizational members decide what to do, assess it, modify it, and determine whether to continue. They do not simply implement something that someone else has designed or decided they should do. Because of this commitment, they experience a strong desire to make the change program work effectively. After all, they are to blame if it goes poorly. The process of collecting data, analyzing alternatives, and generating actions is familiar to most managers. There is frequently an initial enthusiasm for the process. Because they are making decisions that they must live with, individuals engaged in this feedback/adaptation process are motivated to generate valid data about the change program and to go through a careful examination of alternative courses of action.

Enthusiasm depends on the credibility of the assessment process. In organizations where managers have not experienced autonomy in the past and where they find the context to be unpredictable and demanding, there may be a reluctance to assume the responsibility inherent in the feedback/adaptation process. In this climate, establishing a learning community will be much slower and more difficult. Creating a culture for the open exchange of information and joint problem solving is time consuming even in healthy organizations.

Initial enthusiasm can be dampened when the amount of time involved in establishing and carrying out this assessment process becomes apparent. Managers become discouraged by the time they must spend both collecting and reflecting on data. This time, which is essential to the process of guiding the change process, is seen at first as unproductive, particularly when it leads to additional implementation procedures that also consume time. Ironically, either time is the cure for this impatience, or impatience kills the change program. Once confronted by the problems and unanticipated consequences set in motion by the changes, management may either become motivated to spend the time to work them through or decide to abandon the change process altogether.

A design team that has made the commitment actively to assess and steer the change process faces the task of learning how to do this effectively. In addition to learning basic organizational-design concepts and becoming familiar with various approaches to data collection and assessment, the group must become effective problem solvers. Even experienced managers are generally surprised to find how ineffective they are at learning as a group (Argyris and Schön, 1978). When a process consultant facilitates and trains the group, the group must overcome the tendency to turn the change program over to the consultant and thus lose ownership of the outcomes.

Consequences of the Feedback/Adaptation Assessment Model. Although difficult to establish, this approach contributes to effective change in organizations. Local ownership of the design, as well as ongoing refinement and modification of it, are characteristics of successful behavioral change. The change may not resemble what was envisioned early in the process. But through ongoing modification and refinement, congruence can be established between the changes and other aspects of the organizational context. This congruence is necessary if the change program is to become integrated into the organization's normal functioning.

Another consequence of this assessment method is organizational learning. As design teams work through the issues of change and assessment, their understanding of the organization increases, as does their ability to work effectively as a team. One secondary consequence of this learning is that organizational members utilize their knowledge, skill, and understanding in making decisions and designing approaches that fit their specific operating needs. Conducting the assessment process at the local level, with refinement and modification of goals, results in a greater heterogeneity of innovative organizational approaches. Overall, it should also result in greater resource efficiency as both evaluation and implementation resources are expended on innovations that fit more closely with the contextual realities of organizations.

The characteristics, behavioral dynamics, and consequences of the feedback/adaptation assessment model are summarized in Table 21-2.

Summary

Two approaches to assessing organizational change have been described in this chapter. The first, a traditional program approach, stresses rigorous quantitative measurement using an experimental paradigm. Such an approach is designed to provide an answer to the question: "In general, is this an effective treatment?" Emphasis is placed on replicability of a program and on tight control of the experimental design and, by implication, of the implementation process. We have argued that this approach is not suited to complex organizational change. Successful implementation of change programs precludes the kind of external

Table 21-2. Feedback/Adaptation Assessment Model.

	Characteristics	Behavioral Dynamics	Consequences
Goal:	Tailor and adjust the design	Seeking valid, reliable data	Learning
For Whom?	Members of experimenting organization	Motivated to succeed	Design adaptation/implementation
What?	Process of change Self-design	Self-reflection, experimentation	Resource efficiency
Who?	Design team	Generate alternatives	
How?	Ongoing assessment Detailed case analyses	Impatience with time	Heterogeneity of change designs
Measures:	Quantitative Short- and long-term Qualitative Implementation		
Assumptions:	Change is dynamic Differs across organizations Alternative answers		

control and tight specification of treatment that are required for experimental rigor. Furthermore, the conditions of experimentation may set in motion behavioral patterns, such as evaluation apprehension, that distort findings and result in erroneous learning.

The second model of assessing organizational change aims to provide the organization with feedback that is helpful in guiding its own change process. Both quantitative and qualitative data are collected by the organizational members themselves, in order to learn about the short-term and long-term effects of the change program. This information is used to make modifications in the program, including the implementation procedures. In order to effectively conduct this kind of internal assessment, a feedback and learning system must be established to guide the implementation process. The product of this second kind of assessment is a more effective system for organizational innovation and learning. If documented, the results of this assessment process can provide rich and detailed case studies that can serve as examples for organizations contemplating such changes.

When organizations are searching for better ways to do things, it is imperative that they become skilled at implementing and learning from new approaches. Developing an effective feedback and adaptation system can remove some of the risk of innovation by assessing how changes are progressing and by making necessary modifications. Qualitative descriptions of this adaptation process can be of great help to organizations contemplating change. They can provide a much richer description of the nature of organizational change than traditional program assessment methods.

References

Ackoff, R. L. *Creating the Corporate Future.* New York: Wiley, 1981.

Argyris, C., and Schön, D. A. *Organizational Learning: A Theory of Action Perspective.* Reading, Mass.: Addison-Wesley, 1978.

Beckhard, R. "Conversation with Edson W. Spencer and Foster
A. Boyle, Honeywell Corporation." *Organizational Dynamics,* Spring 1983, pp. 21-45.

Campbell, D. T. "Reforms as Experiments." *American Psychologist,* 1969, *24,* 409-429.

Campbell, D. T. " 'Degrees of Freedom' and the Case Study."
In T. D. Cook and C. S. Reichardt (Eds.), *Qualitative and
Quantitative Methods in Evaluation Research.* Beverly Hills,
Calif.: Sage, 1979.

Campbell, D. T., and Stanley, J. C. *Experimental and Quasi-Experimental Designs for Research.* Chicago: Rand McNally,
1966.

Cook, T. D., and Campbell, D. T. *Quasi-Experimentation Design and Analysis Issues for Field Settings.* Chicago: Rand
McNally, 1979.

Cronbach, L. J., and others. *Toward Reform of Program Evaluation: Aims, Methods, and Institutional Arrangements.* San
Francisco: Jossey-Bass, 1980.

Cummings, T. G., and Molloy, E. S. *Improving Productivity
and the Quality of Work Life.* New York: Praeger, 1977.

Doyle, R. J. "Gainsharing: A Total Productivity Approach."
Journal of Contemporary Business, 1982, *2* (2), 57-70.

Goodman, P. S. *Assessing Organizational Change: The Rushton
Quality of Work Experiment.* New York: Wiley-Interscience,
1979.

Judd, C. M., and Kenny, D. A. *Estimating the Effects of Social
Interventions.* Cambridge, England: Cambridge University
Press, 1981.

Kanter, R. *The Change Masters: Innovations for Productivity in
the American Mode.* New York: Simon & Schuster, 1983.

Mohrman, S. A., and Cummings, T. G. "Implementing Quality
of Work Life Programs." In R. Ritvo and A. Sargent (Eds.),
The NTL Management Book. Washington, D.C.: Institute of
Applied Behavioral Science, National Training Laboratories,
1983.

Mohrman, S. A., and Lawler, E. E., III. "Quality of Work Life."
In K. Rowland and G. Ferris (Eds.), *Personnel and Human
Resources Management.* Vol. 2. Greenwich, Conn.: JAI Press,
1984.

Mohrman, S. A., Ledford, G., and Lawler, E. E., III. *Study of Honeywell Participation Groups.* Los Angeles: Center for Effective Organizations, University of Southern California, 1984.

Mohrman, S. A., and Novelli, L., Jr. "Beyond Testimonials: Learning from a Quality Circles Programme." *Journal of Occupational Behavior,* 1984.

Nadler, D. A. "Hospitals, Organized Labor and Quality of Work: An Intervention Case Study." *Journal of Applied Behavioral Science,* 1978, *14* (3), 366–381.

Nadler, D. A., and Lawler, E. E., III. "Quality of Worklife: Perspectives and Directions." *Organizational Dynamics,* 1983, *10* (1), 20–30.

Notz, W. W., Salipante, P. E., and Waters, J. A. "Innovation in Site: A Contingency Approach to Human Resource Development." Unpublished working paper, Department of Administrative Sciences, University of Manitoba, 1976.

Orne, M. T. "On the Social Psychology of the Psychological Experiment: With Particular Reference to Demand Characteristics and Their Implications." *American Psychologist,* 1962, *17,* 776–783.

Ouchi, W. G. *Theory Z: How American Businesses Can Meet the Japanese Challenge.* Reading, Mass.: Addison-Wesley, 1981.

Reich, R. B. *The Next American Frontier.* New York: Times Books, 1983.

Riecken, H. W., and Boruch, R. F. *Social Experimentation: A Method for Planning and Evaluating Social Intervention.* New York: Academic Press, 1974.

Simpson, E. L. "Motorola's Participative Management Program." *National Productivity Review,* 1982–83, *2* (1), 56–63.

Staw, B. M. "The Experimenting Organization: Problems and Prospects." In B. M. Staw (Ed.), *Psychological Foundations of Organizational Behavior.* Santa Monica, Calif.: Goodyear Press, 1977.

Suchman, E. A. *Evaluative Research.* New York: Russell Sage Foundation, 1967.

Walton, R. E. "Quality of Working Life: What Is It?" *Sloan Management Review,* 1973, *14,* 11–21.

Wortman, P. M. "Evaluation Research: A Methodological Perspective." *Annual Review of Psychology,* 1983, *34,* 223–260.

Yankelovich, D. "New Rules in American Life: Searching for Self-Fulfillment in a World Turned Upside Down." *Psychology Today,* 1981, *17* (4), 35–91.

22

Integrating
the Diverse Directions
of the Behavioral Sciences

Peter B. Vaill

"The simplest truth you can ever write about our history," I believe the critic Bernard De Voto once said to Catherine Drinker Bowen, "will be charged and surcharged with romanticism, and if you are afraid of the word you had better start practising seriously on your fiddle." Perhaps it is debatable that an essay such as this chapter should rest on De Voto's principle, but all my experience with the behavioral sciences over the past twenty years confirms the rightness of his judgment for my task. Particularly if we are going to seek *simple* truth, as we must to discuss such a vast subject in a limited space, our search must focus on the essential grounds on which the behavioral sciences rest and on the essential energy from which they draw their spirit. Further, De Voto's call is to write with the same spirit that infuses the subject, and, if this goal is achieved, the mood of this chapter will merely be consistent with the best writing in the behavioral sciences that has gone before it.

It is, of course, the "applied behavioral sciences" with which this chapter is directly concerned, those disciplines and fields that have sought not merely to understand but to change human systems of all kinds. While these disciplines are not found exclusively in professional schools of management, I will further limit the present scope by concentrating mainly on schools of management and their respective client populations of students, practicing managers, and formal organizations. I do not restrict my focus to *business* schools, however, for schools and programs in public administration, educational administration, and health services administration have also involved themselves deeply in the applied behavioral sciences. One of the criticisms that has frequently been made of the applied behavioral sciences in schools of this kind is that these sciences are too heroic, too idealistic, too romantic in just the sense that De Voto urges. Perhaps, therefore, our critics will be happier with the focus of this chapter than will those with whose work it is concerned.

To suggest that a spirit of romanticism has run through the applied behavioral sciences is certainly not to say that this has supplied them with any unifying theme or paradigm. In fact, the spirit has more often been of contention and contradiction. We have seen "East Coast" and "West Coast" approaches, "micro versus macro" approaches, quantitative jousting with qualitative, and confrontational versus accepting intervention styles. Ambivalence about power has been a popular means of name-calling. Empiricism only barely coexists with introspective, armchair methods where an N of 1 is more than sufficient.

A subtler but no less pervasive tension lies in the extent to which one theorist or another is concerned with *organizational* effectiveness, as opposed to the welfare and development of individuals within the organization. Perhaps McGregor best articulated the "integrative" approach in his famous statement that management's job is to show the employees that they can best fulfill their own goals by pursuing the goals of the organization (McGregor, 1960, p. 49). On this point, it is significant that the battle over the possibility of integration still rages in the work of Scott and Hart (1979) and Denhardt (1981), echoing the earlier calls to arms of Argyris (1957) and Whyte (1957).

Another source of tension, perhaps a more chronic one as

the conceptual and stylistic squabbles come and go, stems from the interrelationships among teaching, research, and intervention in organizational affairs. All professional schools hold this troika of missions, but the applied behavioral sciences in management schools may have been going through an especially difficult version of the associated puzzles and contradictions. The difficulty is this: since a significant portion of the subject matter has been about improving human relationships, the subject matter has acted back on the modes of teaching and research and intervention themselves. It is one thing to teach traditionally about participation and quite another to teach participatively about participation. It is one thing to do orthodox research on the situational nature of the manager's role, but "situational" research in which traditional canons of objective, positivist inquiry must be violated because they alienate the investigator from the very setting that he or she is trying to understand is something else entirely. It is hard to be ethically powerful about the ethics of power, hard to be accepting of feedback about one's lecture on feedback.

The social system of the classroom profoundly influences what one can teach on the subject of social systems. Nowhere else in higher education, *ever,* has a community of scholars taken more seriously the truth of the classroom as a social system than have the applied behavioral scientists of the last forty years. They have paid a high price for it, too—in relation to their faculty colleagues, their students, and their clients in organizations. The price, stated colloquially, has been constantly to risk looking silly, unorganized, unsure of what one wants to do. It has been to hear one's highest aspirations for the quality of the learning setting dismissed as a preoccupation with the "touchy-feely" aspects of teaching. In sum, the subject matter is thoroughly self-reflexive: the professional is expected not only to profess but to apply his or her professional wisdom and skill to his or her own behavior as a professional.

Tough-mindedness and ingenuity in this enterprise can be perceived only when one understands the balancing act it entails, and few scholars in the field have succeeded in establishing the credibility of all the various norms they are trying to be re-

sponsive to all at once. "What price human relations?" asked
one of the lions of the marketing faculty of the Harvard Business
School, Malcolm McNair, many years ago as he stood below
his behavioral scientist colleagues on their high wire and
selectively criticized their teetering (Roethlisberger, 1977, pp.
282–286). He thought that *he* was being tough-minded in suggesting
that applied behavioral scientists did not care enough for
what we would today call "the bottom line." He intended his
question rhetorically, and he thought that the answer was obvious.
In fact, his question was and is literally the right one, and
the answer is far from obvious. It has been a stressful business
to pursue the applied behavioral sciences in and out of academe
—and no trade for the bashful.

In the face of all the crosscurrents, criticisms, and contradictions,
there is one story in particular that the applied behavioral
sciences have told themselves to sustain the endeavor, the
story of the essentially scientific nature of their effort. The continued
existence of an academic curriculum in the applied behavioral
sciences and the growth of a profession in the world of
practice have been largely based on the idea that there is indeed
a discipline *here,* that there are indeed theories in the normal
meaning of theory, research findings in their normal meaning,
and academic standards commensurate with other disciplines.
Knowledge does cumulate as the story of science suggests, and
the careers of individual scholars display the growth of competence
in one subfield or another just as in other academic fields.

These and other correlative processes have been "the
story," a story that is told and retold by faculty in doctoral dissertation
defenses, in research proposals to funding agencies, in
deliberations of promotion and tenure committees, in course
descriptions and syllabi, and in all the other places where the
question to the applied behavioral scientist is, "What do you
know? What have you got?" It is a story that is between the
lines of every stand-up presentation—or, perhaps, to be more
accurate, of most stand-up presentations of behavioral science
concepts and research, for there are some curious renegades in
the field who do not subscribe to the story and are willing to
say so out loud.

The story of the applied behavioral sciences *as sciences,* I am saying, has functioned as a litany, in a neutral sense of the term, for explaining what they are about to students, practitioners, colleagues in other fields, and anyone else who is wondering about the soundness of the field. A central thesis of this chapter is that this "story" of the scientific nature of the applied behavioral sciences may have fulfilled important functions from time to time, but it is not their central feature, it never has been, and it will cause progressively more trouble in the future. The "diverse directions of the behavioral sciences" do have themes and continuities and thrilling interrelationships, I will argue, but they are not the stuff of science in its orthodox sense; and further, I will suggest that the road that the story of science is taking us down has atrophy and sterility at its end, if indeed we are not there already!

Let us reflect for a few minutes on the scientific status of some of the building blocks of the applied behavioral sciences. I have to be selective in this effort, and what I select is quite open to accusations of erecting straw men; had I chosen my examples differently, one might claim, I would not be able to say what I do. Well, perhaps, but I do not think so. There may be other ideas than those I discuss whose scientific status is more secure, but the real point of my discussion is what these various ideas *come to* as vehicles for teaching, research, and intervention. No matter how scientific an idea starts out being, it comes to atrophy and sterility when it is handled in the *way* that the applied behavioral sciences have handled their basic ideas. It is to a discussion and critique of this *way of handling ideas* that I now turn.

Theory X and Theory Y—One More Time

Let us begin with what has perhaps been the single most powerful and well-known idea produced by the applied behavioral sciences in the past three decades—Theory X and Theory Y (McGregor, 1960). Is it possible to say anything new about this old war-horse of an idea? I think it is; in fact, I do not think that the three most interesting things about it have been

discussed very much at all. These three things are (1) what the
idea is based on, (2) how McGregor got the idea, and (3) what
the idea is really a theory of. All three of the points, and our inability to discuss them very well, will serve to introduce my
argument about what the "story of science" has been doing to
us. (For readers new to the field, perhaps I do need to emphasize once again that McGregor's idea has had enormous influence. It is one that thousands of managers have heard of, been
trained in, debated, and tried to apply. The book that introduced it is one of the largest-selling management books of all
time. If MBAs of the last twenty-five years remember nothing
else from their management classes, they remember this idea,
however vaguely.)

The simple answer to what Theory X and Theory Y are
based on is "Maslow's Need Hierarchy" (Maslow, 1954), the
idea that there is a predictable sequence in which various kinds
of human needs will influence a person's behavior. The animal
and human research on which Maslow based his concept has
never to my knowledge been seriously criticized by the applied
behavioral sciences. The categories of needs he suggested and
their hierarchical arrangement have been taken pretty much as
given. The form of McGregor's argument was: Since Maslow is
right, we will misunderstand people if we do not realize where
they are on the need hierarchy. Adding a crucial assumption not
contained in the need theory, that people have no natural aversion to work, McGregor then crystallized a way of thinking
about employees that would be consistent with the needs that
Maslow said they had. He called it "Theory Y." It became *the
way to think of people,* as contrasted with Theory X, which was
portrayed as *not the way to think of people.*

Science says that theory should be value free and should
not predispose one to act one way or another toward the world.
In its value-free form, Maslow's need hierarchy could be just as
useful to a Theory X manager as to a Theory Y manager, the
difference being that the one presumably has motives of personal domination over people and the other is interested in fostering an effective work climate. But this is not what happened
in the development of the applied behavioral sciences. Instead,

Theory Y came to be identified as "science-based," and Theory X came to be identified as "science-indifferent." "Science tells us that you should act like Theory Y if you want to be an effective manager"—that has been the story. All kinds of additional imagery got added on through time: Theory Y was "good," X was "bad"; Y managers were "for people," X managers were "against people"; Y managers were "humanistic," X managers were "authoritarian"; and so on, all based on research of unknown quality from another field, enriched with an unsupported assumption about people's willingness to work, and translated into a prescription for action that sounded so right that it tended to become dogma from the hour of its promulgation.

So much for what the idea is based on. How did McGregor get the idea? Well, the answer is simple but unsatisfying: we do not know. We do not know what peculiar conjunction of experience, interests, values, biases, and energies combined themselves in McGregor to produce this quite interesting synthesis. The external details of McGregor's life and professional interests may be of some help, but not decisive. It would help if we knew, for instance, that he was consistently appalled by the way he heard managers talk about their employees—but that is not known one way or another, at least to me.

Orthodox science is willing to let scientists get their ideas in all kinds of crazy ways and in all kinds of crazy places. Popper (1968) declares that induction is not and cannot be a purely logical, accountable process (p. 32), for, however McGregor did what he did, the act was a piece of induction. But orthodox science has a control system, namely, that once a new theory is propounded, it is tested by established methods of research and that "claims" are not to be treated as "knowledge" until the deductive connection between the world of theory and the world of observable events can be shown—until a theory has "proved its mettle," as Popper says (p. 33). This is not what tends to happen in the applied behavioral sciences, and for very good reasons: inductive ideas about human behavior are blendings of observable data and values about the data. Testing of hypotheses flowing from such ideas cannot be merely the attempt to predict the factual portion of such ideas, for, without the companion value judgments woven all through the hypothesis, it can be a relatively empty, even an absurd claim. As everyone who has ever presented Theory X and Theory Y to managers knows, someone *always* sticks up their hand and says, "What about Vince Lombardi? What about General Patton? What about Toscanini? They were able to get people to do things, weren't they? They certainly didn't cater to people's 'needs,' did they?" "That is not the point," the presenter would like to say to such a question but rarely does. "What I am trying to get you to do is *value* your people differently as well as see their psychology differently." The presenter rarely owns up to the value judgments running all through Theory X and Y, because to do so would take the conversation off into the dangerous land of value debate, something most applied behavioral scientists have been loath to address.

Alternatively, the presenter does permit a value debate to get started, but the conclusion is *never,* at least in my experience, that the superiority of Theory Y over X is primarily dependent on agreement with McGregor's values about people and about power. Theory X and Theory Y are still on the final exam or still in the training notebook at the next session, as if the value debate had *never occurred.* Furthermore, although there is this "pressure" toward value debates in the discussion of virtually all concepts in the applied behavioral sciences, the profession has not valued the capacity to engage in value discussion and debate. The capacity has not itself been an object of learning. The capacity to engage in an intelligent discussion of values has been for centuries a mark of the liberally educated person, but the applied behavioral sciences apparently have not realized that their subject matter tests this capacity perhaps as much as or more than any other field. The typical discussion of values in the typical management classroom or training session is rarely more than a bull session and is usually experienced as just that by participants. Values will not be on the final exam; values are not the "competencies to be attained." The difference between Theory X and Theory Y is what one is supposed to remember.

So, in sum, we have Theory Y as an interesting induction,

but resting on an unexamined data base. It generates hypotheses about action in the world that intertwine facts and values, thus rendering such hypotheses untestable by objective testing methods. However, the value content of Theory Y is, at best, mentionable only as a kind of supplementary aspect of the basic assertion and, at worst, is undiscussible, because to discuss values would uncover the nonscientific nature of the original induction. No wonder Theory Y is so frustrating to teach and to learn alike: its substantive roots are hopelessly tangled.

What if we did try to "test Theory X and Theory Y"? Ignoring for the moment the problem of the mixture of facts and values in all hypotheses from Theory X and Theory Y, what could we try to test? The usual answer is, "Does Theory Y 'work'?" However, I think that there is a prior hypothesis in McGregor's idea that, so far as I know, has not been noticed in the twenty-five years since he originally stated it. Curiously, even ironically, it is an unstated hypothesis that gets *disconfirmed* every time Theory X and Theory Y are presented to a group of students or managers. McGregor is regularly proved wrong, and no one notices! For McGregor's idea is not about human motivation and employee needs at all, even though that is the conventional blue-book answer. McGregor's idea is this: "There are two kinds of managers in the world: those who hold Theory X assumptions and those who hold Theory Y assumptions." In moving on quickly to assert the efficacy of one view over the other, attention is diverted from the basic assertion, "there are two kinds of managers in the world." In classrooms and training sessions, there are *always* more than two kinds of managers in the room, and they speak up vociferously. Long before Ouchi (1981), learners were inventing various kinds of "Theory Zs" to deal with the stark dichotomy that their instinct detected as oversimplified but that was so difficult to talk about against the "science" on which McGregor's idea was supposedly based.

In retrospect, McGregor's idea would have been much easier to discuss, and possibly even more fruitful, had he stated his dichotomy as: "There are two kinds of managers in the world: those who have a way of thinking about employees that

is consistent with Maslow's need theory, and everybody else."
But he did not do that, because he was as determined to declare
the punitive, authoritarian style *invalid* as he was to establish an
alternative style. His values led him in this direction.

This lengthy discussion of McGregor is intended to apply
to the vast bulk of ideas that the applied behavioral sciences
have been relying on. I can state in propositional form what I
think has been happening outside of the awareness of the profession, telling itself as it does its story of the scientific nature
of itself.

1. Brilliant inductions about humanity, organizations,
power, groups, communication, change, and so forth have regularly been forthcoming from men and women whose understanding of the world was essentially a clinical one, grounded
in a deep concern for the improvement of the lot of individual
human beings and for the effectiveness of human institutions.

2. Because of the general need for academic respectability and credibility to the outside world (Simon, 1981, p. 130),
these inductions were portrayed as "science," as comparable
with the systematic knowledge that the natural sciences had already established in the public mind as trustworthy.

3. What was *really* interesting about these inductions was
the way these clinical sensitivities work in the personalities of
the men and women producing them. However, these sensitivities were not given very much attention, for several reasons. For
one thing, language for discussing them was largely absent. For
another, while values play a central role, to declare their centrality would undercut the force of the induction. Further, it even
may have seemed vaguely narcissistic to analyze these sensitivities, for the only way to do it really well would be to talk about
oneself. The towering self-descriptions of Carl Rogers and a few
others notwithstanding, few applied behavioral scientists have
been willing to be that open (Rogers, 1961, pp. 273-278; Tannenbaum and Davis, 1970, pp. 129-149).

4. The combination of value-infused ideas emanating
from unexamined and relatively invisible clinical sensitivities,
on the one hand, and operating in a mode giving the appearance
of scientific conduct, on the other, thus arrives at the point of
application innocently but multiply disguised. In the face of

such a confused background of the ideas that the applied behavioral sciences present, it is not surprising that the applied behavioral science culture has come to value a presentation style mixing humor, diffidence, earnestness, and flair. The ideas themselves seem oversimplified and even naive when not vivified with the feeling for them that is so common in the presentation styles of applied behavioral scientists. It is not deception I am talking about, not proselytizing; rather, I am suggesting that the ideas are both abstract content and personal meaning—not one or the other, but both. As content alone, they are relatively commonplace, as can be seen in any standard textbook in the field. In fact, to extend this thought, the electricity is further heightened when the listener/learners have a genuine and conscious need to experience what the idea is saying and promises—that is, when personal meanings of their own mesh with the ideas and personal meanings that the leader is bringing to the session. When a teacher or trainer says, "That was a terrific session," what he or she really means is that the ideas were interesting, he or she was really "on," and the audience was genuinely excited about what they were hearing. The regular occurrence of such events has been the lifeblood of the field.

5. The field is abstract ideas and personal meanings; not one or the other, not one mainly and the other secondarily, not first one, then the other. Thus, the meaning of the phrase "integrating the diverse directions of the behavioral sciences" is quite different from its conventional one. As "ideas-and-meanings," the divergences are more understandable, for they are fed as much by divergences of values as they are by divergences of substance. As the people change in the field, divergences occur. "Integration" of ideas-and-meanings means integration not just of ideas and research findings but of the *community* of investigators, renewed valuing of style differences and the treating of style (meanings) as problematical and evolving, rather than just as "one particular person's way of doing their thing."

Sensitivity Training: A Rueful History

These are learnings that derive from examining the field's interpretation and use of Theory X and Theory Y. A second example will further illuminate some of the difficulties and the opportunities that exist today. The example I have chosen is the method of working with individuals and groups known as "sensitivity training," or variously as "T-groups," "encounter groups," and other names. Even more than Theory X and Theory Y, sensitivity training is now something that most people have heard of, think they understand, know the strengths and weaknesses of, and so forth. Sensitivity training is much more a cultural phenomenon than Theory X and Theory Y, which never got very far outside the world of professional management. Sensitivity training can now be routinely mentioned on TV talk shows and soap operas. It is now even more the stuff of parody than it is regarded as anything of any very central significance in human affairs—basically just one more nutty idea fom the sixties, many people feel, something the "me generation" invented and not to be taken too seriously. Yet here is a kind of philosophy and clinical practice that can still produce profound learning and other experiences of the deepest sort, even among the most jaded and skeptical. However, it is no longer the "thing to do" to go through a group, so the jaded and skeptical are being spared in increasing numbers, and as the generation of great group facilitators we produced in the fifties and sixties passes into retirement, it will soon be possible to be just as lonely in this culture as it ever was, with no place save the corner psychiatrist to talk about it.

My values are showing. I think that sensitivity training is the most original and powerful contribution that the applied behavioral sciences have made to civilized culture. In the next few lines, I want both to elaborate on this judgment and to try to show how the profession's confusion about sensitivity training has pretty much removed whatever operative promise it had. Once again, as with McGregor, I will be discussing some overlooked aspects more than those that have been most often debated. I will not be concerned with whether sensitivity training "works," with the "ethics" of it, or with the alleged psychological aberrations of those who practiced it. In what has been overlooked about sensitivity training lie some clues to our problem of integrating the diverse directions of the behavioral sciences.

I approach the question with some trepidation, however, for, unlike Theory X and Theory Y, sensitivity training has real enemies. The enemies of Theory X and Theory Y attack by yawning; not so with sensitivity training. Furthermore, the many who have known it in one way or another have thought deeply about it, and one hesitates to announce that something new will be said. But, for all the profound thought that individuals have given to sensitivity training, the profession has not been able to sustain the synthesis of theory, practice, research, and humanistic values that marked it at its best—in its golden years, so to speak.

Here are some of the key things that were not well enough understood by it. The first has already been mentioned —the excitement, pro, con, and otherwise, that the idea of sensitivity training generated. Events occurred within and among people in sensitivity training groups to which it was almost impossible to remain indifferent. That these events happened at all was the shock, whether one was a member or observer, a trainer or evaluator, thrilled or appalled. There was a magnetism to the events in a sensitivity training group that was extraordinary. Yet the debate was not about *that*—the debate was over whether it should or should not be happening, what such events "meant," whether it was more a religion than anything else.

It was very difficult to contemplate the social invention itself as a fruit of our values, knowledge, and aspirations, for the demand from friends and foes alike was that we be able to say more about it than just that. To contemplate it as a fruit of a particular profession at a particular moment in history might have told that profession a great deal about itself. It might have helped that profession to see more clearly that it was not a "science" in any conventional sense, that it was a profession "charged and surcharged with romanticism," as De Voto said, that when theory and practice and need did finally conjoin in settings where they could genuinely communicate, quite extraordinary flowerings of thought and feeling were possible, all of which might have suggested to the "diverse behavioral sciences" that this conjoining of theory, practice, need, and congenial setting might be what it was really about as an enterprise.

Perhaps it was not after all an "applied science," with the connotation of a one-way transmission of systematic knowledge and technique from guru-experts to neophytes. The guru-experts never talked to each other about "applying science to group members," but, in its public representation, this image was allowed to persist. To argue against it would have required the guru-experts to admit that they learned as much themselves as they "taught" in sensitivity training groups, that the experience was ever new and enormously fulfilling, that they yearned for a setting such as this where they could get beyond the pretenses and sterilities of normal academic and professional life— that, fundamentally, this was a place where they could fulfill their values. This could not be the "public version" of sensitivity training, for, again, it would have entailed personal and professional risks of unacceptable magnitude. It would have entailed, among other things, admission that one had nothing in particular to profess as content only, but only as "content-and-process," "ideas-and-meanings."

The second thing to be noted about sensitivity training concerns its status as a kind of "laboratory education." In the 1950s and into about the mid-1960s, one heard this phrase constantly in the applied behavioral sciences. The idea was that the learner could learn a great deal about his or her own attitudes and behavior, and about human attitudes and behavior in general, if it were made possible for the learner to *experiment* with different ways of being and acting in relation to others. A great deal was written about this philosophy of learning, and a whole generation of professionals grew up in the context of this philosophy (Schein and Bennis, 1965). Correlative philosophies and techniques of "experiential learning" and "experiential education" emerged and led to a proliferation of training techniques that produced events in the training situation for learners to experience and reflect upon.

But something began to happen in the 1960s, not so much with sensitivity training itself, at least at first, but with these other experiential methods. More and more, these methods began to be used to prove something to the learner, rather than as methods and settings within which the learner could do the experimenting that the original philosophy of laboratory education declared to be so important. I am thinking here of such "exercises" as those concerned with giving feedback to others, bargaining in conflict situations, comparing authoritarian and democratic leadership styles, the conditions under which groups are able to be creative, and so forth. It is a huge range and volume of techniques, many extraordinarily creative and subtle (largely published by University Associates, La Jolla, California, between 1972 and 1983).

In one sense, these techniques can be considered a genuine flowering of the educational spirit, and there is no question that education and training, particularly of adults, is forever changed by these inventions, in contrast to the age-old lecture/ discussion method. But these techniques are only partially the heirs of sensitivity training as it was originally conceived and practiced. Sensitivity training's demonstration of the great learning value of looking at here-and-now events was and is retained in these techniques. Sensitivity training's interest in the process of human relationships has also, for the most part, been carried over in these other kinds of experiential methods. In this sense, the early philosophy of laboratory education and practice of sensitivity training, at the National Training Laboratories, the University of California at Los Angeles, Case Western Reserve, and elsewhere, is the legitimate and indispensable ancestor of all the subsequent experiential techniques that have been invented.

What was most significant of all about sensitivity training, though, has been largely lost in subsequent developments. The core belief of laboratory education is no longer apparent in the experiential education community, and without this core belief (and faith), the meaning of experiential education is transformed into something quite different from and, in my opinion, far less ethical and interesting than the original approaches. This core belief is summed up in a phrase that was present and taken very seriously almost from the beginning: "trust the process." To trust the process as an injunction to the trainer/leader is to free one from the need to *make* anything in particular happen in the training setting. To trust the process as an injunction to the learner is to free one from the need to learn anything in particular from the experience, that is, to free oneself from the mind-compressing question: What am I *supposed* to be learning here?

Trust of the process, I believe, was sensitivity training's great insight into human dynamics—greater than any of the particular learnings that occurred, for the idea of trusting the process was the grounding for the possibility that any real learnings could occur at all. It was not a scientific idea, of course. The wisdom of trusting the process was not really a "research finding." It was some other kind of an induction from the experience of those who sat in these groups, whether as professional trainers or as learner/participants. It was hard-won wisdom, for those who broke the pathways of sensitivity training knew in profound, visceral ways how painful it was to sit there and let things unfold in the group at their own pace and in their own ways. One could not say exactly why what was happening was indeed happening. One did not know what was going to happen next. One had no idea what the "outcomes" were going to be, and at no moment could one prove that things were happening as they "should." All one could say to oneself and to learners was, "trust the process."

Behind this rule of thumb, as it were, were far deeper wisdom and faith about human interaction. This deeper wisdom was about the inherent capacity of the human being to trust, to cherish, to share, to rage at silliness and shallowness and bankrupt values, to be honest, to be helpful, to reach out and be supportive of one's fellow group members as they struggled with the dilemmas of their existence. One did not need to make these things happen; one did not need to exhort oneself and others about the virtues of these qualities, as preachers have done for ages from pulpits. To trust the process was to know that these qualities would emerge if one would just sit down in a sensitivity training group. One did not even need to *intend* to behave in these ways oneself or support them in others. One could sit down in one of these groups in a black, cynical mood and still have these experiences.

Nor, of course, did the principle promise that all things

that happened from moment to moment would be "good" or that all actions by all individual group members would be only of the uplifting sort I have sketched above. In fact, quite the opposite! People said awful things to each other in sensitivity training groups. People sometimes drew bizarre conclusions from group events, about themselves, about others, and about human nature in general. Professional trainers were by no means immune. In fact, it was realized from the beginning that the trainer was hardly more likely to be always "on target" about what was happening than anyone else in the group. That people could, indeed, get confused about the meaning of what was happening and about what they should say or do next was precisely why "trust the process" was such a powerful and such a necessary idea.

For all the power of the idea of trusting the process, it tended to remain as a maxim, rather than as a phenomenon to be explored at deeper levels. *Why* could one trust the process? For the most part, the answer to this day remains implicit, and thus this core principle of laboratory education was vulnerable. There was no manifest reason why the techniques and exercises that proliferated in education and training should give any particular validity to the idea, for its truth was never grounded on anything more than the personal experience of those who participated in sensitivity training groups. As a result, other values than those implicit in the idea of trusting the process flowed in to fill the void. These values were more instrumental and goal-directed values: experiential methods came to be used to achieve particular objectives. As noted earlier, experiential education tended to metamorphose into a set of methods for proving things to learners. It also became a set of methods for making interventions into organizations to solve particular problems. Sensitivity training became "team development" and in this guise was used to further organizational aims.

Once again, the applied behavioral sciences placed themselves in the position of having a science-based technique that would achieve more than techniques that were not grounded in scientific theory and research, or so laypeople were permitted, even encouraged to believe. Of course, as instruments for the attainment of objectives, these techniques began the familiar journey of becoming ever more refined and specialized, with the result that extreme fragmentation is now the rule. The original idea of laboratory education in which the learner would experiment freely within the context of an unfolding social process that could be trusted to yield learning and change has been all but lost. The clinical experience on which these ideas rested and the clinical awarenesses and skills that sustained it never achieved very clear definition, with the result that the idea arose that anyone could use experiential methods—exercises, "instruments," and so on—so that, today, all kinds of people are conducting education and training in these modes with hardly any thought at all of trusting the process. Far from it, in fact: experiential techniques are becoming methods for *controlling* the educational process and are fully as repressive, if that is not too strong a word, as the authoritarian lecture/discussion methods they were originally in opposition to. We cannot know whether these developments would have occurred had the applied behavioral scientists more thoroughly understood and grounded their original inventions in laboratory education. But I think that a substantial share of the blame has to lie at their doorstep.

Theory, research, clinical practice, and congenial setting once combined regularly, as content-and-process, ideas-and-meanings, to produce learning of extraordinary kinds. It is a great tragedy that it is not happening very much anymore. What *is* happening instead is that learners are being taught the ideas we want to teach them—through experiential methods. Whether these ideas are the right ones is not the point. The point is that, by letting this happen, the applied behavioral sciences have committed themselves to continuing to produce ideas that arise elsewhere than in the experience of the learner. These ideas have to seem to be scientific, for, otherwise, there is no reason why the learner should pay any more attention to them than to any other ideas. In particular, the learner's own consciousness and experience beckon, but in having cut themselves off from the deep valuing of the learner's experience that laboratory education originally declared, today's applied behavioral scientists find themselves in the anomalous position of having to challenge and frequently to deny the learner's own experience in favor of the principles they want to impart to the learner. It is a sad and tangled situation.

Active Listening:
"I Hear You Saying That You Feel . . ."

The third and final idea in the applied behavioral sciences that I wish to discuss is what has come to be called "active listening." I have never liked this phrase very much myself, having been introduced to this idea first under the name of "nondirective listening." Others like the phrase "taking the frame of reference of the other," and still others like "empathic understanding." Rogers (1951) himself dropped "nondirective" in favor of "client-centered." In any case, it is the awareness and behavior to which all these phrases refer that I want to talk about.

To be able to understand what another person feels and means has always been one of the cornerstones of the applied behavioral sciences. It is not an exaggeration to say that there is no single ability that is any more important for a professional to possess than this one. There are basically two things that I want to say about it, both of which teach us something further about the integration problem in the "diverse behavioral sciences." Once again, I will be trying to show how our failure to come to grips with the meaning of one of our most central ideas both contributes to our present confusion and blocks the dream of integration.

Both Theory X and Theory Y and sensitivity training have an additional characteristic of central importance to my discussion of active listening. McGregor's argument rests on the assumption that human needs are real and that the managerial attitudes called Theory X and Theory Y are real. Sensitivity training similarly rests on the idea that such a group is a reproducible reality, that a sensitivity training group is virtually a *thing* whose existence can be proved. I consider these beliefs, which are for the most part unexamined, to be erroneous. In permitting them to arise and live, both in the public mind and in professionals' and learners' minds as well, the applied behavioral sciences have made a mistake. This mistake—the misidentification of what is real—is most clearly evident and most clearly damaging in the way it manifests itself on the subject of active listening.

Theory X and Theory Y are about an encounter between a leader/manager and an employee/group member/participant. They are about how the former ought to think about the latter, if a satisfactory work relationship is to result. However, in the way that the idea was originally presented and in the way that it has subsequently been discussed and used, the leader/manager is encouraged to displace his or her understanding of a particular employee to the *category of needs* the employee falls into. Similarly, the leader/manager's awareness of his or her own personal style is displaced to the conceptual categories of Theory X and Y. In other words, the user of McGregor's idea is encouraged to displace reality from concrete, here-and-now persons and relationships to abstract categories about those persons and relationships. The user of McGregor's idea is encouraged to think of a theoretical manager/leader in relation to a theoretical employee/participant and to pretend that *that* relationship is real. It is not.

In permitting a sensitivity training group to become a thing, the applied behavioral sciences unwittingly invited participants and trainers alike to equate an abstract, normative, "typical" group process with the one they were living through in the here and now. Again, the invitation was to displace awareness from the concrete to the abstract. Group members were distracted from what was happening to what was supposed to be happening, given that this was a "thing" called a sensitivity training group. Such distraction is a principal reason why it is hard to trust the process: one worries that the process of this particular group cannot be trusted, because it does not seem to fit what the process is "supposed" to be in a sensitivity training group. Never mind that the only possible reality for any given set of group members is the reality that they are collectively inventing here and now. If a sensitivity group is a known thing, then, participants often feel, there must be something more or something else than what is happening at the moment in the group.

Reification—the attribution of thingness to abstractions—is a problem throughout the applied behavioral sciences. It has been particularly pernicious with respect to these two ideas—Theories X and Y and the nature of a sensitivity training group. It is even more pernicious when we come to active listening. The form that reification has taken in active listening is two-fold: first, the *consciousness* of the active listener and the *skills* of the individual practices have been split into two separate categories; second, the category of skills has received by far the bulk of the attention and has been turned into a normative list of things one is supposed to do to "practice the skill of active listening." Active listening has become a technique. It is paradigmatic as a technique: the process of splitting consciousness from behavioral skill and the subsequent prescription of a normative list of skills have been applied in other areas, such as delegation of authority, giving feedback, and acting as a third-party mediator. One can see the process most clearly, however, in what is called active listening.

The applied behavioral sciences have acted as though one could learn the skills of active listening without caring very much one way or another about the person one is listening to. What is *taught,* what is imparted in briefings, in "skill practice" exercises, and in depictions of the skill in transcripts, are the things one says and does in order to listen actively. Almost never discussed are one's going-in feelings about the person one is listening to or one's feelings as one is trying to listen actively. Carl Rogers, of course, discussed in great detail what went on in him as he tried to empathize with his patients, but no one else has gone to such lengths, and, in particular, no one has spelled out what might happen in you as a practicing manager in a work situation when you start trying to listen actively. The assumption has been that the thing to learn is the skills, not the attitudes and values—the caring—that are fundamentally what undergird every attempt to understand how the world is for another person. Once again, ideas drove out ideas-and-meanings.

It is a scandal that we have permitted active listening to

be reduced to a list of skills and behaviors, a scandal in the practical sense that the idea will not work if one *does not* care deeply about the other person, and a scandal in the ethical sense that, without the injunction that one needs to care about the other's feelings and point of view, the way is opened for the learner to regard active listening as one more tool in the kit to be used when the occasion warrants. Perhaps this puts the matter too strongly, but I think the case can be made that the applied behavioral sciences have permitted active listening to become a method of manipulation, all because we forgot that the practice of it is *both* attitude and action, *both* interest in and interaction with the other person, *both* valuing of and behaving toward the other, *both* idea and meaning.

Once again, the applied behavioral sciences could not bring themselves to say that "you have to care." Again and again, learners have detected this normative theme running through lectures, readings, and exercises on active listening, and again and again, professors and trainers have shied from admitting that active listening makes sense as a technique only when one is genuinely curious about and caring of the other's world. To admit to that takes one off into another one of those bull sessions on values that I described in connection with Theory X and Theory Y. To leave the value issues murky invites the learner to conclude that one should "use" active listening only when it suits one's purposes. The authentic insights that the applied behavioral sciences have achieved about empathy are being turned into impersonal tools.

One could argue that the situation is not nearly so ominous, for, as noted earlier, active listening really works only when one *does* care about the other. Any manager/leader who tries to use it exploitatively will fail, so the argument might go. This is true in the long run, but, in the short run, an understanding of the way people express their feelings can be used to dominate and exploit them. Furthermore, the very fact that active listening for exploitative purposes does *not* work in the long run means that this technique that the applied behavioral sciences are so proud of will ultimately disappoint any learner who tries to use it only as a tool. And once more the profession digs its own grave by failing to be clear, to itself and to its clients, about the values that permeate its overt substance and about the meanings that permeate its ideas.

Once again, the "story of science" that the applied behavioral sciences have told themselves is seen to permit a splitting of values and attitudes from external behaviors, a denial and forgetting of values and attitudes, a pretense that the applied behavioral sciences are a body of knowledge that can be transferred from one person to another independently of consciousness. The best active listeners care about the person they are trying to listen to. Where their caring comes from and how it is sustained and deepened as a process of personal development are left on the margins of awareness and training.

The best active listeners are *exemplars* of an integration of attitude and action. What is to be learned from them is not "how they do it" but how they are as persons. In my opinion, everybody within the profession knows this; it is an utterly commonplace observation. Yet we have not been able to let this commonplace truth be foundational for the development of the field. We have tried to believe that how one is as a person is not that important for the successful "application" of applied behavioral science "knowledge." Yet, in my view, this truncated version of what is involved in "application" of behavioral science ideas will not do. There is just too much clinical evidence that how one *is* as a person makes all the difference in one's ability to work effectively with others.

This brings me to the second main thing that I want to say about active listening and what it teaches us about the problem of integrating the diverse directions of the behavioral sciences. By ignoring the depths of human character with which the attempt to impart active listening techniques confronts us, we not only ignore the professional practitioner as an exemplar; we also ignore the learner of the technique in the complexities of his or her own being. This learner may be anyone from the most naive undergraduate to the most seasoned manager; in either case, the error is the same: we are not able to let ourselves gaze at the learner as existentially grounded in a web of personal feelings and aspirations and situational needs and opportunities. In a word, we cannot let ourselves understand the learner too well. The project of imparting the technique of active listening, or of any other of our facts and methods, prohibits it.

Our technique-oriented communication, deriving from the story of science that we tell ourselves, with its horror of admitting to the interplay of values and moral standards, forces us to discredit the learner's own experience. We find ourselves having to say, in effect: "However well you have learned to relate yourself clearly and caringly to others in the past, to the extent that you do not use explicit methods of active listening, you will not be able to understand the other person." We rarely say it this baldly, of course, for to say it this baldly would plunge us back into the value discussions that we would rather not get into. Instead, we find ourselves having to deny protests from learners such as, "I think I know my people pretty well," "I have my own ways of finding out what's on people's minds," "I think I'm a pretty open and trusting person," "I'm people-oriented," and so forth—all things that learners often feel and say when they are exposed to the techniques of active listening. Some professionals take a benignly paternalistic attitude to such expressions, while others are more confronting and demanding. But few professionals *start* with the assumption that the learner *already* possesses the capacity to "pick up on where another person is coming from," to put it colloquially. In short, we cannot afford to listen too actively to the learner if we are going to keep the focus on learning the technique of active listening, for to listen actively would introduce us not just to the learner's present skills but to the learner's being.

This is why the applied behavioral sciences do not understand the manager's situation in organizational life. The practice of active listening grew up in the two-person therapeutic relationship, in a quiet office, with the phone off the hook, and with the shared project of understanding between the two. The ideas about how understanding occurs in this setting were extracted and transferred to the managerial role, with little if any thought about the differences in the entire relationship and the meanings attached to it between the two (or more) parties involved in the organization where active listening was supposed to occur.

"If I'm going to listen actively," any manager might remark, "I am going to have to do it in the elevator, on the way to or from the parking lot, in meetings and other places where the people I am trying to listen to want *me* to tell *them* something. I am going to have to learn to shift from informing/directing/controlling actions to actions that are more permissive and accepting, because the former are part of my job, too. This is rather stressful on me, among other things. I may have to practice active listening in situations where I have just given the other person some very bad news, where, in other words, I am perceived as the cause of the very hurt feelings that active listening says I am now supposed to be accepting of. As we talk about active listening in this workshop and try to understand how to do it, I hope some of these realities of my situation will be taken into account."

To such a remark, perhaps more extended and coherent than what a manager might actually say but nonetheless plausible for that, the applied behavioral sciences do not have an answer. After forty years of purveying ideas of openness and acceptance to managers, they still do not have an answer, although, of course, individual professionals doubtless have worked out their own responses to such objections. The *core* of knowledge about active listening remains unmodified and unenriched by its encounter with the live situations of live people in a living world. The hypothetical manager quoted here never does get a very good answer to the question, "What about me in my situation?"

Fragmentation: The Consequence of Scientism

The misunderstandings of Theory X and Theory Y, sensitivity training, and active listening that I have discussed lead to fragmentation. By telling itself the "science story," the profession has produced a situation where ideas and techniques could proliferate wildly about all aspects of organizational behavior and development. There is little if any sense of center or integration, because there have been few if any norms and values about remaining centered and integrated.

The story of science abjures doctrine. It believes that the motives of the investigator are irrelevant to the quality of the investigation. It protects itself against investigator bias with an elaborate canon of methodological principles. It wants to keep attention focused on the phenomena, not on the investigator in relation to the phenomena. The investigator is a reporter (tabula rasa), in the final analysis, not an interpreter, which is to say a *valuer*. This is the story of science that the applied behavioral sciences have uncritically adopted from the physical sciences. The crux is that, even though many working professionals are aware of the artificiality of this science story, and even though thousands of investigators and trainers do not *practice* it in the here and now, the story still stands as the official version of what the applied behavioral sciences are.

I have written about this situation extensively elsewhere (Vaill, 1984a, 1984b). A conclusive case can be made for the need for a very different model of inquiry from that developed in the physical sciences. Here, I wish to call attention to a dimension of this different model of inquiry that I have not discussed before and, indeed, that is rarely discussed systematically by anyone (however, see Torbert, 1976).

The *field* is a human enterprise and a system of social processes among academics, professionals, practicing managers, students, and program administrators (for example, deans, managers of human resource development departments, and so on). We learn this way of defining the field from Berger and Luckmann (1966), as well as from many others. This, however, is not just one among many interpretations of the field. It is, I suggest, the single most viable interpretation of the field. It is a *community* of inquiry and planned change that we are talking about, not an abstract collection of theories and research findings. It is a community of ideas and meanings. Without the sense of community and the system of practices that sustain and develop it, the theories and research findings indeed do fragment in all directions. Various persons do become radically cut off from each other, both in modes of practice and, more importantly, in values.

It is the historical mission of the applied behavioral sciences that gives rise to the imperative of community as an organizing and integrating principle. Wrapped up in that word *applied* is a whole perspective on what the organizational world and the persons in it are in need of. It is change and development that the word *applied* refers to. Without a sense of community, values diverge and various members of the field end up at cross-purposes with each other. Communication decreases, comprising canned training sessions and mechanistic consulting interventions. Heavy-handed quantitative evaluation techniques come to provide the criteria for whether some training or consulting action "worked." Subcommunities evolve and bound themselves from each other: Separate schools of thought abound; a gulf arises between "theory" and "practice"; status distinctions between learners and seasoned professionals bedevil the learning process. Perhaps worst of all, knowledge becomes commercialized, and *everyone* becomes preoccupied with what it is worth. Academics develop norms for salaries and consulting fees based on the commercial visibility of the techniques they have created. Clients, unable to question high consulting and training costs directly, displace their attention to "how much bang for the buck" they are going to get from one consultant versus another. "Packaging" becomes an overriding value for any new idea, leading to a proliferation of diagrams and workbooks, videotapes and "interactive software packages," textbooks for a mass college market, and trade books with zippy titles for adult practitioners. Thousands of one- and two-person consulting firms incorporate with grandiose and trendy names and develop a distinctive "schtick" complete with logos and copyrighted workbooks around such ideas as "wellness," "MBO," "culture," "the new age," or whatever it may be.

Students, viewing all this, come into the field thinking of it as a career, with visions of four-digit daily fees and six-digit human resources vice-presidencies dancing through their heads. Students most of all become thus preoccupied with usable knowledge that stands independent of the exemplar professor/trainer through whose consciousness the student initially experiences it. "It's wonderful to have a great teacher, but I have to take something away," goes the litany. "I have to be able to get a job."

Perhaps it is too late; or, at the very least, the externalization of knowledge from the values and consciousnesses that generate it and the degeneration of such knowledge into commercial products have yet a few more years to spin on their dizzy course of fragmentation. But let us proceed on the assumption that it is not too late. In closing this chapter, I wish to mention the features of the field that I think still hold promise for the restoration of the sense of community—investigators in relation to each other and to the phenomena—that I think alone can preserve a *sense* of coherence in the field. For if it is a *community* we are talking about, the "integration" will be not logical but psychological.

1. We take the interplay of our values to be as important as the interplay of our theories, models, and research results. We seek to discover methods for conducting this interplay; we seek to become better at discussing values, and we evolve norms that support the willingness to enter into such discussion. Our assumption is that the car*ing* and care*ful* discussion of values is a pre-eminent quality of professional character.

2. We are suspicious of dualistic thinking in all its forms (Vaill, 1964). The "false dichotomy" is regarded as one of the most divisive of phenomena. In particular, we are suspicious of the dualisms that split abstract from concrete, theorist from theory, and one "school of thought" from another, for each leads to the reification of one half of each pair at the expense of the other.

3. We do not assume that the "applied behavioral sciences" are a cumulating storehouse of knowledge accessible to a small group of cognoscenti, with everyone else in the position of user/consumer. Rather, we assume that the questions we ask of human systems and their development are ever new, that the phenomena of concern are not "finished" but evolving, that a variety of methods and role perspectives and disciplinary backgrounds are "qualified" to contribute to and criticize our work.

4. "Learning" of the applied behavioral sciences is not

regarded as a process of supplanting past attitudes and experiences with more sophisticated, science-based attitudes and experiences. An "agricultural" model of learning and change (Bennis and Slater, 1970) is seen as a more valid view of the learning process than a "replacement" model, where "personal growth" is not just a cliché for learning new skills but a genuine growth of character and deepening of being.

5. We work to create and maintain professional associations and meetings in which the sense of community is the primary value. We do *not* permit such gatherings to be places where academics present papers for their promotion purposes and where professional consultants and trainers hawk their wares. We do not permit such gatherings to become drinking societies and sexual playgrounds. We focus our design skills on creating an ambience of learning and dialogue. We take individual responsibility for the practice of these values, and we energetically invent *new* methods for keeping these values in communication with each other.

6. Commercialization of ideas and methods is tempered by a spirit of amateurism in which providers and users are seen as engaged in a collaborative process of discovery of the applicability of these materials to specific situations. Ideas are not "taken off the shelf and plugged in." New ideas and conceptual models are not reified with vivid graphics that split off the idea from the consciousness and value system that produced it.

7. Work continues on the enterprise of reconceiving what today we call "the applied behavioral sciences" as a community of evolving ideas and meanings in which human values and purposes are kept related to the attempt to discover new empirical facts about the nature of human beings. The core axiom is this: Knowledge about humanity is *humanity's* knowledge of humanity. Humanity's knowledge is *always* "interested" knowledge, that is, knowledge infused with purpose and with value. Therefore, the phenomena reside in the mutual encounter of knower and known, not either in the subjective awareness of knower or in the objective existence of known, not either in values and purposes or in facts and methods. The field is both at once—

ideas and meanings—and, to paraphrase De Voto as quoted at the outset, if we are afraid of this truth, we had better start practicing seriously on our fiddle.

References

Argyris, C. *Personality and Organization.* New York: Harper & Row, 1957.

Bennis, W., and Slater, P. E. *The Temporary Society.* New York: Harper & Row, 1970.

Berger, P. L., and Luckmann, T. *The Social Construction of Reality.* Garden City, N.Y.: Doubleday, 1966.

Denhardt, R. B. *In the Shadow of Organization.* Lawrence, Kans.: Regents Press of Kansas, 1981.

McGregor, D. *The Human Side of Enterprise.* New York: McGraw-Hill, 1960.

Maslow, A. H. *Motivation and Personality.* New York: Harper & Row, 1954.

Ouchi, W. G. *Theory Z: How American Businesses Can Meet the Japanese Challenge.* Reading, Mass.: Addison-Wesley, 1981.

Popper, K. R. *The Logic of Scientific Discovery.* New York: Harper & Row, 1968. (Originally published 1934, rev. 1959.)

Roethlisberger, F. J. *The Elusive Phenomena.* Boston: Division of Research, Harvard Business School, 1977.

Rogers, C. R. *Client-Centered Therapy.* Boston: Houghton Mifflin, 1951.

Rogers, C. R. *On Becoming a Person.* Boston: Houghton Mifflin, 1961.

Schein, E. H., and Bennis, W. G. *Personal and Organizational Change Through Group Methods.* New York: Wiley, 1965.

Scott, W. G., and Hart, D. K. *Organizational America.* Boston: Houghton Mifflin, 1979.

Simon, H. A. *The Sciences of the Artificial.* (2nd ed.) Cambridge, Mass.: MIT Press, 1981.

Tannenbaum, R., and Davis, S. A. "Values, Man, and Organizations." In W. H. Schmidt (Ed.), *Organizational Frontiers and Human Values.* Belmont, Calif.: Wadsworth, 1970.

Torbert, W. *Creating a Community of Inquiry: Conflict, Collaboration, Transformation.* New York: Wiley, 1976.

Vaill, P. B. "The Temptations of Dualistic Thinking in the Behavioral Sciences." Unpublished manuscript, University of California at Los Angeles, Graduate School of Management, 1964.

Vaill, P. B. "OD as a Scientific Revolution." In D. D. Warrick (Ed.), *Contemporary Organization Development.* Glenview, Ill.: Scott, Foresman, 1984a.

Vaill, P. B. "Process Wisdom for a New Age." In J. D. Adams (Ed.), *Transforming Work.* Alexandria, Va.: Miles River Press, 1984b.

Whyte, W. H., Jr. *The Organization Man.* Garden City, N.Y.: Doubleday/Anchor Books, 1957.

Epilogue

———————◆•◆•◆•◆———————

Understanding the Riddle
of People and Organizations

Warren Bennis

Ralph Waldo Emerson would greet old friends he hadn't seen in
a while with this salutation: "What's become clear to you since
we last met?" I've always liked that question, and it seems especially fitting in connection with what I'd like to say about this
book and the three people who put it together, my old friends
and colleagues, Bob, Fred, and Newt. I'd like to tell them and
the readers of this volume what's become clear to me (about
them and their contributions) since we *first* met.

   I recall meeting Bob and Fred (along with their esteemed
colleague, the late Irv Weschler) shortly after receiving my
Ph.D. at M.I.T. It was on the UCLA campus, several years before the Graduate School of Management had erected its own
building, so I know it was before 1960 and roughly thirty years
ago, around 1956 or 1957. We met outside their offices in one
of those presmog days that causes a Bostonian to secretly envy
and openly resent those fortunate enough to live in Southern
California. But it wasn't the sunlight I noticed at first; it was the
light and energy that accompanied their excitement. It was the
beginning of the heydays of what was then referred to as human
relations, the dawning recognition that a decisive change was
taking place at the workplace, that there were some important

practical and conceptual changes in the way people, power, and institutions were construed and valued, that there was a significant shift from viewing the worker as a "cost center" to viewing him or her as a "resource." To this day, our conversations have retained that exuberance—about all manner of things: about the human condition, about living and dying, about war and peace, about ideas and experience, about what is empowering and satisfying and inspiriting. Most of all, I never failed to experience in their presence what F. Scott Fitzgerald inbued one of his favorite characters, Jay Gatsby, with—a "heightened sense of promise." (I met Newt later on; I think it was in 1960, when he took an experimental course that Ed Schein and I taught on leadership, using film as our sole teaching material, at M.I.T.'s Sloan School. He was getting his master's degree in management and enrolled immediately after in the doctoral program, under Tannenbaum's tutelage, at UCLA.)

In retrospect, I can say that the "heightened sense of promise" came from their excitement and ebullience. They reminded me, but only upon reflection, of what one of our greatest twentieth-century physicists, Paul Dirac, once said: "It is more important to have beauty and excitement in one's equations than to have them fit experiments. . . . It seems that if one is working from the point of view of getting beauty and radiance in one's equations, and if one has a really sound insight, one is on a sure line of progress."

To tell the truth, the idea for this book began to crystallize with editorial discussions about the failure of the recent spate of "readers," "proceedings," and "collections of readings" to intelligently meet the development of our field. There was a tendency to carelessly throw together, willy-nilly, all "the names" of individual concerns, differences, and achievements. The theory seems to be that as long as you get the right names, get jazzy sounding if unconnected papers, and always exclude one or two of the most famous as if to symbolize independent thought and judgment, the day's work of keeping up to date is done. This bureaucratic attitude on the part of committees and organizers of "collections" is why the United Nations, originally the meeting place of hope for the nations of the world, eventually became a travesty and a joke. The same charge of general default can be leveled against many of the books that deal with "people and organizations," our editors' main concern.

The editors of this volume strived to find generative meaning rather than a confusing amassment parading as meaning. Instead of looking for the differences among the seemingly never-ending emerging repertoire of concepts, styles, quotations, cross-styles, and images, they decided throughout their work, as represented in this book, to search for some common themes, a few irreducible elements that they elucidate in their introductory chapter.

I should warn the reader before you proceed further: What I have to say about the editors' unique contributions to our understanding of "people and organizations" may not quite correspond to what they believe their contributions to be. Let me say that in another way in order to clarify exactly what I mean about what may likely be a delicate point. The editors adumbrate extremely well in their introduction to this volume the major themes of their work. They group them under four major headings: the human matrix; values and growth; holistic and systems perspectives; and experience, meaning, and alternate realities. Fair enough. No argument about this. The problem is that many others could claim the same conceptual territory. I believe that what is truly *unique* about the UCLA school—and let us make no mistake about that, for clearly Tannenbaum and the others have created a school—has been muted or downplayed by their eclectic grasp.

But before taking a crack at what I consider to be the editors' core contribution to the field they refer to in this book as human systems development, I must, in all fairness to them, stress that the themes that they have emphasized throughout their book and heralded in their introduction have pretty much shaped the parameters of our field. Specifically, I am referring to their emphases on the individual, the small group, the biological (rather than the mechanical) view of systems (that is, *living* systems) and their deep concern with values and how values influence the uses of knowledge.

One way of introducing their unique contribution is to

return, once again, to Ralph Waldo Emerson. Emerson essentially founded a national literature on the basis of a celebration of "the self." In leaving the church that he once referred to as a "mere institution," he gained an individual sense of power that now seems primordial. To go back even further in time, don't forget that the beginning of this American century was grounded in the keen insights of one of the most penetrating observers of America from a European aristocratic, Catholic point of view, Alexis de Tocqueville, who recognized that democracy was the revolutionary proposition of the time and that democracy in America was founded on a faith in the individual that was unprecedented, wonderful, and dangerous. He wrote: "Americans acquire the habit of always considering themselves as standing alone, and they are apt to imagine their whole destiny is in their hands. Thus not only does democracy make every man forget his ancestors, but it hides his descendants, and separates his contemporaries from him; it throws him back upon himself alone, and threatens in the end to confine him entirely within the solitude of his own heart." This now legendary sense of self in America, enunciated so well by Tocqueville and embodied so fervently by Emerson (virtually as a national religion), probably reached its apotheosis in the work of Emerson's devoted younger colleague, Walt Whitman, who once wrote, "I was simmering, simmering, and simmering and Emerson brought me to a boil!" He later spoke of the transcendental self as a "Miracle of miracles beyond statement, most spiritual and vaguest of earth's dreams, yet hardest basic fact, and the only entrance to all facts."

I suppose it would be fair to say that Emerson had labored to provide America a national opportunity to celebrate our insouciant self. But, I would hasten to add, the transcendant self—that shining ether of self-hood that Emerson enshrined—was dimmed for reasons too divertingly complex to go into right now but, by the end of World War I, was almost entirely out.

For Milan Kundera, perhaps the most imaginative novelist writing today (Czech born and now living in Paris), the sign of the decline of the individual being—what marked it for him—

was the celebrated lectures of Edmund Husserl on "the crisis of European humanity," given in 1935, three years before his death. The crisis Husserl spoke of seemed to him so profound that he wondered whether we were in a position to survive it. The root of the crisis lay for him at the beginning of the modern era, in Galileo and Descartes, in the one-sidedness of European science that, in reducing the world to an object with technical and mathematical investigation, had put the world of concrete living beyond its pale. In a speech I recorded, Kundera said: "The rise of science propelled man into the tunnels of specialized knowledge. With every step found in scientific knowledge, the less clearly he could see either the world as a whole or his own self, and he plunged further into what Husserl's pupil, Heidegger, called in a beautiful and almost magical phrase, 'The Forgetting of Being.' Brought up by Descartes to be the master and possessor of nature, man becomes a mere thing before those forces (technology, politics, history) which pass his understanding, exceed his grasp and grasp him. For those forces, man's concrete being, his 'living world' has no value and no interest: it is eclipsed and forgotten." For Tannenbaum and the others, as for Kundera, those sciences concerned with life in organizations tended to ignore "man's being"— which, to Kundera, means "what happens inside," to unmask the secret life of feelings, so to speak. For Kundera, it was Descartes's "thinking self" who is the devil, and perhaps only Cervantes could be his hero.

Please understand. I'm *not* saying or even implying that our editors have ignored the cognitive, the conceptual, the "thinking self." The articles included in this volume, by themselves, should nullify any hint of that. But it seems to me that they came along at a time when much of the writing about organizations (and small groups, for that matter, with some notable exceptions) failed for the most part to examine "what happens inside," failed to discover the individual's rootedness in the past, failed to discover the role of the irrational in human behavior and decision making, failed to query the role of myths that control our movements from the remote past; in short, failed to unmask the secret life of feelings.

These emphases—the irreducibility of the self and the primacy of feelings and their "reality"—characterize a great deal of the work presented here, much of it spearheaded by the editors. One further thought should be added before concluding this essay. Arthur Lovejoy, the historian of ideas, coined the term *metaphysical pathos* to describe the subtle, almost imperceptible, even unconscious attitudes that guide one's theoretical predilections. Nowhere is this temperamental disposition so important to recognize as in the work of those of us who try to understand the riddle of people and organizations. There is only a thin line between what one is and what one wants, between descriptive realities and normative desires. It is true not only, for example, that Hobbes and Freud developed theories different from those of Maslow or Rogers; they also brought to their theories a completely different world view. My own metaphysical pathos tinctures this epilogue as, most certainly, the editors and authors represented here express theirs. And no matter how you turn the page or which page you turn to, there is only one inescapable viewpoint that illuminates the whole—the authors' inability to forget the essence of being, our "living world." The restoration and celebration of the self—that is the centerpiece of the contributions of Bob, Fred, Newt, and all those they have touched.

A novel I just finished—one I enjoyed enormously—has a character in it named Ursula who has an enemy that she calls "jellification"—that congealed state in which, as she says, "You're not fluid anymore. You solidify . . . and from then on your life is doomed to be a repetition of what you've done before." Well, this book should make clear to those of us who have profited enormously from the work of the UCLA school not to worry; "jellification" has been foiled. This school apparently takes its own lessons very seriously. They know about holding on, letting go, and moving on.

Name Index

Subject Index

A

Action: concept of, 448; and knowing, 447-448; knowledge from, 451-452; and patterns, 481-482; and values, 374, 484

Action learning, and interorganizational domains, 188-189

Active listening: in applied behavioral sciences, 565-571; exemplars of, 569; and exploitation, 568-569; and learners, 569-570; and managers, 571; reification of, 567; and skills, 567-569

Adaptability, and organization design, 161-162

Administrative Staff College, career patterns study at, 189

Africa, professionals in, 406

Alignment: concept of, 126-128; and management, 138-139, 140-141; needs for, 129-130

American Association on Mental Deficiency, 509-510, 516

Analysis of Interconnected Decision Areas (AIDA), 177

Applied behavioral sciences: active listening in, 565-571; analysis of integrating, 547-577; background on, 547-551; community imperative in, 573; domains of, 493; epistemology for, 501-508; features of, 574-576; fragmentation of, 571-576; as professional field, 550-551, 572; propositions about, 556-557; reification in, 567; research in, 440-452; as self-reflexive, 549-550; and sensitivity training, 557-565; tensions in, 548-549; and Theory X and Theory Y, 551-557; and values, 435-440, 552, 554, 556, 558, 568, 569, 570, 574. *See also* Human systems development

Appreciation, acts of, and interorganizational domains, 173, 190, 191

Australia, interorganizational domains in, 190, 191, 192

Authenticity value, 6-7, 399-401

Authority value, 402

Autonomy value, 401-402

595